Mon. first 20 pages

STATISTICAL QUALITY CONTROL

STATISTICAL QUALITY CONTROL

Fifth Edition

Eugene L. Grant

Professor of Economics of Engineering, Emeritus
Stanford University

Richard S. Leavenworth

Professor of Industrial and Systems Engineering
University of Florida

McGraw-Hill Book Company

New York   St. Louis   San Francisco   Auckland   Bogotá   Hamburg
Johannesburg   London   Madrid   Mexico   Montreal   New Delhi
Panama   Paris   São Paulo   Singapore   Sydney   Tokyo   Toronto

STATISTICAL QUALITY CONTROL

678910 HDHD 898765432

This book was set in Times Roman. The editor was Julienne V. Brown;
the production supervisor was Donna Piligre; the cover was designed by Edgar Blakeney.

Library of Congress Cataloging in Publication Data

Grant, Eugene Lodewick, date
    Statistical quality control.

    Bibliography: p.
    Includes index.
    1. Quality control-Statistical methods.
I. Leavenworth, Richard S., joint author.
II. Title.
TS156.G7 1980   658.5'68   79-19369
ISBN 0-07-024114-7

CONTENTS

Part 3   Some Related Topics

Appendixes

LIST OF EXAMPLES

PREFACE

This is a practical working manual. It deals primarily with various types of Shewhart control charts and with various types of acceptance sampling systems and procedures. These are simple but powerful techniques that have been widely used in many industries and in many countries throughout the world to improve product quality and to reduce costs. The most effective use of these techniques depends upon their being understood by production and inspection supervisors, by engineers, and by management.

The object has been to write a book that might be immediately useful to all these groups. No attempt has been made to write for the professional statistician or the mathematician. The aim has been to give just enough theory to supply practical working rules that will enable one to recognize the limitations of the methods as well as their many uses.

A special feature of this book is the liberal use of descriptions of actual cases from a number of industries. Each example has been selected to bring out one or more important points. These examples reflect the general viewpoint of the book that the statistical techniques described should be studied primarily as a means to various ends desired by cost-conscious industrial management. A number of the examples deal not only with the behavior of random variables but also with the behavior of people in various manufacturing and industrial situations.

None of the examples is imaginary; they all actually happened. Nevertheless, in certain examples it has been necessary to disguise the source or modify data to protect confidential information; in other examples, some of the actual complications have been omitted to keep the description of the facts fairly short. In general, the points brought out by any such altered or simplified examples are the same ones that would have been appropriate if the examples had given original data and a full description of all the facts.

Just as in previous editions, the changes from the preceding edition have been made in part to improve the presentation of fundamental principles and in part to try to keep the treatment of various topics up to date. Some of the major changes are as follows:

1. The words *defective* and *defect* are no longer used in the portion of this book that deals with various aspects of process control. It is explained in Chapter 1 that the technical meanings of these words differ from their popular meanings and that these differences in meaning have been the source of much confusion and misunderstanding in litigation about product liability.
2. The material in Chapter 5 on rational subgrouping has been expanded and more emphasis has been given to the procedures for making process capability studies.
3. The material on control charts for attributes data has been separated into two chapters. Chapter 7 now deals with control charts for fraction rejected and number of items rejected. Chapter 8 treats control charts for nonconformities (based on the Poisson distribution) and control charts for nonconformities per unit. The treatment of control charts for nonconformities per unit has been expanded.
4. Special process control procedures have been combined into Chapter 9. This affords the instructor an opportunity to expand or contract coverage to fit the circumstances of a particular course. Also, this organization should aid the practitioner seeking special applications of process control techniques.
5. The material in Chapter 18 dealing with life testing has been modified to improve clarity and updated to include recent changes in MIL-STD-781.
6. There are now 486 problems, an increase of 21 per cent from the preceding edition. Almost half of these are entirely new; many of the others have been substantially modified. Just as in the previous editions, answers are given to a number of representative problems, with the thought that this may be helpful to those persons who use the book for home study.

This edition follows the general pattern of the four earlier editions, which were greatly influenced by the viewpoint and philosophy of Dr. W. Edwards Deming. The authors also wish to acknowledge their debt to the late Harold F. Dodge, whose extensive comments had a great influence on the writing of the second and third editions. Their thanks are also due to a number of users of the fourth edition for suggestions for changes and improvements. Particular mention should be made of the suggestions made by Ms. Bonnie Small in her review of the fourth edition and of the suggestions of Mr. Seymour Selig of the Office of Naval Research relative to the coverage of Military Standards. Nevertheless, as in all technical books, the final responsibility for the selection and treatment of material must fall on the shoulders of the authors and they should receive the blame for any deficiencies.

Eugene L. Grant
Richard S. Leavenworth

STATISTICAL QUALITY CONTROL

INTRODUCTION

The long-range contribution of statistics depends not so much upon getting a lot of highly trained statisticians into industry as it does in creating a statistically minded generation of physicists, chemists, engineers, and others who will in any way have a hand in developing and directing the production processes of tomorrow.—W. A. Shewhart and W. E. Deming†

The Control-Chart Viewpoint

One important tool in statistical quality control is the Shewhart control chart. In spite of the apparent simplicity of the control chart, many engineers, production personnel, and inspectors find that its use calls for an entirely new point of view. One purpose of this book is to explain this point of view in some detail. Briefly stated, it is this: *Measured quality of manufactured product is always subject to a certain amount of variation as a result of chance. Some stable "system of chance causes" is inherent in any particular scheme of production and inspection. Variation within this stable pattern is inevitable. The reasons for variation outside this stable pattern may be discovered and corrected.*

The power of the Shewhart technique lies in its ability to separate out these assignable causes of quality variation. This makes possible the diagnosis and correction of many production troubles and often brings substantial improvements in product quality and reduction of spoilage and rework. Moreover, by identifying certain of the quality variations as inevitable chance variations, the control chart tells when to leave a process alone and thus prevents unnecessarily frequent adjustments that tend to increase the variability of the process rather than to decrease it.

---

† W. A. SHEWHART (edited by W. E. DEMING), "Statistical Method from the Viewpoint of Quality Control," p. 49, The Graduate School, Department of Agriculture, Washington, D.C., 1939.

Through its disclosure of the natural capabilities of a production process, the control-chart technique permits better decisions on engineering tolerances and better comparisons between alternative designs and between alternative production methods. Through improvement of conventional acceptance procedures, it often provides better quality assurance at lower inspection cost.

Specification, Production, and Inspection

Before production starts, a decision is necessary as to what is to be made. Next comes the actual manufacturing of the product. Finally it must be determined whether the product manufactured is what was intended. It is convenient to think of all matters related to quality of manufactured product in terms of these three functions of specification, production, and inspection.

Statistical quality control should be viewed as a kit of tools which may influence decisions related to the functions of specification, production, or inspection. Its most effective use generally requires cooperation among those responsible for these three different functions or decisions at a higher level than any one of them. For this reason, the techniques should be understood at a management level that encompasses all three functions.

An Aid to Cooperation

A common complaint among production personnel is that engineers responsible for specifications do not understand production problems. Inspection personnel often complain not only about the poor quality of manufactured product but also about the unreasonableness of specified tolerances. In fact, very frequently inspection practices develop that substitute the inspector's views regarding proper tolerances for those actually specified by the engineers. In many organizations, there is evident need for a basis on which designers, production personnel, and inspectors can understand each other's problems.

In the past many arguments among these three groups have been carried on with more heat than light because of the absence of facts in a form which would provide a basis for agreement. In many cases these facts can be provided by the use of statistical quality control techniques. In fact, statistical quality control provides a common language that may be used by all three groups in arriving at a rational solution of mutual problems.

Some Simple Statistical Tools

Many of the techniques developed by mathematical statisticians for the analysis of data may be used in the control of product quality. The expression *statistical quality control* may be used to cover all uses of statistical techniques for this purpose. However, it often relates particularly to four separate but related techniques that constitute the most common working statistical tools in quality control. These tools are

1. The Shewhart control charts for measurable quality characteristics. In the technical language of the subject, these are described as charts for variables, or as charts for $\bar{X}$† and R (average and range) and charts for $\bar{X}$ and σ‡ (average and standard deviation).
2. The Shewhart control chart for fraction rejected. In the technical language of the subject, this is described as the p chart.
3. The Shewhart control chart for number of nonconformities per unit. In the technical language of the subject, this is described as the c chart.
4. That portion of sampling theory which deals with the quality protection given by any specified sampling acceptance procedure.

This book is primarily an exposition of these four simple techniques. In the use of statistical methods to control product quality, these are the tools for cost reduction and quality improvement that are most widely applied. This is particularly true in the first stages of the use of statistical methods; as people dealing with quality matters acquire statistical sophistication, more advanced statistical methods are also used to good advantage.

Variables and Attributes

An important distinction in the technical language of statistics is that between *variables* and *attributes*. When a record is made of an actual measured quality characteristic, such as a dimension expressed in thousandths of an inch, the quality is said to be expressed by variables. When a record shows only the number of articles conforming and the number of articles failing to conform to any specified requirements, it is said to be a record by attributes.

All manufactured products must meet certain requirements, either express or implied. Many of these requirements may be stated as variables. Examples are dimensions, hardness in Rockwell units, operating temperatures in degrees Fahrenheit, tensile strength in pounds per square inch, per cent of a particular impurity in a chemical compound, weight in pounds of the contents of any container, time in seconds of the blow of a fuse, life in hours of an incandescent lamp. Most specifications of variables give both upper and lower limits for the measured value. Some, such as the per cent of a particular impurity in a chemical compound, may have an upper limit only, whereas others, such as strength, may have a lower limit only. Variables are dealt with in the Shewhart control charts for $\bar{X}$ and R, and for $\bar{X}$ and σ.

---

† The symbol $\bar{X}$ is read as "X bar" or as "bar X." The bar over any symbol always indicates an average. Thus $\bar{X}$ means an average of the X's.

‡ σ is the lowercase form of the Greek letter *sigma*. It is used by statisticians to represent *root-mean-square* or *standard deviation*. It is always read as "sigma." It should not be confused with the Greek capital letter sigma Σ, which mathematicians use to represent summation. The meaning of *root-mean-square deviation* is explained in Chap. 2.

Many requirements are necessarily stated in terms of attributes rather than variables. This applies, for example, to many things that may be judged only by visual examination. The glass cover on a pressure gage either is not cracked or it is. A lithographed label either has a certain desired color or it has not. The surface finish of a piece of furniture either presents a satisfactory appearance or it does not. A spot weld in sheet metal either has not caused cracked edges of the sheets or it has. In general, the thing examined either conforms or does not conform to the specifications.

In addition to numerous quality characteristics that are specified without reference to measurement of any quantity, many characteristics that are specified as measurable variables are inspected merely as conforming or nonconforming to specifications. This applies, for example, to gaging of dimensions of machine parts by go and not-go gages. Attributes are dealt with in the Shewhart control chart for fraction rejected p.

Some Benefits to be Expected from Use of the Shewhart Control Chart for Variables

Trouble is a common state of affairs in manufacturing. Whenever the trouble consists of difficulty in meeting quality specifications that are expressed in terms of variables, the Shewhart control charts for $\bar{X}$ and R are indispensable tools in the hands of the trouble shooter. They provide information on three matters, all of which need to be known as a basis for action. These are

1. Basic variability of the quality characteristic
2. Consistency of performance
3. Average level of the quality characteristic

No production process is good enough to produce all items of product exactly alike. Some variability is unavoidable; the amount of this basic variability will depend on various characteristics of the production process, such as the machines, the materials, the operators. Where both upper and lower values are specified for a quality characteristic, as in the case of dimensional tolerances, one important question is whether the basic variability of the process is so great that it is impossible to make all the product within the specification limits. When the control chart shows that this is true and when the specifications cannot be changed, the alternatives are either to make a fundamental change in the production process that will reduce its basic variability or to face the fact that it will always be necessary to sort out the acceptable product. Sometimes, however, when the control chart shows so much basic variability that some product is sure to be made outside the tolerances, a review of the situation will show that the tolerances are tighter than necessary for the functioning of the product. Here the appropriate action is to change the specifications to widen the tolerances.

Variability of the quality characteristic may follow a chance pattern, or it may behave erratically because of the occasional presence of assignable causes that can be discovered and eliminated. The control limits on the chart are so placed as to disclose the presence or absence of these assignable causes. Although their actual elimination is usually an engineering job, the control chart tells when, and in some instances suggests where, to look. As previously mentioned, the action of operators in trying to *correct* a process may actually be an assignable cause of quality variation. A merit of the control chart is that it tells when to leave a process alone as well as when to take action to correct trouble. The elimination of assignable causes of erratic fluctuation is described as bringing a process *under control* and is responsible for many of the cost savings resulting from statistical quality control.

Even though the basic variability of a process is such that the *natural tolerance range* is narrower than the specified tolerance range, and even though the process is under control, showing a consistent pattern of variability, the product may be unsatisfactory because the average level of the quality characteristic is too low or too high. This also will be disclosed by the control chart. In some cases the correction of the average level may be a simple matter, such as changing a machine setting; in other situations, such as increasing an average level of strength, it may call for a program of research and development work.

Once the control chart shows that a process is brought under control at a satisfactory level and with satisfactory limits of variability, one may feel confident that the product meets specifications. This suggests the possibility of basing acceptance procedures on the control chart, using it to determine whether this happy state of affairs is continuing. Under these favorable circumstances substantial savings are often possible in costs related to inspection. Where inspection consists of destructive tests, it may be possible to reduce the number of items tested, thus saving both in testing cost and in the cost of the product destroyed.

Some Benefits to be Expected from the Use of the Shewhart Control Chart for Fraction Rejected

Most routine inspection of manufactured products is inspection by attributes, classifying each item inspected as either Accepted or Rejected (with possibly a further division of rejects into Spoilage and Rework). This statement applies both to 100% inspection and sampling inspection. In such inspection it is common practice to make a record of the number of items rejected.

The practice of recording at the same time the number of items inspected is not so universal. However, if quality performance at one time is to be compared with that at another time, the record of total number inspected is just as necessary as the record of number rejected. The ratio of the number of items rejected to the number of items inspected is the *fraction rejected*.†

---

† It is commonly expressed as a decimal fraction such as 0.023. The decimal fraction is often multiplied by 100 to convert it into per cent rejected such as 2.3%.

Thus the Shewhart control chart for fraction rejected generally makes use of data that either are already available for other purposes or that can readily be made available. Simple statistical calculations provide control limits that tell whether assignable causes of variation appear to be present or whether the variations from day to day (or lot to lot, vendor to vendor, or whatever the classification basis may be) are explainable on chance grounds.

It will be shown in later chapters that this control chart for attributes (the p chart) is somewhat less sensitive than the charts for variables ($\bar{X}$ and R charts) and does not have as great diagnostic value. Nevertheless, it is an extremely useful aid to production supervision in giving information as to when and where to exert pressure for quality improvement. It is a common experience for the introduction of a p chart to be responsible for substantial reductions in the average fraction rejected. In some instances the p chart will disclose erratic fluctuations in the quality of inspection, and its use may result in improvement in inspection practices and inspection standards. Moreover, the p chart often serves to point out those situations needing diagnosis of trouble by the control chart for variables.

In addition to its use in process control, the p chart may be of great value in dealing with outside vendors. Vendors may differ both in the quality level submitted and in the variability of that quality level. It is particularly desirable to know whether the quality of product submitted by a vendor today is a reliable indication of what may be expected to be submitted next month. The p chart gives useful guidance on this point.

Some Benefits to be Expected from the Use of the Shewhart Control Chart for Nonconformities per Unit

This type of control chart applies to two rather specialized situations. One is the case where a count is made of the number of nonconformities of such type as blemishes in a painted or plated surface of a given area, weak spots in the insulation of rubber-covered wire of a given length, or imperfections in a bolt of cloth. The other is the case of inspection of fairly complex assembled units in which there are a great many opportunities for occurrences of nonconformities of various types, and the total number of nonconformities of all types found by the inspectors is recorded for each unit.

As in other types of control charts, the control limits are set in a way to detect the presence or absence of assignable causes of variation, and they therefore tell when to take action on the process and when not to do so. Experience indicates that erratic variation in inspection standards and inspection practices seems particularly likely to exist in this type of inspection and that the control chart for nonconformities per unit generally proves helpful in standardizing inspection methods.

Although this type of control chart applies only to a limited number of manufacturing situations involving quality, it has broad application to many other types of situations commonly met in everyday life.

Acceptance Sampling

Acceptance inspection is a necessary part of manufacturing and may be applied to incoming materials, to partially finished product at various intermediate stages of the manufacturing process, and to final product. Acceptance inspection may also be carried out by the purchaser of manufactured products.

Much of this acceptance inspection is by sampling. Often 100% inspection turns out to be impracticable or clearly uneconomical. Moreover, the quality of the product accepted may actually be better with modern statistical acceptance sampling procedures than would be the case if the same product were subjected to 100% inspection. Sampling inspection has a number of psychological advantages over 100% inspection. Inspectors' fatigue on repetitive operations may be a serious obstacle to good 100% inspection.

It is common knowledge that on many types of inspection, even several 100% inspections will not eliminate all of the nonconforming product from a stream of product a portion of which does not conform to specifications. The best protection against the acceptance of nonconforming product is, of course, having the product made right in the first place. Good sampling acceptance procedures may often contribute to this objective through more effective pressure for quality improvement than can be exerted with 100% inspection. Some sampling schemes also provide a better basis for diagnosis of quality troubles than is common with 100% inspection.

It should be recognized that although modern sampling acceptance procedures are generally superior to traditional sampling methods established without reference to the laws of probability, anyone who uses acceptance sampling must face the fact that whenever a portion of the stream of products submitted for acceptance does not conform to specifications, some nonconforming items are likely to be passed by any sampling acceptance scheme. The statistical approach to acceptance sampling frankly faces this fact. It attempts to evaluate the risk assumed with alternative sampling procedures and to make a decision as to the degree of protection needed in any instance. It is then possible to choose a sampling acceptance scheme that gives a desired degree of protection with due consideration for the various costs involved.

Use of Examples

Throughout this book there are many descriptions of cases involving use of statistical quality control methods. For convenience in reference, these are numbered consecutively, throughout each chapter.

Before proceeding in Parts One and Two with a detailed description of the tools of statistical quality control explained in this book, it seems advisable to give a general perspective on the subject by illustrating the use of some of the more common tools. Examples 1-1 and 1-2 illustrate the control chart for variables; Example 1-3 illustrates the use of elementary probability theory to evaluate the quality protection given by a common sampling plan.

Example 1-1 $\bar{X}$ **and** R **charts. Experimental control charts for process control**
Facts of the case In the kit of tools provided by statistical quality control, one of the most potent tools for the diagnosis of production problems is the Shewhart control chart for variables. A course in statistical quality control often starts with a brief introduction of this control chart. This chart was the topic for discussion in the third 2-h lecture in an evening course given in the subject.

One of the members of the class was a production supervisor in a small department in a plant which had never before used any statistical quality control methods. After hearing the 2-h lecture, this supervisor, in order to become familiar with the control chart, made an experimental application to one of the operations in the department.

This operation consisted of thread grinding a fitting for an aircraft hydraulic system. The pitch diameter of the threads was specified as 0.4037 ± 0.0013 in. All these fittings were later subject to inspection of this dimension by go and not-go thread ring gages. This inspection usually took place several days after production. In order to minimize gage wear in this inspection operation, it was the practice of the production department to aim at an average value a little below the nominal dimension of 0.4037 in.

To make actual measurements of pitch diameter to the nearest ten-thousandth of an inch, the supervisor borrowed a visual comparator that had been used for other purposes. Approximately once every hour the pitch diameter of five fittings that had just been produced was measured. For each sample of five the average and the range (largest value in sample minus smallest value) were computed. The figures obtained are shown in Table 1-1.

Two charts that are not control charts If these measurements had been made without benefit of the supervisor's introduction to the control-chart technique, the averages for each sample might well have been calculated but probably not the ranges. Figure 1-1 shows two types of charts that are not control charts but that sometimes are made from information of this type. These charts may be of interest to production supervision, but they do not give the definite basis for action that the control chart supplies.

Figure 1-1a shows individual measurements plotted for each sample. It also shows the nominal dimension and upper and lower tolerance limits. With the exception of one fitting in sample 8, all the fittings examined met the specified tolerances.

Figure 1-1b shows the averages of these samples. A chart of this type may be useful to show trends more clearly than one of the type of Fig. 1-1a. However, without the limits provided by the Shewhart technique, it does not indicate whether the process shows lack of control in the statistical sense of the meaning of *control*.†

It should be noted that because Fig. 1-1b shows averages rather than individual values, it would have been misleading to indicate the tolerance limits on this chart. It is the individual article that has to meet the tolerances,

Table 1-1 Measurements of pitch diameter of threads on aircraft fittings

Values are expressed in units of 0.0001 inch in excess of 0.4000 in.
Dimension is specified as 0.4037 ± 0.013 in.

Sample number	Measurement on each item of five items per hour					Average $\bar{X}$	Range R
1	36	35	34	33	32	34.0	4
2	31	31	34	32	30	31.6	4
3	30	30	32	30	32	30.8	2
4	32	33	33	32	35	33.0	3
5	32	34	37	37	35	35.0	5
6	32	32	31	33	33	32.2	2
7	33	33	36	32	31	33.0	5
8	23	33	36	35	36	32.6	13
9	43	36	35	24	31	33.8	19
10	36	35	36	41	41	37.8	6
11	34	38	35	34	38	35.8	4
12	36	38	39	39	40	38.4	4
13	36	40	35	26	33	34.0	14
14	36	35	37	34	33	35.0	4
15	30	37	33	34	35	33.8	7
16	28	31	33	33	33	31.6	5
17	33	30	34	33	35	33.0	5
18	27	28	29	27	30	28.2	3
19	35	36	29	27	32	31.8	9
20	33	35	35	39	36	35.6	6
Totals...						671.0	124

† The word *control* has a special technical meaning in the language of statistical quality control. A process is described as *in control* when a stable system of chance causes seems to be operating. This meaning is developed more fully in Part One of this book. However, the word is often misused and misinterpreted, particularly by those who have been briefly exposed to the jargon of statistical quality control without having had a chance to learn its principles.

For example, a government inspection officer in a certain plant was shown a chart that gave average values of an important quality characteristic of successive lots of a certain item manufactured in this plant. This chart, prepared by one of the inspectors, was similar to Fig. 1-1*b* in showing averages but no control limits. "Any fool could see this process is in control," the officer exclaimed. Later an assistant calculated control limits and plotted them on the chart, showing many points out of control. A few minutes later the inspection officer was overheard giving this advice to the plant manager: "Any fool can see this process is out of control."

As a matter of fact no one—fool or otherwise—can tell by inspection of a chart such as Fig. 1-1*b* whether or not the process is in statistical control.

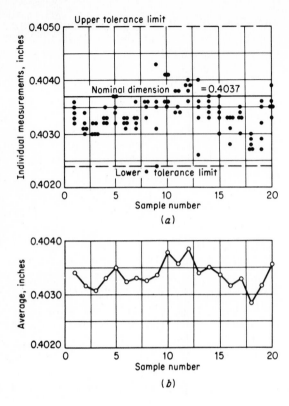

Figure 1-1 Pitch diameter of threads of fitting for aircraft hydraulic system: (*a*) individual measurements; (*b*) averages of samples of five.

not the average of a sample. Averages of samples often fall within tolerance limits even though some of the individual articles in the sample are outside the limits. This was true in sample 8, in which the average was close to the nominal dimension even though one item was below the minimum limit. Therefore, a chart for averages that shows tolerance limits tends to give a false sense of security on the question of whether tolerances have been met. The topic of how to avoid such possible incorrect conclusions from charts for averages is discussed at some length in Chap. 9.

Two control charts Figure 1-2a shows the control chart for averages $\bar{X}$. It will be noted that this is Fig. 1-1b with the addition of control limits and with the elimination of the irregular line connecting the points. Figure 1-2b shows the control chart for range R.

Each of these control charts has a solid line to indicate the average value of the statistic that is plotted. The grand average $\bar{\bar{X}}$ (i.e., the average of the averages) is 33.6 (measured—as in Table 1-1—in units of 0.0001 inch in excess of 0.4000 in). This is the sum of the averages, 671.0, divided by the number of samples, 20. The average of the ranges is 6.2. This is the sum of the ranges, 124, divided by the number of samples, 20.

Each chart also shows two dotted lines marked *upper control limit* and *lower control limit*. The distances of the control limits from the line showing the average value on each chart depend on the subgroup size and the average range $\bar{R}$. The methods for calculating such distances are explained in Chap. 3.

On the $\bar{X}$ chart of Fig. 1-2 this distance is 3.6 for both control limits. The upper control limit is 37.2, 3.6 above the grand average of 33.6, and the lower control limit is 30.0, 3.6 below the grand average.

On the R chart, the control limits are not equidistant from the average range of 6.2; the upper limit is 13.1, and the lower limit is 0.

These limits shown on Fig. 1-2 are what are described in Chap. 4 as *trial limits*. Before projecting them into the future (i.e., past sample 20) to control future production, they need to be slightly modified by methods that are there explained.

The charts show lack of control Three points (samples 10, 12, and 18) are outside the control limits on the chart for averages. Two points (samples 9 and 13) are outside the control limits on the chart for ranges. This indicates the presence of assignable causes of variation in the manufacturing process, i.e., factors contributing to the variation in quality which it should be possible to identify and correct. Of course not much could be done about these past assignable causes, as the control limits were not established until the end of the 20-h record. The control charts in Fig. 1-2 merely give evidence that there should be a good opportunity to reduce the variability of the process.

The dividends from the control chart come in the application of the control limits to future production. The prompt hunting for assignable causes as soon as a point goes out of control gives opportunity for their immediate

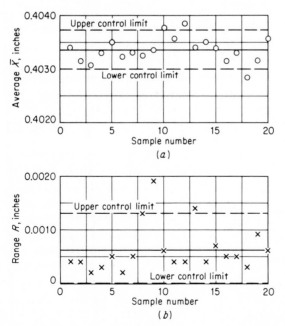

Figure 1-2 Pitch diameter of threads of fitting for aircraft hydraulic system: (*a*) control chart for averages ($\bar{X}$); (*b*) control chart for ranges (R).

discovery. Action may be taken not only to correct them at once but in many cases to prevent their recurrence.

This lack of control was evident to the production supervisor who prepared this chart. A continuation of the chart permitted the identification of the assignable causes of variation in the average—mostly related to machine setting—and the assignable causes of variation in the range—mostly related to carelessness of a particular operator. An effort to prevent their frequent recurrence resulted in a substantial improvement in product uniformity.

Other conclusions from this control chart The simplicity of the control chart is evidenced by the fact that this alert supervisor was able to use it to advantage after receiving only 6 h instruction in statistical quality control with only two of those hours devoted to construction of the control charts for $\bar{X}$ and R. This successful application was to process control, i.e., to the detection and elimination of assignable causes of quality variation. However, several conclusions that might have been suggested by the control-chart analysis were not evident to the supervisor, although they doubtless would have been evident to someone with additional training and experience in this subject. These conclusions, the basis for which will be developed in later chapters, are as follows:

1. If control (in the statistical sense) can be maintained, the natural tolerances of this process appear to be about ± 0.0006 in. Thus, by maintaining statistical control there should be no difficulty in making all the product well within the specified tolerances of ± 0.0013 in.
2. As the practice has been to center the process at a dimension somewhat below the nominal dimension of 0.4037 inch in order to minimize gage wear on 100% inspection with go and not-go thread ring gages, the question arises at what level the process ought to be centered. If statistical control can be maintained, this level must be not less than 0.4030 in to ensure that practically all product be within the specifications. Actually the level shown by the 20-h record was about 0.4034 in. This would be definitely on the safe side if the process could be kept within statistical control. But with the process out of control, there is always danger of nonconforming product regardless of the level.
3. Whenever natural tolerances are within the specification tolerances, consideration should always be given to the advisability of eliminating 100% inspection and substituting sampling inspection with the use of the control chart. In this case, five measurements of the actual dimension at specified intervals might replace 100% inspection with the go and not-go gages, except where the control chart showed lack of control. Such a change should not be made until the control chart had been maintained on this operation for some time with all points falling inside the control limits. Once this change was made, the motive of reducing wear on the ring gages would be eliminated and the nominal dimension of 0.4037 in should be aimed at.

The methods by which one may obtain these conclusions, and similar conclusions of economic importance in other cases, are developed in the following chapters.

Some Comments on Example 1-1

Because management's preconceived ideas on statistical quality control sometimes include a number of misconceptions, it is worth while to make several comments on Example 1-1 directed at these common misconceptions.

1. One misconception is that because the methods are *statistical* they can only be applied where there is a long period of record. Often this is the basis for the feeling that is not worth applying them to new operations that are to be continued for only a few months.

   It should be noted that the necessary data for a successful application in this case were obtained in 20 hours. As a matter of fact, as past records are seldom in a form for the most effective use of the control chart for variables, it is usually necessary to start securing the required data *after* the decision is made to use this technique. The time needed to get enough information to supply a basis for action depends on how long it will take to manufacture enough units for a suitable chart.

2. Another misconception is that the methods are necessarily highly mathematical. This application involved only simple arithmetic.

3. A common misconception is that the methods are so complicated that they cannot be operated by the ordinary production and inspection employees.

   As already pointed out, this particular supervisor made a useful application after only 2 h instruction in the particular technique. This is not to suggest that 2 h is sufficient time to devote to explanation of the control chart for variables; it merely is evidence that the essential features of this method can be explained simply in a short time. As also pointed out, this supervisior missed some of the possible useful conclusions that might have been drawn from the data. The more persons holding positions of responsibility in an organization who understand statistical quality control and the better they understand it, the better the chance for all the possible cost-saving applications to be made.

4. Another misconception is that the techniques are good to use only when you are conscious that you are in trouble.

   It is true that the places where one is conscious of trouble are likely to provide the best opportunities for saving costs. Nevertheless, the techniques often turn up cost-saving opportunities in places where there is no particular awareness of trouble. The possibility in Example 1-1 of substituting sampling inspection by variables for 100% inspection by attributes is an example. The supervisor chose this particular operation somewhat at random in order to provide an opportunity to experiment with the techniques.

5. Still another serious misconception is that effective use of the techniques of statistical quality control may be obtained by applying them only in one department.

In Example 1-1 we have noted that the data secured by the *production* supervisor point to a possibility of a saving in *inspection* costs. Budgetary control systems in industry generally are operated in a way that gives a supervisor credit for a cost saving in the supervisor's own department but not for savings in other departments. In this particular case, if the decision had been made to adopt acceptance sampling by variables at the point of production, with a control chart kept in the production department to be used for process control as well as for acceptance, this decision would have involved the question of whether the measurements were to be made by production or inspection personnel. This question could have been answered only at a management level above both production and inspection. If—as might well have been the case—the decision had been that it was advisable to have the measurements made by production personnel, it would have superficially appeared to *increase* costs in the production department. That is, it would have seemed to increase costs for which the production supervisor was held responsible and to decrease costs in a place where—as a matter of budgetary routine—the supervisor was given no credit.

Without a full understanding by top management, production supervision, and inspection supervision as to the basis of some of the cost savings that may be effected by statistical quality control, it is evident that the routine operations of a budgetary control system may actually prove an obstacle to securing the savings. This topic is explored at greater length in Chap. 19.

Example 1-2 $\bar{X}$ and R charts. Revision of tolerances *Facts of the case* A rheostat knob, produced by plastic molding, contained a metal insert purchased from a vendor. A particular dimension determined the fit of this knob in its assembly. This dimension, which was influenced by the size of the metal insert as well as by the molding operation, was specified by the engineering department as 0.140 ± 0.003 in. Many molded knobs were rejected on 100% inspection with a go and not-go gage for failure to meet the specified tolerances.

A special gage was designed and built to permit quick measurement of the actual value of this dimension. Five knobs from each hour's production were measured with this gage. Table 1-2 shows the measurements obtained on the first 2 days after they were started.

Analysis of the facts by the control-chart technique Figures 1-3b and 1-3c are control charts for $\bar{X}$ and R, respectively, for the 27 samples taken in these 2 days. Figure 1-3a is not a control chart, but—like Fig. 1-1a in Example 1-1—it shows individual measurements.

If we count all the points outside the tolerance limits that are shown on Fig. 1-3a, we find that 42 of the 135 knobs measured failed to meet the

Table 1-2 Measurements of distance from back of rheostat knob to far side of pinhole

Values are expressed in units of 0.001 in. Dimension is specified as 0.140 ± 0.003 in.

Sample number	Measurement on each item of 5 items per hour					Average $\bar{X}$	Range R
1	140	143	137	134	135	137.8	9
2	138	143	143	145	146	143.0	8
3	139	133	147	148	139	141.2	15
4	143	141	137	138	140	139.8	6
5	142	142	145	135	136	140.0	10
6	136	144	143	136	137	139.2	8
7	142	147	137	142	138	141.2	10
8	143	137	145	137	138	140.0	8
9	141	142	147	140	140	142.0	7
10	142	137	145	140	132	139.2	13
11	137	147	142	137	135	139.6	12
12	137	146	142	142	140	141.4	9
13	142	142	139	141	142	141.2	3
14	137	145	144	137	140	140.6	8
15	144	142	143	135	144	141.6	9
16	140	132	144	145	141	140.4	13
17	137	137	142	143	141	140.0	6
18	137	142	142	145	143	141.8	8
19	142	142	143	140	135	140.4	8
20	136	142	140	139	137	138.8	6
21	142	144	140	138	143	141.4	6
22	139	146	143	140	139	141.4	7
23	140	145	142	139	137	140.6	8
24	134	147	143	141	142	141.4	13
25	138	145	141	137	141	140.4	8
26	140	145	143	144	138	142.0	7
27	145	145	137	138	140	141.0	8
Totals..						3,797.4	233

specifications for this dimension. This is approximately 31% nonconforming, a very high figure.

At the same time it is evident that all the points on the $\bar{X}$ chart (chart for averages) and the R chart (chart for ranges) are inside the control limits. The values of averages and control limits are as follows:

$$\bar{\bar{X}} \text{ (grand average)} = \frac{3,797.4}{27}$$

$$= 140.6 \text{ (expressed in units of 0.001 in as in Table 1-2)}$$

$$\bar{R}\ (\text{average range}) = \frac{233}{27} = 8.6$$

$$UCL_{\bar{x}}\ (\text{upper control limit for averages}) = 145.6$$
$$LCL_{\bar{x}}\ (\text{lower control limit for averages}) = 135.6$$
$$UCL_R\ (\text{upper control limit for ranges}) = 18.2$$
$$LCL_R\ (\text{lower control limit for ranges}) = 0$$

This process was evidently in statistical control, even though it was in control with a spread that was unsatisfactory from the standpoint of the specified tolerances of ± 0.003 in. No assignable causes of variability were

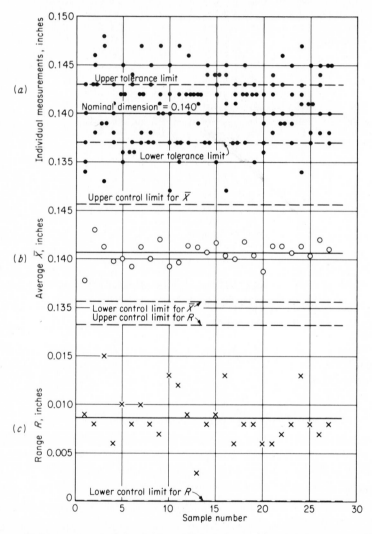

Figure 1-3 Measurements of dimension on rheostat knob: (*a*) individual measurements; (*b*) control chart for averages ($\bar{X}$); (*c*) control chart for ranges (*R*).

indicated. The variations from hour to hour were chance variations; they could not be reduced by hunting for changes which took place from one hour to the next. In a situation of this type, improvement is not likely to be obtained by the plant superintendent's bringing pressure on the department supervisor, or by the supervisor's bringing pressure on the machine operator.

Action based on the control-chart analysis When the quality control engineer in this plant studied the situation, it was discovered that although part of the spread in values of this dimension was due to the inherent variability of the plastic molding operation, the most serious factor was the variability of the metal insert from the outside vendor. Because the part was essential for an important contract and available vendors were scarce, nothing could be done immediately about the variability of the metal insert.

The immediate alternatives were either to continue to eliminate many parts by 100% inspection or to widen the tolerances. The quality control engineer requested the engineering department to review the tolerances. This review showed that the specified tolerances of ± 0.003 in were much narrower than necessary for a satisfactory functioning of the rheostat knob as part of its assembly. After trying knobs with different values of this dimension and judging when the fit was satisfactory, the tolerances were changed to

$$\begin{cases} +0.010 \\ -0.015 \end{cases}$$

It may be noted from inspection of Table 1-2 or Fig. 1-3a that these revised tolerances would have permitted the acceptance of all parts measured in the 27 samples of five there shown. With the change in tolerances and the process shown to be in statistical control, it then became possible to use the control chart as a substitute for 100% inspection of this dimension.

Subsequent work with the vendor resulted in some reduction in the variability of the metal insert. At a later date, assignable causes of variation developed in the plastic molding process; these were promptly detected by the control chart and the conditions corrected. Later it proved satisfactory to reduce the number of parts measured from five every hour to five every 4 h; subsequently this was cut down to five once in 8 h.

This plastic molding operation was carried on intermittently with runs of 2 or 3 days spaced several weeks apart. The control-chart technique is particularly helpful in process control on this type of operation.

Some Comments on Example 1-2

This example affords opportunity for some contrasts with the situation described in Example 1-1 and gives further illustration of some of the uses of the control chart for variables:

1. In Example 1-2 the quality control engineer used the control chart as the

natural weapon to adopt for the diagnosis of trouble. Without the control chart, and with 31% of nonconforming items produced, the most common action is for management to "get tough," bringing pressure on production supervision to do better. The control chart has been described as the substitution of "get smart" for "get tough" in managerial policy in dealing with quality troubles, because it provides supervisors with clues to the causes of correctable day-to-day troubles. In this case, however, the first message of the control chart was to tell management what *not* to do. The chart said, "It's no use to get tough," and it also said, "It's no use to hunt for causes of hour-to-hour or day-to-day variation."

This is the type of situation in which the alternatives presented are (1) to make a fundamental change in the process, (2) to change the specifications, or (3) to resign yourself to the necessity of continuing to try to separate out the acceptable product by 100% inspection. In this case it happened that the specified tolerances had been set arbitrarily without consideration of the particular needs of this assembly; therefore, the appropriate action was to change the specifications.

2. In the situation described in Example 1-2, an active statistical quality control program was in operation. It was in charge of a quality control engineer who reported directly to the works manager. Where the information secured from the analysis of control charts points to action by more than one department, such a plan of organization is often advantageous.

3. The contrast between Examples 1-1 and 1-2 emphasizes the point that *statistical control* is an expression that describes the pattern of variability of the process rather than the past performance of the process in meeting specifications. In Example 1-1, 25% of the samples showed lack of control, whereas only 1% of the product examined failed to meet specifications. In Example 1-2, although none of the samples showed lack of control, 31% of the product failed to meet specifications.

4. The point is made in Example 1-1 that it is always misleading to show tolerance limits on a chart for averages ($\bar{X}$ chart). Example 1-2 emphasizes this point. Even though many of the individual rheostat knobs measured had dimensions greater than 0.143 or less than 0.137 in., no average of a sample of five was outside these tolerance limits. Someone who made a comparison between the tolerance limits and the charted values of $\bar{X}$ might well have reached the incorrect conclusion that all the product examined met the specification of 0.140 ± 0.003 in.

Different Meanings of Two Common Words

The technical meanings of the words *defective* and *defect* as used in the manufacturing industries differ from the common meanings of these words as used in everyday speech. This difference between the technical and popular meanings of these words has been a source of misunderstanding in litigation, particularly in product liability suits.

Among other matters, Example 1-2 illustrates the technical meaning of the word *defective* as used in manufacturing. In this sense, a manufactured part or article is defective if it fails to conform to specifications in some respect. Similarly, a *defect* is a failure of the part or article to conform to some one specification. A manufactured item that is defective may contain only one defect or it may contain two or more defects.

When the measurements shown in Table 1-2 were made, the rheostat knobs appeared to be 31% defective because a certain dimension on 31% of the knobs did not conform to the specification of 0.140 ± 0.003 in. Shortly thereafter, with no change whatsoever in the product, the knobs were 0% defective because the tolerances had been widened to

$$\left\{\begin{matrix} +0.010 \\ -0.015 \end{matrix}\right. .$$

In contrast, when the word *defective* is used in its popular sense as applied to a manufactured article, it means that the article is unsatisfactory with reference to its intended purpose. None of the rheostat knobs in Example 1-2 were defective in the popular sense either before or after the relaxation of tolerances.

In the popular sense of the word, a *defect* of a manufactured article is some characteristic of the article that makes it unsatisfactory for its intended purpose.

The Common Practice of Having a Margin of Safety in Specifications

Chapter 10 of this book is entitled "Some Aspects of Specifications and Tolerances." One of the topics covered in that chapter is the common discrepancy between the values that designers may specify for some particular quality characteristic and the values that are really needed for the satisfactory functioning of a manufactured product in its intended use.

Sometimes, as was the case initially in Example 1-2, the specifications are very much more severe than they really need to be. The quotations from C. G. Darwin and W. B. Rice at the start of Chap. 10 deal with some of the reasons for the frequency of such cases. It should be evident that such great differences between what is specified and what is really needed are rarely, if ever, desirable.

Nevertheless, it is common for specifications to contain *some* margin of safety. More often than not, there is a twilight zone beyond the specification limits within which manufactured product will function satisfactorily in its intended use. Part Two of this book describes a number of widely-used acceptance sampling systems that are based on stipulated allowances for some "per cent defective." In such systems, the word *defective* means "nonconforming to specifications" rather than "unsatisfactory for intended use."

Use of the Words *Defective* and *Defect* in this Book

As previously stated, the difference between the technical meanings of these words and their popular meanings has been a source of misunderstanding in product liability suits. In his Edwards Medal address in 1974 before the American Society for Quality Control, the distinguished past president of the Society, Arthur Bender, Jr., suggested that the best way to avoid such misunderstandings would be to abandon the technical usage of the words.†

Obviously it is impossible for manufacturers to take any action that will change the popular meanings of *defective* and *defect*. The only way the confusion between the technical and popular meanings can be eliminated is to substitute other words or phrases when the technical meanings are intended. An article that does not conform to specifications in some respect can be described as *nonconforming* rather than as *defective*. A failure to conform to a particular specification can be called a *nonconformity* rather than a *defect*. In describing the results of acceptance inspection, it is possible to say *per cent rejected* rather than *per cent defective*.

In the first four editions of this book, the words *defective* and *defect* were used in their technical sense. In this Fifth Edition, the authors have gone part way toward the desirable objective of eliminating this usage.

Part One of this book deals with various aspects of process control, with particular emphasis on the contributions that can be made by the different types of control charts. In this portion of the book, it has been possible to eliminate the words *defective* and *defect* in nearly all cases. However, a few such usages remain in quotations and in the reproduction of certain forms and charts.

Part Two of this book describes a number of acceptance sampling systems that use the words *defective* and *defect* in their technical senses. As long as these words continue to be used in the official documents describing such systems, writers explaining the systems will also need to use the words. Therefore, although *defective* and *defect* have largely been eliminated in Part One, they are used extensively throughout Part Two. In Chap. 12, the introductory chapter of Part Two, we have emphasized the special technical meanings of these words in the literature of acceptance sampling.

In all technical subjects, terminology ought to be as clear as possible. Thus a clarification of the usage of *defective* and *defect* would have been desirable even if it had not been motivated by litigation about product liability. Chapter 19 contains some comments on the economic aspects of product liability in relation to the subject matter of this book.

Example 1-3 Weakness of a common acceptance sampling scheme *Should sampling be used for acceptance?* Two opposite attitudes toward sampling are common in industrial inspection. They are:

1. An uncritical suspicion of all sampling. This is based in part on a belief that a lot may be very different from the sample taken from it.

---

† ARTHUR BENDER, JR., Don't Say THAT!, *Quality Progress*, vol. 7, no. 7, p. 8, July, 1974

2. An uncritical approval of all sampling. This is based on a belief that a lot
   will be like the sample taken from it.

The truth is somewhere between these two viewpoints. Samples may give
a misleading idea of lot quality. On the other hand, it is possible to devise
sampling procedures that do provide a desired quality protection. The basis
for distinguishing bad sampling schemes from good ones is developed
throughout this entire book. At this point it seems worth while to stimulate
curiosity about good sampling schemes by a critical examination of a
common acceptance sampling procedure that is bad.

This common procedure calls for inspecting 5 articles from each lot of 50.
If every article in this 10% sample conforms to specifications, the lot is accepted. If one or more nonconforming articles are found in the sample of 5,
the lot is rejected.

This acceptance procedure gives adequate protection if the articles in a lot
are either all acceptable or all rejectable. (In fact, if the items are either all
acceptable or all rejectable, a sample of one is sufficient.) It gives little protection against product with a moderate percentage of nonconforming articles.

The truth of this latter statement may be demonstrated by assuming that
the product submitted for inspection is, on the average, 4% nonconforming
i.e., on the average there will be 2 nonconforming articles in a lot of 50. Some
lots will contain more; some less. Column B of Table 1-3 shows the number of
lots that would be expected to have each number of nonconforming articles
according to the laws of chance; it is assumed that 1,000 lots are submitted. It
will be noted that the lots submitted vary from 0% nonconforming to 12%
nonconforming. In 1,000 lots with 50 articles in each lot, 50,000 articles are
submitted for acceptance.

Column D gives for each lot quality the relative frequency of having at
least one nonconforming article in a random sample of 5 taken from a lot of
50. The first figure, 0.00, is obvious; there can be no nonconforming article in
the sample if there is none in the lot. The second figure, 0.10, merely states the
reasonable conclusion that if there is only one nonconforming article in a lot
of 50, that article will appear in only 10% of the samples of 5 taken from the
lot. The source of the remaining figures in column D is not so obvious. They
can be calculated by simple probability mathematics as explained in Chap. 6.
Or—for those who are skeptical of unfamiliar mathematics—they may be
checked approximately by a simple experiment such as dealing 5-card hands
from well-shuffled 50-card decks in which certain cards are designated as
nonconforming articles, or by bead-drawing experiments using a sampling
paddle such as the one illustrated in Fig. 20-3.

It is evident that if 10% of the lots are rejected, 90% will be accepted; if
19% are rejected, 81% will be accepted, etc. That is, the sum of the decimals in
columns D and E must be 1.00. Columns F, G, H, and I are derived from the
preceding columns as indicated in the table.

The relationship between the proportion of submitted lots that will be

Table 1-3 Analysis of acceptance sampling plan

Take random sample of 5 from lot of 50. Accept lot if no nonconforming articles are found in sample; reject if one or more nonconforming articles are found. Examine 1,000 lots. Assumed process average is 4% nonconforming.

A Number non-conforming in lot	B Number of lots submitted	C† Number of non-conforming items $A \times B$	D Proportion of lots submitted that will be Rejected	E Accepted	F Number of lots rejected $D \times B$	G Number of lots accepted $E \times B$	H Number of nonconforming articles in rejected lots $A \times F$	I Number of nonconforming articles in accepted lots $A \times G$
0	130	0	0.00	1.00	0	130	0	0
1	270	270	0.10	0.90	27	243	27	243
2	275	550	0.19	0.81	52	223	104	446
3	185	555	0.28	0.72	52	133	156	399
4	90	360	0.35	0.65	32	58	128	232
5	35	175	0.42	0.58	15	20	75	100
6	15	90	0.49	0.51	7	8	42	48
Totals	1,000	2,000	⋯	⋯	185	815	532	1,468

† Column C gives the total number of nonconforming articles in all of the lots in column B for each specified number nonconforming. The total number of nonconforming articles submitted is 2,000. This is 4% of the 50,000 submitted.

22

accepted in the long run (usually referred to as the *probability of acceptance*) and the percentage of nonconforming articles in the submitted lots is shown graphically by the curve in Fig. 1-4. In the language of statistics, such a curve is called an *operating characteristic curve* or, more briefly, an *OC curve*. In the discussion of acceptance sampling in Part Two of this book, we shall have occasion to examine many such curves.

The practical conclusions from the table are obtained from an analysis of the totals of columns *F*, *G*, *H*, and *I*. Column *G* tells that 815 of the lots are accepted; this is a total of 40,750 articles. The significant figure desired is the quality of these accepted lots. Column *I* indicates that they contain 1,468 nonconforming articles. The ratio of 1,468 to 40,750 is 0.036; that is, there are 3.6% of nonconforming articles in the accepted lots.

It is evident that this acceptance procedure has effected a negligible improvement in quality. The incoming quality submitted was 4% nonconforming, and the outgoing quality after inspection is 3.6% nonconforming. To accomplish this small improvement, 185 lots out of the 1,000 submitted were rejected.

The quality of these rejected lots also is a matter of interest. They are, on the average, 5.75% nonconforming; they contain 532 nonconforming articles among their 9,250 articles. In them, each sample of 5 contained at least one

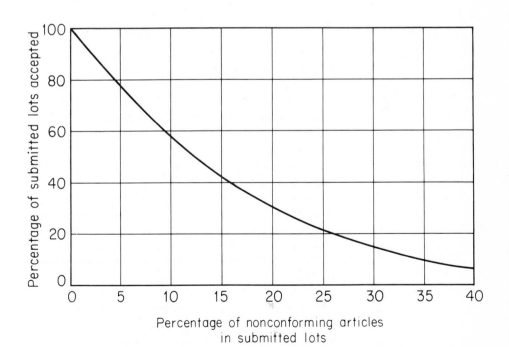

Figure 1-4 Operating characteristic curve for the acceptance sampling plan of Example 1-3.

nonconforming article; calculations based on probability mathematics indicate that 14 of them may be expected to have 2 nonconforming articles in the sample of 5. This is a total of 199 nonconforming articles found in the samples. If these are eliminated from the 185 lots, 333 nonconforming articles will remain among a total of 9,051 articles; this is 3.68% nonconforming. In other words, once the nonconforming articles found in the samples are removed, the quality of the rejected lots is practically as good as that of the accepted lots.

Some Comments on Example 1-3

A serious obstacle to sensible and economic acceptance plans is the illusion that perfection (in the sense of 100% conformity to specifications) is possible as the result of *any* inspection plan. This illusion often is cherished both by those who reject all sampling plans in favor of 100% inspection, and by those who adopt sampling plans that accept a lot if a sample is perfect and reject it if the sample contains one or more nonconforming articles. Perhaps without being conscious of giving the matter any thought, persons who favor the latter view would have confidence that the 815 accepted lots of Table 1-3 were perfect or nearly so because the samples from them were perfect.

In the case of 100% inspection, the belief in perfection through inspection is mistaken for psychological rather than statistical reasons. Where a great many similar items are to be inspected, even several 100% inspections may not weed out every one that does not conform to specifications. Inspection fatigue on repetitive inspection operations may cause even the best inspector to miss some of the nonconforming articles. For instance, a first screening might eliminate 95% of the nonconforming pieces. On the second 100% inspection, the nonconforming items—being less numerous—would be harder to find, and possibly only 90% of those remaining would be eliminated. For the same reason, a third inspection might catch only 80% of those remaining. Although the percentages missed in any given case will depend on the difficulty of the inspection operation and on the skill and diligence of the inspectors, the general principle is sound that if some nonconforming product is submitted for screening inspection, a portion of it is likely to be passed even with several 100% inspections.

Errors in distinguishing between acceptable and rejectable articles are somewhat less likely to occur in sampling inspection than in 100% inspection. There are a number of reasons why this is true. The inspector in sampling inspection obviously has a more responsible assignment; a mistake in classifying an article as satisfactory or unsatisfactory may decide the acceptance or rejection of an entire lot rather than only one article. This greater responsibility tends to influence inspectors to do a better job. Moreover, the greater variety of sampling inspection as compared to 100% inspection tends to cause less inspection fatigue. It is more monotonous and fatiguing to spend all day inspecting one or two kinds of articles than to inspect many different kinds of articles. Because fewer inspectors are needed for sampling inspection, it may be possible to secure better inspectors.

Nevertheless, in spite of these possible advantages over 100% inspection, sampling inspection cannot ensure that all accepted product will conform to specifications. If nonconforming product is included in lots submitted for acceptance under sampling inspection, then, according to the laws of chance, some lots that contain such product are likely to be accepted.

Most sampling plans for lot-by-lot acceptance in small lots that base the decision on each small lot on the evidence of a small sample from that lot are likely to have the same weakness as the plan examined in Table 1-3. Under ordinary conditions the product passed by such a scheme will not be substantially better than the product submitted for examination.

Before such acceptance plans, which often delude the user with a promise of perfection they cannot fulfill, can be discarded in favor of better ones, there must be a recognition of the fact that there is a limit to the degree of perfection to be expected. The question of just what this limit is in any case, i.e., just what is an acceptable quality level, is basically a question of economy. Some methods of getting as good an assurance as possible of this acceptable quality level are explained in Part Two. They require as background some understanding of the principles of the Shewhart control chart, which are developed in Part One.

Many Economy Studies Call for the Viewpoint of Statistical Quality Control

Many decisions on matters related to quality are called for in manufacturing. In making such decisions it is desirable to examine the relative economy of the alternatives under consideration. The techniques of statistical quality control may make a useful contribution to such economy studies.

Consider, for example, the question of the filling of containers—a problem for the food industries and all other industries that package their products. Suppose that government regulations require that all or some specified large percentage of the packages contain at least a certain stipulated weight.† Where a conscientious attempt is made to meet such a specification, it is usually done by overfilling enough to be on the safe side.

But the question always remains, "How much overfill is necessary?" This question is often answered on a practical basis of, "Make it enough so that we avoid trouble with the government inspectors." If these inspectors really do a critical job, the resulting average overfill is likely to be too much for maximum economy.

This is not to say that the economic answer is to be gained by increasing the amount of trouble with the inspectors. It is rather a matter of finding the facts about the variability of weights and analyzing these facts. This can be done by the Shewhart control chart for variables better than by any other known technique.

---

† In the sense used in statistical quality control, a quality of a manufactured product may be any characteristic of that product. Thus the *quantity* of material in a container is a *quality* of the filled container.

Can the variability of the process be reduced without any change in the physical methods being used to fill the containers? In other words, does the process show lack of control (with the word *control* used in its statistical sense)? If so, what are the reasons for the out-of-control points? Perhaps they may be corrected in such a way that they will be unlikely to recur. Or possibly their correction may call for the maintenance of a control chart continuously (rather than briefly as an information-getting and troubleshooting device) with some attendant cost for measurement, clerical labor, and supervision. It may even be necessary to maintain several such charts (for instance, on weights of filled containers, weights of empty containers, density of filling substance).

If out-of-control points can be eliminated, it is obviously possible to work closer to the minimum specification limit and thus reduce the cost of the overfill. This is a matter of balancing the cost of maintaining control against the cost of the extra overfill. The control-chart data giving the basic variability of the process will provide the information for decision as to the average level to be aimed at in order to meet specifications and will thus provide an estimate of the money-saving possible from better control.

If different methods of filling containers are proposed (for example, automatic vs. hand filling, or improved automatic controls vs. controls that are only partially automatic), one element in the cost comparison is the possible difference in the cost of overfill with each method. This requires the use of the Shewhart control chart to estimate the basic variability of each method.

If the specification of minimum filling weights has not been made either by government regulation or by a customer contracting for the product but must be made by the producer, the economic decision becomes even more complicated. Here the question may be the effect on consumer acceptance in a competitive market of occasional shortages below the amount stated on a package. Although it may be difficult or impossible to place a definite money value on this effect, it is extremely helpful to have an idea of the costs associated with various degrees of consumer protection. This information is provided by the control-chart technique.

Statistical Quality Control May Have Useful By-products

The techniques of statistical quality control bring certain desirable results that cannot be achieved as well in any other way. These might be described as the direct benefits of statistical quality control. In addition, the introduction of these techniques into any plant often causes certain desirable changes that might be described as *by-products*. These by-products might have been obtained as well without any use of statistical quality control. Nevertheless, statistical quality control does tend to bring them about.

One such by-product may be the establishment or improvement of inspection standards, with the preparation of definite instructions for each inspection procedure. Another may be the periodic evaluation of departmental performance in quality terms. Still another may be the evaluation of different vendors' quality performance in terms of average fraction rejected, with choice of future vendors based on these findings.

Sometimes an important by-product of statistical quality control may be the establishment of effective process inspection where none has previously existed. In some manufacturing concerns there is little or no process inspection; inspection takes place some days—or even weeks or months—after production with no chance to associate any rejected product with possible causes in the production departments. Statistical quality control, with its emphasis (explained in later chapters) on keeping track of the order of production, tends to call for inspection close to the point of production.

Although the introduction of process inspection is sometimes a by-product, it should be noted that a direct object of statistical quality control is to provide a new tool that makes process inspection more effective. The information obtained by process inspection—either conducted by roving inspectors or by machine operators themselves—is often misused to make too-frequent machine adjustments. As already pointed out under the discussion of the Shewhart control chart for variables, these too-frequent adjustments have the opposite effect from that intended: they increase rather than decrease the variability of the process. In the introduction of statistical quality control, reports such as these are common: "After a week of the control chart we accomplished substantial improvement in product quality by persuading the operator to let the machine run itself rather than changing the settings whenever a critical dimension gets close to the specification limit." "We found the roving inspector was shutting down the machine for resetting three times as often as necessary."

Reasons for Use of the Adjective *Statistical*

Statistics is a word with two quite different meanings. In one sense, it refers to any facts stated in terms of numbers; in this sense it is a plural noun. Thus one may say "Statistics *are* kept in the sales department regarding all branch-office sales." In the other sense, it refers to a body of methods by which useful conclusions can be drawn from numerical data. In this sense it is a singular noun. Thus one may say "Statistics *is* based in large part on the law of large numbers and the mathematical theory of probability." It is in this second sense that the adjective *statistical* is accurately used in the expression *statistical quality control*.

The control of quality of manufactured product is a function that existed long before statistical methods were applied to the analysis of quality data and that exists today whether or not statistical techniques are used. Properly used, the expression *quality control* applies to a function much broader than does the expression *statistical quality control*. The use of *quality control* or *Q.C.* in the sense of *statistical quality control* inevitably leads to confusion as to the meaning of the expression.

In the long run this confusion is likely to be more serious than any troubles introduced by the use of an extra word. For this reason, throughout this book the expression *quality control* is always used in the broader sense of the control of quality of product by whatever methods may be used and the adjective *statistical* is always employed where the control of product quality by statistical methods is referred to.

Many Applications of Statistical Quality Control
Require Only Simple Arithmetic

Although many of the techniques explained in this book are based on the work of mathematical statisticians, some of which involves very advanced mathematics, most of the actual applications described call for nothing more complicated than addition, subtraction, multiplication, and division. Experience shows that the techniques are effectively used by any persons who are able to do these simple arithmetical operations.

The control chart for variables, as originally developed by Shewhart in 1924, called for frequent calculation of squares and square roots in order to obtain standard deviations. This proved to be a definite obstacle to the introduction of the techniques in many places. Subsequent developments by mathematical statisticians made possible the use of the range rather than the standard deviation and substituted a single subtraction for the calculation of the square root of the sum of squares. This made possible shop cooperation in the use of the control chart in many situations where it had previously seemed to be out of the question.

Four Different Levels of Understanding
Statistical Quality Control

In any manufacturing company, government procurement agency, or other organization in which substantial statistical quality control applications are to be made, experience indicates that appropriately there may be four levels of understanding of the subject.

One is the level of understanding the mathematics on which are based the control charts and sampling tables and their relationship to the many other tools for the analysis of data that have been developed by mathematical statisticians. A person on this level should be able to read the literature of mathematical statistics without great difficulty and should have reasonable familiarity with this literature. Persons on this level should be available in any comprehensive statistical quality control program.

The second level is that of general understanding of the principles underlying the various types of control charts and sampling tables. It calls for understanding why these methods work, how to interpret their results, and how to decide which method to use in any particular case.

A third level is that of a broad understanding of the objectives and possible uses of statistical quality control, even though this understanding is not sufficiently detailed and precise to permit close supervision of statistical quality control work. This type of understanding is particularly helpful at higher management levels.

The fourth level calls merely for use of one or more of the techniques on a rule of thumb basis. In any plant in which many applications are made, there will doubtless be a number of inspectors, some machine operators, and possibly one or more clerks on this level.

This book is aimed at the second level. The success of any statistical quality control program is likely to depend on the number of people in an organization who are competent on this level and on the distribution of these people among various departments. The cooperation among departments necessary for the fullest benefits from statistical quality control has been mentioned and is emphasized throughout succeeding chapters. The more persons in inspection supervision, production supervision, methods engineering, tool engineering, engineering design, and top management who understand the basic principles of statistical quality control, the better the opportunity for effective use of these techniques.

This chapter although intended primarily as an introduction for people interested in the second level, is also intended to be helpful to those who are interested only in the third level. Chapter 19 is also suggested as reading for individuals primarily interested in the third level.

Nonmanufacturing Applications of Statistical Quality Control Techniques

Although control charts and statistical types of acceptance sampling procedures were originally developed for use in mass production manufacturing, these techniques are applicable to many other types of activities in business and government. For instance, certain statistical types of acceptance sampling schemes are well adapted to the problem of checking errors in clerical work. Control charts may be applied to many business variables to discover their average values, their range of variation that can be expected as a matter of chance, and the presence or absence of assignable causes of variation. A brief discussion of such applications is given in Chap. 21.

PROCESS CONTROL

WHY THE CONTROL CHART WORKS; SOME STATISTICAL CONCEPTS

There is no such thing as constancy in real life. There is, however, such a thing as a constant-cause system. The results produced by a constant-cause system vary, and in fact may vary over a wide band or a narrow band. They vary, but they exhibit an important feature called stability. Why apply the terms constant and stability to a cause system that produces results that vary? Because the same percentage of these varying results continues to fall between any given pair of limits hour after hour, day after day, so long as the constant-cause system continues to operate. It is the distribution of results that is constant or stable. When a manufacturing process behaves like a constant-cause system, producing inspection results that exhibit stability, it is said to be in statistical control. The control chart will tell you whether your process is in statistical control.—W. E. Deming†

The Need for Understanding Statistical Principles

This chapter and the one that follows deal with the principles behind control charts for variables. Although much good work in statistical quality control has been done by individuals who had only a vague notion of the principles behind the control chart, experience shows that the lack of a clear understanding of these principles may lead to certain costly mistakes that otherwise could be avoided. However, few of the many engineers, production personnel and inspection supervisors who will make use of statistical quality control techniques will be called upon to advance the frontiers of theoretical knowledge. The theory developed in this and subsequent chapters, therefore, will emphasize an *intuitive* approach rather than a purely *mathematical* approach. Much of the theory presented uses ordinary arithmetic with the occasional assistance of algebra. The reader should be aware, however, that the mathematical proofs that back up these intuitive explanations are frequently highly complex and sophisticated.

† W. E. DEMING, Some Principles of the Shewhart Methods of Quality Control, *Mechanical Engineering*, vol. 66, pp. 173–177, March, 1944.

The methods, definitions, and examples that follow are intended to portray the use of statistical theory in quality control work and to stimulate the reader's imagination by suggesting parallel opportunities in the reader's own industry.

Description of Patterns of Variation

As already stated in Chap. 1, variation seems inevitable in nature. Manufacturing processes are no exception to this. Whether one is attempting to control a dimension of a part which is to go into a precision assembly, the resistance of a relay, the acidity of a solution used for dyeing textiles, the weight of the contents of a container, or any other quality of a manufactured product, it is certain that the quality will vary.

It follows that it is necessary to have some simple methods of describing patterns of variation. Statisticians have developed such methods. One useful method involves a *frequency distribution*. Another involves the finding of a measure of the central tendency of a distribution (i.e., an *average*) combined with some measure of the *dispersion*, or spread, of the distribution.

This chapter explains and illustrates these methods of describing patterns of variation. It explains that there may be both stable and unstable patterns of variation; it points out that the practical conclusions to be drawn from frequency distributions, averages, and measures of dispersion depend on the stability of the pattern of variation. The control chart, which is a test for this stability, is illustrated. A further explanation of why the control chart works and detailed instructions as to its use are deferred until later chapters.

Counting the Frequencies of Different Observations

Table 2-1 gives the results of measurements of drained weights† in the canning of tomatoes. Several times during a shift in this particular cannery, a company inspector took from the production line five cans that had been filled and sealed. The inspector opened each can, emptied out and weighed the solid contents, and recorded the results to the nearest half ounce. Table 2-1 shows such measurements covering 11 days of operation on the day shift, a total of 260 measurements.

One way to organize such figures to show their pattern of variation is to count the number of times each value occurs. This may be done conveniently on a check sheet such as Fig. 2-1. The results of such a count are called a *frequency distribution*.

---

† These are drained weights immediately after filling the cans and before processing them. From a control viewpoint, it is advantageous to determine drained weight at this time in order to provide an immediate basis for action whenever the measurements disclose the existence of trouble. Actual specifications for finished product ordinarily relate to drained weights after processing. A necessary part of the control procedure which is not discussed here is a determination of the relationship between drained weights before and after processing.

Table 2-1 Drained weight after filling of contents of size No. $2\frac{1}{2}$ cans of standard grade tomatoes in purée

Weight given in ounces

Sample no.	Date	Hour	Measurement on each can of 5 cans per sample					Average $\overline{X}$	Range R
1	Sept. 21	9:30	22.0	22.5	22.5	24.0	23.5	22.9	2.0
2		10:50	20.5	22.5	22.5	23.0	21.5	22.0	2.5
3		11:45	20.0	20.5	23.0	22.0	21.5	21.4	3.0
4		2:30	21.0	22.0	22.0	23.0	22.0	22.0	2.0
5		5:25	22.5	19.5	22.5	22.0	21.0	21.5	3.0
6	Sept. 22	10:00	23.0	23.5	21.0	22.0	20.0	21.9	3.5
7		1:15	19.0	20.0	22.0	20.5	22.5	20.8	3.5
8		5:00	21.5	20.5	19.0	19.5	19.5	20.0	2.5
9	Sept. 23	9:30	21.0	22.5	20.0	22.0	22.0	21.5	2.5
10		1:15	21.5	23.0	22.0	23.0	18.5	21.6	4.5
11		1:45	20.0	19.5	21.0	20.0	20.5	20.2	1.5
12		3:30	19.0	21.0	21.0	21.0	20.5	20.5	2.0
13	Sept. 25	8:00	19.5	20.5	21.0	20.5	21.0	20.5	1.5
14		10:25	20.0	21.5	24.0	23.0	20.0	21.7	4.0
15		11:30	22.5	19.5	21.0	21.5	21.0	21.1	3.0
16		2:30	21.5	20.5	22.0	21.5	23.5	21.8	3.0
17		3:15	19.0	21.5	23.0	21.0	23.5	21.6	4.5
18		5:30	21.0	20.5	19.5	22.0	21.0	20.8	2.5
19	Sept. 26	2:00	20.0	23.5	24.0	20.5	21.5	21.9	4.0
20		3:00	22.0	20.5	21.0	22.5	20.0	21.2	2.5
21		4:45	19.0	20.5	21.0	20.5	22.5	20.7	3.5
22	Sept. 27	7:30	21.5	25.0	21.0	19.0	21.0	21.5	6.0
23		8:35	22.5	22.0	23.0	22.0	23.5	22.6	1.5
24		10:40	22.5	22.0	22.0	19.5	20.5	21.3	3.0
25		1:45	18.5	22.0	22.5	21.0	21.5	21.1	4.0
26		3:30	21.5	20.5	20.5	16.5	21.5	20.1	5.0
27		4:00	24.0	22.0	17.5	21.0	22.5	21.4	6.5
28		4:40	19.5	22.5	15.5	20.0	22.5	20.0	7.0
29	Sept. 28	7:15	22.0	17.5	21.0	22.0	23.5	21.2	6.0
30		7:45	22.0	20.0	20.5	24.0	21.5	21.6	4.0
31		10:00	22.5	21.0	19.5	21.5	22.5	21.4	3.0
32		1:15	20.0	22.0	20.0	21.5	20.0	20.7	2.0
33		3:30	21.0	19.5	22.0	20.0	20.0	20.5	2.5
34	Sept. 29	9:00	22.5	21.5	21.0	21.5	23.5	22.0	2.5
35		10:50	22.0	21.0	21.0	20.5	21.0	21.1	1.5
36		1:15	25.0	20.0	20.0	20.5	22.5	21.6	5.0
37		2:30	20.5	21.0	21.0	19.0	21.0	20.5	2.0
38		4:10	21.5	22.0	22.0	20.0	21.0	21.3	2.0
39		5:20	21.5	22.0	21.5	20.5	22.5	21.6	2.0
40	Sept. 30	9:30	22.5	24.5	25.5	20.0	21.0	22.7	5.5
41		11:15	21.5	24.0	21.5	21.5	22.5	22.2	2.5
42		2:10	23.0	23.5	21.0	21.5	21.5	22.1	2.5
43		3:30	22.5	19.5	21.5	20.5	20.0	20.8	3.0
44	Oct. 2	8:20	23.5	23.0	24.5	21.5	20.5	22.6	4.0
45		2:30	21.0	21.0	24.5	23.0	22.5	22.4	3.5
46		3:30	24.5	21.5	21.5	22.5	22.5	22.5	3.0
47		5:00	24.0	21.0	24.0	22.0	20.5	22.3	3.5
48	Oct. 3	9:15	23.5	22.5	20.0	20.0	21.0	21.4	3.5
49		10:00	22.0	20.5	21.0	22.5	23.0	21.8	2.5
50		1:00	22.0	23.5	24.0	22.0	22.0	22.7	2.0
51		3:00	23.5	21.0	23.5	21.5	23.0	22.5	2.5
52		4:30	24.5	21.5	21.0	24.5	22.5	22.8	3.5

25.5	*I*
25.0	*II*
24.5	*HH I*
24.0	*HH IIII*
23.5	*HH HH IIII*
23.0	*HH HH IIII*
22.5	*HH HH HH HH HH HH I*
22.0	*HH HH HH HH HH HH IIII*
21.5	*HH HH HH HH HH HH III*
21.0	*HH HH HH HH HH HH HH HH I*
20.5	*HH HH HH HH HH I*
20.0	*HH HH HH HH IIII*
19.5	*HH HH II*
19.0	*HH II*
18.5	*II*
18.0	
17.5	*II*
17.0	
16.5	*I*
16.0	
15.5	*I*

Figure 2-1 Check sheet to determine frequency distribution from data of Table 2-1.

Definitions Relative to Frequency Distributions†

A *grouped frequency distribution* of a set of observations is an arrangement which shows the frequency of occurrence of the values of the variable in ordered classes.

The interval, along the scale of measurement, of each ordered class is termed a *cell*.

The *frequency* for any cell is the number of observations in that cell.

The *relative frequency* for any cell is the frequency for that cell divided by the total number of observations.

Cells and Cell Boundaries

In Table 2-1, each measured weight was recorded to the nearest half ounce, as no greater precision of measurement was required. However, the weight was actually what is called a *continuous variable*. For example, the contents of a given can recorded by this weighing process as weighing 21.0 oz does not necessarily weigh exactly 21 oz. If more precise methods of measurement were used, it might be found to weigh 20.897 or 21.204 oz or any other value which is nearer to 21.0 than it is to 20.5 or 21.5. The statement in the frequency distribution that 41 cans had a

---

† Taken by permission from "Manual on Quality Control of Materials," American Society for Testing and Materials, Philadelphia, 1951. This ASTM manual contained an excellent detailed exposition of matters treated briefly in this chapter.

drained weight of 21.0 oz really means that the weight in each of the 41 cans was somewhere between 20.75 and 21.25 oz. The figure of 21.0 oz is the *mid-point* of a cell the boundaries of which are 20.75 and 21.25.

In grouping data into a frequency distribution, the questions always arise as to how many cells there should be, and where the cell boundaries should be placed. A rough working rule used by statisticians is to aim to have about 20 cells. This is often subject to exceptions dictated by other considerations. The distribution of Fig. 2-1 has 21 cells.

Cell boundaries should be chosen halfway between two possible observations. Cell intervals should be equal. In grouping the data of Table 2-1, the smallest possible cell size is 0.5 oz as measurements were not recorded to any smaller unit. However, if measurements had been made to the nearest 0.1 oz, it might still have been advantageous to use a cell size of 0.5 oz.

Table 2-2 illustrates an appropriate way to present a frequency distribution showing cell mid-points and cell boundaries. It illustrates also the effect of a coarser grouping, using the cell width as 1.0 oz instead of 0.5 oz. With measurements made to the nearest 0.5 oz, no cell size between 0.5 and 1.0 is possible. Thus figures must be grouped into either 21 cells or 11 cells.

Graphic Representation of a Frequency Distribution

Three common ways of graphic presentation of frequency distributions are shown in Fig. 2-2. Of these, the *frequency histogram* of Fig. 2-2a is in some respects the best. In this graph the sides of the columns represent the upper and lower cell boundaries, and their heights (and areas) are proportional to the frequencies within the cells. Figure 2-2b, the *frequency bar chart*, uses bars centered on the mid-points of the cells; the heights of the bars are proportional to the frequencies in the respective cells. Figure 2-2c, the *frequency polygon*, consists of a series of straight lines joining small circles which are plotted at cell mid-points with a height proportional to cell frequencies.

Cumulative Frequency Distributions

It is sometimes advantageous to tabulate the frequencies of values less than or greater than the respective cell boundaries. Table 2-3 illustrates this. It shows both the number of cans and the percentage of cans having less than a given weight.

Such a *cumulative frequency distribution* may be presented graphically in the manner shown in Fig. 2-3a. This type of graph is called an *ogive* because of its similarity to the ogee curve of the architect and the dam designer.

The plotting of relative frequency on a probability scale,† as in Fig. 2-3b, tends to smooth the ogive to something closer to a straight line. It also concentrates somewhat more attention on the extreme variations.

---

† Probability paper is the invention of an engineer, the late Allen Hazen. It can be purchased from most manufacturers of graph paper. The probability scale is so designed that the ogive of a normal curve (explained later in this chapter) will plot on it as a straight line.

Table 2-2 Examples of grouped frequency distributions showing cell mid-points and cell boundaries

Data of Table 2-1 on drained weights of contents of size No. $2\frac{1}{2}$ cans of tomatoes

	a. Finer grouping			b. Coarser grouping	
Cell mid-points	Cell boundaries	Observed frequency	Cell mid-points	Cell boundaries	Observed frequency
	25.75	—		25.75	—
25.5		1			
	25.25	—	25.25		3
25.0		2			
	24.75	—		24.75	—
24.5		6			
	24.25	—	24.25		15
24.0		9			
	23.75	—		23.75	—
23.5		14			
	23.25	—	23.25		28
23.0		14			
	22.75	—		22.75	—
22.5		31			
	22.25	—	22.25		65
22.0		34			
	21.75	—		21.75	—
21.5		33			
	21.25	—	21.25		74
21.0		41			
	20.75	—		20.75	—
20.5		26			
	20.25	—	20.25		50
20.0		24			
	19.75	—		19.75	—
19.5		12			
	19.25	—	19.25		19
19.0		7			
	18.75	—		18.75	—
18.5		2			
	18.25	—	18.25		2
18.0		0			
	17.75	—		17.75	—
17.5		2			
	17.25	—	17.25		2
17.0		0			
	16.75	—		16.75	—
16.5		1			
	16.25	—	16.25		1
16.0		0			
	15.75	—		15.75	—
15.5		1			
	15.25		15.25		1
				14.75	

Total..................... 260   Total..................... 260

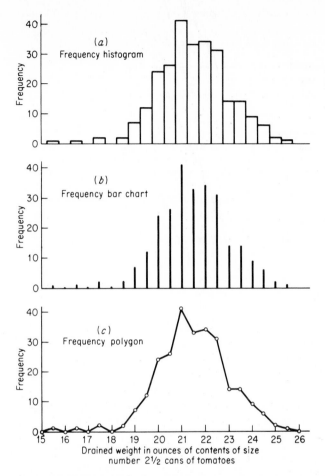

Figure 2-2 Three methods of graphical presentation of a frequency distribution—data of Table 2-2.

Frequency Distributions Often Supply a Basis for Action

A frequency distribution relative to any quality of a manufactured product supplies a useful picture of the way in which that quality has varied in the past. Throughout this book, there are many illustrations of actions that may be taken more intelligently with such a picture than they are likely to be taken without it. Some of these relate to specification of the quality characteristic and its tolerance limits; others to action on the process; still others to the planning of inspection and acceptance procedures.

Example 2-1. A use of a frequency distribution to accomplish a cost saving
Facts of the case In 100% inspection of completed electronic devices, a

Table 2-3 Examples of cumulative frequency distributions

Data of Table 2-1 on drained weights of contents of size No. $2\frac{1}{2}$ cans of tomatoes

Weight, oz	Number of cans having less than given weight	Percentage of cans having less than given weight
25.75	260	100.0
25.25	259	99.6
24.75	257	98.8
24.25	251	96.5
23.75	242	92.3
23.25	228	87.7
22.75	214	82.3
22.25	183	70.4
21.75	149	57.3
21.25	116	44.6
20.75	75	28.8
20.25	49	18.8
19.75	25	9.6
19.25	13	5.0
18.75	6	2.3
18.25	4	1.5
17.75	4	1.5
17.25	2	0.8
16.75	2	0.8
16.25	1	0.4
15.75	1	0.4
15.25	0	0.0

certain critical electrical characteristic was measured on a meter. This meter had a dial gage on which the value of the electrical characteristic was indicated by a pointer. Two fixed red lines were set on the dial, one at the minimum and the other at the maximum specified value. This permitted the inspector to tell at a glance whether or not each device met the specifications, so that the inspector could rapidly sort the nonconforming product from the acceptable product.

Because this characteristic was responsible for a number of rejections and it was desired to study its pattern of variation, the inspector was asked to read the value registered on the dial gage for every device and to make a line on a frequency distribution check sheet indicating this value. One check sheet was made for each shift and sent immediately to the quality control engineer of the plant. These sheets generally looked something like Fig. 2-4.

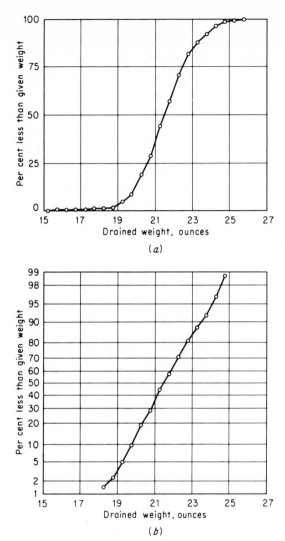

Figure 2-3 Graphical presentation of a cumulative frequency distribution—data of Table 2-3; (*a*) rectangular coordinate ruling; (*b*) probability ruling.

One morning the check sheet from the preceding night shift looked like Fig. 2-5. This not only indicated a great increase in the proportion of nonconforming units but also showed an unusual distribution pattern.

Analysis and action The quality control engineer suspected that this unusual distribution pattern might indicate an inspection error, so went immediately to the inspection station and rescued from the scrap bin the devices rejected on the night shift. They were all retested by the day-shift inspector, and nearly all proved to be satisfactory. It developed that there had been a new inspector on the night shift who had not understood how to operate the test equipment. Several hundred dollars worth of acceptable product was thus saved from the scrap heap. The new night shift inspector was instructed in the correct method of testing so that the mistake would not be repeated.

___

Comment on Example 2-1

Figures 2-4 and 2-5 represent a slightly different form of check sheet from that shown in Fig. 2-1. They are arranged to give a graphic picture of the pattern of variation somewhat like that given by a *frequency histogram* (Fig. 2-2*a*).

In this case the inspector made a record of the frequency distribution with a minimum of clerical labor. The inspector did not actually write down any figures for the measured value of the electrical characteristic but merely made a single line in the appropriate cell on the check sheet each time a measurement was made.

It often happens that a person with some understanding of statistics and with a thorough technical knowledge of a process can make a quick and accurate guess at a reason for trouble from looking at the behavior pattern shown on either a frequency distribution or a control chart. The quality control engineer made such a guess in this case, recognizing Fig. 2-5 as a *bimodal distribution*, that is, one with two cells with high frequencies separated by cells with lower frequencies. This often results from the mixing of two distributions with different modes or averages. From technical knowledge of the testing of electronic devices, the engineer recognized how a particular type of inspection error would have this effect. Guesses made in this way are not always correct, but they have a much better chance of being right than hunches unsupported by any statistical evidence. The subject of analysis of process capability is treated in greater detail in Chaps. 4 and 5.

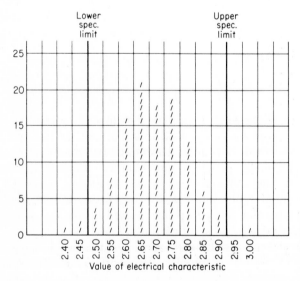

Figure 2-4 Typical check sheet showing frequency distribution of electrical characteristic of electronic device.

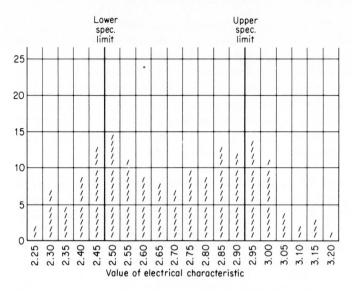

Figure 2-5 This check sheet called for investigation of the reasons for the unusual distribution pattern.

Frequency distributions of samples may be plotted and examined to guide decisions regarding acceptance of lots of product from which the samples are taken. An informal use of a frequency distribution in this manner is described in Example 17-1. The Shainin Lot Plot method, described in Chap. 17, is a formal procedure for acceptance based on analysis of a frequency distribution of a sample of 50 articles.

Averages and Measures of Dispersion

Representation of sample data by means of a frequency distribution is always bulky, frequently time-consuming, and sometimes misleading. Some form of statistical representation is necessary. This always requires at least two numbers, or statistics, one to measure the *central tendency* of the data and another to measure its spread or *dispersion*.

The most commonly used measures of central tendency are the *median*, the *mode*, and the *mean* or, more correctly, the *arithmetic mean*. In popular language, the word *average* usually implies the technical phrase arithmetic mean. Such usage is also common in the literature of quality control and in this book unless otherwise qualified.

The arithmetic mean of a set of n numbers is the sum of the numbers divided by n. Expressed algebraically:

$$\bar{X} = \frac{X_1 + X_2 + X_3 + \cdots + X_n}{n} = \frac{1}{n} \sum_{i=1}^{n} X_i \tag{1}$$

where the symbol $\bar{X}$ (read as "X bar" or, sometimes, as "bar X") represents the arithmetic mean; X_1, X_2, and so forth, represent specific numbers; and the Greek letter Σ (sigma) is the mathematical symbol for the taking of a sum.

The other important measures of central tendency mentioned previously have found relatively less use in quality control. Control charts based on the *median*, which is the magnitude of the middle case when the numbers that make up the sample are arranged by increasing order of magnitude, are discussed in Chap. 9. The *mode* is the magnitude of the case that occurs most frequently, the value corresponding to the high point on a frequency histogram.

Two measures of dispersion that are extremely useful in statistical quality control are the *range* and the *root-mean-square* (RMS) *deviation about the arithmetic mean*. We shall see that the range is of special importance in control charts for variables. In our discussions about the capabilities of manufacturing processes, we shall need to use the RMS deviation as a measure of dispersion.

The range, designated by R in this book,† is the difference between the largest and the smallest of a set of numbers. Expressed algebraically:

$$R = X_{\max} - X_{\min} \tag{2}$$

where $X_{\max}$ is the largest number and $X_{\min}$ is the smallest number in the set.

The RMS (root-mean-square) deviation of a set of numbers from their arithmetic mean is designated in this book by σ (the lowercase form of the Greek letter sigma). Expressed algebraically:

$$\sigma = \sqrt{\frac{(X_1 - \bar{X})^2 + (X_2 - \bar{X})^2 + \cdots + (X_n - \bar{X})^2}{n}}$$

$$= \sqrt{\frac{\Sigma(X - \bar{X})^2}{n}} \tag{3}$$

In our discussion of control charts, an alternate name that we shall use for this RMS deviation will be *standard deviation*. Engineers and physicists will recognize that σ corresponds to the concept in mechanics of radius of gyration about a centroidal axis.

Still another measure of dispersion is the *variance*. This measure is the sum of the squares of the deviations from the arithmetic mean divided by the number of observations, n. In other words, the variance is the square of the RMS deviation. Just as the RMS deviation is comparable to the concept in mechanics of the radius of gyration about a centroidal axis, the variance is comparable to the concept of moment of inertia about such an axis. In many of the derivations in mathematical statistics that deal with the relationship between samples and the universes from which samples are drawn, there are mathematical advantages in the use of the variance as the measure of dispersion.

---

† R is the symbol commonly used in industry in the United States. An alternative symbol for range is w, used in certain British literature on quality control.

A possible source of confusion to persons who read two or more books that deal with principles or applications of statistics may be the different names, symbols, and formulas that different writers use in connection with measures of mean-square deviation. This somewhat troublesome topic is discussed in Chap. 11; it involves the relationship between the dispersion of samples of a finite size and the dispersion of the "universe" from which, in concept, samples are assumed to have been drawn. At this point in our discussion, we have not yet dealt with sampling theory and are merely defining the standard deviation of a set of numbers as the root-mean-square deviation of those numbers.

It is suggested that those readers who have been exposed elsewhere to what seems to them to be a different definition of standard deviation ought to read Chap. 11 at once, but others need have no misgivings if they decide to put off reading Chap. 11 until it is reached in the customary sequence of chapters. Eventually it will be clear that conclusions about the presence or absence of a constant system of chance causes do not depend on the choice of names, symbols, or formulas used for the measure of mean-square dispersion.

Calculation of Average, RMS Deviation, and Range

Computation of the statistics for a small number of observations may be illustrated by reference to the five weights on the first line of Table 2-1 (Sample no. 1).
Using Eq. (1) to find the sample mean:

$$\bar{X} = \frac{1}{n} \sum X$$

$$= \tfrac{1}{5}(22.0 + 22.5 + 22.5 + 24.0 + 23.5) = 22.9$$

Using Eq. (2) to find the range of the sample:

$$R = (X_{\max} - X_{\min}) = (24.0 - 22.0) = 2.0$$

Using Eq. (3) to find the RMS deviation:

$$\sigma = \sqrt{\frac{(22.0 - 22.9)^2 + (22.5 - 22.9)^2 + (22.5 - 22.9)^2 + (24.0 - 22.9)^2 + (23.5 - 22.9)^2}{5}}$$

$$= \sqrt{\frac{0.81 + 0.16 + 0.16 + 1.21 + 0.36}{5}}$$

$$= \sqrt{0.54} = 0.73$$

Note the simplicity in the calculation of R in comparison with that of σ.
A useful alternate form for Eq. (3) is:

$$\sigma = \sqrt{\frac{X_1^2 + X_2^2 + X_3^2 + \cdots + X_n^2}{n} - \bar{X}^2}$$

$$= \sqrt{\frac{\Sigma X^2}{n} - \bar{X}^2} \tag{4}$$

The example calculation using this form for σ is as follows:

$$\sigma = \sqrt{\frac{(22.0)^2 + (22.5)^2 + (22.5)^2 + (24.0)^2 + (23.5)^2}{5} - (22.9)^2}$$

$$= \sqrt{\frac{2,624.75}{5} - 524.41} = \sqrt{524.95 - 524.41}$$

$$= 0.73$$

This form of the equation may prove more convenient, expecially where a desk or pocket calculator or computer is available. It should be noted, however, that more significant figures must be carried along during the calculation. In this example, the fourth and fifth significant figures were the important ones.

Shifting the Origin to Simplify the Arithmetic

One possible trick useful in simplifying the arithmetic and also in reducing the number of significant figures that must be carried throughout the calculations is to shift the measuring scale to a new zero point. For example, a new origin of 20.0 oz could have been chosen for the variable in the preceding calculations. The new variable of interest would be the excess weight above 20 oz. Thus the calculations of $\bar{X}$ and σ would have proceeded as follows:

$$\bar{X} \ (above \ the \ origin \ 20.0) = \frac{2.0 + 2.5 + 2.5 + 4.0 + 3.5}{5} = 2.9$$

$$\bar{X} \ (above \ the \ origin \ 0) = 2.9 + 20.0 = 22.9$$

Had an assumed origin of 23.0 been used:

$$\bar{X} \ (above \ the \ origin \ 23.0) = \frac{-1.0 - 0.5 - 0.5 + 1.0 + 0.5}{5} = -0.1$$

$$\bar{X} \ (above \ the \ origin \ 0) = -0.1 + 23.0 = 22.9$$

Likewise, the addition or subtraction of a constant from all of any set of numbers does not change their RMS deviation. Assuming an origin of 20.0, the calculation of σ becomes:

$$\sigma = \sqrt{\frac{2^2 + 2.5^2 + 2.5^2 + 4^2 + 3.5^2}{5} - 2.9^2}$$

$$= \sqrt{8.95 - 8.41} = 0.73$$

The reader will note a considerable saving in the number of significant figures in this calculation compared with previous calculations of σ.

Calculation of Average and RMS Deviation of Grouped Frequency Distributions—Long Method

Although formulas (1) and (3) might be applied to the actual measured weight in computing the average and standard deviation of the 260 observed weights of Table 2-1, the computation would be time-consuming, and the chances of an error in calculations would be great. To get the average, one would add the 260 individual values

$$\bar{X} = \frac{\Sigma X}{n} = \frac{5,589.5}{260} = 21.498 \text{ oz}$$

The first step in calculating the standard deviation would be the squaring of each of the 260 numbers. This long calculation is not illustrated here.

The same results could be obtained with less effort by considering the numbers grouped into a frequency distribution. This is illustrated in Table 2-4.

The importance of carrying extra significant figures in the calculation of σ by the use of formula (3) is again evident here. For any practical conclusions drawn from the average $\bar{X}$, there would be no need to carry it out to three decimal places as 21.498. However, for correct calculation of σ these three decimal places are necessary. If $\bar{X}$ were rounded off to 21.50 for this calculation, the effect would be to make a 2% error in σ, as σ would then appear to be 1.45 instead of the correct figure of 1.48.

An inspection of Table 2-4 will show that 5,589.5 is necessarily the same sum that would be obtained if the 260 numbers were added one by one, and 120,733.25 is necessarily the same sum that would be obtained if each of the 260 numbers was separately squared and squares were then added. Consider the numbers in any cell of the frequency distribution. For example, consider the cell corresponding to a weight of 20.0 oz. The 24 observations of 20.0 oz, if added one by one, would contribute $24 \times 20.0 = 480$ to the sum of the numbers. As the square of 20 is 400, these 24 observations would contribute $24 \times 400 = 9,600$ to the sum of the squares.

Although less laborious than calculations from the same data without grouping, calculations of the type of Table 2-4 are still wasteful of time. Table 2-4 has been introduced at this point primarily to provide a transition to the common short-cut calculations for frequency distributions from the direct calculations that use the basic formulas defining average and standard deviation. These short-cut calculations are illustrated in Table 2-5. If the reader fully understands Table 2-4, no difficulty should be experienced in understanding Table 2-5.

Calculation of Average and RMS Deviation of Grouped Frequency Distributions—Short Method

Just as the shift of origin simplified the arithmetic in the calculation from ungrouped data, so also may a shift of origin greatly simplify calculations of average and RMS deviation of frequency distributions. Another change in the direction of

Table 2-4 Computation of average and RMS deviation of frequency distribution—long method

Data of Tables 2-1 and 2-2a on drained weights of contents of size No. $2\frac{1}{2}$ cans of tomatoes

Weight, oz (mid-point of cell)	Frequency	Total weight	Squared weight	Sum of squares for cell
X	f	fX	X^2	fX^2
25.5	1	25.5	650.25	650.25
25.0	2	50.0	625.00	1,250.00
24.5	6	147.0	600.25	3,601.50
24.0	9	216.0	576.00	5,184.00
23.5	14	329.0	552.25	7,731.50
23.0	14	322.0	529.00	7,406.00
22.5	31	697.5	506.25	15,693.75
22.0	34	748.0	484.00	16,456.00
21.5	33	709.5	462.25	15,254.25
21.0	41	861.0	441.00	18,081.00
20.5	26	533.0	420.25	10,926.50
20.0	24	480.0	400.00	9,600.00
19.5	12	234.0	380.25	4,563.00
19.0	7	133.0	361.00	2,527.00
18.5	2	37.0	342.25	684.50
18.0	0	0.0	324.00	0.00
17.5	2	35.0	306.25	612.50
17.0	0	0.0	289.00	0.00
16.5	1	16.5	272.25	272.25
16.0	0	0.0	256.00	0.00
15.5	1	15.5	240.25	240.25
Totals.....	260	5,589.5	......	120,734.25

$$\bar{X} = \frac{\Sigma fX}{n} = \frac{5,589.5}{260} = 21.498 \text{ oz.}$$

$$\sigma = \sqrt{\frac{\Sigma fX^2}{n} - \bar{X}^2} = \sqrt{\frac{120,734.25}{260} - (21.498)^2}$$
$$= \sqrt{464.36 - 462.16} = \sqrt{2.20} = 1.48 \text{ oz.}$$

simplification is a change of units; one cell is equal to one unit throughout the calculations. At the end of the calculation in cell units from the assumed origin, the results for average and RMS deviation are converted into units of the original measurements by multiplying by the value of one cell unit. The average is then converted to its original origin by adding the value of the assumed zero point. This is illustrated in Table 2-5.

A further shortcut, which may be used when a rapid calculation is more important than accuracy, may be obtained by grouping the frequencies into larger cells. This could be accomplished by using the grouping of Table 2-2b which has 1 oz rather than 0.5 oz as the cell interval.

Table 2-5 Computation of average and RMS deviation of frequency distribution—short method

Data of Tables 2-1 and 2-2a on drained weights of contents of size No. $2\frac{1}{2}$ cans of tomatoes

Weight, oz, mid-point of cell	Frequency	Deviation in cells from assumed origin		
X	f	d	fd	fd²
25.5	1	9	9	81
25.0	2	8	16	128
24.5	6	7	42	294
24.0	9	6	54	324
23.5	14	5	70	350
23.0	14	4	56	224
22.5	31	3	93	279
22.0	34	2	68	136
21.5	33	1	33	33
21.0	41	0	0	0
20.5	26	− 1	−26	26
20.0	24	− 2	−48	96
19.5	12	− 3	−36	108
19.0	7	− 4	−28	112
18.5	2	− 5	−10	50
18.0	0	− 6	0	0
17.5	2	− 7	−14	98
17.0	0	− 8	0	0
16.5	1	− 9	− 9	81
16.0	0	−10	0	0
15.5	1	−11	−11	121
Totals.....	260		259	2,541

$$\bar{X} \text{ (in cells from assumed origin of 21.0)} = \frac{\Sigma fd}{n} = \frac{259}{260} = 0.996$$

$$\bar{X} \text{ (in original units from true origin)} = \text{Assumed origin} + \frac{\Sigma fd}{n} \text{ (cell interval)}$$

$$= 21.0 + 0.996(0.5) = 21.498 \text{ oz.}$$

$$\sigma \text{ (in cell unit)} = \sqrt{\frac{\Sigma fd^2}{n} - \left(\frac{\Sigma fd}{n}\right)^2} = \sqrt{\frac{2,541}{260} - (0.996)^2}$$

$$= \sqrt{9.773 - 0.992} = \sqrt{8.781} = 2.96$$

$$\sigma \text{ (in original units)} = (\sigma \text{ in cell units)(cell interval)} = 2.96(0.5) = 1.48 \text{ oz.}$$

In all calculations from grouped data, the assumption is made that the true values of the variable are concentrated at the center of the cell in which they fall.†
In the coarse grouping of Table 2-2b, this assumption does not agree with the known facts. For example, in the cell with the mid-point 21.25 it is known that there are 41 occurrences in the lower half of the cell and only 33 in the upper half. In most cases some error will be introduced whenever a coarser grouping is used to shorten computations. In general, it is desirable that the least count of the measuring instrument be such as to permit grouping the data into at least 20 cells.

Inferences About Pattern of Variation to be Drawn from Average and RMS Deviation

It clearly would be advantageous if substantially all the information contained in a frequency distribution could be packed into two figures, such as a measure of central tendency and a measure of the spread or dispersion. Under favorable circumstances it is possible to come close enough to this ideal for many purposes. A practical problem is to judge whether the circumstances are favorable.

Mathematical statisticians have discovered that the best measure of central tendency for this purpose is the *arithmetic mean* (referred to in this book as the *average*). A useful measure of dispersion for this purpose is the *standard deviation*.

The ideal would be to be able to say, given any average and standard deviation, just what proportion of the measurements fell within any specified limits. For example, if $\bar{X}$ were 21.60 mm for some dimension of a manufactured part and σ were 0.05 mm, it would then be possible to tell what proportion of the parts fell between the limits $\bar{X} \pm 2\sigma$, that is, between 21.50 and 21.70 mm. Or it would be possible to tell the proportion that fell between $\bar{X} - 4\sigma$ and $\bar{X} - 2\sigma$, that is, between 21.40 and 21.50 mm, or between any other desired limits. If this could be done, one could completely reconstruct a frequency distribution provided one knew only two figures, its average and its standard deviation.

For this to be possible, the equation of a frequency curve that described the pattern of variation of the particular quality characteristic would need to be fully defined once the average and standard deviation were known. These two numbers are, in fact, sufficient to define the so-called *normal curve*. Many observed frequency distributions of measured qualities of manufactured product, and many other frequency distributions found in nature, do correspond roughly to this normal curve.

---

† By making certain assumptions about the distribution of cases within cells, mathematicians have developed formulas for corrections to be applied to calculations of σ from grouped data. These corrections, known as *Sheppard's corrections*, are explained in most works on mathematical statistics. However, experience with statistics of qualities of manufactured product indicates difficulty in judging whether the assumptions behind these corrections are valid in any particular case; their use sometimes introduces rather than corrects an error. For a pertinent discussion of this point, see W. A. SHEWHART, "Economic Control of Quality of Manufactured Product," pp. 78–79, Van Nostrand Reinhold, Co., Litton Educational Publishing, Inc., Princeton, N.J., 1931. For reasons pointed out by Shewhart, it seems unnecessary to use Sheppard's corrections in most problems in industrial quality control.

The Normal Curve

Figure 2-2a showed a graphical representation of a frequency distribution by means of a frequency histogram. The area contained in each column of the histogram is proportional to the frequency within its cell. If there were enough observed numbers in the frequency distribution, the number of cells might be increased more and more and the width of a cell made smaller and smaller.† The series of steps that constitutes the top of the histogram would then approach a smooth curve. The height of the curve at any point would be proportional to the frequency at that point, and the area under it between any two limits would be proportional to the frequency of occurrence within those limits. Such a curve is called a *frequency curve*.

One can imagine frequency curves of many different shapes. Mathematicians have developed equations that exactly define many common types. The most useful of these curves is the *normal curve*. This curve is variously called the normal law, the normal curve of error, the probability curve, the gaussian curve, the laplacian curve, and the normal distribution curve. Its bell-shaped symmetrical form is illustrated in Fig. 2-9a. Although most of the area under it is included within the limits $\bar{X} \pm 3\sigma$, the curve extends from $-\infty$ (minus infinity) to $+\infty$ (plus infinity). The curve is fully defined by $\bar{X}$ and σ.

The most commonly quoted limits in connection with the normal curve are as follows:

Limits	Per cent of total area within specified limits
$\bar{X} \pm 0.6745\sigma$	50.00
$\bar{X} \pm \sigma$	68.26
$\bar{X} \pm 2\sigma$	95.46
$\bar{X} \pm 3\sigma$	99.73

This means that in those distributions which roughly approximate the normal curve, about two-thirds of the occurrences fall within one standard deviation on either side of the average, all but about 5% within two standard deviations, and practically all fall within three standard deviations.

Table *A*, App. 3, gives to four decimal places the proportion of the total area under the normal curve that occurs between $-\infty$ and any chosen point expressed in terms of multiples of σ on either side of $\bar{X}$. It can be used to find the area between any two chosen points. For example, the area between $\bar{X} + 2.00\sigma$ and $\bar{X} - 1.75\sigma$ is found as follows:

$$\text{Table } A \text{ reading for } +2.00 = 0.9773$$
$$\text{Table } A \text{ reading for } -1.75 = 0.0401$$
$$\text{Area enclosed} = \overline{0.9372}$$

---

† See Fig. 2-6 for an example of a histogram with 61 cells.

Suppose it is desired to check the sum of the frequencies in the cells from 19.5 to 23.0, inclusive, in Table 2-2a with the frequencies expected for the same region from a normal curve having the same $\bar{X}$ and σ. The upper limit of this group of cells is 23.25 (the upper limit of the cell with the mid-point 23.0) and the lower limit is 19.25. These points must be expressed in terms of multiples of σ from $\bar{X}$.

$\sigma = 1.48$ oz.

$$\text{Upper limit} = 23.25 - \bar{X} = 23.25 - 21.50 = 1.75 \text{ oz.} = \frac{1.75}{1.48}\sigma = 1.18\sigma$$

$$\text{Lower limit} = 19.25 - \bar{X} = 19.25 - 21.50 = -2.25 \text{ oz.} = \frac{-2.25}{1.48}\sigma = -1.52\sigma$$

$$\text{Table } A \text{ reading for } +1.18 = 0.8810$$
$$\text{Table } A \text{ reading for } -1.52 = 0.0643$$
$$\text{Area enclosed} = \overline{0.8167}$$

The total frequency in Table 2-2a is 260: this multiplied by the figure of 0.8167 above gives a frequency of 212 cases (i.e., occurrences of the variable) to be expected in cells 19.5 to 23.0 if the distribution were normal. This compares with an actual frequency of

$$14 + 31 + 34 + 33 + 41 + 26 + 24 + 12 = 215$$

cases observed in these cells.

Sampling Statistics and Universe Parameters

Many of the useful actions that may be taken in manufacturing are related to future production rather than completed lots of items. The knowledge that must be gained from the sampling procedure is knowledge of the pattern of variation of the production process from which the sample was drawn.

Statisticians use particular words and phrases to define the unknown pattern of variation from which the known sample has been drawn. It is frequently called the *universe*, *parent distribution*, or *population*. Some of the more recent texts in mathematical statistics refer to it as the *sample space* or *description space*. The true, but unknown, numerical values that describe the universe are called parameters.

In order to draw conclusions about an unknown universe, it is necessary to rely on numerical values derived from samples drawn from that universe. Such numerical values, which include the sample mean, median, RMS or standard deviation, range, variance, and so forth, summarize the information contained in the sample data. Each is referred to as a *statistic* of the sample and may be used to estimate the corresponding *parameter* of the unknown universe.

Use of Prime Notation to Designate a Parameter of a Universe

In the development of the techniques of statistical quality control in the Bell Telephone Laboratories in the 1920s and 1930s, the prime (′) symbol was adopted to identify a parameter of a universe. Thus the symbols $\bar{X}'$ (read "X bar prime") and σ' (read "sigma prime") identify the parametric values of arithmetic mean and standard deviation, respectively, for a given universe.

While statistics literature in general has adopted no uniform standard for notation, the use of the prime notation has been widely adopted in quality control literature and is used in control chart standards of the American National Standards Institute, American Society for Quality Control, and American Society for Testing and Materials.†

While the prime notation may be applied to a known parameter of a universe, as in a bowl drawing experiment where the distribution is known or when analyzing data from all items in a lot, it is more commonly used to indicate a parameter estimated from one or more samples drawn from an unknown universe. Thus $\bar{X}$, the average of a sample of size n, may be used to estimate the parametric mean $\bar{X}'$; and, as will be seen later in this chapter, an estimate of σ', the parametric value of the standard deviation, may be obtained from R or σ.

In some quality control literature, the prime notation is also used to designate an aimed-at or "standard" value adopted to serve as a norm for computing control limits. It is both preferred and recommended, however, that a subscript "0" be added for clarity. Thus an aimed-at value for $\bar{X}'$ should be designated as $\bar{X}'_0$.

Using Samples to Make Estimates About a Universe

Assume that measurements are made on some variable and it is proposed to base some actions on these measurements. In considering the merits of various proposals for action, it usually is helpful to think of the measurements as one or more samples taken from a universe (or perhaps from several universes). If the variable is some quality characteristic of a manufactured product (such as a dimension, weight, or electrical resistance), the universe may be thought of as the potentially unlimited output of the manufacturing process in question. Or, in some instances, the universe may be viewed as a particular lot of manufactured articles from which one or more samples have been taken.

---

† "Guide for Quality Control and Control Chart Method of Analyzing Data, ANSI Standards Z1.1-1975 and Z1.2-1975," American National Standards Institute, New York, 1975.

"Control Chart Method for Controlling Quality During Production, ANSI Standard Z1.3-1975," American National Standards Institute, New York, 1975.

"Definitions, Symbols, Formulas, and Tables for Control Charts, ANSI Standard Z1.5-1971," American National Standards Institute, New York, 1971.

"ASTM Manual on Presentation of Data and Control Chart Analysis," Special Technical Report 15D, American Society for Testing and Materials, Philadelphia, 1976.

It is appropriate to consider the following types of questions before making decisions about proposals for action:

1. Does it appear that we have only one universe? Or, more realistically, is it good enough for practical purposes to take action as if we had a single universe?
2. If the answer to the first question is "Yes," how much do we know about the universe? More specifically what do we know about its centering and dispersion? What are our best estimates of its parameters $\bar{X}'$ and σ', and how satisfactory are these estimates as a basis for action?

Use of Bowl Drawing to Illustrate the Relationship Between a Known Universe and a Series of Samples Under a Constant-cause System

In actual situations, the foregoing questions are relevant because the universes are unknown. However, a good way to obtain a feeling for the rational basis underlying the procedures and formulas used in answering such questions is to conduct an experiment using a known universe.

For example, a number is written on each of a group of physically similar chips. The chips are placed in a bowl, mixed thoroughly, and one chip drawn at random. The number written on this chip is recorded, and the chip replaced in the bowl. The chips are mixed again, and a chip is again drawn and the number is recorded. By repeating this process enough times, a series of numbers may be obtained which, if the chips are stirred well enough between drawings, will have been obtained in a chance or random manner. By examining the behavior of this variable that seems to be influenced only by a constant system of chance causes, it is possible to understand the way in which all constant-cause systems operate.

This type of demonstration is frequently made in courses in statistical quality control. If the chips are all alike, so that each one has as good a chance as any other to be drawn, it is possible to illustrate the meaning of many of the formulas used in control-chart work. These formulas, developed by mathematical statisticians, deal with the relationship between a universe and samples taken from it.

It is appropriate that bowl drawings should be part of explanations of how to use the control chart, as Shewhart used them in the early stages of his work on the applications of statistical methods in manufacturing. In his original treatise on the subject, he gives the data from 4,000 drawings of chips from each of three bowls, one containing a normal universe, one a rectangular universe, and one a triangular universe. The following discussion makes use of the first 400 drawings from Shewhart's normal bowl. (His rectangular and triangular universes are discussed and the results of his drawings from them are briefly summarized later in this chapter.)

Contents of Shewhart's Normal Bowl

Table 2-6 gives the distribution of the markings on the 998 chips in this bowl. Figure 2-6a shows the histogram for this frequency distribution. Figure 2-6b

Table 2-6 Marking on chips in Shewhart's normal bowl†

Marking on chip X	Number of chips	Marking on chip X	Number of chips	Marking on chip X	Number of chips
60	1	39	27	19	22
59	1	38	29	18	19
58	1	37	31	17	17
57	1	36	33	16	15
56	1	35	35	15	13
55	2	34	37	14	11
54	2	33	38	13	9
53	3	32	39	12	8
52	4	31	40	11	7
51	4	30	40	10	5
50	5	29	40	9	4
49	7	28	39	8	4
48	8	27	38	7	3
47	9	26	37	6	2
46	11	25	35	5	2
45	13	24	33	4	1
44	15	23	31	3	1
43	17	22	29	2	1
42	19	21	27	1	1
41	22	20	24	0	1
40	24				

† W. A. SHEWHART, "Economic Control of Quality of Manufactured Product," Appendix II, Tables *A*, *B*, and *C*, Van Nostrand Reinhold Co., Princeton, N.J., 1931. These bowl drawings from Table *A* are used here by permission of the author and publishers. Shewhart's normal bowl contained numbers from −3.0 to +3.0. Numbers from 0 to 60 have been substituted here, to simplify the presentation by elimination of negative numbers and decimals.

shows a more conventional histogram for the same distribution with a coarse grouping into 13 cells rather than 61; it illustrates the effect of coarse grouping on the histogram of a normal distribution.

The average of this symmetrical distribution obviously is 30. The standard deviation may be calculated to be 9.954, or, in round numbers, 10.

In referring to the distribution in this bowl as a normal distribution, we are taking some slight liberties with the normal curve. A true normal curve is continuous, whereas this or any other bowl distribution is discontinuous (or, in the language of statistics, *discrete*). A distribution is discontinuous or discrete if there are intermediate values of the variable that cannot occur. (For example, a chip marked 31 or 32 may be drawn from the bowl but not one marked 31.94279651.)

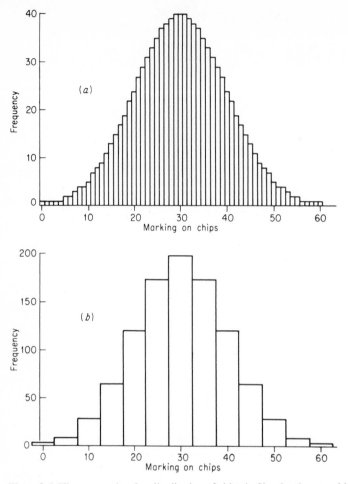

Figure 2-6 Histograms showing distribution of chips in Shewhart's normal bowl.

Moreover, the normal curve extends from $-\infty$ to $+\infty$ even though the percentage of area under the curve outside the 3-sigma limits is very small; a bowl would require several million chips to describe accurately the normal curve out to, say, 5-sigma limits. What can be said about the distribution in Shewhart's normal bowl is that it is as close to a normal distribution as it is possible to get with 998 chips, and that its departure from normality is of no practical significance from the standpoint of the uses to be made of the bowl drawings.

Drawings from Shewhart's Normal Bowl

Table 2-7 gives the results of 400 drawings from Shewhart's bowl of 998 chips. Each time a chip was drawn, it was replaced and the chips stirred before the next drawing. For purposes of analysis, the drawings are shown in subgroups of four.

Table 2-7 400 Drawings from Shewhart's normal bowl arranged into subgroups of four

Numbers of draw-ings	Markings on chips in subgroup				Average $\bar{X}$	Range R	RMS devi-ation σ
1–4	47	32	44	35	39.50	15	6.2
5–8	33	33	34	34	33.50	1	0.5
9–12	34	34	31	34	33.25	3	1.3
13–16	12	21	24	47	26.00	35	12.9
17–20	35	23	38	40	34.00	17	6.6
21–24	19	37	31	27	28.50	18	6.5
25–28	23	45	26	37	32.75	22	8.8
29–32	33	12	29	43	29.25	31	11.2
33–36	25	22	37	33	29.25	15	6.0
37–40	29	32	30	13	26.00	19	7.6
41–44	40	18	30	11	24.75	29	11.1
45–48	21	18	36	34	27.25	18	7.9
49–52	26	35	31	29	30.25	9	3.3
53–56	52	29	21	18	30.00	34	13.3
57–60	26	20	30	20	24.00	10	4.2
61–64	19	1	30	30	20.00	29	11.9
65–68	28	34	39	17	29.50	22	8.2
69–72	29	25	24	30	27.00	6	2.5
73–76	21	37	32	25	28.75	16	6.2
77–80	24	22	16	35	24.25	19	6.9
81–84	28	39	23	21	27.75	18	7.0
85–88	41	32	46	12	32.75	34	13.0
89–92	14	23	41	42	30.00	28	11.9
93–96	32	28	46	27	33.25	19	7.6
97–100	42	34	22	34	33.00	20	7.1
101–104	20	38	27	32	29.25	18	6.6
105–108	30	14	37	43	31.00	29	10.8
109–112	28	29	32	35	31.00	7	2.7
113–116	35	30	37	26	32.00	11	4.3
117–120	51	13	45	55	41.00	42	16.6
121–124	34	19	11	16	20.00	23	8.6
125–128	32	28	41	40	35.25	13	5.4
129–132	14	31	20	35	25.00	21	8.4
133–136	25	44	29	27	31.25	19	7.5
137–140	18	22	20	33	23.25	15	5.8

Table 2-7 400 Drawings from Shewhart's normal bowl arranged into subgroups of four (*Continued*)

Numbers of draw- ings	Markings on chips in subgroup				Average $\bar{X}$	Range R	RMS devi- ation σ
141–144	21	31	39	25	29.00	18	6.8
145–148	17	44	54	13	32.00	41	17.4
149–152	36	48	19	41	36.00	29	10.7
153–156	25	31	38	30	31.00	13	4.6
157–160	35	21	20	34	27.50	15	7.0
161–164	21	22	44	19	26.50	25	10.2
165–168	39	22	24	29	28.50	17	6.6
169–172	40	44	24	18	31.50	26	10.8
173–176	23	25	46	29	30.75	23	9.1
177–180	23	37	44	34	34.50	21	7.6
181–184	36	52	30	28	36.50	24	9.4
185–188	35	23	11	5	18.50	30	11.5
189–192	33	15	40	29	29.25	25	9.1
193–196	18	30	22	25	23.75	12	4.4
197–200	23	30	20	19	23.00	11	4.3
201–204	7	32	36	38	28.25	31	12.5
205–208	29	30	39	31	32.25	10	4.0
209–212	36	12	34	25	26.75	24	9.5
213–216	36	37	39	32	36.00	7	2.5
217–220	38	9	25	39	27.75	30	12.2
221–224	11	44	29	29	28.25	33	11.7
225–228	31	18	31	25	26.25	13	5.4
229–232	22	47	12	27	27.00	35	12.7
233–236	29	24	32	44	32.25	20	7.4
237–240	42	26	32	27	31.75	16	6.3
241–244	29	40	43	29	35.25	14	6.3
245–248	23	22	23	39	26.75	17	7.1
249–252	34	27	52	28	35.25	25	10.0
253–256	27	40	23	24	28.50	17	6.8
257–260	34	38	16	28	29.00	22	8.3
261–264	39	19	39	32	32.25	20	8.2
265–268	42	25	25	42	33.50	17	8.5
269–272	30	25	38	39	33.00	14	5.8
273–276	43	22	10	28	25.75	33	11.9
277–280	17	31	10	16	18.50	21	7.7

Table 2-7 400 Drawings from Shewhart's normal bowl arranged into subgroups of four (*Continued*)

Numbers of draw-ings	Markings on chips in subgroup				Average $\bar{X}$	Range R	RMS devi-ation σ
281–284	40	49	38	37	41.00	12	4.7
285–288	22	39	26	18	26.25	21	7.9
289–292	30	36	34	18	29.50	18	7.0
293–296	41	37	27	32	34.25	14	5.3
297–300	5	20	43	26	23.50	38	13.6
301–304	38	26	38	25	31.75	13	6 3
305–308	27	38	40	33	34.50	13	5.0
309–312	20	23	28	35	26.50	15	5.7
313–316	29	29	34	29	30.25	5	2.2
317–320	25	35	37	42	34.75	17	6.2
321–324	42	59	38	28	41.75	31	11.2
325–328	24	32	22	22	25.00	10	4.1
329–332	38	40	31	52	40.25	21	7.6
333–336	22	52	33	27	33.50	30	11.4
337–340	46	32	20	50	37.00	30	11.9
341–344	27	29	24	15	23.75	14	5.4
345–348	31	26	34	35	31.50	9	3.5
349–352	32	46	30	32	35.00	16	6.4
353–356	35	20	34	46	33.75	26	9.2
357–360	55	25	33	54	41.75	30	13.1
361–364	22	46	52	42	40.50	30	11.3
365–368	14	24	2	43	20.75	41	15.0
369–372	36	52	19	50	39.25	33	13.2
373–376	29	21	17	9	19.00	20	7.2
377–380	33	31	32	18	28.50	15	6.1
381–384	52	34	17	5	27.00	47	17.7
385–388	23	41	21	29	28.50	20	7.8
389–392	28	22	45	21	29.00	24	9.6
393–396	32	27	16	30	26.25	16	6.2
397–400	23	23	27	36	27.25	13	5.3
Totals..					3,007.50	2076	807.8

Table 2-7 gives the average $\bar{X}$, the range R, and the RMS deviation σ for each subgroup.

It is helpful to think of these figures as representing the variation of some quality characteristic of a manufactured product. They might be the last two digits of the measurements of a dimension measured to 0.001 mm. Or they might be the final two digits, showing grams and tenths of grams, of filling weights of a container. Or they might be any other characteristic, such as hardness, tensile strength, electrical resistance, or temperature.

Relationship Between $\bar{X}'$, σ', and the Values of $\bar{X}$

In statistics, the bar above any symbol means an average. Thus $\bar{X}$ is an average of the values of X. In the control chart for variables, each subgroup has its $\bar{X}$. The symbol $\bar{\bar{X}}$ thus refers to an average of the $\bar{X}$ values, i.e., an average of the averages of values of X.

For the 100 subgroups of Table 2-7, $\bar{\bar{X}} = 3{,}007.50/100 = 30.08$. This is very close to 30.00, $\bar{X}'$, the average of the distribution in the bowl. (In fact it is considerably closer to the universe average than would ordinarily be obtained in 400 drawings.) The average of sets of 80 drawings (20 subgroups of 4) may be shown to vary from 28.89 to 31.46. The averages of subgroups of 4 vary from 18.50 to 41.75, and the individual drawings run from 1 to 59.

The more drawings averaged, the more likely it is that their average will be close to the average in the bowl. Or, stated in more general terms, the larger the sample taken from any universe, the more likely it is that the average of the sample will be close to the average of the universe. This would seem to be an acceptable proposition on common-sense grounds even without the support given by statistical theory or by experimental bowl drawings.

Table 2-8 uses an analysis of the 400 drawings from Shewhart's bowl to show how the spread of the averages depends on sample size. These 400 drawings were divided into 200 subgroups of 2, the averages calculated for each subgroup, and a frequency distribution made of the averages. The same was done for subgroups of 4, 8, 16, 40, and 80. To permit easy comparisons of these distributions having different total frequencies, Table 2-8 shows them all expressed in *percentage* of total frequency.

Table 2-8 suggests certain ideas about averages of samples. It is evident that if many random samples of any given size n are taken from a universe, the averages ($\bar{X}$ values) of the samples will themselves form a frequency distribution. This frequency distribution of $\bar{X}$ values is similar to all frequency distributions in having its own central tendency and dispersion or spread, which might be expressed in terms of average and standard deviation. The average $\bar{\bar{X}}$ of such a frequency distribution of $\bar{X}$ values apparently tends to be near $\bar{X}'$, the average of the universe. The spread of this frequency distribution of $\bar{X}$ values seems to depend not only on the spread of the universe but also on the sample size n; the larger the value of n, the less the spread of the $\bar{X}$ values.

Table 2-8 Relative frequencies of $\bar{X}$ values in samples of various sizes from 400 drawings from Shewhart's normal bowl

All frequencies expressed as percentages of total

Cell* boundaries	Distribution in bowl	$\bar{X}$ $n=2$	$\bar{X}$ $n=4$	$\bar{X}$ $n=8$	$\bar{X}$ $n=16$	$\bar{X}$ $n=40$	$\bar{X}$ $n=80$	$\bar{X}$ $n=400$
58.31 – 61.31	0.2							
55.31 – 58.31	0.3							
52.31 – 55.31	0.8							
49.31 – 52.31	1.3	1.0						
46.31 – 49.31	2.4	0.5						
43.31 – 46.31	3.9	2.0						
40.31 – 43.31	5.8	3.5	5					
37.31 – 40.31	8.0	9.0	3	2				
34.31 – 37.31	9.9	11.5	11	8	4			
31.31 – 34.31	11.3	17.0	21	22	32	20	20	
28.31 – 31.31	12.0	18.5	23	34	36	60	80	100
25.31 – 28.31	11.3	12.0	21	26	28	20		
22.31 – 25.31	9.9	11.0	10	4				
19.31 – 22.31	8.0	8.5	3	4				
16.31 – 19.31	5.8	2.0	3					
13.31 – 16.31	3.9	0.5						
10.31 – 13.31	2.4	2.0						
7.31 – 10.31	1.3	1.0						
4.31 – 7.31	0.8							
1.31 – 4.31	0.3							
−1.69 – +1.31	0.2							

* Following the rule that cell boundaries should always be located halfway between two possible values, the cell boundaries for the distribution in the bowl should properly be 58.5 to 61.5, 55.5 to 58.5, etc, rather than 58.31 to 61.31, etc. However, in making frequency distributions of the averages, it was necessary to choose the cells in such a way that no average fell on a cell boundary. In choosing one set of cell boundaries to apply to all the frequency distributions compared in Table 2-8, it was necessary to violate the rule stated.

Statistical theory gives us some very definite information about these matters. It tells us that in the long run the average of the $\bar{X}$ values will be the same as $\bar{X}'$, the average of the universe. And in the long run, the standard deviation of the frequency distribution of $\bar{X}$ values will be $\sigma'/\sqrt{n}$, i.e., the standard deviation of the universe divided by the square root of the sample size. Thus if $n = 4$, the standard deviation of the frequency distribution of the $\bar{X}$ values will tend to be only half as great as the standard deviation of the universe. If $n = 16$, the spread of the frequency distribution of the $\bar{X}$ values will be one-fourth as great as that of the universe. If $n = 400$, it will be one-twentieth as great. A picture of how this works in a sampling experiment may be obtained by comparing the distributions of $\bar{X}$ values given in Table 2-8 with the distribution in the bowl.

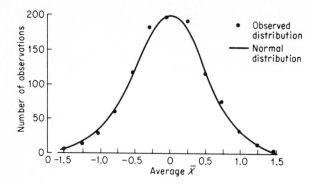

Figure 2-7 The distribution of $\bar{X}$ values from 1,000 samples of four from Shewhart's normal bowl was a very close fit to the normal curve. (*Reproduced by permission from "Economic Control of Quality of Manufactured Product" by W. A. Shewhart, 1931, Van Nostrand Reinhold Co., Litton Educational Publishing, Inc.*)

This standard deviation of the expected frequency distribution of the averages is represented by the symbol $\sigma_{\bar{x}}$. It is referred to in textbooks on statistics as the *standard error of the mean*, or standard error of the average.

Regardless of the form of the universe, whether normal or otherwise, it is true that the expected $\sigma_{\bar{x}} = \sigma'/\sqrt{n}$ and that the expected $\bar{X} = \bar{X}'$. If the universe is normal, statistical theory tells us that the expected frequency distribution of the $\bar{X}$ values will also be normal. This is reinforced by experimental evidence from bowl drawings. Figure 2-7, taken from Shewhart's book,† shows the observed frequencies of averages of 1,000 samples of four from his normal bowl and indicates the excellent fit of this distribution to the normal curve.

As previously stated, any distribution is completely specified if it is known to be normal and its average and standard deviation are known. This means that in sampling from a normal distribution that has a known average and standard deviation, statistical theory gives a complete picture of the expected pattern of variation of the averages of samples of any given size.

Importance of the Normal Curve in Sampling Theory

Even though the distribution in the universe is not normal, the distribution of the $\bar{X}$ values tends to be close to normal. The larger the sample size and the more nearly normal the universe, the closer will the frequency distribution of averages approach the normal curve.

However, even if n is as small as 4 and the universe is far from normal, the distribution of the averages of samples will be very close to normal. Shewhart illustrates this by showing the distributions of averages of 1,000 samples of four from each of two bowls of chips, one containing a rectangular and the other a triangular distribution. Figure 2-8, taken from Shewhart,‡ compares these universes, neither of which even faintly resembles the normal curve, with the close fit of the normal curve to the distribution of averages of samples of four.

---

† Reproduced from SHEWHART, *op. cit.*, p. 181, by permission of the copyright holder.

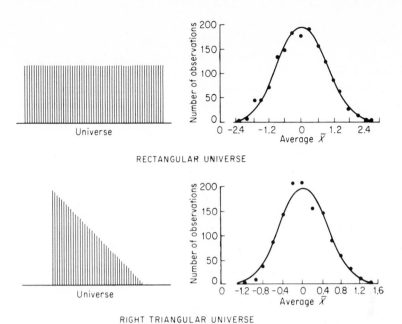

Figure 2-8 Even from rectangular and triangular universes, the distribution of $\bar{X}$ values from samples of four is approximately normal. *(Reproduced by permission from "Economic Control of Quality of Manufactured Product" by W. A. Shewhart, 1931, Van Nostrand Reinhold Co., Litton Educational Publishing, Inc.)*

It has already been stated that many observed distributions of industrial characteristics do correspond roughly to the normal curve. Nevertheless, many others do not. Serious mistakes are often made when it is assumed that the distribution of an industrial quality characteristic is necessarily normal.

---

‡ Reproduced from *ibid.*, p. 182, by permission of the copyright holder. The rectangular universe contained 122 chips, with two chips marked -3.0, two marked -2.9, two marked -2.8, and so on to two marked $+3.0$. The triangular universe contained 820 chips with 40 chips marked -1.3, 39 chips marked -1.2, 38 marked -1.1, and so on to one chip marked $+2.6$.

The main point to be noted here from Fig. 2-8 is that even with a great departure from normality in the universe, the distribution of $\bar{X}$ values with $n = 4$ is approximately normal; in sampling from most distributions found in nature and industry, the distribution of $\bar{X}$ values will be even closer to normal. However, it is of interest to observe that distributions similar to the rectangular and triangular distributions sometimes are found in industry. Although they seldom occur as a result of production alone, they may be found as a result of production followed by 100% inspection. For example, if a production operation gives a distribution on a certain dimension which is roughly normal with a standard deviation of 0.001 and the specified tolerances on the dimension are ± 0.001 cm, it is obvious that only about 68% of the product will meet the specifications. If the production operation accurately centers the dimension at its specified nominal value, about 16% of the product will be rejected by the go gage and another 16% by the not-go gage. The distribution of the accepted product will not be far from rectangular. There will be two distributions something like the triangular, one of the product rejected by the go gage, the other of the product rejected by the not-go gage.

The great practical importance of the normal curve arises even more from its uses in sampling theory than from the fact that some observed distributions are described by it well enough for practical purposes. Of great practical significance is the fact that distributions of averages of samples tend to be approximately normal even though the samples are drawn from nonnormal universes. This very important result of the theory of probability is discussed in greater detail in Chap. 6.

Relationship between σ' and $\bar{\sigma}$

In Table 2-7, the σ of each subgroup was computed by the method explained. The σ values are similar to the $\bar{X}$ values in that they differ greatly from one subgroup to the next; the smallest σ observed was 0.5 and the largest was 17.7. However, one difference between the $\bar{X}$ and σ distributions is evident. Whereas the $\bar{X}$ values tend to be centered at 30, the universe average, the σ values seem to be centered at a considerably lower figure than the universe standard deviation of 9.954.

In the long run, the RMS deviations of samples of any size from a normal universe will follow a chance pattern that can be predicted by mathematics. Statistical theory also predicts the ratio between $\bar{\sigma}$, the average of the RMS deviations of samples of any given size (such as the subgroups of four), and σ', the standard deviation of the universe from which the samples are taken. This ratio, represented by the symbol c_2,† is given in Table B of App. 3.

The value of c_2 for samples of four is 0.7979. This factor may be used to estimate an unknown universe standard deviation σ' from $\bar{\sigma}$, the average observed RMS deviation of any given set of subgroups. From the 100 subgroups of Table 2-7, $\bar{\sigma} = 807.8/100 = 8.078$. This gives an estimate of σ' as

$$\frac{\bar{\sigma}}{c_2} = \frac{8.078}{0.7979} = 10.12$$

Because, in this case, the frequency distribution in the bowl is known, it is possible to compare this estimated σ' of 10.12 with the known σ' of 9.954. The error in estimate is a little less than 2%.

It is of interest to observe that, even with the use of this c_2 factor, the σ of an individual small subgroup gives no reliable information about σ'. For instance, the estimate of σ' from the first subgroup (drawings 1–4) is 6.2/0.7979 = 7.8; from the second subgroup, it is 0.5/0.7979 = 0.6; from the third it is 1.3/0.7979 = 1.6; from the fourth it is 12.9/0.7979 = 16.2, etc.

---

† Insofar as possible, the symbols used in this book are those generally used in statistical quality control work in the United States. Unfortunately, the lowercase form of the letter c is commonly used with three different meanings. c_2 is used for the ratio of $\bar{\sigma}$ to σ'; c is used to represent number of defects in the control chart for nonconformities per unit; c, c_1, and c_2 are used to indicate acceptance numbers in the Dodge-Romig single and double sampling tables described in Chap. 13. The first two uses have the authority of the American National Standards Institute and the American Society for Quality Control; the third is common in the literature and usage of sampling tables. As the possible confusion arising from departure from standard usage seems more serious than the confusion from the use of the same symbol in different ways, c is used in all three senses in this book. The three uses relate to such different situations that the context should always make clear which meaning of c is intended.

If the 100 subgroups are divided into 5 sets of 20 subgroups each, the resulting estimates of σ' are as follows:

Set of subgroups	$\bar{\sigma}$	Estimate of σ'
1–20 (drawings 1–80).........	7.155	8.97
21–40 (drawings 81–160)........	8.49	10.64
41–60 (drawings 161–240)........	8.36	10.48
61–80 (drawings 241–320)........	7.225	9.06
81–100 (drawings 321–400)........	9.16	11.48

Whereas some of the estimates from individual subgroups missed the true σ' by as much as 100%, none of the estimates from the sets of 20 subgroups missed it by more than 16%. The use of all 100 subgroups gave an estimate within 2%. It seems evident that the larger the number of subgroups included in the calculation of $\bar{\sigma}$, the greater should be the confidence in the estimate from $\bar{\sigma}$ of the unknown standard deviation of the universe.

Relationship between σ' and $\bar{R}$

Given n, the sample or subgroup size, statistical theory gives the expected ratio between $\bar{\sigma}$ and σ' in random sampling from a normal universe. Similarly, it gives the expected ratio between the average range $\bar{R}$ and σ'. This latter ratio, designated as d_2, is also given in Table B, App. 3.

One practical use of this d_2 factor is to provide an alternative method of estimating an unknown universe standard deviation σ' from a series of samples or subgroups. It is of interest to compare the estimates of σ' obtained from $\bar{R}$ with those obtained from $\bar{\sigma}$ in the bowl drawings of Table 2-7.

For the 100 subgroups of four, $\bar{R} = 2076/100 = 20.76$. The d_2 factor given for $n = 4$ in Table B is 2.059. Hence the estimate of σ' from $\bar{R}$ is

$$\frac{\bar{R}}{d_2} = \frac{20.76}{2.059} = 10.08$$

If the 100 subgroups are divided into five sets of 20 as was done in the estimates from $\bar{\sigma}$, the estimates of σ' are as follows:

Set of subgroups	$\bar{R}$	Estimate of σ'
1–20 (drawings 1–80).........	18.40	8.94
21–40 (drawings 81–160)........	21.65	10.51
41–60 (drawings 161–240)........	21.65	10.51
61–80 (drawings 241–320)........	18.30	8.89
81–100 (drawings 321–400)........	23.80	11.56

With ranges distributed all the way from 1 to 47, it is evident that estimates of σ' made from a single range could vary all the way from 0.5 to 22.8. The comments regarding the unreliability of estimates of σ' from the σ of a single small sample apply with even greater force to estimates of σ' from a single value of R. The range of one small subgroup gives little information about the standard deviation of the universe.

A comparison of the two estimates of σ' from each set of 20 subgroups shows a close agreement between the estimate based on $\bar{\sigma}$ and the one based on $\bar{R}$.

	Estimate of σ' from $\bar{\sigma}$	Estimate of σ' from $\bar{R}$
First set.............	8.97	8.94
Second set...........	10.64	10.51
Third set............	10.48	10.51
Fourth set...... ...	9.06	8.89
Fifth set............	11.48	11.56

In only one of the five cases is the difference between the two estimates as great as 1% of σ'. In four of the five cases, the estimate of σ' from $\bar{\sigma}$ is a little closer to the true value of σ' (9.954) than is the estimate from $\bar{R}$. On the other hand, the estimate from the $\bar{R}$ of the 100 subgroups, 10.08, happens to be a little closer to the true value than the estimate, 10.12, from the $\bar{\sigma}$ of 100 subgroups. In all cases the differences seem negligible for practical purposes.

A practical point is that it often is much easier† to compute R for a subgroup by making a single subtraction than it is to compute σ by calculating several squares and a square root. In control-chart work, this ease of calculation of R is usually much more important than any slight theoretical advantage that might come from the use of σ as a measure of dispersion of subgroups. However, in some cases where the measurements themselves are costly (for example, destructive tests of valuable items) and it is necessary that the inferences from a limited number of tests be as reliable as possible, the extra cost of calculating RMS deviations of subgroups may be justified.

Other Frequency Curves

The normal curve is useful in many ways in solving practical problems in industry. Some of these ways will be developed in succeeding chapters. Its general pattern, with a concentration of frequencies about a mid-point and with small numbers of

† The statement that it is easier to compute R than σ for a subgroup calls for two reservations. In this statement, "easier" means that the arithmetic is less laborious; hence, less time consuming and less costly. It does not mean that there is any less likelihood of mathematical error in computing R than in computing σ. To compute R, the largest and smallest numbers in a subgroup must first be identified. Whenever an error is made in picking either the largest or the smallest number, the calculated value of R is less than the correct value. Such errors are common in the rapid calculations made for control-chart purposes in industrial plants. As there is no reason for compensating errors making R greater than its true value, computed values of $\bar{R}$ are frequently in error on the low side.

A second reservation is brought about by recent technological developments in desk and pocket calculators. Some of these provide for the automatic calculation of $\bar{X}$ and σ simply by the input of the individual readings. Still others can be programmed by the user to perform these calculations. It is basically easier for such machines to calculate σ for a subgroup than it is for them to calculate R.

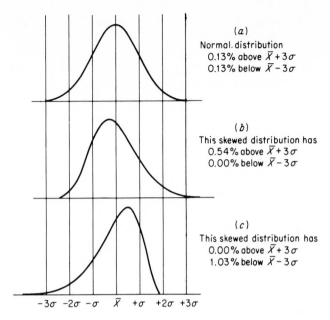

(a)
Normal. distribution
0.13% above $\bar{X} + 3\sigma$
0.13% below $\bar{X} - 3\sigma$

(b)
This skewed distribution has
0.54% above $\bar{X} + 3\sigma$
0.00% below $\bar{X} - 3\sigma$

(c)
This skewed distribution has
0.00% above $\bar{X} + 3\sigma$
1.03% below $\bar{X} - 3\sigma$

-3σ -2σ $-\sigma$ $\bar{X}$ $+\sigma$ $+2\sigma$ $+3\sigma$

Figure 2-9 Normal frequency curve (a), and typical skewed frequency curves (b) and (c).

occurrences at the extreme values, repeats itself again and again. Nevertheless, the normal curve is frequently misused; it is not safe to assume that unknown distributions are necessarily normal.

There are many other frequency patterns which are like the normal in that frequencies decrease continuously from the center to the extreme values but— unlike the normal—are not symmetrical. Extreme values occur more frequently in one direction from the center than in the other. Two such distributions are illustrated in Fig. 2-9b and 2-9c. In the technical language of statistics, these lopsided frequency curves are known as *skewed* curves. Figure 2-9b is skewed to the right; i.e., extreme variations occur more frequently above the mode than below it. Figure 2-9c is skewed to the left. The distribution of weights shown in the graphs of Fig. 2-2 also appears to be somewhat skewed to the left.

What the Average and RMS Deviation of a Set of Numbers Really Tell

It has been pointed out that it would be convenient if the combination of average and RMS deviation could tell us just what proportion of a set of numbers fell within any specified limits. It has also been pointed out that this combination does supply such information in those cases where it is known that the numbers are distributed according to the normal curve.

What do $\bar{X}$ and σ tell if nothing whatever is known about the pattern of variation? One answer to this question is given by *Tchebycheff's inequality*. This mathematical theorem states that more than $1 - (1/t^2)$ of *any* set of finite numbers must fall within the closed range $\bar{X} \pm t\sigma$ (where t is not less than 1). For example, if $t = 3$, this means that more than $1 - (1/3^2)$ or $\frac{8}{9}$ of any set of numbers must fall within the limits $\bar{X} \pm 3\sigma$, where $\bar{X}$ and σ have been computed from the numbers themselves. In other words, less than $\frac{1}{9}$ of the numbers can fall outside these limits. The actual fraction falling outside of $\bar{X} \pm 3\sigma$ may be much less than $\frac{1}{9}$; the Tchebycheff inequality simply states that it cannot be as much as $\frac{1}{9}$. It should be emphasized that this limit of $\frac{1}{9}$ applies to the *sum* of the fractions above an upper limit of $\bar{X} + 3\sigma$ and below a lower limit of $\bar{X} - 3\sigma$.

Usually it is desired to have $\bar{X}$ and σ tell more about a distribution than can be determined from Tchebycheff's inequality. An adaptation of the inequality by Camp and Meidell states that under certain circumstances more than $1 - (1/2.25t^2)$ of any distribution will fall within the closed range $\bar{X} \pm t\sigma$. These circumstances are that the distribution must have only one mode, that the mode must be the same as the arithmetic mean, and that the frequencies must decline continuously on both sides of the mode. Many distributions that are not normal do actually come close enough to meeting these conditions for the Camp-Meidell inequality to be applied with confidence.

The percentages indicated by the normal curve and by the two inequalities are compared as follows:

Limits	If the distribution is roughly normal, *approximately* the following percentages of cases will be *outside* the limits	If the Camp-Meidell conditions apply, *less than* the following percentages of cases will be *outside* the limits	Under any and all circumstances *less than* the following percentages of cases will be *outside* the limits
$\bar{X} \pm 2\sigma$	4.55	11.1	25.0
$\bar{X} \pm 2.5\sigma$	1.24	7.1	16.0
$\bar{X} \pm 3\sigma$	0.27	4.9	11.1
$\bar{X} \pm 3.5\sigma$	0.05	3.6	8.2
$\bar{X} \pm 4\sigma$	0.006	2.8	6.3
$\bar{X} \pm 4.5\sigma$	0.0007	2.2	4.9
$\bar{X} \pm 5\sigma$	0.00006	1.8	4.0

The rules summarized in the foregoing tabulation are given in most books on statistics. It sometimes happens that the readers of such books misinterpret these rules as pertaining to the relationship between the statistics obtained from samples and the parameters of the universes from which the samples are drawn. It should be emphasized that the rules apply merely to any set of numbers, whether the numbers are viewed as constituting a sample or a universe. For example, Tchebycheff's inequality tells us that it is impossible to construct any set of numbers in which 4.0% or more of the numbers are more than five RMS deviations away from the arithmetic mean. Both arithmetic mean and RMS deviation must be calculated from the numbers themselves, using the definitions of mean and RMS deviation we have given in formulas (1) and (3). The user of Tchebycheff's inequality should note that, when $\bar{X}$ and σ are calculated from a sample, then the inequality applies to the distribution of the sample. When known population parameters $\bar{X}'$ and σ' are used, the inequality applies to the universe.

PROBLEMS

2-1 In the production of an electrical device operated by a thermostatic control, five control switches were tested each hour to determine the "on" temperature at which the thermostat actually operated under a given setting. Results of the test over a 4-day production period were as follows:

| Date | Subgroup number | "On" temperature at which thermostatic switch operates (temperature units not specified) | | | | |
		a	b	c	d	e
Apr. 25	1	54	56	56	56	55
	2	51	52	54	56	49
	3	54	52	50	57	55
	4	56	55	56	53	50
	5	53	54	57	56	52
	6	53	47	58	55	54
	7	52	55	54	55	56
	8	56	53	53	54	55
	9	55	52	53	56	55
	10	50	54	53	55	55
Apr. 26	11	57	54	53	52	53
	12	52	52	54	53	55
	13	54	53	55	52	52
	14	54	55	54	53	55
	15	56	53	57	56	54
Apr. 27	16	58	57	56	54	54
	17	55	55	55	56	53
	18	54	57	54	55	54
	19	54	53	56	53	55
	20	53	53	57	54	53
	21	53	55	57	56	55
	22	59	54	53	54	55
	23	54	55	58	55	54
	24	56	53	51	55	59
	25	56	55	55	55	55
Apr. 28	26	54	53	54	55	54
	27	53	52	55	54	53
	28	53	52	53	57	53
	29	53	51	55	50	55
	30	57	54	56	54	55

Using a check sheet similar to Fig. 2-1, make a tally of these 150 measurements to arrange them in a frequency distribution. From this check sheet prepare a table similar to Table 2-2a showing cell mid-points, cell boundaries, and observed frequencies.

2-2 Plot the frequency distribution of Problem 2-1 as a frequency histogram similar to Fig. 2-2a.

2-3 Arrange the frequency distribution of Problem 2-1 into a cumulative frequency distribution similar to the one shown in Table 2-3. Show both "number less than" and "percentage less than" each cell boundary. Plot the ogive on rectangular coordinate paper.

2-4 Find the arithmetic mean and RMS deviation of subgroup 16 of Problem 2-1. Compute the RMS deviation by both formulas (3) and (4). Which method would be more useful for machine calculation? Why?

     Answer: $\bar{X} = 55.8$, $\sigma = 1.6$.

2-5 Find the arithmetic mean and RMS deviation for subgroup 12 of Problem 2-1. Compute the RMS deviation by both formulas (3) and (4). Which method would be more useful for machine calculation? Why?

2-6 Using the long method illustrated in Table 2-4, compute the arithmetic mean and RMS deviation of the frequency distribution data in Problem 2-1.

     Answer: $\bar{X} = 54.23$; $\sigma = 1.88$.

2-7 Using the mean and RMS deviation found in Problem 2-6, determine what proportion of the original data actually fall outside $\bar{X} \pm 3\sigma$. Comment on the differences between this percentage and the three percentages for $\bar{X} \pm 3\sigma$ given in the table on page 68.

     Answer: 0.7%.

2-8 Using the $\bar{X}$ and σ calculated in Problem 2-6, what percentage of the distribution would fall between the limits 51.5 and 57.5 assuming the underlying distribution is approximately normal? Compare this result with the actual results tabulated in Problem 2-1.

     Answer: 88.5%, 90.7%.

2-9 A normal curve has the same average and RMS deviation as those calculated in Problem 2-6. What percentage of the area under the curve will fall between limits of 52.5 and 56.5? Compare this to the percentage of cases observed between these limits in the frequency distribution of Problem 2-1.

2-10 A small electronic device is designed to emit a timing signal of 200 milliseconds duration. In the production of this device, subgroups of five units are taken at periodic intervals and tested. $\bar{X}$ and R are calculated for each subgroup and used to plot control charts. The results of inspection of 125 of these devices are shown in the following table.

     Using a checksheet similar to Fig. 2-1, make a tally of these 125 measurements to arrange them in a frequency distribution. Use cell mid-points of 189.5, 191.5, 193.5, etc. From this check sheet prepare a table similar to Table 2-2a showing cell mid-points, cell boundaries, and observed frequencies.

Subgroup Number	Duration of automatic signal in milliseconds					Average $\bar{X}$	Range R
	Sample letter						
	a	*b*	*c*	*d*	*e*		
1	195	201	194	201	205	199.2	11
2	204	190	199	195	202	198.0	14
3	195	197	205	201	195	198.6	10
4	211	198	193	199	204	201.0	18
5	204	193	197	200	194	197.6	11
6	200	202	195	200	197	198.8	7
7	196	198	197	196	196	196.6	2
8	201	197	206	207	197	201.6	10
9	200	202	204	192	201	199.8	12
10	203	201	209	192	198	200.6	17

(continued)

Subgroup Number	Duration of automatic signal in milliseconds					Average $\bar{X}$	Range R
	Sample letter						
	a	*b*	*c*	*d*	*e*		
11	195	198	196	204	201	198.8	9
12	193	203	197	198	201	198.4	10
13	200	206	208	199	200	202.6	9
14	199	199	197	204	202	200.2	7
15	189	199	205	197	199	197.8	16
16	198	196	199	205	197	199.0	9
17	198	201	201	206	206	202.4	8
18	206	200	190	202	196	198.8	16
19	197	198	198	195	201	197.8	6
20	196	199	197	198	204	198.8	8
21	196	207	203	193	197	199.2	14
22	202	202	206	209	202	204.2	7
23	200	213	196	193	199	200.2	20
24	204	192	198	205	199	199.6	13
25	199	201	194	205	207	201.2	13
Σ						4,990.8	277

2-11 Plot the frequency distribution of Problem 2-10 as a frequency histogram similar to Fig. 2-2a.

2-12 Find the RMS deviation of subgroup 6 of Problem 2-10 by both formulas (3) and (4). Which method would be more useful for machine calculation? Why?

2-13 Find the RMS deviations of subgroups 16 through 20 in Problem 2-10. Use formula (3) to calculate the RMS deviations of subgroups 16 and 17 and formula (4) for subgroups 18 through 20. Which method would be preferable for machine calculation? Why?

2-14 Using the long method illustrated in Table 2-4, compute the arithmetic mean and RMS deviation of the frequency distribution obtained in Problem 2-10.

2-15 Using the short method illustrated in Table 2-5, compute the arithmetic mean and RMS deviation of the frequency distribution obtained in Problem 2-10.

2-16 Using the results of Problem 2-10, plot a frequency histogram and a cumulative frequency curve. Overlay the two curves, one upon the other, using rectangular coordinate paper with the ordinate scale for the histogram on the left side and the ordinate scale for the ogive on the right.

2-17 A normal curve has the same average and RMS deviation as those calculated in Problem 2-14 or 2-15. What percentage of the area under the curve will fall between limits of 190.5 and 210.5? Compare this with the percentage of cases observed between these limits in the frequency distribution of Problem 2-10.

2-18 A normal curve has the same average and RMS deviation as those calculated in Problem 2-14 or 2-15. What percentage of the area under the curve will fall between limits of 194.5 and 208.5? Compare this with the percentage of cases observed between these limits in the frequency distribution of Problem 2-10.

2-19 The high voltage output of a certain power supply used in a copy machine is specified as 350 ± 5 volts dc at 20 milliamps. Subgroups of four power supply units are drawn from the process and inspected approximately every half hour. The data from 25 subgroups are shown in the following table along with the average and range for each subgroup.

Using a check sheet similar to Fig. 2-1, make a tally of these 100 measurements to arrange them in a frequency distribution. Use cell mid-points of 347.0, 347.5, 348.0, 348.5, etc. From this check sheet prepare a table similar to Table 2-2a showing cell mid-points, cell boundaries, and observed frequencies.

Subgroup number	dc-voltage output at 20 mA				Average $\bar{X}$	Range R
	sample letter					
	a	b	c	d		
1	348.5	350.2	348.3	350.3	349.3	2.0
2	351.3	351.2	347.1	349.7	349.8	4.2
3	348.5	350.5	348.5	349.0	349.1	2.0
4	351.4	350.4	348.6	353.2	350.9	4.6
5	349.4	348.0	349.6	351.1	349.5	3.1
6	351.1	348.1	349.2	350.1	349.7	3.0
7	348.3	349.9	350.7	348.5	349.4	2.4
8	349.9	349.1	349.0	349.6	349.4	0.9
9	349.2	348.7	348.8	350.3	349.3	1.6
10	349.2	351.6	351.9	349.2	350.5	2.7
11	350.1	350.5	351.2	347.9	349.9	3.3
12	350.4	350.8	350.3	352.6	351.0	2.3
13	347.7	349.6	348.6	349.3	348.8	1.9
14	349.0	351.1	350.2	348.0	349.6	3.1
15	350.7	349.3	349.3	350.2	349.9	1.4
16	350.0	351.8	352.3	349.8	351.0	2.5
17	350.1	349.8	349.6	349.2	349.7	0.9
18	351.1	350.6	346.9	349.8	349.6	4.2
19	351.4	349.3	349.7	349.6	350.0	2.1
20	348.8	349.6	351.3	349.2	349.7	2.5
21	349.4	350.2	350.2	351.8	350.4	2.4
22	351.7	351.6	349.9	347.1	350.1	4.6
23	350.4	349.0	349.2	349.6	349.6	1.4
24	349.4	348.7	350.3	348.8	349.3	1.6
25	349.6	349.1	349.6	351.2	349.9	2.1
Σ					8,745.2	62.8

2-20 Plot the frequency distribution of Problem 2-19 as a frequency histogram.

2-21 Find the RMS deviation of subgroup 15 of Problem 2-19 by both formulas (3) and (4). Which method would be preferable for machine calculation? Why?

2-22 Find the RMS deviation of subgroup 22 of Problem 2-19 by both formulas (3) and (4). Which method would be preferable for machine calculation? Why?

2-23 Find the RMS deviations of subgroups 6 through 10 of Problem 2-19. Use formula (3) to calculate the RMS deviations of subgroups 6 and 7 and formula (4) for subgroups 8 through 10. Which method would be preferable for machine calculation? Why?

2-24 Using the long method illustrated in Table 2-4, compute the arithmetic mean and RMS deviation of the frequency distribution obtained in Problem 2-19.

2-25 Using the short method illustrated in Table 2-5, compute the arithmetic mean and RMS deviation of the frequency distribution obtained in Problem 2-19.

2-26 Using the results of Problem 2-19, plot a frequency histogram and a cumulative frequency curve. Overlay the two curves, one upon the other, using rectangular coordinate paper with the ordinate scale for the histogram on the left side and the ordinate scale for the ogive on the right.

2-27 A normal curve has the same average and RMS deviation as those calculated in Problem 2-24 or 2-25. What percentage of the area under the curve will fall between limits of 347.25 and 352.75? Compare this with the actual percentage of cases observed between these limits in the frequency distribution of Problem 2-19.

2-28 A normal curve has the same average and RMS deviation as those calculated in Problem 2-24 or 2-25. What percentage of the area under the curve will fall between limits of 348.25 and 351.75? Compare this with the actual percentage of cases observed between these limits in the frequency distribution of Problem 2-19.

2-29 The mean value of the modulus of rupture of a large number of test specimens of green Sitka spruce has been found to be 5,600 lb/in^2.

(*a*) If the RMS deviation is 840 lb/in^2 and the distribution is approximately normal, the modulus of rupture will fall between 5,000 and 6,200 for what percentage of the specimens?

(*b*) For what percentage will it be above 4,000?

(*c*) Below 3,500?

Answer (*a*) 52.5%; (*b*) 97.2%; (*c*) 0.62%.

2-30 Tests of the stiffness of a number of aluminum alloy channels gave the following frequency distribution. Stiffness was measured in "effective *EI* in lb/in^2."

Stiffness	Frequency	Stiffness	Frequency	Stiffness	Frequency
2,640	1	2,440	33	2,280	14
2,600	2	2,400	41	2,240	5
2,560	7	2,360	35	2,200	3
2,520	11	2,320	22	2,160	1
2,480	25				

(*a*) Compute $\bar{X}$ and σ.

(*b*) If a normal distribution had this $\bar{X}$ and σ, what percentage of the distribution would fall below 2,150?

Answer (*a*) $\bar{X} = 2,399.6$; $\sigma = 83.4$; (*b*) 0.14%.

2-31 What proportion of a frequency distribution would you expect to fall outside $\bar{X} \pm 2.8\sigma$ limits:

(*a*) if it is known to be approximately normal?

(*b*) if it is known only that it satisfies the conditions of the Camp-Meidell inequality?

(*c*) if nothing is known about the form of the distribution?

2-32 What proportion of a frequency distribution would you expect to fall outside $\bar{X} \pm 1.6\sigma$ limits:

(*a*) if it is known to be approximately normal?

(*b*) if it is known only that it satisfies the conditions of the Camp-Meidell inequality?

(*c*) if nothing is known about the form of the distribution?

2-33 A manufacturer of electrical products purchases many parts from outside vendors. A lot of 20,000 of a certain small component is received from a new vendor. The receiving inspection department for the manufacturer has taken a random sample of 200 components from this lot and measured the resistance of each component. These resistances in ohms have been arranged into the following frequency distribution:

Cell Boundaries, Ohms	Frequency
88.5–86.5	2
86.5–84.5	5
84.5–82.5	16
82.5–80.5	24
80.5–78.5	40
78.5–76.5	44
76.5–74.5	25
74.5–72.5	22
72.5–70 5	13
70.5–68.5	7
68.5–66.5	2

Compute the average and RMS deviation of this frequency distribution. What percentage of a normal distribution having your computed $\bar{X}$ and σ would fall outside the specification limits 75 ± 10 ohms? If you make the arbitrary assumption that resistances are distributed uniformly throughout each cell, what percentage of the actual distribution fell outside these limits?

Answer (a) $\bar{X} = 77.7$, $\sigma = 4$; (b) 3.5%; (c) 2.9%.

2-34 The contained weight of a certain dry product is labeled as 500 grams. Periodically a sample is taken from the packaging line and the contents are weighed. After 250 samples were weighed and the weight recorded, the following frequency distribution was formed.

Cell boundaries	Frequency	Cell boundaries	Frequency
505.5–506.0	1	501.5–502.0	34
505.0–505.5	2	501.0–501.5	25
504.5–505.0	7	500.5–501.0	17
504.0–504.5	12	500.0–500.5	13
503.5–504.0	25	499.5–500.0	7
503.0–503.5	29	499.0–499.5	4
502.5–503.0	41	498.5–499.0	2
502.0–502.5	30	498.0–498.5	1

(a) Compute $\bar{X}$ and σ of this frequency distribution.

(b) If a normal distribution had this same $\bar{X}$ and σ, what percentage of the distribution would fall below the label weight of 500 grams?

(c) What proportion of the actual frequency distribution fell below the label weight?

(d) What conclusions, if any, can you reach on the question of whether or not the producer was maintaining good statistical control of this quality characteristic? Explain your answer.

THREE

WHY THE CONTROL CHART WORKS; SOME EXAMPLES

Statistical methods serve as landmarks which point to further improvement beyond that deemed obtainable by experienced manufacturing men. Hence after all obvious correctives have been exhausted and all normal logic indicates no further gain is to be made, statistical methods still point toward a reasonable chance for yet further gains; thereby giving the man who is doing trouble shooting sufficient courage of his convictions to cause him to continue to the ultimate gain, in spite of expressed opinion on all sides that no such gain exists.—G. J. Meyers, Jr.†

The Use of Control Charts to Judge Whether or Not a Constant System of Chance Causes Is Present

Control charts for $\bar{X}$, R, and σ supply a basis for judgment on a major question of practical importance. This question might be phrased in different ways, such as, "Were all these samples drawn from the same bowl?" or "Is there one universe from which these samples appear to come?" or "Do these figures indicate a stable pattern of variation?" or "Is this variation the result of a constant-cause system?" or merely "Do these measurements show statistical control?"

Any rule that might be established for providing a definite "Yes" or "No" answer to these questions is bound to give the wrong answer part of the time. The decision where to draw the line between a "Yes" and a "No" answer must be based on the expected action to be taken if each answer is given.

In quality control in manufacturing, the answer, "No, this is not a constant-cause system," leads to a hunt for an assignable cause of variation, and an attempt to remove it, if possible. The answer, "Yes, this is a constant-cause system," leads to leaving the process alone, making no effort to hunt for causes of variation. The rule for establishing the control limits that will determine the "Yes" or "No"

---

† G. J. MEYERS, JR., Discussion of E. G. Olds, On Some of the Essentials of the Control Chart Analysis, *Transactions, American Society of Mechanical Engineers*, vol. 64, pp. 521–527, July, 1942.

answer in any case should strike an economic balance between the costs due to two kinds of errors—the error of hunting for trouble when it is absent (whenever the " No " answer is incorrect) and the error of leaving a process alone because of not hunting for trouble when it really is present (whenever the " Yes " answer is incorrect).

Any rule for establishing control limits for use in manufacturing should be a practical one based on this point of economic balance. In this book, we follow the common practice in the United States of using so-called 3-sigma limits. Experience indicates that in most cases 3-sigma limits do actually strike a satisfactory economic balance between these two types of errors. (Although, in principle, the choice of limits is a problem of minimizing the sum of certain costs, there are great practical difficulties in making good estimates of the relevant unit costs.)

Stable and Unstable Patterns of Variation

Figure 2-1 presented a frequency distribution of the 260 drained weights of contents of cans of tomatoes obtained over an 11-day period. At first glance, it might appear that this distribution presents a satisfactory picture of a pattern of variation that existed throughout that 11 days.

Such a statement is not necessarily true. It may be that the pattern of variation has gone through several changes during the period. The first question that must be answered is whether there was a stable pattern. If there is evidence of a lack of stability, it may be true that the 260 weights represent samples from a number of different universes that existed at different times. The resulting frequency distribution, in this case, would represent a weighted average of the various universes that existed at the times the samples were taken.

Whenever a frequency distribution is to be used as a basis for estimating the capabilities of a manufacturing process, making a proposed change in the process, or reviewing specifications, the control chart becomes an important tool in establishing stability. Once stability has been established, the analyst may feel relatively confident that he is measuring one universe and not a weighted average of many. *The order in which the measurements were made should always be preserved in recording data for a frequency distribution.*

Use of the Control Chart in Interpretation of a Frequency Distribution

Figure 3-1 shows the control charts for $\bar{X}$ and R for the basic data on drained weights contained in Table 2-1. None of the $\bar{X}$ points is outside the control limits; one of the 52 points for R is outside the limits. Application of secondary rules based on the theory of runs, discussed later in this chapter and in Chap. 6, indicate some slight shifts during the 11-day period. While usage of these data to estimate $\bar{X}'$ and σ' might be subject to question, it does not necessarily follow that this much departure from a constant pattern of variation is unsatisfactory from a practical standpoint. Many production processes never do as well.

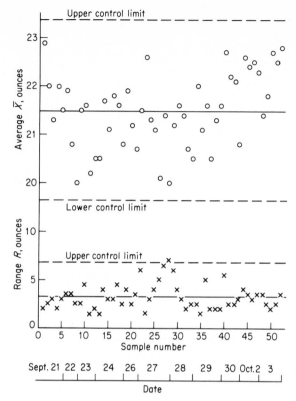

Figure 3-1 $\bar{X}$ and R control charts for drained weights of contents of cans of tomatoes—data of Table 2-1.

The $\bar{X}$ Chart for Drawings from Shewhart's Normal Bowl

It has already been pointed out in Chap. 2 that the distribution of the $\bar{X}$ values of random samples drawn from one universe tends to be normal when the sample size is four or more, even though the universe is not normal. It has also been pointed out that nearly all the cases (all but 0.27%) in a normal distribution will fall within 3-sigma limits on either side of the average.

It follows that as long as a series of samples (or subgroups) are really random samples from one universe, their averages will nearly always fall within limits $\bar{X}' \pm 3\sigma_{\bar{x}}$. This is illustrated by Fig. 3-2 which is a control chart for the averages of 100 samples of 4 from Shewhart's normal bowl, using data of Table 2-7. No points fall outside the control limits of 45 and 15. In Shewhart's 1,000 drawings of samples of four from this bowl, only 2 of the 1,000 points fell outside these control limits.†

---

† It is of interest to examine the distribution of markings on chips as given in Table 2-6. These markings extended from 0 to 60, with 60 of the 998 chips below 15 and another 60 above 45. Obviously in any random series of drawings, occasional subgroups of 4 will contain chips with numbers low enough for the average to be below 15; others will have the average above 45. The point to be emphasized is that if the chips are drawn in a random manner, the laws of chance operate in a way that these averages below 15 or above 45 will be infrequent. Whenever one of these infrequent events occurs, the control chart will seem to say, "The universe has changed; look for trouble," when in reality the composition of the universe is unchanged and no trouble can be found.

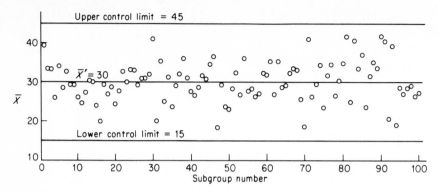

Figure 3-2 Control chart for $\bar{X}$ for 100 subgroups of four drawn from Shewhart's normal bowl.

In Fig. 3-2, the central line on the chart could be set at 30, that is, at $\bar{X}'$, the known average of the universe. The 3-sigma limits could be based on a calculation from the known value of σ', the standard deviation in the bowl, which in round numbers was 10. The standard error of the average

$$\sigma_{\bar{X}} = \frac{\sigma'}{\sqrt{n}} = \frac{10}{\sqrt{4}} = 5$$

The 3-sigma limits were therefore $3\sigma_{\bar{X}} = 3(5) = 15$ on either side of the average of 30. This placed the upper control limit at 45 and the lower control limit at 15.

It is not strictly accurate to say that in the long run 3-sigma limits on an $\bar{X}$ chart will show points out of control only 27 times in 10,000 (that is, 0.27% of the time) provided the universe is really unchanged. This would be strictly true only if the distribution of the $\bar{X}$ values were exactly normal and the control limits were based on known values of $\bar{X}'$ and σ'. Actually, although the distribution of $\bar{X}$ values is roughly normal, it is not exactly so unless the universe is normal; the 3-sigma limits are necessarily calculated from the observed data rather than from parameters of the universe. Hence 3-sigma limits may give false indications of lack of control somewhat oftener than is indicated by the normal curve.

Nevertheless, such false indications of lack of control will be infrequent. The 3-sigma limits seldom make the error of indicating trouble (i.e., indicating an assignable cause of variation) when there is no trouble to be found. If points on the $\bar{X}$ chart fall outside 3-sigma limits, there is good reason for confidence that they point to some factor contributing to quality variation that can be identified.

Calculation of 3-sigma Limits on Control Charts for $\bar{X}$

The use of Tables B, C, and D of App. 3 for the calculation of control limits may be illustrated by using the first 20 subgroups of the bowl drawings of Table 2-7.

After calculating the averages and ranges of subgroups, the next step in the calculation of limits is to find $\bar{\bar{X}}$ and $\bar{R}$. For the first 20 subgroups, these are

$$\bar{\bar{X}} = \frac{\Sigma \bar{X}}{20} = \frac{577.75}{20} = 28.9$$

$$\bar{R} = \frac{\Sigma R}{20} = \frac{368}{20} = 18.4$$

If Table B is to be used, the next step is to estimate σ'. For this it is necessary to find in Table B the d_2 factor for the subgroup size. In this case $n = 4$, and Table B gives $d_2 = 2.059$.

$$\text{Estimate of } \sigma' = \frac{\bar{R}}{d_2} = \frac{18.4}{2.059} = 8.94$$

Then $3\sigma_{\bar{x}}$ can be calculated from the relationship $\sigma_{\bar{x}} = \sigma'/\sqrt{n}$:

$$3\sigma_{\bar{x}} = \frac{3\sigma'}{\sqrt{n}} = \frac{3(8.94)}{\sqrt{4}} = 13.4$$

$$\text{Upper Control Limit}_{\bar{x}} = \bar{\bar{X}} + 3\sigma_{\bar{x}} = 28.9 + 13.4 = 43.3$$

$$\text{Lower Control Limit}_{\bar{x}} = \bar{\bar{X}} - 3\sigma_{\bar{x}} = 28.9 - 13.4 = 15.5$$

The two steps in the calculation of $3\sigma_{\bar{x}}$ might be consolidated as

$$3\sigma_{\bar{x}} = \frac{3\bar{R}}{d_2\sqrt{n}} = \frac{3}{2.059\sqrt{4}}\bar{R} = 0.73\bar{R} = 0.73(18.4) = 13.4$$

To shorten the calculation of control limits from $\bar{R}$, this factor $3/d_2\sqrt{n}$, the multiplier of $\bar{R}$ in the preceding calculation, has been computed for each value of n from 2 to 20 and tabulated in Table C of App. 3. This factor is designated A_2. The formulas for 3-sigma control limits on charts for $\bar{X}$ then become

$$UCL_{\bar{x}} = \bar{\bar{X}} + A_2\bar{R}$$

$$LCL_{\bar{x}} = \bar{\bar{X}} - A_2\bar{R}$$

If control limits are to be calculated from $\bar{\sigma}$ rather than from $\bar{R}$, the calculations for the first 20 subgroups of Table 2-7 are as follows:

$$\bar{\bar{X}} = 28.9$$

$$\bar{\sigma} = \frac{\Sigma \sigma}{20} = \frac{143.1}{20} = 7.155$$

Using the c_2 factor from Table B to estimate σ',

$$\text{Estimate of } \sigma' = \frac{\bar{\sigma}}{c_2} = \frac{7.155}{0.7979} = 8.97$$

$$3\sigma_{\bar{x}} = \frac{3\sigma'}{\sqrt{n}} = \frac{3(8.97)}{\sqrt{4}} = 13.5$$

$$UCL_{\bar{x}} = 28.9 + 13.5 = 43.4$$

$$LCL_{\bar{x}} = 28.9 - 13.5 = 15.4$$

As in the calculation from $\bar{R}$, the two steps in the calculation of $3\sigma_{\bar{x}}$ can be consolidated as

$$3\sigma_{\bar{x}} = \frac{3\bar{\sigma}}{c_2\sqrt{n}} = \frac{3}{0.7979(\sqrt{4})}\bar{\sigma} = 1.88(7.155) = 13.5$$

To shorten the calculations for control limits from $\bar{\sigma}$, this factor $3/c_2\sqrt{n}$, the multiplier of $\bar{\sigma}$ in the above calculation, has been computed for each value of n from 2 to 25, thence by 5s to 100, and tabulated in Table D of App. 3. This factor is designated A_1. The formulas for 3-sigma control limits using this factor are

$$UCL_{\bar{x}} = \bar{\bar{X}} + A_1\bar{\sigma}$$

$$LCL_{\bar{x}} = \bar{\bar{X}} - A_1\bar{\sigma}$$

For those situations where it is desired to calculate control limits directly from known or standard values of σ' and $\bar{X}'$, the factor $3/\sqrt{n}$ has been computed and tabulated in Table E, App. 3. This factor is designated as A. The formulas for 3-sigma control limits using this factor are

$$UCL_{\bar{x}} = \bar{X}' + A\sigma'$$

$$LCL_{\bar{x}} = \bar{X}' - A\sigma'$$

As applied to the control chart of Fig. 3-2, using the known values $\bar{X}' = 30$ and $\sigma' = 10$ and the value $A = 1.50$ given by Table E for a sample size of 4,

$$UCL_{\bar{x}} = 30 + 1.50(10) = 45.0$$

$$LCL_{\bar{x}} = 30 - 1.50(10) = 15.0$$

The various equations for central lines and 3-sigma limits on control charts for $\bar{X}$, R and σ are assembled for convenient reference in Table 3-1. The factors (such as A, A_1, etc.) referred to are given in Tables B to E of App. 3. The reader will note that the spread of the limits on $\bar{X}$ charts as well as on R or σ charts depends on the process dispersion. Limits on all the charts may be calculated directly from a known or assumed σ' or by estimating σ' either from $\bar{R}$ or $\bar{\sigma}$. In most cases in industrial practice, limits are computed from $\bar{R}$.

Table 3-1 Equations for computing 3-sigma limits on Shewhart's control charts for variables

(Table references for required factors pertain to App. 3)

Method	$\bar{X}$ chart	R chart	σ chart
σ' and $\bar{X}'$ known or assumed	Central line $= \bar{X}'$ $UCL_{\bar{x}} = \bar{X}' + A\sigma'$ $LCL_{\bar{x}} = \bar{X}' - A\sigma'$ See Table E	Central line $= d_2\sigma'$ $UCL_R = D_2\sigma'$ $LCL_R = D_1\sigma'$ See Tables B & E	Central line $= c_2\sigma'$ $UCL_\sigma = B_2\sigma'$ $LCL_\sigma = B_1\sigma'$ See Tables B & E
σ' and $\bar{X}'$ estimated respectively from $\bar{R}$ & $\bar{\bar{X}}$	Central line $= \bar{\bar{X}}$ $UCL_{\bar{x}} = \bar{\bar{X}} + A_2\bar{R}$ $LCL_{\bar{x}} = \bar{\bar{X}} - A_2\bar{R}$ See Table C	Central line $= \bar{R}$ $UCL_R = D_4\bar{R}$ $LCL_R = D_3\bar{R}$ See Table C	
σ' and $\bar{X}'$ estimated respectively from $\bar{\sigma}$ & $\bar{\bar{X}}$	Central line $= \bar{\bar{X}}$ $UCL_{\bar{x}} = \bar{\bar{X}} + A_1\bar{\sigma}$ $LCL_{\bar{x}} = \bar{\bar{X}} - A_1\bar{\sigma}$ See Table D		Central line $= \bar{\sigma}$ $UCL_\sigma = B_4\bar{\sigma}$ $LCL_\sigma = B_3\bar{\sigma}$ See Table D

Control Charts for Range and RMS Deviation

A general formula for the control limits on the $\bar{X}$ chart is $\bar{X}' \pm 3\sigma_{\bar{x}}$. Similarly, general formulas for control charts for measures of subgroup dispersion are:

1. For the R chart, ... $\bar{R} \pm 3\sigma_R$
2. For the σ chart, ... $\bar{\sigma} \pm 3\sigma_\sigma$

However, when these three formulas are applied to the calculation of lower control limits, such limits will turn out to be less than 0 where n is 6 or less for the R chart and where n is 5 or less for the σ chart. Because R and σ cannot be less than 0, the lower limit is not used in these cases.

Figure 3-3 shows control charts for σ and R for the 100 subgroups of four given in Table 2-7. Limits on these charts were calculated using the respective values of $\bar{\sigma}$ and $\bar{R}$ found in Table 2-7 and calculated by the equations indicated in Table 3-1.

$$UCL_\sigma = B_4\bar{\sigma} = 2.27(8.08) = 18.3$$

$$LCL_\sigma = B_3\bar{\sigma} = 0(8.08) = 0$$

$$UCL_R = D_4\bar{R} = 2.28(20.8) = 47.4$$

$$LCL_R = D_3\bar{R} = 0(20.8) = 0$$

The similarity between the variation from subgroup to subgroup shown in the σ

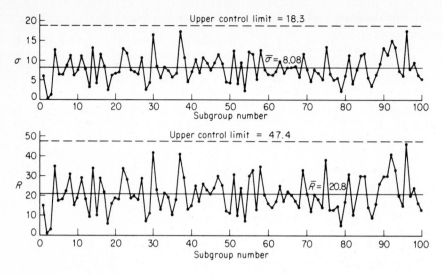

Figure 3-3 Control charts for RMS deviation and range—drawings from Shewhart's normal bowl.

and R charts is emphasized here by the use of lines† connecting the successive points. It seems clear that these two charts tell practically the same story. Either one may be used in any instance to tell the story; there is no need to use both.

In subsequent illustrations throughout this book, only one measure of subgroup dispersion will be calculated. Usually this will be R, although occasionally it may be σ. The purpose of calculating both R and σ for the subgroups in Table 2-7 was to illustrate that R and σ were alternative measures of the same thing, that they led to similar estimates of σ', similar control limits on $\bar{X}$ charts, and similar control charts showing subgroup dispersion.

In practical control-chart work in industry, R rather than σ should nearly always be used as a measure of subgroup dispersion. As has already been stated, this is partly because R is easier to compute. Equally important is the advantage that R is easier to explain; almost everyone can understand range, whereas many people have difficulty understanding RMS or standard deviation.

R as a measure of subgroup dispersion is always necessary to provide a basis for calculating limits on a control chart for $\bar{X}$ and to permit estimates of σ'. However, the control chart for R is sometimes omitted where experience shows that R seldom goes out of control even though $\bar{X}$ does so frequently.

---

† In practical control-chart work in industry, the points on $\bar{X}$ and R charts are sometimes connected and sometimes not. In this book points on the charts are not connected except in special cases such as Fig. 3-3. Generally speaking, experience shows that the connection of points on control charts for variables is likely to lead to their misinterpretation, particularly by many people who are not familiar with the principles behind the control chart. It is usually advantageous if control charts for $\bar{X}$ and R do not look like ordinary trend charts.

Estimates of σ' from $\bar{R}$ and $\bar{\sigma}$ from Various Subgroup Sizes in a Controlled Process

The preceding discussion of $\bar{X}$ charts makes it clear that the width of the band between upper and lower control limits depends entirely on the variability within the subgroups, which we have measured either by the average range $\bar{R}$ or the average standard deviation $\bar{\sigma}$. Both $\bar{R}$ and $\bar{\sigma}$ lead to estimates of σ', the standard deviation of the universe. It is of interest to examine data from a controlled process to see whether subgroup size seems to influence these estimates of σ'.

As the chips were drawn one by one from Shewhart's bowl and as each chip drawn was replaced and the chips stirred before the next drawing, there is no natural subgroup size; it is permissible to group the drawings into subgroups of any size. To illustrate the effect of different sizes of subgroups, the 400 drawings have been divided into subgroups of 2 and 8 as well as 4, and values of R and σ have been computed for each subgroup. (The individual R and σ values for subgroups of 2 and 8 are not shown here.) $\bar{R}$ and $\bar{\sigma}$ for subgroup sizes of 2 and 8 have been computed for each set of 80 drawings as well as for the entire 400 drawings. σ' has been estimated from each value of $\bar{R}$ and $\bar{\sigma}$ using the appropriate d_2 and c_2 factors from Table B.

Table 3-2 gives the estimates of σ' for each set of 80 drawings and for the entire 400 drawings, using $\bar{R}$ and $\bar{\sigma}$ as estimators and using the three different subgroup sizes. The fairly close agreement among the different estimates of σ' from any given set of drawings is striking. The variation in estimates of σ' from one set of 80 drawings to another is evidently much greater than the variation among the different estimates from any set. It would seem that, at least from the standpoint of estimating the dispersion of the universe, many different subgroup sizes are acceptable.

(Incidentally, it will be noted that $\bar{R}$ and $\bar{\sigma}$ give identical estimates of σ' for the subgroup size of 2. The σ of a subgroup of 2 obviously is half the range of the subgroup. c_2 is therefore half of d_2 and $\bar{\sigma}$ is half of $\bar{R}$.)

Table 3-2 Comparison of estimates of universe standard deviation σ' based on subgroup sizes of 2, 4, and 8

(Known value of $\sigma' = 9.95$)

Drawings	Estimates of σ' Subgroup size of 2		Estimates of σ' Subgroup size of 4		Estimates of σ' Subgroup size of 8	
	From $\bar{R}$	From $\bar{\sigma}$	From $\bar{R}$	From $\bar{\sigma}$	From $\bar{R}$	From $\bar{\sigma}$
1–80	8.62	8.62	8.94	8.97	9.24	8.98
81–160	10.75	10.75	10.51	10.64	10.50	10.58
161–240	9.73	9.73	10.51	10.48	9.76	9.89
241–320	8.86	8.86	8.89	9.06	8.85	9.02
321–400	11.68	11.68	11.56	11.48	11.98	12.17
1–400	9.93	9.93	10.08	10.12	10.07	10.13

Although satisfactory estimates of σ' may be made with various subgroup sizes, there often are good reasons why some one particular subgroup size may be the best to use in any given instance. Various considerations entering into the choice of subgroup size are discussed in Chaps. 4 and 5.

The Distribution of the Standard Deviation

Gen. Leslie Simon,† in his presentation of sampling by variables, introduces his subject with the following quotation from De Morgan's "A Budget of Paradoxes":

> Great fleas have little fleas upon their backs to bite 'em,
> And little fleas have lesser fleas, and so ad infinitum.

Whether or not De Morgan was right about the fleas, a somewhat parallel idea certainly applies to distribution theory in mathematical statistics. Universes seem to give nourishment to many other distributions that have less spread, such as distributions of averages, standard deviations, and ranges. And just as each universe has its average and standard deviation, so also does each distribution of averages, standard deviations, or ranges have its own average and standard deviation.

† L. E. SIMON, "An Engineers' Manual of Statistical Methods," p. 41, John Wiley & Sons, Inc., New York, 1941.

Table 3-3 Distribution of relative frequencies of standard deviations of samples of 2, 4, and 8 from 400 drawings from Shewhart's normal bowl
(All frequencies expressed as percentages of total)

Cell boundaries	Values of σ		
	$n = 2$	$n = 4$	$n = 8$
19.95–21.95	1.0		
17.95–19.95	0.5		
15.95–17.95	1.0	3	2
13.95–15.95	2.5	1	4
11.95–13.95	4.0	9	6
9.95–11.95	5.5	16	22
7.95– 9.95	13.5	13	30
5.95– 7.95	16.0	33	26
3.95– 5.95	15.5	17	10
1.95– 3.95	20.0	6	
0.00– 1.95	20.5		

The reader may get a feeling for what is meant by *the distribution of standard deviations* by examining three such frequency distributions compared in Table 3-3. This table, based on the 400 bowl drawings and the computed values of σ for the three subgroup sizes, shows how the distribution pattern of σ changed with change in subgroup size. It is evident that for $n = 2$, the distribution of values of σ centers considerably below the universe standard deviation of 10, and that as n increases this centering approaches closer to the universe standard deviation. The spread of the distribution of σ seems to decrease as n increases. The distribution of σ is evidently not symmetrical (and therefore cannot be normal), particularly for low values of n.

Unfortunately, statistical theory cannot give us such useful generalizations about the distribution of σ as it can about the distribution of $\bar{X}$. In the case of the distribution of $\bar{X}$, theory gave the expected average $(\bar{X}')$ and the expected standard deviation $(\sigma'/\sqrt{n})$, both of which were independent of the form of the universe. Moreover, theory told us that if the universe distribution were normal the distribution of $\bar{X}$ values would be normal regardless of sample size, and that even if the universe distribution were not normal, the distribution of $\bar{X}$ values would approach normality as sample size increased.

However, if the universe is normal, statistical theory can tell us the expected average and the expected standard deviation of the distribution of σ. As has already been pointed out, in samples from a normal universe the expected average $\bar{\sigma}$ is $c_2 \sigma'$.† A commonly used approximate estimate of σ_σ, the expected standard deviation of the distribution of σ for samples from a normal universe, is $\sigma'/\sqrt{2n}$. It is also known that as n increases, the distribution of σ becomes closer and closer to a symmetrical distribution.

Theoretical knowledge of the distribution of σ in samples from a normal universe is the basis for 3-sigma limits on the control chart for σ. The central line on the control chart is set at $\bar{\sigma}$. The limits are set at $\bar{\sigma} \pm 3\sigma_\sigma$.

The approximate value of σ_σ for a normal universe is

$$\sigma_\sigma = \frac{\sigma'}{\sqrt{2n}} \tag{1}$$

Modern statistical theory gives the exact value as‡

$$\sigma_\sigma = [2(n-1) - 2nc_2^2]^{1/2} \frac{\sigma'}{\sqrt{2n}} \tag{2}$$

† Where

$$c_2 = \sqrt{\frac{2}{n}} \frac{[(n-2)/2]!}{[(n-3)/2]!}$$

In this formula, the symbol ! means factorial. See Chap. 6 for an explanation of factorials.

‡ See "Manual on Quality Control of Materials," p. 111, American Society for Testing Materials, Philadelphia, Pa., 1951. See also FREDERICK MOSTELLER, On Some Useful "Inefficient" Statistics, *The Annals of Mathematical Statistics*, vol. 17, pp. 377–408, December, 1946.

When n is large, the difference between equations (1) and (2) is negligible. Equation (2) is the basis for the control limit factors where n is 25 or less; Eq. (1) is used where n exceeds 25.

When 3-sigma limits on a σ chart are calculated from an observed $\bar{\sigma}$, they are

$$UCL_\sigma = \bar{\sigma} + 3\sigma_\sigma = B_4\bar{\sigma}$$

$$LCL_\sigma = \bar{\sigma} - 3\sigma_\sigma = B_3\bar{\sigma}$$

When limits are based on a known or assumed value of universe standard deviation σ', they are

$$UCL_\sigma = c_2\sigma' + 3\sigma_\sigma = B_2\sigma'$$

$$LCL_\sigma = c_2\sigma' - 3\sigma_\sigma = B_1\sigma'$$

In computing σ_σ for the B_4 and B_3 factors given in Table D of App. 3, σ' is assumed to be $\bar{\sigma}/c_2$. The B_2 and B_1 factors are given in Table E.

The Distribution of the Range

Although no simple formula gives either the expected average range $\bar{R}$ or the standard deviation of the range σ_R, statistical theory does give the ratio of these figures to universe standard deviation σ' in sampling from a normal universe. Theory also fully defines the expected distribution of R in sampling from a normal universe.†

When 3-sigma limits are calculated from an observed $\bar{R}$, they are

$$UCL_R = \bar{R} + 3\sigma_R = D_4\bar{R}$$

$$LCL_R = \bar{R} - 3\sigma_R = D_3\bar{R}$$

When limits are based on a known or assumed value of universe standard deviation, σ', they are

$$UCL_R = d_2\sigma' + 3\sigma_R = D_2\sigma'$$

$$LCL_R = d_2\sigma' - 3\sigma_R = D_1\sigma'$$

The ratio $\bar{R}/\sigma'$, designated d_2, is given in Table B of App. 3. The factors necessary to calculate control limits appear in Tables C and E.

A Modification of d_2 When Relatively Few Subgroups Are Available

In estimating σ' from $\bar{R}$, we have used the fraction $\bar{R}/d_2$. The mathematical theory underlying the d_2 factor assumes that sampling has been from a normal universe.

---

† See SIMON, *op. cit.*, p. 204, and E. S. PEARSON, "The Probability Integral of the Range in Samples of n Observations from a Normal Population," *Biometrika*, vol. 32, 1942. See also N. L. JOHNSON and FRED LEONE, "Statistics and Experimental Design," Vol. I, John Wiley & Sons, New York, 1964.

Table 3-4 Ratio d_2^* of expected $\bar{R}$ to σ' in averaging ranges of various numbers of subgroups of 5 from a normal universe

Number of Subgroups of 5	d_2^*
1	2.474
2	2.405
3	2.379
5	2.358
6	2.353
8	2.346
10	2.342
12	2.339
20	2.334
∞	2.326

The d_2 factor depends on the subgroup size. For example, it is 2.326 for a subgroup size of 5.

Strictly speaking, the validity of the exact value of the d_2 factor assumes that the ranges have been averaged for a fair number of subgroups, say 20 or more. Where only a few subgroups are available, a better estimate of σ' is obtained by using a factor that writers on statistics have designated as d_2^* (read as "dee-sub-two-star"). Table 3-4, adapted from Military Standard 414 of the U.S. Department of Defense, illustrates the dependence of this factor on the number of subgroups in the special case where the subgroup size is 5.

In the ordinary construction of control charts for quality control in industry, it is good enough for practical purposes to use factors based on d_2 rather than on d_2^*. However, in certain other statistical applications it is desirable to use d_2^*. The only such application included in this book is in Chap. 17 in our discussion of Military Standard 414 for acceptance sampling by variables.

Acheson Duncan has tabulated values of d_2^* for subgroup sizes from 2 to 15 and for numbers of subgroups from 1 to 15.†

Contribution of the Control Chart to Elimination of Causes of Trouble

As pointed out and briefly illustrated in Chap. 1, actions based on the control chart for variables are of many kinds. Some of these actions, particularly those related to specifications and tolerances and to acceptance procedures, need to start from evidence that a process is in control. For such actions, it is satisfactory to understand the behavior of constant-cause systems.

---

† A. J. DUNCAN, "Quality Control and Industrial Statistics," 4th ed., p. 950, Richard D. Irwin, Inc., Homewood, Ill., 1974.

Other useful actions start from evidence of the control chart that a process is out of control. Trouble shooting in manufacturing is a particularly important example of this. In this type of control-chart application, the control chart sometimes says, "Leave this process alone," and at other times it says, "Hunt for trouble and try to correct it."

A major virtue of the control chart is that it tells—within reasonably satisfactory limits—*when* to hunt for the cause of variation. It is always helpful to know *when*; sometimes this may be sufficient to indicate *where* to look. Nevertheless, there is often a fair amount of hard work between the decision to hunt for trouble and the actual discovery and correction of the cause of the trouble. This fact is responsible for H. F. Dodge's frequently quoted statement that "Statistical quality control is 90% engineering and only 10% statistics."†

The control chart unaided cannot put its finger on exactly *where* the cause of trouble can be found. Nevertheless, users of the control-chart technique sometimes develop an ability to diagnose causes of production troubles with surprising accuracy. This ability usually depends on a combination of an understanding of the principles of the control chart with an intimate knowledge of the particular manufacturing processes to which the control chart is applied.

No general book on statistical quality control can supply the necessary knowledge of various manufacturing processes. However, some guidance may be given on the statistical aspects of interpretation of the control chart for purposes of trouble shooting. We shall try to provide this guidance by examining several general ways in which lack of control may occur and noting the effect of each on the appearance of control charts for $\bar{X}$ and R.

Lack of Statistical Control Implies a Shift in the Universe

Drawing chips from a bowl is a helpful analogy in clarifying what really happens when a manufacturing process shows lack of control. The system of chance causes in operation at any particular moment corresponds to the universe, that is, to the distribution of chips in the bowl. The items actually manufactured at that moment correspond to a sample drawn from that bowl or universe. When points fall

---

† This statement has sometimes been misinterpreted to belittle the practical contributions of statistics in industrial quality control.

When statistics—by means of the control chart or otherwise—points to the need to hunt for trouble, it often is true that 90% of the hard work remains to be done; the tough engineering job of hunting for causes and eliminating them is still ahead. In cases where this trouble shooting has led to spectacular reductions in scrap and rework, these cost reductions would not have been made without the hard engineering work. It is sometimes forgotten that neither would they have been made without the statistics.

A fair analogy is to think of the use of the control chart in trouble shooting as a chain with ten links. One of them is the statistical link; the other nine are engineering links. From the standpoint of the strength of the chain, weakness in the statistical link is just as serious as weakness in one of the engineering links.

outside the limits on the control charts, this is evidence that the universe has changed; it is as if samples were being drawn from a different bowl.

Usually the items *produced* in any period constitute a much larger sample from the universe than do the items actually *measured* for control-chart purposes during the same period. Thus the control chart gives evidence not only regarding the universe (that is, the chance cause system operating) but also regarding the items produced that were not measured.

A Classification of Ways in which Lack of Control May Occur

Because lack of control corresponds to the substitution of a new bowl, a classification of different types of lack of control may be thought of as a classification of ways in which two bowls may differ in their distribution of chips. It is helpful to give separate consideration to three ways in which universes may differ, as follows:

1. They may differ in average only.
2. They may differ in dispersion only.
3. They may differ in both average and dispersion.

Shifts in universe average influence the control charts for $\bar{X}$ and R in one way; shifts in universe dispersion influence them in another way.

Shifts in the universe may be sustained shifts over a period of time, as if many subgroups were drawn from one bowl and then many more drawn from another bowl. Or shifts may be frequent and irregular as if there were a great many bowls with the drawings from each bowl continued for periods of different lengths. Or shifts may be gradual and systematic.

In Fig. 3-4, the frequency curves are intended to represent the universe or bowl, i.e., the chance cause system in operation at any moment. Figure 3-4a shows a situation in which the universe continued for a while at one average, then shifted for a while to a higher average, and finally was brought back to the original average. Figure 3-4b shows a situation in which the universe average varies erratically and universe dispersion remains constant. Figure 3-4c shows the universe average gradually increasing. Figure 3-4d shows a situation in which, although the universe average remained unchanged, the universe dispersion doubled. Figure 3-4e shows universe average and dispersion both varying erratically.

Changes in Universe Average

A common type of lack of control observed in manufacturing is a shift in universe average with little or no change in universe dispersion. In such cases, the control chart is often of great value to the machine setter, helping the setter to center the machine setting in order to produce at a desired process average. This type of lack of control is shown on the $\bar{X}$ chart; unless the changes in universe average take place within a subgroup, the R chart will show control.

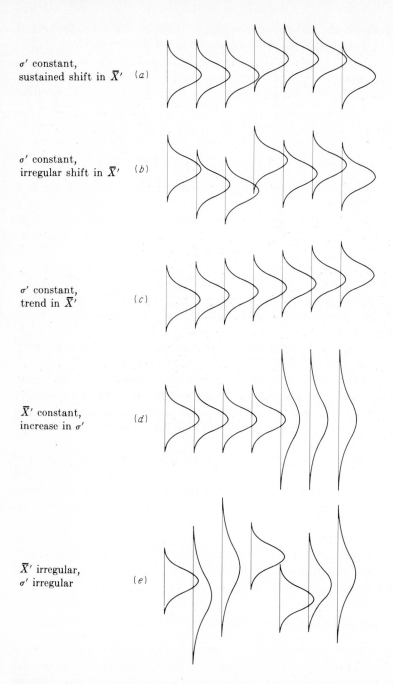

σ' constant,
sustained shift in $\bar{X}'$ (a)

σ' constant,
irregular shift in $\bar{X}'$ (b)

σ' constant,
trend in $\bar{X}'$ (c)

$\bar{X}'$ constant,
increase in σ' (d)

$\bar{X}'$ irregular,
σ' irregular (e)

Figure 3-4 Chance cause systems (represented here by frequency curves) may change in different ways;
(a) sustained shift in universe average with constant spread; (b) irregular shifts in universe average with
constant spread; (c) steady trend in universe average with constant spread; (d) change in universe
spread with no change in average; (e) irregular changes in both average and spread.

In those cases where the main reason for keeping a control chart is to detect changes in the universe average, the appropriate scheme of selection of subgroups differs from those cases in which the control chart has several purposes, including acceptance inspection. Various possible schemes of subgrouping and the basis of their selection are discussed in Chap. 5.

Because, as previously explained, control limits are set far enough from the central line on the chart for there to be very few points outside the limits without a real change in the universe, small shifts in universe average will not cause many points to fall out of control. For this reason, it is often useful to supplement the evidence given by the position of the points relative to the control limits by evidence given by tests based on the statistical theory of runs or sequences.

Some Tests for Lack of Control Based on Runs of Points above or below the Central Line on the Control Chart

Considerable work has been done by mathematicians on the development of various types of statistical tests based on the theory of runs. Many of these tests involve a complete tabulation of all the runs, long and short alike, in any definite sequence of observations. Such tests provide useful tools for the study of research data.

In order to detect shifts in a universe parameter in the common applications of control charts in manufacturing, the most practical plan is to use a few simple rules that depend only on the extreme runs. The following are suggested:

Consider that grounds exist for suspicion that the universe parameter has shifted:

Whenever in 7 successive points on the control chart, all are on the same side of the central line.

Whenever in 11 successive points on the control chart, at least 10 are on the same side of the central line.

Whenever in 14 successive points on the control chart, at least 12 are on the same side of the central line.

Whenever in 17 successive points on the control chart, at least 14 are on the same side of the central line.

Whenever in 20 successive points on the control chart, at least 16 are on the same side of the central line.

The theoretical basis for these rules is discussed in Chap. 6.

The sequences mentioned in each of these rules will occur as a matter of chance, with no change in the universe, more frequently than will a point outside of 3-sigma control limits. (In fact, such sequences did occur in the 400 drawings from Shewhart's normal bowl.) For this reason they provide a less reliable basis for hunting for trouble than does the occurrence of a point outside of control limits.

Moreover, if all of these different rules are used to judge whether the universe

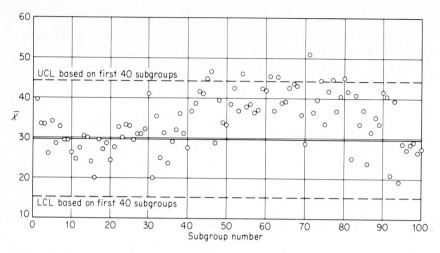

Figure 3-5 $\bar{X}$ chart showing sustained shift in universe average.

parameter has shifted, the chances of the false indication of a shift are greater than if only one of the rules is used.†

Sequences of points on one side of a central line can be useful in relation to possible action on the control chart even where they are not used for hunting for trouble in the process. They are particularly helpful in the special case where the lower control limit is zero. For instance, a reduction in the value of σ' calls for a change in the location of the upper and lower control limits on the $\bar{X}$ chart and a change in the center line and limits on the R chart. But in all R charts for which the subgroup size is not more than six, it is impossible for the change in σ' to be shown by a point falling below the lower control limit of 0. However, an indication of the decrease in process dispersion can be obtained by applying the theory of runs.

Certain other applications of the theory of runs to the interpretation of control charts are discussed in Section I of Chap. 9.

Sustained Shift in Universe Average

In the control chart for $\bar{X}$ given in Fig. 3-5, the universe varied in the manner indicated in Fig. 3-4a. The universe average for the first 40 subgroups was 30; for the next 40 subgroups it was 40; for the final 20 subgroups it went back to 30. The universe standard deviation was 10 throughout the entire period.

Figure 3-5 was made by adding 10 to each drawing from the 161st to the 320th in Table 2-7. This has the same effect as if subgroups 41 to 80 were drawn from a bowl in which each chip was marked with a number 10 higher than a correspond-

---

† See S. W. ROBERTS, "Properties of Control Chart Zone Tests," *Bell System Technical Journal*, vol. 37, pp. 83–114, January, 1958.

ing chip in the distribution described in Table 2-6. Of course, subgroups 1 to 40 and 81 to 100 were drawn from the bowl described in Table 2-6. Figure 3-5 is similar to Fig. 3-2 except that points 41 to 80 have been raised 10 units. However, the control limits are drawn on Fig. 3-5 as if they were established by the $\bar{X}$ and R of the first 40 subgroups.

During the period in which the universe average has changed, namely, subgroups 41 to 80, occasional points are above the upper control limit. Tests based on the theory of runs also give clear evidence that the universe average has shifted.

This shift in average was equal to one standard deviation of the universe. It is obvious that the greater this shift in the average, the stronger will be the evidence of lack of control, and the sooner the shift is likely to be detected by the control chart.

When sustained shifts of process average occur *after* the control limits have been established, they result in all the out-of-control points falling outside *one* control limit, and all suspicious runs occurring on the *same* side of the central line. However, if the shift occurs *during* the period from which the control limits were established, the evidences of lack of control shift from one side to the other at the time of shift in process average.

No R chart has been given to accompany the $\bar{X}$ chart of Fig. 3-5. With this type of shift in process average, the R chart gives no indication of lack of control. It is evident that without a change of universe dispersion, the dispersion within the subgroups will not be affected.

Examples 3-1 and 3-2 illustrate situations involving shifts in process average.

Example 3-1 Shift in process average of acidity of dye liquor *Facts of the case* In the dyeing of woolen yarns, it is desirable to control the acidity of the dye liquor. Unless the dye liquor is sufficiently acid, the penetration of color is unsatisfactory; on the other hand, a too-acid liquor affects the durability of the products made from the yarn. Acidity is conveniently measured as pH (hydrogen ion concentration). A low pH corresponds to high acidity, and vice versa. In any dyeing operation there is a band of pH values within which the best results as to both color penetration and durability are obtained. A control chart for pH is helpful in maintaining acidity within the desired band.

Such a control chart is shown in Fig. 3-6. On this chart are plotted the average $\bar{X}$ values of pH of dye liquor from five Hussong kettles used for the dyeing of blanket wool. Table 3-5 gives the actual $\bar{X}$ and R values for the period of approximately 5 weeks covered by this chart. Generally, two determinations of pH were made from each kettle every day, although a few days show one or three determinations.

The central line on the chart at $\bar{X}' = 4.22$ and the control limits of 4.05 and 4.39 were established by previous data. This process average and dispersion had proved to be satisfactory from the standpoint of the desired characteristics of the dye liquor. The chart is plotted with high acidity (i.e., low pH) at the top of the graph.

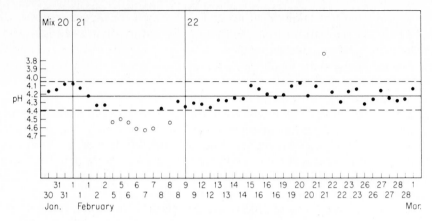

Figure 3-6 Control chart for average ($\bar{X}$) for pH of dye kettles.

Table 3-5 pH of dye liquor used for dyeing of blanket wools

Date	$\bar{X}$	R	Date	$\bar{X}$	R
Jan. 30	4.17	0.14	Feb. 14a	4.25	0.11
31a	4.15	0.30	14b	4.26	0.26
31b	4.08	0.20	15a	4.10	0.18
Feb. 1a	4.07	0.09	15b	4.14	0.23
1b	4.13	0.10	16a	4.20	0.52
1c	4.22	0.24	16b	4.24	0.17
2a	4.33	0.65	19a	4.21	0.46
2b	4.33	0.17	19b	4.11	0.20
5a	4.54	0.58	20a	4.07	0.40
5b	4.50	0.22	20b	4.22	0.12
6a	4.54	0.22	21a	4.11	1.34
6b	4.61	0.18	21b	3.72	0.96
7a	4.63	0.44	22a	4.18	0.35
7b	4.61	0.20	22b	4.29	0.31
8a	4.37	0.23	23a	4.17	0.20
8b	4.54	0.23	23b	4.14	0.13
8c	4.29	0.32	26a	4.32	0.26
9a	4.35	0.62	26b	4.26	0.08
9b	4.31	0.28	27a	4.16	0.51
12a	4.32	0.20	27b	4.25	0.25
12b	4.36	0.40	28a	4.28	0.09
13a	4.27	0.40	28b	4.26	0.15
13b	4.28	0.38	Mar. 1	4.14	0.11

(Averages and ranges of subgroups composed of samples from five Hussong kettles)

Analysis and action The acidity of the dyeing solution depends not only on the constituents put into the dye liquor but also on the characteristics of the wool being dyed. From time to time it is necessary to use wools from sources that have different characteristics. Although blends of wools from various sources are made, successive blends will differ somewhat from one another.

On February 1 a new blend of entirely different wools was introduced. Immediately the acidity dropped. On February 5, after the old surplus stock had been used up, acidity fell below the control limit and continued out of control thereafter until corrective measures were taken on February 8. At this time the amount of acid introduced into the dye liquor was changed. Although after this all points fell within the control limits, the run of points below the central line indicated that the previous average was not restored until February 15.

Thereafter, with the exception of a brief departure from control on February 21, the pH values continued in satisfactory control. The temporary difficulty on February 21 was traced to two batches of improperly neutralized carbonized (baked with concentrated sulphuric acid) stock. Such stock is acid in relation to stock normally used.

Example 3-2 Shift in quality level of steel castings *Facts of the case* Certain specially treated steel castings were required to meet rigid requirements as to strength and ductility. As part of the acceptance procedure for these castings, the purchaser required that two tensile specimens from each heat be tested to destruction in the testing laboratory. Specifications regarding the results of these tests covered tensile strength, yield point, per cent elongation, and reduction in area. $\bar{X}$ and R charts were maintained on yield point and per cent elongation. Whenever these charts showed control for a sufficient number of heats and the tests were otherwise satisfactory, the amount of required testing was reduced to two specimens from every fourth heat.

The tests did in fact show control at a satisfactory level for a number of months. Suddenly points on both $\bar{X}$ charts went out of control.

Analysis and action The responsible supervisors in the production department were sure no changes had been made in production methods. Nevertheless, all the following heats continued out of control on the $\bar{X}$ charts. An attempt was made to throw the blame on the testing laboratory; however, tests made by other personnel on other machines showed the points continuing to fall out of control. This condition continued for some time despite pressure brought by supervisors on operating personnel. Finally someone remarked that a change in the source of quench water for heat treatment had been made just before the time when the first points fell out of control. Although no one believed that this could be the source of the trouble, as a last resort the original source of quench water was restored. Immediately the results of tensile tests of specimens from subsequent heats gave points that fell within the original control limits. From this time on, the process continued in control at the original satisfactory level.

Comments on Examples 3-1 and 3-2

These examples describe cases in which the average values of the measured quality definitely moved outside control-chart limits. Even though in such cases the actual trouble shooting may encounter many difficulties, from a statistical viewpoint these are the simplest types of examples. In fact, when such cases are described in presenting the advantages of control-chart techniques, the question is likely to be asked, "Would not the need for action have been just as clear from the tests as a matter of common sense even if there had been no control chart? Just how did the control chart itself really help?"

This question implies that the tests would have been carried out and that their results would have been conveniently available for analysis, regardless of whether or not a control chart was used. This assumption is often contrary to the facts. Experience shows that the use of the control chart sometimes leads to a more systematic program of testing and measurement; it nearly always leads to a tabulation of test results in a way that makes them more readily available as a basis for action.

But the control chart's contribution to effective action in cases like Examples 3-1 and 3-2 does not depend on any stimulus that it may have given to more systematic procedures in making and recording measurements of quality. The control chart provides a graphic presentation of quality history that gives a clearer picture than could be obtained from any tabulation of test data. Of course the primary contribution of the control chart to such trouble shooting lies in the information given by the control limits. These provide rules for action that are much more definite and much more reliable than any so-called "common-sense" judgments. When the control chart shows a long period of control followed by several points out of control, the evidence is conclusive that there is a discoverable cause of variation. Such evidence may be followed with confidence in the face of assertions, such as those in Example 3-2, that no change has really taken place. Moreover, the limits provide a definite basis for judgment as to whether or not the cause of trouble has been corrected.

It will be noted that in Example 3-2 the production personnel first insisted there was no trouble; the cause of trouble was found only because some individual whose job was entirely outside production insisted that the hunt be continued. This example is not intended to suggest that an outsider using the control chart can succeed where those intimately connected with production will fail. What the outsider provided here was *insistence* that the source of trouble could be found; the actual identification of the source was made by individuals connected with production.

Experience shows that those closest to production sometimes have blind spots with respect to certain sources of trouble. A quality control engineer with wide experience states that in production conferences regarding processes which the control chart shows have gone out of control, it is common for someone close to the production operation to state "It may be cause A or cause B or cause C. One thing I am sure of is that it isn't cause D." In such instances, about half the time the source of trouble turns out to be cause D.

Examples 3-1 and 3-2 are alike in that it was the evidence of the control chart as to *when* the process went out of control that was the basis of discovering *why* it went out of control.

Example 3-2 illustrates a case in which a purchaser's control chart gave guidance to a vendor. This is a common occurrence and often leads to the use of the control-chart technique by the vendor.

Example 3-1 represents a common situation characteristic of the food industry, the chemical industry, and the ceramic industry as well as the textile industry. This is the situation in which some variation in raw material quality is inevitable. In spite of this variation (such as that of wool from different sources) it is desired to maintain a certain quality level (as of pH of dye liquor) at some stage of the manufacturing operations. This quality level may in itself not be a quality of the finished product, but, as in the case of the dye liquor, may influence various desired qualities of the product.

In the case of Example 3-1, control limits on the $\bar{X}$ chart were set on the basis of a previous $\bar{R}$ of 0.30. No R chart was kept, as previous experience had indicated that troubles were always with process average and not with process dispersion. However if an R chart is plotted for the data of Table 3-5, it will show lack of control on February 2 and 21. Both cases coincide with times when $\bar{X}$ went out of control and result from an unequal influence on different members of the subgroup by a change in the process average. To use the analogy of drawing from a bowl, it is as if while switching from one bowl to another, a few subgroups were drawn with some chips from the old bowl and the remaining chips from the new bowl.

Frequent Irregular Changes in Universe Average with Constant Universe Standard Deviation

Figure 3-7 is derived from the data of Table 2-7 in a way intended to produce an illustration of the effect of numerous changes in the universe average. Table 2-7 gave drawings from a bowl with a constant average of 30 and standard deviation of 10. Figure 3-7 uses these drawings for the first 50 subgroups. The remaining 50 subgroups show irregular variation in universe average, with the amount and duration of each shift having been determined from a table of random numbers. The universe standard deviation continued at 10 throughout all 100 subgroups.

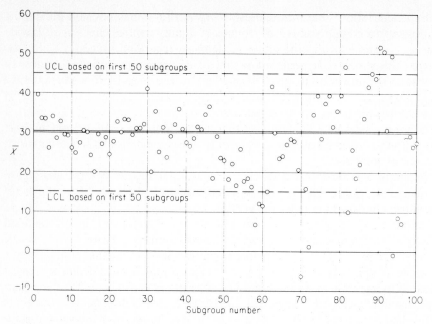

Figure 3-7 $\bar{X}$ chart showing the effect of frequent irregular changes in universe average.

The averages used were as follows:

Subgroups	Universe Average
1–50	30
51–57	20
58–61	10
62	45
63–69	25
70–72	5
73–81	35
82–85	15
86–93	40
94–96	10
97–100	30

This type of situation is often a result of carelessness in machine setting. As indicated in Fig. 3-7, it results in points falling outside *both* control limits on the $\bar{X}$ chart. If the shifts in universe average occur between subgroups and never happen to fall within a subgroup, the R chart will continue to show control regardless of the variations shown on the $\bar{X}$ chart.

At first glance it might seem that a situation such as that pictured in the control chart of Fig. 3-7 should always be a cause for action on the manufacturing process. However, this is not necessarily true. It all depends on the relationship between the specified tolerances, on the one hand, and the constant universe dispersion and the fluctuations of the universe average on the other.

Assume, for example, that the data of Table 2-7 referred to the final two digits of a dimension measured to thousandths of a centimeter; let us say a figure of 27 in Table 2-7 would correspond to a dimension of 21.527 cm. If the engineering specification were 21.53 ± 0.03, it would be evident that the tolerances were so tight that careful attention would always have to be paid to machine setting; any points falling out of control limits on the $\bar{X}$ chart would indicate that some product was being made outside tolerance limits. On the other hand, if the engineering specification were 21.53 ± 0.10, the situation shown in Fig. 3-7 would not have caused any rejected product; in this case there would be quite a range of possible carelessness in machine setting without causing any product to fall outside the tolerances.

In control of dimensions in manufacturing, the great usefulness of the control charts for $\bar{X}$ and R is in those situations where the specification tolerances are tight compared to the inherent variability of the manufacturing process. Fortunately, in most manufacturing operations this is true of only a small proportion of specified dimensions.

Shift in Universe Dispersion with No Change in Universe Average

The inherent variability of a process may change from time to time even though there is no change in the process average. On any process where the skill and care of the operator is an important factor, a common cause of increase in variability is a change from one operator to another who is less skillful or less careful. In fact, an operator's skill and care may sometimes vary from day to day or from hour to hour.

This type of shift in universe is illustrated in Fig. 3-8, which has been adapted from the data of Table 2-7. For the first 40 subgroups, universe standard deviation is 10; for subgroups 41 to 80, universe standard deviation is 20; for the final 20 subgroups it is 10 again. The universe average has been held constant at 30 throughout. Figure 3-8 gives both $\bar{X}$ and R charts. Both charts show lack of control, with more points outside control limits on the R chart than on the $\bar{X}$ chart. Extreme runs above the central line on the R chart also give strong evidence of lack of control.

The central lines and control limits on Fig. 3-8 have been set using the data from the first 40 subgroups. If they had been set using the data from the first 80 subgroups, $\bar{R}$ would have been larger and the limits on both the $\bar{X}$ and R charts would have been wider. With these limits fewer points would have fallen outside the control limits. However, the higher value of the central line on the R chart would have introduced other evidence of lack of control in the form of extreme runs below the central line.

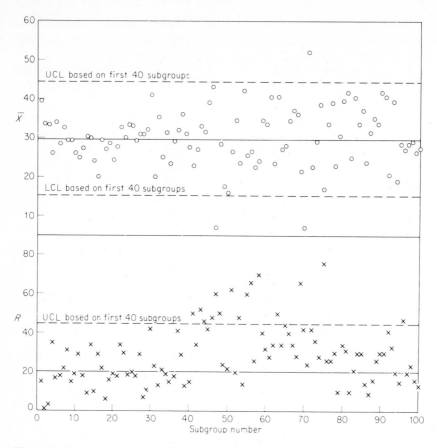

Figure 3-8 Control charts for $\bar{X}$ and R showing the effect of a sustained shift in universe dispersion.

The Importance of the R Chart Depends on the Type of Production Process

Many production processes tend to have relatively uniform dispersion even though the process centering changes from time to time. In such processes, lack of statistical control will be detected from the $\bar{X}$ chart; the R chart adds relatively little useful information.

In contrast, there are many other production processes in which it is difficult to maintain uniform process dispersion; in such processes the R chart may be an extremely useful tool for process control. A generalization, subject to exceptions, is that such variability of process dispersion is particularly likely to be found in those processes where the skill of the operator is important. Generally speaking, the first step in improving such processes should be to try to bring the process dispersion into statistical control.

The following interesting wartime quotation from a publication of the British Ministry of Labour and National Service and the Ministry of Production deals with the circumstances in which the range chart is useful in controlling the operation of machine tools:†

It has often been said that quality control technique is not likely to prove of much value when applied to jobs in which the human element plays a major part in controlling the quality of the product.

The saving in inspection costs and personnel which often results from the introduction of quality control has been so extensively publicised that there has been a tendency to lose sight of the real object of the system, which is to improve quality, increase uniformity, reduce or prevent the production of scrap, and to provide a running commentary on the performance of machines and operators, invaluable for shop floor investigations and factory planning. This demands a fundamentally different approach to the subject. It is not a question, in the first place, of relying on a control chart to do our inspection for us. No control chart should ever be relied upon in this way until it has given abundant evidence that such reliance is justified. It is, in the first place, a question of using the control chart to give such information to, and keep such a check upon, operators and setters that the quality of the product is improved. If the improvement (as often happens) is so significant that the percentage of rejects at gauging inspection is found to be held invariably at an acceptable level, then of course, there is a clear case for reducing or eliminating the gauging inspection, but this is a consequence of the introduction of quality control, not its original objective. Incidentally, many factories have found that control charts and measuring equipment easily pay for themselves even though inspection cost is not reduced at all. It may even be increased, particularly when first introducing quality control.

Charts for hand-operated jobs should be interpreted rather differently from those on fully automatic machines. The ranges of samples from a reasonably good auto are often found to vary very little. It is the points on the chart for means that tend to wander. In other words, an automatic machine can usually produce a uniform product at least for a short period, and it is tool wear and setter's adjustments that need to be controlled, not the basic variability of the machine. In fact, so stable is the range chart often found to be on an automatic job, that some firms are not even bothering to plot it at all, on the grounds that it tells them nothing but what they know already, namely that, so long as the machine is properly set and adjusted, its product will be satisfactory. It is the mean chart which is the setter's chart. Should the ranges of samples from an auto be found out of control, it is quite a serious matter, for it indicates some breakdown in the basic operating characteristics of the machine, and will possibly mean that some actual repair, replacement or overhaul is necessary, as distinct from mere setting or adjustment.

On a hand-operated job, however, the position is rather different. We still have our chart of sample means to give information to the setter, but our main sources of error are likely to be the shortcomings of the operator herself. These errors are usually of a random nature—too long a dwell on one component, not long enough on another; odd, erratic performances of all kinds, due to lack of concentration or skill on the part of the operator. Such errors, when present, will result in an increase in the variability of the product and will be detected by the large ranges of the samples taken during the periods of bad workmanship. It is, thus, the chart of ranges which needs watching in this instance. It should be regarded as the operator's own personal chart, and everything possible should be done to encourage the operator herself to regard it in this way. It is a running commentary on her work—a chart standing always right before her eyes on which are recorded, faithfully and inevitably, for all the world to see, her careless slips and faults—as well as her long runs of good production.

† Quality Control on Hand-operated Machines, *Production and Engineering Bulletin*, vol. 3, pp. 25–31, January, 1944.

Effect of Gradual Reduction in Process Dispersion on Control Limits on $\bar{X}$ and R Charts

On processes where the skill and care of the operator have a major influence on process dispersion, the mere introduction of a control chart often causes a gradual reduction in the dispersion of the quality characteristic charted. Example 4-2 in the next chapter describes a case where this happened. Such a change is a useful contribution of the control chart to improved quality, even though this contribution does not depend on the use of the chart as a statistical tool to diagnose the causes of troubles.

Nevertheless, such cases create certain practical problems in the interpretation of the control chart for R. As long as the subgroup size is six or less, the lower control limit on the R chart is always zero regardless of the value of $\bar{R}$. Thus, with the usual size of subgroups, a decrease in universe dispersion cannot be reflected in points falling below the lower control limit on the R chart. Here reliance must be placed on regular reviews of the value of $\bar{R}$ used to set limits on both the $\bar{X}$ and R charts. Often the need to review $\bar{R}$ is suggested by extreme runs below the central line on the R chart. It should be remembered that whenever, because of evidence of a decrease in universe dispersion, the value of $\bar{R}$ used in computing control limits is recalculated and reduced, this tightens the control limits on the $\bar{X}$ chart as well as on the R chart.

Changes in Universe Average and Universe Dispersion

When universe dispersion as well as universe average is shifting, it is obvious that lack of control will be indicated in both charts, the R chart as well as the $\bar{X}$ chart. Such a condition was illustrated in Fig. 1-2 of Example 1-1. This state of affairs is common in the first stages of the use of the control chart for variables for analysis of many manufacturing operations.

Where several assignable causes of variation exist, the elimination of some of the causes will decrease the number of out-of-control points but will not eliminate all of them. In such circumstances, the continuance of some points out of control may be discouraging to anyone anxious for quick results. Rather than causing discouragement, the control chart is better viewed as an indication that further improvement is possible and as an incentive to keep hunting for more sources of trouble.

Assignable Causes of Variation May Be Due to Errors of Measurement

In Example 3-2, the production department first tried to lay the blame on faulty inspection as the source of the indication of lack of control. This common production alibi proved to be wrong. Nevertheless, there is always the possibility that it may be right.

It should be emphasized that the control-chart analysis, like any other statistical test, is applied to a set of numbers. Anything that affects these numbers affects the control chart. The numbers are influenced by variations in the measurements, just as they are influenced by variations in the quality characteristic being measured. The universe from which samples are being drawn is the result of a cause system that includes measurement causes as well as production causes.

Therefore, an error in measurement may be an assignable cause of variation in the figures resulting from the measurements. In describing the various types of lack of control, reference was made to production situations that might give rise to each type. Similarly, each might have been associated with some sort of inspection error. An error in setting a measuring device may make a sudden shift in universe average. Frequent errors in setting may make irregular shifts in the average. Some types of wear of measuring devices may increase universe dispersion. Other types of wear may give rise to trends in averages.

Interpreting Patterns of Variation on $\bar{X}$ and R Charts

An important aspect of the use of control charts is the interpretation of the many patterns that they may exhibit. In addition to the standard rule for looking for trouble, we have also discussed secondary or supplementary rules based on the theory of runs.

In the examples and discussions presented, an intimate knowledge of the process being controlled was vital to the effective use of the control chart. The control chart tells *when* to look for trouble but it cannot, by itself, tell *where* to look or *what* cause will be found.

Figure 3-9 illustrates some of the patterns that are frequently seen on control charts and states some possible causes of these patterns. Studies performed at Bell Telephone Laboratories during the summer of 1964 categorized the most frequent causes of trouble.† Developed as an aid to training young inspectors and engineers, the listed causes should be used only as a guide to possible action, not as an authoritative listing of *the* causes of trouble.

The Causing of Product Variability by Too-frequent Adjustment of the Process Centering

In certain types of manufacturing processes, the greatest value of an $\bar{X}$ chart may be that it tells the operator when to leave the process alone. Many processes are similar to the ones illustrated in Fig. 3-4a, b, and c in having a fairly constant process dispersion under ordinary circumstances combined with a tendency of the process centering to shift. In a number of such processes, the process centering can be changed by one or more simple machine adjustments made by the operator.

---

† The authors are indebted to Dr. Richard L. Patterson, University of Michigan, for supplying the basic data for Fig. 3-9. A more complete discussion of recognition of patterns on control charts is contained in the "Statistical Quality Control Handbook," Western Electric Company, New York, 1956.

Some causes affecting $\bar{X}$ chart
(stable variability)

Some causes affecting R chart

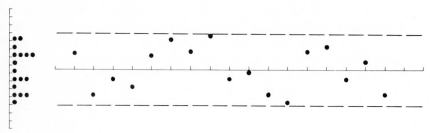

(a) *Recurring cycles*

1. Temperature or other recurring changes in physical environment
2. Worker fatigue
3. Differences in measuring or testing devices which are used in order
4. Regular rotation of machines or operators
5. Merging of subassemblies or other processes

1. Scheduled preventive maintenance
2. Worker fatigue
3. Worn tools

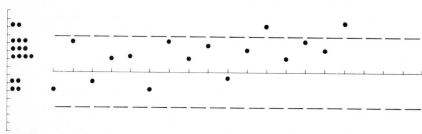

(b) *Trends*

1. Gradual deterioration of equipment which can affect all items
2. Worker fatigue
3. Accumulation of waste products
4. Deterioration of environmental conditions

1. Improvement or deterioration of operator skill
2. Worker fatigue
3. Change in proportions of subprocesses feeding an assembly line
4. Gradual change in homogeneity of incoming material quality

Figure 3-9 Some interpretations of patterns of $\bar{X}$ and R charts.

Some causes affecting $\overline{X}$ chart
     (stable variability)   Some causes affecting R chart

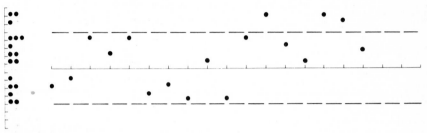

(c) *Jumps in process level*

1. Change in proportions of materials or subassemblies coming from different sources
2. New worker or machine
3. Modification of production method or process
4. Change in inspection device or method

1. Change in material
2. Change in method
3. Change in worker

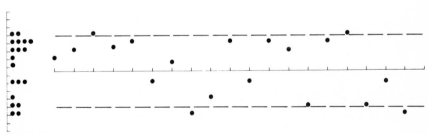

(d) *High proportion of points near or outside limits*

1. Over control
2. Large systematic differences in material quality
3. Large systematic differences in test method or equipment
4. Control of two or more processes on same chart

1. Mixture of materials of distinctly different quality
2. Different workers using a single R chart
3. Data from processes under different conditions plotted on same chart

Figure 3-9 (*continued*)

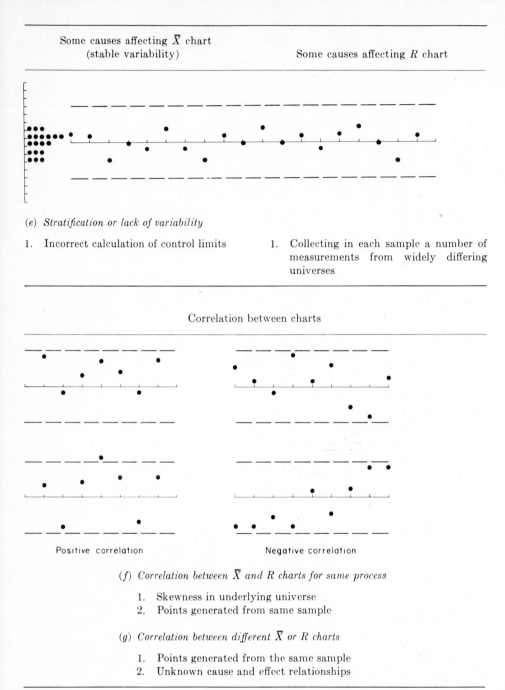

Some causes affecting $\bar{X}$ chart
(stable variability)

Some causes affecting R chart

(e) *Stratification or lack of variability*

1. Incorrect calculation of control limits

1. Collecting in each sample a number of measurements from widely differing universes

Correlation between charts

Positive correlation

Negative correlation

(f) *Correlation between $\bar{X}$ and R charts for same process*

1. Skewness in underlying universe
2. Points generated from same sample

(g) *Correlation between different $\bar{X}$ or R charts*

1. Points generated from the same sample
2. Unknown cause and effect relationships

Figure 3-9 (*continued*)

Without the restraining influence exerted by a control chart, operators frequently have a tendency to adjust the process too often. Example 3-3 describes a case where this occurred.

Example 3-3 Use of $\bar{X}$ chart to prevent too-frequent changes in process centering *Facts of the case* One of the steps in manufacturing an assembled article was to fill a certain component with a specified weight of a certain dry powder. The specification might be described as $W \pm T$, where W is the desired average weight and T is the allowable tolerance. Several thousand components per hour were filled by an automatic machine. The average filling weight could be increased or decreased by a simple adjustment of the machine. The practice of the operator—working under instructions from a supervisor—was to take one filled component at random every half hour or so, empty the component, and weigh its powder contents on an accurate balance. Whenever the weight of this sample of one fell below W, the machine was adjusted to give a higher weight; whenever the weight fell above W, the machine was adjusted to give a lower weight. Many of the samples caused some machine adjustment.

Subsequent inspection of finished product showed a substantial fraction of the product falling outside the specified limits of $W \pm T$. One of the persons supervising the operation commented that this failure to meet specifications took place "in spite of the careful attention we are giving to machine adjustment."

Analysis and action When an engineer familiar with control-chart techniques joined the staff of this manufacturing plant, this was the first operation to which $\bar{X}$ and R charts were applied. Samples of 5 were taken at intervals over a considerable period of time during which no machine adjustment was permitted. Control charts showed that the process was close to being in statistical control. Thereafter the control charts were continued on a regular basis. The operator was instructed to make no machine adjustments as long as points fell within control limits. It turned out that the process was one that ordinarily stayed in statistical control for a fairly long period without requiring adjustment. Not only did it prove possible to hold all product within the original specification limits; the tolerance limits were later narrowed in a way that improved the performance of the assembled product. It was evident that the "careful attention" to machine adjustment had been the cause of unnecessarily large variation in product quality.

Comment on Example 3-3

Although in fact the example describes one particular case, the reader might interpret it as giving a rough description of many similar cases that have occurred in a wide variety of manufacturing plants. Whenever process adjustments are

Table 3-6 Calculations of adjustments to centering of Shewhart's normal bowl, drawings 141–156. It is assumed that samples of one have been taken and an adjustment made whenever observed value falls above or below 30

Bowl drawing number	Marking on chip	Correction to chip marking (preceding F minus 30)	Adjusted chip value $(B + C)$	Change in process centering based on adjusted chip value (30 minus D)	Revised process centering (preceding F plus E)
A	B	C	D	E	F
					30
141	21	0	21	+ 9	39
142	31	+ 9	40	−10	29
143	39	− 1	38	− 8	21
144	25	− 9	16	+14	35
145	17	+ 5	22	+ 8	43
146	44	+13	57	−27	16
147	54	−14	40	−10	6
148	13	−24	−11	+41	47
149	36	+17	53	−23	24
150	48	− 6	42	−12	12
151	19	−18	1	+29	41
152	41	+11	52	−22	19
153	25	−11	14	+16	35
154	31	+ 5	36	− 6	29
155	38	− 1	37	− 7	22
156	30	− 8	22	+ 8	30

made based on criteria that do not recognize the inherent variability of a manufacturing process, there is danger that these adjustments will be too frequent and that they will increase the amount of product variability. One quality control consultant described this type of condition as a "sitting duck."

A simple model based on a sequence of drawings from Shewhart's bowl may help the reader to visualize what was happening in Example 3-3 before the introduction of the control charts. Assume that with no machine adjustments, filling weights follow the distribution shown in Table 2-7, with a centering at 30 and a spread from 0 to 60. (These figures might represent the final two digits of a weight expressed, say, in thousandths of a gram.) Whenever the centering of the distribution is raised or lowered, all other values of the distribution are raised or lowered by an equal amount.

Table 3-6 uses drawings 141 to 156 from Shewhart's bowl to illustrate the adjustments to the process entering that would have been made if an adjustment had been made whenever a single observed value fell above or below the desired value of 30. Each observed value from the original bowl is increased or decreased to correspond to the difference between the current process centering and 30. The arithmetic of the table should be self-explanatory. It will be observed from column E that changes are being made at every observation. It will be observed from column F that these changes are introducing considerable variability into the centering of the process.

A Possible View of the Question Answered by a Control Chart

The following discussion uses the $\bar{X}$ chart as an example, assuming the special case in which the universe dispersion remains constant and the universe average may shift. However, the points that are brought out in the discussion are equally applicable to other types of charts and to cases where changes occur in the dispersion.

The 100 subgroups from Shewhart's bowl listed in Table 2-7 and charted in Fig. 3-2 gave control limits on the $\bar{X}$ chart of approximately 45 and 15. Suppose the 101st subgroup has an $\bar{X}$ of 43. Should we interpret this as telling us that the universe has changed (possibly by the substitution of a set of chips that has an $\bar{X}'$ of more than 30)? Our control-chart limits answer this question with a "No." However, if the $\bar{X}$ for the 101st subgroup should be 48, the answer would be "Yes."

Either the universe has changed or it has not changed. We are in the position of having to make a judgment on this point based on the evidence of the $\bar{X}$ of a sample of 4. Sometimes this judgment will be correct; sometimes it will be incorrect.

If we conclude that the universe has changed when it really is unchanged, this conclusion is described by writers on statistics as a Type I or α error. If we conclude that the universe has not changed when it really has changed, this conclusion is described as a Type II or β error.

With limits on an $\bar{X}$ chart at $\bar{\bar{X}} \pm 3\sigma_{\bar{X}}$, it is evident that Type I errors will be infrequent. On the other hand, if moderate changes in the centering of the process occur, Type II errors may happen fairly often. The existence of Type II errors with 3-sigma limits and a moderate shift in $\bar{X}'$ may be illustrated by looking back at Fig. 3-5, where we assume that $\bar{X}'$ shifted from 30 to 40 for subgroups 41 to 80. This was a shift of approximately one standard deviation. Only 9 of the $\bar{X}$ values for subgroups 41 to 80 fell outside the limits that had been established on the basis of subgroups 1 to 40; the first point outside limits did not occur until subgroup 45.

Modern statistical theory provides many different tests of hypotheses that samples come from the same or different universes. Control charts used in manufacturing may be thought of as relatively simple statistical tests; there are many tests of greater complexity and sophistication. A dilemma in all such tests is to strike some sort of rational balance between Type I and Type II errors. There are good reasons why the common practice in manufacturing is to set control-chart limits far enough apart so that Type I errors will be rare.

Some Practical Aspects of the Tightness of Limits on Control Charts Used in Manufacturing

A typical action based on out-of-control points on control charts for variables is to hunt for the source of trouble. Such hunting was illustrated in Examples 3-1 and 3-2. Sometimes a process may be shut down until it is believed that the assignable cause of variation has been found and corrected.

It is rare for a manufacturing process to behave for long periods of time like the drawing of chips from a bowl. At best, small changes in any process may be expected to occur from time to time—in the centering of the process and possibly in its dispersion and the form of the frequency distribution of any quality characteristic. The assignable causes of such small changes may be extremely difficult to find.

Moreover, trouble, in the sense of assignable causes of substantial changes in quality, is a common state of affairs in manufacturing. Even those large changes that cause nearly all points to fall outside 3-sigma limits may require much hunting and hard work before the assignable causes are found. This was illustrated in Example 3-2.

Under such circumstances, it seldom pays to hunt for trouble without a strong basis for confidence that trouble is really there. The real basis for the use of 3-sigma limits on control charts for variables in industrial quality control is experience that, when closer limits, such as 2-sigma, are used, the control chart often gives indication of assignable causes of variation that simply cannot be found whereas, when 3-sigma limits are used and points fall out of control, a diligent search will usually disclose the assignable causes of variation.

Although wide limits, such as 3-sigma, are generally appropriate, special circumstances arise where narrower limits may be desirable. In principle, the tightness of control limits is an economic problem involving the balancing of the various economic consequences of different possible limits. If enough information about the relevant costs and other economic matters were available in each case, the tightness of limits could be tailormade for each control chart. Unfortunately, all the relevant economic information is rarely obtainable.

Reducing the Chance of a Type II Error by Increasing the Subgroup Size

Consider an $\bar{X}$ chart in the type of case illustrated in Fig. 3-5, where σ' remains constant and $\bar{X}'$ changes. A decision to use relatively wide limits, such as 3-sigma, ensures that Type I errors will be rare. This is true regardless of subgroup size.

However, the larger the subgroup size, the narrower the limits on the $\bar{X}$ chart and the greater the sensitivity of the $\bar{X}$ chart to shifts in $\bar{X}'$.† In other words, an

---

† Generally speaking, the advantages of the $\bar{X}$ chart cannot be obtained with a subgroup size of one. Nevertheless, some writers have misrepresented the control-chart technique by analyzing the sensitivity of such charts to changes in $\bar{X}'$ on the assumption (not explicitly stated) that all Shewhart charts use one as the subgroup size. For example, see Fig. 5 in H. M. TRUAX, Cumulative Sum Charts and Their Application to the Chemical Industry, *Industrial Quality Control*, vol. 18, no. 6, p. 21, December, 1961.

increase in subgroup size reduces the frequency of Type II errors without the penalty of too frequent Type I errors.

Cases sometimes arise where relatively large subgroup sizes are justified by the need for prompt detection of small shifts in $\bar{X}'$. But there are usually good reasons for the common practice by favoring subgroup sizes of 4 or 5. Various aspects of the question of subgroup size are discussed further in Chaps. 4 and 5.

Basis of Selection of Subgroups

The discussion throughout this chapter has implied *time* of production as the basis for selection of rational subgroups. This is a natural and logical basis, but, for reasons explained in Chap. 5, it is not always a sufficient one. As pointed out there, the conclusions to be drawn from any control chart depend on the basis of selection of subgroups; a process may appear to show control with one plan of subgrouping and not show control with some other plan.

Moreover, there are many situations in which the order of production is no longer known but where it is still possible to use the control chart to advantage. Some comments on this are made in Chap. 9.

PROBLEMS

3-1 Control charts for $\bar{X}$ and R are maintained on a certain dimension of a manufactured part, measured in inches. The subgroup size is 4. The values of $\bar{X}$ and R are computed for each subgroup. After 20 subgroups, $\Sigma \bar{X} = 41.340$, and $\Sigma R = 0.320$. Compute the values of the 3-sigma limits for the $\bar{X}$ and R charts, and estimate the value of σ' on the assumption that the process is in statistical control.
          Answer: 2.079, 2.055; 0.0360, 0; 0.0078.

3-2 Control charts for $\bar{X}$ and R are maintained on the shear strength in pounds of test spot welds. The subgroup size is 3. The values of $\bar{X}$ and R are computed for each subgroup. After 30 subgroups, $\Sigma \bar{X} = 12,930$, and $\Sigma R = 1,230$. Compute the values of the 3-sigma limits for the $\bar{X}$ and R charts, and estimate the value of σ' on the assumption that the process is in statistical control.
          Answer: 472.8, 389.2; 105.4,0; 24.2.

3-3 Control charts for $\bar{X}$ and σ are maintained on the breaking strength in pounds in a certain destructive test of a particular type of ceramic insulator used in vacuum tubes. The subgroup size is 15. The values of $\bar{X}$ and σ are computed for each subgroup. After 12 subgroups, $\Sigma \bar{X} = 1,307$, and $\Sigma \sigma = 191.5$. Compute the values of the 3-sigma limits for the $\bar{X}$ and σ charts, and estimate the value of σ' on the assumption that the process is in statistical control.
          Answer: 122.0, 95.8; 25.05, 6.86; 16.8.

3-4 Control charts for $\bar{X}$ and R are maintained on dissolved iron content of a certain solution in parts per million (ppm). After 125 hourly samples have been drawn and analyzed, the data are organized into 25 subgroups of 5 measurements each maintaining the time order of sampling. From these data, $\Sigma \bar{X} = 390.8$ and $\Sigma R = 84$. Find the values of 3-sigma control limits for $\bar{X}$ and R and estimate the value of σ' for this process under the assumption that the process is in control.

3-5 The specification on the process described in Problem 3-4 calls for no more than 18 ppm dissolved iron in the solution. Assuming a normal distribution underlies the process and that the process continues to be in statistical control with no change in average or dispersion, what proportion of the sample measurements may be expected to exceed this specification?

3-6 Control charts for $\bar{X}$ and σ are maintained on the resistance in ohms of a certain rheostat coil based on a subgroup size of five. After 30 subgroups, $\Sigma \bar{X} = 58,395$ and $\Sigma \sigma = 1,356$.

(a) Determine the central lines and 3-sigma control limits for this process.

(b) Estimate the value of σ' assuming that the process is operating in statistical control.

(c) Assuming that the distribution generated by the process is approximately normal, what proportion of the rheostat coils meets specifications of $2,000 \pm 150$ ohms?

3-7 In order to meet government regulations, the contained weight of a product must at least equal the labeled weight 98% of the time. Control charts for $\bar{X}$ and σ are maintained on the weight in ounces of the contents using a subgroup size of 10. After 20 subgroups, $\Sigma \bar{X} = 731.4$ and $\Sigma \sigma = 9.16$. Compute 3σ control limits for $\bar{X}$ and σ and estimate the value of σ' assuming the process is in statistical control. If the label weight is 36 oz, and assuming the process generates a normal distribution, does it meet federal requirements?

Answer: 37.04, 36.10; 0.788, 0.128; 0.496; No, 12.5% out.

3-8 Control charts for $\bar{X}$, R, and σ are to be maintained on drawings from a bowl of chips the distribution of which is approximately normal. The subgroup size is 4. $\bar{X}'$ is 40.00 and σ' is 6.00. Assume the 3σ limits are to be based on $\bar{X}'$ and σ'. Compute the value of the upper control limit, the central line, and the lower control limit for $\bar{X}$, R, and σ charts, respectively.

Answer: 49, 40, 31; 28.2, 12.36, 0; 10.86, 4.79, 0.

3-9 After the bowl drawing referred to in Problem 3-8 has continued for some time, a frequency distribution is made of the $\bar{X}$ values. Estimate the average and standard deviation of this distribution. A frequency distribution is also made of the σ values. Estimate the average and standard deviation of this distribution.

Answer: 40, 3; 4.79, 2.12.

3-10 The statement is made on page 83 that the standard deviation of a subgroup of 2 is always half the range. Explain why this is true.

3-11 Use the factors in Table B to determine the values of A, A_1, and A_2 for a subgroup size of 3.

3-12 Use the factors in Table B to determine the values of A, A_1, and A_2 for a subgroup size of 8.

3-13 Use the factors in Table B and the approximation of σ_σ given on page 85 to determine the factors B_1, B_2, B_3 and B_4 for a subgroup size of 10.

3-14 Use the factors in Table B and the approximation of σ_σ given on page 85 to determine the factors B_1, B_2, B_3, and B_4 for a subgroup size of 8.

3-15 Compute 3σ control chart limits for $\bar{X}$, R, and σ for drawings 201 through 300 (25 subgroups) from Shewhart's normal bowl in Table 2-7. Estimate the value of σ' using both ΣR and $\Sigma \sigma$. Is a state of statistical control indicated for these 25 values of $\bar{X}$, R, and σ? If these control limits are used for charting the last 25 subgroups (drawings 301 through 400), is there any reason to conclude that the two groups of drawings might not come from the same universe? Explain your answer.

3-16 $\bar{X}$ and R charts have been maintained on a certain quality characteristic. All points have fallen within control limits on both charts. A sudden change in the process occurs that increases $\bar{X}'$ by $1.5\sigma'$ but does not change σ'. In answering the following questions, assume that the quality characteristic is normally distributed both before and after the change and that the control limits are based on observations made before the shift in process centering.

(a) If the subgroup size is 3, approximately what percentage of points would you expect to fall outside control limits on the $\bar{X}$ chart because of the change in $\bar{X}'$?

Answer: 34.4%.

(b) Answer the same question assuming a subgroup size of 5.

Answer: 63.8%.

(c) Answer the same question assuming a subgroup size of 8.

Answer: 89.3%.

3-17 Plot control charts for $\bar{X}$ and R for the data in Problem 2-1. Does this process appear to be in control?

3-18 Calculate 2σ control limits for $\bar{X}$ from the Shewhart normal bowl data given in Table 2-7. What proportion of the mean values would you expect to fall outside these limits purely by chance? What proportion actually fall outside the 2σ limits? Comment on your results.

Answer: 40.2, 20.0; 4.55%; 9%.

3-19 Calculate the position of the central lines and control limits for $\bar{X}$ and R charts for the data of Table 3-5, assuming that no information prior to January 30 was available. Plot both $\bar{X}$ and R charts with these limits. Comment on the difference between the results so obtained and the results shown in Fig. 3-6.

3-20 Compute control limits for $\bar{X}$ for Fig. 3-5, basing the limits on the first 80 subgroups rather than on the first 40. For these 80 subgroups $\bar{\bar{X}} = 34.7$ and $\bar{R} = 20.0$. What change does this make in the points falling outside the control limits?

3-21 On page 99 it is stated that a specification of 21.53 ± 0.10 permits a considerable range of carelessness in machine setting but that a specification of 21.53 ± 0.03 calls for close attention to machine setting. Explain this statement. If necessary, refer to Tables 2-6 and 2-7 and Fig. 3-7 in your explanation.

3-22 Compute control limits for $\bar{X}$ and R for Fig. 3-8, basing the limits on the first 80 subgroups rather than the first 40. For these 80 subgroups $\bar{\bar{X}} = 29.50$ and $\bar{R} = 30.00$. What points fall outside the control limits? Are there any significant extreme runs above or below the central line?

3-23 Why is it that an increase in universe dispersion with no change in universe average throws the $\bar{X}$ chart out of control as well as the R chart?

3-24 The $\bar{X}$ and R charts of Fig. 1-2, Example 1-1, show lack of control. Of the various types of shifts in the universe illustrated in Fig. 3-4, which ones might be expected to result in control charts such as these? Explain.

3-25 You are shown what purports to be a control chart for $\bar{X}$ on a certain quality characteristic of a manufactured product. This control chart contains 50 subgroups. You observe that all the $\bar{X}$ values are close to the central line on the chart and none are near the 3-sigma limits. In fact, when you draw 1-sigma limits (only one-third of the distance from the central line to the control limits shown), all the points fall within these narrow limits.

Would such a chart make you suspicious that something was wrong? Why? What possible explanations occur to you that might account for an $\bar{X}$ chart of this type?

3-26 $\bar{X}$ and R charts have been maintained on a certain quality characteristic. All points have fallen within control limits on both charts. A sudden change in the process occurs that decreases $\bar{X}'$ by $1.0\sigma'$ but does not change σ'. In answering the following questions, assume that the quality characteristic is normally distributed both before and after the change and that the control limits are based on observations made before the shift in process centering.

    (a) Approximately what percentage of points would you expect to fall outside control limits on the $\bar{X}$ chart because of the change in $\bar{X}'$ if the subgroup size is 4?

    (b) Answer the same question assuming the subgroup size is 6.

    (c) Answer the same question assuming the subgroup size is 9.

    (d) Relate the answers to the above questions to Type II error and the effect of subgroup size on the detection of shifts in $\bar{X}'$ on the $\bar{X}$ chart.

3-27 Control charts for $\bar{X}$ and σ are maintained on the resistance in ohms of a certain electronic device. The subgroup size is 10. After 25 subgroups, $\Sigma\bar{X} = 110.371$ and $\Sigma\sigma = 1.846$. Compute the values of the central lines and 3-sigma control limits for these charts.

3-28 On the assumption that the process described in Problem 3-27 is operating in statistical control, estimate the value of σ' for the process. What proportion of the product would you expect to meet specifications of 4.50 ± 0.25 ohms if the process is assumed to generate a normal distribution?

3-29 Control charts for $\bar{X}$ and R are maintained on a critical dimension in a certain manufacturing process. The subgroup size is five. After 25 subgroups, $\Sigma\bar{X} = 562.5$ mm, and $\Sigma R = 90.0$ mm. Compute the values of the central lines and 3-sigma control limits for this process. Estimate the value of σ' on the assumption that the process was operating in a state of statistical control.

3-30 A textile mill's development group determines that it must have a fiber which, among other properties, has a minimum tensile strength of 1.800 grams in 95% of the fiber used. Manufacturer A offers to supply such a fiber and a contract is arranged.

(a) Manufacturer A knowns that the standard deviation (σ') of its process is 0.015 grams. What minimum aimed-at value of the mean $(\bar{X}'_0)$ is required to assure compliance with the contract? Assume that statistical control will be maintained and that the distribution of tensile strength is approximately normal.

(b) Control charts for $\bar{X}$ and σ are to be maintained based on a subgroup size of 6. Determine the central lines and control limits for these charts.

3-31 Government regulations require that the net contained weight of a certain product must equal the labeled weight 98% of the time. Control charts for $\bar{X}$ and σ are maintained on the weight in grams of the contents using a subgroup size of 8. After 25 subgroups, $\Sigma\bar{X} = 25,335.0$ grams and $\Sigma\sigma = 184.0$ grams. Compute the central lines and 3-sigma limits for these control charts.

3-32 If the labeled weight is one kilogram in the situation described in Problem 3-31, does the product meet government specifications? Explain your answer. What percentage of the product would you expect to meet the labeled weight?

3-33 $\bar{X}$ and R charts based on a subgroup size of 5 have been maintained on a process for a long period of time. During the past month, no points have fallen outside the control limits. The resulting month's data yields $\bar{\bar{X}} = 0.7505$ and $\bar{R} = 0.0045$.

(a) Estimate the current value of σ' for this process.

(b) Ten of the last eleven points on the R chart are above the central line. Based on this evidence, does the process appear to be operating in statistical control?

3-34 Mark 500 chips as follows:

Marking	Frequency	Marking	Frequency	Marking	Frequency
28	1	22	58	16	22
27	2	21	73	15	11
26	5	20	78	14	5
25	11	19	73	13	2
24	22	18	58	12	1
23	39	17	39		

Place the chips in a bowl and stir thoroughly. Draw five chips and record the readings. Replace the chips, stir thoroughly, and draw five more. Repeat this until you have a record of 50 subgroups of 5 each. Compute $\bar{X}$ and R for each subgroup as you go along, and plot a control chart. After the first 20 subgroups, compute control limits and put them on the chart. After the 50 subgroups have been drawn, compute $\bar{R}$ for the entire set of 50. From this estimate σ'. Compute the true σ' from the distribution in the bowl and compare with the σ' estimated from the drawings.

3-35 Mark 500 chips as follows:

Marking	Frequency	Marking	Frequency	Marking	Frequency
32	1	26	58	20	22
31	2	25	73	19	11
30	5	24	78	18	5
29	11	23	73	17	2
28	22	22	58	16	1
27	39	21	39		

Continue the control charts for $\bar{X}$ and R that we started in Problem 3-34 by drawing 25 subgroups of 5 chips each from this new bowl. Replace the chips after each drawing. Continue to use the control limits established in Problem 3-34. How many points fall out of control on each chart? Do you get any extreme runs on either side of the central line? What has happened to universe average and universe dispersion?

3-36 Mark 500 chips as follows:

Marking	Frequency	Marking	Frequency	Marking	Frequency
36	1	25	24	14	19
35	1	24	29	13	15
34	1	23	33	12	11
33	1	22	36	11	8
32	2	21	39	10	6
31	4	20	40	9	4
30	6	19	39	8	2
29	8	18	36	7	1
28	11	17	33	6	1
27	15	16	29	5	1
26	19	15	24	4	1

Continue the control charts for $\bar{X}$ and R that were started in Problem 3-34 by drawing 25 subgroups of 5 chips each from this new bowl. Replace the chips after each drawing. Continue to use the control limits established in Problem 3-34. (For purposes of this problem neglect your drawings in Problem 3-35.) How many points fall out of control on each chart? Do you get any extreme runs on either side of the central line? What has happened to universe average and universe dispersion?

FOUR

DIRECTIONS FOR SIMPLE $\bar{X}$ AND R CHARTS

"... the $\bar{X}$ and R chart is the most sensitive control chart for tracing and identifying causes. The R pattern is read first, and from this it is possible to identify many causes directly. The $\bar{X}$ pattern is read in the light of the R chart, and this makes it possible to identify other causes. Finally, the $\bar{X}$ pattern and R pattern are read jointly, which gives still further information."†

Outline of Necessary Steps in Connection with Using the Control Charts for $\bar{X}$ and R for any Quality Characteristic of Manufactured Product

It is helpful to visualize the decisions and calculations that must be made and the actions that must be taken as occurring in a sequence somewhat as follows.

I. Decisions preparatory to the control charts
    A. Some possible objectives of the charts
    B. Choice of the variable
    C. Decision on the basis of subgrouping
    D. Decision on the size and frequency of subgroups
    E. Setting up the forms for recording the data
    F. Determining the method of measurement
II. Starting the control charts
    A. Making the measurements
    B. Recording the measurements and other relevant data
    C. Calculation of average $\bar{X}$ for each subgroup
    D. Calculation of range R for each subgroup
    E. Plotting the $\bar{X}$ chart
    F. Plotting the R chart

---

† *Statistical Quality Control Handbook*, Western Electric Company, Inc., New York, 1956, p. 11.

III. Determining the trial control limits
    A. Decision on required number of subgroups before control limits are calculated
    B. Calculation of $\bar{R}$, the average of the ranges
    C. Calculation of upper and lower control limits for R
    D. Calculation of $\bar{\bar{X}}$, the average of the $\bar{X}$ values
    E. Calculation of upper and lower control limits for $\bar{X}$
    F. Plotting the central lines and limits on the charts
IV. Drawing preliminary conclusions from the charts
    A. Indication of control or lack of control
    B. Apparent relationship between what the process is doing and what it is supposed to do
    C. Actions suggested by the control chart
  V. Continuing to use the charts
    A. Revision of central line and control limits for R
    B. Revision of central line and control limits for $\bar{X}$
    C. Use of the charts for action on the process
    D. Use of the charts for acceptance
    E. Use of the charts for action on the specifications

I DECISIONS PREPARATORY TO THE CONTROL CHARTS

Some Possible Objectives of the Charts

In general, where control charts for variables, either $\bar{X}$ and R or $\bar{X}$ and σ, are undertaken, some or all of the following purposes are present:

1. To analyze a process with a view to one or more of the following objectives:
    a. To secure information to be used in establishing or changing specifications or in determining whether a given process can meet specifications. This was illustrated in Example 1-2.
    b. To secure information to be used in establishing or changing production procedures. Such changes may be either elimination of assignable causes of variation or fundamental changes in production methods that may be called for whenever the control chart makes it clear that specifications cannot be met with present methods. Production changes of one or the other of these types are referred to in Examples 1-1, 3-1, 3-2, and 4-1 to 4-3.
    c. To secure information to be used in establishing or changing inspection procedures or acceptance procedures, or both. This objective is referred to in Examples 1-1, 1-2, 3-2, and 4-1 to 4-3.
2. To provide a basis for current decisions during production as to when to hunt for causes of variation and take action intended to correct them, and when to leave a process alone. This is nearly always one of the purposes of any control chart for variables.

3. To provide a basis for current decisions on acceptance or rejection of manufactured or purchased product. This is illustrated in Examples 3-2 and 4-1 and discussed further in Chap. 16. Sometimes, as in Example 3-2, the control chart is undertaken primarily for this purpose. Often when it is undertaken for other purposes, there is a hope that, as time goes on and the other purposes are accomplished, it will ultimately be possible to reduce inspection costs by using the control chart for variables for acceptance. This was actually accomplished in Example 1-2. It was suggested as a possibility in the comments on Example 1-1.
4. To familiarize personnel with the use of the control charts. Although this would seem to be a legitimate purpose only in the early stages of the use of statistical quality control techniques in any organization, control charts undertaken for this purpose often disclose opportunities for cost savings.

Choice of the Variable

The variable chosen for control charts for $\bar{X}$ and R must be something that can be measured and expressed in numbers, such as a dimension, hardness number, tensile strength, weight, etc. The real basis of choice is always the prospect of reducing or preventing costs. From the standpoint of the possibility of reducing *production* costs, a candidate for a control chart is any quality characteristic that is causing rejections or rework involving substantial costs. From the *inspection and acceptance* standpoints, destructive testing always suggests an opportunity to use the control chart to reduce costs. Expensive analytical procedures also suggest the possibility of reducing inspection costs with the control charts.

In general, if acceptance is on a sampling basis and the quality tested can be expressed as a measured variable, it is likely to be worth while to examine inspection costs to form a basis for judgment as to the possibilities of reducing these costs by basing acceptance on the control chart for variables. Where 100% inspection takes place on an attributes basis, as with go and not-go gages, the chances for savings in costs depend on considerations outlined in Chap. 19.

Frequently the best chances to save costs are in places that would not be suggested either by an examination of costs of spoilage and rework or of inspection costs. These depend on the use of the control chart to analyze a process. The discussion in Chap. 1 of the problem of filling containers illustrates this type of opportunity. Concealed costs often exist that are not apparent in any cost statement.

In the introduction of the control-chart technique in any organization, the choice of the right variables is often troublesome (see Example 10-5). Occasionally the large number of possible variables is a source of confusion. One large manufacturing plant counted several hundred thousand specified dimensions on the many parts going into its products. Obviously only a very small fraction of these were legitimate candidates for control charts for $\bar{X}$ and R. In selecting variables for initial application of the control-chart technique, it may be important not only to choose those with opportunities for cost savings but to select carefully a type of saving that everyone in a supervisory or managerial capacity will readily accept as being a real saving. This usually—although not always—suggests starting where the spoilage and rework costs are high.

Decision on the Basis of Subgrouping

The key idea in the Shewhart method is the division of observations into what Shewhart called *rational subgroups*. The success of the Shewhart technique depends in large measure on the discrimination used in the selection of these subgroups. The principles of subgroup selection are discussed at length in Chap. 5.

Generally speaking, subgroups should be selected in a way that makes each subgroup as homogeneous as possible and that gives the maximum opportunity for variation from one subgroup to another. As applied to control charts on production, this means that it is of vital importance not to lose track of the order of production. Particularly if the primary purpose of keeping the charts is to detect shifts in the process average, one subgroup should consist of items produced as nearly as possible at one time; the next subgroup should consist of items all produced at a single later time; and so forth.

This basis of subgrouping was illustrated in Examples 1-1 and 1-2 in which five items constituting one subgroup were produced in succession at about 8 o'clock; five items constituting the next subgroup were produced in succession at about 9 o'clock; none of the items produced between the 8 and 9 o'clock subgroups were measured for purposes of the control charts. With this scheme of subgrouping, it sometimes is desirable that the exact time of choosing a sample should vary a bit one way or the other from the stipulated time and that this variation should not be predictable by the operator. For instance, the 9 o'clock sample might be taken one day at 9:10 and the next day at 8:45. It is better if the operator is not able to be sure in advance just which items are to be selected as the sample for inspection.

This desirable scheme of subgrouping to make each sample as homogeneous as possible may sometimes need to be modified either because of practical difficulties in taking homogeneous samples or because the control chart is intended to serve several different purposes. For instance, if one of the purposes of a control chart is to provide a basis for acceptance, it may be desirable to have each subgroup as nearly representative as possible of the production over a given period of time. For this purpose it would be better to inspect five items selected at random from the production in some given period of time than to inspect five items produced in succession at the beginning or end of the period. Or, if each item takes a considerable period of time to produce, it may be more convenient for the items inspected for each subgroup to be spaced approximately uniformly over the production of a given period. This is illustrated in Example 4-2.

Decision on the Size and Frequency of Subgroups

Shewhart suggested four as the ideal subgroup size. In the industrial use of the control chart, five seems to be the most common size. Because the essential idea of the control chart is to select subgroups in a way that gives minimum opportunity for variation *within* a subgroup, it is desirable that subgroups be as small as possible. On the other hand, a size of four is better than three or two on statistical grounds; the distribution of $\bar{X}$ is nearly normal for subgroups of four or more even though the samples are taken from a nonnormal universe; this fact is helpful in the interpretation of control-chart limits. A reason sometimes advanced for the use of five is ease of computation of the average, which can be obtained by multiplying the sum by two and moving the decimal point one place to the left.

Subgroups of two or three may often be used to good advantage, particularly where the cost of measurements is so high as to veto the use of larger subgroups.

Larger subgroups such as 10 or 20 are sometimes advantageous where it is desired to make the control chart sensitive to small variations in the process average. The larger the subgroup size, the narrower the control limits on charts for $\bar{X}$ and the easier it is to detect small variations; this is true only if subgroups are selected in a way that these variations in process average occur between and not within subgroups. Generally speaking, the larger the subgroup size, the more desirable it is to use standard deviation rather than range as a measure of subgroup dispersion. A practical working rule is to use $\bar{X}$ and σ charts rather than $\bar{X}$ and R charts whenever the subgroup size is greater than 15.

In certain problems of process control, the issue of subgroup size may be viewed as an economic problem that is closely related to the issue of the tightness of control limits, which was examined briefly in Chap. 3.

In the introduction of the control-chart technique in any organization, charts for variables are often applied to data already collected for some other purpose. Often it is wise to start the control charts with no change in the method of collecting data, putting off any changes that might improve the control charts until such time as the charts have proved their usefulness to management. In such cases the subgroup size is likely to be determined by the way in which the data are collected. Sometimes this involves variable subgroup sizes; methods of determining limits and plotting charts for these are explained in Chap. 9.

Where the control-chart analysis is applied to past data already tabulated, this may necessitate much larger subgroups than would ordinarily be selected. This is illustrated in Chap. 9.

No general rules may be laid down for frequency of subgroups. Each case must be decided on its own merits, considering both the cost of taking and analyzing measurements and the benefits to be derived from action based on the control charts. In the initial use of a control chart for analyzing a process, it may be desirable to arrive at conclusions quickly by taking frequent samples. Later on, after the troubles have been diagnosed and corrected and the function of the control chart has become the maintenance of process control on current production, it may be advisable to reduce the frequency of sampling. This was illustrated in Example 1-2, in which the frequency of sampling was ultimately reduced from one sample every hour to one sample every 8 h.

The frequency of taking a subgroup may be expressed either in terms of time, such as once an hour (as in Examples 1-1 and 1-2), or as a proportion of the items produced, such as 5 out of each 100 (as in Example 4-3).

Setting Up the Forms for Recording the Data

Although the exact details of forms used will vary from one organization to another, two general types of forms are in common use. Both types are shown in Example 4-3 near the end of this chapter. The type shown in Fig. 4-7, in which the successive measurements in each subgroup are recorded one below the other, avoids the necessity of mental arithmetic (or calculations on scratch paper) in figuring averages.

Figure 4-8 shows the other common type of form, in which each line contains all the measurements in one subgroup. This type avoids the necessity of copying the $\bar{X}$ and R values to compute the grand averages and generally allows room for more subgroups on a page. Where only the final two digits of the measurement are subject to variation, the mental arithmetic involved in obtaining averages is not complicated.

All forms need spaces for indicating the item measured, the unit of measurement, and other relevant information. It is particularly important to provide opportunity for remarks regarding any production changes (for example, changed machine setting, changed operator, tool sharpened, etc.), inspection changes, or other matters observed by the quality control inspector that might give clues to the causes of any out-of-control points.

Determining the Method of Measurement

Decision must be made as to the measuring instruments to be used and the way in which the measurements are to be made. Usually it is desirable to prepare definite written instructions on this point.

II STARTING THE CONTROL CHARTS

Making and Recording the Measurements and Recording Other Relevant Data

The actual work of the control chart starts with the first measurements. As emphasized in the preceding chapter, it should always be remembered that the information given by the control chart is influenced by variations in measurement as well as by variations in the quality characteristic being measured. Any method of measurement will have its own inherent variability; it is important that this not be increased by mistakes in reading measuring instruments or errors in recording data. It is also important that notes be made about any occurrences which, if the control chart later shows lack of control, might provide help on the investigation of assignable causes of variation.

Calculation of Average $\bar{X}$ for Each Subgroup

As already explained, the measurements in each subgroup are added together and the sum is divided by the number of items in the subgroup.

$$\bar{X} = \frac{X_1 + X_2 + X_3 + \cdots + X_n}{n} = \frac{1}{n} \sum X$$

Calculation of the Range R for Each Subgroup

The highest and lowest numbers in the subgroup must first be identified. With large subgroups it is helpful to mark the highest value with the letter H and the lowest with the letter L. The range is computed by subtracting the lowest value from the highest.

Plotting the $\bar{X}$ and R Charts

Many $\bar{X}$ and R charts have already been illustrated in the preceding chapters and many others are given throughout this book. Such charts are often plotted on rectangular cross-section paper having 8 or 10 rulings to the inch. Profile paper may also be used. Some special forms developed for this purpose have used rulings similar to profile paper, with vertical lines spaced $\frac{1}{6}$ in apart and horizontal lines spaced $\frac{1}{20}$ in apart.

The vertical scale at the left is used for the statistical measures $\bar{X}$ and R. The horizontal scale is used for subgroup numbers. Dates, hours, or lot numbers may also be indicated on the horizontal scale. Each point may be indicated on the chart by a dot, circle, or cross. In this book the general practice is to use a circle for points on $\bar{X}$ charts and a cross for points on R charts; there are some exceptions, however. There is no standard practice in industry in this regard. Points on control charts may or may not be connected. In this book they are not connected except where the connecting line serves some definite purpose or where published charts having connecting lines are being reproduced.

Points on both $\bar{X}$ and R charts should be kept plotted up to date. This is particularly important where the charts are posted in the shop and are used by machine operators, setters, and supervisor.

As explained in Chap. 3, the objectives of the control chart can sometimes be fully served by the $\bar{X}$ chart alone. In such cases the R chart may be omitted.

III DETERMINING THE TRIAL CONTROL LIMITS

Decision on Required Number of Subgroups Before Control Limits are Calculated

The determination of the minimum number of subgroups required before control limits are calculated is a compromise between a desire to obtain the guidance given by averages and control limits as soon as possible after the start of collecting data and a desire that the guidance be as reliable as possible. The fewer the subgroups used, the sooner the information thus obtained will provide a basis for action but the less the assurance that this basis for action is sound.

On statistical grounds it is desirable that control limits be based on at least 25 subgroups. Moreover, experience indicates that the first few subgroups obtained when a control chart is initiated may not be representative of what is measured later; the mere act of taking and recording measurements is sometimes responsible for a change in the pattern of variation.

For these reasons, if 25 subgroups can be obtained in a short time, it is desirable to wait for 25 or more subgroups; this would be true, for example, where a new subgroup was measured every hour.

However, where subgroups are obtained slowly there is a natural desire on the part of those who initiated the control charts to draw some conclusions from them within a reasonable time. This impatience for an answer frequently leads to the policy of making preliminary calculations of control limits from the first 8 or 10 subgroups, with subsequent modification of limits as more subgroups are obtained.

Calculation of Trial Limits

First it is necessary to compute the average range $\bar{R}$. This is the sum of the ranges of the subgroups divided by the number of subgroups. The D_3 and D_4 factors from Table C, App. 3, should then be used to calculate control limits for R

$$UCL_R = D_4 \bar{R}$$

$$LCL_R = D_3 \bar{R}$$

Then $\bar{\bar{X}}$, the average of the $\bar{X}$ values, should be computed. This is the sum of the $\bar{X}$ values divided by the number of subgroups. The A_2 factor from Table C, App. 3, should be used to calculate control limits for $\bar{X}$

$$UCL_{\bar{X}} = \bar{\bar{X}} + A_2 \bar{R}$$

$$LCL_{\bar{X}} = \bar{\bar{X}} - A_2 \bar{R}$$

The trial limits thus obtained are appropriate for analyzing the past data which were used in their calculation. They may require modification before extending them to apply to future production.

The preceding formulas for limits for $\bar{X}$ and R assume a constant subgroup size. Chapter 9 explains the necessary calculations where the subgroup size is variable.

Plotting the Central Lines and Limits on the Charts

The central line on the R chart should be drawn as a solid horizontal line at $\bar{R}$. The upper control limit should be drawn as a dashed horizontal line at the computed value of UCL_R. If the subgroup size is seven or more, the lower control limit should be drawn as a dashed horizontal line at LCL_R. If the subgroup size is six or less, the lower control limit for R is zero.

The central line on the $\bar{X}$ chart should be drawn as a solid horizontal line at $\bar{X}$. The upper and lower control limits for $\bar{X}$ should be drawn as dashed horizontal lines at the computed values.

IV DRAWING PRELIMINARY CONCLUSIONS FROM THE CHARTS

Indication of Control or Lack of Control

Lack of control is indicated by points falling outside the control limits on either the $\bar{X}$ or R charts. Some users of the control charts identify such out-of-control points by a special symbol. For instance, if each point is represented by a circle, a cross is made in the circles designating out-of-control points; if each point is represented by a dot, a circle may be drawn around the dot for out-of-control points.

When, because points fall outside the control limits, we say a process is "out of control," this is equivalent to saying, "Assignable causes of variation are present; this is not a constant-cause system." As explained in Chap. 3, with 3-sigma limits we can make this statement with considerable confidence that it is correct; a constant-cause system will seldom be responsible for points falling outside control limits.

In contrast to this, when all points fall inside the control limits we cannot say with the same assurance, "*No* assignable causes of variation are present; this *is* a constant-cause system." No statistical test can give us this positive assurance. When we say, "This process is in control," the statement really means, "For practical purposes, it pays to act as if no assignable causes of variation were present."

Moreover, even in the best manufacturing processes, occasional errors occur that constitute assignable causes of variation but that may not constitute a basis for action. This fact may lead to various practical working rules on the relationship between satisfactory control and the number of points falling outside limits.

One such rule is to consider not more than 1 out of 35, or 2 out of 100 points outside control limits as evidence of control.†

Even though all points fall within control limits, lack of control may be indicated by runs of seven or more points in succession on the same side of the central line, or by the presence of other extreme runs such as were listed in Chap. 3.

The actions suggested by the evidence of the control chart depend on the relationship between what the process is doing and what it is supposed to do. That is, the apparent pattern of variation as shown by the control chart needs to be compared with the specifications. This comparison is simplest if the process appears to be in control.

Interpretation of Processes in Control

With evidence from the control chart that a process is in control, we are in a position to judge what is necessary to permit the manufacture of product that meets the specifications for the quality characteristic charted. The control chart data give us estimates of

1. The centering of the process ($\bar{X}'$ may be estimated from $\bar{\bar{X}}$).
2. The dispersion of the process (σ' may be estimated as $\bar{R}/d_2$).

The discussion in Chap. 2 made it clear that estimates of $\bar{X}'$ and σ' are subject to sampling errors. For this reason, any conclusions obtained from a short period (such as 25 points on the control chart) must be regarded as tentative, subject to confirmation or change as the control chart is continued and as more evidence becomes available. However, the reasonable thing to do at any stage in the proceedings is to make the best interpretation possible of the data already available. Once it is evident what actions are suggested by this interpretation, a decision can be made whether action should be taken at once or whether it should await more data. In applying the following analysis of processes in control, the limitations of the current estimates of $\bar{X}'$ and σ' should always be kept in mind.

In Chap. 2 it was pointed out that practically all (all but 0.27%) of a normal distribution falls within limits of $\bar{X}' \pm 3\sigma'$; i.e., for practical purposes the spread of the distribution may be thought of as approximately $6\sigma'$. In the preliminary analysis of control-chart data, there is hardly enough evidence to permit judgment as to whether the distribution is approximately normal. Certainly the evidence is seldom sufficient to tell whether 0.27% or 0.6% or 1.1% or some other small percentage of the distribution will fall outside $\bar{X}' \pm 3\sigma'$. Evidence of the exact form of the frequency distribution and the percentage of the distribution outside these limits may be obtained only after a long accumulation of data under control. In

---

† "Control Chart Method of Controlling Quality during Production. ANSI Standard Z1.3–1958," (Reaffirmed 1975) p. 18, American National Standards Institute, New York, 1975.

the meantime a satisfactory rough guide to judgment is provided by the assumption that $6\sigma'$ is a measure of the spread of the process.

Actions based on the relationship between the specifications and the centering and dispersion of a controlled process depend somewhat on whether there are two specification limits, a maximum or upper limit U and a minimum or lower limit L, as is always true of dimensions, or only one specification limit, either U or L, as might be true of a specified minimum tensile strength, or minimum weight of the contents of a container, or maximum per cent of a particular chemical impurity. Some of the various possible situations that may exist with two limits are shown in Figs. 4-1 to 4-3. Some situations that may exist with a single limit are shown in Figs. 4-4 to 4-6.

Possible Relationships of a Process in Control to Upper and Lower Specification Limits

When a controlled process must meet two specification limits on individual values, U and L, all possible situations may be grouped into three general classes, as follows:

1. The spread of the process ($6\sigma'$) is appreciably less than the difference between the specification limits ($U - L$).
2. The spread of the process ($6\sigma'$) is approximately equal to the difference between the specification limits ($U - L$).
3. The spread of the process ($6\sigma'$) is appreciably greater than the difference between the specification limits ($U - L$).

The first situation is illustrated in Fig. 4-1, in which the specification limits are shown by the upper and lower horizontal lines. Frequency curves A, B, C, D, and E indicate various positions in which the process might be centered. With any of the positions A, B, or C, practically all the product manufactured will meet the specifications as long as the process stays in control.

In general, the conditions represented in Fig. 4-1A, B, and C represent the ideal manufacturing situation. When the control chart shows that one of these conditions exists, many different possible actions may be considered; the choice among the various actions is a matter of relative economy.

For example, it may be considered economically advisable to permit $\bar{X}$ to go out of control if it does not go too far; that is, the distribution may be allowed to move between positions B and C. This may avoid the cost of frequent machine setups and of delays due to hunting for assignable causes of variation that will not be responsible for unsatisfactory product. In Chap. 9, the use of so-called "modified control limits" for this purpose is explained.

Or, where acceptance has been based on 100% inspection, it may be economical to substitute acceptance based on the control chart for $\bar{X}$ and R.

Or, if there is an economic advantage to be gained by tightening the specification limits, such action may be considered.

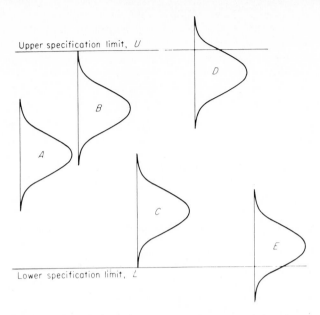

Figure 4-1 Some cases where the spread of a process is less than the difference between specification limits.

If none of these things is to be done, it may be economical to discontinue the use of the control chart, or at least to increase the time interval between control-chart inspections. The larger the ratio of $U - L$ to the process spread $(6\sigma')$, the more favorable is the situation to getting good product without assistance from any control chart.

With the process in position D of Fig. 4-1, some product will fall above the upper specification limit; in position E some product will fall below the lower specification limit. In either case the obvious action is to try to change the centering of the process, bringing it closer to position A. Once this has been done, consideration may be given to the various actions just enumerated.

The second type of situation is illustrated in Fig. 4-2. Only if the process is exactly centered between the specification limits, as in position A, will practically all the product conform to the specifications. If the distribution shifts away from this exact centering, as in B or C, it is apparent that some of the product will fall outside the specification limits.

Here the obvious action is to take all steps possible to maintain the centering of the process. This usually calls for continuous use of the control charts for $\bar{X}$ and R with subgroups at frequent intervals and immediate attention to points out of control. If fundamental changes can be made that reduce process dispersion, they will ease the pressure. Consideration should also be given to the question of whether the tolerances are tighter than is really necessary.

The third type of situation is illustrated in Fig. 4-3. Here the specification limits are so tight that even with the process in control and perfectly centered as in

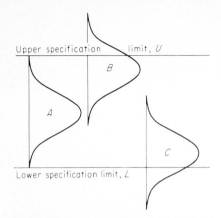

Figure 4-2 Some cases where the spread of a process is approximately equal to the difference between specification limits.

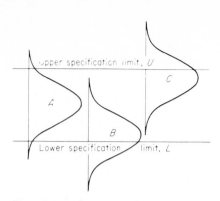

Figure 4-3 Some cases where the spread of a process is greater than the difference between specification limits.

position A, some nonconforming product will be made. This calls for a review of tolerances, as was illustrated in Example 1-2. It also calls for effort to make fundamental changes that will reduce process dispersion. It is still important to maintain the centering of the process; the curves in positions B and C show how a shift in process average will increase the nonconforming percentage.

If 100% inspection is possible, the nonconforming product may be sorted out and eliminated. (This is subject to the limitations of the human error involved in any 100% inspection.) But if such 100% sorting is impossible because acceptance is based on destructive tests, there is no chance to obtain product all of which conforms to specifications. The alternatives are to make fundamental changes in the process in order to reduce the process dispersion or to widen the specification limits to fit the process.

However, in some cases (for example, certain dimensions of mating parts, certain electrical characteristics of electrical components) a twilight zone exists just beyond the specification limits within which a moderate percentage of out-of-tolerance articles may be used without causing trouble; this situation usually calls for continued action to maintain the centering of the process.

Possible Relationships of a Process in Control to a Single Specification Limit

The key to the most useful classification of the situations involving two specification limits was the process dispersion. A similar key to the classification of situations involving a minimum limit is the position of $\bar{X}' - 3\sigma'$ with respect to L. Again three situations may be considered:

1. The low value of the process distribution ($\bar{X}' - 3\sigma'$) is appreciably above L. This is illustrated in Fig. 4-4.

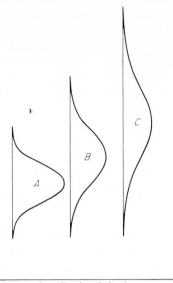

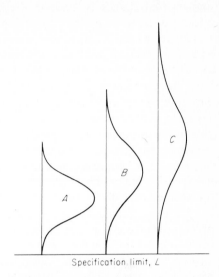

Figure 4-4 Some cases where the low value of the process distribution is above the specification minimum.

Figure 4-5 Some cases where the low value of the process distribution is approximately at the specification minimum.

2. The low value of the process distribution $(\bar{X}' - 3\sigma')$ is approximately at L. This is illustrated in Fig. 4-5.
3. The low value of the process distribution $(\bar{X}' - 3\sigma')$ is appreciably below L. This is illustrated in Fig. 4-6.

The first situation is one in which there is a margin of safety, the second is one in which the specification is just barely met as long as the process stays in control,

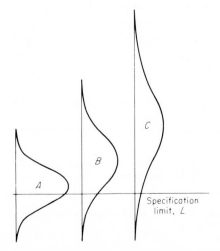

Figure 4-6 Some cases where the low value of the process distribution is below the specification minimum.

and the third is one in which some nonconforming product is inevitable unless a fundamental change is made in the process. The fundamental change may be either a decrease in process dispersion or an increase in the process average.

Three curves, A, B, and C, with different dispersions have been shown in Figs. 4-4 to 4-6 to emphasize the interrelationship of process average, process dispersion, and specification minimum limit. All three distributions, A, B, and C, have the same low value. However, distribution B with a greater dispersion must have a greater process average than A for the low points to be at the same level; similarly C must have a greater process average than B. It is evident that the greater the dispersion, the higher must be the average for the entire distribution to fall above the specification minimum limit. This relationship between average and dispersion is an important matter related to costs in many instances; for example, in the filling of containers a reduction in dispersion may reduce cost by reducing the average overfill.

On the other hand, the less the dispersion the more important it is that the process average not go out of control. This is illustrated by comparing distributions A and C in Figs. 4-5 and 4-6. In Fig. 4-6 both process averages have shifted an equal amount below their position in Fig. 4-5. However, the proportion of bad product, as indicated by the area of the distribution below the specification limit, is much greater in A than in C.

The preceding discussion has related to a single lower specification limit L, with no upper limit. Similar reasoning would apply if there were an upper limit with no lower limit.

Relationships between Processes out of Control and Specification Limits

If the control chart shows lack of control one obvious step is to hunt for the assignable causes of variation and try to correct them. Some guidance was given in Chap. 3 on the statistical aspects of detection of assignable causes.

It is also pertinent to enquire into the process centering and dispersion that may be expected if control is obtained. If the out-of-control points on the R chart are eliminated, what evidence does the control chart give about process dispersion? In view of this process dispersion and of the specification limits, where ought the process average to be? The same type of analysis of the relationship between process average, process dispersion, and specification limits that was discussed for controlled processes is appropriate for processes not yet brought under control. The practical differences are that it may not be certain whether control can actually be attained and that there is less basis for confidence in the estimates of $\bar{X}'$ and σ' at which control might be attained.

Some Specific Suggestions about Preliminary Conclusions and Actions Based on the Control Charts

If the charts show control, estimate σ' as $\bar{R}/d_2$. If there is an upper specification limit, compare $\bar{\bar{X}} + 3\sigma'$ with U. If there is a lower specification limit, compare

$\bar{\bar{X}} - 3\sigma'$ with L. If there are two specification limits, also compare $6\sigma'$ with $U - L$. Determine from these comparisons which type of condition is applicable of the various types illustrated in Figs. 4-1 to 4-6. Consider the possible actions suggested in our discussion of these figures.

If the charts show lack of control, try to judge from the charts and all other pertinent information what may be the assignable causes and whether or not it is likely they can be eliminated. After removing the subgroups that showed lack of control on the R chart, calculate a revised $\bar{R}$ and new control limits for R. If these limits show additional subgroups out of control, remove those subgroups and repeat the calculation. Estimate σ' as $\bar{R}/d_2$, using the final revised $\bar{R}$ after all out-of-control values of R have been eliminated. Consider this as a value of σ' that might conceivably be obtained if the process were brought into control.

Consider whether or not the process average can readily be set at any desired level. (In some cases, as in dimensions resulting from machining operations, this may be merely a matter of machine setting; in other cases, as in tensile strengths or percentages of chemical impurities, this may be a difficult matter involving costly changes in the process.) If so, decide on the desired value of $\bar{X}'_0$ at which to aim, assuming that control could be attained with σ' as estimated. If not, in the light of the known value of $\bar{\bar{X}}$, decide on an attainable $\bar{X}'_0$. Use the values of $\bar{X}'_0$ and σ' thus obtained as a basis for an analysis of the relationship of the specification limits to the process average and dispersion.

Decisions as to whether to take action now on the basis of the control-chart data already at hand, or to defer action until more data are obtained, should give weight to the uncertainties in the estimates of $\bar{X}'$ and σ' and to the costs and possible consequences of the proposed action.

Example 4-1 describes a case in which control charts on product received from two vendors were used to diagnose entirely different sources of trouble in the production processes of the different vendors.

Example 4-1 Use of control charts by a purchaser to help a vendor improve his process *Facts of the case* A manufacturer of electronic devices had trouble with the cracking of a certain small cross-shaped ceramic insulator used in the device. The cracking generally took place after the manufacturing operations were nearly completed and did so in a way that made it impossible to salvage the unit. Hence the costs resulting from each cracked insulator were many times the price of an insulator. Moreover, the cracking of some insulators during manufacturing operations suggested that others might be likely to crack under service conditions.

In an effort to improve the situation, all incoming insulators of this type were given 100% inspection. This inspection included a proof load test in which the inspector applied a more or less standardized finger pressure in an effort to break each insulator. This 100% inspection failed to decrease the percentage of units rendered defective by cracked insulators.

A simple testing device was then constructed to measure the actual strength in flexure by testing insulators to destruction. From each incoming lot of insulators, 25 were tested. As the insulators came from two vendors, control charts for $\bar{X}$ and σ were maintained for each vendor. The tests showed that both vendors had approximately the same percentage of defective insulators. However, the control charts indicated that the explanations for the defectives were totally different in the two cases.

Vendor A had high average strength but complete lack of anything resembling statistical control. Vendor B had excellent statistical control but at a level such that an appreciable part of the frequency distribution was below the required minimum strength.

This diagnosis of the situation was brought to the attention of both vendors. They were encouraged to exchange information about production methods. Certain techniques used by vendor A (largely related to mixing and molding the clay) were adopted by vendor B to try to raise his average strength. Certain techniques used by vendor B (largely related to control of temperature and humidity during firing) were adopted by vendor A to try to bring his process into control. Both vendors established control charts to help in the maintenance of control. As a result of these actions, both vendors brought their product into control at a satisfactory level and the trouble with the cracking of the insulators was eliminated.

V CONTINUING TO USE THE CHARTS

Revision of Central Lines and Control Limits

The trial control limits served the purpose of determining whether past operations were in control. The continuing use of the control chart, with each out-of-control point used as a possible basis for hunting for an assignable cause of variation and taking action to eliminate that cause, may require revised limits.

If the process has been in control with both average and dispersion satisfactory from the standpoint of the specification limits, the trial control limits should be extended to apply to future production. As more data accumulate, the limits may be reviewed from time to time and revised whenever necessary. It is desirable to establish regular periods for this review, such as once every week, once every month, once every 25, 50, or 100 subgroups.

If the dispersion has been in control, as evidenced by the R chart, but the average $\bar{X}$ has been out of control, the trial central line and trial limits on the R chart should continue to be used, and control limits on the $\bar{X}$ chart should continue to be a distance of $A_2 \bar{R}$ on either side of the central line. The location of the revised central line on the $\bar{X}$ chart calls for a decision whether this should be at an aimed-at level (sometimes called a standard level), designated as $\bar{X}'_0$, or whether it should be based on the past data, a revision of $\bar{X}$. When making this choice it should be recognized that wherever the central line (i.e., the assumed process average for the purposes of the control chart) is placed, a point outside control limits is interpreted as meaning, "This variation is more than would be expected as a matter of chance if the assumed process average is maintained."

If the process average may be changed by a fairly simple adjustment of the manufacturing process, such as a machine adjustment influencing a dimension, it is nearly always desirable to decide on a standard or aimed-at value $\bar{X}'_0$. This aimed-at process average should be determined by consideration of the relationship between process average, process dispersion, and specification limits, along the lines already discussed. Where there are upper and lower specification limits and product falling outside one limit may be reworked whereas product falling outside the other limit must be scrapped, the aimed-at average should be chosen with due consideration for the difference between costs of spoilage and rework.

Unless the process average can be changed by a definite adjustment, $\bar{\bar{X}}$ is likely to be the result of a complex set of factors, with the influence of each factor not clearly known. In such instances, a control chart based on an aimed-at value of $\bar{X}'_0$ which was different from the past $\bar{\bar{X}}$ might show many points out of control; these out-of-control points would simply indicate that the aim had been poor without giving much help in correcting the aim. For this reason it is more sensible in such cases to use the past $\bar{\bar{X}}$ as the new central line, or possibly a revised $\bar{\bar{X}}$ corrected by the elimination of the past out-of-control points. Then if different changes in the process are undertaken one after another with the purpose of finding a way to bring the process average to a new desired level, the control chart based on the past process average will give evidence whether each change constitutes an assignable cause of variation from past performance. If these assignable causes move the process average closer to the desired average, they should be continued rather than eliminated. Each change that is continued may call for a new central line on the $\bar{X}$ chart based on the changed performance.

Where the R chart shows that the process dispersion is out of control, it is desirable to estimate the value of $\bar{R}$ and σ' that might be attained if the dispersion were brought into control. This estimate is necessary even though it cannot be made with great assurance that it is correct. One possible method is to eliminate the values of R above the control limits and make a new calculation of $\bar{R}$. If new limits calculated from this $\bar{R}$ throw more points above the control limits, the calculation of a revised $\bar{R}$ may be repeated again. This method is illustrated in Example 4-3.

This revised $\bar{R}$ may be used as the new central line on the R chart, as the basis for calculating the new limits on the R chart and as the basis for calculating $A_2 \bar{R}$ to get the distance of the control limits from the central line on the $\bar{X}$ chart. This has the effect of tightening the limits on both the R and $\bar{X}$ charts, making them consistent with a σ' that may be estimated from the revised $\bar{R}$ as $\bar{R}/d_2$. This σ' may also serve as a basis for a preliminary analysis of the relationship among process average, process dispersion, and specification limits, as outlined in our discussion of Figs. 4-1 to 4-6.

Where both R and $\bar{X}$ are out of control and new limits on the $\bar{X}$ chart are to be based on an aimed-at $\bar{X}'_0$, the calculation of the revised $\bar{R}$ should be made before making a decision regarding the value of $\bar{X}_0'$ to be used. This is illustrated in Example 4-3.

Revised limits should be reviewed from time to time as additional data are accumulated.

Use of the Control Chart as a Basis for Sorting Sub-Lots into Homogeneous Grand Lots

If some quality of a manufactured product shows unsatisfactory variability and if the control chart shows that lack of control is responsible for this variability, the natural action seems to be to make a strong effort to bring about a state of control. However, it may turn out that for some reason it is impracticable to achieve control. Sometimes a satisfactory alternative may exist in the sorting of sub-lots of product into grand lots that seem to be statistically homogeneous. The variability from one grand lot to another may then become the basis for different correction factors somehow applied in the use of each grand lot. Conceivably, even though control could actually be obtained at a cost, it might be more economical to carry out this sorting.

This sorting is a possible procedure, for example, in the case of artillery ammunition. Experience shows that the variation in ballistic properties from one lot to another may be greater than the variation within any lot. (In other words, the averages show lack of statistical control.) Successive lots, the samples from which under ballistic tests all fall within control-chart limits, may be treated as sub-lots of one grand lot. Different corrections in the powder charge, or in the firing tables used by the artilleryman, could then be made for each grand lot.

In the case of chemical or bacteriological tests that different laboratories make of the same product, experience shows it is often impracticable to get control. The variation from one laboratory to another will be greater than the variation in successive tests made by any one laboratory. Here also, correction factors might be applied to the results given by any laboratory that did not seem to be part of the grand lot.†

Although the control chart provides the best way to sort sub-lots into homogeneous grand lots, it sometimes happens that people who do not fully understand the principles behind the control chart use it for sorting in ways that are incorrect. This point is illustrated in Example 4-2.

Example 4-2 An unsound proposal for sorting product into classes *Facts of the case* This example is adapted from an actual case with slight modifications intended to disguise the source and to simplify the situation in a way that will concentrate attention on the important principle involved.

---

† See Example 5-2 for an ingenious application of this correction factor technique to a manufacturing problem.

A certain munitions product, which for purposes of this story will be called the XYZ-77, was subject to destructive testing in order to determine a particular quality characteristic. Four of these XYZ-77s from each lot of 500 were tested to establish a basis for acceptance. Control charts were plotted using each set of four tests as a subgroup. These exhibited good control with only an infrequent point falling outside control limits.

The specifications stated that the average value of this quality characteristic should be 540. Tolerances were ± 20. It proved possible to hold the average (i.e., $\bar{\bar{X}}$ on the control chart) at 540. The upper control limit on the $\bar{X}$ chart was 549; the lower control limit was 531. This indicated that 3σ limits on individual values were 558 and 522. From this it seemed reasonable to believe that, if the distribution were normal or nearly so, as long as control was maintained practically all the product would fall within the specification limits of 560 and 520. As the process showed good control, this was a very satisfactory state of affairs.

Suddenly there was a demand for some XYZ-77s that would hold the much closer tolerances of 540 ± 6. Not all the product was required to meet these specifications, but it was desired that a substantial portion of it do so.

One of the team who had been working with the control chart had a suggestion that was thought would solve the problem. It called for no change in production methods, and for a continuance of destructive testing of four out of each lot of 500 with the control chart carried on as before. However, it was proposed to add two new inner limits to the control chart. These were to be set at a distance from $\bar{\bar{X}}$ equal to the tolerance limits divided by $\sqrt{n}$. This meant inner limits at $540 \pm 6/\sqrt{4}$, i.e., at 543 and 537.

It was further proposed that whenever the average of a sample plotted within these inner limits, the lot was to be classified as meeting the new specifications of 540 ± 6. Whenever the average of the sample plotted within control limits but above 543 or below 537, the lot was to be classified as meeting the original specifications of 540 ± 20.

Comment on Error in Reasoning Involved in Example 4-2

This suggestion could not have been made except by someone who had completely misunderstood the correct interpretation of the control chart.

When $\bar{X}$ and R charts for some quality characteristic of a manufactured product exhibit control over a long period, this means that the successive subgroups behave like random samples drawn from a single bowl. The existence of control indicates that for all practical purposes the bowl was unchanged throughout the period. If, as in Example 4-2, each subgroup is a small sample from a large lot, the evidence is that the large lots are practically alike. The variation from one subgroup to another is simply a chance variation to be expected in random sampling.

With all points on the control chart for $\bar{X}$ falling between control limits of 549 and 531, the fact that the sample from one lot has an $\bar{X}$ of 545 and the sample from the next lot has an $\bar{X}$ of 540 is an indication that the lots are *alike*, not that they are different. It is only in the case of lack of control that the control chart can be used to sort lots into grand lots having different dispersions or different averages.

In Example 4-2, the control chart gave conclusive evidence that the manufacturing process, as it was then carried on, could not meet the proposed new tolerance of ± 6. If 100% inspection were possible, the product meeting these close tolerances (about two-thirds of the total product if the distribution were approximately normal) could be sorted from the product not meeting the tolerances. As the test was destructive, this was not possible. It was necessary, therefore, either to make some fundamental change in the manufacturing process that would reduce the variability of the product, or to devise some nondestructive test that gave substantially the same information as the destructive test and would thus permit 100% inspection.

Use of the Control Charts for Action on the Process

In continuing the use of the control charts, there may be three different kinds of action on the process, as follows:

1. Action to remove assignable causes of variation that are brought to attention by out-of-control points.
2. Action to establish the process average.
3. Action to establish the process dispersion.

Once a process is brought into control with a satisfactory average and dispersion, an important purpose of the control chart is to help continue this happy state of affairs. The most common routine use of the control chart for variables is for this purpose. This involves simply leaving a process alone as long as it stays in control, and hunting for and removing assignable causes of variation whenever the control charts show lack of control. Uses of the control chart for this purpose were illustrated in Examples 3-1 and 3-2.

Actions to establish a process average at some desired level follow the lines that we have suggested. It should be emphasized that whenever an aimed-at value $\bar{X}'_0$ is used for the central line on the control chart, there should be an actual effort made to aim at that value in the manufacturing process itself. It does no good to put such a line on the control chart unless this forms a basis for action by those who carry out the manufacturing operations.

Actions to reduce process dispersion often call for fundamental changes in machine or methods. Action may also be undertaken to match various process dispersions with different jobs to be undertaken. The information given by control charts about the natural tolerances that will be held by various machines or various production methods may make it possible to fit the process dispersion to the job in hand. Operations calling for close tolerances may be assigned to the machines that will hold the close tolerances, and operations on which wide toler-ances are satisfactory may be assigned to those machines that will hold only wide tolerances. This use of the control chart in production planning may be its chief contribution in some jobbing shops.

Control Charts for Variables in Relation to Acceptance Inspection

Our discussion of the interesting and important subjects of the strategy and tactics of acceptance inspection and acceptance sampling is deferred until Part Two of this book.

We shall see there that one useful concept in acceptance sampling is that an overall decision with respect to the acceptance or rejection of a manufacturing process often is superior to a series of unrelated decisions regarding acceptance or rejection of separate lots of product. Control charts may give evidence that a process is in statistical control with satisfactory centering and dispersion and thus provide a rational basis for the acceptance of the process.

In Part Two we shall see that another useful concept is that the best way to obtain satisfactory product is to have it made right in the first place—that it usually is difficult or impossible to "inspect quality into a product." We have already noted cases in Examples 3-2 and 4-1 in which the feedback of information obtained from control charts played an important part in the diagnosis of troubles that were interfering with the making of satisfactory product.

Use of the Charts for Action on the Specifications

The control charts for variables may influence specifications in two ways.

They may be used to determine the capabilities of a manufacturing process before the specification limits are set. This is often a sensible procedure. This is discussed in Chap. 10.

They may also be used to give evidence that, because of the inability of a manufacturing process to meet existing specification limits even when it is in control, a review of specification limits is called for.

A general principle applicable here is that the basis of all specification limits should be the prospective use of the part or product for which the limits are specified. Ideally, all specification limits should be exactly right from the stand-point of what is really needed. Actually, as illustrated in Example 1-2, many specification limits are made tighter than really necessary, often because no time or effort has been given to finding out what is necessary. Moreover, in most cases there is no one right value of specification limits which can be settled indepen-dently of cost factors involved; these cost factors cannot be properly judged without information regarding the capabilities of the manufacturing process such as is given by the control chart. For these reasons, many cases exist in which the appropriate conclusion from the control chart is to change the specifications.

Example 4-3 Milling a slot in an aircraft terminal block. An example to illustrate the steps in the use of $\bar{X}$ and R charts on a manufacturing operation *Decisions preparatory to the control chart* High percentages of rejections for many of the parts made in the machine shop of an aircraft company indicated the need for examination of the reasons for trouble. As most of the rejections were for failure to meet dimensional tolerances, it was decided to try to find the causes of trouble by the use of $\bar{X}$ and R charts.

These charts, which of course required actual measurement of dimensions, were to be used only for those dimensions which were causing numerous rejections. Among many such dimensions, the ones selected for control charts were those having high costs of spoilage and rework, and those on which rejections were responsible for delays in assembly operations. Although the initial purpose of all the $\bar{X}$ and R charts was to diagnose causes of trouble, it was anticipated that some of the charts would be continued for routine process control and possibly for acceptance inspection.

This example deals with one of these dimensions, the width of a slot on a duralumin forging used as a terminal block at the end of an airplane wing spar. The final machining of this slot width was a milling operation. The width of the slot was specified as $0.8750 \begin{vmatrix} +0.0050 \\ -0.0000 \end{vmatrix}$ in. The designing engineers had specified this dimension with a unilateral tolerance because of the fit requirements of the terminal block; it was essential that the slot width be at least 0.8750 in and desirable that it be as close to 0.8750 as possible.

Most of the aircraft parts produced in this machine shop were large parts fabricated in lots the size of which varied from a few hundred to several thousand. It was felt that practical considerations called for a single decision as to the method of subgrouping and the size and frequency of sample to apply to all the $\bar{X}$ and R charts to be used. One limiting factor was the small number of available personnel for the control-chart inspection in relation to the number of control charts it was desired to keep. On this basis it was decided that for each chart the sample inspected would be approximately 5% of the total production of the part in question. Because of the many general considerations favoring five as the subgroup size, this size was adopted. It was considered essential that, wherever possible, all measurements be made at the point of production. As lots of five of these large parts did not accumulate at the machine, it was decided that one part would be measured out of approximately every 20 produced, and that a subgroup would consist of five such measurements.

The type of form used for recording the data is illustrated in Fig. 4-7. It was chosen as a result of the decision to measure many of the dimensions to the nearest ten-thousandth of an inch: it was believed that with so many significant figures, delays and errors would be introduced by any type of form calling for much mental arithmetic. If measurements had been made only to thousandths of an inch, the other type of form would have been appropriate.

$\bar{X}$ AND R CONTROL CHART DATA SHEET

Product _Terminal block_ ____ Dept No. _78_ _____ Order No. _54321_

Characteristic _Width of slot_ _____

Unit of measurement _0.0001 in. over 0.8000_ Specified limits { _0.8800 in_ ___ Max. _0.8750 in._ ___ Min.

Subgroup No.	1	2	3	4	5	6	7			$\bar{X}$	R
a	772	756	756	744	802	783	747		1	770	85
b	804	787	773	780	726	807	766		2	750	54
c	779	733	722	754	748	791	753		3	751	51
d	719	742	760	774	758	762	758		4	765	36
e	777	734	745	774	744	757	767		5	756	76
Total	3851	3752	3756	3826	3778	3900	3791		6	780	50
Average, $\bar{X}$	770	750	751	765	756	780	758		7	758	20
Range, R	85	54	51	36	76	50	20		8	771	38
Date or time	3/7	3/7	3/7	3/8	3/8	3/8	3/9		9	748	16
Subgroup No.	8	9	10	11	12	13	14		10	717	25
									11	737	36
a	788	757	713	716	746	749	771		12	740	36
b	750	747	730	730	727	762	767		13	769	38
c	784	741	710	752	763	778	785		14	772	20
d	769	746	705	735	734	787	772		15	768	13
e	762	747	727	751	730	771	765		16	777	27
Total	3853	3738	3585	3684	3700	3847	3860				
Average, $\bar{X}$	771	748	717	737	740	769	772				
Range, R	38	16	25	36	36	38	20		12,129	621	
Date or time	3/9	3/9	3/10	3/10	3/10	4/2	4/2		Calculation of limits		
Subgroup No.	15	16							$\bar{\bar{X}} = 12,129 \div 16 = 758$		
a	771	767							$\bar{R} = 621 \div 16 = 39$		
b	758	769							$A_2\bar{R} = .58(39) = 23$		
c	769	770							$UCL_{\bar{X}} = \bar{\bar{X}} + A_2\bar{R}$		
d	770	794							$= 758 + 23 = 781$		
e	771	786							$LCL_{\bar{X}} = \bar{\bar{X}} - A_2\bar{R}$		
Total	3839	3886							$= 758 - 23 = 735$		
Average, $\bar{X}$	768	777							$UCL_R = D_4\bar{R}$		
Range, R	13	27							$= 2.11(39) = 82$		
Date or time	4/3	4/3							$LCL_R = D_3R = 0$		

Figure 4-7 $\bar{X}$ and R data sheet for Example 4-3.

This is illustrated in Fig. 4-8, in which the same measurements as in Fig. 4-7 have been recorded to the nearest thousandth of an inch.

The method of inspection to secure data for each $\bar{X}$ and R chart was stated in written instructions. In the case of the slot width of the terminal block, this was to measure the width with a micrometer at two specified positions in the slot. The recorded slot width was the average of these two measurements.

RECORD SHEET FOR X̄ & R CHART

Material or part name __*Terminal block*_____ Part No. __*1-2345*__
Characteristic measured __*Width of slot*_____ Plant __*6*____ Dept. __*78*____
Unit of measurement __*0.001 in. over 0.800*_____ Recorded by __*J. S.*____

Series No.	Date pro- duced	Measurements on each of five items in series					X̄ Av. of items	R Range of items	Record of inspection
		A	B	C	D	E			
1	3/7	77	80	78	72	78	77.0	8	
2		76	79	73	74	73	75.0	6	
3		76	77	72	76	74	75.0	5	
4	3/8	74	78	75	77	77	76.2	4	
5		80	73	75	76	74	75.6	7	
6		78	81	79	76	76	78.0	5	
7	3/9	75	77	75	76	77	76.0	2	
8		79	75	78	77	76	77.0	4	
9		76	75	74	75	75	75.0	2	
10	3/10	71	73	71	70	73	71.6	3	
11		72	73	75	74	75	73.8	3	
12		75	73	76	73	73	74.0	3	
13	4/2	75	76	78	79	77	77.0	4	Operator's check measure-
14		77	77	78	77	76	77.0	2	ments have been made
15	4/3	77	76	77	77	77	76.8	1	on hot part.
16		77	77	77	79	79	77.8	2	Instructed to wait until part
17									has cooled before making
18									check measurement, and to
19									center process at 0.8775 inches
20									
	Totals						1212.8	61	

$$\bar{\bar{X}} = \frac{1212.8}{16} = 75.8$$

$$\bar{R} = \frac{61}{16} = 3.8$$

$$A_2\bar{R} = 0.58(3.8) = 2.2$$

$$D_4\bar{R} = 2.11(3.8) = 8.0$$

$$\begin{cases} UCL_{\bar{X}} = 75.8 + 2.2 = 78.0 \\ LCL_{\bar{X}} = 75.8 - 2.2 = 73.6 \end{cases}$$

$$\begin{cases} UCL_R = 8.0 \\ LCL_R = 0 \end{cases}$$

Figure 4-8 An alternate form of $\bar{X}$ and R data sheet.

Starting the control charts The actual measurements for the first 16 sub-groups are shown in Fig. 4-7. This number of subgroups corresponds to a production order for 1,600 of these terminal blocks. Averages and ranges were calculated as shown in Fig. 4-7 and were plotted as shown in Fig. 4-9.

At the time of the twelfth subgroup, before the completion of this production order and before the calculation of central line or control limits, the quality control inspector noticed that the machine operator was occasionally checking performance by a micrometer measurement on width of slot on a terminal block which had just come off the machine. As the block was still hot from the milling operation, this dimension as measured by the operator was

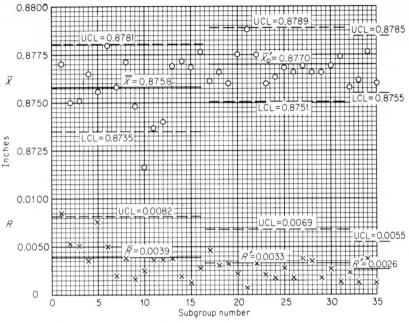

Figure 4-9 $\bar{X}$ and R control charts for Example 4-3.

too high because of the expansion of the metal due to temperature. Moreover, the operator was influenced by the unilateral tolerance to aim at a dimension at or very slightly above the nominal dimension of 0.8750 in.

Even without a central line or control limits, it was evident from the chart and the data sheet that this was producing many slots that were too narrow. After the twelfth subgroup the operator was instructed to make check measurements on parts that had cooled to room temperature and to aim at a dimension of 0.8775, halfway between the upper and lower tolerance limits. This was reflected in the results in subgroups 13 to 16.

Determining the trial control limits Calculation of trial control limits was made after the first 16 subgroups which completed the production order. As shown in Fig. 4-7, this was done using the A_2 and D_4 factors and formulas from Table C, App. 3. These trial control limits are shown for the first 16 subgroups in the control charts in Fig. 4-9.

Drawing preliminary conclusions from the charts Subgroup 1 is above the upper control limit on the R chart. Subgroup 10 is below the lower control limit on the $\bar{X}$ chart. Moreover, the last 10 of the 16 points on the R chart all fall below the central line. It is evident that the measurements obtained are not the result of a constant system of chance causes.

If subgroup 1 is eliminated from consideration, $\bar{R}$ for the remaining 15 subgroups is 536/15 = 36. This gives as the revised upper control limit

$$D_4\bar{R} = 2.11(36) = 76$$

Subgroup 5 falls exactly on the control limit.

A common experience on hand-operated machines, where the dispersion of a controlled process is dependent in part on the care taken by the operator, is that the introduction of the control chart increases the care taken by the operator and thus reduces process dispersion. For this reason the ranges of the first few subgroups may not be representative of what may be expected as time goes on. The general appearance of this R chart with its run of the last 10 points below $\bar{R}$ suggests this as probably true of the slot width. Hence a second revision of $\bar{R}$, with subgroup 5 eliminated, seems reasonable. This gives $\bar{R} = 460/14 = 33$; i.e., $\bar{R} = 0.0033$ in.

From this second revision of $\bar{R}$ an estimate may be made of σ', the process standard deviation that might be anticipated if the process were controlled in the future. This estimate of $\sigma' = \bar{R}/d_2 = 0.0033/2.326 = 0.0014$ in. If this should be the value of σ', the natural tolerance or spread of the controlled process, $6\sigma'$, will be

$$6(0.0014) = 0.0084$$

This spread may be compared with the tolerance spread:

$$U - L = 0.8800 - 0.8750 = 0.0050$$

It is evident that the natural tolerance of this process is considerably greater than the specified tolerance. Unless the process dispersion can be reduced, it is evident that even though the process can be brought into control a high percentage of nonconforming product will be produced.

It is evident that this situation is like the one shown in curve B of Fig. 4-3, namely, the dispersion is too wide and the process average ($\bar{\bar{X}} = 0.8758$) is too low. It is also evident that the process average is capable of adjustment; the instructions given to the operator after subgroup 12 seemed definitely to raise the average. At first glance, it would seem that the most desirable thing to do is to aim at minimum rejections by trying to hold the process in control at an average midway between the upper and lower specification limits, namely, at 0.8775.

However, this conclusion fails to give weight to the fact that a slot that is too narrow can be widened but a slot that is too wide cannot be narrowed. In other words, rework is less costly than spoilage. It is therefore desirable to center the process at a level that results in few slots over the upper specification limit of 0.8800 in, even though a number may be under the lower specification limit of 0.8750 in. The upper 3-sigma limit on individual values might be placed at 0.8800 to make a trial calculation of the aimed-at $\bar{X}'_0$. If this is done

$$\bar{X}'_0 + 3\sigma' = 0.8800$$

$$\bar{X}'_0 + 3(0.0014) = 0.8800$$

$$\bar{X}'_0 = 0.8758$$

By chance, this is exactly the $\bar{\bar{X}}$ of the first 16 subgroups. It is evident that such a centering will continue to result in considerable rework.

Experience on similar jobs indicates that it is reasonable to expect that process dispersion may be further reduced. Hence it seems wise to center the process somewhat above 0.8758. Just how much above depends on how much improvement is expected and on the relative costs of spoilage and rework. A figure of 0.8770 was selected.

Continuing to use the charts For the continuation of the control chart for the next production order, which started several weeks later, the central line was set as $\bar{X}'_0 = 0.8770$. The 3-sigma control limits were based on assuming $\sigma' = 0.0014$. Using Table E of App. 3,

$$UCL_{\bar{x}} = \bar{X}'_0 + A\sigma' = 0.8770 + 1.34(0.0014) = 0.8789$$

$$LCL_{\bar{x}} = \bar{X}'_0 - A\sigma' = 0.8770 - 1.34(0.0014) = 0.8751$$

$$UCL_R = D_2\sigma' = 4.92(0.0014) = 0.0069$$

$$\text{Central Line}_R = d_2\sigma' = 2.326(0.0014) = 0.0033$$

$$LCL_R = D_1\sigma' = 0$$

(As σ' was estimated from an $\bar{R}$ of 0.0033, the same limits would have been obtained using the factors and formulas from Table C of App. 3, with an $\bar{R}$ of 0.0033.)

These limits are shown for subgroups 17 to 32 on the control charts of Fig. 4-9. The averages and ranges of these subgroups were as follows: (As in the data sheet shown in Fig. 4-7, $\bar{X}$ is in units of 0.0001 in above 0.8000 and R is in units of 0.0001 in.)

Subgroup number	$\bar{X}$	R
17	761	47
18	766	31
19	760	32
20	775	22
21	788	7
22	775	32
23	760	21
24	763	18
25	768	27
26	766	17
27	769	38
28	766	35
29	766	17
30	769	26
31	774	14
32	758	24
Totals.........	12,284	408

None of the pieces inspected for control-chart inspection in subgroups 17 to 32 fell outside the specification limits. The average values for these 16 subgroups are

$$\bar{\bar{X}} = \frac{12,284}{16} = 768 \text{ (i.e., 0.8768 in.)}$$

$$\bar{R} = \frac{408}{16} = 26 \text{ (i.e., 0.0026 in.)}$$

It is evident that there has been a further narrowing of the process dispersion. This should be recognized by a revision of control limits starting with subgroup 33. As there seems to be no reason for a change in the aimed-at average, these revised control limits should be computed from an $\bar{X}_0'$ of 0.8770 and an $\bar{R}$ of 0.0026, using the factors from Table C of App. 3.

$$UCL_{\bar{X}} = \bar{X}_0' + A_2\bar{R} = 0.8770 + 0.58(0.0026) = 0.8785$$

$$LCL_{\bar{X}} = \bar{X}_0' - A_2\bar{R} = 0.8770 - 0.58(0.0026) = 0.8755$$

$$UCL_R = D_4\bar{R} = 2.11(0.0026) = 0.0055$$

$$LCL_R = D_3\bar{R} = 0$$

These limits are shown on the control chart of Fig. 4-9 as applying to subgroups 33, 34, and 35. With $\bar{R}$ reduced to 0.0026, the estimate of σ' is now

$$\frac{0.0026}{2.326} = 0.0011 \text{ in}$$

If control can be maintained at this level, $\bar{X}' + 3\sigma' = 0.8803$ and $\bar{X}' - 3\sigma' = 0.8737$. This indicates that a small amount of spoilage and a moderate amount of rework will still be produced; however, the situation is greatly improved as compared to that which existed before the start of the control chart. As time went on it proved possible to maintain control and to decrease $\bar{R}$ (and σ') further to the point where nearly all the product fell within specification limits.

In situations where the specification limits are as tight as this in relation to the process dispersion, it is not appropriate to use the control chart for acceptance as a substitute for 100% inspection. Neither was this a situation in which the tolerance limits could be widened; the required fit of the part properly controlled the specifications despite the fact that the natural tolerance of the process seemed to be wider than the specified tolerance.

Comment on Example 4-3

The reader should be warned against the inference that a reduction in universe dispersion can always be readily attained, even though it was actually attained in this case. Although such reduction in σ' is possible in certain machine-shop operations in which the skill and care of the operator are controlling factors, it is not possible in many operations on automatic machines where the process dispersion is almost entirely a matter of what the machine will do and of the variability of the materials being machined. Neither is it possible in operations on many quality characteristics other than dimensions.

Example 4-3 has been explained at some length. The purpose of this full explanation has been not only to show forms and computations involved in the simple control charts for $\bar{X}$ and R, but also to show the way in which judgment enters into interpretation of these charts and into the action based on this interpretation.

A point to be emphasized is that no fixed rules may be laid down regarding the appropriate action based on interpretation of a control chart. The person who makes decisions about action, whether a quality control engineer, supervisor, methods engineer, or machine operator, must understand both the process being analyzed and the general principles underlying the control-chart analysis. Even though all situations may be grouped into a few simple classes from the statistical viewpoint, each actual case is somewhat different from all others; decisions regarding action are economic decisions that should be based on all the facts of each particular case.

It is recommended that all users of $\bar{X}$ and R charts examine the American National Standards Institute pamphlets on control charts referred to in Chap. 2. The presentation of the subject in this and the two preceding chapters has been greatly influenced by these standards.

PROBLEMS

4-1 The dimension referred to in Problem 3-1 is specified as 2.050 ± 0.020. If the dimension falls above U, rework is required; if below L, the part must be scrapped. If the process is in statistical control and normally distributed, what can you conclude regarding its ability to meet specifications? Can you make any suggestions for improvement?

Answer: About 35% rework, 0% scrap.

4-2 In Problem 3-2 the specified minimum strength for a weld is 370 lb. If the process is in statistical control and normally distributed, what can you conclude regarding its ability to meet this specification?

Answer: 0.59% below 370.

4-3 In Problem 3-3 $L = 90$ lb. If the process is in statistical control and normally distributed, what can you conclude regarding its ability to meet this specification?

Answer: 13% below 90.

4-4 Problem 3-17 involved the plotting of $\bar{X}$ and R charts for the 30 subgroups of Problem 2-1. All points on the $\bar{X}$ chart fell within the control limits; one point on the R chart fell outside the limits. Compute a revised $\bar{R}$ eliminating this out-of-control value of R. From this revised $\bar{R}$, estimate the value of σ' that might be expected if the process dispersion could be held under statistical control.

Answer: 4.07, 1.75.

The specification for the "on" temperature of this thermostatically controlled switch is 54 ± 4. If the process could be centered at 54 with the σ' you have just estimated, and if statistical control could be maintained, what percentage of switches would you expect to fall outside these specification limits? Assume that the normal distribution is applicable. Among the 150 switches observed, how many actually fell outside the specification limits?

Answer: 2.2%, 2.7%.

4-5 Automatic machinery is used to fill and seal ten-ounce cans of a certain liquid product. The process standard deviation is 0.20 oz. To ensure that every can meets or exceeds this 10 oz minimum, the company has set a target value for the process of 11.0 oz.

(a) At this process average of 11 oz, what per cent of the cans will have less than 10.5 oz of product? Assume contained weights are normally distributed.

(b) If the quality control section samples these cans in subgroups of four, what will 3σ control limits be for the $\bar{X}$ chart?

(c) Assuming that $\pm 3\sigma'$ natural tolerance limits on the process cover virtually all of the filled cans, what is the minimum value to which the process average may be lowered in order to ensure that virtually no cans are filled with less than a minimum of 10 oz?

Answer: 0.62%; 11.3, 10.7; 10.6.

4-6 (a) Compute the central lines and 3-sigma control limits for $\bar{X}$ and R charts for the data of Problem 2-10.

(b) Plot the control charts and determine if the process is in control.

4-7 This is a continuation of Problem 4-6.

(a) Estimate the value of σ' from the range data of Problem 2-10.

(b) How does this estimate of σ' compare to the value of σ calculated in either Problem 2-14 or 2-15? Explain your answer based on the conclusions drawn in Problem 4-6.

4-8 This is a continuation of Problem 4-6.

(a) Estimate the value of σ' from the range data of Problem 2-10.

(b) Assuming that the distribution of timing signal is approximately normal, what proportion of the devices would you expect to meet specifications of 190.5 and 210.5 milliseconds?

(c) What proportion of the devices tested actually met these specifications?

4-9 This is a continuation of Problem 4-6.

(a) If the mean of the distribution shifts to 205 milliseconds, compute the probability that the shift will not be detected on the $\bar{X}$ chart on the first subgroup after the shift occurs. Assume no change in σ' and base your analysis on the $\bar{X}$ control limits found in Problem 4-6.

(b) Assuming a normal distribution of timing signals, what proportion of nonconforming devices would be produced at this new value of the mean?

4-10 (a) Compute the central lines and 3-sigma control limits for $\bar{X}$ and R charts for the data of Problem 2-19.

(b) Plot the control charts and determine if the process is in control.

4-11 This is a continuation of Problem 4-10.

(a) Estimate the value of σ' from the range data of Problem 2-19.

(b) How does this estimate of σ' compare to the value of σ calculated in either Problem 2-24 or 2-25? Explain your answer based on the conclusions drawn in Problem 4-10.

4-12 This is a continuation of Problem 4-10.

(a) Estimate the value of σ' from the range data of Problem 2-19.

(b) Assuming that the distribution of voltage output is approximately normal, what proportion of the units would you expect to meet specifications of 347.25 and 352.75 volts?

(c) What proportion of the units tested actually met these specifications?

4-13 This is a continuation of Problem 4-10.

(a) If the mean of the distribution shifts to 347 volts, compute the probability that the shift will not be detected on the $\bar{X}$ chart on the first subgroup plotted after the shift takes place. Assume no change in σ' and base your analysis on the $\bar{X}$ control limits calculated in Problem 4-10.

(b) Assuming a normal distribution of voltage output, what proportion of nonconforming units would be produced at this new value of the mean?

4-14 A certain product is manufactured to a specification of 120.0 ± 5.0 for one of the quality characteristics. At present, the estimated process average is 120.0 and the standard deviation is 1.50.

(a) Compute the 3σ control limits for an $\bar{X}$ and R chart based on a subgroup size of 4.

(b) What per cent of the product will not meet specifications if the process average suddenly shifts to 121.0 assuming a normally distributed product?

Answer: 122.25, 117.75, 7.05, 0; 0.38%.

4-15 At the end of Example 1-1, three conclusions are stated with no explanation of the analysis on which these conclusions were based. Explain the calculations that may be made to provide the basis for these three conclusions.

4-16 A control chart has been used to monitor a certain process during a considerable period of time. The process is sampled in subgroups of four at intervals of about two hours, and the $\bar{X}$ control chart has 3σ control limits of 121.0 and 129.0 with the target $\bar{X}_0$ at 125.0.

(a) If this product is sold to a user who has a specification of 127.0 ± 8.0, what per cent of the product will not meet this specification assuming a normally distributed output?

(b) If the target value of this process can be shifted without effect on the process standard deviation, what target value would minimize the amount of product being produced outside the specification values?

(c) At this new target value, what per cent of the product will not meet the required specifications?

Answer: 1.22%; 127; 0.27%

4-17 Manufacture is initiated on a new feed pipe to be used as a water line in a particular heater. To monitor the length of the pipe, $\bar{X}$ and R control charts were initiated based on 25 subgroups of four samples each. For these 25 subgroups, $\Sigma\bar{X} = 500$ and $\Sigma R = 51.474$. What should the 3σ control limits be for the $\bar{X}$ and R charts?

Answer: 21.5, 18.5, 4.7, 0.

4-18 In Example 4-3, if the slot width were below the lower specification limit of 0.8750, the part could be reworked to bring it within specifications. However, if above 0.8800, it would have to be scrapped. After the first 16 subgroups, an estimate was made that the standard deviation σ' of a controlled process would be 0.0014. This called for an $\bar{X}'$ of 0.8758 if the process average were to be $3\sigma'$ below the upper specification limit. However, the decision was made to aim at 0.8770 as the process average.

(a) If the distribution of slot width were normal with σ' of 0.0014, approximately what percentage of rework could be expected if $\bar{X}'$ were 0.8758?

(b) With $\bar{X}'$ at 0.8770, what percentage of spoilage would be expected? What percentage of rework?

(c) In what way do the answers in (a) and (b) suggest an economic basis for establishing the process average in cases of this type?

(d) How would your decision as to process average to be aimed at in Example 4-3 be influenced if you knew that terminal blocks with slot widths up to 0.8830 had been accepted by the plant salvage committee for use in the airplane and had been used satisfactorily?

Answer: (a) 28.4%; (b) 1.61%, 7.66%.

4-19 The following data were obtained over a 10-day period to initiate $\bar{X}$ and R control charts for a quality characteristic of a certain manufactured product that had required a substantial amount of rework. All the figures apply to product made on a single machine by a single operator. The subgroup size was 5. Two subgroups were taken per day.

Subgroup number	$\bar{X}$	R	Subgroup number	$\bar{X}$	R
1	177.6	23	11	179.8	9
2	176.6	8	12	176.4	8
3	178.4	22	13	178.4	7
4	176.6	12	14	178.2	4
5	177.0	7	15	180.6	6
6	179.4	8	16	179.6	6
7	178.6	15	17	177.8	10
8	179.6	6	18	178.4	9
9	178.8	7	19	181.6	7
10	178.2	12	20	177.6	10

(a) Determine trial control limits for the $\bar{X}$ and R charts.

(b) What preliminary conclusions about statistical control can you draw from your observation and analysis of the data and of the control charts? Justify these conclusions. Does it seem reasonable that the introduction of the control charts may have had some influence on the process? Why or why not?

(c) The specified requirements for the quality characteristic are given as 171 ± 11. If a product falls below the L of 160, it must be scrapped, whereas if it falls above the U of 182, it may be reworked. Because scrapping an article is much more costly than rework, it is desired to hold scrap to a low figure without causing excessive rework. The process average can be shifted by a relatively simple machine adjustment. What would you suggest as the aimed-at value for process centering in the immediate future? Why?

(d) The $\bar{X}$ and R charts are to be continued. What would you recommend as the new limits on these charts? Show your calculations and explain your reasoning.

4-20 A fair percentage of a certain product requires costly rework operations to change a certain quality characteristic after the product has been rejected by the manufacturer's 100% final inspection. Rework is possible whenever the value of this quality characteristic falls above the upper specification limit. If the value falls below the lower specification limit, the product must be scrapped.

$\bar{X}$ and R control charts have been initiated and maintained for 50 subgroups of 5 each with samples taken from production every 2 h. The specification requirements for the measured quality characteristic are 119 ± 10. The process appears to be in statistical control with an $\bar{X}'$ of 124 and a σ' of 5. The 3-sigma control limits on the $\bar{X}$ chart are 130.7 and 117.3; the 3-sigma control limits on the R chart are 24.6 and 0. On the assumption that the quality characteristic is normally distributed, approximately what percentage of nonconforming product is being produced? How much of this can be reworked?

Answer: 16.0%; 15.9%.

4-21 In the case described in Problem 4-20 various persons in the manufacturing organization examined the new control charts. Among the numerous suggestions for changes were the following:

(a) Alter the specification limits so that the upper limit U is the upper control limit of 130.7 and the lower limit L is the lower control limit of 117.3.

(b) Use 2-sigma instead of 3-sigma limits on the $\bar{X}$ chart. In this way, both limits on the $\bar{X}$ chart will be within the present specification limits of 119 ± 10.

(c) Take samples every hour rather than every 2 h.

(d) Increase the sample size from 5 to 10. It is pointed out that this change will bring the limits on the $\bar{X}$ chart within the specification limits.

Discuss the merits of these suggestions, indicating the circumstances, if any, under which you believe each suggestion might be helpful in reducing the trouble (high rework cost) that led to the initiation of the control charts. Describe any other possible types of action that you believe might help the manufacturer to improve this operation. What information not given in the statement of Problem 4-20 would you want before recommending any particular type of action? Why would you want this information?

4-22 In a certain manufacturing process, $\bar{\bar{X}} = 178$ and $\bar{R} = 10$. The subgroup size is five.

(a) Find control chart limits for the $\bar{X}$ and R charts.

(b) Estimate σ' on the basis that the process is in control.

(c) Specifications on this product are 165 ± 20. What fraction nonconforming is currently being produced assuming the distribution of product is approximately normal?

(d) Is this process capable of meeting specifications? Explain your answer.

4-23 Control charts for $\bar{X}$ and R, based on a subgroup size of 4, are to be used to control a process. The standard deviation of this process is 10. An aimed-at value of the mean $(\bar{X}_0)$ is to be 250.

(a) Determine control limits for the $\bar{X}$ and R charts.

(b) Determine the probability of a point falling within the $\bar{X}$ chart control limits if the actual $\bar{X}'$ is $0.5\sigma'$ below the aimed-at value of 250.

(c) If it is $1.0\sigma'$ below 250.

(d) If it is $2.0\sigma'$ below 250.

(e) If it is $2.5\sigma'$ below 250.

(f) Sketch these probabilities as a function in the location of the true mean (horizontal scale) and comment on the usefulness of this diagram in relation to the detection of shifts in the mean.

4-24 The high-voltage output of a certain power supply unit for copy machines is specified as 350 ± 5 volts dc. Subgroups of four units are drawn approximately every hour and tested. After 30 subgroups, $\Sigma \bar{X} = 10,560.0$ and $\Sigma R = 86.5$.

(a) Determine control limits for $\bar{X}$ and R charts and estimate the value of σ'.

(b) Assuming the process is in control and that variation in the product follows a normal distribution, what proportion of defective product is being made?

4-25 (a) Can the process described in Problem 4-24 meet specifications if it is recentered at 350?

(b) Calculate the control limits for $\bar{X}$ and R based on recentering at 350.

(c) If these new control limits are used but no adjustment is made in the process, compute the Type II error probability that this fact will not be detected on the first subgroup plotted against the new control limits.

4-26 An automatic screw machine turns out round-head bolts with a specified shank diameter of 9.00 ± 0.04 mm. The process has been operating in control at an estimated $\bar{X}'$ of 9.00 mm and an $\bar{R}$ of 0.0206 mm. The subgroup size is four.

(a) Calculate the $\bar{X}$ and R chart control limits.

(b) If the mean of the process shifts to 9.02 mm, compute the Type II error probability that the shift will not be detected on the first subgroup drawn after it occurs.

(c) What proportion of defective product is being produced at this new value of $\bar{X}'$ assuming the product is normally distributed?

4-27 The bursting strength of test specimens of a certain cardboard material has been found by a manufacturer to be 100 pounds with a σ' of 20 pounds.

(a) Using a subgroup size of four, what control limits would be used on $\bar{X}$ and R charts?

(b) What are the natural tolerances of the process?

(c) Assuming the mean of the process shifts to 90 pounds compute the probability that it will not be detected on the first subgroup drawn after the shift occurs.

4-28 Specifications on a certain part are 155.0 ± 20.0. The subgroup size is five. After 50 subgroups, $\Sigma \bar{X} = 7,660.0$ and $\Sigma R = 880.0$.

(a) Determine control limits for $\bar{X}$ and R charts.

(b) Assuming the process is in control and that the product is approximately normally distributed, what fraction of nonconforming items is being produced?

(c) If the process is recentered to exactly 155, what fraction nonconforming will be produced?

4-29 A certain process with a σ' of 0.0010 has been statistically controlled at a mean of 0.0360. The product is currently sold to two users who have different specifications. User A's specifications are 0.0380 ± 0.0040; those of user B are 0.0360 ± 0.0040.

(a) Assuming a normal distribution of product, what per cent of product does not meet user A's requirements?

(b) What per cent does not meet user B's requirements?

(c) The suggestion is made that the process be adjusted to an $\bar{X}'_0$ of 0.0370. Determine, in terms of per cent nonconforming for each user, the effect of this shift. Do you consider it desirable? Why or why not?

4-30 The diameter of one end of a gyro drive shaft is subject to statistical control using $\bar{X}$ and R charts. After 30 subgroups of 5 shafts each have been examined, $\Sigma \bar{X} = 34,290$ and $\Sigma R = 330$.

(a) Determine the control chart limits for $\bar{X}$ and R.

(b) Estimate the mean, $\bar{X}'$, and standard deviation, σ', of the process assuming that it is in statistical control.

(c) What are the natural tolerances of this process?

4-31 Specifications on the process described in Problem 4-30 are $1,140 \pm 10$. Shafts with diameters less than 1,130 must be scrapped; shafts with diameters greater than 1,150 can be reworked but the rework operation must be done by skilled lathe operators. The resulting rework cost is as great as the direct cost of manufacture.

(a) Determine the percentage of rework and of scrap product assuming a normal distribution for the process.

(b) 100 percent inspection has been carried on up to this point. What would be your advice regarding the level of inspection, centering, etc., for the immediate future?

(c) A Material Review Committee, made up of representatives from the plant and the customer, has decided that shafts can be used successfully with diameters as large as 1,155. How would this information affect your decisions in (b)?

4-32 $\bar{X}$ and R charts are used to control a process by drawing subgroups of five units every two hours. Specifications on one critical characteristic are $2,119 \pm 10$. Product over specs may be reworked; if undersized, it must be scrapped. After 50 subgroups, $\Sigma \bar{X} = 106,200.0$ and $\Sigma R = 581.5$.

(a) Determine 3-sigma control limits for $\bar{X}$ and R charts.

(b) Assuming that the process is in control and normally distributed, estimate σ' and determine the per cent of product that must be reworked and that must be scrapped.

4-33 (a) In the situation described in Problem 4-32 someone suggests that the specifications be changed such that the upper spec limit, U, equals the upper control limit on the $\bar{X}$ chart, and the lower spec limit, L, equals the lower control limit. Assuming that this change would be accepted by the design department, do you think it is a good suggestion? Why or why not?

(b) Someone else suggests that the problem can be solved by merely changing from 3-sigma to 2-sigma control limits on the $\bar{X}$ chart. Is this a good suggestion? Why or why not?

(c) A supervisor points out that, by changing the subgroup size from 5 to 10, both control limits easily will fall within specifications. Comment on this suggestion.

(d) Suggest an approach that you believe would be desirable. What further investigations are indicated?

4-34 Control charts for $\bar{X}$ and R are maintained on the shear strength in pounds of test spot welds based on a subgroup size of three. After 30 subgroups, $\Sigma \bar{X} = 12,930$ and $\Sigma R = 1,230$.

(a) Compute the values of 3-sigma control limits for $\bar{X}$ and R.

(b) Assuming the process is in control, estimate σ'.

(c) After some period of time, $\bar{X}'$ shifts to 467.3. Compute the Type II error probability that this shift will go undetected on the first subgroup drawn after the shift occurs.

(d) The minimum test specification on this weld is 365 pounds. Comment on the ability of the process to meet this specification taking into consideration the estimate of σ' found in (b) and the shift indicated in (c).

4-35 Specifications on a certain item are 150 ± 10 grams. $\bar{X}$ and R control charts are maintained based on a subgroup size of five. After 25 subgroups have been drawn, $\Sigma \bar{X} = 3,830$ and $\Sigma R = 440$.

(a) Determine the control limits for $\bar{X}$ and R charts.

(b) Assuming the process is in control and generates a normal distribution, what proportion of product does not meet specifications?

(c) Determine the natural tolerances of the process and comment on its capability to meet specifications.

4-36 $\bar{X}$ and R charts have been maintained on a certain quality characteristic. All points have fallen within limits on both charts. A sudden shift occurs in the process that increases $\bar{X}'$ by $1.5\sigma'$. Assuming that the quality characteristic is normally distributed both before and after the shift, that σ' remains constant, and that the control limits were determined prior to the shift:

(a) Approximately what percentage of points would you expect to fall outside the upper control limit on the $\bar{X}$ chart if the subgroup size is five?

(b) Answer (a) for a subgroup size of nine.

(c) Comment on the effect that subgroup size has on the ability of the $\bar{X}$ chart to detect shifts in $\bar{X}'$.

(d) Comment briefly on the effect of this type of shift on a σ or R chart.

(e) Why is it that a shift in universe dispersion with no change in universe average may cause $\bar{X}$ to show lack of control as well as R?

4-37 A plot of Type II error probability as a function of shift magnitude in multiples of σ' is a useful tool in illustrating the sensitivity of various control charting schemes. Assuming a normal distribution, find the probability of Type II error for an $\bar{X}$ chart for shift magnitudes of $0^+\sigma'$, $0.5\sigma'$, $1.0\sigma'$, $1.5\sigma'$, and $2\sigma'$ for the following cases:

   (a) 3-sigma control limits and a subgroup size of 5.
   (b) 2-sigma control limits and a subgroup size of 5.
   (c) 3-sigma control limits and a subgroup size of 16.
   (d) Sketch these three curves on a single graph with Type II error probability on the ordinate scale and shift magnitude on the abscissa. Discuss these curves.

FIVE

RATIONAL SUBGROUPING; ANALYZING AND CONTROLLING VARIATION

... The ultimate object is not only to detect trouble but also to find it, and such discovery naturally involves classification. The engineer who is successful in dividing his data initially into rational subgroups based upon rational hypotheses is therefore inherently better off in the long run than the one who is not thus successful.—W. A. Shewhart†

The Information Given by the Control Chart Depends on the Basis Used for Selection of Subgroups

One possible view of a control chart is that it provides a statistical test to determine whether the variation from subgroup to subgroup is consistent with the average variation within the subgroups. If it is desired to determine whether or not a group of measurements is statistically homogeneous (i.e., whether they appear to come from a constant system of chance causes), subgroups should be chosen in a way that appears likely to give the maximum chance for the measurements in each subgroup to be alike and the maximum chance for the subgroups to differ one from the other.

This may be demonstrated in a striking way. Take a set of measurements which have been subgrouped according to order of production and which show definite lack of control as based on the evidence of $\bar{X}$ and R charts. Write each measurement on a chip, put the chips in a bowl, mix them thoroughly, and draw the chips out one by one without replacement. Record the values written on the chips in the order drawn. Plot $\bar{X}$ and R charts from these recorded values. If you have done a good job of mixing the chips, these new charts will show control. By this mixing you have substituted chance causes for the original assignable causes as a basis for the differences among subgroups.

---

† W. A. SHEWHART, "Economic Control of Quality of Manufactured Product," p. 299, 1931, by Litton Educational Publications, Inc., quoted here by permission of Van Nostrand Reinhold Company.

The basis of subgrouping calls for careful study, with a view to obtaining the maximum amount of useful information from any control chart. As already pointed out, the most obvious rational basis for subgrouping is the order of production.

Two Schemes Involving Order of Production as a Basis for Subgrouping

Where order of production is used as a basis for subgrouping, two fundamentally different approaches are possible:

1. The first subgroup consists of product all produced as nearly as possible at one time; the next subgroup consists of product all produced as nearly as possible at a later time; and so forth. For example, if the subgroup size is five, the quality control inspector who makes measurements at hourly intervals may measure the last five items that were produced just before each hourly visit to the machine. This is possible on machine parts, for example, if the parts are placed in trays in the order of production. Otherwise the same result may be obtained by the inspector waiting for five items to come off the machine and measuring them as they come.
2. One subgroup consists of product intended to be representative of all the production over a given period of time; the next subgroup consists of product intended to be representative of all the production of approximately the same quantity of product in a later period; and so forth. Where product accumulates at the point of production, the inspector may choose a random sample from all the product made since the last visit. If this is not practicable, there might be five visits (if $n = 5$) approximately equally spaced over a given production quantity or time, with one measurement made at each visit; these five measurements constitute one subgroup.

The first method follows the rule for selection of rational subgroups of permitting a minimum chance for variation within a subgroup and a maximum chance for variation from subgroup to subgroup. It can be expected to give the best estimate of a value of σ' that represents the ideal capabilities of a process obtainable if assignable causes of variation from one subgroup to another can be eliminated. Moreover, it provides a more sensitive measure of shifts in the process average; it makes the control chart a better guide to machine setting or to other actions intended to maintain a given process average. Thus the first method is more ideally suited to analysis of a process and to process control.

However, if subgrouping is by the first method and a change in process average takes place after one subgroup is taken and is corrected before the next subgroup, the change will not be reflected in the control chart. For this reason, the second method is sometimes preferred where one of the purposes of the control chart is to influence decisions on acceptance of product. In such cases a question to be asked before choosing between the two schemes is whether or not two compensating shifts in process average are really likely to occur between subgroups. If so, and if there is no other way to detect bad product that might be produced between subgroups (for instance, failure of a part to fit into an assembly), the second method of subgrouping is desirable in spite of the other advantages of the first method. In machining operations, such compensating shifts between subgroups are more likely to occur in hand-operated machines than on automatic machines.

Where the second method of subgrouping is used, the interpretation of points out of control on the R chart is somewhat different from that in the first method. With the second method a shift in the process average during the period covered by a subgroup may cause out-of-control points on the R chart even though there has been no real change in the process dispersion.

The choice of subgroup size should be influenced, in part, by the desirability of permitting a minimum chance for variation within a subgroup. In most cases, more useful information will be obtained from, say, five subgroups of 5 than from one subgroup of 25. In large subgroups, such as 25, there is likely to be too much opportunity for a process change within a subgroup. Nevertheless, if process changes do not occur within subgroups, large subgroup sizes have the advantage mentioned in Chap. 3 of reducing the risk of so-called Type II errors in interpreting control charts. Whenever relatively large subgroup sizes are used for this purpose, it is particularly desirable to use the first method of subgrouping.

In many cases where the first method of subgrouping is really better, it may be necessary to use the second method because of practical reasons associated with the taking of the measurements. This was illustrated in Example 4-3.

Objectives of an Analysis of Process Capability

Part One in this book emphasizes the use of statistical techniques to control on-going production. In many instances, however, examples and discussions focus on the problems of starting a new process or of introducing control techniques into an existing process.

The basic statistical problem in process quality control is that of establishing a state of control over the manufacturing process and then maintaining that state of control through time. Of no less importance is the problem of adjusting the process to the point where virtually all of the product output meets specifications. This second problem is the realm of capability analysis. That is, once a state of control has been established, attention turns to the question: Is the output meeting specifications and, if not, can the process be adjusted to a level where it will?

Actions that result in a change or adjustment in a process are frequently the result of some form of capability study. As is discussed throughout Part One of this book, the comparison of natural tolerance limits with specification limits and the natural tolerance range with the specification range may lead to any of the following possible courses of action:

1. *No action.* If the natural tolerance limits fall well within the specification limits, usually no action will be required. Frequently in such cases, control may be relaxed; a modified control chart, discussed in Chap. 9, or a p chart, the subject of Chap. 7, may be substituted for the conventional $\bar{X}$ and R charts.

2. *Action to adjust centering.* When the natural tolerance range is about the same as the specification range, a relatively simple adjustment to the centering of the process may be all that is necessary to bring virtually all product within specifications.

3. *Action to reduce variability.* This is usually the most complex action. In those cases where several product streams merge into one line prior to inspection, similar to examples discussed in this chapter, action may involve the relatively uncomplicated task of bringing the several streams under control separately at some standard $\bar{X}'_0$. In other cases, a complex analysis of the sources of variation may be required resulting in changes of methods, tooling, materials, and/or equipment.

4. *Actions to change specifications.* This is a design decision but one that should not be ignored by quality control personnel. Simply because specifications are stipulated in writing does not necessarily mean they are inviolate. On the other hand, quality control and manufacturing personnel cannot callously ignore them without running the risk of causing real trouble. There is a limit, however, to the amount of time and investment that should be put into the types of analyses and adjustments discussed in action (3) before design groups should be made aware of the problem. In some cases, specifications may be set tighter than necessary. In others, slight design changes may be less costly, or more feasible, than changes in machinery or tooling. It may be feasible on occasion totally to redesign the product unit within the manufacturer's capability to produce. Needless to say, there are important economic trade-offs between action items (3) and (4) that require close coordination among design, manufacturing, and quality control functions.

5. *Resignation to losses.* When all else fails, management must be content with a high loss rate. Attention, at this point, focuses on scrap and rework costs, the economical level of control that should be exercised over the production process, and the costs associated with screening all product realizing that some nonconforming product still is likely to be accepted. It is most important in this case to have good estimates of the form and shape of the distribution of product as an aid to proper process centering.

The reader should note that, in nearly all cases, the resulting decisions are management decisions. One or another course of action may be recommended by quality control or production personnel but the decision will be made and funded by higher management.

Sources of Variability†

Much of the discussion of process capability will concentrate on the analysis of sources of variability. It is worthwhile, therefore, to consider the possible sources

---

† This breakdown of process variability was suggested by the procedures described in "The Span Plan Method, Process Capability Analysis," by LEONARD A. SEDER and DAVID COWAN, American Society for Quality Control, Milwaukee, Wisconsin, Pub. No. 3, 1956.

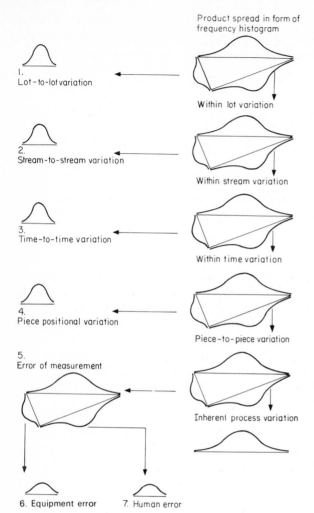

Product spread in form of frequency histogram

1.
Lot-to-lot variation

Within lot variation

2.
Stream-to-stream variation

Within stream variation

3.
Time-to-time variation

Within time variation

4.
Piece positional variation

Piece-to-piece variation

5.
Error of measurement

Inherent process variation

6. Equipment error   7. Human error

Figure 5-1 Diagram of breakdown of sources of variability in manufactured product. This figure is suggested by and similar to Figure 6 in L. A. Seder and D. Cowan, *The Span Plan Method, Process Capability Analysis*, Pub. No. 3, 1956, American Society for Quality Control, Milwaukee, Wis., 53203.

of variation in manufactured product. In doing so, it is helpful to view these sources in a manner similar to that shown in Figure 5-1.

The long-term variation in product, for convenience termed the *product spread*, may be measured from a histogram made up from inspection data taken over a substantial period of time. If the process is shifting, there will be some difference between the process average, and possibly standard deviation, from lot to lot. One of the objectives of control charting is to eliminate, or markedly reduce, this *lot-to-lot* variability.

The effects of *stream-to-stream* variability will be discussed at length later in this chapter. Suffice it to say here that the distribution of product flowing from several streams, such as gang-machining operations, multiple-cavity molds, several individual machines, etc., is formed of a weighted average of the distributions of each individual producing unit. The variability of this weighted average will frequently be much greater than the variabilities inherent in the individual streams. In order to eliminate this source of variability, it may be necessary to analyze each producing entity separately.

A main objective of control charting is to minimize the *time-to-time* variation that is listed as the next factor contributing to product spread. The types of control charts that are maintained, for example separate $\bar{X}$ and R charts on each product stream, will depend on the spread of the process at each level and the need to minimize each of the contributing factors discussed so far.

In many cases, physical inspection measurements may be taken at a great many different points on a given unit. For example, the diameter of a shaft may be measured at an infinite number of points around its diameter and across its length. Measuring at several points, therefore, need not lead to consistent results due to out-of-roundness and/or tapering. Such differences are referred to as *piece positional* variability. Significant piece positional variation may necessitate changes in tooling, material, or machinery.

A considerable portion of Chap. 10 is devoted to problems of *inherent error of measurement*. There are many examples in modern industry where the inherent error of measurement constitutes a significant portion of the apparent product spread. Many situations require very expensive electronic and optical measuring devices in order to minimize this source of variability.

The remaining source of variability is the piece-to-piece variability of a single production entity, the *inherent process capability*. It is frequently referred to as the instant reproducibility of the machine and represents the ultimate capability of the production facility operating under virtual laboratory conditions.

One very important factor is still missing from this discussion of sources of variability. That factor is the interaction that takes place between man and machine. In this case, *man-machine interaction* refers not only to the interaction between the machinist and the machine but also between the inspector and the inspection device. In semiautomated or fully automated cases, this effect may be minimal or virtually nonexistent. There are many instances, however, where to ignore the person in the system would be to ignore the largest single source of variability.

Order of Production is Not Always a Sufficient Basis for Subgrouping

The reason why order in time is a good basis of subgrouping is that its use tends to disclose assignable causes of variation that come and go. However, there may be other assignable causes of variation that are not disclosed merely by taking subgroups in the order of production.

Two or more apparently identical machines may have different process averages, different process dispersions, or other differences in their patterns of variation. If these machines contribute to a stream of product in a way that subgroups taken from that stream contain approximately constant numbers from each machine, the differences among the machines will not be disclosed by the control charts. The principle here is that assignable causes, if they are to be indicated by the charts, must influence some but not all of the subgroups.

For this reason, consideration often needs to be given to the question of different subgroups for different machines each doing the same operation, or for different spindles on the same machine, or for different cavities in a mold, or for different operators or different inspectors or different shifts. In some cases separate control charts may be needed rather than merely separate subgroups.

The extent to which it pays to make this type of breakdown is a matter for judgment in each individual case. The decision depends on whether it is normally difficult or easy to meet specified tolerances, on the costs of keeping and analyzing the control charts, on whether it is practicable or economical to correct certain known assignable causes of variation, and on other matters that vary from case to case. One case in which it did pay to make this breakdown is described in Example 5-1.

Example 5-1 Setting of thermostatic controls. Compensation for the differences between operators *Facts of the case* Thermostatic controls for an electrical device were all adjusted on two banks of units which soak the thermostats at a given temperature level. After soaking for a few minutes, each thermostat was adjusted by an operator until a light flashed on the adjusting unit; a lock nut was subsequently put on the control to hold this adjustment. Each bank of units required its own operator. These controls were produced on two shifts. Thus four operators used two banks of units.

The specifications stated the temperatures at which the thermostatically controlled switches should turn the electrical device on and off and gave tolerances for these temperatures. Each finished device was checked by a testing set operating on the go and not-go principle to determine whether these tolerances were met. Whenever an out-of-tolerance thermostat was found on this final inspection, it had to be removed from the completed device, reset, and reassembled into the device.

Several weeks might elapse between the original adjustment of a thermostatic control and its final assembly into a completed device. Hence it was not economical to depend only on the 100% inspection at final assembly as a check on the thermostat setting; any continued systematic error in setting could be responsible for many defective thermostats before it was detected at final assembly and hence could cause much costly rework.

For this reason, samples of the thermostatic controls were taken immediately after setting and checked on a test panel that permitted the measurement of actual on and off temperatures. Control charts for $\overline{X}$ and R were plotted. At first the scheme of subgrouping was to take five thermostats that had just been set; a subgroup would generally contain some thermostats adjusted by each of the two operators on the current shift.

This proved successful in detecting trouble from time to time and in obtaining prompt correction of the trouble. Usually the assignable causes were of a type that could be corrected by maintenance work on one of the adjusting banks.

Analysis and action However, even when the process stayed in control, some of the thermostats were outside specified tolerances. With σ' estimated from the $\bar{R}$ of the control charts, the tolerance spread $U - L$ appeared to be about $5\sigma'$.

It was decided to use a plan of subgrouping by operators and by adjusting banks; all the thermostats in any subgroup came from one operator and one bank. This disclosed the fact that on each shift the thermostats from one operator showed a consistently higher average on and off temperature than those from the other operator. By shifting operators from one bank to the other it was determined that this was a personal difference between operators and not a difference between banks. It was evidently a difference in reaction time to the flashing of the light in the adjusting unit.

The temperature levels in the adjusting banks were then established in a way that allowed the difference in temperature level to compensate for the difference between the "hot" and "cold" operators. The scheme of subgrouping by operators reduced $\bar{R}$ and σ'. The change in temperature level of the banks to compensate for differences between operators tended to keep the same process average for all operators and thus kept the process in control with the narrower control limits. As the new σ' was about $\frac{5}{6}$ of the previous σ', the tolerance spread $U - L$ was now six times the new σ'. With careful attention to routine use of the control charts to prevent shifts in the process average, it was now possible to make all the thermostats within tolerances and to avoid rework costs at final assembly.

Comment on Example 5-1

In this example, order in time was a necessary but not a sufficient basis for subgrouping. After it proved possible to compensate for differences in operators, a single chart was maintained with each subgroup representing a single bank and one operator. Separate control charts were not maintained on each machine-operator combination. If the tolerances had not been so tight compared to the dispersion of the process, it would not have been necessary to go to the extra trouble of keeping subgroups by operators.

Need for Discrimination in the Selection of Subgroups

Where there is trouble in meeting tolerances and control is shown by a control chart based merely on the order of production, it may still be possible to diagnose and correct trouble by changing the basis of subgrouping or by keeping separate charts for different sources of measurements, such as different machines, different spindles on the same machine, or different operators. But because such breakdowns usually increase the costs of taking and analyzing data, it may pay to avoid them in cases where tolerances are easily held most of the time.

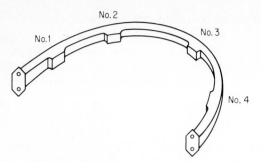

Figure 5-2 Half-ring engine mount.

Moreover, there is no point in continuing to take subgroups in a way that has the effect of disclosing assignable causes of variation that it is impracticable or uneconomical to remove. The need for discrimination in selection of subgroups is illustrated in Example 5-2.

Example 5-2 Thickness of pads on half-ring engine mount. An example in which subgroups were taken in a way that made evidence of lack of control have no practical value *Facts of the case* Figure 5-2 shows a rough sketch of a half-ring that was part of an assembly used in connection with the mounting of an airplane engine. This half-ring contained four contact pads. It was desired to control the thickness of these pads. All four pads were machined at the same time and were supposed to have the same thickness.

The thickness of each pad was measured with a micrometer to the nearest ten-thousandth of an inch. The four pads on one half-ring were considered to be one subgroup. The measurements for 36 half-rings are shown in Table 5-1. The $\bar{X}$ and R charts plotted from these measurements are shown in Fig. 5-3.

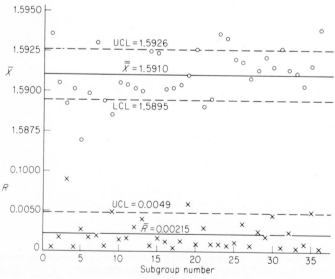

Figure 5-3 $\bar{X}$ and R charts for thickness of pads on half-ring engine mount—data of Table 5-1.

Table 5-1 Thickness of each of pads on half-ring engine mount
(Measurements in units of 0.0001 in above 1.5000 in)

Half-ring number	Pad 1	Pad 2	Pad 3	Pad 4	$\bar{X}$	R
1	933	937	938	935	936	5
2	897	898	915	913	905	18
3	840	900	900	930	892	90
4	900	905	902	900	902	5
5	879	852	873	871	869	27
6	903	890	892	908	898	18
7	930	940	930	920	930	20
8	890	895	897	895	894	7
9	890	900	850	900	885	50
10	900	915	900	905	905	15
11	901	916	901	900	904	16
12	920	890	905	895	902	30
13	920	890	910	880	900	40
14	929	921	924	928	925	8
15	927	914	925	931	924	17
16	907	896	895	908	901	13
17	902	900	903	905	902	5
18	903	900	914	900	904	14
19	870	930	920	920	910	60
20	925	930	920	930	926	10
21	880	895	910	885	892	30
22	890	900	895	895	895	10
23	940	935	930	940	936	10
24	930	935	938	930	933	8
25	915	921	918	927	920	12
26	895	930	925	925	919	35
27	910	907	905	913	909	8
28	905	916	902	928	913	26
29	925	930	910	925	922	20
30	924	928	882	927	915	46
31	925	931	924	930	927	7
32	900	905	925	925	914	25
33	910	910	915	910	911	5
34	900	905	900	910	904	10
35	900	950	920	900	918	50
36	940	938	940	938	939	2
Totals..					32,781	774

These charts appeared to show the process badly out of control. However, a more critical consideration of the matter showed that it was practically certain this type of subgrouping would show lack of control, and that this showing of lack of control did not provide a useful guide to action.

Control charts answer the question, "Is the variation among the sub-groups consistent with the variation within the subgroups?" With subgroups taken as they were, this question might have been phrased, "Is the variation among the half-rings consistent with the variation from pad to pad within each half-ring?" The answer, "No," given by the control chart might have been guessed without help from any control charts. That is, it was to be expected from the fact that the four pads on any half-ring were machined together; it was reasonable to expect more variation among the half-rings than among the pads. Moreover, it was no help to know that this was true, as nothing could be done about it by attention to out-of-control points.

Comment on Example 5-2

In this case what might have appeared at first glance to be a natural plan of subgrouping was, in fact, an unsatisfactory plan. The subgroup was actually taken as four pads on one half-ring. Four control charts, one for each pad, might well have been used.

Many situations exist like Example 5-2. In such situations the decision regarding the number of control charts to be used cannot be made without studying the behavior of the variables and having a clear idea of the objectives of the charts. For example, pad thicknesses at the four locations had tended to vary in unison, with an increase or decrease at one location accompanied by equal increases or decreases at the other locations. Thus a single chart for one location would have served to control the general thickness.

If the variations from one location to another had been completely unrelated, it is clear that one chart could not have done the job. Actual situations are nearly always somewhere between these two extremes. Whether one chart or several are required depends on the degree of relationship (in statistical language, the correlation) between the fluctuations at the several points and on the tightness of the tolerances.

In the situation described in Example 5-2, a slight change in tooling resulted in a reduction in the variation of pad thickness from pad to pad within a half-ring. It then proved satisfactory to use a single control chart on which the variable was thickness of pad 2, and a subgroup consisted of the measured thickness of this pad from four successive half-rings.

It may be remarked that it is always an advantage if one control chart can be made to do the work of four. Not only is there a saving in the cost of clerical labor in computing and charting; the practical difficulties in having charts analyzed and in securing action based on that analysis are also reduced. It is easier to get people to study one chart and take action on it than it is to get them to study four related charts and take action on them.

Sometimes in this type of situation a practical answer may be to take enough data to permit the several control charts to be made, but actually to keep only one chart as a routine matter. Then if at any time the situation calls for critical study, the data will be available for the construction of the other charts for purposes of analysis.

Identification on a Control Chart of Different Sources of Subgroups

In Example 5-1, subgrouping was finally by operators and by banks of adjusting units. Four sources of subgroups were possible, namely, operator *A* and bank 1, operator *B* and bank 2, operator *C* and bank 1, and operator *D* and bank 2. However, subgroups for all four combinations were plotted on the same control chart. It is common for different subgroups to come from different shifts and is not unusual for them to come from different machines or different operators.

In all such cases it is desirable to differentiate the various subgroup sources on the control charts, so that any consistent differences may be readily observed by someone looking at the charts. This may be done by the use of different types of symbols (such as circles, dots, and crosses) or different colors to represent each source of subgroups.

Steps in the Analysis of Process Capability

The basic steps that appropriately may be taken in performing a capability study are given in the following paragraphs. Unfortunately, no two studies are identical; therefore, certain of these steps may be eliminated or the order may be changed to suit the needs of the particular situation. A good knowledge of both the techniques to be used and the operation of the manufacturing process is required. Each study must be planned ahead of time. Decisions must be made regarding sampling procedures, timing, and collection of data, and data must be recorded in such a manner that there will be no confusion as to how, where, or when they were taken.

1. *Establish control over the process.* The statistical tests discussed in this book begin with the premise that samples are being drawn from a single universe. Until this supposition has been proven, estimates of the parameters of the distribution underlying the process are virtually meaningless. All of the pitfalls regarding rational subgrouping apply with special emphasis to capability studies.
2. *Analyze process data.* Estimates are made of the process average and dispersion, and frequency histograms may be plotted in order to get a feel for the form of the distribution of product. This step may be carried out whether or not control is indicated. Even though control is not indicated, a frequency histogram gives an indication of the product spread. When combined with control-chart information, prime candidates for reduction of this spread may become apparent.

3. *Analyze sources of variation.* Study of the component sources of variation and their magnitudes may range from relatively simple tests to extremely complicated experimental designs carried on over long periods of time. This is the point at which knowledge of the characteristics of the manufacturing process becomes most important. Utilizing the general outline illustrated in Fig. 5-1, the analyst should determine those factors and operations that are most likely to be contributing to the process spread. Data collection is then planned in such a way as to isolate these potential sources and evaluate them first. Since the results of any part of the capability study may suggest further investigation in other directions, it is important carefully to identify the timing and source of all measurements. This may make it possible to go back and recombine data based on insights gained from the planned study.

Example 5-3 Process capability study of glass stresses in glass-to-wire seal
Facts of the case This study is concerned with the preservation of integrity of glass-to-wire seals on certain miniature electrical resistance components. Finished bare components are sealed in a glass envelope in a semivacuum on infrared heat source assembly machines. During the sealing process, an inert forming gas flows through the forming head to ensure an inert atmosphere within each unit of product when the seal is completed. Each assembly machine has four head positions and thus can handle four product units at a time.

Integrity of the seals is predicted based upon measuring stress in the glass seals once the test units have cooled. These stresses are either tension or compression. Tension occurs at the inside of the seal next to the wire while compression occurs at the outer surface of the seal. Both stresses are measured by means of a polariscope which measures the angle of retardation in degrees produced by the stress lines, of a light source passed through a seal. Previous study had shown that angles of retardation between 7.5 and 25.0 degrees and 0 and 30.0 degrees under tension and compression, respectively, would adequately protect the integrity of the seals.

Analysis Initially, samples were collected from each machine twice daily. The tension and compression in both top and bottom seals were measured and recorded. The data collected were plotted on $\bar{X}$ and R charts by assembly head position for each machine. A subgroup size of two, comprised of the two samples taken during one day, was used. These charts showed wide variation from machine head to machine head as well as from day to day on any one head position.

The next step in the analysis was to isolate a single machine for experimental purposes. Control charts for the next 12 subgroups of two taken from each of the four head positions are shown in Fig. 5-4. In order to simplify discussion of the analysis, only the test results of the top seals are presented. Similar results, analyzed concurrently, were obtained for the bottom seals. It can be seen from the very apparent pattern on the $\bar{X}$ charts that something causes temporary shifts in level and that the cause appears to affect all heads

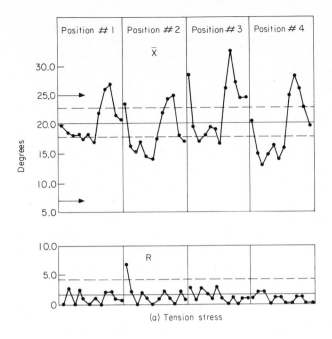

(a) Tension stress

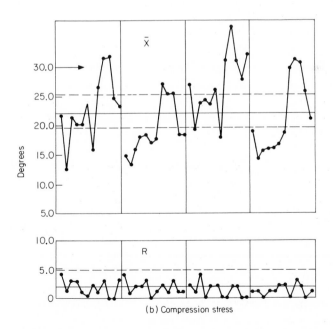

(b) Compression stress

Figure 5-4 Stress in glass-to-wire seal by polariscope analysis of angle of retardation, machine no. 1, top seal.

at the same time. However, the R chart for each requirement remains essentially stable. This indicates that the changes in level are likely to be controllable shifts. That is, whatever affects one seal tends to affect all seals in the same way.

Of the substantial number of variables that could affect the process, observation indicated that the least controlled was the flow rate of the inert forming gas. Thus, the next step was to evaluate the effect of this one variable on stress characteristics. Three series of samples were run at carefully controlled flow rates using a single head on the test machine, a single rack of glass from the same melt, and product units from the same lot. The results of these tests are shown in Fig. 5-5 for the three selected flow rates of 2.6, 4.2, and 5.8 liters per minute.

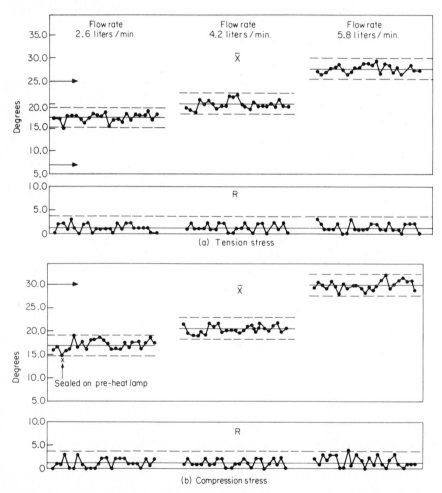

Figure 5-5 Effect of varied flow rate of forming gas on glass-to-wire seal. Analysis of angle of retardation by polariscope, machine no. 1, head position no. 1.

From the control-chart patterns it readily can be seen that variations in the forming-gas flow rate is a prime factor having a significant effect on the level of stresses in the end seals. Also, the charts show a positive correlation between forming-gas flow rate and the level of stress; that is, when forming-gas flow rate is increased, both tension and compression are increased.

Action Further samples were taken from the production floor in much the same manner as in the first test. However, as each sample was taken, the flow rate of the forming gas was measured. These data were plotted as a function of flow rate indicating a nearly linear relationship between forming-gas flow rate and stress in the glass seals. This enabled the engineers to establish tolerances on forming-gas flow rate necessary to maintain stress requirements within engineering limits. These limitations introduced no problems in the ability to make satisfactory seals in all other respects.

A means for limiting forming-gas flow rate was designed and installed on all of the machines. Control-chart data since the installation of these controls show that the stress requirements have been maintained at a satisfactory level.

Discussion of Example 5-3

It is the usual case that the need for a process capability study is evidenced by a high rate of defective production. In this case, the failure of glass-to-wire seals was evidenced by a foreshortened life of the resistance devices. The ultimate result of the study was a much more uniform product in general and the virtual elimination of the problem.

It need not always be the case that savings can only be made at obvious trouble spots. Paul C. Clifford has reported a case in which a process capability study was run on what appeared to be a satisfactory process.[†] Substantial savings in the consumption of zinc on a multiline wire galvanizing operation were accomplished in addition to increasing the uniformity of product.

In Example 5-3, careful observation of the process during early stages of study allowed the engineers to bypass many of the factors contributing to variation discussed previously in this chapter. Attention was quickly directed to the main contributing factor. This was facilitated in large part by the lack of uncontrolled variation in subgroup ranges.

The final point should be made that the factory floor can seldom operate with the precision of a laboratory experiment. Once the parameters of the problem were determined, engineering judgment was required to establish feasible tolerances on the process. Further, engineering design work was required to develop the automatic control device to control the flow rate of the forming gas. Quality control was able to define the problem but did not, by itself, solve it.

[†] PAUL C. CLIFFORD, A Process Capability Study Using Control Charts, *Journal of Quality Technology*, vol. 3, no. 3, July, 1971.

Stages in the Analytical Procedure

Normally, a capability study proceeds in stages. As implied by the discussion of the steps in the procedure, these stages usually proceed from those involving simpler tests and adjustments to those involving more complex and, therefore, more expensive changes.

Usually the study will terminate as soon as the adjusted production spread is comfortably less than the specification range; in short, as soon as the immediate problem is solved. In the long run, this may be an unfortunate result. A basic knowledge of the capability of manufacturing and testing equipment, verified and adjusted from time to time as more data become available, can be of great help to the design, manufacturing, and quality control functions in setting specifications, costing-out contracts and new products, production planning, and decisions regarding the purchase of new facilities. This is in addition to its usual value in setting standards for control charts on new production runs.

PROBLEMS

5-1 In Problems 4-30 and 4-31 you were asked to analyze the capability of a process to meet specifications. Assume that, after the initial analysis called for, you observe the process during the time that the next 10 sample subgroups are drawn. The parts are being made on three different semiautomatic machines. Finished parts move on a single conveyor to the inspection station where each unit is measured as it arrives. Five successive measurements comprise a subgroup. At the suggestion of the supervisor, operators occasionally take a part and check it themselves, adjusting their machine as seems appropriate.

(a) What is your opinion of the estimates of $\bar{X}'$ and σ' found in Problem 4-30 assuming that these procedures were followed when the first 30 subgroups were formed?

(b) What suggestions would you make relative to the formation of subgroups and analysis of process capability?

(c) What suggestions would you make relative to manufacturing procedures?

5-2 Specifications on the dimension of a certain part are 101.550 ± 0.200. Parts produced outside specifications must be scrapped. Two automatic screw machines produce these parts at a rate of 100 units per hour each. Items from both machines are discharged into a single tote box from which the inspector selects a subgroup of 5 parts every half-hour. Adjustments to both machines are made only on the approval of the inspector.

(a) After 50 subgroups have been drawn $\Sigma\bar{X} = 72.25$ and $\Sigma R = 8.80$. To simplify the arithmetic, 100 has been subtracted from each value of X. Determine the control limits for $\bar{X}$ and R.

(b) Assuming no points are outside the control limits on either chart and no significant runs are apparent, based on a normal distribution of this characteristic what would you estimate the fraction nonconforming to be?

(c) Recentering the process would reduce this estimate of fraction nonconforming to what level?

(d) How would you approach the task of improving this process capability study?

5-3 In Example 5-1, why should $\bar{R}$ have been decreased by the change in the method of subgrouping? With the subgrouping by operators but with no change in the temperature levels of the adjusting banks to compensate for the differences among operators, what would have been the appearance of the $\bar{X}$ and R charts? With the original plan of subgrouping, how was it that the differences between operators did not cause points to go out of control on the $\bar{X}$ chart?

5-4 In Example 5-2 someone made the suggestion that the variable ($\bar{X}$) used for the control charts should be the average of the four pad thicknesses on a half-ring, and that a subgroup should consist of four such averages. What objection can you see to this suggestion?

5-5 Prepare $\bar{X}$ and R control charts for the thickness of pad 2 in Table 5-1, Example 5-2. Use a subgroup size of 3. This will give you 12 subgroups. Discuss the difference between the results you obtain and those indicated in Fig. 5-3.

5-6 Prepare $\bar{X}$ and R control charts for the thickness of pad 3 in Table 5-1, Example 5-2. Use a subgroup size of 3. This will give you 12 subgroups. Discuss the difference between the results you obtain and those indicated in Fig. 5-3.

5-7 Prepare $\bar{X}$ and R control charts for the thickness of pad 4 in Table 5-1, Example 5-2. Use a subgroup size of 3. This will give you 12 subgroups. Discuss the difference between the results you obtain and those indicated in Fig. 5-3.

5-8 One convenient method for plotting data such as that of Table 5-1, Example 5-2, is on what has been termed a group control chart. The technique is only valid when there are no significant differences among the σ's of the producing units (measured in pad thicknesses, in this case) that cannot be corrected. $\bar{X}$ and R for each subgroup for each source are calculated but it is only the highest and lowest values of $\bar{X}$ and R that are plotted. Usually, the high values will be connected by straight lines as will the low values, and the producing source that yielded the high and low values will be identified on the chart. Plot group control charts for $\bar{X}$ and R for the data of Table 5-1 using a subgroup size of 4. This will give you 9 subgroups for each pad.

5-9 Visit a manufacturing plant in which multiple machine or multiple spindle operations are performed. Discuss the operation with production and inspection personnel. Prepare a short report describing the operation, the critical measured characteristics, potential causes of nonconformance, and how you would proceed with a process capability study. Prepare to discuss your results in class.

SIX

SOME FUNDAMENTALS
OF THE THEORY OF PROBABILITY

*There are many difficulties and troubles with which a factory management has to
contend—dies which wear; bearings that get loose; stock which is undersize,
oversize, or dirty; loose fixtures; careless, tired, or untrained employees. For
these reasons it would seem that there is no mathematical method which takes into
account all these factors. However there is a kind of mathematics which is applicable in just such conditions, and that is the mathematics of probability.—L. T.
Rader†*

Probability Has a Mathematical Meaning‡

The statement that tomorrow will probably be a hot day is perfectly clear and
understandable, whether you agree with it or not. So also is the statement that
Smith is more likely than Jones to receive a promotion. In general, the word
probability and its derivative and related words such as *probable, probably, likelihood, likely,* and *chance* are used regularly in everyday speech in a qualitative sense
and there is no difficulty in their interpretation.

But consider a statement that the probability is 0.98 that the shear strength of
a spot weld will be above 480 lb if two 0.040-gage test strips of duralumin are
welded on Sciaky machine No. 18 provided statistical control is maintained on the
welding operation. Or a statement that if a sample of 5 is taken at random from a
lot of 50 pieces that contains exactly 3 nonconforming pieces, the probability is
0.724 that the sample will contain no nonconforming pieces. In such statements,
probability is used in its quantitative or mathematical sense. It is evident that some
special explanation of the meaning of *probability* is necessary before these statements can be understood. A critical consideration will show that the two statements not only call for more explanation but that they need somewhat different
explanations.

---

† L. T. RADER, Putting Quality into Quantity, *American Machinist*, vol. 87, pp. 92–93, Oct. 28, 1943.
‡ The explanation of probability developed in the initial articles of this chapter was considerably
influenced by a volume of mimeographed notes on the subject prepared by Paul Coggins and R. I.
Wilkinson for use in an out-of-hour course given for engineers of the New York Telephone Company.

Two different traditional definitions of *probability* in its mathematical sense may be given. One may be described as the *frequency definition*, the other as the *classical definition*.

Traditional Definitions of Probability

From the standpoint of its useful applications in industry, probability may be thought of as relative frequency in the long run. This may be phrased somewhat more precisely as follows:

Assume that if a large number of trials be made under the same essential conditions, the ratio of the number of trials in which a certain event happens to the total number of trials will approach a limit as the total number of trials is indefinitely increased. This limit is called the probability that the event will happen under these conditions.

Mathematically, this definition may be expressed as follows: Let the letter E represent the occurrence of some event and $n(E)$ represent the total number of times E occurs in n trials. Then the probability of the event E, $P(E)$, equals $n(E)/n$ as n increases without bound.

It may be noted that this limit is always a fraction (or decimal fraction), which may vary from 0 to 1. A probability of 0 corresponds to an event that never happens under the described conditions; a probability of 1 corresponds to an event that always happens.

It is because *probability* describes relative frequency in the long run that the concept is so useful in practical affairs. But its use would be severely limited if the only way to estimate any probability were by a long series of experiments. Most mathematical manipulations of probabilities are based on another definition, which may be stated as follows:

If an event may happen in a ways and fail to happen in b ways, and all of these ways are mutually exclusive and equally likely to occur, the probability of the event happening is a/(a + b), the ratio of the number of ways favorable to the event to the total number of ways.

This is called the *classical definition*. It represents the approach to the subject developed by the classical writers on the mathematics of probability, many of whom wrote particularly about probabilities associated with games of chance. Experience shows that where properly used, this definition permits the successful forecasting of relative frequency in the long run without the necessity of a long set of trials prior to each forecast.

The statement in the preceding article about the probability of a given strength for spot welds could only be justified on the basis of a considerable record of measurements of spot-weld strength from Sciaky machine No. 18; it would be impossible to enumerate a number of equally likely ways in which the strength could be above or below 480 lb. On the other hand, the statement about the sample of 5 from the lot of 50 is based on a counting of equally likely ways in which the sample of 5 might contain no nonconforming articles or one or more such articles; even though not based on the evidence of actual trials, a statement of this sort may be made with strong confidence that the stated probability is really the relative frequency to be expected in the long run.

Axiomatic Definition of Probability

It is possible to raise philosophical and practical objections to both the traditional definitions of probability. For example, in the frequency definition how long a series of trials should one have to estimate relative frequency in the long run? In the classical definition, how can one tell which ways are equally likely? Such types of objections have led many of the modern writers on probability to view probability merely as a branch of abstract mathematics developed from certain axioms or assertions. The establishment of any relationship between actual phenomena in the real world and the laws of probability developed from the axioms is viewed as an entirely separate matter from the mathematical manipulations leading to the probability theorems.†

In spite of the different definitions that have been used by mathematicians, the same probability theorems are developed from all the definitions. Generally speaking, persons who use control charts, acceptance sampling procedures, and other statistical techniques in industry will find it satisfactory to think of probability as meaning relative frequency in the long run.

A Simple Example Relating the "Equally Likely" and "Relative-Frequency" Concepts

Table 2-7 gave the actual numbers on each of the first 400 chips drawn from Shewhart's normal bowl. In the technical language of statistics (as first explained in Chap. 1), we describe the data of Table 2-7 as having been recorded "by variables."

To illustrate certain aspects of the two traditional definitions of probability (and also to illustrate several other matters to be discussed later in this book), it will be helpful to classify the same data "by attributes." The reader will recall that a record by attributes merely classifies observations as conforming or failing to conform to certain specified requirements. Let us assume that the drawing of chips from Shewhart's bowl corresponds to a manufacturing process and that any chip numbered 20 or less represents a nonconforming product. (The process capability in relation to an L of 20.5 is similar to the one shown in distribution B of Fig. 4-6.)

An examination of the markings on the chips (shown in Table 2-6) tells us that 170 of the 998 chips are marked 20 or less. If we assume that each of the 998 chips is equally likely to be drawn (a reasonable assumption when the chips are alike and are mixed thoroughly after each drawing), the classical definition gives us $\frac{170}{998} = 0.17034$ as the probability of drawing a nonconforming item.

---

† For a clear discussion of the relationship of the axiomatic definition of probability to the two traditional definitions, see G. P. WADSWORTH and J. G. BRYAN, "Applications of Probability and Random Variables," 2ed, pp. 2–9, McGraw-Hill Book Company, Inc., New York, 1974.

In Table 6-1 the first 400 drawings from Shewhart's bowl that were shown in Table 2-7 have been divided into successive subgroups of 10, with the number nonconforming recorded for each subgroup. For the purpose of illustrating the relative-frequency concept of probability, the final three columns of the table (designated E, F, and G) are the ones of interest. These columns record the total number observed, the total number of nonconforming items found, and the ratio of total nonconforming items to total observed. The last figure (from column G) is plotted in Fig. 6-1.

Column G and Fig. 6-1 illustrate the meaning of the "limit" referred to in the frequency definition of probability. Under the special circumstances of the bowl drawing experiment, we know the true fraction nonconforming in the bowl to be 0.17034. Obviously a single draw could give us only 0 or 1 as an estimate of this fraction. If the first draw happens to be a conforming item (as it did), the estimate will continue to be 0 until the first nonconforming item is drawn; thereafter it will always be between 0 and 1. Similarly, the only estimates obtainable from a draw of 5 are 0, 0.2, 0.4, 0.6, 0.8, and 1.0. It seems clear that we need a fair number of drawings before we can expect the relative frequency to give us a satisfactory estimate of the fraction nonconforming in the bowl.

However, another matter that may not be so evident is the special meaning attached to the word *limit* in the frequency definition of probability. This is not a limit in the conventional mathematical sense of a function always getting closer and closer to the limit as some variable increases or decreases even though the limit is never quite reached with any finite value of the variable. It is rather what is called a *statistical limit* (or, sometimes, a *stochastic limit*).† It will be noted from

† For a graph showing a statistical approach to a limit in 1,000 drawings with a new value of relative frequency computed after each drawing, see W. A. SHEWHART, " Economic Control of Quality of Manufactured Product," p. 438, 1931 by Litton Educational Publishing, Inc., Van Nostrand Reinhold Company.

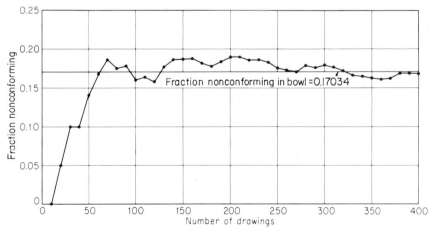

Figure 6-1 Cumulative estimates of fraction nonconforming from 400 drawings, considered by tens, from Shewhart's bowl (assuming that a chip numbered 20 or less is a nonconforming item).

Table 6-1 Example of successive estimates of relative frequency based on 400 drawings from Shewhart's normal bowl

(A chip marked 20 or less is designated as a nonconforming item. Observations are considered in subgroups of 10. Fraction nonconforming in bowl is 0.17034)

Sub-group number (A)	Size of sub-group (B)	Number of non-conforming items in subgroup (C)	Fraction non-conforming in subgroup (D)	Cumulative number observed (E)	Cumulative number of non-conforming items (F)	Cumulative fraction non-conforming (G)
1	10	0	0.0	10	0	0.000
2	10	1	0.1	20	1	0.050
3	10	2	0.2	30	3	0.100
4	10	1	0.1	40	4	0.100
5	10	3	0.3	50	7	0.140
6	10	3	0.3	60	10	0.167
7	10	3	0.3	70	13	0.186
8	10	1	0.1	80	14	0.175
9	10	2	0.2	90	16	0.178
10	10	0	0.0	100	16	0.160
11	10	2	0.2	110	18	0.164
12	10	1	0.1	120	19	0.158
13	10	4	0.4	130	23	0.177
14	10	3	0.3	140	26	0.186
15	10	2	0.2	150	28	0.187
16	10	2	0.2	160	30	0.188
17	10	1	0.1	170	31	0.182
18	10	1	0.1	180	32	0.178
19	10	3	0.3	190	35	0.184
20	10	3	0.3	200	38	0.190
21	10	2	0.2	210	40	0.190
22	10	1	0.1	220	41	0.186
23	10	2	0.2	230	43	0.187
24	10	1	0.1	240	44	0.183
25	10	0	0.0	250	44	0.176
26	10	1	0.1	260	45	0.173
27	10	1	0.1	270	46	0.170
28	10	4	0.4	280	50	0.179
29	10	1	0.1	290	51	0.176
30	10	3	0.3	300	54	0.180
31	10	1	0.1	310	55	0.177
32	10	0	0.0	320	55	0.172
33	10	0	0.0	330	55	0.167
34	10	1	0.1	340	56	0.165
35	10	1	0.1	350	57	0.163
36	10	1	0.1	360	58	0.161
37	10	2	0.2	370	60	0.162
38	10	4	0.4	380	64	0.168
39	10	2	0.2	390	66	0.169
40	10	1	0.1	400	67	0.168

column *G* of Table 6-1 and from Fig. 6-1 that the computed figure for relative frequency passes through the true proportion nonconforming of 0.17034 several times.

Of course, the more observations we make, the smaller the influence of the most recent observation on the computed figure for relative frequency. Intuitively, it seems reasonable that the greater the number of observations used in computing a relative frequency, the better will be our estimate of an unknown true relative frequency in a bowl (or other source of our observations). It seems sensible to have more confidence in an estimate from, say, 400 observations than in one from, say, 100 observations. Nevertheless, this does not mean that 100 observations could not, by chance, give us an excellent estimate of the proportion of nonconforming items in the bowl and 400 observations could not, by chance, give us a poorer estimate.

Incidentally, it should be mentioned that the reader should not attach any significance to the fact that in Fig. 6-1 the relative frequencies start at zero and gradually work *up* to a value close to the proportion nonconforming in the bowl. The early estimates might as readily have been too high, and the relative frequencies could have worked *down* to somewhere near the true value.

If we do not know the true fraction nonconforming in the bowl (the usual condition), the best we can do is to use the relative frequency up to the most recent observation as our estimate of the probability.

However, in the usual case where we have only the observations and no other information about the "bowl" from which the observations are made, it always is appropriate to consider the question of whether all the observations came from the same bowl (or the same other source). In other words, were all the observations made "under the same essential conditions?" There is no meaningful relative frequency in the long run if a bowl that contains a different distribution has been substituted for the initial bowl at some time during the observations. The reader will recognize that control charts constitute one type of test to judge whether a constant system of chance causes have been operating during a period of observation. The *p* chart, explained in Chap. 7, is specifically applicable to fraction rejected. Chapter 11 examines some general aspects of the relationship between control-chart techniques and estimates of values of various probabilities in industry.

Modern Concepts of Probability Theory

Modern writers in the field of probability theory prefer a foundation in set theory as a basis for the development of probability theorems. This foundation rests on the few relatively simple axioms, or definitions, presented in the following paragraphs.

First, we shall define the set of all possible outcomes of an experiment or test as the *probability space* for the experiment and designate the probability space by *S*. In Fig. 6-2, each of the boxes (*a*), (*b*), (*c*), and (*d*) represents a probability space.

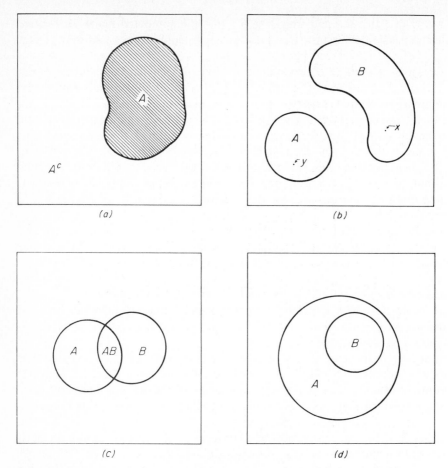

Figure 6-2 Venn diagrams illustrating probability spaces, events, and elementary outcomes.

Since the probability of any event occurring in S is between 0 and 1, the probability of S must equal 1 since S includes all possible outcomes. The first axiom therefore states:

$$P(S) = 1 \tag{1}$$

As examples of probability spaces, consider the following:

1. Tossing a coin. The set of all possible outcomes includes getting a head or a tail, assuming that the coin cannot land on end, or:

$$S = \{H, T\}$$

2. Tossing a single die. S, in this case, contains the discrete numerical quantities 1, 2, 3, 4, 5, and 6; or:

$$S = \{1, 2, 3, 4, 5, 6\}$$

3. Life of a vacuum tube. S includes the continuous time scale from $t = 0$ to $t = \infty$.

Correspondingly, it is impossible for any outcome outside the probability space to occur. In the language of probability, this impossible outcome is termed a *null* outcome and usually designated Φ (the Greek capital letter phi). Thus:

$$P(\Phi) = 0 \tag{2}$$

An *event*, which will be designated by a capital letter other than the letter S, is a subset of outcomes contained within S. In Fig. 6-2, the areas designated A and B are events.

The points x and y in Fig. 6-2b may also be termed events but are of a somewhat different nature and will be discussed in subsequent paragraphs.

Since an event is a subset of the probability space, S, the probability of an event is greater than (or equal to) zero and less than (or equal to) one. That is:

$$0 \le P(A) \le 1 \tag{3}$$

Consider the examples used previously in describing probability spaces.

1. Tossing a coin. If we let the event A equal the obtaining of a head on the tossing of a coin, then:

$$A = \{H\}$$

which is a subset of $S = \{H, T\}$.
2. Tossing a single die. In this case we may describe several events. For example, the event A may be described as the occurrence of a 1, 2, or 3 on the toss. That is:

$$A = \{1, 2, 3\} \text{ which is a subset of:}$$

$$S = \{1, 2, 3, 4, 5, 6\}$$

or A might be:

$$A = \{1, 4, 6\}, \text{ or}$$

$$A = \{5\}$$

In this latter case, A is an event and also an *elementary outcome* since the occurrence of a single face of the die is the smallest unit into which we can divide the probability space with probability finite and greater than 0.
3. Life of a vacuum tube. In this case we are concerned with time which is an event measured on a continuous scale from $t = 0$ to $t = \infty$. We may then describe an event A, for example, where

$$A = \{0 \le t \le 400 \text{ h}\} \qquad \text{(the life, } t, \text{ is between 0 and 400 hours)}$$

or another event B where

$$B = \{100 \text{ h} \le t \le 1000 \text{ h}\} \qquad \text{(life is between 100 and 1000 hours)}$$

or

$$C = \{t \geq 1000 \text{ h}\} \qquad \text{(life is greater than or equal to 1000 hours)}$$

An *elementary outcome* is the occurrence of an event which is the smallest unit into which the probability space may be divided. Two elementary outcomes x and y are illustrated on the Venn diagram, Fig. 6-2b. The probability of an elementary outcome from any given experiment is always greater than or equal to zero (≥ 0). Using our previous examples:

1. Tossing a coin. The smallest units into which we can divide the probability space (S) are:

$$S = \{H, T\}$$

Note that these single-point outcomes are *mutually exclusive*. That is, if either outcome does occur (e.g., a head turns up), then the other cannot occur simultaneously (we cannot also get a tail).
2. Tossing a single die. The probability space, in this case, may be divided into six mutually exclusive single-point outcomes.

$$S = \{1, 2, 3, 4, 5, 6\}$$

Each of these outcomes is an elementary outcome with finite probability of occurrence. Note that each may also be called an event, in which case the six events are also mutually exclusive.
3. Life of a vacuum tube. The smallest unit into which we may divide the life of a vacuum tube, or alternately divide the continuous time scale, is an infinitely small unit.

As an example, the measured life may be 413.69 hours. This measurement is limited by the capability of the measuring instrument which has, in reality, measured the life, t, somewhere between:

$$413.68499 \cdots \leq t \leq 413.69499 \cdots$$

The nature of continuous scales dictates that, for practical purposes, we divide them into reasonable nonoverlapping segments. Several examples of this type of procedure were discussed in Chap. 2 in forming the cells and cell boundaries for calculating frequency distributions. That discussion indicated that as cell boundaries became narrower the expected frequency became smaller. The same logic applies to mathematical statements about outcomes of experiments measured along a continuous scale. As the range of the outcome becomes narrower, and approaches 0, the probability of the outcome becomes smaller and approaches zero.†

---

† Writers sometimes say that the probability of a precise single-point outcome on a continuous scale *is* 0. This statement is made merely for reasons of simplicity. The null or impossible event is the only event that has probability *equal to* 0. All other events are, by implication at least, defined over some finite range and therefore have some finite probability of occurrence.

Mutually Exclusive Events

Two events are mutually exclusive if the occurrence of one event precludes the occurrence of the other. The Venn diagrams in Fig. 6-2 illustrate some events which are mutually exclusive and some which are not.

In Fig. 6-2a the set S contains two events, the event A and the event A^c (read A complement) which is the event that A does not occur. Mathematically

$$S = A + A^c$$

by definition; then

$$P(S) = P(A) + P(A^c) = 1 \qquad (4)$$

Thus the probability that any event A, defined in the probability space S, plus the probability of *not* A, A^c, equals the probability of S, which is always 1; or

$$P(A^c) = P(S) - P(A) = 1 - P(A) \qquad (5)$$

In Fig. 6-2b, the events A and B are also mutually exclusive since the occurrence of A precludes B from occurring. As an example, the following events may be defined for the tossing of a single die:

$$S = \{1, 2, 3, 4, 5, 6\}$$

$$A = \{1, 2, 3\}$$

$$B = \{5, 6\}$$

The definitions of A and B also define their complements:

$$A^c = \{4, 5, 6\} = S - A$$

$$B^c = \{1, 2, 3, 4\} = S - B$$

Further, the definitions of A and B may be used to define the *compound events:*

1. both A and B $AB = \{\Phi\}$
2. both A^c and B^c $A^c B^c = \{4\}$
3. both A and B^c $AB^c = \{1, 2, 3\}$
4. both A^c and B $A^c B = \{5, 6\}$

When the die is rolled, one of the faces, one of the elementary outcomes between one and six, will turn up. Note, however, that in no case will the outcome fall within the event A *and* within B. Thus the *compound event* AB is impossible (a *null* event).

This statement leads directly to the definition of mutually exclusive events. *Given any two events A and B, each of which has some finite probability of occurrence, if the compound event AB is an impossible event* (Φ) *then A and B are mutually exclusive.* Thus, if

$$AB = \Phi, \text{ then}$$

$$P(AB) = P(\Phi) = 0 \qquad (6)$$

The events A and B in Fig. 6-2c and Fig. 6-2d are not mutually exclusive. In Fig. 6-2d, in fact, the event B is fully contained within the event A. Thus the event AB equals the event B, and:

$$P(AB) = P(B)$$

Dividing a Probability Space into Mutually Exclusive Events

Description of the occurrence of events in Fig. 6-2c is not simple; the event A could occur, or the event B, or the compound event AB.

Suppose it were desired to describe an event that is composed of at least one of events A or B. It would be necessary to include the portion of the probability space covered by A and also that covered by B. Since there is an area of overlap, AB, adding area A directly to area B would result in double counting of the area AB. The solution is obvious. In order to avoid double counting, the area AB is subtracted from the sum of areas A and B. This statement is precisely the definition of the *union* of two events;

$$A \cup B = A + B - AB$$

and may be extended by similar logic to the union of three or more events. Stated in terms of the probabilities of the respective events,

$$P(A \cup B) = P(A) + P(B) - P(AB) \tag{7}$$

The reader should note that Fig. 6-2b illustrates the special case of expression (7) where $AB = \Phi$. Thus the union of two *mutually exclusive* events A and B may be expressed:

$$P(A \cup B) = P(A) + P(B) \text{ if } AB = \Phi \tag{8}$$

It is usually convenient in application to divide a probability space into a set of mutually exclusive events in order to make use of the simplicity of the expression for union of events given in Eq. (8).

The probability space in Fig. 6-2c may be so divided as follows:

1. Only event A occurs.
2. Only event B occurs.
3. Both A and B occur.
4. Neither A nor B occurs.

Consider first the compound event AB. AB can occur only if the outcome lies within both the events A and B. AB may, therefore, be *conditioned* upon A having occurred or it may be *conditioned* upon B having occurred. That is:

$$P(AB) = P(B \mid A)P(A) = P(A \mid B)P(B) \tag{9}$$

The first expression is read as "the probability of AB equals the probability of B, given A has occurred, times the probability of A. The vertical line stands for the word *given* and the expression $P(B\,|\,A)$ is the *conditional probability* of the event B given A.

Figure 6-2c may now be divided into the four mutually exclusive events previously listed.

1. Only event A occurs. In order to isolate A, it is necessary to form the compound event A and *not* B, or AB^c. Mathematically, this is the *intersection* of A and B^c, or

$$AB^c = A - AB$$

   and

$$P(AB^c) = P(A) - P(AB) = P(A) - P(B\,|\,A)P(A)$$

2. Only event B occurs. The same argument may be used in this case resulting in

$$A^cB = B - AB$$

   and

$$P(A^cB) = P(B) - P(AB) = P(B) - P(A\,|\,B)P(B)$$

3. Both A and B occur. From the previous discussion, this is the compound event AB, and

$$P(AB) = P(A\,|\,B)P(B) = P(B\,|\,A)P(A)$$

4. Neither A nor B occurs. This is the compound event *not* A (A^c) and *not* B (B^c), A^cB^c. By the laws of set theory, it can be shown that the intersection of the complements of two events equals the complement of the union of the events themselves. That is:

$$A^cB^c = (A \cup B)^c$$

   thus

$$P(A^cB^c) = P[(A \cup B)^c] \tag{10}$$

   Using expressions (5), (7) and (10),

$$P(A^cB^c) = P[(A \cup B)^c] = 1 - P(A) - P(B) + P(AB)$$

If the four mutually exclusive and exhaustive events have been properly defined, the sum of their respective probabilities should be one. That is, if

$$S = AB^c + A^cB + AB + A^cB^c$$

then

$$P(S) = P(AB^c) + P(A^cB) + P(AB) + P(A^cB^c)$$

Making the appropriate substitutions;

$$P(S) = P(A) - P(AB) + P(B) - P(AB) + P(AB) + 1 - P(A) - P(B) + P(AB)$$

$$= 1$$

Consider the tossing of a single die for which the following events, and their respective probabilities, are defined:

$$S = \{1, 2, 3, 4, 5, 6\} \qquad P(S) = 1$$
$$A = \{2, 3, 4\} \qquad P(A) = \tfrac{3}{6}$$
$$B = \{4, 5\} \qquad P(B) = \tfrac{2}{6}$$
$$AB = \{4\} \qquad P(AB) = \tfrac{1}{6}$$

Either intuitively or by enumeration, the mutually exclusive and exhaustive set may be defined as follows:

1. $AB^c = \{2, 3\}$
2. $A^cB = \{5\}$
3. $AB = \{4\}$
4. $A^cB^c = \{1, 6\}$

Assuming that the die is not loaded and each face is as likely to turn up as any other, application of the classical definition of probability yields:

1. $P(AB^c) = \tfrac{2}{6}$
2. $P(A^cB) = \tfrac{1}{6}$
3. $P(AB) = \tfrac{1}{6}$
4. $\underline{P(A^cB^c) = \tfrac{2}{6}}$
   $P(S) = 1$

Alternately, the same results could have been found using only the defined events and their respective probabilities. In this case, the defined outcomes are:

1. $P(S) = 1$
2. $P(A) = \tfrac{3}{6}$
3. $P(B) = \tfrac{2}{6}$
4. $P(AB) = \tfrac{1}{6}$

Using the previous derivations of the four mutually exclusive and exhaustive subsets:

1. $\qquad P(AB^c) = P(A) - P(AB) = \tfrac{3}{6} - \tfrac{1}{6} = \tfrac{2}{6}$
2. $\qquad P(A^cB) = P(B) - P(AB) = \tfrac{2}{6} - \tfrac{1}{6} = \tfrac{1}{6}$
3. $\qquad P(AB) = \qquad\qquad\qquad\qquad\qquad \tfrac{1}{6}$
4. $\qquad P(A^cB^c) = 1 - P(A) - P(B) + P(AB)$
   $\qquad\qquad\quad = 1 - \tfrac{3}{6} \quad - \tfrac{2}{6} \quad + \tfrac{1}{6} = \tfrac{2}{6}$

If the set is formed of mutually exclusive events, then the union of the set may be found as the sum of their respective probabilities. Furthermore, if the set of events exhausts the probability space, the sum of their respective probabilities will be one. Thus

$$P[(AB^c) \cup (A^cB) \cup (AB) \cup (A^cB^c)] = P(AB^c) + P(A^cB) + P(AB) + P(A^cB^c)$$
$$= \tfrac{2}{6} + \tfrac{1}{6} + \tfrac{1}{6} + \tfrac{2}{6} = 1$$

The probabilities defined for the events A, B, and AB could also be used to find the conditional probabilities $P(B|A)$ and $P(A|B)$. Rearranging formula (9):

$$P(B|A) = \frac{P(AB)}{P(A)} = \frac{\frac{1}{6}}{\frac{3}{6}} = \frac{1}{3}$$

$$P(A|B) = \frac{P(AB)}{P(B)} = \frac{\frac{1}{6}}{\frac{2}{6}} = \frac{1}{2}$$

Thus, if A has already occurred, the face on the die must read 2, 3, 4. In order for B to occur also, the face must be 4 which can happen in only one of three ways. $P(B|A)$, therefore, must equal $\frac{1}{3}$. A similar argument may be used to describe $P(A|B)$.

Some Theorems of the Theory of Probability

Three important theorems, derived in texts on mathematical statistics from a set theoretical base, are here stated and illustrated by reference to the drawings from Shewhart's normal bowl discussed in Chap. 2.

Theorem 1 The addition theorem or theorem of total probabilities The probability of the occurrence of either one or any number of mutually exclusive events is the sum of the probabilities for the separate events.

As an example, consider the drawing of a single chip from Shewhart's normal bowl. The events A and B are defined as follows:

$$A = \text{a chip marked 50}$$

$$B = \text{a chip marked 51}$$

Assuming that any one of the 998 chips in the bowl is as likely to be drawn as any other, and, since there are 5 chips marked 50 and 4 marked 51,

$$P(A) = \tfrac{5}{998}$$

$$P(B) = \tfrac{4}{998}$$

The occurrence on a single draw of a chip marked either 50 or 51 is the union of the events A and B. Thus

$$P(A \cup B) = P(A) + P(B)$$

$$= \tfrac{5}{998} + \tfrac{4}{998} = \tfrac{9}{998}$$

where A and B are mutually exclusive.

Theorem 2 The theorem of compound probabilities or multiplication theorem If a compound event be made up of a number of separate and independent subevents, and the occurrence of the compound event be the result of each of the subevents happening, the probability of occurrence of the compound event is the product of the probabilities that each of the subevents will happen.

Returning to the Shewhart normal bowl example, consider a case in which two chips are drawn in succession with the second drawn after the first has been returned to the bowl. The events A and B are defined as:

A = occurrence of a chip marked 50 on the first draw

B = occurrence of a chip marked 50 on the second draw

In this case, $P(A) = P(B) = \frac{5}{998}$ because there are 5 chips marked 50 and a total of 998 chips in the bowl at each draw. The two draws, or events, are *independent* since the occurrence of one does not affect the probability of occurrence of the other. The event of drawing a chip marked 50 on both draws is the compound event AB and has probability:

$$P(AB) = P(A)P(B) = \left(\tfrac{5}{998}\right)\left(\tfrac{5}{998}\right)$$
$$= 25/996{,}004$$

Theorem 3 The multiplication theorem for conditional probabilities If a compound event is made up of two (or more) dependent subevents, the probability of occurrence of the compound event is the product of the probability of the first multiplied by the probability that if the first has occurred the second will also happen.

Consider the successive drawings from Shewhart's normal bowl discussed following Theorem 2. The definitions of events A and B were based on replacement of the first chip before drawing the second. If the first chip had not been replaced, the bowl would have been partially exhausted and, if event A had occurred, there would be only 4 chips marked 50 remaining. The probability of B, therefore, will depend on the results of the first drawing and the occurrence of A. Thus, if

$$P(A) = \tfrac{5}{998}$$
$$P(B|A) = \tfrac{4}{997}$$
$$P(B|A^c) = \tfrac{5}{997}$$

then

$$P(AB) = P(A)P(B|A)$$
$$= \left(\tfrac{5}{998}\right)\left(\tfrac{4}{997}\right)$$
$$= 20/995{,}006$$

Note that this conditional form could have been used to describe the case explained following Theorem 2. The example could have been stated:

$$P(A) = \tfrac{5}{998}$$

$$P(B\,|\,A) = \tfrac{5}{998}$$

$$P(AB) = P(A)P(B\,|\,A)$$

$$= \left(\tfrac{5}{998}\right)^2$$

Theorem 2, therefore, is a special case of Theorem 3 where the events A and B are independent. The mathematical statement equating the two cases yields the definition of *statistical independence*. Thus:

$$P(AB) = P(A)P(B\,|\,A) = P(A)P(B)$$

if and only if $P(B\,|\,A) = P(B)$, that is, the two events are independent.

Infinite and Finite Universes

Early in this book, there was a brief introduction to certain aspects of acceptance sampling by attributes. Example 1-3 dealt with a process in which there was a constant probability 0.04 of producing a nonconforming item. The output from this process was submitted for acceptance inspection in lots of 50 items. From each lot of 50 items, a random sample of 5 items was inspected. If there were no nonconforming items in the sample of 5, the lot was accepted; otherwise it was rejected.

Example 1-3 analyzed one weakness of this acceptance sampling procedure by showing that the product accepted would be, on the average, little better than the product submitted. Numbers computed by the mathematics of probability were used in developing this conclusion.

Although the point was not brought out in the discussion in Chap. 1, this example illustrated both the concept of an infinite or unlimited universe and the concept of a finite or limited universe. The distinction between these two concepts is important in any explanation of the mathematics of probability.

In effect, column B of Table 1-3 gives the respective probabilities of various numbers of nonconforming items in lots of 50 from a process in which the probability of a nonconforming item is 0.04. (For instance, the statement that in the long run 275 lots out of 1,000 will have exactly 2 nonconforming items is another way of saying that the probability of exactly 2 such items is 0.275.) The probabilities in column B were based on the concept of an *infinite* universe; each lot of 50 was assumed to be a random sample from an unlimited number of items 4 per cent of which are nonconforming.

In contrast, the probabilities in column E of Table 1-3 are based on the concept of samples of 5 from *finite* universes of 50 items. For the purpose of Example 1-3, it was necessary to know the respective probabilities of acceptance when lots of 50 contained various numbers of nonconforming items.

We shall see that in computing desired probabilities for problems in industrial quality control, there will be many cases where we assume an infinite universe for each case where we assume a finite universe. In part, this will be because, as in column B of Table 1-3, the assumption of an infinite universe is correct in principle for the particular application. In part, also, this will be because probability calculations involving large finite universes are often quite burdensome; in many such cases, simpler calculations assuming an infinite universe give results that are close enough for practical purposes.

Nevertheless, some aspects of the subject are easier to understand if an explanation of the mathematics of probability starts with examples that assume relatively small finite universes. We shall therefore examine a number of cases of sampling from finite universes before proceeding to the more important and more general subject of sampling from an infinite universe.

Formula for Combinations

For the solution of many problems in probability it is necessary to know how many different sets of r objects can be chosen from n objects.

For example, consider a lot of 50 pieces from which a sample is to be drawn. How many different ordered sets of 5 can be drawn? (That is, how many sets are possible which differ either in the pieces included or in the order in which the pieces were drawn?) The first draw might be any one of 50; the next, any one of the remaining 49; the next, any one of 48; the next, any one of 47; and the final draw any one of 46. The total number of possible ordered sets is obviously the product of these numbers; this is called the number of *permutations*. The symbol P_5^{50} is read "the number of permutations of 50 things taken 5 at a time." This is

$$P_5^{50} = (50)(49)(48)(47)(46) = 254{,}251{,}200$$

In general, the number of permutations of n things taken r at a time is given by the formula

$$P_r^n = (n)(n-1)(n-2) \cdots (n-r+1) = \frac{n!}{(n-r)!}$$

Here the expression $n!$, read as "factorial n" or "n factorial," is used for the product of the first n integers. By definition, $0! = 1$. From this an expression may be written for the number of permutations of n things taken all at a time.

$$P_n^n = n!$$

Sets without regard to the order of drawing are called *combinations*. To find the number of different combinations of 5 that may be drawn from a lot of 50, it may first be noted that any one combination of 5 has $5! = (5)(4)(3)(2)(1) = 120$ possible permutations. As each combination includes 120 possible permutations, the total number of combinations can be computed by dividing the total number of permutations by 120.

$$C_5^{50} = \frac{50!}{5!\,45!} = \frac{(50)(49)(48)(47)(46)}{(5)(4)(3)(2)(1)} = \frac{254{,}251{,}200}{120} = 2{,}118{,}760$$

In general, the number of combinations of n things taken r at a time is given by the formula

$$C_r^n = \binom{n}{r} = \frac{n!}{r!\,(n-r)!}$$

Application of the Combination Formula to Probability Problems

Example 1-3 gave some probabilities associated with the common sampling acceptance procedure of inspecting five articles from each lot of 50. With the use of the combination formula, it is now possible to illustrate how such probabilities are computed.

Consider a lot of 50 articles containing 3 nonconforming articles. A sample of 5 is selected at random from the lot. What are the respective probabilities of 0, 1, 2, and 3 nonconforming articles occurring in the sample of 5?

The total number of different samples of 5 has already been calculated as 2,118,760. If the sample is selected at random, all these may be considered to be equally likely. To compute the respective probabilities we must find how many of these different possible samples contain exactly 0, 1, 2, and 3 nonconforming articles.

Consider a sample containing 0 nonconforming articles. Such a sample must come from the 47 articles that conform to specifications. From these articles the number of different possible samples of 5 is

$$C_5^{47} = \frac{47!}{5!\,42!} = \frac{(47)(46)(45)(44)(43)}{(5)(4)(3)(2)(1)} = 1{,}533{,}939$$

A sample containing exactly one nonconforming article must include 4 articles from the 47 acceptable ones and 1 article from the 3 rejectable ones. Thus there are

$$C_4^{47}C_1^3 = \frac{47!\,3!}{4!\,43!\,1!\,2!} = \frac{(47)(46)(45)(44)}{(4)(2)} = 535{,}095$$

A sample containing exactly 2 nonconforming articles must include 3 articles from the 47 good ones and 2 articles from the 3 bad ones. Of such samples, there are

$$C_3^{47}C_2^3 = \frac{47!\,3!}{3!\,44!\,2!\,1!} = \frac{(47)(46)(45)}{2} = 48{,}645$$

A sample containing exactly 3 nonconforming articles must include 2 articles from the 47 good ones and all 3 bad articles. There are

$$C_2^{47}C_3^3 = \frac{47!}{2!\,45!} = \frac{(47)(46)}{2} = 1{,}081$$

The respective probabilities are

$$P_0 = \frac{1{,}533{,}939}{2{,}118{,}760} = 0.72398$$

$$P_1 = \frac{535{,}095}{2{,}118{,}760} = 0.25255$$

$$P_2 = \frac{48{,}645}{2{,}118{,}760} = 0.02296$$

$$P_3 = \frac{1{,}081}{2{,}118{,}760} = 0.00051$$

$$\text{Total} \quad = \overline{1.00000}$$

(Here P_0 means the probability of exactly 0 nonconforming articles, P_1 means the probability of exactly 1 nonconforming article, etc.)

As the probabilities of all the mutually exclusive alternatives have been computed, their sum must be unity. This check should be made for all such calculations.

Use of Logarithms of Factorials

Factorials are very large numbers. For instance $15! = 1{,}307{,}674{,}368{,}000$. In dealing with many problems in probability, it is convenient to use logarithms of factorials such as those given in Table H, App. 3.†

As an illustration, consider the calculation of P_0 from the preceding discussion.

$$\frac{C_5^{47}C_0^3}{C_5^{50}} = \frac{47!\,45!}{42!\,50!}$$

---

† For factorials of numbers above 1,000, use the first term of Stirling's approximation to the factorial: $n! = n^n e^{-n}\sqrt{2\pi n}$. Here e is 2.71828. See T. C. FRY, "Probability and Its Engineering Uses," 2d ed., pp. 121–124, D. Van Nostrand Company, Inc., Princeton, N.J., 1965. Many small pocket calculators can calculate up to 69! directly making use of tables of factorials of quantities up to 69 unnecessary.

Solving this problem by logarithms of factorials from Table *H*,

log 47!	59.4127	
		115.4905
log 45!	56.0778	
log 42!	51.1477	
log 50!	64.4831	115.6308
log P_0		$9.8597 - 10$

and $P_0 = 0.724$

The example used in the preceding discussion involved drawing a sample of size $n = 5$ from lot of size $N = 50$ which contained $D = 3$ nonconforming items. The probabilities associated with drawing d nonconforming items in the sample were calculated where d varied from 0 to 3. Such problems are sufficiently common that the mathematical formula describing them has been named the *Hypergeometric Probability Law.*

This law of probability may be stated as follows:

$$p(d \mid N, D, n) = \frac{C_d^D C_{n-d}^{N-D}}{C_n^N} = \frac{\binom{D}{d}\binom{N-D}{n-d}}{\binom{N}{n}}$$

which says: *the probability of d nonconforming items in a sample of size n is equal to the product of the possible combinations of nonconforming items, (C_d^D), times the possible combinations of conforming items, (C_{n-d}^{N-D}), divided by the possible combinations of samples of size n that can be drawn from lots of size N, (C_n^N). N, D, and n are parameters of the probability law;* they must be known, or hypothesized, ahead of time.

The vertical line in $p(d \mid N, D, n)$ stands for *given that,* and the statement itself reads: The probability of d occurring given that N, D and n are specified.

The previous statement of the hypergeometric probability law is usually referred to as the *probability density function* (p.d.f.) or *mass function.* While tables of such functions are published by many sources, *cumulative density functions,* or *cumulative distribution functions* (c.d.f.) are more common and frequently more useful.

As an illustration of the use of the cumulative distribution functions, consider the example $N = 50$, $D = 3$, $n = 5$ used previously. We would like to find the probability that no more than one nonconforming item will be found in the sample of five. To do so, two terms of the hypergeometric probability law will have to be calculated and summed. In general, the mathematical expression is

$$P(d \le c \mid N, D, n) = \sum_{d=0}^{c} \frac{\binom{D}{d}\binom{N-D}{n-d}}{\binom{N}{n}}$$

Substituting the values for the example,

$$P(d \le 1 \mid 50, 3, 5) = \sum_{d=0}^{1} \frac{\binom{3}{d}\binom{50-3}{5-d}}{\binom{50}{5}}$$

$$= \frac{\binom{3}{0}\binom{47}{5}}{\binom{50}{5}} + \frac{\binom{3}{1}\binom{47}{4}}{\binom{50}{5}}$$

$$= 0.724 + 0.253 = 0.977$$

If the value $c = 1$ were used as an acceptance number for a plan that specified testing samples of five drawn from lots of 50 items, then lots containing three nonconforming items would be accepted with probability equal to 0.977.

Changes in Probabilities Due to Partial Exhaustion of a Lot by a Sample

The problems in the two preceding articles that were solved with the help of the combinatorial formula might also have been solved by computing the probabilities on each draw and applying the theorem of conditional probabilities.

This may be illustrated by again considering the calculation of the probability that a sample of 5 will contain 0 nonconforming items if drawn from a lot of 50 containing 3 such items. The probability that the first article drawn will be acceptable is $\frac{47}{50}$. If the first draw is acceptable, the probability that the second will be acceptable is $\frac{46}{49}$. If the first and second are both acceptable, the probability that the third will be acceptable is $\frac{45}{48}$, etc. This gives the probability that all 5 are acceptable as

$$P_0 = \left(\frac{47}{50}\right)\left(\frac{46}{49}\right)\left(\frac{45}{48}\right)\left(\frac{44}{47}\right)\left(\frac{43}{46}\right) = \left(\frac{45}{50}\right)\left(\frac{44}{49}\right)\left(\frac{43}{48}\right) = 0.72398$$

It is evident that, because each new drawing changes the proportion of acceptable and rejectable articles in the remaining portion of the lot, the probability changes from draw to draw. This partial exhaustion of the lot by the sample is recognized by the above type of calculation, or by calculations that use the combinatorial formula in the way previously illustrated. However if the lot is large enough compared to the sample, the change in probability from one draw to the next is of negligible importance. Consider a sample of 5 taken from a lot of 5,000 containing 300 nonconforming items. The probability that this sample contains 0 nonconforming items is

$$P_0 = \left(\frac{4700}{5000}\right)\left(\frac{4699}{4999}\right)\left(\frac{4698}{4998}\right)\left(\frac{4697}{4997}\right)\left(\frac{4696}{4996}\right) = 0.73381$$

For all practical purposes, this is $(4700/5000)^5$ or $(0.94)^5$ which equals 0.73390.

The foregoing calculation provides a good transition from the case of the finite universe to the case of the infinite universe. It is evident that in taking a small sample from a finite universe of 5,000 items 6 per cent nonconforming, no appreciable error is introduced if calculations are simplified by assuming that the probability of a nonconforming item is 0.06 on every draw. In other words, calculations are made assuming an infinite universe 6 per cent nonconforming. We shall introduce the subject of the infinite universe by examining the very useful binomial distribution.

The Binomial as a Probability Distribution

Probability problems in which the probability of occurrence of an event may be assumed to be constant may be solved by the use of a formula that depends on the familiar binomial theorem. The reader may recall from algebra that

$$(a + b)^n = a^n + na^{n-1}b + \frac{n(n-1)}{(2)(1)} a^{n-2}b^2$$

$$+ \frac{n(n-1)(n-2)}{(3)(2)(1)} a^{n-3}b^3 + \frac{n(n-1)(n-2)(n-3)}{(4)(3)(2)(1)} a^{n-4}b^4 + \cdots$$

This binomial expansion is the basis of a probability distribution that is of great importance in statistical quality control.

Let p' be the symbol for the constant probability that a particular event will happen. In applications to statistical quality control, this generally is the probability of a rejectable article (i.e., an article nonconforming to specifications).

Let q' be the symbol for the probability that the same event will not happen. In applications to statistical quality control, this generally is the probability of an acceptable article (i.e., an article conforming to specifications). Because $p' + q' = 1$, it follows that $q' = 1 - p'$.

As a specific example let p', the fraction nonconforming in a large number of articles, be 0.06. Then $q' = 0.94$. Consider the respective probabilities of the various possible number of rejectable articles in samples of 5 drawn from this large number.

By the multiplication theorem, it is obvious that the probability of zero rejectable articles in a sample of five

$$P_0 = (0.94)(0.94)(0.94)(0.94)(0.94) = (0.94)^5$$

Similarly, the probability of 5 rejectable articles is

$$P_5 = (0.06)(0.06)(0.06)(0.06)(0.06) = (0.06)^5$$

Consider the probability of exactly one rejectable article. This article might be any one of the five in the sample. The probability that the first is rejectable and the other four are acceptable is

$$(0.06)(0.94)(0.94)(0.94)(0.94) = (0.94)^4(0.06)$$

The probability that the first is acceptable, the second rejectable, and the last 3 acceptable is

$$(0.94)(0.06)(0.94)(0.94)(0.94) = (0.94)^4(0.06)$$

Similar statements may be made about the respective probabilities of the third, fourth, and fifth articles being rejectable with the others acceptable. By the addition theorem, the probability that some one of the articles is rejectable is the sum of these five separate probabilities

$$P_1 = 5(0.94)^4(0.06)$$

The probability that the first two articles are rejectable and the last three acceptable is

$$(0.06)(0.06)(0.94)(0.94)(0.94) = (0.94)^3(0.06)^2$$

The various ways in which exactly 2 of the articles might be rejectable (D) and the other 3 acceptable (G) may be enumerated as follows:

D	D	G	G	G		G	D	G	D	G
D	G	D	G	G		G	D	G	G	D
D	G	G	D	G		G	G	D	D	G
D	G	G	G	D		G	G	D	G	D
G	D	D	G	G		G	G	G	D	D

The probability of each of these is $(0.94)^3(0.06)^2$.

Therefore the probability that some two of the five articles will be rejectable is

$$P_2 = 10(0.94)^3(0.06)^2 = 0.0299 \ldots$$

It was not really necessary to enumerate the ten ways in which exactly two of the articles might be rejectable and the other three acceptable. This is evidently the problem of the number of different sets of two articles that can be selected from five, i.e., the number of combinations of five things taken two at a time.

$$C_2^5 = \frac{5!}{3!\,2!} = \frac{(5)(4)}{2} = 10$$

Similarly, the coefficient 5 in the expression for P_1 is the number of combinations of five things taken one at a time, C_1^5.

Table 6-2 Illustration of the binomial as a probability formula
(Probability of exactly r occurrences in n trials)

r	General expression	Value when $p' = 0.06$ and $n = 5$
0	$C_0^n q'^{n-0} p'^0 = q'^n$	$(0.94)^5 = 0.7339040224$
1	$C_1^n q'^{n-1} p'^1 = nq'^{n-1} p'$	$5(0.94)^4 (0.06) = 0.2342246880$
2	$C_2^n q'^{n-2} p'^2 = \dfrac{n!}{2!(n-2)!} q'^{n-2} p'^2$	$10(0.94)^3 (0.06)^2 = 0.0299010240$
3	$C_3^n q'^{n-3} p'^3 = \dfrac{n!}{3!(n-3)!} q'^{n-3} p'^3$	$10(0.94)^2 (0.06)^3 = 0.0019085760$
4	$C_4^n q'^{n-4} p'^4 = \dfrac{n!}{4!(n-4)!} q'^{n-4} p'^4$	$5(0.94)(0.06)^4 = 0.0000609120$
5	$C_5^n q'^{n-5} p'^5 = \dfrac{n!}{5!(n-5)!} q'^{n-5} p'^5$	$(0.06)^5 = 0.0000007776$
Total.......	....	$= 1.0000000000$

In general, the probability of exactly r occurrences in n trials of an event that has a constant probability of occurrence p' is

$$C_r^n q'^{n-r} p'^r = \frac{n!}{r!(n-r)!} q'^{n-r} p'^r = \binom{n}{r} q'^{n-r} p'^r$$

The above is a generalized term of the binomial expansion, applying to all terms of the binomial. This should be clear from examination of Table 6-2, which illustrates the binomial as a probability formula.

In the literature of statistics, the binomial as a probability distribution is frequently described as the Point Binomial or as the Bernoulli Distribution.

Average and Standard Deviation of the Binomial

If a product is 6% rejectable ($p' = 0.06$) and many samples of 5 are drawn from this product, it seems obvious that the expected average number of rejectable items per sample will be $(5)(0.06) = 0.3$. This may be verified in a particular case by a calculation using the binomial distribution of Table 6-2.

Number of rejectable items*	Relative frequency, that is, probability of occurrence	Rejectable items × relative frequency
0	0.7339040224	0.0000000000
1	0.2342246880	0.2342246880
2	0.0299010240	0.0598020480
3	0.0019085760	0.0057257280
4	0.0000609120	0.0002436480
5	0.0000007776	0.0000038880
Totals	1.0000000000	0.3000000000

* Average number of rejectable items $= 0.3/1 = 0.3$.

Where many sets of n trials are made of an event with a constant probability of occurrence p', the expected average number of occurrences in the long run is np', i.e., np' is the average of the binomial. Translated into terms of a problem in statistical quality control, if many random samples of size n are taken from a product having a fraction rejectable p', the expected average number of rejectable items per sample is np'.

In mathematical terms, np' is the *expected value*, or *mathematical expectation*, of x where $x = 0$ if an item is acceptable and $x = 1$ if it is rejectable. The expected value of x can be developed directly from the binomial formula by recognition of the fact that the mathematical expectation, $E(x)$, is a first degree operator equivalent to center of gravity in mechanics. In general terms, this operator can be expressed as follows:

$$E(x) = \int_{-\infty}^{+\infty} xf(x)\, dx \qquad \text{where } x \text{ is continuous}$$

or

$$E(x) = \sum_x xp(x) \qquad \text{where } x \text{ is discrete}$$

Since the binomial is a discrete distribution, we shall use the second form. Designating r as equal to the number of rejectable items found in a sample of size n which is p' fraction rejectable, the expected value of r can be found from

$$E(r) = \sum_{r=0}^{n} r \binom{n}{r} p'^r (1 - p')^{n-r}$$

where

$$\sum_{r=0}^{n} \binom{n}{r} p'^r (1 - p')^{n-r} = 1$$

This summation may be written

$$\sum_{r=1}^{n} np' \binom{n-1}{r-1} p'^{r-1} (1 - p')^{(n-1)-(r-1)}$$

and, since n and p' are constant parameters of the distribution, they may be moved outside the summation sign leaving

$$np' \sum_{r=1}^{n} \binom{n-1}{r-1} p'^{(r-1)} (1 - p')^{(n-1)-(r-1)}$$

Returning to the original expansion of the binomial:

$$(a + b)^n = \sum_{k=0}^{n} \binom{n}{k} a^k b^{n-k}$$

$$\sum_{r=1}^{n} \binom{n-1}{r-1} p'^{(r-1)} (1 - p')^{(n-1)-(r-1)} = (p' + (1 - p'))^{n-1} = 1$$

Therefore

$$E(r) = np'$$

and, since the mathematical expectation is a linear operator,

$$E\left(\frac{r}{n}\right) = p'$$

That is, the expected value of the number of rejectable items found divided by the sample size is the parametric value of the fraction rejectable.

The expression for standard deviation of the frequency distribution that results from the binomial is derived in standard works on mathematical statistics.[†]
It is $\sqrt{np'q'} = \sqrt{np'(1-p')}$.

In the case where n is 5 and p' is 0.06, the standard deviation is

$$\sqrt{5(0.06)(0.94)} = \sqrt{0.282} = 0.531037$$

The standard deviation given by the formula may be checked by the following calculation from the distribution:

Fraction rejectable	Number of rejectable items	Rejectable items squared	Relative frequency	Relative frequency × rejectable items squared
0.00	0	0	0.7339040224	0.0000000000
0.20	1	1	0.2342246880	0.2342246880
0.40	2	4	0.0299010240	0.1196040960
0.60	3	9	0.0019085760	0.0171771840
0.80	4	16	0.0000609120	0.0009745920
1.00	5	25	0.0000007776	0.0000194400
Total				0.3720000000

$$\sigma = \sqrt{0.372 - (0.3)^2} = \sqrt{0.372 - 0.09} = \sqrt{0.282} = 0.531037$$

For purposes of mathematical development, the expression for standard deviation will be developed from the mathematical expectation of the variance, $(\sigma'_{np})^2$.

$$(\sigma'_{np})^2 = \text{Var}\ (r) = E[(r - np')^2]$$

This expression is related to the moment of inertia, or second moment about the center of gravity, from mechanics. Notice, also, that the expression inside the expectation operator, which itself is a linear operator, is a second degree expression. The variance operator, therefore, is a second degree mathematical operator.

[†] For example, see W. MENDENHALL, and R. L. SCHAEFFER, "Mathematical Statistics with Applications," Duxbury Press, North Scituate, Mass., 1973, pp. 94–95.

This fact will prove useful later in developing expressions for the standard deviation of p' and $\bar{X}'$.

Using the binomial distribution, it is desired to find the expected value of $(r - np')^2$, where r, n, and p' were defined previously.

$$E[(r - np')^2] = E[r^2 - 2r(np') + (np')^2] = E(r^2) - 2E[r(np')] + E(np')^2$$

The foregoing paragraph showed that

$$E(r) = np'$$

from which we may deduce that

$$E(np') = np'$$

and

$$E(np')^2 = (np')^2$$

Thus the expression for variance yields

$$E[(r - np')^2] = E(r^2) - (np')^2$$

leaving $E(r^2)$ yet to be found.

The mathematical expectation equation may again be applied, where, for convenience, r^2 is set equal to $r(r - 1) + r$. Thus

$$E(r^2) = E[r(r - 1)] + E(r)$$

$$= \sum_{r=0}^{n} r(r - 1)\binom{n}{r}p'^r(1 - p')^{n-r} + \sum_{r=0}^{n} r\binom{n}{r}p'^r(1 - p')^{n-r}$$

$$= n(n - 1)p'^2 \sum_{r=2}^{n} \binom{n - 2}{r - 2}p'^{(r-2)}(1 - p')^{(n-2)-(r-2)} + np'$$

$$= n(n - 1)p'^2 + np'$$

Substituting this result into the expression for variance,

$$\text{Var}(r) = n(n - 1)p'^2 + np' - (np')^2$$

$$= np' - np'^2 = np'(1 - p')$$

and the standard deviation is

$$\sigma'_{np} = \sqrt{np'(1 - p')}$$

It is important to distinguish between the average number of occurrences of the event in n trials np' and the relative proportion of occurrence or probability of occurrence p'. In statistical quality control, this is a distinction between average number of rejectable items in the samples and the average fraction rejectable. In any sample, the fraction rejectable is the number of rejectable items divided by the sample size n. The standard deviation of the fraction rejectable is, of course, the standard deviation of the number of rejectable items, $\sqrt{np'q'}$, divided by the sample size n. This is

$$\sigma'_p = \frac{\sqrt{np'q'}}{n} = \sqrt{\frac{p'q'}{n}} = \sqrt{\frac{p'(1-p')}{n}} = \frac{\sqrt{p'(1-p')}}{\sqrt{n}}$$

This is an important formula in connection with the control chart for fraction rejected. Its mathematical development may be drawn from

$$(\sigma'_p)^2 = \text{Var}\left(\frac{r}{n}\right) = E\left\{\left[\left(\frac{r}{n}\right) - p'\right]^2\right\}$$

In this case, however, it is much easier to work with the second degree variance operator than with the first degree expectation operator.

Any constant may be drawn outside a second degree operator merely by squaring the constant; thus

$$\text{Var}\left(\frac{r}{n}\right) = \left(\frac{1}{n}\right)^2 \text{Var}(r)$$

and, since the Var (r) has previously been derived,

$$\text{Var}\left(\frac{r}{n}\right) = \left(\frac{1}{n}\right)^2 np'(1-p')$$

$$= \frac{p'(1-p')}{n}$$

yielding

$$\sigma'_p = \sqrt{\frac{p'(1-p')}{n}}$$

An Experimental Example of the Meaning of the Average and Standard Deviation of the Binomial

The data of Table 6-1 may be used to clarify certain aspects of the foregoing formulas. Consider columns C and D of that table. Both apply to the results of samples of 10. Because each chip drawn was replaced before the next drawing, the binomial is applicable in principle; there was a constant probability p' of drawing a nonconforming item.

Column C gives the number of nonconforming items in each sample of 10.

The result of the 40 samples may be arranged into a frequency distribution as follows:

Number of nonconforming items	Frequency
4	3
3	7
2	9
1	16
0	5
	40

If we calculate the average and standard deviation of this distribution, we find the average to be 1.675 and the standard deviation to be 1.127. (The method illustrated in Table 2-5 is appropriate for these calculations.) If we use the formulas for average and standard deviation that have been given for numbers of occurrences, we can find the expected values of these statistics if we are able to obtain a great many such samples of 10. The expected average

$$np' = 10(0.17034) = 1.7034$$

The expected standard deviation

$$\sqrt{np'(1 - p')} = \sqrt{10(0.17034)(0.82966)} = 1.189$$

In this particular experiment, the observed values seem fairly close to the expected values.

Column D of Table 6-1 gives the fraction nonconforming in each sample of 10. The fractions nonconforming may be summarized into the following frequency distribution:

Fraction nonconforming	Frequency
0.4	3
0.3	7
0.2	9
0.1	16
0.0	5
	40

The similarity to the previous frequency distribution is apparent. The average and standard deviation of the distribution of fractions nonconforming are 0.1675 and 0.1127, respectively. Obviously each figure is $\frac{1}{10}$ of the corresponding figure from the distribution of numbers of nonconforming items. In general, in a binomial distribution these statistics of a distribution of fractions of occurrences will be $1/n$ times the corresponding statistics of numbers of occurrences. The expected average fraction of occurrences is, of course, the p' of 0.17034. The expected standard deviation is

$$\sqrt{\frac{p'(1 - p')}{n}} = \sqrt{\frac{(0.17034)(0.82966)}{10}} = 0.1189$$

The Binomial as a Basis for Approximate Estimates of Probabilities in Sampling from Finite Lots

The binomial describes the situation that exists when the probability of a nonconforming item is constant from draw to draw. As already pointed out, this is never quite true in sampling from finite lots. Nevertheless, the binomial often provides a good enough approximation to serve as a practical basis for judgments about various sampling plans.

In the preceding discussion, the binomial example was carried to many decimal places. This was necessary to illustrate how np' and $\sqrt{np'q'}$ gave exact results for the average and standard deviation of the binomial distribution. However, practical calculations for industrial quality control never require so many decimal places. For the common calculations to judge the quality protection given by alternative sampling plans, three decimal places, or in some instances only two decimal places, are adequate.

Our illustration of the use of the combination formula gave the probabilities of 0, 1, 2, and 3 nonconforming items in drawing samples of 5 from lots of 50 that were 6% nonconforming. Table 6-2 gave the probabilities of 0, 1, 2, 3, 4, and 5 nonconforming items in drawing samples of 5 from an infinite lot that was 6% nonconforming. Where these probabilities are expressed only to three decimal places, the differences between them do not seem to be serious.

Nonconforming items	Probabilities from lot of 50	Probabilities from infinite lot
0	0.724	0.734
1	0.252	0.234
2	0.023	0.030
3	0.001	0.002

In general, the more the lot tends to be exhausted by the sample the greater will be the difference between the correct probabilities and the approximate ones computed by the binomial theorem on the assumption of an infinite lot. From the standpoint of practical action based on these probabilities, it may well be true that it is satisfactory to assume that the probabilities that apply to an infinite lot also apply to samples of five from finite lots of 50 or more.

The Poisson Distribution as an Approximation to the Binomial

Calculations involving the use of binomials are often burdensome; this is particularly true if many terms are involved and if n is large. Fortunately, a simple approximation may be obtained to any term of the binomial. This approximation, called *Poisson's Exponential Binomial Limit*, is referred to more briefly in statistical literature as "the Poisson law," "Poisson distribution," or simply as "the Poisson." The larger the value of n and the smaller the value of p', the closer is the Poisson approximation. It is admirably suited to the solution of many problems that arise in industrial quality control.

The Poisson formula may be derived from the binomial theorem in the following manner. In the binomial formula, let $c' = np'$, then

$$\frac{n!}{r!\,(n-r)!}\,p'^r(1-p')^{n-r} = \frac{n!}{r!\,(n-r)!}\left(\frac{c'}{n}\right)^r\left(1-\frac{c'}{n}\right)^{n-r}$$

$$= \left(\frac{n!}{(n-r)!\,n^r}\right)\left(\frac{c'^r}{r!}\right)\left(1-\frac{c'}{n}\right)^{n}\left(1-\frac{c'}{n}\right)^{-r}$$

At this stage, the *limit* of each term is taken allowing n to go to infinity and holding $c' = np'$ constant.

$$\lim_{n\to\infty}\left(\frac{n!}{(n-r)!\,n^r}\right) = 1$$

$$\lim_{n\to\infty}\left(\frac{c'^r}{r!}\right) = \left(\frac{c'^r}{r!}\right)$$

$$\lim_{n\to\infty}\left(1-\frac{c'}{n}\right)^{n} = e^{-c'}$$

where e is 2.71828^+, the base of natural or napierian logarithms.

$$\lim_{n\to\infty}\left(1-\frac{c'}{n}\right)^{-r} = 1$$

Thus, as n increases without bound, the limiting case of the binomial distribution, stated

$$B(r\,|\,n,\,p') = \binom{n}{r}p'^r(1-p')^{n-r}$$

is the Poisson distribution

$$P(r\,|\,c' = np') = \frac{c'^r}{r!}\,e^{-c'}$$

$$= \frac{(np')^r}{r!}\,e^{-np'}$$

It will be remembered that np' is the average value of the expected number of occurrences. For ordinary use in discussion of the Poisson throughout this book, c' is used for this average instead of np'.

Use of Tables and Diagrams for Solution of Poisson Problems

Molina's tables[†] give individual terms and summation terms of the Poisson formula to six decimal places for values of $c'(np')$ up to 100. Table G in App. 3 of this book gives summation terms to three decimal places. Figure 6-3, taken from Dodge and Romig,[‡] also gives summation values; the figure may be read to two decimal places, with some uncertainty in the second place.

In Table G the values of c' go by intervals of 0.02 from 0 to 0.10, by intervals of 0.05 from 0.10 to 1.00, by intervals of 0.1 from 1.0 to 2.0, by intervals of 0.2 from 2.0 to 8.0, by intervals of 0.5 from 8.0 to 15.0, and by intervals of 1 from 15 to 25. The approximate Poisson distribution corresponding to any value of c' under 25 that is not given in Table G may be obtained by interpolation between the distributions for the two adjacent values of c' that are given in the table. Such an interpolation is illustrated in Table 6-3, in which c' is 5.28. Each value for 5.28 is assumed to be 0.4 (that is, $[5.28 - 5.20]/[5.40 - 5.20]$) of the way from the 5.20 value to the 5.40 value. Such a linear interpolation in Table G will generally give values that are either correct or in error by not more than one unit in the third decimal place.

In addition to illustrating the use of Table G, Table 6-3 gives values of the Poisson summation as read from Fig. 6-3. As both Table G and Fig. 6-3 give only summations of terms, the individual Poisson terms must be obtained by subtracting the adjacent summation terms. This has been done in Table 6-3.

The Poisson as a Distribution in its Own Right

The Poisson can be used to save labor of calculation both in probability problems to which the binomial is directly applicable and in other problems to which the binomial provides a satisfactory approximation. But this is not the limit of usefulness of the Poisson. Certain types of frequency distributions occur in nature, both in industrial quality control work and elsewhere, that are closely fitted by the Poisson. The situations to which it has been shown to be applicable are so numerous and so diversified that the Poisson has sometimes been called the law of small numbers. Some representative examples are shown in Table 6-4.

Table 6-4a§ is based on 33 years of records for 10 rainfall stations widely

---

[†] E. C. MOLINA, "Poisson's Exponential Binomial Limit," D. Van Nostrand Company, Inc., Princeton, N.J., 1942.

[‡] H. F. DODGE and H. G. ROMIG, "Sampling Inspection Tables," 2d ed., Fig. 2-6, John Wiley & Sons, Inc., New York, 1959.

[§] E. L. GRANT, Discussion of "Rainfall Intensities and Frequencies," by A. J. SCHAFMAYER and B. E. GRANT, *Transactions, American Society of Civil Engineers,* vol. 103, p. 388, 1938.

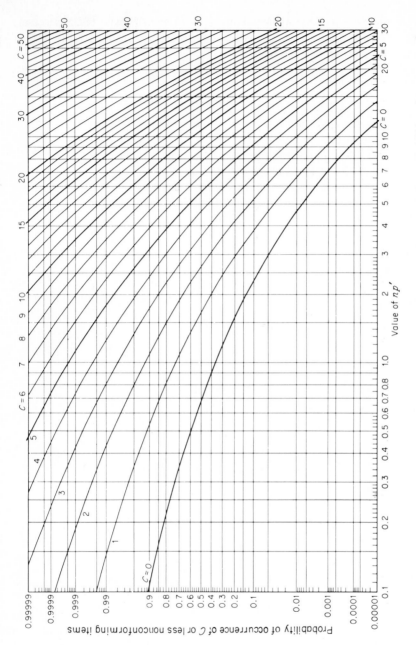

Figure 6-3 Cumulative probability curves for Poisson's exponential binomial limit. For determining probabilities of occurrence of c or less nonconforming items in a sample of n items selected from an infinite universe in which the fraction nonconforming is p'. (*Reprinted by permission from H. F. Dodge and H. G. Romig, "Sampling Inspection Tables," 2d ed., fig. 2-6, John Wiley & Sons, Inc., New York, 1959.*)

Table 6-3 Illustration of estimation of terms of Poisson by use of tables and diagrams

$n = 240$ $p' = 0.022$ $np' = c' = 5.28$

| | Probability of c or less occurrences | | | | Estimates from Fig. 6–3 | |
| | Summation terms from Table G | | Interpolated summation terms for $c' = 5.28$ | Probability of exactly c occurrences for $c' = 5.28$ | Summation terms | Individual terms |
	for $c' = 5.2$	for $c' = 5.4$				
0	0.006	0.005	0.006	0.006	0.005	0.005
1	0.034	0.029	0.032	0.026	0.03	0.025
2	0.109	0.095	0.103	0.071	0.10	0.07
3	0.238	0.213	0.228	0.125	0.23	0.13
4	0.406	0.373	0.393	0.165	0.39	0.16
5	0.581	0.546	0.567	0.174	0.57	0.18
6	0.732	0.702	0.720	0.153	0.72	0.15
7	0.845	0.822	0.836	0.116	0.83	0.11
8	0.918	0.903	0.912	0.076	0.91	0.08
9	0.960	0.951	0.956	0.044	0.96	0.05
10	0.982	0.977	0.980	0.024	0.98	0.02
11	0.993	0.990	0.992	0.012	0.992	0.012
12	0.997	0.996	0.997	0.005	0.997	0.005
13	0.999	0.999	0.999	0.002	0.999	0.002
14	1.000	1.000	1.000	0.001	0.9996	0.0006

scattered throughout the midwestern United States. It gives the number of 10-min. periods in a year having half an inch or more of rainfall. c is the number of such cloudbursts in a station-year; the frequency is the number of station-years having respectively 0, 1, 2, 3, 4, and 5 such excessive rainstorms. The average number of such storms per station-year, $\bar{c}$, is 1.2. Table 6-5 shows the close agreement between the frequencies observed for the 330 station-years and the frequency computed by the Poisson for the same average and the same number of station-years.

Table 6-4b is the classic example of the Poisson series that has been quoted in many books on probability and statistics. It was compiled by Bortkewitsch, who wrote on the subject of the Poisson law in 1898. He found from the records of the Prussian army the number of men killed by the kick of a horse in each of 14 cavalry corps in each of 20 successive years, and after discarding the records for 4 corps that were considerably larger than the others, treated the rest as one series of samples. c is the number of Prussians killed in this way in a corps-year. The frequency is the number of corps-years having exactly c cavalrymen killed. This was the first example of the applicability of the Poisson to accident statistics.

Table 6-4 Examples of distributions to which the Poisson law is applicable

(a) Excessive Rainstorms

c	Frequency
0	102
1	114
2	74
3	28
4	10
5	2

(b) Deaths from Kick of a Horse

c	Frequency
0	109
1	65
2	22
3	3
4	1

(c) Lost Articles

c	Frequency
0	169
1	134
2	74
3	32
4	11
5	2
6	0
7	1

(d) Vacancies in the U.S. Supreme Court

c	Frequency
0	59
1	27
2	9
3	1

(e) Calls from Group of 6 Coin-box Telephones

c	Frequency
0	8
1	13
2	20
3	37
4	24
5	20
6	8
7	5
8	2
9	1

(f) Errors in Alignment Found at Aircraft Final Inspection

c	Frequency	c	Frequency
0	0	10	2
1	0	11	5
2	0	12	2
3	1	13	3
4	4	14	1
5	3	15	2
6	6	16	1
7	7	17	0
8	7	18	1
9	5		

Table 6-4c gives the number of articles turned in per day to the lost and found bureau of a large office building (excluding Sundays and holidays, and June, July, and August, when there might be a considerable reduction in the average population of the building).† The frequency is the number of days with exactly c lost articles turned in.

Table 6-4d shows the vacancies in the United States Supreme Court, either by death or resignation of members, from 1837 to 1932.‡ The frequency is the number of years in which there were exactly c vacancies.

† Tables 6-4c and 6-4e are taken from FRANCES THORNDIKE, Applications of Poisson's Probability Summation, *The Bell System Technical Journal*, vol. 5, pp. 604–624, October, 1926.

‡ W. A. WALLIS, The Poisson Distribution and the Supreme Court, *Journal of the American Statistical Association*, vol. 31, p. 376, June, 1936.

Table 6-5 Comparison of observed frequencies with theoretical frequencies by the Poisson

(Data of Table 6-4a on excessive rainstorms)

c	Observed frequency in 330 trials	Total number of rainstorms	Summation terms of Poisson, $c' = 1.2$	Individual terms of Poisson, $c' = 1.2$	Expected frequency in 330 trials
0	102	0	0.301	0.301	99
1	114	114	0.663	0.362	119
2	74	148	0.879	0.216	71
3	28	84	0.966	0.087	29
4	10	40	0.992	0.026	9
5	2	10	0.998	0.066	2
6	0	0	1.000	0.002	1
	330	396	. . . . .	1.000	330

$$\bar{c} = {}^{396}\!/_{330} = 1.20$$

Table 6-4e shows the number of telephone calls per 5-min interval from a group of six coin-box telephones in a large railway terminal. The data were taken for the period from noon to 2 P.M. for seven days, not including a Saturday or Sunday. The frequency is the number of 5-min intervals in which exactly c calls were originated.

Table 6-4f gives the numbers of errors in alignment discovered by inspectors at the time of final inspection of an airplane. The frequency is the number of planes for which exactly c such errors were listed on the inspector's "squawk sheet."

At first impression, these six Poisson illustrations may seem to have very little similarity to one another. However, a more critical examination shows they have very definite characteristics in common. In each, a count was made of the number of occurrences of an event which had many opportunities to occur but which was extremely unlikely to occur at any given opportunity. There were many 10-min periods in a year; it was unlikely any particular one would bring a cloudburst of half an inch or more of rain. There were many contacts between a cavalryman and a horse during a year of history of a cavalry corps; it was unlikely the horse would make a fatal kick at any particular contact. There were many people passing through the large office building during a day; it was unlikely that any one person would find a lost article and turn it in to the lost and found bureau, etc.

In all these cases, there is the concept of the existence of a large n and a small p', even though it may be impossible to assign definite values to either n or p'. Even in cases where it is not impossible to determine definite values of n and p', it may simply be of no advantage to determine n and p' and to calculate a binomial based on them; the Poisson will serve as well.

It will be noted that in all instances an effort has been made to keep constant a quantity that might be called *the area of opportunity for occurrence*. Thus the 4 cavalry corps that were much larger than the other 10 were eliminated from the tabulation of deaths of cavalrymen; the days in which the office building was believed to have a less than normal population were eliminated from the tabulation of articles turned in to the lost and found bureau; the record of calls from the group of coin-box phones was limited to an apparently homogeneous 2-h period in the middle of the day and Saturdays and Sundays were eliminated.

By similar reasoning, it would not have been appropriate to combine alignment "squawks" observed on two airplanes of different designs.

Average and Standard Deviation of the Poisson

The average and standard deviation of the Poisson distribution are $c' = np'$ and $\sqrt{c'} = \sqrt{np'}$, respectively. These parameters may be derived by considering the Poisson either as the limiting case of the binomial or as a distribution in its own right.

The mean and standard deviation of the binomial were found to be np' and $\sqrt{np'(1-p')}$, respectively. In the limiting case where $c' = np'$, a constant,

$$\text{mean} = np' = c'$$

$$\sigma'_c = \sqrt{np'(1-p')}$$

$$= \sqrt{c'\left(1 - \frac{c'}{n}\right)}$$

$$= \sqrt{c'}$$

Considered in its own right, the mean of the Poisson may be derived from

$$E(r) = \sum_{r=0}^{\infty} r \frac{c'^r}{r!} e^{-c'} = c'$$

and the standard deviation from

$$\sigma'_c = \sqrt{\text{Var}(r)} = \sqrt{c'}$$

where

$$\text{Var}(r) = E[(r - c')^2] = \sum_{r=0}^{\infty} r^2 \frac{c'^r}{r!} e^{-c'} - c'^2$$

The Poisson is therefore a distribution for which the standard deviation, $\sqrt{c'}$, is always the square root of the average, c'.

The Normal Distribution

The basic probability distribution underlying the calculation of Shewhart control-chart limits for variables data is the *normal* or *gaussian* distribution. The mathematical formula for this distribution is

$$f(z) = \frac{1}{\sqrt{2\pi}} e^{-z^2/2} \, dz$$

A plot of this function over its full range $-\infty$ to $+\infty$ produces the familiar symmetrical bell-shaped curve. It is a continuous curve over its full range and has a mean value of zero and a standard deviation of one. Fortunately, almost the entire area under this curve lies on the range of z between -3 and $+3$. Table A of App. 3 tabulates the area under this curve from $-\infty$ to the value of z indicated in the left-hand column, i.e., from $z = -3.59$ to $z = +3.59$. The mathematical formula for the table values is

$$F(z) = \int_{-\infty}^{z} \frac{1}{\sqrt{2\pi}} e^{-z^2/2} \, dz$$

In mathematical terms, the table is referred to as a tabulation of the cumulative left-hand standard normal curve, designated $N(0, 1)$.

For practical usage, however, it is necessary to convert from mean values and standard deviations other than zero and one, respectively. This procedure, called *normalizing*, involves substituting

$$z = \left(\frac{X - \bar{X}'}{\sigma'} \right)$$

into the general formula, yielding

$$F(z) = \int_{-\infty}^{(X - \bar{X}')/\sigma'} \frac{1}{\sqrt{2\pi}} e^{-z^2/2} \, dz$$

Thus the values read from the table represent the area under the curve from $-\infty$ to $z = (X - \bar{X}')/\sigma'$.

Two important mathematical relationships may be developed from the mean $\bar{X}'$ and standard deviation σ' of the normal distribution. First, the expected value of the average of a sample of size n equals the expected value of an individual measurement $\bar{X}'$. This may be demonstrated as follows:

$$E(\bar{X}) = E\left[\frac{1}{n} \sum X_i \right]$$

and, since E is a linear operator,

$$E(\bar{X}) = \frac{1}{n} E(\sum X_i)$$

$$= \frac{1}{n}(n\bar{X}')$$

$$= \bar{X}'$$

The second important relationship is that between the variance of distribution of sample averages and that of the distribution of individual items $(\sigma')^2$. Remembering the Var is a second degree operator,

$$\text{Var}(\bar{X}) = \text{Var}\left[\frac{1}{n}\sum X_i\right]$$

$$= \frac{1}{n^2}\text{Var}(\sum X_i)$$

$$= \frac{1}{n^2}\sum \text{Var}(X_i)$$

$$= \frac{1}{n^2}(n\sigma'^2)$$

$$= (\sigma')^2/n$$

Thus the standard deviation of the distribution of sample averages is equal to the standard deviation of the distribution of individual measurements divided by the square root of the sample size. This relationship has already been extensively used in the development of $\bar{X}$ control charts.

The Central Limit Theorem

From the standpoint of process control, the *Central Limit Theorem* is one of the most powerful tools of mathematical statistics. It has and will be used extensively throughout this book. Simply stated, the theorem says:

Irrespective of the shape of the distribution of a universe, the distribution of average values, $\bar{X}$'s, of subgroups of size n, $(\bar{X}_1, \bar{X}_2, \bar{X}_3, \ldots, \bar{X}_k)$, drawn from that universe will tend toward a normal distribution as the subgroup size n grows without bound.

Thus we may use the normalized statistic $z = \sqrt{n}(\bar{X} - \bar{X}')/\sigma'$ and a normal table such as Table A of App. 3 to evaluate probabilities related to the distribution of sample averages.

The reader will immediately recognize that this statistic forms the basis of the $\bar{X}$ chart. The fact is that n does not have to be very large before the normal distribution may be applied. This fact was discussed at some length in Chap. 2 and illustrated in Figs. 2-7 to 2-9 using samples of four drawn from normal, rectangular, and triangular universes, respectively.

The mathematical proof of the central limit theorem is beyond the scope of this book. The discussion and illustrations in Chap. 2 clearly demonstrate not only the fact but also the speed at which the limit is approached.

The Normal Curve as an Approximation to the Binomial

One of the several common derivations of the normal curve is as a limit of the binomial distribution as n is increased indefinitely. The greater the value of n, the better the estimate of the binomial that can be made from a normal curve area table such as Table A, App. 3. It should be recognized, however, that the normal curve is always a symmetrical distribution. The binomial is symmetrical only in the special case where $p' = \frac{1}{2}$. For a given value of n the normal curve gives a better approximation when p' is close to $\frac{1}{2}$ than when p' is close to 0 or 1. However, if n is large enough—say in the hundreds or more—the normal curve may be used for a wide range of values of p' and will give an approximation to the binomial that is good enough for practical purposes in many problems in industrial sampling. Where p' is close to 0 or 1, the approximation will be considerably less reliable in the extreme tails of the distribution than near the center of the distribution. In previous mathematical expectation calculations the following relationships were found:

Distribution	Expected value	Standard deviation
Normal	$\bar{X}'$	σ'
Binomial	np'	$\sqrt{np'(1 - p')}$

The form for z, any deviate in the standard normal table, was

$$z = \frac{X - \bar{X}'}{\sigma'}$$

which may be approximated to the binomial by substituting the binomial statistics equivalent to $\bar{X}'$ and σ'. This substitution leads to

$$z = \frac{X - np'}{\sqrt{np'(1 - p')}}$$

A problem remains, however, in relating the mathematical form of the normal curve, a continuous function, to that of the binomial, a discrete function. That is, given some discrete value, r, the binomial formula

$$P(r) = \binom{n}{r} p'^r (1 - p')^{n-r}$$

has some finite value. The corresponding mathematical operation with the normal curve function yields nothing; that is,

$$P(z = r) = \int_{(r-np')/\sqrt{np'(1-p')}}^{(r-np')/\sqrt{np'(1-p')}} \frac{1}{\sqrt{2\pi}} e^{-z^2/2} \, dz = 0$$

An approximation method for circumventing this problem is to use the area under the normal curve from $r - \frac{1}{2}$ to $r + \frac{1}{2}$. Therefore, we designate

$$z_1 = \frac{r - np' - 0.5}{\sqrt{np'(1 - p')}}$$

$$z_2 = \frac{r - np' + 0.5}{\sqrt{np'(1 - p')}}$$

and

$$P(z = r) = F(z_2) - F(z_1)$$

$$= \int_{z_1}^{z_2} \frac{1}{\sqrt{2\pi}} e^{-z^2/2} \, dz$$

The method of using Table A to approximate the binomial is illustrated in the following example.

Samples of 45 are being taken from a stream of products. This product is, on the average, 25% nonconforming in the sense that one-fourth of the product normally fails to conform to a particularly severe specification that is being applied as part of the acceptance procedure. The following two questions are representative of the two types of probability calculations that might be required:

1. What is the probability that a sample of 45 will contain 13 nonconforming items?
2. What is the probability that a sample of 45 will contain 13 or more nonconforming items?

It is evident that the binomial distribution is applicable and that $n = 45$ and $p' = 0.25$. To answer question 1 by calculation from the binomial distribution itself, it must be recognized that $r = 13$.

$$P(13) = \binom{n}{r} p'^r (1 - p')^{n-r}$$

$$= \frac{45!}{13! \, 32!} (0.25)^{13} (0.75)^{32}$$

$$= 0.1093$$

The actual calculation of this 0.1093 value may require the use of logarithms of factorials from Table H, App. 3, as well as the use of a table of ordinary logarithms such as Table J.

To approximate this answer from Table A, it is first necessary to compute the average and standard deviation of the binomial distribution.

$$np' = 45(0.25) = 11.25$$

$$\sqrt{np'(1 - p')} = \sqrt{45(0.25)(0.75)} = 2.905$$

These values may now be substituted into the formulas previously developed.

$$z_1 = \left(\frac{13 - 11.25 - 0.5}{2.905}\right) = 0.4303$$

$$z_2 = \left(\frac{13 - 11.25 + 0.5}{2.905}\right) = 0.7745$$

The approximation of $P(13)$ may be taken from Table A.

$$
\begin{aligned}
F(z_2) &= F(0.7745) = 0.7807 \\
F(z_1) &= F(0.4303) = -0.6665 \\
P(13) & = 0.1142
\end{aligned}
$$

This figure, 0.1142, is an approximation to the correct figure of 0.1093, the probability of exactly 13 nonconforming items under the stated conditions.

A fairly long and tedious calculation is required to find the correct answer to question 2 regarding the probability of 13 or more nonconforming items. It is necessary to calculate 33 terms of the binomial corresponding to values of r from 13 to 45 inclusive and to take the sum of these terms. A somewhat shorter calculation, still fairly long, requires the evaluation of the 13 terms corresponding to values of r from 0 to 12 inclusive, the summation of these terms, and the subtraction of the sum from 1.

In the present instance these long calculations can be avoided by the use of "Applied Mathematics Series No. 6, Tables of the Binomial Probability Distribution," published by the Government Printing Office and available from the Superintendent of Documents, Washington, D.C. This volume, containing 387 large pages, gives to seven decimal places both the individual values and the summation values of the terms of the binomial where n is 49 or less. The values of p' go from 0.01 to 0.50 by intervals of 0.01. The table for $r = 13$ and $n = 45$ gives the correct answer to question 2 as 0.3251992.†

The approximate answer that the normal curve gives for question 2 requires only a slight modification of the calculations already made to answer question 1. It has already been pointed out that, as applied to a continuous distribution such as the normal curve, the probability of exactly 13 nonconforming items should be

---

† For additional individual and summation values of the binomial, see H. G. ROMIG, "50–100 Binomial Tables," John Wiley & Sons, Inc., New York, 1953. This publication of the Bell Telephone Laboratories covers values of n from 50 to 100 by steps of 5. Extensive tables of summation values are given in "Cumulative Binomial Probability Distribution," Harvard University Press, Cambridge, Mass., 1955. This Harvard volume includes values of n from 100 to 200 by steps of 10, from 200 to 500 by steps of 20, and 500 to 1,000 by steps of 50.

interpreted as meaning the probability of from 12.5 to 13.5 nonconforming items. It follows that the probability of 13 or more nonconforming items should be interpreted to mean the probability of 12.5 or more. It has already been calculated that 0.6665 of a normal distribution having the same $\bar{X}'$ and σ' as this particular binomial will be below 12.5. It follows that the approximate probability of 13 or more nonconforming items is $1 - 0.6665 = 0.3335$.

Deciding on the Method to be Used for Calculating Probabilities in Industrial Sampling Problems

In the attributes inspection of industrial product, each item either conforms to specifications or fails to conform. In sampling for acceptance purposes, the decision on acceptance or rejecton of the product sampled will commonly depend on the number of nonconforming items in the sample or samples. In judging the merits of any proposed sampling acceptance scheme, it is appropriate to calculate the probabilities of acceptance assuming a number of different percentages of nonconforming items in the product sampled. Some calculations of this type have already been illustrated; many more are given in the chapters on acceptance sampling by attributes.

In one type of problem it is specified that a random sample of size n is to be drawn from a lot of size N containing a specified percentage of nonconforming items. It is desired to find the probability that the sample will contain exactly r nonconforming items or, perhaps, r or more or r or less. In this type of problem, the theoretically correct answer requires consideration of lot size N as well as sample size n. Methods of making such calculations were illustrated on pages 187–190; probabilities so calculated are described as *hypergeometric* probabilities. As pointed out on page 191, in problems of this type it is often good enough for practical purposes to assume that the sample is drawn from an infinite lot rather than from a finite lot and to use the binomial to give an approximation to the desired hypergeometric probabilities.

In another type of problem the random sample of size n is assumed to be drawn from a stream of product containing a specified percentage of nonconforming items. Here the binomial is applicable in principle rather than as an approximation.

For many of the problems involving either hypergeometric probabilities or the binomial, the required calculations may be long and time-consuming. This is particularly true if n is large and probabilities must be calculated for many different possible numbers of nonconforming items in order to solve a problem dealing with "r or more" or "r or less." In solving such problems it is necessary to decide whether to use an approximate method that saves computational time even though it gives answers that are not quite correct. If some approximate method is to be used, a choice must be made among the various approximate methods.

No simple general rules can be laid down as to when to use approximate methods. It is always a matter of balancing the saving in the time and cost of calculations against the error introduced by the approximation. The following suggestions are merely intended to give some general guidance.

1. In principle, hypergeometric probabilities are required whenever a sample is drawn from a finite lot of stated size N. The decision on whether to compute hypergeometric probabilities or to assume an infinite lot should be influenced by the size of N, by the ratio n/N, and by the number of values of r for which calculations are required. If N is more than 1,000, the fact that log factorials are not available makes the calculation of such probabilities very time-consuming; where N is small, say 20 or less, it is easy to compute such probabilities even without the aid of logarithms. The smaller the ratio of sample size to lot size, the less the error introduced by assuming that the sample is drawn from an infinite lot. The amount of time saved by an approximation is relatively small if calculations are required for only one or two values of r and much greater if many values of r are involved. A possible rule of thumb is to view the binomial as giving an acceptable approximation to hypergeometric probabilities whenever n/N does not exceed 0.1.†

2. Whenever the binomial applies in principle or is considered to give a satisfactory approximation to hypergeometric probabilities, the decision must be made among (a) calculation by the binomial, (b) use of the Poisson distribution as an approximation to the binomial, and (c) use of the normal curve as an approximation to the binomial. For anyone who has the sets of binomial tables that we have mentioned, it is simple to use the binomial for the values of n and p given in the tables. Without these tables, or for values of n and p not given, a decision for or against calculation by the binomial depends in part on the number of terms to be evaluated. If many terms are to be evaluated in an "r or more" or "r or less" type of problem, it is usually more practical to use an approximate method.

3. The great timesaver in all such calculations is the Poisson distribution. With a table such as Molina's table or Table G or with a diagram such as Fig. 6-3, approximate answers can be obtained very rapidly. This statement applies to calculations of the probability of exactly r occurrences as well as to "r or more" or "r or less" occurrences. In many industrial sampling problems, the approximate values given by the Poisson distribution are good enough. The larger the n and the smaller the p', the closer the approximate answer will be to the true probability.

4. The normal curve as an approximation to the binomial gives a more rapid answer than the Poisson approximation only when the np' of the problem is greater than the maximum np' in the available Poisson table or diagram. (This maximum is 25 in Table G, 30 in Fig. 6-3, and 100 in Molina's tables.) The normal curve is somewhat better adapted to rapid calculation of cumulative terms than of individual terms. The larger the n and the nearer the p' to 0.5, the closer the approximate answer will be to the true probability. A rough working rule of thumb is to avoid using the normal curve as an approximation to the binomial whenever np' is less than 5.

---

† For some 700 pages of tables giving hypergeometric probabilities, see G. J. LIEBERMAN and D. B. OWEN, "Tables of the Hypergeometric Probability Distribution," Stanford University Press, Stanford, Calif., 1961.

Theory of Extreme Runs

If, in tossing a coin, the probability of a head on one toss is $\frac{1}{2}$, the probability of heads on both of two successive independent tosses is $(\frac{1}{2})^2$. Similarly, the probability of heads on all of seven successive independent tosses is $(\frac{1}{2})^7 = \frac{1}{128}$. As the probability of tails on every toss for 7 tosses is also $\frac{1}{128}$, the probability of a run of either 7 heads or 7 tails in any given set of 7 tosses is $\frac{1}{128} + \frac{1}{128} = \frac{1}{64}$.

The *median* of a set of numbers has been defined (Chap. 2) as the mid-number, the one so located that half the numbers are above it and the other half below it. If numbers were written on a set of chips, the probability is $\frac{1}{2}$ that a single chip drawn at random would fall above the median. Or if measurements are made on a quality characteristic that is statistically controlled, the probability is $\frac{1}{2}$ that any one measurement will be above the universe median. Whenever a frequency distribution is symmetrical, the median and average (arithmetic mean) are the same. In this case, the probability is $\frac{1}{2}$ that any one measurement will fall above the universe average, or that the average of any subgroup will fall above the universe average. Extreme runs of subgroup averages above or below the universe average are as likely as extreme runs of heads or tails in coin tossing. Thus the probability is $\frac{1}{64}$ that 7 successive subgroup averages will fall on the same side of the universe average.

This type of reasoning is the basis for the rules given in Chap. 3 regarding interpretation of extreme runs on a control chart. For example, if the probability is assumed as $\frac{1}{2}$ that any subgroup average will fall above the universe average, the probability that at least 10 out of 11 subgroups would fall on the same side of the universe average can be computed by adding the first two and last two terms of the binomial, $(\frac{1}{2} + \frac{1}{2})^{11}$.

P_{11}, the probability of all 11 above $\quad = \left(\dfrac{1}{2}\right)^{11} \quad = \dfrac{1}{2048}$

P_{10}, the probability of exactly 10 above $\quad = 11\left(\dfrac{1}{2}\right)^{10}\left(\dfrac{1}{2}\right) = \dfrac{11}{2048}$

P_1, the probability of exactly 10 below (1 above) $\quad = 11\left(\dfrac{1}{2}\right)\left(\dfrac{1}{2}\right)^{10} = \dfrac{11}{2048}$

P_0, the probability of all 11 below (0 above) $\quad = \left(\dfrac{1}{2}\right)^{11} \quad = \dfrac{1}{2048}$

The probability that 10 or more out of 11 will fall on the same side of the universe average $\quad = \dfrac{24}{2048}$

$\dfrac{24}{2048} = 0.0117$, or approximately $\dfrac{1}{85}$

As many distributions of industrial quality characteristics are not symmetrical, it is not strictly correct to state that the probability is always $\frac{1}{64}$ that, with no change in the universe, 7 successive subgroup averages will be on the same side of the universe average, or that the probability is always $\frac{1}{85}$ that at least 10 out of 11 will be on the same side. Just as the control chart limits are best interpreted as rules for action rather than as means of estimating exact probabilities, so also should the extreme runs mentioned in Chap. 3 be interpreted in this way.

As pointed out in Chap. 3, these runs may be expected to occur as a matter of chance with no change in universe average oftener than would a departure from 3-sigma limits. The relative frequencies of the runs and the out-of-control points may be judged by noting that, assuming a normal universe, the probability of a point outside 3-sigma limits is 0.0027 or about $\frac{1}{380}$. If it were desired to set up rules for extreme runs that were as unlikely as departures from 3-sigma limits, such runs could readily be calculated. For example, 9 points in a row on the same side of the average have a probability of $\frac{1}{256}$; 10 points have a probability of $\frac{1}{512}$.

Significant extreme runs are not necessarily with reference to the central line of the control chart. It is suggested in Chap. 9 that two points in succession on the same side of a 2-sigma limit constitutes an extreme run that is a more significant indication of an assignable cause than a single point outside of 3-sigma limits. The statement may be verified by the following calculations. If the probability of one point *above* the *upper* 2-sigma limit is 0.0228, the probability of two in a row is $(0.0228)^2 = 0.00052$. As the probability of two points in a row *below* the *lower* 2-sigma limit is also 0.00052, the probability of two points in succession outside the *same* 2-sigma limit (either above the upper limit or below the lower limit) is $0.00052 + 0.00052 = 0.00104$, or about $\frac{1}{960}$.†

PROBLEMS

NOTE: In all of the following problems, use the method that is correct in principle unless the problem statement specifies the use of an approximate method.

6-1 What is the probability that a single draw from Shewhart's normal bowl will yield a chip marked 29, 30, or 31? See Table 2-6 for the distribution in this bowl.

   Answer: $\frac{120}{998}$.

6-2 If two successive draws from Shewhart's normal bowl are made with the first chip drawn replaced before the second draw, what is the probability that a 30 will be obtained on both draws?

   Answer: 1,600/996,004.

6-3 If two successive draws are made with the first chip drawn not replaced before the second draw, what is the probability that a 30 will be obtained on both draws?

   Answer: 1,560/995,006.

6-4 A sample of 3 is to be selected from a lot of 20 articles. How many different samples are possible?

   Answer: 1,140.

6-5 A sample of 30 is to be selected from a lot of 200 articles. How many different samples are possible?

   Answer: 4.096×10^{35}.

† Probability tests may also be applied to runs in which each value is greater (or less) than the preceding value. For probability tables and a diagram applicable to this type of run, see P. S. OLMSTEAD, Distribution of Sample Arrangements for Runs Up and Down, *Annals of Mathematical Statistics*, vol. 17, pp. 24–33, March, 1945.

6-6 What is the probability of getting exactly 3 sixes in a throw of 6 dice? What is the probability of 3 or more sixes?

Answer: 0.0536; 0.0623.

6-7 What are the respective probabilities of getting 0, 1, 2, 3, 4, 5, 6, and 7 heads in a toss of 7 coins? Assume the probability of heads in one toss to be $\frac{1}{2}$.

Answer: $\frac{1}{128}$; $\frac{7}{128}$; $\frac{21}{128}$; $\frac{35}{128}$; $\frac{35}{128}$; $\frac{21}{128}$; $\frac{7}{128}$; $\frac{1}{128}$.

6-8 From past records it is estimated that the probability that a flood of 10,000 sec-ft or more will occur in any year on a certain stream is $\frac{1}{5}$. What is the probability that such a flood will occur at least once in the next 5 years?

Answer: 0.672.

6-9 Bill proposes the following dice game to Jack. Jack will throw 5 dice. If 3 or more of them do not turn up the same face (i.e., 3 or more sixes, 3 or more fives, etc.), Bill wins and Jack will pay him 10 cents. If 3 or more of the 5 dice do turn up the same face, Jack wins and Bill will pay him 40 cents. What is the probability that Jack will win? As the game is proposed, who has the best of the bet?

Answer: 0.213; odds of 4 to 1 are favorable to Jack, as fair odds would be 3.69 to 1.

6-10 (*a*) How many different hands of 13 cards might you have out of a standard deck of 52 playing cards?

(*b*) What is the probability of a 13-card hand without an ace, king, queen, or jack?

(*c*) What is the probability of a 13-card hand containing all four aces?

(*d*) What is the probability of a 13-card hand containing one or more aces?

Answer: (*a*) 635,013,560,000; (*b*) 0.00364; (*c*) 0.00264; (*d*) 0.696.

6-11 In the discussion on probability spaces and events, several illustrations were given of the formation of events. For each of the experiments below, define the probability space by listing all possible elementary outcomes. Also list all of the events that can be defined on each space. Illustrate the elementary outcomes and the probability of each.

(*a*) The tossing of a single coin.

(*b*) The tossing of a single die.

(*c*) The simultaneous tossing of two coins.

(*d*) The tossing of a pair of dice.

6-12 A random sample of 4 is to be selected from a lot of 12 articles, 3 of which are nonconforming. What is the probability that the sample will contain exactly 1 nonconforming article?

Answer: $\frac{28}{55}$.

6-13 A random sample of 20 is to be selected from a lot of 150 articles, 15 of which are nonconforming. What is the probability that the sample will contain 2 or more nonconforming articles?

Answer: 0.627.

6-14 A controlled manufacturing process is 0.2% nonconforming. What is the probability of finding 2 or more nonconforming pieces among 100 pieces?

Answer: 0.017.

6-15 Use the Poisson distribution to obtain an approximate answer to Problem 6-14.

Answer: 0.018.

6-16 A random sample of 10 articles is taken from a stream of product 2% nonconforming. What is the probability that the sample will contain no nonconforming articles?

Answer: 0.817.

6-17 An acceptance plan calls for the inspection of a sample of 75 articles out of a lot of 1,500. If there are no nonconforming articles in the sample, the lot is accepted; otherwise it is rejected. If a lot 1% nonconforming is submitted, what is the probability that it will be accepted? Solve this using the Poisson as an approximation.

Answer: 0.472.

6-18 An acceptance plan calls for the inspection of a sample of 115 articles out of a lot of 3,000. If there are 6 or less nonconforming articles in the sample, the lot is accepted; with 7 or more it is rejected. If a lot 5% nonconforming is submitted, what is the probability that it will be rejected? Solve using the Poisson as an approximation.

Answer: 0.354.

6-19 If the probability is 0.033 that a single article will be nonconforming, what are the respective probabilities that a sample of 100 will contain exactly 0, 1, 2, 3, 4, 5, 6, 7, 8, 9, 10, and 11 nonconforming articles? Assume that the Poisson is a satisfactory approximation to the binomial in this case and solve by interpolation in Table *G*.

Answer: 0.037; 0.122; 0.201; 0.2205; 0.182; 0.1205; 0.0655; 0.0315; 0.013; 0.0045; 0.002; 0.0005.

6-20 If the probability is 0.25 that a single article will not conform to a special severe specification, what is the probability that a sample of 50 will contain exactly 15 nonconforming articles?

Answer: 0.089.

6-21 Using the normal curve as an approximation to the binomial, answer the question in Problem 6-20. Also find the approximate probability of 15 or more nonconforming articles.

Answer: 0.094; 0.257.

6-22 Using the Poisson as an approximation to the binomial, answer the question in Problem 6-20. Also find the approximate probability of 15 or more nonconforming articles.

Answer: 0.081; 0.275.

6-23 (*a*) A sample of 5 is selected from a lot of 30 articles. How many different samples are possible?

(*b*) A sample of 30 is selected from a lot of 180 articles. How many different samples are possible?

(*c*) Discuss the problem of answering the foregoing questions by solving them on a calculator or computer.

6-24 If two successive draws from Shewhart's normal bowl (see Table 2-6) are made with the first chip drawn replaced before the second draw, what is the probability that a 25 will be obtained on both draws? Find the probability of a 25 on both draws if the first chip drawn is not replaced before the second draw.

6-25 Solve Problem 6-24 using draws of a chip marked 16 rather than marked 25.

6-26 Solve Problem 6-24 using draws of a chip marked 10 rather than marked 25.

6-27 A die has two sides painted red, two painted black and two painted yellow. Define the elementary outcomes and the probability space. What probabilities would you assign to each elementary outcome?

6-28 (*a*) If the die described in Problem 6-27 is rolled three times, what is the probability that a yellow side appears only on the third roll?

(*b*) only on the fifth roll in five rolls?

(*c*) within the first three rolls?

6-29 In a hand of 13 cards drawn from a standard 52-card deck, what is the probability of exactly 6 diamonds?

6-30 One urn contains two white and three black balls; a second urn contains four white and two black balls.

(*a*) If one ball is chosen from each urn, what is the probability that they will be the same color?

(*b*) If an urn is selected at random, what is the probability that a ball drawn from that urn will be black?

(*c*) If an urn is selected at random and two balls are drawn (without replacement) from it, what is the probability that they will both be the same color?

6-31 Assuming that the ratio of one sex to total children is exactly $\frac{1}{2}$, what is the probability that in a family of five children.

(*a*) All will be of the same sex?

(*b*) The three oldest will be boys and the two youngest will be girls?

(*c*) Exactly two of the children will be boys?

6-32 Two balls are drawn from an urn containing two white, three black, and five green balls. What is the probability that the first is white and the second black, assuming the first ball is not placed back in the urn before the second is drawn? What is the probability assuming the first ball is placed back in the urn before the second is drawn?

6-33 In a hand of 13 cards drawn from a standard 52-card deck, what is the probability that the hand contains exactly seven spades and exactly five clubs? What is the probability given the added stipulation that the seven spades include the ace, king, queen, and jack?

6-34 What is the probability that if a lot of 50 items contains three nonconforming items (6% nonconforming), a random sample of five items will contain all three of them? Exactly two? One or less? What is the sum of these probabilities?

6-35 If the probability is 0.06 that a single article is nonconforming in a continuous manufacturing process, what are the respective probabilities that 0, 1, 2, 3, 4, and 5 articles are nonconforming in a random sample of five items taken from the process?

6-36 Use the Poisson approximation to the binomial to solve Problem 6-35. Comment on the difference in results so obtained.

6-37 Use the normal approximation to the binomial to solve Problem 6-35. Comment on the difference in results so obtained.

6-38 The probabilities computed in Problem 6-35 constitute a binomial distribution. (Why?) Compute the average and standard deviation of this binomial following the tabular pattern given in the calculations on pages 193 and 195. Compare these calculated values with values given by the formulas np' for the mean and $\sqrt{np'(1 - p')}$ for the standard deviation.

6-39 Random samples of 80 items are drawn from a continuous process which is known to produce 30% nonconforming items. Determine the probability of finding exactly 15 nonconforming items in a sample:

(a) Using the exact binomial distribution.
(b) Using the normal approximation to the binomial.
(c) Using the Poisson approximation to the binomial.
(d) Comment on the relative accuracy of the approximations.

6-40 Change Problem 6-39 so that the probability sought is that of more than 15 nonconforming items in a sample rather than exactly 15. Do not attempt to solve part (a), but comment on the difficulties presented in making an exact binomial calculation in this case.

6-41 Make a calculation similar to Table 6-5 to compare the observed frequencies of Table 6-4c with the theoretical frequencies of the Poisson.

6-42 Derive the mean and standard deviation for the Poisson distribution following the mathematical expectation procedure.

Hint: The pattern of the derivation follows very closely that used to derive the mean and standard deviation for the binomial.

6-43 A lot of 60 items contains 15 nonconforming items. A random sample of 20 items is drawn and 5 nonconforming items (the expected average number of nonconforming items in a sample of 20) are found.

(a) Use the exact hypergeometric distribution to find the probability of this event.
(b) Use the binomial approximation to the hypergeometric to estimate this probability.
(c) Use the Poisson approximation to estimate this probability.
(d) Use the normal approximation to estimate this probability.
(e) Comment on the relative accuracy of the various approximation formulas in this case.

6-44 Consider the sampling plan for which the lot size is 40, the sample size is 8, and lot acceptance is based on finding no more than one nonconforming item.

(a) On the assumption that the lot is 20% nonconforming, use the correct formula to find the probability that the lot will be accepted.
(b) Use a Poisson approximation to find the probability that the lot will be accepted.
(c) Comment on the relationship between the answers found in (a) and (b).

6-45 A large number of samples of 250 items each are taken from a process generating 10% nonconforming items.

(*a*) What is the expected number of nonconforming items per sample?

(*b*) What is the upper limit of the number of nonconforming items in a sample that you would expect to find exceeded only 5% of the time assuming no shift in the process average? Use the normal approximation to the binomial to find the limit.

(*c*) Solve part (*b*) using the Poisson approximation to the binomial.

6-46 In Chap. 3, several "decision rules" related to the theory of extreme runs are presented. The statement was: "whenever in *n* successive points on a control chart, at least *r* are on the same side of the central line," where:

	n	r
(*a*)	7	7
(*b*)	11	10
(*c*)	14	12
(*d*)	17	14
(*e*)	20	16

Assume the probability to be $\frac{1}{2}$ that a subgroup average will fall above the central line. If there has been no shift in the universe average, what probability is associated with the random occurrence of each of these events?

6-47 Assuming that the probability is 0.0559 that a point will randomly fall above a $1.5\sigma_{\bar{X}}$ limit on a control chart for $\bar{X}$ if the universe average has not shifted, develop a decision rule similar to that shown in Problem 6-46(*a*) based on the theory of runs that yields a probability of occurrence approximately equivalent to that in Problem 6-46(*a*).

6-48 Certain shipments of insulators were subject to inspection by a high-voltage laboratory. One of the important tests was a destructive one. The procedure adopted for inspection was as follows: Select six insulators at random from the large lot and test them. If all six pass the test, accept the lot. If two or more fail the test, reject the lot. If only one insulator fails, take a second sample of six insulators. If all six insulators in the second sample pass the test, accept the lot; otherwise reject it.

(*a*) What is the probability of accepting lots in which 5% are nonconforming?

(*b*) What is the probability of acceptance if 25% are nonconforming? Comment on the effectiveness of the procedure.

6-49 A stipulated acceptance procedure calls for examining 12 articles from a lot of 1,000 articles. If none of the 12 articles are classified nonconforming, the lot is accepted; otherwise it is rejected. Assume that a lot containing 10% nonconforming articles is submitted for acceptance.

(*a*) Using hypergeometric probabilities, compute the probability of acceptance.

(*b*) Using the binomial distribution as an approximation to the method that is correct in principle, compute the approximate probability of acceptance.

(*c*) Using the Poisson distribution as an approximation to the binomial, compute the approximate probability of acceptance.

(*d*) Using the normal distribution as an approximation to the binomial, compute the approximate probability of acceptance.

6-50 Solve Problem 6-49 changing the lot size from 1,000 to 50 and making no other change in the problem statement.

6-51 Discuss your results in Problems 6-49 and 6-50 in relation to the question of which approximation, if any, to use in computing such probabilities of acceptance.

6-52 In the situation described in Problem 3-4, assume that the mean of the process shifts to 18 ppm dissolved iron before the next subgroup is drawn. What is the Type II error probability that this shift will go undetected on the next subgroup plotted on the $\bar{X}$ chart? Assume no change takes place in the dispersion of the process.

6-53 In the situation described in Problem 3-33, the control limits for $\bar{X}$ and R were based on an estimate of σ' of 0.0015 and an aimed-at value of $\bar{X}'_0$ of 0.7500. Based on this past month's data, what is the probability that any given point would have fallen outside the previously established $\bar{X}$ chart limits?

THE CONTROL CHART FOR FRACTION REJECTED

Some time ago when we first began to get steamed up about this matter of statistical control, we called on a number of large automotive parts manufacturers with the intention of getting production records from which simple control charts could be plotted. The results were quite startling. In the first place, even the well-managed plants which ordinarily have all kinds of records found that they had no record of the percentage defective by lots. Some information was available, of course, but it was woefully inadequate and could not be used to indicate past experience. The tragic thing about it all is that the executives in these several plants had assured the writer that they had specific data on their quality control and knew exactly the range in process average. In several instances, further investigation revealed that the process average was considerably higher than they had estimated, in fact much higher than permissible.—Joseph Geschelin†

Some Practical Limitations of the Control Charts for Variables

In spite of the advantages of the $\bar{X}$ and R charts, both as powerful instruments for the diagnosis of quality problems and as a means for routine detection of sources of trouble, it is evident that their use is limited to only a small fraction of the quality characteristics specified for manufactured products.

One limitation is that they are charts for *variables*, i.e., for quality characteristics that can be measured and expressed in numbers. Many quality characteristics can be observed only as *attributes*, i.e., by classifying each item inspected into one of two classes, either conforming or nonconforming to the specifications.

Moreover, even for those many quality characteristics that can be measured, the indiscriminate use of $\bar{X}$ and R charts would often be totally impracticable, as well as uneconomical. For example, the inspection department in one manufacturing plant had the responsibility for checking over 500,000 dimensions. Although

† JOSEPH GESCHELIN, Statistical Method Points to Process Control by Spotting Variables in Manufacture, *Automotive Industries*, vol. 67, pp. 166–169, Aug. 6, 1932.

any one of these dimensions could have been measured as a variable and was therefore a possible candidate for $\bar{X}$ and R charts, it is obvious that there could not be 500,000 such charts. No dimension should be chosen for $\bar{X}$ and R charts unless there is an opportunity to save costs—costs of spoilage and rework, inspection costs, costs of excess material—or otherwise to effect quality improvements that would in some way more than compensate for the costs of taking the measurements, keeping the charts, and analyzing them.

Control Charts for Attributes

There are several different types of control charts that may be used in either of the cases described in the foregoing paragraphs:

1. the p chart, the chart for fraction rejected as nonconforming to specifications
2. the np chart, the control chart for number of nonconforming items
3. the c chart, the control chart for number of nonconformities
4. the u chart, the control chart for number of nonconformities per unit

The c chart and the u chart are discussed in Chap. 8.

The cost of collecting data for attributes charts is likely to be less than the cost of collecting data for $\bar{X}$ and R charts, because the attributes chart generally uses data already collected for other purposes. $\bar{X}$ and R charts on the other hand require special measurements for control-chart purposes. The cost of computing and charting may be less since one attributes chart may apply to any number of quality characteristics observed at an inspection station, whereas separate $\bar{X}$ and R charts are necessary for each measured quality characteristic.

In addition to the cost advantages that may be gained, the use of attributes control charts provides management with useful records of quality history. Many managerial decisions need to be based on a knowledge of the quality level currently maintained and on prompt information about changes that occur in the quality level. In government contract work, such information may be required in order to demonstrate capability to meet requirements both prior to award of a contract and later during fulfillment.

The Control Chart for Fraction Rejected

The most versatile and widely used attributes control chart is the p chart. This is the chart for the fraction rejected as nonconforming to specifications (the so-called fraction defective). It may be applied to quality characteristics that can be observed only as attributes. It may also be applied to quality characteristics that are considered as attributes—for example, dimensions checked by go and not-go gages—even though they might have been measured as variables. As long as the result of an inspection is the classification of an individual article as accepted or rejected, a single p chart may be applied to one quality characteristic or a dozen or a hundred.

Fraction rejected, p, may be defined as the ratio of the number of nonconforming articles found in any inspection or series of inspections to the total number of articles actually inspected. Fraction rejected is nearly always expressed as a decimal fraction.

Per cent rejected is $100p$, that is, 100 times the fraction rejected. For actual calculation of control limits, it is necessary to use the fraction rejected. For charting, and for general presentation of results to shop personnel and to management, the fraction is generally converted to per cent.

The Binomial as a Probability Law that Determines the Fluctuations of Fraction Rejected

Suppose 10,000 beads of the same size and density are placed in a container. Of these, 9,500 are white and 500 red. White may be considered to represent articles that conform to specifications and red to represent nonconforming articles. Let samples of 50 beads be drawn at random from this container. If the 50 beads are replaced after each sample has been drawn and all beads are thoroughly mixed before the next drawing, the theory of probability enables us to calculate the relative frequency in the long run of getting exactly 0, 1, 2, 3, 4, 5, etc. red beads. As explained in Chap. 6, the binomial gives a very close approximation to these probabilities. If the container held an infinite number of beads, 5% of which were red, the binomial would apply exactly.

Any one sample of beads drawn from the container is a sample from a very large quantity of beads 5% red. As a matter of chance, variations in the number of red beads are inevitable from sample to sample. In a similar way, we may think of a day's production (or other lot) of any manufactured article or part as a sample from a larger quantity with some unknown fraction that do not conform to specifications. This unknown universe nonconforming fraction depends upon a complex set of causes influencing the production and inspection operations. As a matter of chance, the nonconforming fraction in the sample may vary considerably. As long as the nonconforming fraction in the universe remains unchanged, the relative frequencies of nonconforming fractions in the samples may be expected to follow the binomial law.

Control Limits for the p Chart

As a general mathematical model, the Shewhart control chart model with 3-sigma limits may be expressed as

$$UCL_y = E(y) + 3\sigma_y$$

$$\text{Central Line}_y = E(y)$$

$$LCL_y = E(y) - 3\sigma_y$$

where y is the random variable, or control statistic, to be plotted on the control chart, for example, $\bar{X}$, R, p, c, and so forth, $E(y)$ is the expected value of the statistical variable, and σ_y is the standard deviation of the variable y.

In the case of the control chart for $\bar{X}$, the basic model becomes

$$UCL_{\bar{X}} = \bar{X}' + 3\sigma_{\bar{X}}$$

$$\text{Central Line}_{\bar{X}} = \bar{X}'$$

$$LCL_{\bar{X}} = \bar{X}' - 3\sigma_{\bar{X}}$$

where the statistical variable $y = \bar{X}$, $E(y) = \bar{X}'$, and

$$\sigma_y = \sigma_{\bar{X}} = \sigma'/\sqrt{n}$$

The reader will remember that the distribution of the statistic $y = \bar{X}$, even with small subgroup sizes, tends toward a normal distribution because of the power of the central limit theorem. Since the chance (probability) that an exactly normally distributed random variable will fall outside either 3-sigma control limit is 0.0027, such an occurrence purely by chance on an $\bar{X}$ chart would be very rare indeed.

The $\bar{X}$ chart, however, is the only instance in the application of the Shewhart control chart model for which the distribution of the random variable can be shown to tend toward the normal distribution. In all other cases—for example, the R chart, σ chart, p chart, etc.—it is sufficient to simply say that the chance occurrence of a point falling outside 3-sigma limits would be very unlikely.†

The mean, or expected value, of the binomial is p' and its standard deviation is $\sqrt{p'(1 - p')/n}$ (see Chap. 6). Thus, 3-sigma limits for the p chart are

$$UCL_p = p' + 3\sqrt{\frac{p'(1 - p')}{n}} = p' + 3\frac{\sqrt{p'(1 - p')}}{\sqrt{n}}$$

$$LCL_p = p' - 3\sqrt{\frac{p'(1 - p')}{n}} = p' - 3\frac{\sqrt{p'(1 - p')}}{\sqrt{n}}$$

The prime notation has the same meaning as stated previously with respect to control charts for variables. It refers to the parametric, or universe, value of the statistic in question. When combined with the subscript o (that is, p'_o), it refers to the standard or aimed-at value chosen for control chart purposes.

In cases where a standard value is not used, the observed value, $\bar{p}$, may be. The

---

† This is not to say that it is impossible to associate probability values with points outside control limits for charts other than the $\bar{X}$ chart. Such calculations are very tedious and time consuming, especially in p chart applications with varying sample size, and contribute little to the application of the basic decision rule. The general statement may be made, however, that they are of the same order of magnitude as the probabilities of a point falling outside 3-sigma limits in drawing from a normal universe.

observed value is necessarily used in the calculation of trial control limits. In these cases, the control limits are

$$UCL_p = \bar{p} + 3\sqrt{\frac{\bar{p}(1 - \bar{p})}{n}} = \bar{p} + 3\frac{\sqrt{\bar{p}(1 - \bar{p})}}{\sqrt{n}}$$

$$LCL_p = \bar{p} - 3\sqrt{\frac{\bar{p}(1 - \bar{p})}{n}} = \bar{p} - 3\frac{\sqrt{\bar{p}(1 - \bar{p})}}{\sqrt{n}}$$

Industrial practice in the use of the p chart generally bases control limits either on 3-sigma or some other multiple of sigma. Except for very small subgroups, the calculation of probability limits (such as described for $\bar{X}$, R, and σ charts in Chap. 9) for a p chart is too burdensome a job. However, if probability limits are desired, they may be obtained for probability levels of 0.005 and 0.995, and for 0.1 and 0.9, by the use of Simon's I_Q charts.†

As in the case of the $\bar{X}$ and R charts, the use of 3-sigma limits rather than narrower or wider limits is a matter of experience as to the economic balance between the cost of hunting for assignable causes when they are absent and the cost of not hunting for them when they are present. Although in most cases 3-sigma limits are best, special cases arise in which the use of narrower limits, such as 2-sigma, is desirable. The need for narrower limits arises out of the use of the p chart as an instrument for executive pressure on quality.

Problems Introduced by Variable Subgroup Size

The larger the subgroup, the more likely it is that the fraction nonconforming in the subgroup will be close to the fraction nonconforming of the universe. This obvious general principle is expressed in mathematical terms by the statement that the standard deviation of p, like the standard deviation of $\bar{X}$, varies inversely with $\sqrt{n}$.

For both the $\bar{X}$ chart and the p chart, the appropriate 3-sigma control limits depend on the subgroup size (see Fig. 9-1). The practical difference is that because most measurements used for $\bar{X}$ charts are taken for control-chart purposes, it is usually possible to keep subgroup size constant. Most p charts, on the other hand, use data taken for other purposes than the control chart; where subgroups consist of daily or weekly production, the subgroup size is almost certain to vary.

As a practical matter, whenever subgroup size is expected to vary, a decision must be made as to the way in which control limits are to be shown on the p chart. There are three common solutions to this problem, as follows:

---

† L. E. SIMON, "An Engineers' Manual of Statistical Methods," John Wiley & Sons, Inc., New York, 1941, particularly chaps. III and IV. It should be noted that General Simon uses Q, rather than p, to represent fraction defective.

1. Compute new control limits for every subgroup, and show these fluctuating limits on the control chart. This is illustrated in the first two months of the four months shown in Example 7-1.

2. Estimate the average subgroup size for the immediate future. Compute one set of limits for this average and draw them on the control chart. Whenever the actual subgroup size is substantially different from this estimated average, separate limits may be computed for individual subgroups. This is particularly necessary if a point for an unusually small subgroup falls outside control limits. This scheme is illustrated in the final two months of the period shown in Example 7-1. Estimates of future average subgroup size must be revised from time to time; where each day's production is one subgroup, it is customary to revise these estimates monthly.

3. Draw several sets of control limits on the chart corresponding to different subgroup sizes. A good plan is to use three sets of limits, one for expected average subgroup size, one close to the expected minimum, and one close to the expected maximum. In Example 7-1, for instance, limits might be drawn corresponding to subgroup sizes of 1,000, 2,500, and 4,000. This scheme is not satisfactory unless the data are shown on the same sheet with the control chart, with the figures for each subgroup on the same line with the plotted point for the subgroup, so that the subgroup size may be seen at a glance. Because with this scheme it is not immediately evident from inspection of the chart which

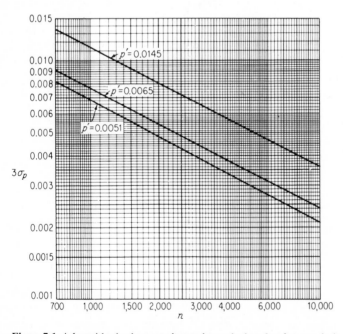

Figure 7-1 A logarithmic chart can be used to calculate $3\sigma_p$ for any desired value of p'.

points are out of control, it is desirable to use a special symbol to mark out-of-control points. For instance, if a dot were used for each point on the chart, a circle might be drawn around the dot for each point out of control.

Simplifying the Computation of Control Limits

The chief objection raised to separate calculation of correct control limits for each subgroup is the time consumed by such calculations. Actually, even modestly priced electronic pocket or desk calculators provide for automatic extraction of square roots, thus such calculations should take very little time. Once the value of $3\sqrt{p'_o(1 - p'_o)}$ has been computed to apply to all control limits for some period of time, the division of this quantity each day by $\sqrt{n}$ is a simple task.

It is sometimes desirable to prepare special tables or graphs to be used by inspection personnel on the shop floor. Table F in App. 3 is an example of tabulated control limits covering a broad range of standard values of per cent rejected and subgroup sizes. When the range of values of p'_o and n can be estimated ahead of time, special purpose tables may be prepared in an engineering office. Linear interpolation for intermediate values is usually accurate enough for practical purposes.

Diagrams prepared on graph paper provide an alternative method for visually obtaining values of $3\sigma_p$ for a range of values of n. For any given value of p'_o, the values of $3\sigma_p$ as a function of n plot as a straight line on logarithmic paper.† This is illustrated in Fig. 7-1, which shows such straight lines for the three values of $\bar{p}$ and p'_o used in Example 7-1. The curve for any desired value of p' may be obtained by computing $3\sigma_p$ for two values of n, plotting on logarithmic paper the two points so defined and connecting these two points by a straight line. For example, for $p' = 0.0145$ and $n = 900$, $3\sigma_p$ is $0.359/\sqrt{900} = 0.01197$. For $n = 4,900$,

$$3\sigma_p = 0.359/\sqrt{4,900} = 0.00513$$

These two points may be plotted and connected by a straight line. The straight lines for all values of p'_o are parallel to one another. Thus lines for additional values of p'_o, such as 0.0065, may be added to the diagram by computing the coordinates of a single point and drawing a line through that point parallel to the original line.‡

---

† Note:

$$3\sigma_p = \frac{3\sqrt{p'(1 - p')}}{\sqrt{n}}$$

$$\log 3\sigma_p = \log 3\sqrt{p'(1 - p')} - \tfrac{1}{2} \log n$$

If, for any given value of p', $\log 3\sigma_p$ is plotted on rectangular coordinate paper as a function of $\log n$, it is evident from this equation that the resulting curve will be a straight line with a slope of $-\tfrac{1}{2}$ and an intercept of $\log 3\sqrt{p'(1 - p')}$. Such a plotting on rectangular coordinate paper is equivalent to plotting $3\sigma_p$ as a function of n on paper having a logarithmic ruling.

‡ A variety of special-purpose probability slide rules and graph papers are available from James R. King, Team, Tamworth, New Hampshire, 03886.

Example 7-1 Illustration of calculations necessary for control chart for fraction rejected *Facts of the case* This example applies to a 4-month record of daily 100% inspection of a single critical quality characteristic of a part for an electrical device. It is intended chiefly as an illustration of how control limits are calculated with variable production, and of the setting and revision of standard values for fraction rejected.

When, after a change in design, the production of this part was started early in June, the daily fraction rejected was computed and plotted on a chart. At the end of the month, the average fraction rejected $\bar{p}$ was computed. Trial control limits were computed for each point. A standard value of fraction rejected p'_o was then established to apply to future production. During July new control limits were computed and plotted daily based on the number of parts n inspected during the day. A single set of control limits was established for August, based on the estimated average daily production. At the end of August, a revised p'_o was computed to apply to September, and the control chart was continued during September with this revised value.

Calculation of trial control limits Table 7-1 shows the number inspected and the number rejected as nonconforming to specifications each day during June. The fraction rejected each day is the number of parts rejected divided by the number inspected that day. For example, for June 6, $p = 31/3,350 = 0.0093$. The per cent rejected is $100p = 0.93\%$.

At the end of the month, the average fraction rejected $\bar{p}$ is computed. It should be emphasized that the correct way to calculate $\bar{p}$ is to divide the total number rejected in the period by the total number of parts inspected during the period. Whenever the subgroup size (in this case, the daily number inspected) is not constant, it is incorrect to average the values of p.

The standard deviation was calculated based on this observed value of $\bar{p}$, 0.0145. Note that the value of $3\sqrt{\bar{p}(1-\bar{p})}$ was calculated only once to apply to all calculations of control limits. Thus, for June 6, the 3-sigma limits are $\pm 0.3586/\sqrt{3,350}$, or ± 0.0062.

The daily values of p and the control limits for each day are shown in Fig. 7-2. In this figure, per cent rejected ($100p$) rather than fraction rejected has been plotted. Because per cent rejected is more readily understood by both shop and administrative personnel, it is usually desirable for fraction rejected to be converted to per cent rejected for all plotting.

Determination of standard value p'_o If all the points fall within the trial control limits, the standard value p'_o may be assumed to be equal to $\bar{p}$.

Here many points fell outside the trial control limits. In such cases, the decision as to the value of p'_o to be used calls for judgment as to what process average fraction rejected can be maintained in the future, provided the occasional assignable causes of bad quality can be eliminated. An aid to such judgment may be obtained by computing a revised value of $\bar{p}$, eliminating the days on which p fell above the upper control limit.

With these days, June 7, 12, 13, and 22, eliminated, the remaining number

Table 7-1 Computation of trial control limits for control chart for fraction rejected

(Data on a single quality characteristic of a part of an electrical device)

Date	Number inspected n	Number rejected	Fraction rejected p	$3\sigma = \dfrac{3\sqrt{\bar{p}(1-\bar{p})}}{\sqrt{n}}$	UCL $\bar{p} + 3\sigma$	LCL $\bar{p} - 3\sigma$
June 6	3,350	31	0.0093	0.0062	0.0207	0.0083
7	3,354	113	0.0337	0.0062	0.0207	0.0083
8	1,509	28	0.0186	0.0092	0.0237	0.0053
9	2,190	20	0.0091	0.0077	0.0222	0.0068
11	2,678	35	0.0131	0.0069	0.0214	0.0076
12	3,252	68	0.0209	0.0063	0.0208	0.0082
13	4,641	339	0.0730	0.0053	0.0198	0.0092
14	3,782	12	0.0032	0.0058	0.0203	0.0087
15	2,993	3	0.0010	0.0066	0.0211	0.0079
16	3,382	17	0.0050	0.0062	0.0207	0.0083
18	3,694	14	0.0038	0.0059	0.0204	0.0086
19	3,052	8	0.0026	0.0065	0.0210	0.0080
20	3,477	27	0.0078	0.0061	0.0206	0.0084
21	4,051	44	0.0109	0.0056	0.0201	0.0089
22	3,042	70	0.0230	0.0065	0.0210	0.0080
23	1,623	12	0.0074	0.0089	0.0234	0.0056
25	915	9	0.0098	0.0119	0.0264	0.0026
26	1,644	1	0.0006	0.0088	0.0233	0.0057
27	1,572	22	0.0140	0.0090	0.0235	0.0055
28	1,961	3	0.0015	0.0081	0.0226	0.0064
29	2,440	3	0.0012	0.0073	0.0218	0.0072
30	2,086	1	0.0005	0.0079	0.0224	0.0066
Totals	60,688	880				

$$\bar{p} = \frac{\text{Total number rejected}}{\text{Total number inspected}} = \frac{880}{60,688} = 0.0145$$

$$3\sqrt{\bar{p}(1-\bar{p})} = 3\sqrt{(0.0145)(0.9855)} = 0.3586$$

of rejects is 290 and the remaining number inspected is 46,399. The revised $\bar{p} = 290/46,399 = 0.0063$.

After consideration of this and of the previous record on similar parts of slightly different design, it was decided to assume $p'_o = 0.0065$.

Calculation of control limits based on standard fraction rejected, p'_o Table 7-2 gives the daily numbers inspected and rejected during July and shows the calculation of control limits based on the standard fraction rejected. This calculation appears to be almost identical with that shown in Table 7-1. The value of p'_o is used in the calculation of limits in Table 7-2 wherever $\bar{p}$ was used in Table 7-1.

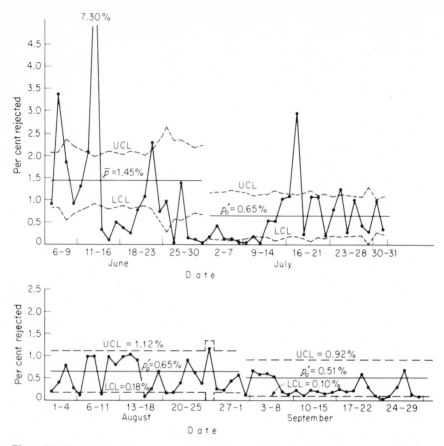

Figure 7-2 Control chart for per cent rejected—4 months' production of an electrical device.

The practical difference is that where $\bar{p}$ is used, no control limits can be computed until $\bar{p}$ is known; *i.e.*, not until the end of the period. Where a standard value p'_o is established in advance, the limits can be computed each day and drawn on the control chart as the day's point is plotted. In this way, the control chart provides a basis for immediate action whenever a point goes outside the control limits.

Establishment of control limits based on expected average subgroup size Although the correct position of 3-sigma control limits on a p chart depends on subgroup size (in this case, a subgroup is the number of parts inspected each day), the calculation of new limits for each new subgroup consumes some time and effort. Where the variation in subgroup size is not too great (for example, where the maximum and minimum subgroups are not more than 25% away from the average) it often may be good enough for practical purposes to establish a single set of control limits based on the expected average subgroup size. In this way, limits may be established at the start of a period (for instance, a month) and projected ahead for the entire period.

Table 7-2 Computation of daily control limits based on standard value of fraction rejected p'_o

(Data on a single quality characteristic of a part of an electrical device)

Date	Number inspected n	Number rejected	Fraction rejected p	$3\sigma = \dfrac{3\sqrt{p'_o(1-p'_o)}}{\sqrt{n}}$	UCL $p'_o + 3\sigma$	LCL $p'_o - 3\sigma$
July 2	2,228	4	0.0018	0.0051	0.0116	0.0014
3	2,087	9	0.0043	0.0053	0.0118	0.0012
5	2,088	3	0.0014	0.0053	0.0118	0.0012
6	1,746	2	0.0011	0.0058	0.0123	0.0007
7	2,076	1	0.0005	0.0053	0.0118	0.0012
9	2,164	1	0.0005	0.0052	0.0117	0.0013
10	2,855	5	0.0018	0.0045	0.0110	0.0020
11	2,560	5	0.0020	0.0048	0.0113	0.0017
12	2,545	14	0.0055	0.0048	0.0113	0.0017
13	1,874	1	0.0005	0.0056	0.0121	0.0009
14	2,329	24	0.0103	0.0050	0.0115	0.0015
16	2,744	30	0.0109	0.0046	0.0111	0.0019
17	2,619	77	0.0294	0.0047	0.0112	0.0018
18	2,211	5	0.0023	0.0051	0.0116	0.0014
19	1,746	19	0.0109	0.0058	0.0123	0.0007
20	2,628	28	0.0107	0.0047	0.0112	0.0018
21	2,366	5	0.0021	0.0050	0.0115	0.0015
23	2,954	23	0.0078	0.0044	0.0109	0.0021
24	2,586	32	0.0124	0.0047	0.0112	0.0018
25	2,790	8	0.0029	0.0046	0.0111	0.0019
26	2,968	30	0.0101	0.0044	0.0109	0.0021
27	3,100	13	0.0042	0.0043	0.0108	0.0022
28	1,359	4	0.0029	0.0065	0.0130	0.0000
30	3,940	39	0.0099	0.0038	0.0103	0.0027
31	3,138	11	0.0035	0.0043	0.0108	0.0022
Totals	61,701	393				

Standard fraction rejected p'_o is 0.0065

$3\sqrt{p'_o(1-p'_o)} = 3\sqrt{(0.0065)(0.9935)} = 0.241$

At the end of July the situation was reviewed to consider the possibility of doing this. It was decided that daily output was well enough stabilized to justify the use of a single set of control limits during August. Average daily production during July had been $61,701/25 = 2,468$. The estimated average daily output during August was 2,600; this was assumed as the value of n for calculation of control limits. As $\bar{p}$ during July had been $393/61,701 = 0.0064$, no change was made in the p'_o of 0.0065. The calculations for the control limits for August are shown in Table 7-3.

Whenever control limits are set in this way on an expected average value of n, any points on the control chart that are either outside the limits or just

Table 7-3 Record of daily fraction rejected with control limits computed on standard daily production and on standard value of fraction rejected, p_o'

(Data on a single quality characteristic of a part of an electrical device)

Date	Number inspected n	Number rejected	Fraction rejected p	Date	Number inspected n	Number rejected	Fraction rejected p
Aug. 1*	3,068	6	0.0020	Sept. 1†	2,539	3	0.0012
2	776	3	0.0039	3	2,425	16	0.0066
3	2,086	16	0.0077	4	1,537	9	0.0059
4	3,652	10	0.0027	5	2,852	17	0.0060
6	2,606	3	0.0012	6	2,953	16	0.0054
7	2,159	21	0.0097	7	2,649	5	0.0019
8	2,745	27	0.0098	8	2,835	4	0.0014
9	2,606	3	0.0012	10	2,752	6	0.0022
10	2,159	21	0.0097	11	892	1	0.0011
11	2,745	22	0.0080	12	3,186	7	0.0022
13	3,114	30	0.0096	13	2,646	5	0.0019
14	1,768	18	0.0102	14	2,714	4	0.0015
15	3,208	29	0.0090	15	2,878	5	0.0017
16	2,629	2	0.0008	17	2,384	6	0.0025
17	3,576	9	0.0025	18	2,639	5	0.0019
18	2,262	15	0.0066	19	3,160	7	0.0022
20	3,294	5	0.0015	20	1,895	11	0.0058
21	3,026	5	0.0017	21	4,287	13	0.0030
22	2,713	10	0.0037	22	2,917	3	0.0010
23	2,687	24	0.0089	24	2,479	1	0.0004
24	3,824	23	0.0060	25	1,991	2	0.0010
25	3,265	12	0.0037	26	3,280	10	0.0030
27	1,205	14	0.0116	27	2,195	15	0.0068
28	3,035	7	0.0023	28	2,570	3	0.0012
29	2,793	6	0.0021	29	3,323	3	0.0009
30	3,295	14	0.0042				
31	3,227	18	0.0056				
Totals	73,523	373		Totals	65,978	177	

* For August:

Estimated average daily production is 2,600
Standard fraction rejected, p_o', is 0.0065

$$3\sigma = \frac{3\sqrt{p_o'(1 - p_o')}}{\sqrt{n}} = \frac{3\sqrt{(0.0065)(0.9935)}}{\sqrt{2,600}} = 0.0047$$
$$UCL = p_o' + 3\sigma = 0.0065 + 0.0047 = 0.0112$$
$$LCL = p_o' - 3\sigma = 0.0065 - 0.0047 = 0.0018$$

† For September:

Estimated average daily production is 2,700
Standard fraction rejected, p_o', is 0.0051
$$3\sigma = 0.0041$$
$$UCL = 0.0051 + 0.0041 = 0.0092$$
$$LCL = 0.0051 - 0.0041 = 0.0010$$

inside the limits require more critical examination to see whether the limits as drawn really apply to these points. Whenever the subgroup size is larger than the assumed average value of n, the true limits are inside those drawn. Whenever the subgroup size is smaller, the true limits are outside.

Such a calculation was made for August 27, when p was 0.0116. This is above the upper control limit of 0.0112 which was computed for the assumed daily production of 2,600. A revised upper control limit for this day based on the actual production of 1,205 is 0.0134. The revised limits for this day are indicated on the control chart (Fig. 7-2); they show that the point was actually not out of control.

Further revision of p_o' During August, the average fraction rejected $\bar{p}$ was $373/73,523 = 0.0051$. No points fell above the upper control limit. This value, 0.0051, was therefore assumed as p_o' to apply to September. Control limits for September were based on an estimated average subgroup size of 2,700. (Daily production during August had been $73,523/27 = 2,723$.) Daily values for September with calculated control limits are shown in Table 7-3 and plotted in Fig. 7-2.

The process quality during September improved even more. Although only two points fell below the lower control limit during the month, confirmation of the existence of a new better level of quality was given by an extreme run for eleven points—from September 7 to 19—below the central line. For the month, the process average $\bar{p}$ was $177/65,978 = 0.0027$. This justified a further downward revision of p_o' to 0.0027 for October. The data and the control chart for October are not shown here.

Outline of Necessary Steps in Connection with Control Chart for Fraction Rejected

It will be helpful in gaining a full understanding of the procedures followed in Example 7-1 to review the decisions and calculations that must be made and the actions which must be taken in initiating and operating a control chart for attributes data. The major events occur in a sequence somewhat as follows:

  I. Decisions preparatory to the control chart
    A. Determination of the purpose of the chart
    B. Selection of inspection station and quality characteristics to be charted
    C. Decisions on the selection of subgroups
    D. Choice of type of chart to be used (p or np)
    E. Decision regarding calculation of control limits
    F. Setting up the forms for recording and charting the data
  II. Starting the control chart
    A. Recording the data
    B. Calculation of the subgroup control statistics (p)
    C. Calculation of the average value of the control statistic ($\bar{p}$)

I. DECISIONS PREPARATORY TO THE CONTROL CHART

A. Determination of the Purpose of the p Chart

As applied to 100% inspection, a control chart for fraction rejected may have any or all of the following purposes:

1. To discover the average proportion of nonconforming articles or parts submitted for inspection over a period of time.
2. To bring to the attention of management any changes in this average quality level.
3. To discover those out-of-control high spots that call for action to identify and correct causes of bad quality.
4. To discover those out-of-control low spots that indicate either relaxed inspection standards or erratic causes of quality improvement which might be converted into causes of consistent quality improvement.
5. To suggest places for the use of $\bar{X}$ and R charts to diagnose quality problems.

The p chart as applied to sampling inspection on a lot-by-lot basis may have any or all of the purposes cited for 100% inspection. An additional purpose usually is:

6. To afford a basis for judgment whether successive lots may be considered as representative of a process. This judgment may properly influence the severity of acceptance criteria. This matter is discussed in Chap. 14.

Example 7-2 An illustration of the selection of quality characteristics for charts for fraction rejected *Facts of the case* In this example, the product manufactured was an automatic pressure switch used to open and close a valve in a gas line in order to maintain gas pressure within given limits. An inspection station was located in the assembly line just before the cover was bolted onto this device. This was not final inspection in the sense that it involved a check of the overall functioning of the device. However, it was the final chance before the completion of the device to identify a number of nonconformities that would prevent the functioning of a completed pressure switch.

At this inspection station 31 different possible nonconformities to specifications might be observed. A device for which the inspector finds one or more nonconformities is a *reject*. For each reject, the inspector's record sheet showed the particular nonconformities found, designated by initials or some other appropriate symbol (such as *BL* for broken lead, *DR* for defective receptacle, etc.).

When the *p* chart was first applied at this inspection station, the average proportion rejected was around 15%. It was decided to start with 11 *p* charts. A chart was maintained for each of the following nine nonconformities: (1) points off; (2) broken lead; (3) defective receptacle; (4) defective bar; (5) high tube; (6) cracked base; (7) loose bar; (8) close bar; and (9) defective tube. The other 22 of the 31 possible nonconformities were grouped together in a single chart (10) for miscellaneous. In addition, a chart was kept for total per cent rejected. The total number of rejects recorded from any day's inspection might, of course, be less than the total nonconformities observed because a device containing two or more nonconformities would be classified as only one reject. For this reason, the fraction rejected shown on the total chart was generally less than the sum of the fractions rejected shown on the 10 constituent charts.

Prompt attention to out-of-control points on some of the charts resulted in a substantial improvement in the average quality. In a short time, "points off" was reduced from 4.5% to 0.5% and "total rejects" reduced from 15% to 9%. After the charts had been in operation for three months, it was decided that separate charts for individual nonconformities could be abandoned except for the three quality characteristics that were giving the most trouble. Several months later the total rejects level was reduced to 3%. After this time only a single control chart for total fraction rejected was used.

In the establishment of these control charts, a problem was created by the fact that all rework as well as all new work was inspected at this station. Experience showed that the chances of rejection of a reworked article were considerably greater than the chances of rejection of a new article. There was a tendency on the part of the production department to accumulate rework for several days; then a large number of reworked devices would come to the inspection station on the same day. If these had been included in the inspection record, the days receiving considerable rework would have shown lack of control. Moreover, the average quality level would have appeared to be worse than it really was, because of the inclusion of two or more rejections of the same article. And the number of items inspected would have appeared to be greater than the total production. For these reasons, the maintenance of the control chart made it necessary to put special tags on all rework items and to keep separate inspection records for inspection of rework. The results of this rework inspection were not included in the control-chart data.

B. Comments on Selection of Inspection Stations and Quality Characteristics to be Charted

It is a common practice for a *p* chart to be applied at an inspection station where many different quality characteristics are to be checked. In such cases, a decision must always be made on the question faced in Example 7-2, i.e., whether to have one control chart or several. A single control chart is the most common solution, with the thought that any investigation of the causes of rejections may look to the supporting data on the inspection record sheet.

Occasionally, however, it will pay to use separate control charts for certain selected nonconformities. Nearly always it is true that troubles with different quality characteristics differ in their influence on costs. Some nonconformities may be corrected by simple inexpensive rework operations; others require costly rework; others involve the scrapping of the article inspected. Separate control charts may help to concentrate attention on those nonconformities that are responsible for the greatest costs. A single control chart that includes all nonconformities observed at an inspection station will have its variations (and its showings of lack of control) influenced more by the most common causes of rejection than by the most costly ones.

In some cases it may pay to have one control chart for spoilage and another for rework. This may be true, for example, in checking dimensions with go and not-go gages, where rejection by the go gage means rework, and rejection by the not-go means spoilage (or vice versa, depending on the dimension to be checked).

Another possible breakdown for control-chart purposes may be on the basis of the effect of a nonconformity on the functioning of a part or product. An example is the classification into critical, major, minor, and incidental defects, mentioned first at the end of Chap. 10 and discussed at greater length in Chap. 14. This breakdown is most common where acceptance sampling plans use acceptance criteria that depend on the seriousness of a nonconformity to specifications.

In all cases, the determination of which inspection stations should employ *p* charts should be based on a consideration of whether the accomplishment of the various purposes seems likely to have a sufficiently favorable effect on costs to justify the expense of maintaining the chart.

C. Decision on the Selection of Subgroups

As in the case of the Shewhart control chart for variables, in the control chart for fraction rejected the most natural basis for selecting rational subgroups is the order in which production takes place.

A common basis for subgrouping is the one illustrated in Example 7-1 in which each subgroup consisted of the items inspected in a day. This is a good basis wherever the inspection operation is an integral part of the production process, so that the order of inspection is substantially the same as the order of production. Sometimes a control chart showing daily per cent rejected may be supplemented by charts showing weekly and monthly figures. The daily chart may be used as a basis for current action on the manufacturing process by production supervisors, methods analysts, and operators; the weekly chart may be used by manufacturing executives such as department heads; the monthly chart may be used in quality reports to top management.

Where production is not on a continuous basis, a satisfactory alternative basis of subgrouping may be to consider each production order as one subgroup.

In the sampling inspection of a large lot of purchased articles from a single source, it is often desirable to use the p chart as a test for homogeneity in order to judge whether the sample may be considered to be representative of the entire lot. For example, consider the receipt of a shipment of 100,000 bolts packed in 50 containers each holding 2,000 bolts. Even though the purchaser of the bolts has no way of knowing the order of production, there is a strong likelihood that the bolts have not been thoroughly mixed since production took place. If 50 bolts were taken at random from each box of 2,000, and tested for conformity to specifications, each such sample of 50 would be an appropriate rational subgroup for use in a p chart. If the control chart showed control, the conclusion would be either that (1) the bolts had been well mixed, or (2) although not well mixed, they came from a production process that was in statistical control. Either conclusion would be satisfactory from the standpoint of considering the 2,500 bolts inspected as representative of the lot of 100,000.

In all control charts, rational subgroups should be selected in a way that tends to minimize the chance for variation within any subgroup. A possible assignable cause of variation in any inspection operation is difference in inspectors. This is particularly true in inspection by attributes. In visual inspection, where judgment plays an important part, there is a great chance for differences among inspectors. Even with go and not-go gages, inspectors may differ considerably. If each sub-group is taken in a way to reflect the work of only one inspector, the p chart may sometimes be used as a useful check on inspection standards.

D. Choice Between Chart for p and Chart for np

The choice among the control chart techniques for attributes data is based par-tially upon convenience in interpretation of the chart and partially upon the choice of the probability distribution that best fits the circumstances. In Example 7-1, the p chart was appropriate because the number of items inspected varied daily and the statistic of interest was the fraction (or per cent) rejected. Thus a charting technique based on the binomial distribution was a rational choice.

Whenever subgroup size is variable, the control chart must show the fraction rejected (or proportion rejected) rather than the actual number of rejects. If actual numbers of rejects were plotted, the central line on the chart (as well as the limits) would need to be changed with every change in subgroup size. However if subgroup size is constant, the chart for actual numbers of rejects may be used. Such a chart is called a chart for *np* or *pn*. (The fraction rejected *p* was obtained by dividing the actual number of rejects by the subgroup size *n*. The actual number of rejects may therefore be represented by *np*, the quantity which, divided by *n*, gives *p*.)

A chart for *np* may be used for data such as those shown in Table 7-4. This table gives the results of inspection of a sheet-metal part for an aircraft turbo-supercharger skin. The part was inspected after being shaped by means of a drop hammer.

As explained in Chap. 6, the standard deviation of the *number* of occurrences in *n* trials of an event with a constant probability of occurrence p' (in other words, the standard deviation of the *number* of rejects) is $\sqrt{np'(1 - p')}$. The standard deviation of the *proportion* of occurrences (in other words, the *fraction* rejected) is $\sqrt{p'(1 - p')/n}$. Thus the appropriate model for 3-sigma control limits on an *np* chart is

$$UCL_{np} = np' + 3\sqrt{np'(1 - p')}$$

$$LCL_{np} = np' - 3\sqrt{np'(1 - p')}$$

Since no standard value for *p* was established for the data in Table 7-4, the average fraction rejected $\bar{p}$ is used as the best available estimate of p'.

Figure 7-3 shows a chart for *np* for the data of Table 7-4. If a chart for *p* were drawn for the same data, it would look exactly like the chart for *np* except for the graduations on the vertical scale. Each unit on the vertical scale would represent $\frac{1}{200}$ (that is, $1/n$) as much as it does on the chart for *np*. It is evident that there is no fundamental difference in the appearance of the *np* and the *p* charts or in the information they give.

Where subgroup size is constant, there might be two possible reasons for preferring an *np* chart to a *p* chart. One reason is that the *np* chart saves one calculation for each subgroup, the division of number of rejects by subgroup size to get *p*. The other reason is that some people may understand the *np* chart more readily.

However, it often happens that in a manufacturing plant there are many places where, because of variable subgroup size, only a *p* chart is applicable, and a few places where, because subgroup size is constant, either type of chart may be used. In such cases, the possibility of confusion from having two types of charts might outweigh the slight advantage of the *np* chart, and it would be better to use the *p* charts even for constant subgroup size.

E. Decision Regarding Calculation of Control Limits

For any *p* chart with variable subgroup size, a decision must be made whether to compute new control limits for each subgroup or to adopt one of the less accurate methods that have been described.

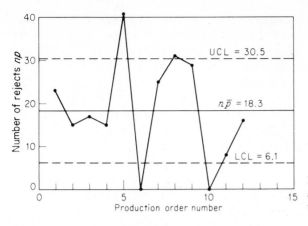

Figure 7-3 An *np* chart shows actual numbers of rejects rather than per cent rejected.

Table 7-4 Calculations for control chart for number of rejects, *np*

(Inspection in drop-hammer department of sheet-metal part)

Production order number	Lot size n	Number of rejects. np
1	200	23
2	200	15
3	200	17
4	200	15
5	200	41
6	200	0
7	200	25
8	200	31
9	200	29
10	200	0
11	200	8
12	200	16
Totals......	2,400	220

$$n\bar{p} = \frac{220}{12} = 18.3$$

$$\bar{p} = \frac{220}{2,400} = 0.0917$$

$$3\sigma_{np} = 3\sqrt{n\bar{p}(1-\bar{p})}$$
$$= 3\sqrt{(200)(0.0917)(0.9083)}$$
$$= 12.2$$

$$UCL = n\bar{p} + 3\sigma_{np} = 18.3 + 12.2 = 30.5$$
$$LCL = n\bar{p} - 3\sigma_{np} = 18.3 - 12.2 = 6.1$$

In making this decision, it should be recognized that only the separately computed limits are really correct. The objections raised in some manufacturing plants to separately computed limits have been twofold, namely, (1) the difficulty (and therefore, cost) of their calculation, and (2) the difficulty in explaining to many of the people who see the control charts the reasons why control limits vary from day to day.

The difficulties and costs of separate calculations of control limits for each subgroup tend to be overestimated. As already explained, there are a number of ways in which the job of making these computations can be simplified. With proper organization of the calculations, the extra costs of computing separate limits may be negligible.

On the other hand, where the p charts are posted in places available to shop personnel, there are real difficulties in explaining varying control limits. (Sometimes it may be even harder to explain them to the top executives than to the machine operators.) This may be a good reason for establishing one set of limits based on expected average subgroup size, particularly if such limits do not have to be changed frequently and if variations in subgroup size are not so great as to call for numerous calculations of separate limits for individual subgroups (such as the one shown in Fig. 7-1 for August 27). However, where subgroup sizes vary enough so that numerous variations in limits are inevitable, it may be better practical psychology to have everyone get used to the idea that control limits *always* vary with subgroup size, rather than to have control limits seem to vary in some cases and not in others.

F. Setting up the Forms for Recording and Charting the Data

Figure 7-4 illustrates a form used for recording data for a control chart for fraction rejected. This form contains space for all the information which is essential for preparing the control chart itself.

RECORD SHEET FOR p CHART

Name of product or part_____ Part No._____
Characteristics measured _____
Inspection station_____ Recorded by _____

Lot No.	Date	Number inspected	No. of rejects	Percent rejected	Control limits		Remarks
					Upper	Lower	

Figure 7-4 A simple form for p chart data.

LOT BY LOT
SAMPLING RECORD

PART No. _03001570_

DESCRIPTION _Cap, Pa, .005 mf 25%_

_600 V_

VENDOR

SAMP. PLAN No. _DR-7_

SUMMARY PERIOD _3 mos._

DEFECTS IN FIRST SAMPLE

	1949 YEAR DATE	REC. REPORT No.	LOT SIZE	FIRST SAMPLE SS₁	DEF.	TOTAL SAMPLE SS₁+SS₂+	TOTAL DEF.	Out of tol. on high side	Out of tol. on low side	Wrong lead length	Pin holes in wax coating						INSPECTOR'S INITIALS	DISPOSITION OF LOT PASS, REJECT, ETC.	REMARK No.
1	8/15	0014	1000	35	0												TH	P	
2	8/25	0090	700	35	0												BK	P	
3	9/5	0170	1500	50	1	150	3	1									BK	(R)	1
4	9/20	0220	1800	50	1	150	2		1								CD	P	
5	10/5	0278	1250	35	1	105	1										TH	P	
6	10/22	0315	1155	35	2			1	1								BK	(R)	2
7	10/31		7405	240	5			2	1	1	1								3
8																			
9	11/1	0407	1200	35	0												TH	P	
10	11/13	0438	1500	50	0												TH	P	
11	11/29	0500	2100	50	0												BK	P	
12	12/5	0539	2900	50	4			2	2								BK	(R)	4
13	12/10	0581	3500	75	0												TH	P	
14	12/17	0644	2700	50	0												TH	P	
15	1/8	0773	2005	50	1				1								TH	P	
16	2/1		15905	360	5														3
17																			
18	2/3	0838	1550	50	0												CD	P	
19	2/21	0907	1275	35	0												CD	P	
20	3/5	0982	1475	50	0												TH	P	
21																			
22																			
23																			
24																			
25																			

REMARKS:
1. _Returned to vendor._
2. _Rush – Balance of lot inspected._
3. _Entered into summary report._
4. _Rejection waived on lead lengths. 100% electrical inspection of lot._

Figure 7-5 Record of attributes inspection including columns showing different types of nonconformities observed. (*Reproduced from Carl L. Gartner, " Quality Control in Television Receiver Manufacturing," Industrial Quality Control, November, 1951.*)

Often it is desirable that information regarding the particular nonconformities observed be included in a record sheet showing items inspected and numbers of items rejected. Figure 7-5 illustrates a sampling record form containing columns giving this type of information. This form was used by Allen B. DuMont Laboratories, Incorporated, and is reproduced from an article by C. L. Gartner, Quality Control in Television Receiver Manufacturing, in the November, 1951, issue of *Industrial Quality Control.*

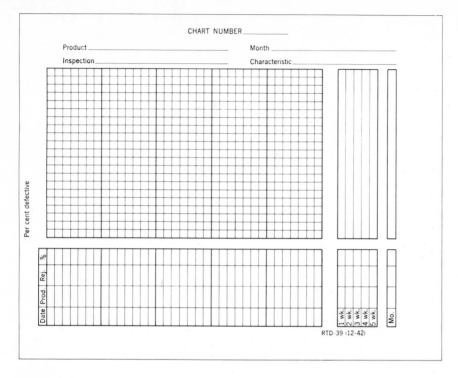

Figure 7-6 This form combines *p* chart data with a control chart. *(Courtesy of General Electric Company.)*

The chart itself may be plotted to advantage on coordinate paper with a "profile" type of ruling.

A compact presentation is provided by a combination of data sheet and control chart in one form such as is illustrated in Fig. 7-6. This particular form shows weekly figures as well as daily figures.

II. STARTING THE CONTROL CHART

Essential Steps in the Control Chart

The steps in starting the control chart were illustrated in Example 7-1. Briefly stated, they are:

A. *Record the data* for each subgroup on number inspected and number of rejects. Any occurrences that might be clues to an explanation of points out of control or to changes in the quality level should be noted on the data sheet as supplementary remarks.

B. *Compute p for each subgroup*

$$p = \frac{\text{number of rejects in subgroup}}{\text{number inspected in subgroup}} = \frac{np}{n}$$

C. *Compute $\bar{p}$, the average fraction rejected*

$$\bar{p} = \frac{\text{total number of rejects during period}}{\text{total number inspected during period}} = \frac{\Sigma np}{\Sigma n}$$

Wherever practicable, it is desirable to have data for at least 25 subgroups before computing $\bar{p}$ and establishing trial control limits.

D. *Compute trial control limits* for each subgroup based on the observed average fraction rejected, $\bar{p}$.

E. *Plot each point as obtained.* Plot trial control limits as soon as calculated and note whether the process appears to be in control.

It often happens that when the decision is made to use a *p* chart for any manufacturing operation, data are available for the period immediately past. If so, the steps just outlined should be applied to this past record. This permits putting the *p* chart to work at once as an effective instrument for process control and avoids a period for which no control limits are currently available.

III. CONTINUING THE CONTROL CHART

A. Selecting a Standard Fraction Rejected

The *p* chart is not, as generally used, merely a test for the presence or absence of assignable causes of variation. It is also a basis for judging whether the quality level is at some desired objective.

In the setting of a standard fraction rejected, p'_o, the two purposes sometimes seem to be in conflict. For example, if p'_o should be set at 0.02 and if the process actually is in statistical control (i.e., there are no assignable causes of variation from subgroup to subgroup) at a substantially higher fraction rejected, such as 0.05, the majority of the points on the control chart may fall above the upper control limit. With the *p* chart used to establish a standard quality level, points may be expected to fall outside control limits for either of two reasons, (1) the existence of assignable causes of variation, or (2) the existence of a quality level that is different from the assumed standard p'_o. This interpretation of the *p* chart should be kept in mind in the establishment and revision of the standard fraction rejected p'_o.

When a preliminary period has been completed and trial limits have been computed on the basis of $\bar{p}$, the control chart may show any condition from an excellent state of control with all points falling within control limits to an apparently hopeless absence of control with very few points within limits.

If the chart shows control, p'_o should be assumed equal to $\bar{p}$. This is generally desirable even though $\bar{p}$ is considered too high a fraction rejected to be satisfactory in the long run. For any standard really to be accepted by production personnel as a basis for action, there needs to be evidence that the standard is attainable. As illustrated in Example 7-1, p'_o may later be reduced as soon as efforts to improve the general quality level have resulted in lower values of $\bar{p}$.

If the chart shows apparently hopeless absence of control, it is generally better to continue the p chart for a time without any control limits (and without any standard value of fraction rejected) until the situation can be somewhat improved. For control limits to be respected, there needs to be evidence that it is possible to stay within the control limits most of the time. Until such evidence exists, the drawing of control limits on a p chart can be of little help and may hurt the control-chart program by creating a state of mind antagonistic to control limits.

In most cases, the control chart for the preliminary period will show a condition somewhere between the two extremes of perfect statistical control and complete absence of control. There will be a few points outside control limits, even though the majority fall within limits. This common situation was illustrated in Example 7-1. In such cases, the best procedure is to eliminate the points above the upper control limit and then to recompute $\bar{p}$. (In Example 7-1, this revised $\bar{p}$ was 0.0065 in contrast to the original $\bar{p}$ of 0.0145.) Judgment may then be applied to the revised $\bar{p}$ when establishing the standard fraction rejected p'_o to be used in the immediate future.

B. Calculation of Control Limits

Once p'_o is established, 3-sigma control limits are computed based on this standard value.

Where subgroup size is variable, limits should be computed separately for each subgroup unless some plan for approximate limits is adopted such as one of those described earlier in this chapter.

In some instances management may elect to use tighter limits than 3-sigma. If 2-sigma limits are to be used, the figure 2 is substituted for 3 in the appropriate formulas.

C. Plotting the Points and Limits

As soon as the data are obtained, points and limits should be plotted promptly on the control chart. Promptness is particularly important where the charts are posted in the shop where they may be seen by operating personnel and supervisors.

In charts exhibited in the shop, it is often desirable to omit the lower control limit. It is almost impossible to make clear to some operating people just why a point should be classed as out of control when it refers to quality that is better than the standard.

In the discussion of the $\bar{X}$ and R charts, it was stated that it is generally desirable not to draw lines connecting the points which represent the successive subgroups. The contrary is true in the case of the p chart; a line connecting the points is usually helpful in interpretation of the chart. Such a line assists in the interpretation of trends; this may be almost as important on the p chart as the interpretation of control limits.

D. Interpretation of Lack of Control

There may be erratic changes in the quality level for an occasional subgroup even though quality is otherwise maintained at the standard fraction rejected p_o'. Such changes are shown by points outside control limits and are evidence of assignable causes of variation.

In most p charts that extend over any considerable length of time, there are also definite sustained shifts of average fraction rejected to a new level either better or worse than standard. A shift to a better level was illustrated in Example 7-1. Such departures from the standard fraction rejected p_o' are often evident merely from inspection of the control chart without application of any formal statistical tests. Extreme runs above or below the central line, as well as points outside control limits, may be used to provide tests that supplement observation of the chart.

For purposes of a statistical test, any consecutive set of subgroups may be combined into a single subgroup. In this way the average fraction rejected of a set of subgroups may be tested to see whether it varies by more than 3-sigma from the standard fraction rejected.

For instance, the September data in Example 7-1 might be tested to see whether the observed fraction rejected during September, 0.0027, may be explained as a chance variation from a process which has its average at the assumed p_o' of 0.0051. With all September combined into a single subgroup, the subgroup size n is 65,978. The lower control limit corresponding to this subgroup size and to a p_o' of 0.0051 is computed as follows:

$$LCL = p_o' - \frac{3\sqrt{p_o'(1 - p_o')}}{\sqrt{n}} = 0.0051 - \frac{3\sqrt{(0.0051)(0.9949)}}{\sqrt{65,978}}$$

$$= 0.0051 - 0.0008 = 0.0043$$

It is evident that the September figure of 0.0027 is a long way outside the limits. (The difference of 0.0024 between the p_o' of 0.0051 and the actual p of 0.0027 is really a 9-sigma difference.) As this makes it clear that a new improved quality level has been established, it is possible to proceed with confidence to set a new value of p_o'.

E. Periodic Review and Revision of p_o'

The standard fraction rejected should be reviewed from time to time. This might be done at irregular intervals whenever there seems to be enough evidence to justify a change. Where many p charts are being used, it is usually better practice to ensure periodic review by establishing a regular review period. In Example 7-1, this review period was once a month. Where a subgroup consists of one day's production, it may be satisfactory to have a 2 months' review period, with half the charts reviewed each month. Where subgroups consist of production orders or of lots submitted for inspection, the frequency of subgroups will influence the proper length of the review period. This period might then be stated as once every 20 subgroups, once every 40 subgroups, etc.

Whenever there is sustained evidence of a decrease in average per cent rejected and it is clear that this decrease reflects real quality improvement rather than relaxed inspection, it is a good idea to revise p'_o downward. This helps to supply an incentive to hold this new and better level. On the other hand, where there is sustained evidence of a poorer quality level, the quality control engineer should be reluctant to revise p'_o upward. An upward revision should not be made without evidence that changes have taken place that seem to make it inevitable that, with the same attention to quality as before, the per cent rejected will increase. Some possible changes of this type are tighter specification limits, more adequate enforcement of existing limits by inspectors, and poorer incoming materials. The value of p'_o should not be increased merely on the basis of a poorer quality level that seems to have resulted from reduced attention to quality on the part of production personnel.

IV. REPORTS AND ACTIONS BASED ON THE CONTROL CHART

A. Action to Bring a Process Into Control at a Satisfactory Level

Experience shows that the mere introduction of a p chart often causes some quality improvement. This improvement may result from the influence of the chart in focusing the attention of production personnel on the quality level and may have no relation to the actual use of the control limits. This influence is most likely to be effective when the chart is new.

In the long run, much of the quality improvement attributable to the use of the p chart will come from concentration of attention on assignable causes of trouble indicated whenever a point on the chart falls above the upper control limit. Such out-of-control points are known as "high spots." Often they are reported to production supervisors and to management in regular forms known as "high spot reports."

Frequently the discovery and correction of assignable causes of poor quality are really technical jobs. In such cases, it may do no good merely to bring pressure on the production supervisor by means of a high spot report. The supervisor may already know of the trouble; what is needed is technical help in discovering its causes.

For this reason, any p chart program may need to be reinforced by methods engineers or other technical specialists who are available to give immediate attention to the most urgent high spots. In this connection, it should be emphasized that the only clue given by the p chart as to the *cause* of lack of control is the *time* at which lack of control was observed. This is in contrast to the $\bar{X}$ and R charts which, as pointed out in Chap. 3, are often very effective instruments for the diagnosis of the causes why product fails to meet specifications. The p chart, therefore, may point to the place for effective use of $\bar{X}$ and R charts.

Low spots on the control chart (i.e., points below the lower control limit) call for a different kind of attention from that given to high spots. They sometimes point to faulty inspection and may indicate the necessity of providing better inspection standards or securing better inspectors. In other cases they may be worth examining to find the reasons why quality for one subgroup was so much better than the standard; a knowledge of these reasons may help to bring about more permanent quality improvement.

B. Review of Design and Specifications in Relation to the Capabilities of a Production Process

The control chart for p may exhibit fairly good control over a period of time, but this control may be at an average fraction rejected that is too high to be satisfactory. This suggests that the situation can be improved only by fundamental changes of some sort.

Such a fundamental change might be in the design of the product. For example, a p chart used in the manufacture of an oxygen pressure gage gave an average fraction rejected which was too high. It was suggested that this might be corrected by the use of a somewhat heavier Bourdon tube in the gage. When this change in design was made, the average fraction rejected was immediately reduced to half of its previous figure.

Or it might be a change in specifications. For instance, a review of the needs of the product might indicate that tolerances were tighter than necessary on certain dimensions.

Or it might be a change in the production process through the substitution of new tooling or new machinery.

These matters may call for joint study of the problem by representatives of design, production, and inspection.

C. Information to Management Regarding the Quality Level

The facts obtained for purposes of a p chart constitute information that should always be available to management. But—as suggested in the quotation at the start of this chapter—frequently this information is not available in any form.

The usual difficulty is that although numbers of rejects may have been recorded regularly, no record shows the numbers inspected for each group of rejects. To compare quality levels at different times, it is necessary to know the fractions rejected at the various times. Every fraction has a numerator and a denominator. The numerator, number of rejects, is commonly recorded. The denominator, number inspected, is often omitted. One great advantage of the *p* chart is that it requires the denominator as well as the numerator to be recorded and thus supplies information to management regarding the current quality level and the changes in that level.

In a plant where there are a number of departments, and many control charts for fraction rejected are maintained in each department, it may be desirable to prepare charts which in some way summarize all the *p* charts in each department. Such summary charts may be useful to top executives who would not have time to examine each individual *p* chart.

Sensitivity of the *p* Chart

In order to make effective use of the control chart for fraction rejected as a help in process control, there must be some rejects in the sample observed. It is obvious that the better the quality, the larger must be the sample in order to find some rejects in the majority of the samples. If only 0.1% of the product is rejected, the sample must be at least 1,000 before there will be an average of one reject per sample. In contrast, a sample of 5 will give an average of one reject per sample if 20% of the product is rejectable. It is evident that with very good quality the *p* chart is useful in detecting lack of control only if the sample is large; with poor quality, the *p* chart may be useful with small samples.

In addition, the larger the sample, the more closely it may be expected to reflect the universe. Consider, for example, samples of various sizes drawn from product that is 2% rejectable. A sample of 5 will generally be either 0 or 20% nonconforming (that is, it will contain either 0 or 1 rejects). A sample of 20 will generally be from 0 to 10% nonconforming. A sample of 100 will generally be from 0 to 6% nonconforming. A sample of 2,000 will generally be from 1.06 to 2.94% nonconforming. A sample of 50,000 will generally be from 1.81 to 2.19% noncon-forming. In the preceding statements, "generally" applies to 3-sigma limits. For this reason, the smaller the subgroup size, the less sensitive is the *p* chart to changes in the quality level and the less satisfactory it is as an indicator of assignable causes of variation.

Where it is desirable to use a control chart for a single measurable quality characteristic and a choice must be made between the *p* chart and the $\bar{X}$ chart, it is important to recognize that the $\bar{X}$ chart will give useful results with a much smaller sample. From a statistical point of view, variables are much superior to attributes; actual measurements on a few parts are as good as gagings on many parts with go and not-go gages.

p Charts Are Not Suitable for All Data on Fraction Rejected

Control limits on the *p* chart are based on the use of the binomial as a probability distribution. As explained in Chap. 6, the binomial assumes a constant probability of occurrence of whatever event is under consideration—in the case of the *p* chart, a constant probability of occurrence of a rejected article or part. If the probability is to be constant from one article to another, each article must be a separate unit independent of the preceding and succeeding articles. With this probability constant, rejections will tend to occur at random rather than in bunches. As long as successive articles continue to be independent of one another and the quality level does not change, practically all the points on the *p* chart will fall within 3-sigma limits.

In some instances, however, it is obvious from the way in which manufacturing or inspection operations are carried on that successive units measured are not independent of one another. In such cases, most of the points on a conventional *p* chart may fall outside control limits. Here the control-chart limits tell—quite correctly—a fact that is already evident without the control chart, namely, that the probability of one article being rejected is influenced by whether or not the immediately preceding articles were rejectable. If this fact is already known and it is evident that nothing can be done about it, the information given by the *p* chart limits is of no practical help. The use of the *p* chart with conventional limits may even do harm, as it may tend to discredit the control chart in the minds of operating personnel and thus handicap the use of the control chart in cases where it would really be helpful.

Four representative cases where conventional *p* charts were unsuitable because of the foregoing type of difficulty are described in the following paragraphs:

1. In the manufacture of a certain type of rubber belt, a large mold was used that produced 2,300 belts at one time. Conditions of curing varied throughout the mold; if one belt was rejectable, it was likely that many of the adjacent belts also would be rejectable.

2. In the manufacture of a certain type of pile floor covering, daily figures were recorded for total yards produced and for the total yardage of output that was classified as substandard. In this case an imperfection that caused the classification of product as substandard might persist through many successive yards; rejectable yards were not independent of one another. Moreover, there was no natural unit of counting the product (no *n* for the binomial); for instance, feet or meters might have been used as readily as yards.

3. In the sheet-metal inspection booth of a large aircraft factory, records were kept showing daily numbers of parts inspected and numbers rejected. An average of 160,000 parts per day was inspected. Some 1,250 different parts—including practically everything of sheet metal that went into the airplane—were subject to this inspection. Over a period of time the rejections averaged about 3%. Because of the many different parts that passed through this booth, with different cause systems affecting the different parts, it was evident that the probability of a rejectable item could not be constant from part to part. Control limits based on a *p'* of 0.03 and an *n* of 160,000 would have been 0.0313 and 0.0287. Actual daily fractions rejected varied from about 0.05 to about 0.01.

4. In the 100% inspection of detonators in an ammunition plant, inspection was performed in lots of 10,000. The average fraction rejected was 0.0223. This gave

control limits of 0.0268 and 0.0178. Actual lot fractions rejected varied from 0.055 to 0.008 with approximately two-thirds the points falling outside the control limits. A study of the production process made it evident that quite different cause systems were influencing the different lots.

Even though the conventional p chart cannot be used to advantage in situations like these, it may still be desirable to keep a quality record in the form of a chart that will be available to production supervision and to management. Generally speaking, this may be done to best advantage simply by plotting per cent rejected without control limits.

PROBLEMS

7-1 An electronics company manufactures several types of cathode ray tubes on a mass production basis. During the past month, tube Type A has caused considerable difficulty. The following table contains data from 21 days of this troublesome period. Compute 3σ control limits for a p chart for this tube. 100 units are inspected each day.

Day	Tube type A fraction rejected	Day	Tube type A fraction rejected
1	0.22	12	0.46
2	0.33	13	0.31
3	0.24	14	0.24
4	0.20	15	0.22
5	0.18	16	0.22
6	0.24	17	0.29
7	0.24	18	0.31
8	0.29	19	0.21
9	0.18	20	0.26
10	0.27	21	0.24
11	0.31		

7-2 A certain product is given 100% inspection as it is manufactured, and the resultant data are summarized by the hour. In the following table, 16 hours of data are recorded. Calculate the variable control limits of a p chart using 3σ control limits and indicate the values that are out of control.

Hour	Number of units inspected	Number of units outside specs
1	48	5
2	36	5
3	50	0
4	47	5
5	48	0
6	54	3
7	50	0
8	42	1
9	32	5
10	40	2
11	47	2
12	47	4
13	46	1
14	46	0
15	48	3
16	39	0

7-3 Example 7-1 states that "because the daily production is not constant, it would be incorrect to average the values of p." Compute the correct value of $\bar{p}$ from the following data:

Lot	Number inspected	Number of units outside specs	p
1	1,200	18	0.015
2	750	40	0.053
3	150	26	0.173
4	75	15	0.200
5	225	23	0.102
Total	2,400	122	

Compare your correct $\bar{p}$ with the unweighted average value of p. Why do the two figures differ? Why is the unweighted average value of p an unsatisfactory measure of the process average fraction nonconforming?

7-4 A manufacturer purchases small bolts in cartons that usually contain several thousand bolts. Each shipment consists of a number of cartons. As part of the acceptance procedure for these bolts, 400 bolts are selected at random from each carton and are subjected to visual inspection for certain nonconformities. In a shipment of 10 cartons, the respective percentages of rejected bolts in the samples from each carton are 0, 0, 0.5, 0.75, 0, 2.0, 0.25, 0, 0.25, and 1.25. Does this shipment of bolts appear to exhibit statistical control with respect to the quality characteristics examined in this inspection?

  Answer: $UCL_p = 0.016$; $LCL_p = 0$.

7-5 An item is made in lots of 200 each. The lots are given 100% inspection. The record sheet for the first 25 lots inspected showed that a total of 75 items did not conform to specifications.

  (a) Determine the trial control limits for an np chart.

(b) Assume that all points fall within the control limits. What is your estimate of the process average fraction nonconforming p'?

(c) If this p' remains unchanged, what is the probability that the 26th lot will contain exactly 7 nonconforming units? That it will contain 7 or more nonconforming units?

Answer: (a) $UCL_{np} = 8.157$, $LCL_{np} = 0$; (b) 0.015; (c) 0.022, 0.034.

7-6 Daily inspection records are maintained on production of a special-design electronic device. 100 items have been inspected each day for the past 21 days. A total of 546 items failed during a particularly severe heat stress test. The four highest and lowest values of p are:

Highest	Lowest
0.46	0.18
0.33	0.18
0.31	0.20
0.31	0.21

(a) Compute 3σ trial control limits for a p chart. Is the process operating in control?

(b) Recommend an aimed-at value of p_o' and 3σ control limits for continued use of the p chart.

7-7 The test results described in Problem 7-6 are from a special severe heat stress chamber which is designed in such a way that 25% of the product will fail when, in fact, it is satisfactory for its intended use. If the minimum stress specification is 750 units and the process standard deviation is known to be 12 units, what should be the lower limit of the test? Assume this stress characteristic to be normally distributed.

7-8 A large number of samples of 200 items each are taken from a process that has a percentage nonconforming of 10%.

(a) What is the expected average number of noncomforming units per sample?

(b) Find the 3σ control limits for an np chart to control this process.

(c) What is the upper limit in the number of nonconforming items in a sample that, in the long run, you would expect to find exceeded only 5% of the time? Use a Poisson approximation.

7-9 The Selector Corporation produces synthetic and natural gut casings for a process meat packer. Natural gut materials are visually inspected upon receipt, graded, and sent to processing. After processing, all finished casings are tested under pressure on a special device to ensure a specified strength before shipping to the meat packer. During the past month 25 lots of 500 casings each have been subjected to 100% inspection. A total of 1,000 casings burst during test.

(a) Find 3σ limits for a control chart for p.

(b) Assuming that all points fall within these limits, what is your estimate of the process average fraction nonconforming, p'?

7-10 In the manufacture of certain special duty transformers, units are required to meet a number of specifications related to temperature rise, output voltages, voltage and current ripple, on-off recovery times, etc. Approximately 200 units are produced and subjected to a final inspection daily. At the end of 20 working days, 230 units have been rejected out of 4,150 units produced and inspected.

(a) Determine 3σ trial control limits for a p chart based on the estimated average daily production of 200 units.

(b) Only one point on the control chart falls outside limits. On that day, 30 nonconforming units were found in 200 units inspected. Investigation uncovered the fact that a voltage pot setting was being incorrectly adjusted. What aimed-at values of p_o' and control limits would you recommend for the following period based on an average daily production of 200 units?

7-11 The new item startup procedure of a certain electronics plant calls for 100 per cent inspection for at least first four months or until process control is established at an acceptable level of nonconforming product. A total of 960 units were found to not meet specifications during the first 20 working days. The number of units produced during this time period was 31,985.

Determine trial control limits for a p chart based on the average number of units produced per day.

7-12 After the control limits found in Problem 7-11 were plotted on the p chart, three points were found to be above the UCL. On these days, a total of 4,950 items were produced and 232 nonconforming units found.

(a) What value of an aimed-at p_o' would you recommend for the next production period?

(b) Give a general formula for calculating control limits during the next production period. Reduce this formula to the point that only n needs to be found in order to plot the limits.

7-13 In Problem 7-8b, find the probability that a shift to 20% nonconforming product will be detected on the first sample drawn after the shift occurs.

7-14 Assume that the process described in Problem 7-11 was found to be in control but that the level of nonconforming product shifts from 3% to 4.5%.

(a) Use Table A to estimate the probability that this shift will be detected on the first subgroup drawn after the shift occurs. Base this calculation on the average value of n found in Problem 7-11.

(b) What is the probability that this shift will be detected within the first three subgroups drawn?

7-15 A manufacturer wishes to maintain a process average of 1% nonconforming product or less. 1,500 units are produced per day and two day's runs are combined to form a shipping lot. It is decided to sample 250 units each day and use an np chart to control production.

(a) Find the 3σ control limits for this process.

(b) Assume the process shifts from 1% to 3% nonconforming product. Use Table G to find the probability that the shift will be detected as the result of the first day's sampling after the shift occurs.

(c) What is the probability that the shift described in (b) will be caught within the first three days after it occurs?

7-16 A parts manufacturer requires that 100% final inspection be performed during the first three months of production on any new or modified part. A total of 750 items were found to be nonconforming to specifications in the first 50 lots of a new item produced in lots of 500 units.

(a) Compute 3σ trial control limits for an np chart for this process.

(b) If the process average remains unchanged, what is the probability that the 51st lot will contain more than 20 nonconforming units?

(c) If the process average value of np increases by 8, what is the probability that the 51st lot inspected will exceed the upper control limit found in (a)? Use Table G.

7-17 Receiving inspection is performed on a certain high-volume part using a p chart based on a standard value (p_o') of 0.02, 3σ limits, and a standard sample size of 50.

(a) Compute control limits for the chart.

(b) A group of lots are received from a process that was generating 5% nonconforming product. What is the probability that this higher value of p' will not be detected within the first five lots inspected? Use Table G.

7-18 For a given period, $100p'$ is 2.20. Daily production is expected to vary from 400 to 1,000. Table F, App. 3, gives values of upper and lower control limits for values of $100p'$ of 2.00 and 2.50, and for subgroups of 400, 500, 600, 800, and 1,000. Interpolate between the values for 2.00 and 2.50 and prepare a table showing upper and lower control limits for subgroup size of 400, 500, 600, 800, and 1,000 for a standard per cent rejected of 2.20.

7-19 In your table for a standard per cent rejected of 2.20 which you prepared in Problem 7-18, interpolate to get upper and lower control limits for $n = 425$, 650, and 925.

EIGHT

THE CONTROL CHART FOR NONCONFORMITIES

Some processes in nature exhibit statistical control. Radioactive disintegration is an example. The distribution of time to failure of vacuum tubes and of many other pieces of complex apparatus furnish further examples. But a state of statistical control is not a natural state for a manufacturing process. It is instead an achievement, arrived at by elimination one by one, by determined effort, of special causes of excessive variation. W. Edwards Deming†

The Place of the c Chart in Statistical Quality Control

The $\bar{X}$ and R control charts may be applied to any quality characteristic that is measurable. The control chart for p may be applied to the results of any inspection that accepts or rejects individual items of product. Thus both these types of charts are broadly useful in any statistical quality control program.

The control chart for nonconformities, generally called the c *chart*, has a much more restricted field of usefulness. In many manufacturing plants there may be no opportunities for its economic use, even though there are dozens of places where $\bar{X}$ and R charts and p charts can be used advantageously.

Nevertheless, there are certain manufacturing and inspection situations in which the c chart is definitely needed. To decide whether or not to use a c chart in any individual case, it is first necessary to determine whether its use is appropriate from the viewpoint of statistical theory. If so, then it is necessary to judge whether the c chart is really the best technique to use for the purpose at hand.

---

† W. EDWARDS DEMING, "On Some Statistical Aids Toward Economic Production," *Interfaces*, vol. 5, no. 4, August, 1975, The Institute of Management Sciences, Providence, R.I., p. 5.

Distinction between a Nonconforming Article and a Nonconformity

As already explained, a *nonconforming article* (a *defective* in the restricted technical sense of the word) is an article that in some way fails to conform to one or more given specifications. Each instance of the article's lack of conformity to specifications is a *nonconformity* (a *defect* in the restricted technical sense of the word). Every nonconforming article contains one or more nonconformities. Where it is appropriate to make a total count of the number of nonconformities in each article, or in each group of an equal number of similar articles, it may be reasonable to use a control chart technique based on the Poisson distribution. This means using either a *c* chart or a *u* chart.

The *np* chart, which was explained in Chap. 7, applies to the number of rejected items in subgroups of constant size. In contrast, the *c* chart applies to the number of nonconformities in subgroups of constant size. Each subgroup for the *c* chart usually is a single article; the variable *c* is the number of nonconformities observed in one article. But a *c* chart subgroup may be two or more articles. It is essential only that the subgroup size be constant in the sense that the different subgroups have substantially equal opportunity for the occurrence of nonconformities. When the opportunity for occurrence of nonconformities changes from subgroup to subgroup, the *u* chart for nonconformities per unit is available.

Limits for the *c* Chart Are Based on the Poisson Distribution

Chapter 6 explained that Poisson's Exponential Binomial Limit was useful not only as a limit of the binomial but also as a probability distribution in its own right. Table 6-5 illustrated a number of examples of this. In all these examples, a count was made of the number of occurrences of some event that had many opportunities to occur but that was extremely unlikely to occur at any given opportunity.

In many different kinds of manufactured articles, the opportunities for nonconformities are numerous, even though the chances of a nonconformity occurring in any one spot are small. Whenever this is true, it is correct as a matter of statistical theory to base control limits on the assumption that the Poisson distribution is applicable. The limits on the control chart for *c* are based on this assumption. Some representative types of nonconformities to which the *c* chart may be applied are as follows:

1. *c* is the number of nonconforming rivets in an aircraft wing or fuselage.
2. *c* is the number of breakdowns at weak spots in insulation in a given length of insulated wire subjected to a specified test voltage.
3. *c* is the number of surface imperfections observed in a galvanized sheet or a painted, plated, or enameled surface of a given area.
4. *c* is the number of "seeds" (small air pockets) observed in a glass bottle.
5. *c* is the number of imperfections observed in a bolt of cloth.
6. *c* is the number of surface imperfections observed in a roll of coated paper or a sheet of photographic film.

Limits on Control Charts for c

The standard deviation of the Poisson is $\sqrt{c'}$ (see Chap. 6). Thus 3-sigma limits on a c chart are as follows:

$$UCL = c' + 3\sqrt{c'}$$
$$LCL = c' - 3\sqrt{c'}$$

When a standard value of average number of nonconformities per unit, c'_o, is not used, c' may be estimated as equal to the observed average $\bar{c}$. This is always done in the calculation of trial control limits. In this case the control limits are

$$UCL = \bar{c} + 3\sqrt{\bar{c}}$$
$$LCL = \bar{c} - 3\sqrt{\bar{c}}$$

As the Poisson is not a symmetrical distribution, the upper and lower 3-sigma limits do not correspond to equal probabilities of a point on the control chart falling outside limits even though there has been no change in the universe. This fact has sometimes been advanced as a reason for the use of probability limits on c charts. The use of 0.995 and 0.005 probability limits has been favored.†

The position of limits corresponding either to these probabilities or to any other desired probabilities may readily be determined either from Fig. 6-3 or from Table G in App. 3. The use of this figure and this table is explained in Chap. 6.

The theoretical conditions for the applicability of the Poisson distribution call for the count of the number of occurrences of an event that has an infinite number of opportunities to occur and a very small constant probability of occurrence at each opportunity. (For practical purposes, "infinite" may be interpreted as meaning very large.) As already emphasized, the area of opportunity for occurrence at each count of occurrences must remain constant. However, as we have noted, the count may be of the occurrence of all of several different events, each with its own very large number of opportunities to occur and each with a different small probability of occurrence at every opportunity.

In a large proportion of the applications of the Poisson to industrial quality control (or, for that matter, to all other practical affairs), it is possible to pick minor flaws in the theoretical applicability of the Poisson to the actual situation. It may be evident that the number of opportunities for the occurrence of a nonconformity (or other event being counted) falls far short of being infinite. Or it may be clear that the unknown probability of occurrence of a nonconformity is

---

† A diagram on logarithmic paper giving these limits is shown in "Control Chart Method of Controlling Quality During Production, American Standard Z1.3–1958," p. 16, American Standards Association, New York, 1958. In August, 1966, the name of the American Standards Association was changed to USA Standards Institute. In turn, this was changed to American National Standards Institute (ANSI) in October, 1969. Index identification numbers of these standards were not changed. This standard was reaffirmed by ANSI in 1975. Another diagram which shows these limits on rectangular coordinate paper is given in L. E. SIMON, "An Engineers' Manual of Statistical Methods," p. 73, John Wiley & Sons, Inc., New York, 1941.

not quite constant. Or it may not be possible to keep the area of opportunity exactly constant. As long as these are only minor failures to meet the exact conditions of applicability, the results obtained by assuming that the Poisson is applicable are likely to be good enough for practical purposes.

Slight departures of the actual distribution from the true Poisson usually will cause the standard deviation to be slightly greater than $\sqrt{\bar{c}}$. Limits based on $3\sqrt{\bar{c}}$ may really be at a little less than 3-sigma. This fact in itself generally does not justify discarding $3\sqrt{\bar{c}}$ or $3\sqrt{c'_o}$ as a basis for calculating limits. In some situations to which the c chart is applied, such as records of numbers of nonconformities observed in inspections of complex assemblies, this use of limits a little tighter than 3-sigma may actually be desirable. As pointed out in Chap. 3, the economic basis of any control-chart limits is experience that the procedures used for their computation strike a satisfactory balance between the costs of two kinds of errors, namely, looking for assignable causes when they are really absent, and not looking for them when they are really present.

In general, the c chart limits used in this book are based on $3\sqrt{\bar{c}}$ or $3\sqrt{c'_o}$.

Example 8-1 Control chart for nonconformities *Facts of the case* Table 8-1 gives the numbers of errors of alignment observed at final inspection of a certain model of airplane. Figure 8-1 gives the control chart for these 50 observations. The alignment errors observed on each airplane constitute one subgroup for this chart.

The total number of alignment errors in the first 25 ships was 200. The average $\bar{c}$ is 200/25 = 8.0. Trial control limits computed from this average are as follows:

$$UCL = \bar{c} + 3\sqrt{\bar{c}} = 8 + 3\sqrt{8} = 16.5$$

$$LCL = \bar{c} - 3\sqrt{\bar{c}} = 8 - 3\sqrt{8} = \text{negative, therefore no } LCL$$

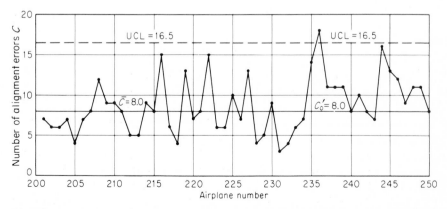

Figure 8-1 Control chart for nonconformities, c. Data on aircraft alignment errors observed at final inspection.

Table 8-1 Aircraft alignment errors observed at final inspection

Airplane number	Number of align-ment errors	Airplane number	Number of align-ment errors
201	7	226	7
202	6	227	13
203	6	228	4
204	7	229	5
205	4	230	9
206	7	231	3
207	8	232	4
208	12	233	6
209	9	234	7
210	9	235	14
211	8	236	18
212	5	237	11
213	5	238	11
214	9	239	11
215	8	240	8
216	15	241	10
217	6	242	8
218	4	243	7
219	13	244	16
220	7	245	13
221	8	246	12
222	15	247	9
223	6	248	11
224	6	249	11
225	10	250	8
Total.........	200	Total.........	236

Whenever calculations give a negative value of the lower control limit of a control chart for attributes, no lower control limit is used. In effect, the chart will exhibit only an upper control limit.

As none of the first 25 points on this chart is outside the trial control limits based on these points, the standard number of defects c_o' may be taken as equal to $\bar{c}$ and the control chart continued for the following period with a central line of 8.0 and an upper control limit of 16.5.

One point (airplane No. 236) out of the next 25 is above the upper control limit. The average during this period was $236/25 = 9.44$. (Even omitting the out-of-control value, the average is 9.08.) Of the final 16 points corresponding to airplanes 235 to 250, 12 are above the standard c_o', 3 are exactly at the standard, and only one is below. It seems evident that there has been a slight but definite deterioration in quality (or increase in the strictness of inspection) during this period.

Comment on Example 8-1

In a case such as this, the previously established standard value of c_o' should nearly always be continued despite the evidence of quality deterioration. The principle stated in the preceding chapter regarding the p chart also applies to the c chart, namely, that the standard value should not be revised in the direction of poorer quality merely because production personnel seem to be giving less attention to quality. On the other hand, if a definite tightening up of inspection standards had the effect of making quality *seem* poorer, even though it was really no worse than before, an upward revision of c_o' might be justified.

Many of the comments and suggestions relative to the p chart on pages 233 to 248 obviously apply also to the c chart and do not need to be repeated here. It should be emphasized that extreme runs should be looked for in the c chart, just as in the other control charts. Other significant patterns in the data should also be noted.

The Combination of Poisson Distributions

In discussing the setting of control limits, it was stated that small departures of the actual distribution from the true Poisson usually will cause the standard deviation to be slightly greater than $\sqrt{\bar{c}}$. This departure from theoretical justification exists in all applications in which mixtures of inspection units each with different areas of opportunity for nonconformities are included. The effect of this departure is discussed in the following paragraphs.

Assume that the average number of surface imperfections observed in a piece of enameled ware of a certain size is 0.5 and that the frequency of these imperfections follows the Poisson law. If 1,000 such pieces are examined, the expected frequencies of the various numbers of imperfections may be determined from Table G, App. 3, to be as follows:

Number of Imperfections	Frequency in 1,000 Observations
0	607
1	303
2	76
3	12
4	2
Total...............	1,000

Now assume that the average number of surface imperfections is 1.5 in another piece of enameled ware having three times the area of the first. The expected frequencies of various numbers of imperfections in 1,000 pieces are as follows:

Number of Imperfections	Frequency in 1,000 Observations
0	223
1	335
2	251
3	125
4	47
5	15
6	3
7	1
Total...............	1,000

Suppose that these two pieces of enameled ware pass the same inspection station and that the results of the inspection are recorded with no identification of whether the imperfections were observed on the small or the large pieces. If 1,000 pieces of each size pass the station, the expected frequencies in the total of 2,000 will be the sum of the two frequency distributions just given. The average number of surface imperfections per observed piece will of course be 1.0, the average of 0.5 and 1.5.

However, this combined distribution will not follow the Poisson law. This may be demonstrated by comparing it with the expected frequency distribution of 2,000 observations on a quality characteristic which does follow the Poisson law and which has an average value $\bar{c}$ of 1.0. Clearly, if the standard deviation of the mixed distribution is calculated from the data in the second column, the result will be numerically greater that the same calculation made from the data of the third column.

Number of imperfections	Expected frequencies in 2,000 observations	
	1,000 observations with $\bar{c} = 0.5$ and 1,000 observations with $\bar{c} = 1.5$	2,000 observations with $\bar{c} = 1.0$
0	830	736
1	638	736
2	327	368
3	137	122
4	49	30
5	15	6
6	3	2
7	1	0
Totals......	2,000	2,000

On the other hand, assume that one small and one large piece of enameled ware are fastened together in an assembly. If many such assemblies are made and inspected for surface imperfections, the average number of imperfections per assembly will, of course, be $0.5 + 1.5 = 2.0$. If the pairing of the small and large pieces is done at random, the frequency distribution of the number of imperfections in the assemblies will follow the Poisson law. (This statement can be proved mathematically. However, no simple demonstration of it is given here, similar to the demonstration just given that the sum of two Poisson distributions having different averages is not a Poisson.)

These two illustrations show one kind of combination of Poisson distributions that *does not* yield a Poisson distribution, and another combination of Poisson distributions that *does*. In the first case, two products, for which the area of opportunity for a nonconformity was different, passed the same inspection station. This situation is analogous to merging the output of two production lines prior to inspection. The average that may be expected to result from the combination is the *weighted average* of the two processes. That is:

$$c'_{comb} = \frac{n_1 c'_1 + n_2 c'_2}{n_1 + n_2} = \frac{1,000(0.05) + 1,000(1.5)}{1,000 + 1,000} = 1.0$$

The result is a distribution that *does not* follow the Poisson law and *does not* have a standard deviation equal to that for the Poisson where $c' = 1.0$.

In the second case, where assembly is assumed to take place at random, the resulting combination forms what is called a *linear combination* of random variables each of which follows the same law. This situation may be explained by first considering the drawing of a unit from Part 1, one of the smaller dishes, for example. This dish has d_1 imperfections. We can *expect* that, upon drawing a dish at random from Part 2, the larger dish, and assembling it with the dish selected from Part 1, the combination will have $d_1 + c'_2$ total imperfections. Expanding this concept to cover all random assemblies of Part 1 and Part 2, any assembly at random may be *expected* to have $c'_1 + c'_2$ total imperfections. By definition, this type of combination is called a *linear combination* where

$$c'_{comb} = c'_1 + c'_2 = 0.5 + 1.5 = 2.0$$

and will be Poisson distributed with a standard deviation equal to $\sqrt{c'_{comb}}$ if the parts that make up the assembly are Poisson distributed. Problem 8-2 at the end of this chapter demonstrates the theory just discussed.

Because the control chart for c uses limits based on the Poisson, the preceding remarks on various ways of combining Poisson distributions have a bearing on industrial quality control. They indicate that if Poisson limits are to be used, care should be taken to keep approximately constant the area of opportunity for the occurrence of a nonconformity. However, the c chart need not be restricted to a single type of nonconformity but may be used for the total of many different kinds of nonconformities observed on any unit. This adds another field of usefulness to those listed already, namely, a count of the total number of nonconformities of all types in complex assemblies such as tractor subassemblies, radio receiving sets, sewing machines, etc.

Conditions Favorable to the Economic Use of the Control Chart for Nonconformities

The c chart has been used to advantage in four different types of situation, as follows:

1. It has been applied to a count of nonconformities all of which must be eliminated following 100% inspection. In this use, the c chart is primarily an instrument for reducing cost of rework incident to correcting the nonconformities and to a lesser extent for reducing costs of inspection incident to identifying the nonconformities. The chart serves to keep management and production supervisors informed about the current quality level, indicates whether or not the process appears to be in control, and serves as a basis for executive pressure to improve the general quality level and to eliminate out-of-control points. The c chart applied in this way sometimes calls attention to the lack of definite inspection standards or to irregularities in the application of inspection standards. A typical example of this kind of use of the c chart is its application to nonconformities of all types observed in inspection of subassemblies and final assemblies of many complex products.
2. Where a certain number of nonconformities per unit are tolerable, even though it is desired to hold their number to a minimum, the c chart may be applied to periodic samples of production. Here the chief objective is the improvement of the quality of outgoing product, leading possibly to fewer rejections by customers' inspection and to a generally better consumer acceptance of the product. Like the application to 100% inspection, this use of the c chart gives management up-to-date information on the quality level and helps to increase uniformity of product by putting pressure on out-of-control points. A typical example of this kind of use is found in a paper mill in which a sample consisting of one roll of coated paper per shift is carefully examined for surface defects.
3. It has been applied for special short studies of the variation of quality of a particular product or manufacturing operation.
4. It has been applied to sampling acceptance procedures based on defects (i.e., nonconformities) per unit. This application is referred to in Chap. 14.

Adaptations of the c Chart to Variations in the Area of Opportunity for a Nonconformity

The quantity c is the number of nonconformities observed in some specified inspection. Often this inspection is of a single unit of product, such as an airplane, a radio set, a coil of wire, or a roll of coated paper. In this common case where the subgroup size is unity, c is both the number of nonconformities and the number of nonconformities per unit. As already explained, the units should be alike in size and in the apparent likelihood of the existence of a nonconformity, in order that the area of opportunity for a nonconformity be constant from unit to unit.

However, it is not really necessary that the subgroup be a single unit of product. The unit for control-chart purposes (i.e., the subgroup) may be 10 product units, or 100, or any convenient other number. Total nonconformities for each subgroup may be plotted just as if the subgroup were a single unit of product. Control charts for c using a fixed multiple of units are frequently used when the probability of a nonconformity is so small that a single unit of product is likely to have no nonconformities. As long as the number of product units does not change from subgroup to subgroup and each unit is essentially indentical to all others, no special problem is created.

Whenever there is an evident change in the area of opportunity for occurrence of a nonconformity from subgroup to subgroup, the conventional c chart showing only total number of nonconformities is not applicable. It is necessary to create some standard measure of the area of opportunity. For example, if a number of units constitute a subgroup of size n, where n varies from subgroup to subgroup, defects per unit (c/n) may be an appropriate control statistic. In such cases, if total defects observed in each subgroup were plotted, the central line on the chart as well as the control limits would have to change from one subgroup to another. This would make the chart confusing and hard to interpret.

The symbol u is used to represent nonconformities per unit c/n where c is the count of nonconformities found and n may be number of items, or whatever standard is used to establish the constant area of opportunity for the occurrence of a nonconformity. The central line on the u chart will be u' with standard 3-sigma limits of:

$$UCL = u' + \frac{3\sqrt{u'}}{\sqrt{n}}$$

$$LCL = u' - \frac{3\sqrt{u'}}{\sqrt{n}}$$

Control limit lines on such a chart will vary with subgroup size, just as they do on the $\bar{X}$ chart and the p chart. When a standard value of u is to be used, u'_o is substituted for u' into the previous equations. When the average value $\bar{u}$ from a series of subgroups is to be used for trial control limits to test for a constant chance cause system and estimate u', $\bar{u}$ is found from:

$$\bar{u} = \frac{\Sigma c}{\Sigma n} = \frac{\text{total nonconformities found}}{\text{total units inspected}}$$

and the trial control limits are:

$$UCL = \bar{u} + \frac{3\sqrt{\bar{u}}}{\sqrt{n}}$$

$$LCL = \bar{u} - \frac{3\sqrt{\bar{u}}}{\sqrt{n}}$$

It should be noted that the statistic u does not follow the Poisson distribution.† However, the statistic nu does. Thus probabilities may be associated with specific points falling within or outside control limits using Table G in App. 3 and using the values of n for the individual subgroups.

Example 8-2 illustrates the calculations required for this adaptation of the chart for nonconformities.

Example 8-2 A control chart for nonconformities per unit with variable subgroup size *Facts of the case* This is an application to nonconformities observed in aircraft subassembly. The problem of the variable subgroup size was created by the difference in the number of employees on the three shifts. These were roughly in the ratio of 3 on the day shift to 2 on the swing and 1 on the graveyard shift. The number of units assembled in each production center varied from shift to shift in something like this proportion and also showed some variation from day to day.

Table 8-2 gives the record of the number of nonconformities (which, in this aircraft plant, were picturesquely described as *squawks*) recorded by the inspection department for each shift in one production center for a period of 8 days. The number of units produced is also given. In order to measure this production on each shift, the establishment of a system of weighting different assembly operations was required. For example, if one production center carried out operations 251, 252, and 253, it might happen that on one day, because of the irregular flow of parts to the department, the day shift would work chiefly on operations 251 and 252; the swing shift might concentrate on 253. On another day, this might be reversed. By giving each operation an appropriate weighting factor, the actual production on the different operations may be converted to an equivalent number of production units, as follows:

Assembly operation number	Weighting factor	Production on assembly operation	Equivalent units produced on shift
251	0.45	6	2.7
252	0.30	8	2.4
253	0.25	4	1.0
	1.00	...	6.1

---

† In Chap. 6 it was shown that the statistic c was Poisson distributed with mean equal to c' and standard deviation equal to the square-root of the mean, $\sqrt{c'}$. It therefore follows that since the standard deviation of u is equal to $\sqrt{u'}/\sqrt{n}$, the square-root of its mean divided by $\sqrt{n}$, u cannot be Poisson distributed.

Table 8-2 Computation of control-chart limits for data on nonconformities observed on aircraft subassemblies

Standard value of nonconformities per unit u'_o is 3.2

Date	Shift	Non-conformities observed on shift c	Units produced n	Non-conformities per unit u	$3\sigma = \dfrac{3\sqrt{u'_o}}{\sqrt{n}}$	$UCL = u'_o + 3\sigma$	$LCL = u'_o - 3\sigma$
June 9	D	13	6.0	2.2	2.2	5.4	1.0
	S	12	4.3	2.8	2.6	5.8	0.6
	G	7	2.9	2.4	3.2	6.4	0.0
11	D	19	5.5	3.5	2.3	5.5	0.9
	S	14	4.4	3.2	2.6	5.8	0.6
	G	9	2.0	4.5	3.8	7.0	0.0
12	D	18	5.5	3.3	2.3	5.5	0.9
	S	13	4.0	3.2	2.7	5.9	0.5
	G	6	2.0	3.0	3.8	7.0	0.0
13	D	24	6.1	3.9	2.2	5.4	1.0
	S	15	4.9	3.1	2.4	5.6	0.8
	G	6	2.9	2.1	3.2	6.4	0.0
14	D	16	6.6	2.4	2.1	5.3	1.1
	S	11	4.1	2.7	2.7	5.9	0.5
	G	20	2.5	8.0	3.4	6.6	0.0
15	D	16	4.3	3.7	2.6	5.8	0.6
	S	29	4.2	6.9	2.6	5.8	0.6
	G	3	2.2	1.4	3.6	6.8	0.0
16	D	21	6.1	3.4	2.2	5.4	1.0
	S	20	4.2	4.8	2.6	5.8	0.6
	G	2	1.8	1.1	4.0	7.2	0.0
17	D	14	2.9	4.8	3.2	6.4	0.0
	S	10	1.9	5.3	3.9	7.1	0.0
	G	3	1.0	3.0	5.4	8.6	0.0
Totals		321	92.3				

That is, these operations actually carried out on the shift are judged to be equivalent to carrying out all three of the required assembly operations on 6.1 airplanes.

In Table 8-2, c, the total nonconformities observed on each shift, is divided by n, the number of equivalent units produced, to get nonconformities per unit, u. In plotting the value of u on the control chart (Fig. 8-2), a different symbol is used for each shift. The standard value of nonconformities per unit u'_o of 3.2 was established by past performance; this is used as the central line on the control chart. Table 8-2 shows the calculation of the upper and lower control limits for each subgroup.

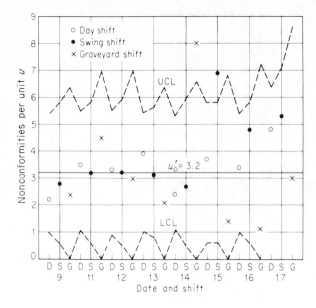

Figure 8-2 Adaption of c chart to variable subgroup size—data of Table 8-2.

Comment on Example 8-2

The comparison in one chart of the performance of the three shifts may improve the general quality level by stimulating competition among the shifts. Moreover, if one shift is out of line with the others, such a chart will make this fact quickly evident to management.

If no consideration had been given to the advantages of combining the shifts on one chart and separate charts had been kept for each shift, the slight variations in subgroup size within each shift from day to day might have been neglected. Each chart might then have been a conventional c chart showing number of nonconformities and having constant limits. Or, if it were desired to express quality in terms of nonconformities per unit, constant limits might have been plotted based on average subgroup size.

The points in Fig. 8-2 have not been connected. If they were to be connected, it would be better to draw separate lines for each shift rather than a single line connecting all the points. If the symbols used for the three shifts differ enough from one another, the chart is more easily read if the points are not connected. A good plan is to use a different color for each shift.

This is one of the many cases where, even though the strict applicability of the Poisson distribution might be questioned by a statistical theorist, the limits based on the Poisson are good enough for practical purposes. The Poisson might be questioned because the equivalent production units depend on the weighting factors adopted for the various assembly operations. Ideally, the weighting factors should be chosen in a way to be proportional to the relative frequency of nonconformities in each of the assembly operations being weighted. Actual weighting, based on some such factor as standard direct labor hours for each operation, may measure this well enough in most instances unless certain of the assembly operations are much more difficult than others.

Probability Limits for c and u Charts

Table G in App. 3 may be used to find control chart limits for c and u charts based on probability limits. For example, the standard value used in Example 8-1 was $c_o' = 8.0$. Entering Table G at a c' of 8.0, the following cumulative probabilities are obtained for pertinent values of c:

c	Probability
1	0.003
2	0.014
15	0.992
16	0.996

If symmetrical 0.995 and 0.005 upper and lower control limits are desired, then the finding of 0 or 1 nonconformities should result in a point below the lower control limit; likewise, the finding of 16 or more nonconformities should result in a point above the upper control limit. Finding from 2 to 15 nonconformities should result in a point within the control limits. A convenient setting of these limits would be:

$$UCL_c = 15.5$$

$$LCL_c = 1.5$$

In setting noninteger limits, there can be no confusion as to whether a point plot lies within or outside the limits.

Two observations should be made about the calculation of these probability limits. First, they are not 0.995 and 0.005 symmetrical probability limits. They are 0.992 and 0.003 probability limits. Interpolation between $c = 15$ and $c = 16$ and again between $c = 1$ and $c = 2$ will not make them symmetrical because the count of nonconformities is integer-valued. If c' is relatively small, it is possible to come close to the desired probabilities, but it is not possible to obtain them exactly.

The second observation is that these limits are different from those found in Example 8-1; in this case, narrower. Thus use of these limits will not always lead to the same conclusions about statistical control or the same estimates of c'.

Table G may also be used to find probability limits for the u chart in Example 8-2. Suppose approximate 0.995 and 0.005 probability limits are desired. As previously explained, u' is not Poisson distributed but nu' is. Thus, for the G shift on June 11, $nu' = (2.0 \times 3.2) = 6.4$ and from Table G we can read:

c	Probability
0	0.002
1	0.012
13	0.994
14	0.997

Appropriate control limits are:

$$UCL_u = 13.5/2.0 = 6.75$$

$$LCL_u = 0.5/2.0 = 0.25$$

The same general comments may be made about the results of this application of probability limits as were made about the c chart application. The probabilities associated with points out of control are not exactly those desired and they are not exactly symmetrical.

The u Chart for Nonconformities per Multiple Units

An adaptation of the u chart useful in clerical as well as industrial application is the ku chart for nonconformities per multiple production units. An example of this type of chart involves counts of mistakes made per 100 manhours worked. Where nonconformities (or mistakes) are very infrequent and the count of units produced is very large, it is necessary to scale the data if useful charts are to be prepared. The control statistic may be defined:

$$ku = \frac{c}{n/k} = \frac{\text{no. of nonconformities}}{\text{no. of units/scaling factor}}$$

where k is the scaling factor; for example, 100 manhours where n is the total manhours in the subgroup.

The formulas for control limits are:

$$UCL = ku' + 3\sqrt{\frac{ku'}{n/k}}$$

$$LCL = ku' - 3\sqrt{\frac{ku'}{n/k}}$$

A standard value u_o' or and average value $\bar{u}$ developed from sampling may be substituted as appropriate for u' in the above formulas.

For a process with a standard value of 4 mistakes per 100 manhours worked, a subgroup of 250 manhours would have control limits of:

$$UCL = 4 + 3\sqrt{\frac{4}{250/100}} = 7.79$$

$$LCL = 4 - 3\sqrt{\frac{4}{250/100}} = 0.21$$

Listing Individual Nonconformities on the Form
Containing a c or u Chart

If not too many different types of nonconformities are possible, it sometimes is a good idea to combine a c or u chart with a record of the number of nonconformities observed of each type. Figure 8-3 is such a chart. It will be noted that, although this is a u chart, the sample size, 10, is constant. This chart, applicable to sewing machine cabinet covers, is reproduced from an article by Robert Chateaneuf of The Singer Manufacturing Co., St. John's, Quebec, Canada.†

The Introduction of a Control Chart May Motivate Quality Improvement

Incidentally, Fig. 8-3 illustrates a common occurrence when a chart for p, np, c, or u is first applied to a product. This occurrence is a substantial improvement in the average quality level with this improvement unrelated to any actions taken on points outside the control limits. Such an improvement usually is caused by factory personnel taking an increased interest in the quality characteristics being charted. Sometimes this type of improvement, unrelated to statistical techniques, is the most useful consequence of the introduction of a control chart.

It will be observed that, although neither section of Fig. 8-3 shows any points outside control limits, the average number of defects per unit in the second section of the chart is less than one-third of the average number shown in the first section some 15 months earlier. The author states that this improvement was secured "through better handling, a greater desire to produce quality, and a superior polishing operation."

Adaptation of the c Chart to Quality Rating

Some defects (i.e., nonconformities) are more serious than others. In an overall picture of quality by departments to be presented to management, there may be an advantage in weighting defects according to some scale that measures their seriousness. Such a plan has been in use for many years in the Bell Telephone System. The classes of defects used are described by H. F. Dodge, as follows:‡

> *Class "A" Defects*—Very serious.
>> Will render unit totally unfit for service.
>> Will surely cause operating failure of the unit in service which cannot be readily corrected on the job, e.g., open induction coil, transmitter without carbon, etc.
>> Liable to cause personal injury or property damage.

---

† ROBERT CHATEANEUF, Modern QC Pays Off in Woodwork, *Industrial Quality Control*, vol. 17, no. 3, pp. 19–25, September, 1960.

‡ H. F. DODGE, A Method of Rating Manufactured Product, *The Bell System Technical Journal*, vol. 7, pp. 350–368, April, 1928. This article, which has been reprinted as Bell Telephone Laboratories Reprint B-315, gives clear detailed directions for the use of such a plan based on demerits per unit.

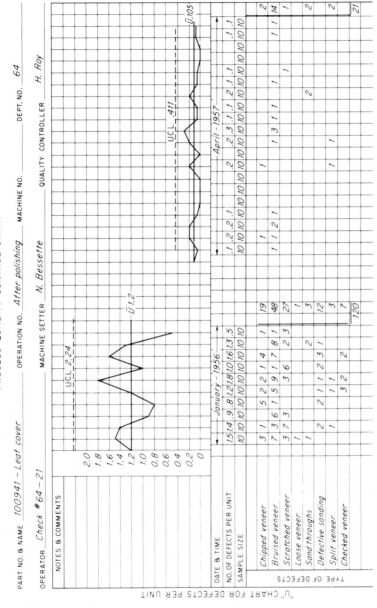

Figure 8-3 Example of u chart showing numbers of blemishes of various types on sewing machine cabinet covers. (*Reproduced from Robert Chateauneuf, "Modern QC Pays Off in Woodwork," Industrial Quality Control, vol. 17, no. 3, pp. 19–25, September, 1960.*)

270

Class "B" Defects—Serious.

Will probably, but not surely, cause Class *A* operating failure of the unit in service.

Will surely cause trouble of a nature less serious than Class *A* operating failure, e.g., adjustment failure, operation below standard, etc.

Will surely cause increased maintenance or decreased life.

Class "C" Defects—Moderately serious.

Will possibly cause operating failure of the unit in service.

Likely to cause trouble of a nature less serious than operating failure.

Likely to cause increased maintenance or decreased life.

Major defects of appearance, finish, or workmanship.

Class "D" Defects—Not serious.

Will not cause operating failure of the unit in service.

Minor defects of appearance, finish, or workmanship.

Once such a classification of all defects is established, demerits may then be assigned to each class of defect. Control charts may be plotted for demerits per unit rather than for defects per unit. The reader is referred to Dodge's paper cited in the footnote on page 269 for the details of this variation of the *c* chart.†

Quality rating schemes based on demerits per unit may be an important feature of both vendor rating and quality audit procedures.

Use of $3\sqrt{c'}$ for Approximate Calculation of Control Limits in Situations Involving the Binomial Distribution

It often happens that a quick calculation of control limits is useful in some situation where no actual control chart has been plotted. If this is needed in any case to which the binomial is applicable as a probability distribution, it is handy to remember that the standard deviation of the Poisson $\sqrt{c'}$ is an approximation to $\sqrt{np'(1-p')}$. Even though the binomial itself is only an approximation to the correct probability obtainable by the use of combinatorial formulas, $3\sqrt{c'}$ often provides a basis for rapid mental arithmetic about control limits that may be good enough for practical purposes.

For example, assume that product submitted under a purchase contract has been 0.4% nonconforming. The question is raised as to what variation in number of nonconforming items may be expected in lots of 1,000. The expected average number of such items in such lots is obviously 4. As $3\sqrt{4} = 6$, the answer is that nonconforming items might generally be expected to fall between 0 and 10 in lots of 1,000. The occurrence of 11 or more nonconforming items in such a lot would be evidence of an assignable cause of variation.

---

† See also the following:

H. F. DODGE and M. N. TORREY, A Check Inspection and Demerit Weighting Plan, *Industrial Quality Control*, vol. 13, no. 1, pp. 5–12, July, 1956, and reprinted in *Journal of Quality Technology*, vol. 9, no. 3, July, 1977. This article states the demerit weights, used since the early 1930s, as Class *A*—100, Class *B*—50, Class *C*—10, and Class *D*—1.

D. A. HILL, Control of Complicated Products, *Industrial Quality Control*, vol. 8, no. 4, pp. 18–22, January, 1952.

Applicability of c Chart Technique in Fields Other than Industrial Quality Control

Like all control charts, the c chart gives evidence regarding the quality level, its variability, and the presence or absence of assignable causes of variation. This is useful information as a basis for action in many other fields besides industrial quality control. The universal nature of the Poisson distribution as the law of small numbers makes the c chart technique broadly useful.

For example, it may be applied to such diverse phenomena as clerical errors, industrial accidents, and highway accidents. In all these fields, action should often be based on evidence of assignable causes of variation, and it is important to note changes in the average value of the variable being studied. A discussion of such nonproduct applications of the c chart is included in Chap. 21.

PROBLEMS

8-1 The following table gives the numbers of missing rivets noted at aircraft final inspection:

Airplane number	Number of missing rivets	Airplane number	Number of missing rivets	Airplane number	Number of missing rivets
201	8	210	12	218	14
202	16	211	23	219	11
203	14	212	16	220	9
204	19	213	9	221	10
205	11	214	25	222	22
206	15	215	15	223	7
207	8	216	9	224	28
208	11	217	9	225	9
209	21				

Find $\bar{c}$, compute trial control limits, and plot a control chart for c. What value of c'_o would you suggest for the subsequent period?

Answer: $UCL_c = 25.28$ (25.5); $LCL_c = 2.80$ $(2.5.)$; $c'_o = 12.96$

8-2 Page 260 gives the expected frequencies in 2,000 observations, 1,000 of which came from a Poisson distribution with $\bar{c} = 0.5$ and 1,000 from a Poisson distribution with $\bar{c} = 1.5$. Find the standard deviation of this distribution.

The $\bar{c}$ of this combined distribution is, of course, 1.0. Assume that a c chart is established with the upper control limit at $3\sqrt{\bar{c}}$ above the central line on the chart. Consult the table on page 260 to see how many of the 2,000 observations would fall above this upper limit. What objections can you see to the use of a single control chart in this type of situation?

8-3 Use Table G, App. 3, to find 0.995 and 0.005 probability limits for a c chart when $c' = 5.8$. Also when $c' = 12.0$.

Answer: 12.5, 0.1; 21.3, 3.5.

8-4 Use Table G, App. 3, to find 0.95 and 0.05 probability limits for a c chart when $c' = 4.2$. Also when $c' = 9.5$.

    Answer: 7.4, 0.6; 14.4, 4.2.

8-5 A control chart for nonconformities per unit u uses probability limits corresponding to probabilities of 0.975 and 0.025. The central line on the control chart is at $u' = 2.0$. The limits vary with the value of n. Determine the correct position of these upper and lower control limits when $n = 5$.

    Answer: 3.30, 0.70.

8-6 A c chart is used to monitor the number of surface imperfections on sheets of photographic film. The chart presently is set up based on a $\bar{c}$ of 2.6.

    (*a*) Find 3σ control limits for this process.

    (*b*) Use Table G to determine the probability that a point will fall outside these control limits while the process is actually operating at a c' of 2.6.

    (*c*) If the process average shifts to 4.8, what is the probability of not detecting the shift on the first sample taken after the shift occurs?

8-7 Solve Problem 8-6 using 0.01 and 0.99 probability limits rather than 3σ limits. What is the actual probability of a Type I error in this case as opposed to the planned probability 0.02?

8-8 Explain the difference in the results obtained in Problem 8-6 and 8-7.

8-9 A c chart is used to monitor surface imperfections on porcelain enameled water heater cabinets. Each cabinet is checked for nonconformities of a certain grade and the count entered on the c chart. Two limits are used on the chart; a control limit at $+3\sigma$ and a warning limit at $+2\sigma$. If a point falls above the control limit or two points in a row fall between the warning limit and the control limit, the process is stopped until the problem is corrected. The central line is set at an aimed-at value of c'_o of 2.5.

    (*a*) Find the values of the warning limit and the control limit.

    (*b*) If the process suddenly shifts to a mean value of 5, what is the probability that a point will fall above the control limit?

    (*c*) Under the circumstance described in part (*b*), what is the probability that two points in a row will fall between the warning limit and the control limit?

    (*d*) What is the combined probability of detection of this shift within the first two units inspected after the shift occurs?

8-10 A textile manufacturer initiates use of a c chart to monitor the number of imperfections found in bolts of cloth. Each bolt is the same length, width, weave, and fiber composition. A total of 191 imperfections were found in the last 25 bolts inspected. The four highest and lowest counts were:

Count of imperfections	
Highest	Lowest
22	4
19	4
14	5
12	5

    (*a*) Calculate 3σ control limits for this process.

    (*b*) Is this process in control? If not, what aimed-at values of c'_o and control limits would you recommend for the next period?

8-11 (*a*) Solve Problem 8-10 using 0.025 and 0.975 probability limits rather than 3σ limits (Table G).

    (*b*) Explain the difference in the conclusions arrived at in part (*a*) and those arrived at in Problem 8-10.

8-12 Both 3σ control limits and 2σ warning limits are used on a c chart. The decision rules state that an out-of-control condition will be declared if: (1) one point falls outside a 3σ limit; or (2) two points in succession fall between a given set of warning and control limits (e.g., between $+2\sigma$ and $+3\sigma$). The aimed-at value of c_o' is 15.

(a) Calculate the warning and control limits.

(b) If the process mean suddenly shifts downward to a c' of 8.0, what is the probability that the next value of c plotted will fall below the lower control limit?

(c) In the circumstances described in part (b), what is the probability that the next two values of c will fall between the lower warning and control limits?

(d) What is the combined probability that the shift described in part (b), will be detected within the next two samples?

8-13 A u chart is to be used to control a corrugated paper product line. End product is produced in rolls of varying length 48 inches wide. Nonconformities include surface imperfections, improper gluing, improper tension setting on the corrugated inner core, etc. The control statistic is nonconformities per 100 ft with one roll constituting a sample. After 20 rolls have been inspected, the total count of nonconformities is 340 in a total of 9,300 ft. inspected.

(a) Find the value of $\bar{u}$ in nonconformities per 100 ft.

(b) Set up the formulas for 3σ control limits and reduce them to the most convenient form for calculating specific limits.

(c) Find the control limits for the following three representative samples and determine if the points are in control.

Length of roll (ft)	Count of nonconformities
250	7
500	34
150	11

8-14 The hydraulic shop of a large aircraft maintenance facility maintains control charts on maintenance workers based on maintenance errors per standard manhour required to refurbish hydraulic parts. Since assemblies of many sizes and degrees of complexity flow through the shop, no other measure of quality performance seems feasible. A chart is maintained on each worker based on a random sampling of five items daily. The inspector records the item description code, the worker code, number and type code for errors found, and the standard manhours required to refurbish the assembly. Each day the statistic d/n is plotted on the worker's control chart where d is the number of errors found in 5 assemblies and n is the total manhours required for the 5 assemblies.

(a) After the first 4 weeks of operation, the record for one worker is $\Sigma d = 21$ and $\Sigma n = 54$. Determine the central line and 3σ control limits for this worker's chart. Reduce the calculation to the simplest form for direct calculation of the limits.

(b) On a certain day during the four-week period, $d = 2$ errors and $n = 4.3$ standard manhours. Make the necessary calculations to determine if the point for this day falls within control limits.

8-15 A manufacturer wishes to operate a control chart on nonconformities found per 100 units produced where each point on the chart represents the output of a shop for a day. Production in a certain shop varies from 800 to 1,500 units per day. The average number of nonconformities per 100 units for the past three months is 4.6.

(a) Set up the general formula for 3σ control limits for this process and reduce it to its simplest form.

(b) Calculate the control limits for a day during which 900 units are produced.

(c) Someone suggests that a simpler control chart model could be used. The suggestion is that c be defined as the number of nonconformities found during a given day divided by the number of hundreds of units produced during a day. The average value $\bar{c}$ could then be obtained by averaging the values of c and the model $\bar{c} \pm 3\sqrt{\bar{c}}$ used to calculate control limits. Discuss why this suggestion is inappropriate. Calculate control limits for this model based on an average $\bar{c}$ of 4.6 and compare these results with those found in part (b).

8-16 The manager of a dye plant for 65-35 dacron polyester fabric for the garment industry believes that the plant will lose a most important contract if the rate of dye imperfections exceeds 4 per 100 yards of material more than 2 per cent of the time.

(a) Use Table G to find an aimed-at value of u'_o to be used as a central line for a control chart to monitor this process.

(b) Calculate 3σ control limits for a bolt of material which is 500 yards in length.

8-17 Assume that the centering of the process described in Problem 8-15 shifts from 4.6 nonconformities per 100 units to 7.6.

(a) What is the probability that this shift will be detected on the first subgroup plotted after the shift occurs? Use Table A and assume 900 units were produced on that day.

(b) What would be the probability of detection if 1,500 units had been produced on that day?

(c) Discuss the difference in the results you obtained in parts (a) and (b).

8-18 Solve Problem 8-1 using 0.025 and 0.975 (95%) probability limits rather than 3σ limits. Use Table G to find these control limits. Explain why the conclusion reached in determining a prospective aimed-at value c'_o differs from that reached in Problem 8-1.

8-19 Listed in the following table are the number of bolts of cloth produced on a daily basis in a small textile mill and the corresponding number of imperfections found in these bolts. Use these data to estimate u' and then compute trial control limits for a u chart.

Day	Bolts of cloth produced	Number of imperfections
1	20	27
2	20	23
3	20	30
4	21	28
5	22	29
6	22	31
7	23	37
8	33	29
9	23	36
10	21	27

8-20 Solve Problem 8-19 using 0.025 and 0.975 (95%) probability limits rather than 3σ limits. Derive these limits by the use of Table G.

NINE

SOME SPECIAL
PROCESS CONTROL PROCEDURES

You need not be a mathematical statistician to do good statistical work, but you will need the guidance of a first class mathematical statistician. A good engineer, or a good economist, or a good chemist, already has a good start, because the statistical method is only good science brought up to date by the recognition that all laws are subject to the variations which occur in nature. Your study of statistical methods will not displace any other knowledge that you have; rather, it will extend your knowledge of engineering, chemistry, or economics, and make it more useful.—W. E. Deming†

Some Miscellaneous Topics

This chapter deals with a number of more or less unrelated topics that should be covered in any presentation of statistical methods for process control. Some of these are forms of the Shewhart technique for process control that vary slightly from the simple $\bar{X}$, R, and p charts described in the preceding chapters. Other topics deal with schemes for plotting and analysis which are based on other statistical procedures or were devised with principal objectives other than control of a manufacturing process. The material is divided into eight subtopics in order to emphasize its relationship to other topics presented in this book.

I. SOME SPECIAL TOPICS ON SHEWHART CONTROL CHARTS FOR VARIABLES

Control Charts with Variable Subgroup Size

Wherever possible it is desirable to have a constant subgroup size. If this cannot be done, the limits on both $\bar{X}$ and R charts (or $\bar{X}$ and σ charts) should be variable

---

† W. E. DEMING, "Some Principles of the Shewhart Methods of Quality Control," *Mechanical Engineering*, vol. 66, pp. 173–177, March, 1944.

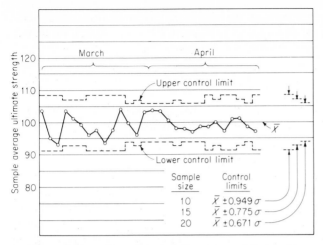

Figure 9-1 $\bar{X}$ chart illustrating variation of control limits with sample size. The variable X is the ultimate strength of suspension insulators.

limits. Such variable limits are illustrated in the $\bar{X}$ chart of Fig. 9-1,† which shows limits corresponding to subgroup sizes of 10, 15, and 20 for ultimate strength of suspension insulators.

Once σ' has been estimated, these limits for various sample sizes may be obtained by using the factors and formulas of Table E, App. 3. Where the data used to estimate σ' include subgroups of various sizes, a satisfactory working rule (although not precisely correct as a matter of statistical theory) is to calculate R/d_2 for each subgroup, using the appropriate d_2 factor from Table B, App. 3, for the size of the subgroup in question. The estimate of σ' is the average of these values of R/d_2. If standard deviation, rather than range, is the measure used for subgroup dispersion, σ/c_2 may be computed for each subgroup; the estimate of σ' is the average value of σ/c_2.

R Charts or σ Charts where $\bar{X}$ Charts are not Appropriate

In some cases subgroups may be comparable in their dispersion even though not comparable in their averages. This is true, for example, of many standard chemical analyses that are made in duplicate, triplicate, or quadruplicate. Each two, three, or four analyses of a given sample may be thought of as a subgroup. If samples having somewhat different chemical content are analyzed, the averages of the subgroups are not comparable. The dispersion of the subgroups, however, reflects the ability of an analyst and an analytical procedure to reproduce results by several similar determinations. The control chart for R or σ provides a basis for

† Reproduced from J. J. TAYLOR, Statistical Methods Applied to Insulator Development and Manufacture, *Transactions, American Institute of Electrical Engineers*, vol. 64, pp. 495–499, July, 1945.

judging whether this dispersion seems to be influenced by a constant-cause system. Calculations for the central lines and control limits for R or σ are no different from such calculations for any other control charts.

$\bar{X}$ and σ Charts with Large Subgroups

It sometimes happens that data are at hand on averages and standard deviations of some measured variable from a number of different sources. It may be desired to apply a test for homogeneity to these figures to see if there is clear evidence that the different sources seem to represent different cause systems. The control charts for $\bar{X}$ and σ constitute a simple test for this purpose.

For example, in a certain manufacturing plant it was desired to compare the strength and uniformity of spot welds made on nine apparently identical machines. A number of specimen welds of sheet aluminum alloy of a certain gage were made on each machine. The ultimate strength of each weld was determined by testing to destruction in a shear testing machine. The averages and standard deviations of the welds from each machine were tabulated in a report summarizing this investigation. They are shown in Table 9-1. Because the investigator was not acquainted with the Shewhart techniques, no record was preserved of the order of production of welds or of order of measurement.

The shear strengths from each machine constitute one rational subgroup. The subgroups are large, ranging from 111 to 128. With such large subgroups, the c_2 factor (see Table B) is practically unity, and the best estimate of σ' (that is, $\bar{\sigma}/c_2$) becomes $\bar{\sigma}$. A_1 therefore becomes $3/\sqrt{n}$, B_4 becomes $1 + (3/\sqrt{2n})$, and B_3 becomes $1 - (3/\sqrt{2n})$. These expressions, stated in Table D, are evident from the explanation of the A_1, B_4, and B_3 factors as given in Chap. 3.

Where the subgroup sizes are different, it may be advisable to use weighted averages for the calculation of $\bar{X}$ and $\bar{\sigma}$. The formulas for these are as follows:

$$\bar{\bar{X}} = \frac{n_1 \bar{X}_1 + n_2 \bar{X}_2 + n_3 \bar{X}_3 + \cdots + n_m \bar{X}_m}{n_1 + n_2 + n_3 + \cdots + n_m}$$

$$\bar{\sigma} = \sqrt{\frac{n_1 \sigma_1^2 + n_2 \sigma_2^2 + n_3 \sigma_3^2 + \cdots + n_m \sigma_m^2}{n_1 + n_2 + n_3 + \cdots + n_m}}$$

However, unless the differences in subgroup size are large, the calculations are simpler and the results are nearly the same if $\bar{X}$ is estimated as the simple unweighted average of the $\bar{X}$ values and $\bar{\sigma}$ is estimated as the simple unweighted average of the σ values. No absolute rule may be given as to when this simplification is satisfactory; a rough rule is to figure unweighted averages unless the largest subgroup is at least twice the smallest. It is clearly satisfactory to compute unweighted averages for the data of Table 9-1. Thus

$$\bar{\bar{X}} = \frac{\bar{X}_1 + \bar{X}_2 + \bar{X}_3 \cdots + \bar{X}_m}{m} = \frac{6{,}435}{9} = 715$$

$$\bar{\sigma} = \frac{\sigma_1 + \sigma_2 + \sigma_3 \cdots + \sigma_m}{m} = \frac{572}{9} = 64$$

Table 9-1 Shear strengths of spot welds made by nine different machines

Machine	Number of tests n	Average shear strength, lb $\bar{X}$	Standard deviation σ
A	128	743	63
B	127	695	47
C	126	711	67
D	114	668	51
E	126	736	80
F	126	791	58
G	126	686	50
H	111	801	92
J	119	604	64
Totals............	1,103	6,435	572

The question now arises whether, because of the different subgroup sizes, different limits should be computed for each subgroup. Again the computations are much simpler if one set of limits is computed based on average subgroup size. This simplification is usually satisfactory for a start; separate limits for individual subgroups may be calculated later for any doubtful cases. The average subgroup size $\bar{n}$ must be computed

$$\bar{n} = \frac{1,103}{9} = 123$$

The factors A_1, B_4, and B_3 may now be computed

$$A_1 = \frac{3}{\sqrt{n}} = \frac{3}{\sqrt{123}} = 0.27$$

$$B_4 = 1 + \frac{3}{\sqrt{2n}} = 1 + \frac{3}{\sqrt{246}} = 1.19$$

$$B_3 = 1 - \frac{3}{\sqrt{2n}} = 1 - \frac{3}{\sqrt{246}} = 0.81$$

From these factors, the control limits may be computed

$$UCL_{\bar{X}} = \bar{\bar{X}} + A_1\bar{\sigma} = 715 + 0.27(64) = 732$$

$$LCL_{\bar{X}} = \bar{\bar{X}} - A_1\bar{\sigma} = 715 - 0.27(64) = 698$$

$$UCL_{\sigma} = B_4\bar{\sigma} = 1.19(64) = 76$$

$$LCL_{\sigma} = B_3\bar{\sigma} = 0.81(64) = 52$$

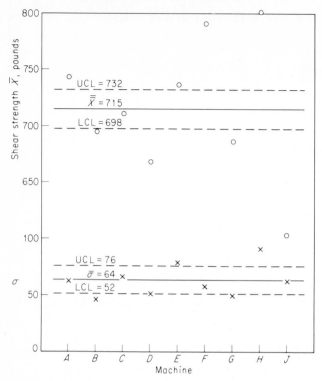

Figure 9-2 $\bar{X}$ and σ control charts for shear strength of spot welds—data of Table 9-1.

These limits are plotted on the control charts of Fig. 9-2. Both charts definitely show lack of control; in fact, only one point falls within the control limits on the $\bar{X}$ chart. It is quite evident that even though these spot-welding machines are identical in their design, they perform differently both with regard to average strength and uniformity of strength of welds.

It should be remarked in passing that a tabulation of averages and standard deviations of large numbers of measurements such as that in Table 9-1 is of little value for prediction without the knowledge that each source of measurements is itself in control. For example, without any evidence of control on machine A, it is not safe to assume that the strength of future spot welds on machine A will fall within limits suggested by the average of 743 lb and the standard deviation of 63 lb. It would have been much better if the order of production had not been lost and the results on each machine had been subjected to the control-chart analysis.

Warning Limits on Control Charts

Some writers on statistical quality control have advocated the use of two sets of limits on $\bar{X}$ charts. The outer limits, sometimes called *action limits*, are the conventional limits, usually at 3-sigma, or—if 0.002 probability limits are used—at 3.09 sigma. The inner limits are recommended as *warning limits* and are usually at 2-sigma, or—if 0.05 probability limits are used—at 1.96 sigma. The use of probability limits is discussed in Sec. IV of this chapter.

On the conventional $\bar{X}$ chart with only one set of limits, the chart seems to give only two kinds of advice. It either says, " Look for trouble," or it says, " Leave the process alone." This has the virtue of definiteness. However, any such definite advice is sure to be wrong part of the time. Limits placed at 3-sigma or 3.09-sigma are seldom wrong when they say, " Look for trouble," but are much oftener wrong when they say, " Leave the process alone."

The inner limits or warning limits seem to add a third kind of advice. This might be phrased, " Start being suspicious that trouble is brewing."

At first thought, the idea of having warning limits on $\bar{X}$ charts may seem attractive. Nevertheless, there is a sound reason for the common practice of having only one set of limits and having these limits at or near 3-sigma. This reason is the greater definiteness of a single set of limits. Two sets of limits tend to be confusing with regard to the exact action to be taken when a point falls between the inner and the outer limits. This is particularly true if many of the people in a manufacturing plant who are using the $\bar{X}$ and R control charts as a basis for action are not fully clear as to the principles underlying these charts. Inner limits will be exceeded at least 5% of the time as a matter of chance. If a single point just outside the inner limits is to be used as a basis for hunting for trouble there is bound to be unproductive hunting which may tend to destroy confidence in the control charts. Usually in a manufacturing plant so much trouble really exists that it does not pay to hunt for trouble without strong evidence that it is present.

Nevertheless, even though inner limits should not be drawn on most control charts, they can be extremely useful in the sophisticated interpretation of control charts by people who understand control-chart theory. Here the clue to action is given not by a *single* point outside either of the inner limits, but rather by two or more points, both outside the same inner limit. This is really a matter of sizing up extreme runs; it is somewhat comparable to the interpretation of extreme runs on the same side of the central line that was explained on page 91. For example, 2 points in succession outside the same inner limit on an $\bar{X}$ chart give even stronger evidence of a shift in process average than a single point outside the outer limit. Two points out of 3 beyond one inner limit, 3 out of 7, or 4 out of 10, may all be considered as appropriate grounds for action.

However, this type of interpretation may be made by the quality control engineer or other qualified individual without confusing matters for colleagues by having inner limit lines actually drawn on all $\bar{X}$ charts. When a suspicious sequence of points is observed close to a conventional 3-sigma limit, the quality control engineer may imagine an inner limit two-thirds of the distance from the central line to the control limit. Or, if this is too much strain on the imagination, such a line may be drawn lightly on the portion of the chart to be studied.

Problems of Detecting Small but Sustained Shifts

The use of the theory of runs to identify shifts in the universe was discussed briefly in Chap. 3. Later, in Chap. 6, the method of calculating the approximate probabilities associated with runs of points on one side of the central line of an $\bar{X}$ chart was presented. Such tests may be useful because an $\bar{X}$ chart with 3-sigma limits and a small subgroup size (e.g., two to five) is not sensitive to small shifts in the process centering.

Consider an example in which a controlled and correctly centered process shifts to a new centering $\frac{1}{2}\sigma'$ greater than the old centering. σ' remains constant through the shift and the centering holds constant at the new level after the shift. A combination rule is used which says look for trouble if either of these conditions occurs:

1. A point falls outside the control limits
2. Eight points in a row fall between the central line and one control limit

Assuming subgroups of four drawn from a normally distributed universe, the probability that a single point will fall outside a given control limit is 0.00135 and the probability that a point will fall between the central line and one control limit is 0.49865 when the process is correctly centered. After the $\frac{1}{2}\sigma'$ shift, the respective probabilities increase to 0.0228 and 0.8186.

Under the rules as stated, it is conceivable that either rule could signal the shift on the first sample after the shift. That is, a single point could fall outside the upper 3-sigma control limit (with probability 0.0228) or the eighth point in a row could be between the central line and the upper control limit (with probability 0.8186) if the previous seven points before the shift had fallen in the same region (with probability 0.49865^7). Thus the combined probability of detection on the first sample after the shift is:

$$0.0228 + (0.49865)^7(0.8186) = 0.0291$$

The probability of detection on the second sample is the probability of not detecting the shift on the first sample multiplied by the sum of the probabilities of a point outside the upper 3-sigma limit and eight points in a row between the central line and the upper limit, or:

$$0.9709[0.0228 + (0.49865)^6(0.8186)^2] = 0.0321$$

The probability of detection by the second sample is the sum of the respective individual probabilities, or:

$$0.0291 + 0.0321 = 0.0612$$

The following tabulation shows the respective probabilities of detection on the first eight sample subgroups and the cumulative probabilities to and including the subgroup listed.

Subgroup number	Probability of detection	
	on that subgroup	by that subgroup
1	0.0291	0.0291
2	0.0321	0.0612
3	0.0328	0.0985
4	0.0456	0.1441
5	0.0585	0.2026
6	0.0778	0.2804
7	0.1048	0.3852
8	0.1380	0.5232

Some companies have formalized the use of the theory of runs into standard operating procedures. The following paragraphs describe the procedure used by Western Electric Company as published in the company's *Statistical Quality Control Handbook*.†

The general procedure calls for connecting lines between plotted points, somewhat easing the visual problem of identifying runs on a chart. In addition to the usual 3-sigma control limits, and the companion rule that a single point outside a limit indicates a shift, the area between the central line and each limit is divided into three zones, *A*, *B*, and *C*. Each zone has a specific decision rule for points falling within or beyond that zone.

Zone *A* lies between 2-sigma and 3-sigma above and below the central line. A shift in the process average is signaled when two out of three points fall within or beyond Zone *A*. Zone *B* lies between 1-sigma and 2-sigma on either side of the central line. A shift in the process average is signaled in this case if four out of five points fall within or beyond Zone *B*. Zone *C* lies between the central line and 1-sigma on either side. A shift in the process average is signaled if eight points in a row fall within or beyond Zone *C*. The reader will note that the Zone *C* rule is equivalent to the rule discussed earlier in this section; that is, eight points in a row on one side of the central line.

---

† *Statistical Quality Control Handbook*, Western Electric Company, Inc., 1956, sec. I, part B and sec. II, part F. This book is available to the public but only through the company. Copies may be purchased by writing the Manager, Quality Assurance, 222 Broadway, New York, 10038.

These rules may be condensed as follows:

Zone	Rule	Proportion in zone assuming normal distribution	Probability of Type I error when using rule
	1 point beyond limit	0.00135	0.00135
$UCL_{\bar{x}}$			
A	2 of 3 in Zone A or beyond	0.02135	0.0015
B	4 of 5 in Zone B or beyond	0.1360	0.0027
C	8 in a row in Zone C or beyond	0.3413	0.0039
$\bar{X}'$			

The foregoing table is adapted by permission from the Western Electric *Statistical Quality Control Handbook*. The figures in the two right-hand columns are based on an $\bar{X}$ chart with 3-sigma limits and drawings from a normal universe. It should be noted that there is a degree of redundancy in the rules. For example, the rule for Zone A includes the possibility that at least one of the two points in or beyond the zone will fall beyond the 3-sigma limit. Such an occurrence would automatically signal a shift, thus nullifying the effect of the zone rule.

The probabilities shown apply to Type I error; that is, when the process is operating in control and correctly centered. The sum of the probabilities associated with the use of each rule, 0.0094, is an approximation of the Type I error associated with their joint application, but somewhat overstates the true probability because of the aforementioned interaction between decision rules.

We have made specific mention of several combinations of decision rules that may be used in control charting to detect shifts in this and preceding articles in this book. Examples of the types of calculations that may be useful in approximating the effectiveness of these combination rules have been illustrated. It should be noted, however, that the real justification of the use of rules based on runs such as those adopted by Western Electric is similar to the justification of the use of 3-sigma limits on $\bar{X}$ and R charts; namely, that experience indicates that, in general, when the rules say "hunt for trouble," a source of trouble can be found. When the rules say "leave the process alone," it often happens that no source of trouble (i.e., no assignable cause of variation) can be discovered.

The Problem of Misinterpretation of the Relationship between Control-chart Limits and Specification Limits

One source of confusion appears almost universally wherever the control chart for $\bar{X}$ is introduced on production operations. Whenever specifications apply to individual values (as is always true of dimensions and usually true of other quality characteristics), the specification limits tend to be confused with the control-chart limits. This confusion often exists in the minds of shop personnel, inspectors, engineers, and even managers. It leads to a diversity of troubles.

It has already been pointed out in Chap. 4 that where the specification tolerances are tighter than the natural tolerances (i.e., than the 3-sigma limits on individual values), some nonconforming product is sure to be made even by a controlled process. A controlled process may also make nonconforming product if the process average is not properly centered with respect to upper and lower specification limits or properly located with respect to a single specification limit. Thus there may be many cases where the control chart shows the process in control and some of the product is bad. If this is not understood, the control chart may give a false assurance that all is well.

If specification limits are drawn on the $\bar{X}$ control chart, there is a natural tendency to compare the subgroup *averages*, plotted on the chart, with the specification limits. This sometimes leads to the false conclusion that whenever an average plots within specification limits, all the product is within specifications.

A misinterpretation opposite to this is also made occasionally. This is to compare measured individual values with the control limits that apply to averages, and to conclude that trouble exists whenever an individual value is outside the limit for averages.

The spread of the control limits for averages is less than the spread of individual values. It is therefore often less than the spread of the specification limits. This condition sometimes leads to the incorrect conclusion that the use of the $\bar{X}$ chart amounts to the use of working tolerances that are closer than the specification tolerances.

The ideal preventive for these various errors is for the people who use the control chart to understand clearly that averages are different from individual values and that control limits mean something entirely different from specification limits. In this book the first illustrations of the $\bar{X}$ chart were deliberately chosen in a way to bring this out. The reader may recall the contrast between Examples 1-1 and 1-2. In Example 1-1 practically all the product was within specification limits even though there were many points out of control. In Example 1-2 much of the product did not conform to specifications even though all points were within control limits. Some such illustrations are desirable in any introduction of personnel to the $\bar{X}$ control chart, not only in the short in-plant courses frequently given to production and inspection supervisors but also in presentation of the technique to individuals.

Unless all of the people exposed to $\bar{X}$ charts are familiar with control-chart principles, any specification limits for individual values drawn on such charts may constitute a troublesome source of misunderstanding.

Plotting Subgroup Totals

One scheme that has been used in many plants is to plot on the control chart the sum of the n measurements in each subgroup rather than the average of these measurements. Where totals are plotted, the values on the chart do not appear to shop personnel as if they were comparable with specification limits; hence there is little chance for confusion on this point.

This type of chart is merely a conventional $\bar{X}$ chart with the scale magnified n times. The values for the central line and limits are the $\bar{X}$ chart values multiplied by n. Any conclusions to be drawn from the $\bar{X}$ chart may also be drawn from the chart for totals.

This variation of the $\bar{X}$ chart is particularly useful where a machine operator is using the control chart under definite instructions to leave the machine settings alone as long as a process shows control and to stop production and get help from some definite source (for example, the machine setter or the maintenance department) whenever a point goes out of control.

A minor advantage of the chart for totals is a saving of the arithmetical operation of dividing the total of each subgroup by the subgroup size. A minor limitation is that the method should not be used where the subgroup size is variable.

II. SOME RELATED SPECIAL PROCEDURES

Charts for Individual Measurements

Where charts for averages are misunderstood by shop personnel, one possible way to avoid this misunderstanding is not to plot averages at all but rather to plot individual measurements. Figures 1-1a and 1-3a are charts of this type. Specification limits applying to individual measurements are, of course, properly shown on such charts.

If sampling is by subgroups, as illustrated in Figs. 1-1a and 1-3a, universe standard deviation σ' may be estimated from $\bar{R}$. Control limits for individual measurements may then be drawn at $\bar{X}' \pm 3\sigma'$. A point outside such limits may be considered as evidence of an assignable cause of variation.

Such a chart may be better than nothing, but it is much less satisfactory than a conventional $\bar{X}$ chart based on a subgroup size of 4 or 5. If the limits on a chart for individual values are set at $\bar{X}'$ (or $\bar{\bar{X}}$) $\pm 3\sigma'$, the chart is relatively insensitive to substantial shifts in process average. Although greater sensitivity to such shifts may be gained by the use of narrower limits, such sensitivity is gained only by increasing the chance of false indications of lack of control (so-called Type I errors). Unless a chart for individual measurements is accompanied by a range chart, it is difficult to discover whether there have been changes in process dispersion. In general, charts for individual measurements are inferior to conventional control charts because they fail to give as clear a picture of changes in a process or as quick evidence of assignable causes of variation.

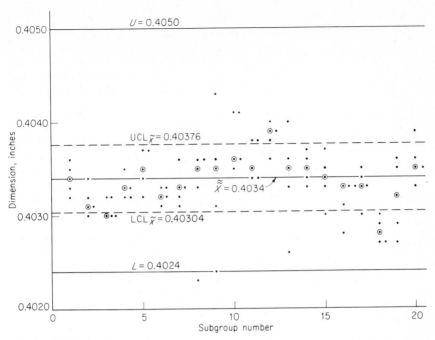

Figure 9-3 Control chart for medians superimposed on chart showing individual measurements and specification limits—data of Example 1-1.

Combination of Chart for Individual Measurements and Chart for Medians

If it is desired to plot individual measurements, it is suggested that a control chart also be plotted that reflects the central tendency of subgroups ($\bar{X}$, median, or midrange). Such a chart might be separate. However, the control chart for central tendency might also be superimposed on the chart for individual measurements.

A convenient plan for such superimposed charts is to combine a chart for individual measurements with a chart for medians. The convenience of the median chart for this purpose is greatest where the subgroup contains an odd number of measurements such as 3, 5, or 7. If so, the median may be quickly identified and circled as shown in Fig. 9-3.† The data charted are from Example 1-1. A discussion of control charts for subgroup medians, including the method of calculating control limits, is contained in subsequent sections of this chapter.

On such a combined chart, the individual values may be examined with reference to the tolerance limits shown on the chart and the circled medians may be examined with reference to the control limits for medians.

---

† This figure is adapted, with some changes, from a similar chart in P. C. CLIFFORD's article, Control Charts without Calculations: Some Modifications and Some Extensions, *Industrial Quality Control*, vol. 15, no. 11, pp. 40–44, May, 1959.

Control Charts for Medians within Subgroups
Using Medians of Statistics of Sets of Subgroups

Enoch B. Ferrell of Bell Telephone Laboratories has proposed the use of the midrange as the measure of central tendency of each subgroup. He has also proposed that the estimate of the central tendency of a universe be based on the median of the midranges of a set of subgroups and that the estimate of universe dispersion be based on the median of the ranges of the same set of subgroups.[†]

The midrange of a set of numbers is the average (arithmetic mean) of the maximum and minimum numbers in the set. The reader will recall that the median was defined in Chap. 2 as the magnitude of the middle case—the value that has half the observations above it and half below it.

Paul C. Clifford has suggested modifying Ferrell's procedure.[‡] Medians of subgroups are used rather than midranges. The median of the subgroup medians (or, alternatively, the median of the individual observations) is used as the estimate of the central tendency of the universe. Just as in Ferrell's procedure, the median of the ranges is used as an estimate of universe dispersion.

Table 9-2 gives factors for 3-sigma limits for charts for subgroup medians.

[†] E. B. FERRELL, Control Charts Using Midranges and Medians, *Industrial Quality Control*, vol. 9, pp. 30–32, March, 1953. Equations and factors for midrange charts are given in this article.

[‡] P. C. CLIFFORD, Control Charts without Calculations: Some Modifications and Some Extensions, *Industrial Quality Control*, vol. 15, no. 11, pp. 40–44, May, 1959.

Table 9-2 Factors and formulas for 3-sigma limits for control charts for medians of subgroups using median range as a measure of subgroup dispersion
(Reproduced from P. C. Clifford, Control Charts without Calculations: Some Modifications and Some Extensions, *Industrial Quality Control*, vol. 15, no. 11, pp. 40–44, May, 1959)

n	A_5	n	A_5
		6	0.562
2	2.224	7	0.520
3	1.265	8	0.441
4	0.829	9	0.419
5	0.712	10	0.369

$$UCL_X = \tilde{\tilde{X}} + A_5 m(R)$$
$$LCL_{\tilde{x}} = \tilde{\tilde{X}} - A_5 m(R)$$

These factors assume that sampling has been from a normal universe. One wavy line over an X (that is, $\tilde{X}$) is used to indicate a subgroup median. Two wavy lines over an X (that is, $\tilde{\tilde{X}}$) indicate the median of a set of subgroup medians.

An advantage of the median as a measure of central tendency of a subgroup is that it can be found quickly with no arithmetic for subgroups containing odd numbers of observations such as 3 or 5. A characteristic of the median as a measure of a central tendency is that it gives no weight to the extent of the extremity of extreme values in a subgroup. For instance, consider subgroup 8 in Table 1-1; the X values are, respectively, 23, 33, 36, 35, and 36. The extreme value 23 influences the subgroup average (arithmetic mean) of 32.6 and the midrange of 29.5. In contrast, the median value of 35 is no different from the median that would have existed if the first X had been, say, 33.

When the central tendency of subgroups is charted, the foregoing characteristic of the median usually is a disadvantage as compared with charting $\bar{X}$. Nevertheless, this characteristic of the median might conceivably be viewed as an advantage if for some reason it were desired to give little weight to occasional "wild shot" values in individual measurements.

Figure 9-3 illustrated the combination of a chart for medians with a chart for individual values.

III. A GENERAL TEST FOR HOMOGENEITY

The Control Chart as a General Test for Homogeneity

It is impossible to give too much emphasis to the importance of keeping track of the order of production whenever measurements are made of any quality of manufactured product. Ideally, measurements should be planned with this in view. Practically this may not be possible. This is particularly true when a purchaser wishes to apply the control-chart analysis to an incoming shipment of product regarding which there is no knowledge of the order of production.

Suppose, for instance, that an aircraft manufacturer receives a shipment of 100,000 bolts packed in 50 boxes each containing 2,000 bolts. Wishing to test 200 of these for some quality, such as Rockwell hardness number or tensile strength, the manufacturer will naturally pick four bolts from each of the 50 boxes.

Suppose the results of these tests are plotted on $\bar{X}$ and R charts, with the four bolts from each box constituting a subgroup, and these control charts show a state of control. The interpretation of this showing of control is not the same as if the basis of subgrouping had been the order of production. Here the control charts are simply a test for homogeneity. This homogeneity may have been obtained by a constant-cause system during production with the bolts packed in boxes in order of production, or it may have been obtained by a thorough mixing of the bolts before they were packed even though they came from several different cause systems.

The control-chart analysis may also be applied to data already at hand that were taken with no thought of the control chart, provided there is some rational basis for subgrouping. Here also the control charts are a general test for homogeneity. For example, they have been applied by Shewhart to published data regarding the determination of fundamental physical constants such as the velocity of light.† This type of application in a manufacturing setting is illustrated in Fig. 9-2 in an example dealing with the shear strength of spot welds.

IV. PROBABILITY LIMITS FOR CONTROL CHARTS FOR VARIABLES

Two Questions for Decision Regarding Control Limits on Charts for $\bar{X}$, R, and σ

Two topics that often have been debated among statisticians, as well as among persons engaged in quality control work in industry, are as follows:

1. Shall control-chart limits be described as multiples of the standard deviation of the statistic charted or in terms of the estimated probabilities associated with the limits?
2. How far apart ought the limits to be spaced, all things considered?

The first question is primarily one of semantics. We have already suggested that, in principle, the second question is primarily an economic one.

Probability Limits on $\bar{X}$ Charts

If we assume that $\bar{X}$ values follow the normal distribution when all samples have been taken from the same universe, we can use Table A to find the multiple of $\sigma_{\bar{X}}$ associated with any stipulated probabilities. The reader will recall that in Chap. 2 it was pointed out that $\bar{X}$ values are normally distributed when the universe is normal; they are approximately normal even from nonnormal universes when the sample size is 4 or more.

For instance, if it is desired that the probability be 0.001 that without a change in the universe a point will fall above the upper control limit, we look in Table A for the multiplier of σ corresponding to 0.001. This is 3.09. Because the factors A_2, A_1, and A in Tables C, D, and E are based on 3-sigma limits, it is merely necessary to multiply them by $3.09/3 = 1.03$ to obtain corresponding factors based on 0.001 probability limits. It should be remembered that to the probability of 0.001 that a

---

† W. A. SHEWHART (edited by W. E. DEMING), "Statistical Method from the Viewpoint of Quality Control," p. 68, The Graduate School, Department of Agriculture, Washington, 1939.

point will fall above the upper limit must be added the equal probability of 0.001 that a point will fall below the lower limit. This means a probability of 0.002 of a point outside limits, or 0.998 within limits. The British particularly have used limits based on 3.09σ.

Or if it is desired that the probability be 0.025 that a point fall above the upper limit (corresponding to 0.05 that it fall outside limits), Table A gives 1.96 as the appropriate multiple of σ. The multiplier to be applied to the A_2, A_1, and A factors is then $1.96/3 = 0.653$. Factors based on 1.96σ have been used by the British as inner control limits or warning limits.

Probability Limits on Charts for R and σ

The distribution of $\bar{X}$ values, which is normal or approximately so, is symmetrical. Therefore probability limits on an $\bar{X}$ chart are like 3-sigma limits in being equidistant from the central line on the chart. In contrast, because the distributions of R and σ are not symmetrical even when the universe is normal, it is necessary to have separate factors for the upper and lower control limits if the probabilities of extreme variations are to be made equal. Table 9-3 gives such factors for probability limits for σ charts; Table 9-4 gives them for R charts. Three sets of symmetrical probabilities (giving unsymmetrical limits) are 0.001 and 0.999, corresponding to a 0.002 probability that with no change in the universe a point will fall outside of the limits; 0.005 and 0.995, corresponding to a 0.01 probability of a point falling outside; and 0.025 and 0.975, corresponding to an 0.05 probability of a point falling outside.

Table 9-3 gives multipliers for the assumed or estimated value of σ' to obtain limits on a chart for σ. σ' may be estimated as $\bar{\sigma}/c_2$.

Table 9-3 Factors for probability limits to be used in control charts for RMS deviation

(To obtain limits, multiply the estimated value of σ' by the B factor with subscript corresponding to the desired probability)

Size of subgroup n	Lower limits			Upper limits		
	$B_{.001}$	$B_{.005}$	$B_{.025}$	$B_{.975}$	$B_{.995}$	$B_{.999}$
2	0.00	0.00	0.02	1.59	1.99	2.33
3	0.03	0.06	0.13	1.57	1.88	2.15
4	0.08	0.13	0.23	1.53	1.79	2.02
5	0.13	0.20	0.31	1.49	1.72	1.92
6	0.19	0.26	0.37	1.46	1.67	1.85
7	0.23	0.31	0.42	1.44	1.63	1.79
8	0.27	0.35	0.46	1.42	1.59	1.74
9	0.31	0.39	0.49	1.40	1.56	1.70
10	0.34	0.42	0.52	1.38	1.54	1.67

Table 9-4 Factors for probability limits to be used in control charts for range

(To obtain limits, multiply the estimated value of σ' by the D factor with the subscript corresponding to the desired probability)

Size of subgroup n	Lower limits			Upper limits		
	$D_{.001}$	$D_{.005}$	$D_{.025}$	$D_{.975}$	$D_{.995}$	$D_{.999}$
2	0.00	0.01	0.04	3.17	3.97	4.65
3	0.06	0.13	0.30	3.68	4.42	5.06
4	0.20	0.34	0.59	3.98	4.69	5.31
5	0.37	0.55	0.85	4.20	4.89	5.48
6	0.53	0.75	1.07	4.36	5.03	5.62
7	0.69	0.92	1.25	4.49	5.15	5.73
8	0.83	1.08	1.41	4.60	5.25	5.82
9	0.97	1.21	1.55	4.70	5.34	5.90
10	1.08	1.33	1.67	4.78	5.42	5.97

Table 9-4 gives multipliers for the assumed or estimated value of σ' to obtain limits on a chart for R.† σ' may be estimated as $\bar{R}/d_2$.

It should be emphasized that the probabilities given for these limits are strictly accurate only when sampling from a normal universe. They are also based on the assumption that a σ' estimated from the data is the true universe standard deviation. For practical control-chart work in industry, where the exact form of the universe is hardly ever known and control limits are often based on the evidence of short series of observations, it must be recognized that these probabilities are approximate rather than exact and may often be substantially in error.

Differing Viewpoints on How to Describe the Limits on Control Charts for Variables

Two points of view are found regarding the best way to describe limits on control charts for $\bar{X}$, R, and σ.

One viewpoint is that the appropriate decision to make in setting limits is the numerical value of a probability. This should be the probability that, with no change in the universe, a point will fall within the control limits (or, alternately, without the limits). The advocates of this point of view have usually adopted 0.998 as the desired probability of falling within limits of $\bar{X}$ charts. This has led to limits of $\bar{X}$ (or $\bar{X}'$) $\pm 3.09\sigma_{\bar{X}}$.

An alternate point of view is that, even if the probability associated with any limits could be known accurately, the exact numerical value of the probability is

---

† For extensive tables of the percentage points of the distribution of values of R when sampling from a normal universe, see H. L. HARTER, Tables of Range and Studentized Range, *The Annals of Mathematical Statistics*, vol. 31, no. 4, pp. 1,122–1,147, December, 1960.

only of incidental interest. The important matter is that there be a definite basis for the establishment of limits and that this basis form a suitable guide to the actions that are to be based on the control charts.

In comparing these viewpoints, the reader should recognize that it really is not the exact value of the probability that constitutes a basis for action. For instance, it would be practically impossible to have any sense of the difference between the effect of probabilities of 0.0010 and 0.00135 that a point would fall above the upper control limit by chance. The real basis for acceptance of control limits, whether called 3-sigma limits or something else, is experience that the operational procedure involved in their computation gives limits that provide a satisfactory basis for action. As far as the practical use of $\bar{X}$ charts in manufacturing is concerned, it makes very little difference whether limits are at 3 sigma or at 3.09 sigma and it makes even less difference whether they are called 3-sigma limits or probability limits. Both types of limits are used in the same manner and give very nearly the same results.

Some Special Aspects of Probability Limits on Control Charts for R and σ

Although probability limits on $\bar{X}$ charts are like 3-sigma limits in being equidistant from the central line, probability limits on charts for R are not equally spaced with reference to the central line. The lack of symmetry of the distribution of σ values for small samples was illustrated in Table 3-3, page 84. R values are similar to σ values in having a decidedly skewed distribution with small samples.

A point emphasized by some advocates of probability limits is that for the common subgroup sizes of 5 or less, the lower 3-sigma limit is zero on these charts. In contrast, for the probabilities given in Tables 9-3 and 9-4, a subgroup size of 3 or more will give a lower control limit greater than zero.

V. CONTROL CHARTS FOR MOVING AVERAGES

The Use of Control Limits for Moving Averages

In manufacturing plants many schemes other than the Shewhart control chart have been used for plotting data on quality characteristics. For example, a chemical plant may maintain charts on which are plotted the results of daily analyses made to determine the percentages of certain chemical constituents in its incoming materials, product in process, and finished product. A common variation of this is to plot moving averages rather than daily values. The moving average is particularly appropriate in continuous process chemical manufacture when applied to quality characteristics of raw materials and product in process. The smoothing effect of the moving average often has an effect on the figures similar to the effect on the product of the blending and mixing that take place in the remainder of the production process.

Table 9-5 Calculation of moving average and moving range

(Data on per cent of unreacted CaO at an intermediate stage in a chemical manufacturing process)

Date		Daily value	3-day moving total	3-day moving average	3-day moving range	Combination (for conventional control charts)
Sept.	1	0.24				
	2	0.13				
	3	0.11	0.48	0.160	0.13	A
	4	0.19	0.43	0.143	0.08	B
	5	0.16	0.46	0.153	0.08	C
	6	0.17	0.52	0.173	0.03	A
	7	0.13	0.46	0.153	0.04	B
	8	0.17	0.47	0.157	0.04	C
	9	0.10	0.40	0.133	0.07	A
	10	0.14	0.41	0.137	0.07	B
	11	0.16	0.40	0.133	0.06	C
	12	0.14	0.44	0.147	0.02	A
	13	0.17	0.47	0.157	0.03	B
	14	0.15	0.46	0.153	0.03	C
	15	0.20	0.52	0.173	0.05	A
	16	0.26	0.61	0.203	0.11	B
	17	0.16	0.62	0.207	0.10	C
	18	0.00	0.42	0.140	0.26	A
	19	0.18	0.34	0.113	0.18	B
	20	0.18	0.36	0.120	0.18	C
	21	0.20	0.56	0.187	0.02	A
	22	0.11	0.49	0.163	0.09	B
	23	0.30	0.61	0.203	0.19	C
	24	0.21	0.62	0.207	0.19	A
	25	0.11	0.62	0.207	0.19	B
	26	0.17	0.49	0.163	0.10	C
	27	0.18	0.46	0.153	0.07	A
	28	0.13	0.48	0.160	0.05	B
	29	0.28	0.59	0.197	0.15	C
	30	0.16	0.57	0.190	0.15	A
Oct.	1	0.14	0.58	0.193	0.14	B
	2	0.16	0.46	0.153	0.02	C
	3	0.14	0.44	0.147	0.02	A
	4	0.10	0.40	0.133	0.06	B
	5	0.13	0.37	0.123	0.04	C
	6	0.20	0.43	0.143	0.10	A
	7	0.14	0.47	0.157	0.07	B
	8	0.10	0.44	0.147	0.10	C
	9	0.18	0.42	0.140	0.08	A
	10	0.11	0.39	0.130	0.08	B
	11	0.08	0.37	0.123	0.10	C
	12	0.12	0.31	0.103	0.04	A
	13	0.13	0.33	0.110	0.05	B
	14	0.12	0.37	0.123	0.01	C
	15	0.17	0.42	0.140	0.05	A
	16	0.10	0.39	0.130	0.07	B
	17	0.09	0.36	0.120	0.08	C

In the introduction of Shewhart techniques into chemical plants, it may be desirable not to disturb the custom of plotting moving averages. However it is appropriate to apply control limits to such moving average charts and to add charts for moving ranges. The calculations for these limits and the interpretation of these charts are similar to the conventional $\bar{X}$ and R charts but differ in certain respects.

Table 9-5 illustrates the calculation of moving averages and moving ranges. The figures given are the daily analyses of percentages of unreacted lime (CaO) at an intermediate state in a continuous manufacturing process. The average given for September 3 is the average of the percentages on the first, second, and third; the average for the fourth is the average of the values on the second, third, and fourth; and so forth. (From a technical statistical viewpoint, the average should always be plotted at the *mid-point* of the period; for instance, the average of the first, second, and third should be assigned to the second, not to the third. In this case, however, practical psychology takes precedence over statistical correctness. The reason for the common practice in manufacturing of assigning the moving average to the final date rather than to the middle date is to have the average always seem up to date rather than behind time.) The calculation of a 3-day moving average is simplified by carrying a moving total to which is added each day the algebraic difference between the value today and the value 3 days ago.

The daily values are plotted in Fig. 9-4a; the moving averages in Fig. 9-4b. A comparison of these two graphs shows the effect of the moving average in smoothing the curve. The more successive points averaged, the greater this smoothing effect and the more the curve emphasizes trends rather than point-to-point fluctuations. The moving range for the same data is plotted in Fig. 9-5a.

The control limits in Figs. 9-4 and 9-5 are computed from an $\bar{X}'$ of 0.17 and an $\bar{R}$ of 0.065. These figures were established on the basis of the record of the two preceding months. The calculation of limits uses the factors and formulas of Table C, App. 3.

If the same data had been subgrouped for conventional $\bar{X}$ and R charts with a subgroup size of three, the decision as to the date of starting the subgroups would have been entirely arbitrary. The first subgroup might have been September 1, 2, and 3; the next the fourth, fifth, and sixth; and so forth; this is identified in Table 9-5 as combination A. Or September 2, 3, and 4 might have been combined; this is combination B. Or September 3, 4, and 5; this is combination C.

A moving average chart with $n = 3$ is as if the points from three conventional $\bar{X}$ charts were superimposed. That is, Fig. 9-4b combines the points of Fig. 9-4c, d, and e. Similarly, the moving range chart Fig. 9-5a combines the points in the three conventional R charts, Fig. 9-5b, c, and d.

It follows that the interpretation of a point outside control limits on moving average and moving range charts is the same as a point outside control limits on conventional $\bar{X}$ and R charts. However, because successive points on moving average and moving range charts are not independent of one another, the interpretation of several points in a row outside control limits is obviously not the same. For example, three points in a row outside control limits in Fig. 9-5a

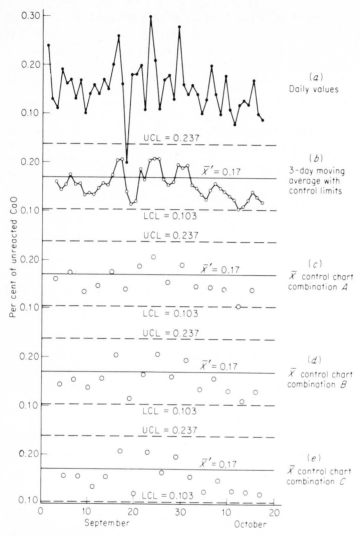

Figure 9-4 Per cent of unreacted CaO. Comparison of (a) daily values, (b) graph of three-day moving average, and (c), (d), and (e) the three $\bar{X}$ control charts combined in the moving average graph (b).

correspond roughly to one point outside limits on each of the conventional R charts, Fig. 9-5b, c, and d. Similarly, runs above or below the central line do not have the same significance on moving average and moving range charts as on conventional $\bar{X}$ and R charts.

As pointed out in previous chapters, whenever a shift in universe average occurs *within* a subgroup rather than *between* subgroups, the R chart tends to show lack of control. Changes of short duration that do not persist through one entire subgroup may be shown only on the R chart and not on the $\bar{X}$ chart. In Figs. 9-4 and 9-5, the indications of lack of control are on the R chart.

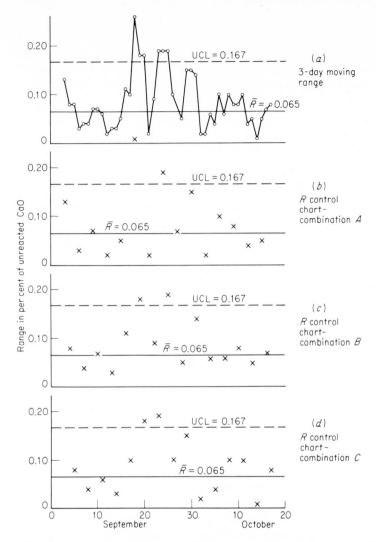

Figure 9-5 Comparison of graph for three-day moving range with the three R control charts combined in the moving range graph—data from Table 9-5.

Combination of Chart for Individual Measurements and Moving Range Chart†

In some processes, it is common to have single measurements spaced some time apart. A case in point was the chemical process with one measurement per day

---

† A good discussion of this topic, with several examples, is given in "A.S.T.M. Manual on Presentation of Data and Control Chart Analysis," STP 15D, pp. 99, 130–133, American Society for Testing and Materials, Philadelphia, 1976.

that is used in Table 9-5 and Figs. 9-4 and 9-5 to illustrate charts for moving averages and moving ranges.

Under such circumstances, it may be desired to plot X values rather than to smooth the day-to-day fluctuations by plotting moving averages. The individual X values from Table 9-5 were shown without control limits in Fig. 9-4a. To add 3-sigma control limits for individuals to such a chart, it is necessary to compute $\bar{X}' \pm 3\sigma'$, with σ' estimated from the moving range as $\bar{R}/d_2$. With the standard $\bar{X}'_o$ of 0.17 and the standard $\bar{R}$ of 0.065 for subgroups of 3 used in Figs. 9-4 and 9-5, the upper and lower control limits for individual X values are 0.285 and 0.055, respectively. If these limits had been added to Fig. 9-4a, this figure would have been a control chart for individual values.

Even though the moving $\bar{X}$ is not used in such a case, it is necessary to use the moving range as a measure of process dispersion. The "A.S.T.M. Manual on Quality Control of Materials" recommends a subgroup size of two for the moving range in connection with such a chart for individual values.

VI. $\bar{X}$ CHART WITH A LINEAR TREND

$\bar{X}$ Charts for Trended Universe Average with Constant Standard Deviation

In some machining operations, tool wear occurs at a uniform rate over the period of use of the tool. This tool wear may be one of the factors influencing the average value of some dimension of the product manufactured and may be responsible for a trend in this average. Where subgroups are selected in a way that spaces them uniformly with respect to this wear, control charts for $\bar{X}$ may look something like Fig. 9-6. The R chart, however, is likely to remain in control yielding a constant estimate of σ'.

The central line and control limits for the $\bar{X}$ chart, in such a case, should be sloping rather than horizontal. The slope of the central line, or universe average, and σ', estimated from $\bar{R}$, are determined from the measurements themselves. Once known, it becomes possible to determine the initial setting and length of run that together will give the maximum period between machine settings consistent with the specified tolerances. The methods of making the required calculations are illustrated in Example 9-1.

Example 9-1 Determining the initial machine setting when a trend is expected in the value of a dimension *Facts of the case* On certain operations in one machine shop, it was a common experience for a definite steady trend in the average value of dimensions of machined parts to be caused by rapid tool wear. On many specified dimensions the spread of the specification limits, $U - L$, was substantially greater than the natural tolerance range of the process, $6\sigma'$. This provided an ample margin of safety against the production of nonconforming product as long as the machine setting held the average value of the dimension somewhere close to a point midway between the specification limits. However, the tendency of the average value of a dimension to shift rapidly as a result of tool wear called for frequent new setups to restore the average value to its desired position. Each new setup involved appreciable costs, both for setup expense and for idle machine time.

The introduction of the control-chart point of view provided a basis for reducing the frequency of setups. The situation here was essentially the one illustrated in Fig. 3-4c. The average value of the frequency distribution of the variable X (in this case, a dimension) shifted at an approximately uniform rate, but the shape of the frequency distribution and its dispersion (measured by σ') did not change. From control-chart data properly taken, it was possible to estimate σ'. It was also possible to estimate the rate of change of the average $\bar{X}$ and to express this rate of change in terms of an equation.

The estimate of σ' made it possible to determine the aimed-at average value for an initial setup to permit the maximum run between setups. The estimate of the rate of change of the dimension provided a basis for decision as to the required frequency of new setups. Once σ' and the rate of change of X were estimated for a particular operation, it proved possible to use this information on new jobs. Even jobs involving relatively short runs were benefited, as many such jobs were completed with a single setup in contrast to the two or three setups usually required for similar jobs before the use of the control chart.

Fitting a trend line to an $\bar{X}$ chart Consider the following values of $\bar{X}$ and R for a dimension specified as 0.644 ± 0.004 in. Subgroups of five components were measured every half-hour.

Subgroup number	$\bar{X}$	R
1	0.6417	0.0011
2	0.6418	0.0016
3	0.6424	0.0010
4	0.6431	0.0015
5	0.6433	0.0009
6	0.6437	0.0010
7	0.6433	0.0014
8	0.6436	0.0004
9	0.6441	0.0006
10	0.6444	0.0011
11	0.6456	0.0009
12	0.6457	0.0007
13	0.6454	0.0009
Totals.........	8.3681	0.0131

$$\bar{\bar{X}} = \frac{8.3681}{13} = 0.6437$$

$$\bar{R} = \frac{0.0131}{13} = 0.0010$$

Certain precautions should be taken in the collection of data to be used for the calculation of a trend line and control limits. The production between successive subgroups should be approximately constant.† The components included in a subgroup should be produced in succession so that the trend will have little effect on the range of a subgroup.

On the conventional $\bar{X}$ chart, the central line is horizontal. With an upward trend of $\bar{X}$ values, the central line must be a sloping line. The position of this central line may be described by an equation of the form $\bar{X} = a + bh$, with the symbol h used to represent the subgroup number (preferably with a revised subgroup numbering using the middle subgroup as the origin). a is the value of $\bar{X}$ when $h = 0$, and b is the slope of the line. The method of least squares provides a satisfactory way of finding the values of a and b corresponding to any given set of measurements.‡

Under certain special circumstances, computing a least squares trend line is a very simple operation. These circumstances are that the observed values of the variable plotted on the vertical axis of the chart (in this case, values of $\bar{X}$) are uniformly spaced along the horizontal axis of the chart (in this case, on the scale of subgroup numbers h); that there are an odd number of observed values; and that the origin on the horizontal axis is taken as the mid-point of that axis (that is, the 0 value of h is assumed at the middle subgroup). Under these circumstances $a = \bar{\bar{X}}$, and $b = \Sigma h\bar{X}/\Sigma h^2$. The method of calculation is illustrated in Table 9-6.

For simplicity in calculations, the $\bar{X}$ values in Table 9-6 are expressed in units of 0.0001 in excess of 0.6400. The equation $\bar{X} = 37.0 + 3.29h$ is, of course, expressed in these units. In terms of the actual dimension in inches, the equation becomes $\bar{X} = 0.6437 + 0.000329h$.

To plot this line on the control chart (Fig. 9-6), it is necessary to locate two points on the line and connect them.

$$\text{For example, for } h = -6, \ \bar{X} = 0.6437 + (0.000329)(-6) = 0.6417$$
$$\text{for } h = +6, \ \bar{X} = 0.6437 + (0.000329)(6) = 0.6457$$

Interpreting the control chart as a basis for action The control limits are sloping lines parallel to the central trend line. The upper control limit is $A_2\bar{R}$ above the trend line, and the lower control limit is $A_2\bar{R}$ below it. In this case,

---

† If the total production up to each subgroup were recorded, it would be possible to plot $\bar{X}$ as a function of production even though the production were not uniform from subgroup to subgroup. In such a case, however, the fitting of a least squares trend line is somewhat more complicated than is the simple method illustrated in Table 9-6. Methods of fitting least squares lines in such cases are explained in standard texts on statistical methods.

‡ Although fair results may often be obtained by drawing a trend line by eye on the chart, the personal equation enters into such fits to the extent that no two people are likely to agree exactly. As the least squares line is so easy to compute in this special case, it will generally pay to take the slight additional time required to obtain the least squares fit.

Table 9-6 Calculation of equation of least squares trend line for $\bar{X}$
($\bar{X}$ expressed in units of 0.0001 in excess of 0.6400)

Subgroup number	Revised subgroup number	Subgroup average		
	h	$\bar{X}$	$h\bar{X}$	h^2
1	−6	17	−102	36
2	−5	18	− 90	25
3	−4	24	− 96	16
4	−3	31	− 93	9
5	−2	33	− 66	4
6	−1	37	− 37	1
7	0	33	0	0
8	1	36	36	1
9	2	41	82	4
10	3	44	132	9
11	4	56	224	16
12	5	57	285	25
13	6	54	324	36
Totals.. ..	0	481	599	182

$$a = \bar{\bar{X}} = \frac{481}{13} = 37.0$$

$$b = \frac{\Sigma h\bar{X}}{\Sigma h^2} = \frac{599}{182} = 3.29$$

$$\bar{X} = a + bh = 37.0 + 3.29h$$

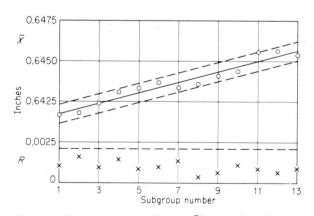

Figure 9-6 Illustration of trend line on $\bar{X}$ chart—Example 9-1.

$A_2 \bar{R} = 0.58(0.0010) = 0.0006$. Figure 9-6 shows sloping limits plotted at this distance from the central line.

To decide on the value of the average dimension to be aimed at in the initial machine setting, it is first necessary to estimate σ'. This is $\bar{R}/d_2 = 0.0010/2.326 = 0.00043$. The tolerance spread $U - L$ may then be compared with σ'. In this case

$$U - L = 0.6480 - 0.6400 = 0.0080$$

This is equal to $18.6\sigma'$.

A decision must then be made as to how many multiples of σ' the initial setting should be from the lower specification limit. In some instances this might be $3\sigma'$; in others, it might be a greater multiple of σ' such as $4\sigma'$. Where the tolerance spread is great enough to allow a considerable run between settings, as in this case, the additional margin of safety involved in the use of $4\sigma'$ is likely to be justified. The same multiple of σ' should be used to determine the time of a new setup. Using $4\sigma'$ in this case, we obtain the following directions: On initial setup, aim at

$$\bar{X} = L + 4\sigma' = 0.6400 + 0.0017 = 0.6417$$

Make a new setup when trend line $= U - 4\sigma' = 0.6480 - 0.0017 = 0.6463$.

The slope of the trend line, $b = 0.000329$, is the expected change in average dimension from one subgroup to the next. The interval between setups may be estimated as $(0.6463 - 0.6417)/0.000329 = 14$ subgroup intervals. With subgroups spaced half an hour apart, this indicates that a new setup is required every 7 h.

Discussion of Example 9-1

When a point falls outside control limits on an $\bar{X}$ chart with a sloping central line, there are two possible interpretations. One is the conventional one that an assignable cause of variation is responsible for the point falling outside the limits. The other is that the limits are based on a trend line that is wrong. For example, a control chart might be started for a new job using a slope of a trend line determined from a previous similar job; it might turn out that the jobs were really sufficiently different for the slopes to differ. As another example, tool wear is a factor that does not necessarily operate at a uniform rate; on jobs where the rate of change of the average value of a dimension is variable, no straight line fitted to $\bar{X}$ values will provide a satisfactory central line for a control chart.

VII. PATROL INSPECTION BY p CHART

Special Adaptation of the p Chart for Patrol Inspection

The reader will recall that the fraction rejected control chart requires a substantially larger sample size than does the $\bar{X}$ chart in order to maintain the same level of sensitivity to shifts in the process. Two aspects of sample size determination require a special adaptation of the p chart if it is to be an effective instrument for process control where a high level of quality must be maintained. First, some rejects must be *expected* to show up in the sample. If, for example, the process operates at 0.5% rejected, a sample size of 200 is required before there will be an average of one reject per sample. This factor would suggest the use of a rather large sample size.

Second, the larger the sample size, the more likely it is that a shift will occur during the drawing of the sample. The result, of course, would be an increased chance that shifts occurring between samples would go undetected.

In cases where it is necessary to use inspection by attributes and still detect small changes in the process, circumstances may require the use of small samples. Here the only way in which a p chart or np chart may be used to advantage is by artificially creating a pseudo bad quality level by applying acceptance standards for control-chart purposes which are much more severe than those really imposed by the specifications. That is, there may be established a special severe definition of a "defective" which is used only for purposes of process control by means of the control chart. In this way, the small sample size is not such an obstacle to the use of a control chart based on inspection by attributes.

This scheme has been applied advantageously in certain types of electrical testing and in ballistic testing. In Great Britain it has been applied to dimensional control. Example 9-2 describes an application taken from British literature.†

Example 9-2 Process control by np chart based on gage tolerances that are tighter than specification tolerances *Facts of the case* This example deals with an internal diameter specified as 1.008 ± 0.0035 in. Actual measurements were made on 100 components. These showed control with an estimated σ' of 0.0011. The following calculations show the relationship between the natural tolerances of the process and the specification tolerances:

$$U - L = 1.0115 - 1.0045 = 0.0070 \text{ in}$$

$$6\sigma' = 6(0.0011) = 0.0066 \text{ in}$$

As the tolerance spread was barely greater than $6\sigma'$, it was evident that the centering of the dimension must be maintained accurately at the nominal dimension of 1.008.

A special quality control gage was made with not-go and go dimensions as 1.00925 and 1.00675, respectively. These limits were at $\bar{X}' \pm 1.14\sigma'$. If the distribution were normal and perfect statistical control were maintained with

---

† Quantity Control by Limit Gauging, *Production and Engineering Bulletin*, vol. 3, pp. 433–437, October, 1944. This article also contains other examples and gives general directions for the application of this technique to dimensional control. See also A. E. MACE, The Use of Limit Gages in Process Control, *Industrial Quality Control*, vol. 8, no. 4, pp. 24–31, January, 1952.

the dimension centered at its nominal value, approximately 25% of the product would be rejected by this quality control gage, even though substantially all the product would be within specification limits.

Samples of 10 were used with this quality control gage. A variation of the np chart was used. The upper half of this chart showed the number rejected by the not-go gage and the lower half showed the number rejected by the go gage. In accordance with the British practice, warning limits as well as action limits were used on this chart.

Figure 9-7 shows a comparison of this chart for number of defectives with an $\bar{X}$ chart based on actual measurements of the same components which were gaged with the special go and not-go gage. This applies to a period when the process was out of control. It will be observed that the lack of control was readily apparent from this np chart, with even more points showing out of control than on the chart for averages.

Comment on Example 9-2

In some manufacturing plants, patrol inspection is carried out with go and not-go gages having tighter tolerances than the gages used for acceptance or rejection of finished product. This may provide a good opportunity for the use of the type of np chart shown in Fig. 9-7.

The appropriate value of p' for use in setting control limits on this np chart is not necessarily the average value $\bar{p}$ as determined from the work gages. For best results, it is necessary to estimate σ', the universe standard deviation. (In Example 9-2 this estimate was made by actual measurements on 100 components.) This permits differentiation of circumstances where the centering of a dimension must be closely controlled from those circumstances where the average value may be permitted to shift.

Figure 9-8 illustrates the case in which the centering of a process may not shift without producing defective product. If samples of ten are to be used, the gage limits should be set so that each shaded portion of the area under the frequency

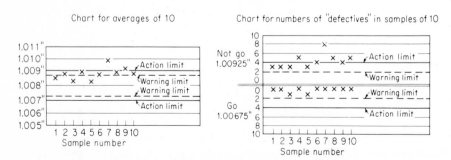

Figure 9-7 Comparison of charts for $\bar{X}$ and np for out-of-control period—Example 9-2. (*Reproduced from "Quality Control by Limit Gauging," Production and Engineering Bulletin, October, 1944.*)

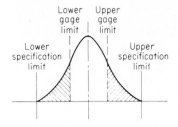

Figure 9-8 Relationship between special severe gage limits and specification limits when manufacturing processes can just work to specification limits.

curve (representing satisfactory product rejected by the work gage) includes 10 to 15% of the total area under the curve. In this case, if the centering is maintained, the "defectives" observed by the go portion of the work gage will be approximately equal to those observed by the not-go portion of the gage. If the sum of the shaded areas in Fig. 9-8 is 25% of the area under the frequency curve, p' is 0.125 for the go chart and 0.125 for the not-go chart. If the centering of the process is maintained, the observed $\bar{p}$ values will be practically the same as these p' values.

Figure 9-9 illustrates the case in which the centering of a process may be allowed to shift through a considerable range. If control-chart limits are to be set to permit this shift, p' should be based on the ratio of each shaded area to the total area under the frequency curve, just as was done in the case illustrated by Fig. 9-8. However, in Fig. 9-9, the actual fraction rejected by the work gages might be considerably less than in Fig. 9-8; that is, $\bar{p}$ might be less than the value of p' used for establishing control limits.

In Example 9-2, the tolerance range used for the special quality control gage (0.0025) was about one-third the total range permitted by the specifications (0.0070). This is approximately the best ratio for cases of the type illustrated in Fig. 9-8. For cases such as illustrated in Fig. 9-9, the tolerance range on the work gage should be a larger fraction of the tolerance range permitted by the specifications; the greater the permissible shift in process average, the greater the best value of work gage range to specification range.

Generally speaking, more useful information can be secured from $\bar{X}$ and R charts than can be obtained by the use of np charts using small samples with a

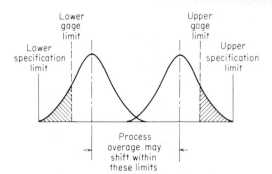

Figure 9-9 Relationship between special severe gage limits and specification limits when manufacturing process has a margin to spare.

special severe definition of a defective for control-chart purposes. The chief practical advantage of this type of *np* chart over the $\bar{X}$ and *R* charts is that the *np* chart may occasionally be applied to the results of patrol inspection with little or no change in the way this inspection is being carried on. In such circumstances, the *np* chart may involve lower costs for securing data and a minimum amount of training of personnel and changing of inspection procedures. Unless these conditions favorable to the *np* chart are present, the $\bar{X}$ and *R* charts are usually preferable.

VIII. COMBINING PROCESS CONTROL AND PRODUCT ACCEPTANCE

Reject Limits for Averages on $\bar{X}$ Charts

One possible method of showing the relationship between $\bar{X}$ values and the specification limits that apply to individual items is through the use of *reject limits* for averages.† If the assumption is made that σ' is known and will not change and that practically all the product will fall within limits of $\bar{X}' \pm 3\sigma'$ (or, for that matter, $\bar{X}' \pm$ any other desired multiple of σ'), it is easy to calculate the highest and lowest values of $\bar{X}'$ that will permit practically all of the product to fall within specification limits. The reject limits for averages are certain control-chart limits that would be appropriate if $\bar{X}'$ should be at each of these computed values. The derivation of these reject limits is explained here. Their application to acceptance inspection is discussed in Chap. 17.

Figure 9-10 illustrates the development of such limits. Assume the universe in its highest acceptable position with universe average *exactly* $3\sigma'$ below the upper specification limit. On an $\bar{X}$ chart with subgroup size *n*, the upper control limit $UCL_{\bar{x}}$ will be $3\sigma'/\sqrt{n}$ above the universe average. This will evidently be the highest possible satisfactory value of the upper control limit and is designated as the Upper Reject Limit for averages, abbreviated as $URL_{\bar{x}}$.

The distance of $URL_{\bar{x}}$ below the upper specification limit for individual values is obviously $3\sigma' - (3\sigma'/\sqrt{n})$. This may be expressed as $[3 - (3/\sqrt{n})]\sigma'$. This factor $[3 - (3/\sqrt{n})]$ is designated as *V*. Table 9-7 gives values of *V* corresponding to values of *n* from 2 to 25. By a similar process of reasoning which assumes the universe in its lowest acceptable position, it may be shown that the Lower Reject Limit for averages, $LRL_{\bar{x}}$, is $V\sigma'$ above the lower specification limit.

If an $\bar{X}$ chart shows a state of statistical control and both control limits fall within the two reject limits, this means that as long as control is maintained all is

---

† A. J. WINTERHALTER, Development of Reject Limits for Measurements, *Industrial Quality Control*, vol. 1, no. 4, pp. 12–15, January, 1945; vol. 1, no. 5, pp. 12–13, March, 1945. See also Engineering Data Book, Sec. 29, "Statistical Methods in Quality Control," issued Sept. 22, 1943, Hunter Pressed Steel Co., Lansdale, Pa. See also R. A. FREUND, "Acceptance Control Charts," *Industrial Quality Control*, October, 1957.

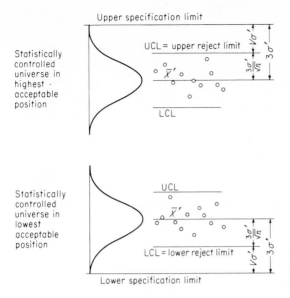

Figure 9-10 Relationship among specification limits, control limits, and reject limits.

well; practically all the product will fall within specification limits. If the $UCL_{\bar{x}}$ falls above the $URL_{\bar{x}}$, or if the $LCL_{\bar{x}}$ falls below the $LRL_{\bar{x}}$, the conclusion is that even though control is maintained, some of the product manufactured will fall outside specifications. In this way, limits telling the conformance of individual values with specifications may be placed on the chart for averages.

Table 9-7 Values of V, factor for reject limits, for different values of n subgroup size

n	V	n	V	n	V
2	0.88	10	2.05	18	2.29
3	1.27	11	2.09	19	2.31
4	1.50	12	2.13	20	2.33
5	1.66	13	2.17	21	2.35
6	1.78	14	2.20	22	2.36
7	1.87	15	2.23	23	2.37
8	1.94	16	2.25	24	2.39
9	2.00	17	2.27	25	2.40

Upper reject limit$_{\bar{x}}$ = U (upper specification limit) − $V\sigma'$
Lower reject limit$_{\bar{x}}$ = L (lower specification limit) + $V\sigma'$

$$V = 3 - \frac{3}{\sqrt{n}}$$

Modified Control Limits

One step beyond the use of reject limits *and* control limits on $\bar{X}$ charts is the use of reject limits *in place of* control limits. Reject limits used in this way have been called *modified control limits*. They have been applied particularly to control of dimensions. Their use is practical only where the spread of the process (frequently estimated as $6\sigma'$) is appreciably less than the difference between the two specification limits $(U - L)$.

The idea behind the modified control limits is to permit limited shifts in the process average in cases where the difference between the two specification limits is substantially greater than the spread of a controlled process. This is intended to avoid the cost of stopping production to hunt for trouble whenever the shifts in process average are not sufficient to cause the production of nonconforming product. It is as though in Fig. 9-10 the process were to be allowed to vary from the position marked "highest acceptable position of universe" to that marked "lowest acceptable position."

However, in the use of modified control limits a larger margin of safety is sometimes introduced than that given by the assumption that the spread of the process is $\pm 3\sigma'$ from the process average. One British practice is to set such limits at a distance from the specification limits equal to $3.09\sigma' - (1.96\sigma'/\sqrt{n})$. This gives multipliers of σ' of 1.70, 1.97, 2.10, and 2.21 for $n = 2, 3, 4,$ and 5, respectively; this contrasts with the more common practice in the United States of using the respective V factors of 0.88, 1.27, 1.50, and 1.66 given in Table 9-7 for the same subgroup sizes.

Modified control limits seem to have proved particularly useful as applied to intermittent short production runs in machining operations where process dispersion $(6\sigma')$ has been determined from previous runs. The more $(U - L)$ exceeds $6\sigma'$, the greater the permissible latitude in machine setting. The use of modified control limits may simplify the problem of maintaining machine settings that are good enough for practical purposes.

Nevertheless, where the only limits shown on $\bar{X}$ charts are modified control limits, the users of these charts should recognize that the charts fail to disclose the presence or absence of statistical control in the manufacturing process. Moreover, the protection given by the reject limits depends on a good estimate of σ'; after this estimate has been made, the process dispersion must remain in statistical control. Whenever process dispersion behaves erratically, reject limits or modified control limits are not appropriate. For this reason, a chart for R should supplement any $\bar{X}$ chart using reject limits or modified control limits.

PROBLEMS

I. Some special topics on Shewhart control charts for variables

9-1 A certain company manufactures electronic components for use in television sets. One particular component is made to a critical length of 0.450 in. Based on past production experiences, the standard deviation of this dimension is 0.010 in. Because of the critical nature of the dimension, the quality control group maintains warning limits on the $\bar{X}$ control chart as well as the normal 3σ control limits. The $\bar{X}$ chart is based on subgroups of four samples, and warning limits are maintained at two standard deviations from the mean.

Compute the warning limits and the control limits for the $\bar{X}$ chart.

Answer: 0.460, 0.440; 0.465, 0.435.

9-2 Problem 9-1 asked for the calculation of both warning limits and control limits for an $\bar{X}$ chart. Using those data:

(a) What is the probability that a subgroup average will exceed the upper warning limit but not exceed the upper control limit when the process is correctly centered?

(b) The quality control supervisor has a policy that he should be notified immediately if two successive subgroup averages exceed one of the warning limits or if one subgroup average exceeds either of the control limits. What is the probability that, when there has been no change in the process, the quality control supervisor will have to be notified based on:

1. two successive subgroup averages falling between the upper warning limit and upper control limit.
2. a subgroup average exceeding the upper control limit.

(c) If the process average suddenly shifts to 0.460 with no change in the standard deviation, what is the probability that two successive points will exceed the upper warning limit but not exceed the upper control limit?

Answer: (a) 0.0214; (b) 0.0005, 0.0014; (c) 0.1165.

9-3 Calculate control limits and plot an $\bar{X}$ chart for the data of Table 9-1. Base your calculations on the exact sample size, n, for each subgroup rather than the average value, 123. Does using the exact values of n lead to any different conclusions from interpreting your chart than those reached from interpretating the $\bar{X}$ chart in Fig. 9-2?

9-4 In the manufacture of the balance wheel for a speed control device, finished wheels are tested for dynamic balance on a test stand at 6,000 r/min. If a vibration force in excess of 85 g cm/s² results, the balance must be remachined.

Because of the critical nature of this test, control charts for $\bar{X}$ and R are maintained using a subgroup size of four. Warning limits at $\pm 2\sigma$ are used as well as standard 3σ control limits. The process has been operating in control at an estimated $\bar{X}'$ of 74 g cm/s² and a σ' of 3.4.

(a) Calculate control limits for both the $\bar{X}$ and R charts and warning limits for the $\bar{X}$ chart.

(b) With the process centered as indicated, what is the probability that two successive points will fall between the UCL and the UWL on the $\bar{X}$ chart?

9-5 In the situation described in Problem 9-4, the mean of the process suddenly shifts to 78 g cm/s².

(a) At this new mean level, what proportion of the balance wheels will exceed the 85 g cm/s² limit assuming a normal distribution of this characteristic?

(b) What is the probability that this shift in $\bar{X}'$ will be detected on the first subgroup after the shift occurs?

(c) What is the probability that the shift will be detected on the first two subgroups based only upon two successive points falling between the UCL and the UWL?

(d) What is the combined probability of detecting this shift within the first two subgroups plotted?

9-6 For a certain process, the natural tolerance range exceeds the specification range. Slight changes in centering will therefore result in substantial product being produced outside specifications. Someone has suggested the use of 1σ warning limits in addition to 3σ control limits on an $\bar{X}$ chart. A shift in process is assumed to have occurred if: (1) a point falls outside one of the 3σ control limits; or (2) three points in a row fall outside one of the warning limits.

(a) What is the probability that the application of rule (2) will lead to hunting for trouble when none exists (Type I error)?

(b) Assuming an upward shift in $\bar{X}'$ of $0.5\ \sigma'$ and a subgroup size of 4, what is the probability that the application of rule (2) will lead to *not* detecting the shift on the first three subgroups drawn after the shift occurs (Type II error)?

9-7 Both 3σ control limits and 2σ warning limits are maintained on an $\bar{X}$ chart for the internal diameter of a shock tube assembly. The aimed-at value is 35.50 mm and σ' is 0.25 mm. The subgroup size is 5.

(a) Calculate the control and warning limits for an $\bar{X}$ chart for this process.

(b) Calculate the control limits for an R chart to control dispersion.

(c) If the actual mean of the process is 35.70 mm, find the probability that any given point would fall above the UCL and the probability that two points in succession would fall between the UWL and the UCL.

9-8 In a certain manufacturing process, $\bar{\bar{X}} = 178.46$ and $\bar{R} = 9.8$. The subgroup size is 5, and standard 3σ control limits are used. If seven consecutive points all fall above (or below) $\bar{\bar{X}}$, the process average is assumed to have shifted.

(a) If $\bar{X}'$ is 178.46, what is the probability of seven consecutive points falling on one side of $\bar{\bar{X}}$ (Type I error)?

(b) If $\bar{X}'$ shifts to 182.00 what is the probability of seven consecutive points falling on one side of $\bar{\bar{X}}$ (i.e., not making a Type II error).

9-9 Prepare a control chart for subgroup totals for the data of Problem 2-10.

9-10 Prepare a control chart for subgroup totals for the data of Problem 2-19.

9-11 An $\bar{X}$ chart used to monitor a particular quality characteristic has an $\bar{X}$ value of 32.0 and $3\sigma_{\bar{x}}$ limits at 30.5 and 33.5. The product is sampled in subgroups of four. The analyst considers that a quality characteristic is out of control if one subgroup falls outside either of the control limits or if seven successive subgroup averages fall on one side of the central line.

(a) Estimate the $\bar{X}'$ and σ' of the process.

(b) With the process in control and assuming a normal distribution, what is the probability that seven successive subgroup averages will fall on the upper side of the central line?

(c) If the process average shifts from 32.0 to 32.9 with no change in σ', what is the probability that the next seven successive values of $\bar{X}$ will fall on the upper side of the central line? Assume that the $\bar{X}$ of the subgroup immediately preceding the shift fell below the central line.

(d) In the circumstances described in (c), what is the probability that at least one $\bar{X}$ value in the next seven subgroups will fall above the upper control limit on the $\bar{X}$ chart?

II. Some related special procedures

9-12 Plot individual measurements and a superimposed chart for medians using the data of Problem 2-1. The chart should be similar to Fig. 9-3 except that no specification limits are required. Base 3σ control limits for the medians on the median of the ranges.

9-13 Plot individual measurements and a superimposed chart for medians using the data of Problem 2-10. The chart should be similar to Fig. 9-3 except that no specification limits are required. Base 3σ control limits for the medians on the median of the ranges.

III. A general test for homogeniety

9-14 Tests of tensile strengths of malleable iron castings from four foundries gave the following results:

Foundry	Number of tests	Average tensile strength lb/in^2	Standard deviation
A	54	58,400	1,600
B	60	57,000	1,550
C	71	57,700	1,190
D	49	56,900	2,080

Use the methods explained in the discussion of Table 9-1 to plot $\bar{X}$ and σ charts to judge whether there is clear evidence that the different foundries represent different cause systems. Use simple unweighted averages to determine $\bar{\bar{X}}$ and $\bar{\sigma}$, and base your limits on average subgroup size.

9-15 Solve Problem 9-14 using the correct weighted averages for $\bar{\bar{X}}$ and $\bar{\sigma}$ and base your limits on the correct values of n. How does your solution in this case compare with that arrived at from interpreting the results in Problem 9-14?

9-16 A textile manufacturer has six lines producing fiber thread for which one important characteristic is tensile strength. Data obtained over the past ten days have been summarized in the following table.

Machine	Number of tests	Average tensile strength	Standard deviation
1	56	2.34	0.11
2	70	2.39	0.16
3	75	2.25	0.18
4	102	2.34	0.11
5	86	2.38	0.09
6	90	2.37	0.08

Using the methods explained in the discussion of Table 9-1, plot $\bar{X}$ and σ charts for these test data and judge whether there is clear evidence that the different machines represent different chance cause systems. Use simple unweighted averages to determine $\bar{\bar{X}}$ and $\bar{\sigma}$ and base the control limits on the average sample size.

IV. Probability limits on control charts for variables

9-17 Assume that probability limits rather than 3-sigma limits are to be used for the data of Example 1-2. Where would these limits be on the $\bar{X}$ and R chart:

   (a) If the probability of a point falling outside the limits in sampling from a normal universe were to be 0.002?

   (b) If this probability were to be 0.01?

   (c) If this probability were to be 0.05?

   Answer: (a) $UCL_{\bar{X}} = 145.7$; $LCL_{\bar{X}} = 135.5$.

9-18 Find 95% probability limits for $\bar{X}$ and R control charts for the data of Problem 2-10. Does the process appear to be operating in control?

9-19 Calculate 95% and 99% probability limits for $\bar{X}$ and R control charts for the data of Problem 2-19. Is there any difference in the interpretation of the results based on the use of the two different sets of control limits?

9-20 Control charts for $\bar{X}$ and σ are maintained on the weight in ounces of the contents of a cereal container. The subgroup size is 10. After 18 subgroups, $\Sigma\bar{X} = 595.8$ and $\Sigma\sigma = 8.24$.

    (a) Compute 3σ control limits for the $\bar{X}$ chart and estimate the value of σ'.

    (b) A decision is made to use 95% probability limits on the $\bar{X}$ chart rather than 3σ limits. What would be the locations of these limits?

    (c) If the mean shifts to 33.4, what is the probability of detecting this shift on the first subgroup after the shift occurs if the 3σ limits are used?

    (d) What is the probability of detecting the shift described in (c) if 95% probability limits are used?

V. Control limits for moving averages

9-21 Calculate three-point moving averages and ranges for the first 20 drawings from Shewhart's normal bowl in Table 2-7. Find 3σ control limits for an $\bar{X}$ and an R chart and comment on whether or not the "process" appears to be in control.

9-22 For purposes of computing control limits in the moving average illustration of Table 9-5 and Figs. 9-4 and 9-5, $\bar{R}$ was assumed as 0.065. From this $\bar{R}$ what would be your estimate of σ'? Assuming $\bar{X}'$ as 0.17, what are 3σ limits on individual daily values? If these limits were drawn on Fig. 9-4a, on what dates would points fall outside control limits? How does this compare with the dates on which points fell outside control limits on the moving range chart, Fig. 9-5a? How do you explain this relationship?

9-23 Summarized below are daily analyses of CO_2 as CaO at an intermediate stage in a chemical manufacturing process. Compute 3-day moving averages and moving ranges for these data and establish $\bar{X}$ and R control chart limits for monitoring this process basing the control limits on a standard process average of 0.660 and an $\bar{R}$ of 0.075.

Date	Per cent CO_2 as CaO	Date	Per cent CO_2 as CaO	Date	Per cent CO_2 as CaO
May 1	0.53	14	0.65	27	0.71
2	0.62	15	0.59	28	0.68
3	0.63	16	0.60	29	0.74
4	0.54	17	0.69	30	0.66
5	0.50	18	0.65	31	0.67
6	0.50	19	0.65	June 1	0.67
7	0.51	20	0.67	2	0.68
8	0.53	21	0.71	3	0.72
9	0.56	22	0.78	4	0.70
10	0.64	23	0.82	5	0.67
11	0.57	24	0.82	6	0.69
12	0.56	25	0.88	7	0.68
13	0.55	26	0.82		

VI. $\overline{X}$ chart with a linear trend

9-24 A certain manufacturing process has exhibited a linear increasing trend. Sample averages and ranges for the past 15 subgroups, taken every 15 minutes in subgroups of 5 items, are given in the following table.

Subgroup	Average	Range	Subgroup	Average	Range
1	198.8	7	9	209.2	7
2	197.6	2	10	207.8	16
3	204.6	10	11	210.0	9
4	203.8	12	12	214.4	8
5	205.6	17	13	211.8	16
6	204.8	9	14	211.8	6
7	205.4	10	15	213.8	8
8	210.6	9			

Fit the linear trend line to these data and plot a trended $\overline{X}$ control chart with 3σ limits.

9-25 Specifications on the process in Problem 9-24 are 200 ± 20. The process may be stopped at any time and readjusted. If upon readjustment the mean is to be set exactly $3\sigma'$ above the lower specification and the process is to be stopped for readjustment when the mean reaches a level exactly $3\sigma'$ below the upper specification;

(a) Calculate the aimed-at starting and stopping values of $\overline{X}'$; and

(b) estimate the duration of a run between adjustments.

9-26 The following data are from a machining operation that exhibits a steady trend in the average dimension of the items processed. The subgroup size is four, the four samples being taken in succession at 30-minute intervals and measured in millimeters.

Subgroup	$\overline{X}$	R
1	31.42	0.10
2	31.49	0.13
3	31.57	0.04
4	31.71	0.08
5	31.83	0.11
6	31.89	0.05
7	32.00	0.09
8	32.13	0.14
9	32.19	0.07
10	32.30	0.10
11	32.39	0.11
12	32.51	0.13
13	32.64	0.12

(a) Determine the equation of a least squares trend-line fitted to the $\overline{X}$ values.

(b) Determine the 3σ control limits for an $\overline{X}$ chart.

(c) If the dimensions of the part are specified as 32.00 ± 0.75, estimate σ' and express the tolerance spread $(U - L)$ as a multiple of the estimated σ'.

(d) What would you recommend as the aimed-at value of $\bar{X}'_o$ in the initial setting if this is to be $3\sigma'$ above the lower specification limit?

(e) If a new setup is to be made when the value of the central line on the $\bar{X}$ chart is $3\sigma'$ below the upper specification limit, what would you estimate as the length of a production run before a new setup is required?

9-27 A certain dimension was specified as 0.8250 ± 0.0050 in. Experience indicated that tool wear caused a fairly steady trend in the average dimension of parts made on the required type of machining operation. The following values of $\bar{X}$ and R were obtained from subgroups of 4 parts taken from the machine at half-hour intervals:

Subgroup number	$\bar{X}$	R
1	0.8220	0.0004
2	0.8228	0.0007
3	0.8233	0.0005
4	0.8232	0.0010
5	0.8235	0.0011
6	0.8241	0.0012
7	0.8244	0.0014
8	0.8248	0.0004
9	0.8251	0.0005
10	0.8253	0.0013
11	0.8257	0.0003
12	0.8257	0.0008
13	0.8265	0.0011
14	0.8260	0.0010
15	0.8270	0.0007

Determine the equation of a least squares trend line fitted to the $\bar{X}$ values. Plot an $\bar{X}$ chart similar to Fig. 9-6 using slope 3-sigma limits parallel to the trend line.

Estimate σ' and express the tolerance spread $(U - L)$ as a multiple of the estimated σ'. What would you recommend as the aimed-at value of $\bar{X}'_o$ in the initial setting if this is to be at $4\sigma'$ above the lower specification limit? If a new setup is to be made when the value of the central line on an $\bar{X}$ chart is $4\sigma'$ below the upper specification limit, what would you estimate as the length of a production run before a new setup is required?

VII. Patrol inspection by p chart

9-28 In the testing of a certain ballistic characteristic of ammunition, it is desired that all values of this quality characteristic fall between 2,720 and 2,900 units. The quality characteristic has been tested on a variables basis with a sample of 4 taken from each lot. $\bar{X}$ and R charts have been plotted from past samples. The R chart has shown excellent statistical control with an $\bar{R}$ of 51 units. The $\bar{X}$ chart has shown a decided lack of statistical control. This lack of control of $\bar{X}$ is to be expected because past experience with other ammunition has indicated that it is very difficult to control the centering of the production process with respect to this particular quality characteristic.

It has been determined that it will be considerably more economical to test 16 items on an attributes basis than 4 items on a variables basis. In this connection it is decided to maintain an np chart similar to the right-hand chart in Fig. 9-7. For purposes of this chart it is desired to conduct the go and not-go testing using special severe test limits similar to the upper and lower gage limits shown in Fig. 9-9. These severe limits are to be established so that the appropriate p' is 0.15 for the "above limits" chart (corresponding to the not-go chart of Fig. 9-7) and is also 0.15 for the "below limits" chart (corresponding to the go chart of Fig. 9-7).

(*a*) With specification limits of 2,720 and 2,900 as stated, what should be the values of these special severe test limits?

(*b*) With 16 items tested in each sample, where should the action limits (3-sigma limits) be placed on the np chart?

Answer: 2,851.4, 2,768.6; 6.68.

9-29 It is decided to prepare a set of special patrol inspection "go" and "not-go" gages for process control of a critical machining operation. Specifications call for a dimension of 9.650 ± 0.150 cm. Previous application of $\bar{X}$ and R charts indicates an estimate of σ' of 0.045 cm and an approximate normal distribution of product when the process is in control. The patrol inspection gages are to be set at $+1\sigma'$ for the "go" gage and $-1\sigma'$ for the "not-go" gage.

(*a*) Calculate the gage limits.

(*b*) What proportion of the units should not fail each of these tests when the process is correctly centered?

(*c*) Calculate the control limits for the np charts for each gage based on a subgroup size of 12.

9-30 On a certain part, one critical dimension is the diameter of a reamed hole, 3.650 ± 0.020 mm. $\bar{X}$ and R charts have been used to control the process. This characteristic has shown itself to be nearly normally distributed with an estimated σ' of 0.005 mm. It is decided to convert to control charts for np using specially severe "go" and "not-go" gages set at the nominal dimension minus and plus one σ', respectively.

(*a*) What should be the limits on these gages?

(*b*) If the process is correctly centered, what proportion of product can be expected to not pass the test for each individual gage?

(*c*) If a subgroup size of eight is used, what should be the central lines and control limit values on each of the pair of np charts?

VIII. Combining process control and product acceptance

9-31 The specifications for a certain quality characteristic are 220 ± 20. It is decided to initiate $\bar{X}$ and R control charts with the $\bar{X}$ chart based on reject limits. Past evidence indicates that, although the centering of the process shifts from time to time, the dispersion tends to remain constant with a σ' of about 9 units.

With a subgroup size of 4, $URL_{\bar{X}} = 240 - 1.5(9) = 226.5$. $LRL_{\bar{X}} = 200 + 1.5(9) = 213.5$. (See Table 9-7.) $UCL_R = 4.70(9) = 42.3$. $LCL_R = 0$. (See Table E.)

The control chart is initiated. In the first 50 subgroups no points on the R chart are outside the control limits. On the $\bar{X}$ chart, 4 points are above the upper reject limit and 3 points are below the lower reject limit. The analyst who proposed the charts concludes that the process is "badly out of statistical control."

Discuss the foregoing case with reference to control-chart principles. Is this the type of case in which you would recommend the use of reject limits? Why or why not?

9-32 A certain dimension is specified in inches as 3.5100 ± 0.0050. Control charts for $\bar{X}$ and R indicate that the $\bar{X}$ chart shows lack of statistical control but the R chart always shows control. From the R chart the estimate of σ' is 0.0010. If the aimed-at process average $\bar{X}'_o$ is to be 3.5100, what should be the upper control limit for $\bar{X}$ with a subgroup size of 4? What should be the upper reject limit on the $\bar{X}$ chart assuming the use of 3-sigma reject limits?

Answer: $UCL_{\bar{X}} = 3.5115$; $URL_{\bar{X}} = 3.5135$.

9-33 A product is manufactured to meet an upper specification limit of 150.0 and a lower specification limit of 100.0. The process standard deviation is 5.00, and the product is sampled in subgroups of size four. Both $\bar{X}$ and R charts are maintained to monitor the product quality. Assume the distribution of the process follows the normal curve.

(a) To ensure that no more than 0.135% of the product fails to meet each specification limit, what must the control limits of the highest and lowest acceptable $\bar{X}$ charts be?

(b) Determine reject limits for a modified $\bar{X}$ chart. How do these limits compare with those found in (a)?

(c) Calculate the central line and control limits for an R chart for monitoring the dispersion of this process.

(d) If the R chart were to suddenly indicate a lack of control, i.e., an upward shift of σ', what effect would this have on the solutions to (a) and (b)?

Answer: (a) 142.5, 128.5, 122.5, 107.5; (b) 142.5, 107.5; (c) 10.30, 23.5, 0.

9-34 The thickness of fiber clutch pads for a certain device must be controlled within specifications of 0.360 ± 0.015 cm. These pads are formed in a semiautomatic machine with an estimated σ' of 0.002 cm. It is suggested that reject limits be used for an $\bar{X}$ chart rather than standard 3σ control limits about the nominal dimension of 0.360 cm. The subgroup size is 4.

(a) Use Table 9-7 to calculate the reject limits.

(b) What would be the central line and control limits to control dispersion of the process using subgroup ranges?

(c) It is suggested that, since the factor V, used to find the reject limits in (a), relies heavily on the assumption of a normal distribution of this product characteristic, the factor 3 be replaced by 4 in the multiplier of σ' in the formula. Thus $3\sigma_{\bar{x}}$ reject limits would be based on maintaining the process $4\sigma'$ away from specifications. What would be the reject limits in this case?

9-35 A product is manufactured to meet an upper specification limit of 150 and a lower specification limit of 100. The process standard deviation is 5, and product is sampled in subgroups of 4 items. In answering the following questions, assume the distribution of product at any given time is approximately normal.

(a) Is this process an acceptable candidate for reject limits? Why or why not?

(b) Assuming the answer to part (a) is affirmative, what would be the location of the reject limits?

(c) Calculate the central line and control limits for an R chart to control the dispersion of this process.

(d) If the R chart were suddenly to indicate lack of control, i.e., an upward shift in σ', what effect would this have on the answers to parts (a) and (b)?

(e) Your superior tells you that reject limits are to be used but that the process mean should not be allowed to shift any closer to either specification limit than $4\sigma'$. Revise the reject limits found in (b) to take this new requirement into account.

9-36 A shop decides to use reject limits on a modified control chart for $\bar{X}$ for both product acceptance and for process control. A random sample of 6 items is drawn from a storage cradle and inspected. If the value of $\bar{X}$ falls outside the reject limits, the tote box is screened for nonconforming units. Previous analysis indicates that this dimension is approximately normally distributed when held in control with an estimated σ' of 3.62 mm. The specification range $(U - L)$ is 50.0 mm.

(a) Is this process a reasonable candidate for using reject limits?

(b) Calculate the reject limits when $U = 1,040$ mm and $L = 990$ mm.

(c) If the process is operating at an actual mean value of 1,035 mm, what fraction defective is being produced?

(d) What is the probability of detection on any given subgroup when $\bar{X}'$ is 1,035 mm?

SOME ASPECTS OF SPECIFICATIONS
AND TOLERANCES

... It looked as if some of the tolerances were assigned much closer than should be necessary, and I started to try to find out how they had been fixed. To accomplish this, on every occasion when I met an engineer I asked him how he decided the tolerances in his branch of the subject; I fear I bored a great many people at this time. I got a variety of answers which sometimes explained things a bit, but often not at all, and though I discussed it with quite a number of men, many of them occupying prominent places in different branches of the profession, I came away with the impression that scarcely any of them were really interested in the subject of tolerances. To exaggerate the picture which I got as the result of my inquiry, I concluded that in designing a new machine the chief engineer drew it freehand with dimensions to the nearest inch, and sent it to the draughtsman to work out the detail to the nearest thousandth, who then gave it to his junior assistant to mark in the tolerances. Instructions were certainly always given that tolerances should be as easy as possible, but only lip service was done to them, and the junior assistant, anxious not to get himself into trouble, would, as a general rule, think of the smallest number he knew and then halve it.—C. G. Darwin†

Design and Inspection Specifications

The three functions in manufacturing of specification, production, and inspection were mentioned in Chap. 1. In any discussion of acceptance inspection, it is helpful to recognize the distinction between a design specification and an inspection specification. This distinction was clearly pointed out by Shewhart.‡ The design specification deals with what is desired in a manufactured article; in other words, it deals with the so-called specification function. In contrast, the inspection specification deals with the means of judging whether what is desired is actually obtained; in other words, it deals with the inspection function.

---

† C. G. DARWIN, Statistical Control of Production, *Nature*, vol. 149, pp. 573–575, May 23, 1942.
‡ W. A. SHEWHART, Some Aspects of Quality Control, *Mechanical Engineering*, vol. 56, pp. 725–730, December, 1934.

Some Problems in the Enforcement of Design Specifications

Although the following quotation from William B. Rice relates to the specification of dimensional tolerances and their enforcement some years ago, it describes a condition that may occur at any time with respect to many different types of quality characteristics.†

In many machine shops and metal working plants there have grown up over a period of years certain practices with regard to tolerances which can well bear re-examination. The blueprints may call for one tolerance; inspection gages may allow another usually wider tolerance, and the foreman may be even more liberal. Each of the three parties views the operation from a different standpoint. The engineer sees the problem as one of design; the inspector tries to maintain an acceptable quality; the foreman is under pressure to produce in quantity. Much of the spoilage and reworking which cost American industry so much in time, money and man-power arise from a failure to coordinate the viewpoints of the designing, inspection and production departments.

One reason why engineers, foremen and inspectors have different ideas about what tolerances should be permitted is that there are several ways in which inspection can be done. Take as an illustration a half-inch turning on a four-spindle automatic screw machine. If four successive pieces are taken off the same spindle, the diameters of the four turnings will probably vary by less than a thousandth of an inch. If, however, one turning is taken off each spindle, the measurements may vary by as much as two thousandths. Again, suppose that a run of 50,000 turnings has been completed; if a large sample (say 1,000) is taken at random from the entire lot, the difference between the largest and smallest diameters measured may be six or seven thousandths.

Another reason for disagreement is that the dimensions of the work which can actually be produced depend upon many factors. A new machine will hold more closely than an old one; skilled workers can do more accurate work than green hands can; experienced foremen are able to get better results than untried men in supervisory jobs; material, too, has a strong bearing on quality, as have the kind and quantity of tooling, personnel relationships, morale, pay, and a thousand other factors which come and go, fluctuating throughout the process in usually unpredictable fashion.

In general, product or design engineers often seem to do their planning and drafting with reference to somewhat ideal conditions, assuming good machines, well-trained workers and skilled supervision, or else they use reference tables which may tacitly assume such factors. Therefore tolerances on blueprints tend to be conservative and are sometimes actually impossible to meet with any degree of economy in the manufacturing process. Nearly ideal conditions may be attained during some small part of the process, but almost never for any extended period of time.

Production men, on the other hand, knowing from experience that a careless operator, a soft spot in the steel, a slight mis-adjustment of the tools, a loose collet or any one of a multitude of other troubles will cause an automatic to do out-of-tolerance work, are inclined to ask for more liberal tolerances; if these are not forthcoming they just "do the best they can." Unfortunately they do not always stop to figure how they can make that best better. Being human, and under pressure to turn out large volume, they are prone to accept what they have as the best they can get.

The process inspector, caught in the crossfire of these opposing interests, usually has to compromise. The workmen on the floor, with whom the inspector is in daily contact, argue that too strict adherence to blue-print standards will slow down or even stop production, and that another thousandth won't make any difference anyway. The engineering department, more

† W. B. RICE, Setting Tolerances Scientifically, *Mechanical Engineering*, vol. 66, pp. 801–803, December, 1944.

remote but exerting its influence through the blue-print which the inspector sees and uses constantly, calls for certain dimensions to which all pieces must adhere. Who can blame the inspector for letting an occasional out-of-tolerance piece go by under such conditions?

Two dangers arise, however, under such circumstances. First, neither the inspector nor the foreman knows every step in the manufacturing process, hence their judgment as to what can and what cannot be allowed to pass is usually poor. Second, laxity is encouraged which may destroy the validity and nullify the value of inspection. The idea of concrete, objective standards which result in usable articles economically produced should be basic to the inspection function. Violating this idea undermines the fundamental purpose of inspection.

Some Bad Consequences of Careless Setting of Specification Limits

The quotation at the beginning of this chapter was taken from an address by Dr. C. G. Darwin, Director of the British National Physical Laboratory, given at a joint meeting of the Institutions of Civil, Mechanical, and Electrical Engineers. These two quotations from Darwin and Rice reflect the fact that specification limits are often set by designers with little or no critical consideration of the various problems involved. In some instances, this may be because designers are too absorbed in other matters to have time to give much attention to tolerances. Lacking time and information, designers feel they are on the safe side by not being too liberal in their tolerances. They often feel that they can count on complaint from production and inspection to tell them of any cases where tolerances turn out to be tighter than can be held by production.

In other instances, the use of unnecessarily tight tolerances may be a deliberate policy on the part of designers. They may be conscious of the difference between the blueprint tolerances and those which actually are enforced. Therefore, in order actually to get what they think they need, these designers tend to specify closer tolerances than they believe are necessary.

As Rice suggests, an unfortunate result of this policy may be the creation of lack of respect for specifications on the part of production and inspection personnel. Sometimes it is critically important that specifications be met. Production and inspection personnel, tending to ease up a bit on any tolerances that are difficult to meet, and not understanding the reasons behind the designer's specifications, may ease up as readily on the critical ones as on those less important. On the other hand, enforcing tolerances that are really too tight tends to increase costs.

Statistical Methods May Help in Setting Better Specification Limits

The designer's considerations in establishing any specification limits may be classified into three groups, namely, (1) those related to the service needs of the article or part for which specifications are being written, (2) those related to the capabilities of the production process to produce to any given specification limits, and (3) those related to the means to be used for determining whether the specifications are actually met by the product.

The fundamental basis of all specification limits is, of course, the service need of the part or article. This is not primarily a statistical matter. However, it often happens that the service need can be judged more accurately with the aid of statistical methods. The viewpoint that every quality characteristic is a frequency distribution is always helpful. This is particularly true in matters involving the interrelationships of specification limits. The usefulness of statistics in this respect is illustrated later in this chapter in Examples 10-2 and 10-3.

There is no use specifying desired tolerances on any quality characteristic without some prospect that these tolerances can be met. Whenever production methods will not meet the proposed tolerances, this fact needs to be known and considered before such tolerances are adopted. The inability of any process to meet its quality specifications is sure to be responsible for extra costs. These may be costs of spoilage and rework, or of changing to another more expensive production process, or—in the case of dimensional tolerances—costs incident to giving up the idea of interchangeable manufacture and adopting selective fitting of parts. If such costs are to be undertaken, this should be done deliberately after weighing the facts rather than unconsciously because the capabilities of a production process are unknown. One of the major contributions of statistical quality control to design can be in the information the control chart gives about the capacity of a production process to meet any given tolerances. This point was a major topic of Chap. 5 and is expanded later in this chapter.

The third matter which was stated as relevant in setting specification limits is the means to be used for determining whether the specification limits are actually met. The relevance of the inspection specification in determining the design specification is not always understood. Both design engineers and inspection executives sometimes say, "It is the designer's job to specify what is needed; it is the inspector's job to devise tests and acceptance procedures to find out whether the designer's specifications have been met; let each stick to his own job." This fails to take into account the fact that, although the designer may not devise tests and acceptance procedures, he should not be indifferent to the tests and acceptance procedures that are to be applied. These constitute useful information for the designer for the same reason that he should know something about the capabilities of the production process; both influence the likelihood of obtaining what is specified. This point is developed throughout Part Two of this book.

Use of Information from Control Charts as an Aid in Judging Process Capabilities

If there is difficulty in producing within existing specification limits, the $\bar{X}$ and R charts provide a method of finding out why. They tell whether a process is in control, and, if so, at what average value and with what dispersion. If a long enough record of controlled production is available, a picture may be obtained of the form of the frequency distribution of the quality characteristic. All this provides a basis for judging whether or not it is possible to meet existing specifications without a fundamental change in the production process. As emphasized in the comments on Example 1-2, this information should be available in any review of a request for more liberal tolerances. As pointed out in Chap. 5, the method that was used for choosing rational subgroups may be of great importance in interpreting control charts to judge process capabilities.

In setting specification limits on new designs, considerable help may be obtained from $\bar{X}$ and R charts on past production operations similar to those which are to be employed, even though there is no control-chart information directly applicable to the new design. For such past control-chart data to be used effectively, design engineers must understand control-chart principles, and there must be some plan of organization that makes control-chart information readily available to them.

Some Common Methods of Interpretation of a Pilot Run as a Basis for Setting Tolerances

In the development of any new design of a manufactured product, it is often possible to improve the design and avoid production difficulties by means of a pilot run. If production methods used on this pilot run are similar to those which are to be used later in actual quantity production, it is good sense to use the pilot run to review the proposed specifications limits for the various quality characteristics. Thus it may be possible to anticipate and avoid situations in which the design tolerances are closer than can be met by the production departments.

The number of units produced in such a pilot run will depend on the costs involved, and might vary from two or three to several thousand. Suppose 100 units are produced, and actual measurements are made on each unit for every quality characteristic for which tolerances have been proposed. What tabulations and calculations are required relative to the measurements on each quality characteristic? How should the measurements be interpreted with regard to the setting of tolerances? Different individuals might answer these questions in different ways.

Without benefit of any statistical analysis, a common answer might be to take the highest and lowest measured values on the pilot run as indicating the upper and lower limits of the production process.

Someone who had been introduced to conventional elementary statistics, including frequency distributions and the normal curve, might reject this simple method as unsatisfactory. Instead he might group the measurements into a frequency distribution and compute the average and standard deviation. He might then compute 3-sigma limits on either side of the average and state that such limits would include practically all the items produced. Or he might even go so far as to make the precise statement that they will include 99.73% of the items produced.

The individual who has been introduced to the Shewhart control chart will be inclined to insist that the order of production of the units in the pilot run of 100 not be lost sight of. The measurements might then be divided into rational subgroups—perhaps 25 subgroups of four, and might then be tested for control by means of charts for $\bar{X}$ and R or $\bar{X}$ and σ. If no points fall outside control limits, σ'

might be estimated, either as $\bar{R}/d_2$ or $\bar{\sigma}/c_2$. Then $\bar{\bar{X}} \pm 3\sigma'$ will give an estimate of upper and lower limits for individual values in a controlled process—the so-called "natural tolerances" of the process. The individual who has made these calculations might state that if control is maintained, practically all the items produced will fall within these estimated natural tolerance limits. Or, as in the case of the frequency distribution analysis, he might go farther and state that 99.73% of the cases will fall within these limits.

Errors in Common Interpretations of a Pilot Run

All these methods of interpreting a pilot run miss the point to some extent. The frequency distribution method is likely to be better than taking as the limits merely the upper and lower measured values in the pilot run. The control-chart method is much more realistic than the frequency distribution method, in that it recognizes that there is no basis for an inference that a frequency distribution from an uncontrolled process will repeat itself. But no method of analysis can be found which justifies the positive statements that the process will hold within certain limits.

The justifiable statement is a negative one to the effect that without a fundamental change in the process it will be impossible to hold the process within limits closer than certain specified values. The control-chart method provides the basis for such a statement if the process is in control. If the proposed tolerances are closer than such limits, it is clear that either the tolerance range must be widened, or the process must be changed, or, if 100% inspection is possible, the decision must be made to accept the inevitability of producing some nonconforming product and doing a 100% sorting job of separating good from bad.

Even though no positive statement can be justified that a production process will hold within given limits, a positive decision must be made by the designer regarding the tolerances to be specified. In using the evidence of the pilot run to help in this decision, the designer should recognize that even though the natural tolerances as computed from $\bar{\bar{X}} \pm 3\sigma'$ happen to be within the proposed specification limits, this fact does not *ensure* that these proposed limits can always be met. The estimate of what tolerances actually can be held is partly a matter of statistics and partly a matter of engineering judgment.

The statistical questions involved deal with the reliability of estimates from a limited sample and with the form of the frequency distribution from a controlled process. Not a great deal can be told about the exact shape of a frequency curve from the evidence of a short pilot run, such as one providing only 100 measured values. It would take tens of thousands of values all in control to define the extreme portions of a frequency curve well enough to justify a statement such as one that in the long run 99.73% of the values will fall within certain specified limits. As explained in Chap. 2, skewed distributions of industrial quality characteristics often have several times 0.27% of the distribution outside one 3-sigma limit even though none of the distribution is outside the other 3-sigma limit.

The questions of engineering judgment involved in estimating what tolerances can be held deal with the difficulties of maintaining statistical control in the light of such matters as expected tool wear, operator variability, variability of incoming materials, and so forth. Any differences between the conditions of the pilot run and those of actual production should also be considered.

Example 10-1 Establishment of tolerance limits by pilot runs *Facts of the case* Nearly all the product of a company manufacturing electronic devices was sold to one customer. New designs of devices were continually being developed. In each new design, it was necessary to establish tolerances on the many different measurable quality characteristics. With regard to many of the characteristics, the usual practice had been for the customer to set specification limits at the design value $\pm 10\%$. It nearly always happened that when the device got into production there would be difficulty in meeting some of the tolerance limits that had been specified in this way.

After this manufacturer had started to use statistical quality control in connection with production operations, the control chart was applied to the analysis of the pilot runs used in development work on new devices. This analysis disclosed those characteristics for which the $\pm 10\%$ tolerances seemed likely to cause trouble. It also disclosed other characteristics for which it seemed probable that tolerances could be held much closer than $\pm 10\%$, so that some specified tolerances might be tightened where it was advantageous to do so. On this basis, definite suggestions were made to the customer regarding tolerances for all quality characteristics. These suggestions were usually accepted. As a result, specifications on new designs were better adapted to the capabilities of the production process, the percentage defective was reduced, and increased uniformity was obtained on certain important quality characteristics.

Two Statistical Theorems of Great Importance in the Interrelationship of Tolerances

A dimension on an assembled product may be the sum of the dimensions of several parts. Or an electrical resistance may be the sum of several electrical resistances of parts. Or a weight may be the sum of a number of weights of parts. In this common situation, what should be the relationship of the tolerances of the parts to the tolerances of the sum? This question may be answered with the aid of a theorem of mathematical statistics that is extremely useful in many problems of quality control. This theorem states that the standard deviation of the sum of any number of independent variables is the square root of the sum of the squares of the standard deviations of the independent variables.

$$\sigma'_{\text{sum}} = \sqrt{(\sigma'_1)^2 + (\sigma'_2)^2 + (\sigma'_3)^2 + \cdots + (\sigma'_n)^2}$$

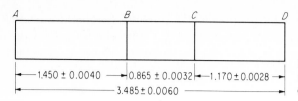

Figure 10-1 Dimension *AD* is built up from the assembly of parts having dimensions *AB*, *BC*, and *CD*.

For example, consider an assembly containing a dimension, *AD*, which is the sum of the dimensions of parts *AB*, *BC*, and *CD* (see Fig. 10-1). Assume that the dimension of each part is statistically controlled with averages and universe standard deviations as follows:

	$\bar{X}'$	σ'
AB	1.450	0.0010
BC	0.865	0.0008
CD	1.170	0.0007

Assume that upper and lower specification limits are at 4-sigma distance from the average. Specifications are then as follows:

	Specification	U	L	Tolerance range, $U - L$
AB	1.450 ± 0.0040	1.4540	1.4460	0.0080
BC	0.865 ± 0.0032	0.8682	0.8618	0.0064
CD	1.170 ± 0.0028	1.1728	1.1672	0.0056
Total........	....	3.4950	3.4750	0.0200

Someone considering merely the specified tolerances and not the distribution pattern of the dimensions might conclude that the appropriate specification for the overall dimension *AD* was 3.485 ± 0.010. This conclusion is incorrect because it fails to recognize the probability aspects of the situation. If the assembly of the parts is at random, large *AB* parts are just as likely to be assembled with small *BC* parts as with large ones. If the probability is small of the occurrence of an extreme maximum value of one part, the probability that three parts all having maximum values will be assembled together is very much smaller. The probabilities of all kinds of combinations of parts are reflected in a simple way by the formula for the standard deviation of the sum of independent variables

$$\sigma'_{AD} = \sqrt{(\sigma'_{AB})^2 + (\sigma'_{BC})^2 + (\sigma'_{CD})^2}$$
$$= \sqrt{(0.0010)^2 + (0.0008)^2 + (0.0007)^2} = 0.0015$$

If the specification limits for the sum AD, like the limits for the parts, are placed at 4-sigma distance from the average, the specifications for AD will be 3.485 ± 0.006. This ± 0.006 is in sharp contrast with the ± 0.010 obtained by simple addition of the allowable maximum and minimum values of the parts.

Some individuals in a manufacturing plant may find it difficult to believe that the laws of chance make the appropriate tolerance range for an assembly less than the sum of the tolerance ranges for the component parts. To convince them, it may be helpful to make an experimental verification of the theorem for the standard deviation of the sum of independent variables. Such an experiment at Westinghouse Electric Corporation is reported by Epstein.[†] Fifty of each of three components of an assembly were drawn at random from storage lots. These were gaged and averages and standard deviations of the dimensions of each component were obtained. The 3-sigma limits on assembled dimensions were then predicted by formula. The components were then selected at random and assembled, and the assemblies were gaged. The 3-sigma limits on the dimensions of the assemblies checked closely with the limits predicted by the use of statistical theory.

Whenever it is reasonable to assume that the tolerance ranges of the parts are proportional to their respective σ' values, such tolerance ranges may be combined by taking the square root of the sum of the squares. Thus

$$(U - L)_{AD} = \sqrt{[(U - L)_{AB}]^2 + [(U - L)_{BC}]^2 + [(U - L)_{CD}]^2}$$
$$= \sqrt{(0.0080)^2 + (0.0064)^2 + (0.0056)^2} = 0.012$$

The actual situation in setting tolerance limits is often the reverse of the one just described. Frequently the desired tolerance range is known for the overall quality characteristic (such as a dimension, electrical resistance, weight, etc.) and the problem is to set tolerance ranges on the component parts that can be expected to produce the desired range on the whole. This may be determined without much difficulty by trial-and-error solution of the formula. However, a direct solution is possible if the standard deviations of the various parts are assumed to be equal. In this case the formula for the standard deviation of the sum of n independent parts becomes

$$(\sigma'_{\text{sum}}) = \sqrt{n(\sigma'_{\text{part}})^2}$$

From this, it is evident that

$$(\sigma'_{\text{part}}) = \sqrt{\frac{(\sigma'_{\text{sum}})^2}{n}}$$

If tolerance ranges are assumed proportional to standard deviations,

$$(U - L)_{\text{part}} = \sqrt{\frac{[(U - L)_{\text{sum}}]^2}{n}}$$

† B. EPSTEIN, Tolerances in Assemblies, *American Machinist*, vol. 90, no. 1, pp. 119–121, Jan. 3, 1946.

Another useful theorem† of mathematical statistics deals with the standard deviation of the difference between independent variables, which is as follows:

$$\sigma'_{1-2} = \sqrt{(\sigma'_1)^2 + (\sigma'_2)^2}$$

It will be noted that the standard deviation of the difference is the same as the standard deviation of the sum. Example 10-3 gives an illustration of the use of this difference theorem in a problem involving the interrelationship between nominal dimensions.

A word of caution is called for on the application of these useful theorems to tolerance problems. The theorems assume independence of the variables being added and subtracted. In some assembly operations this independence does not exist. For example, suppose a dimension on an assembled product is the combined thickness of four metal washers. If these washers all come from the same production process and are assembled in the order of production, the thickness of the four washers in any assembly will not be independent of one another unless the process of producing them is in strict statistical control. Otherwise there will be a tendency for thick washers to be assembled together in some assemblies and thin washers assembled together in others. If this tendency exists, the theorem for the standard deviation of the sum of independent variables is not applicable to the problem of setting tolerances on the over-all dimension.

Example 10-2 Tolerances at intermediate stages in manufacturing electrical cable *Facts of the case* The manufacture of armored electrical cable requires a number of operations, such as insulation of wire, spinning strands of insulated wire together, applying various types of insulating and water-resisting coatings, and applying the armored covering. Customers' specifications on dimensions apply only to the finished diameter. However, in order to meet specified tolerances on the finished diameter, it is desirable to set tolerance limits on the diameters after each of the manufacturing operations. Such limits, properly established, should be helpful to the various manufacturing departments. In order that the limits be respected, they should represent a practical goal at each stage of manufacturing, and they should be set in such a way that departure from the intermediate limits really causes difficulty in meeting specifications on the completed product.

In the case where an arbitrary guess is used as the basis for such tolerance limits on intermediate diameters, it is likely that the limits so established will be inconsistent with one another. At one stage in manufacturing, they may be tighter than it is practicable to hold. At another, the manufacturing departments may believe that even though the intermediate tolerances are not met, it will still be possible to make enough corrections in the remaining operations to meet the overall specification. If the intermediate tolerances have these

---

† For a simple proof of these two theorems, see MENDENHALL, W., and R. L. SCHAEFFER, "Mathematical Statistics with Applications," Duxbury Press, North Scituate, Mass., 1973, pp. 185–188.

faults, they may not be respected by the manufacturing departments. If a customer's specified tolerances on final diameter are tight and are enforced, this state of mind on the part of the manufacturing departments may result in a substantial percentage of rejected product.

A rational approach to a consistent set of tolerance limits would require an estimate of the natural tolerances of each operation. For example, if operation 3 increases the diameter from 0.300 to 0.500 inches, an $\bar{X}$ control chart might be maintained on which the variable was the increase of diameter produced by operation 3. This would give a basis for estimating $6\sigma'$ for operation 3. The $6\sigma'$ values for the increase in diameter from each of the other operations might be similarly estimated. An analysis of the tolerances should then start with the specification limits on the final diameter and work backward operation by operation.

This is illustrated in Table 10-1. The figures used in this table have been modified from an actual case in a way that serves to conceal any confidential information. The calculations in this table start with the assumption that it is desired that the specified tolerance range of 0.050 on the final diameter should represent $6\sigma'$. The tolerance range at the start of the last operation (operation 8) is computed to be consistent with this specification and with the natural tolerance of the final operation (0.016). A similar calculation is made for each preceding operation. The calculations depend on the use of the theorem for the standard deviation of the sum of two variables

$$\sigma'_{sum} = \sqrt{(\sigma'_1)^2 + (\sigma'_2)^2}$$

In this case, σ'_{sum} (the universe standard deviation of the final diameter) and σ'_2 (the universe standard deviation of the last operation) are known or assumed, and it is desired to find a consistent σ' for the diameter just before the final operation. Hence

$$\sigma'_1 = \sqrt{(\sigma'_{sum})^2 - (\sigma'_2)^2}$$

Table 10-1 is representative of the first of a series of trial calculations for setting the tolerances on the intermediate operations. It uses (column C) an allowance of $6\sigma'$ for each operation from operation 8 to operation 2. This results in a computed tolerance range for operation 1 of 0.015, whereas the $6\sigma'$ tolerance range of operation 1 is 0.008. Thus, if the computed specifications of column I were to be adopted, this would amount to allowing a little over $11\sigma'$ range for operation 1 and only a $6\sigma'$ range for each of the other seven operations. It is evident that a second trial calculation is necessary.

This new calculation might be based on an arbitrary increase of all the column C figures by some selected percentage. In this way each of the eight operations would be treated alike with regard to the increased latitude allowed in the tolerances. Or, if experience indicated that it was difficult to maintain control on two of the operations and easy to maintain control on the other six, the entire increase in latitude of tolerances might be thrown into an increase in the column C figures for the two operations on which control was

Table 10-1 Example of trial computation of tolerance limits at intermediate stages in manufacture of electrical cable

(Final diameter specified as 0.750 in ± 0.025)

Operation number	Nominal diameter range at completion of operation	Estimated natural tolerance range $(6\sigma')$ of increase in diameter due to operation	Specified tolerance range of diameter at completion of operation $X_{max} - X_{min}$	Computed squared tolerance range	C^2	$E - F$	Computed tolerance range before start of operation $\sqrt{G}$	Computed specification at start of operation
A	B	C	D	E	F	G	H	I
8	0.750	0.016	0.050	0.002500	0.000256	0.002244	0.047	0.710 ± 0.023
7	0.710	0.021	0.047	0.002244	0.000441	0.001803	0.042	0.640 ± 0.021
6	0.640	0.018	0.042	0.001803	0.000324	0.001479	0.038	0.585 ± 0.019
5	0.585	0.007	0.038	0.001479	0.000049	0.001430	0.038	0.550 ± 0.019
4	0.550	0.013	0.038	0.001430	0.000169	0.001261	0.036	0.500 ± 0.018
3	0.500	0.028	0.036	0.001261	0.000784	0.000477	0.022	0.300 ± 0.011
2	0.300	0.016	0.022	0.000477	0.000256	0.000221	0.015	0.100 ± 0.007
1	0.100	0.008	0.015	0.000221	0.000064	0.000157		

difficult. Several trial calculations might be required to obtain a satisfactory set of computed specifications. The test of a consistent set is agreement between the computed tolerance range for operation 1 and the figure shown in column C for the estimated natural tolerance range of this operation. Or, stated a little differently, the final computed figure in column G (shown as 0.000157 in Table 10-1) should be zero.

Example 10-3 An illustration of the statistical relationship among specified nominal dimensions, tolerances, and fits and clearances

Facts of the case Many hand tools used by mechanics involve sockets and attachments. Rice describes a study[†] made to determine the difference between the specified nominal dimensions of the socket and the corresponding attachment, and to establish the tolerances for each dimension. He explains, as follows:

"The socket has a square hole into which the end of the attachment fits. There is a ball and spring assembled on the male square (attachment) which

---

† W. B. Rice, Setting Tolerances Scientifically, *Mechanical Engineering*, vol. 66, pp. 801–803, December, 1944.

catches in a ball check hole in the female square (socket) so that the two tools become a single driving unit. Important dimensions are: On sockets, the inside dimension of the female square; on attachments, the width across the flats and the height of the ball.... In actually working out this problem, there were several variables involved, but for the sake of clarity in presentation only the distance across male and female squares will be considered. The type of attachment studied was an extension, a straight metal bar with a male square at one end.

"The first step was to make several hundred random assemblies of finished sockets and extensions to determine what maximum and minimum clearances between male and female squares were necessary for practical use in a mechanic's work. This was done by a field survey. When the effect of ball height and other variables were removed, it was found on the $\frac{1}{2}$-in drive series that a minimum of 0.004 in and a maximum of 0.015 in clearance between male and female squares were required."

Rice explains that this study of consumer requirements was followed by a study of the variability of the dimensions of the sockets and extensions as they were then being produced. Shewhart control charts for variables were maintained on each dimension until a state of control has been reached and the natural tolerances determined.

For the extensions (male squares) the average dimension $\bar{\bar{X}}_M$ was 0.5005 in. The standard deviation σ'_M of this dimension (as estimated from $\bar{R}/d_2$) was 0.0015 in. For the sockets (female square) the average dimension $\bar{X}_F$ was 0.5120 in. The standard deviation σ_F was 0.0010 in. The distribution curves for these two dimensions were approximately normal. This is illustrated graphically in Fig. 10-2a.

Establishing the nominal dimensions for sockets and extensions As shown in Fig. 10-2a, the $3\sigma'$ limits for the individual extensions are 0.496 and 0.505. The $3\sigma'$ limits for sockets are 0.509 and 0.515. If it is assumed that, because the distributions are approximately normal, practically all the values will fall within limits of $\pm 3\sigma'$, it is evident that there will practically never be found an extension and socket with less than the desired clearance of 0.004 in. The maximum extension dimension is 0.505 in and the minimum socket dimension is 0.509 in.

On the other hand, it is clear that occasionally an extension will be paired with a socket with more than the maximum desired clearance of 0.015 in. The minimum extension dimension is 0.496 in, whereas the maximum socket dimension is 0.515 in.

It therefore appears that the existing setting of the nominal dimensions of extensions and sockets at 0.5005 and 0.5120 in, respectively, tends toward fits that are too loose. Generally speaking, the tighter the fit, as long as there is enough clearance for extensions actually to go into sockets, the better satisfied the mechanic will be and the better the reputation of the line of tools. Hence consideration should be given to a possible decrease in the difference between the nominal dimensions.

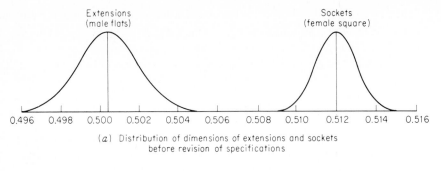

(a) Distribution of dimensions of extensions and sockets
before revision of specifications

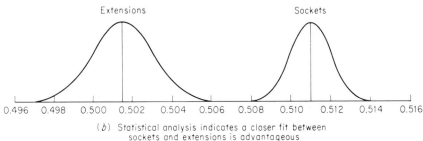

(b) Statistical analysis indicates a closer fit between
sockets and extensions is advantageous

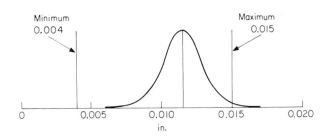

(c) Distribution of the clearance between extensions
and sockets before revision of specifications

Figure 10-2 Frequency curves representing distribution of dimensions of sockets and extensions. Example 10-3.

Rice suggests that the principle governing the decision of how far to go in the change of nominal dimensions may be found in the answer to the question, "What risk does the manufacturer want to take that, somewhere, sometime, a mechanic will pick up a socket and extension with less than 0.004 in ... clearance between them?"

The theorem for the standard deviation of the difference of two independent variables may be used advantageously to estimate this risk associated with any given difference between the nominal dimensions.† This standard

---

† From this point on, the analysis presented here differs slightly from that given by Rice.

deviation is

$$\sigma'_{F-M} = \sqrt{(\sigma'_F)^2 + (\sigma'_M)^2} = \sqrt{(0.0010)^2 + (0.0015)^2} = 0.0018$$

The existing average clearance between sockets and extensions is

$$\bar{\bar{X}}_F - \bar{\bar{X}}_M = 0.512 - 0.5005 = 0.0115$$

If, as in this case, both variables are distributed normally, the difference between the variables (that is, the clearance between sockets and extensions) will also be distributed normally. From this fact the probabilities may be calculated of a smaller clearance than the minimum desired value of 0.004 and of a larger clearance than the maximum desired value of 0.015.

A clearance of 0.004 is a departure of 0.0075 (that is, $0.0115 - 0.004$) from the average clearance. This is $0.0075/0.0018$ or 4.17 times σ'_{F-M}. The probability of as great a departure in one direction from the average is so small that it is outside the limits of Table A, App. 3, but may be determined from a six-place table of normal curve areas to be 0.000015. Thus too tight a fit might be expected about one time in 67,000.

A clearance of 0.015 is a departure of 0.0035 from the average clearance. This is 1.94 times σ'_{F-M}. The probability of such a departure is given by Table A as 0.0262, or about one time in 38.

The distribution of this clearance between sockets and extensions is illustrated in Fig. 10-2c. This figure shows the dimension centered on the nominal dimension 0.0115, prior to revision of specifications, and with upper and lower natural tolerances of 0.0169 and 0.0061, respectively. Probabilities associated with clearance less than 0.004 and greater than 0.015 may be changed simply by shifting the distribution of differences to the left, that is, by narrowing the difference between the nominal dimensions of the distributions of the individual parts as shown in Fig. 10-2b. Calculations for other assumed clearances between average dimensions give the following probabilities of fits that are too tight or too loose:

$\bar{\bar{X}}_F - \bar{\bar{X}}_M$, in.	Probability of smaller clearance than 0.004 in	Probability of larger clearance than 0.015 in
0.0115	0.0000 +	0.0262
0.011	0.0001 −	0.0132
0.0105	0.0002 −	0.0062
0.010	0.0004	0.0027
0.0095	0.0011	0.0011
0.009	0.0027	0.0004
0.0085	0.0062	0.0002 −
0.008	0.0132	0.0001 −
0.0075	0.0262	0.0000 +

This type of probability analysis supplies a rational basis for a decision as to the difference between the nominal dimensions. It is clear that the existing average clearance of 0.0115 should be somewhat reduced. A reduction of 0.002 to 0.0095 in gives a probability of 0.0011 (about 1 chance in 900) that a socket and extension selected at random will have a smaller clearance than the desired minimum of 0.004. In deciding whether or not to adopt this average clearance of 0.0095 it is also helpful to observe that if it is adopted, the probability of a clearance of 0.003 in is 0.0002—, and the probability of a clearance of 0.002 in is negligible. All these probabilities are subject to the limitation that they assume statistical control of the production process and a normal distribution of the quality characteristics involved.

If 0.0095 is adopted as the average clearance, it remains to establish the average value of the nominal dimension. If this were to be 0.511 for the sockets, the nominal dimension of extensions would be 0.5015. Figure 10-2*b* shows the relative positions of the frequency curves if these values are adopted.

If 100% inspection is to be used, the tolerances on extensions should be specified as ±0.045 and on sockets as ±0.030. For reasons that are subsequently explained, if sampling inspection is to be employed somewhat tighter tolerance limits may be desirable.

A Useful Diagram for Dealing With Overlapping Frequency Distributions

Examples 10-2 and 10-3 represent special cases of a common type of problem. R. W. Hanna and E. C. Varnum of Barber-Colman Company have commented on certain practical aspects of this problem as follows:†

> It is common practice for many engineers to specify dimensions for mating parts which differ appreciably so that there is essentially no chance of interference, i.e., little chance of getting pairs which will not assemble. However this method of avoiding interference can result in the equally disturbing problem of extreme looseness of fit.
>
> Consider, too, what happens sometimes when mating parts are delivered to the assembly floor with greatly overlapping distributions. Under general inspection procedures in many plants both types would be subjected to a 100% screening and the pieces found in the overlapping regions would be removed for correction or scrapping. In this way the assembly floor is assured of good mating parts but at an unnecessarily high cost in inspection, rework, and scrap.

Figure 10-3 is a diagram prepared by Hanna and Varnum to determine the probability of interference when two normal distributions overlap. Their directions for the use of the diagram are as follows:

† R. W. HANNA and E. C. VARNUM, Interference Risk When Normal Distributions Overlap, *Industrial Quality Control*, vol. 7, pp. 26–28, September, 1950.

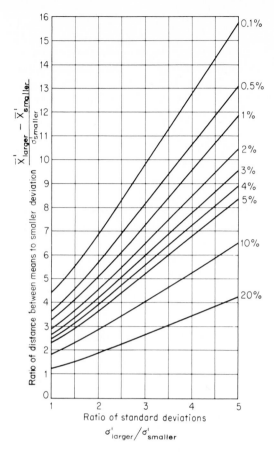

Figure 10-3 Probability of interference of two overlapping frequency distributions. (*Reproduced from R. W. Hanna and E. C. Varnum, "Interference Risk When Normal Distributions Overlap," Industrial Quality Control, vol. 7, pp. 26–28, September, 1950.*)

(1) Divide the larger standard deviation by the smaller; (2) locate this value on the lower scale; (3) subtract the means, or averages; (4) divide this difference by the smaller standard deviation; (5) locate the result of the division in (4) on the vertical scale; (6) find the point which is above the lower scale value and to the right of the vertical scale value; (7) determine the interference risk from the per cent curves passing nearest this point.

If it is desired to assume a given risk of interference, Fig. 10-3 may be used to determine the distance between the $\bar{X}'_o$ values that should be specified by the designer. For example, suppose it is desired to accept a risk of interference of 0.1%. If the two distributions have equal standard deviations, the distance between the $\bar{X}'_o$ values should be about $4.5\sigma'$. If one standard deviation is twice as large as the other, the distance should be about seven times the smaller standard deviation.

This Hanna-Varnum diagram may be used in place of calculations such as those made in Example 10-3 for the probability of clearances less than or more than any stated values. For example, with

$$\bar{\bar{X}}_F - \bar{\bar{X}}_M = 0.0085 \text{ in}$$

the probability of a smaller clearance than 0.004 in was computed to be 0.0062. To use Fig. 10-3 for this calculation, subtract the stated minimum clearance, 0.004 in, from the distance between the average values, 0.0085 in. This difference is 0.0045 in. Compute the ratio of this difference to the smaller standard deviation, 0.0010 in. This ratio is 4.5. Enter Fig. 10-3 using this 4.5 figure in combination with the ratio of the standard deviations, 1.5. The probability falls between the 0.5% and 1.0% lines; interpolation indicates an approximate value of 0.6% (that is, 0.006).

To illustrate the application of Fig. 10-3 to the determination of the probability of a fit looser than some stated value, consider the case where

$$\bar{\bar{X}}_F - \bar{\bar{X}}_M = 0.0115 \text{ in}$$

and it is desired to find the probability of a clearance larger than 0.015 in. Subtract 0.0115 in from 0.015 in, obtaining a difference of 0.0035 in. The ratio of this difference to the smaller standard deviation, 0.0010 in, is 3.5. For the ratio of standard deviations of 1.5, Fig. 10-3 shows the probability to fall between the 2% and 3% lines. Interpolation indicates a close check with the probability of 0.0262 computed in Example 10-3.

Precision, Reproducibility, and Accuracy of Methods of Measurement†

The only way in which the value of any quality characteristic—dimensions, hardness, tensile strength, weight, percentage of chemical impurity, etc.—may be determined is by some form of measurement. If measuring devices and those who used them were perfect, it would be possible to make a direct determination of the variability of the true values of the measured quality characteristic. Actually, the measured values reflect errors of measurement as well as variation in the quantity measured.

The phrase *method of measurement* may be thought of as including not only the measuring devices and the procedures specified for their use but also their manipulation by the particular user or users. Any method of measurement of an industrial quality characteristic may be expected to have some pattern of variability. Under favorable conditions this pattern may be observed by repeating a measurement many times on a quality characteristic that remains unchanged. For instance, Fig. 10-4 shows a frequency distribution obtained from 100 micrometer measurements all on the thickness of the same steel strip.‡ Different methods of measurement will have different patterns of variation.

The *precision* of a method of measurement refers to its variability when used to make repeated measurements under carefully controlled conditions. Where practicable, as in the case referred to in Fig. 10-4, these repeated measurements

---

† The meanings of these three terms are not standardized among writers on errors of measurement. Regardless of the terminology used, it is important to distinguish among these three concepts.

‡ Taken from "Dimensional Control," p. 19, The Sheffield Corporation, Dayton, 1942.

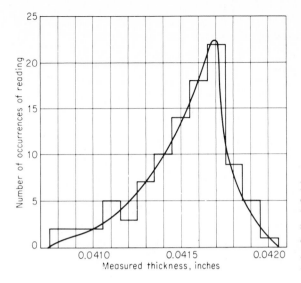

Figure 10-4 Frequency distribution of 100 micrometer measurements of the same dimension made by the same experienced inspector. (*Reproduced from "Dimensional Control," published by the Sheffield Corporation, Dayton, 1942.*)

should be made on a single quality characteristic of one particular article. Otherwise, as in chemical tests or other destructive tests, they should be made on a homogeneous sample. A numerical measure of precision is the standard deviation of the frequency distribution that would be obtained from such repeated measurements. This may be referred to as $\sigma'_{\text{error of measurement}}$.

The *reproducibility* of a method of measurement refers to the consistency of its pattern of variation. This may be judged to best advantage by control charts for $\bar{X}$ and R or $\bar{X}$ and σ. Where repeated measurements show erratic patterns of variation, the method of measurement used is not reproducible. Any statement regarding the precision of a method of measurement implies that the method of measurement is reproducible.

The *accuracy* of a method of measurement refers to its absence of bias—to the conformity of its results to the true value of the quality characteristic being measured. In an accurate method, the average value obtained from a set of measurements should differ from the true value by not more than would be expected as a chance variation in the light of the precision of the particular method. A practical difficulty in judging accuracy is that the only way to find the "true" value is by some other method of measurement. Presumably the method employed to determine the true value should be a method of high precision that is believed to be without bias.

In our initial discussion of the control chart for variables as applied to an industrial process, it was pointed out that an industrial quality characteristic will have (1) basic variability; (2) consistency of performance, that is, presence or absence of statistical control; and (3) an average level. This is also true of a method of measurement. In the foregoing discussion, *precision* refers to basic variability, *reproducibility* to consistency, and *accuracy* to average level.

Relationship between the Variability of Measured Values and the Precision of the Method of Measurement

The variability observed in measured values of dimensions, hardness, tensile strength, and other quality characteristics of industrial product is due in part to the variability of the product and in part to the variability inherent in the method of measurement. It is helpful to think of a measured value as the sum of two variables, the quantity measured and the error of measurement.

As these two variables are likely to be independent of one another, the formula for the standard deviation of the sum of two independent variables may be used to advantage. For this purpose it might be written

$$\sigma'_{\text{measured value}} = \sqrt{(\sigma'_{\text{true value}})^2 + (\sigma'_{\text{error of measurement}})^2}$$

This formula always supplies a useful point of view toward any problem involving errors of measurement. Its numerical use in solving practical problems depends on obtaining a reliable estimate of the magnitude of the standard deviation of chance errors of measurement.

One possible numerical application of the formula for standard deviation of the sum of two variables is in the determination of tolerance limits that are intended to allow for errors of measurement as well as for fluctuations in the true value of a quality characteristic. Another is in judging the ratio of the variability of true values to the variability of measured values. This latter application is illustrated in Example 10-4.

Example 10-4 Influence of chance errors of measurement on variability of measured values *Facts of the case* In a chemical plant, the method employed for laboratory analysis of the nonvolatile content of a certain product was not the most precise one possible. It was a rapid and economical method that was considered satisfactory by the laboratory director. Nevertheless, whenever a laboratory analysis showed the product to be outside specification limits, the production department was inclined to place the blame on the lack of precision of the laboratory methods rather than on any fault in the manufacturing operations. For this reason, a change to a more precise method was under consideration.

A determination of the precision of the analytical procedure indicated that the standard deviation of the error of measurement was 3.3 units. A control chart on the measured value for the manufactured product supplied an estimate that when the process remained in control σ' was 9.5 units. These values were substituted in the formula given above to estimate the σ' of the true value, as follows:

$$9.5 = \sqrt{(\sigma'_{\text{true value}})^2 + (3.3)^2}$$
$$\sigma'_{\text{true value}} = \sqrt{79.36} = 8.9$$

This indicated that the chance errors inherent in this analytical procedure caused the measured values to be about 7% more variable than they would have been if the analytical procedures had always given perfect results. The adoption of a more precise analytical procedure with a standard deviation of two-thirds the existing one would have reduced the variability of the measured values by about 3%, as shown by the following calculation:

$$\sigma'_{\text{measured value}} = \sqrt{(8.9)^2 + (2.2)^2} = 9.2$$

On the basis of this analysis, it was decided to continue with the less accurate and more economical analytical procedure.

Establishing Manufacturing Tolerances in the Consumer Goods Industries

A situation that is common in many industries is clearly described by Beckwith.[†] He classifies the possible conditions with regard to customer inspection of final product into two groups, namely:

(1) Where the product is not subject to immediate, systematic, and quantitative evaluation of quality and, therefore, is not subject to systematic acceptance and rejection. (2) Where the product is subject to immediate, systematic, and quantitative evaluation of quality and, therefore, is subject to systematic acceptance or rejection.

His comments on the first condition are as follows:

Condition No. 1 has been quite general in the textile industry in the past; that is, goods are produced, but the consumer, in general, does not make immediate systematic, and quantitative determination of their conformity to quality standards. Instead, the manufacturer is forced to maintain quality by the customer's longtime, haphazard, qualitative experience with the manufacturer's output. If, through good manufacturing methods, quality (for example, wear life of a fabric) is maintained at a standard level ±10%, it is not likely that increasing uniformity of product to ±5% will be readily discerned by the individual consumer. Therefore, if a manufacturer is enjoying a profitable business with a quality variation of ±10%, the arguments toward adoption of methods and processes designed to give a more uniform production having ±5% variation are somewhat abstract, even though it might prove over a period of years to show savings because of lower claims for defective merchandise. In such situations the need for close control or statistical control of quality is not readily apparent, unless it happens that competitors adopt quality-control techniques which give better products.

    Although many such situations exist in textile mills today, there are still cogent arguments for adoption of statistical quality control in these mills. The relationship of each department in a mill to the next one in the manufacturing operation is that of producer and consumer. The picking department produces prepared wool for its consumer, the card room; the card room, for the spinning room; the spinning room for the dyehouse. Even though there may be no testing at these points or systematic attempts to evaluate quality, nevertheless the production of each department is subject to immediate, systematic, and somewhat quantitative evaluation of the product in the next department. If stock is not well picked, the card room will complain and point

† O. P. BECKWITH, A Fresh Approach to Quality Control, *Textile World*, vol. 94, pp. 79–82, January, 1944.

to higher costs necessary because card speeds must be reduced to process the insufficiently opened and blended stock. If the roving is not well carded, the spinning department complains of allowances that must be made to spinners for their lowered production. Thus, it is seen that even in mills where the need for closely controlling final product quality is not sufficient to induce action by management, closely controlling quality within departments of the mill can be appreciated and the economies effected demonstrated relatively quickly.

This quotation illustrates the way in which the establishment of specification limits on certain quality characteristics at intermediate stages in manufacturing operations may be used to reduce costs and to assist management in controlling the relationship among the various manufacturing departments. It is evident that the only practical basis for such limits is the evidence of past performance in a period in which quality was considered to be satisfactory. Such manufacturing tolerance limits may best be established on the basis of the evidence of control charts. Conformity to the limits may also be determined to best advantage by the use of control charts.

Various Meanings of Quality of Manufactured Product in Relation to Design and Inspection Specifications

In the popular sense of the word, particularly as applied to consumer products, the word *quality* means general excellence. More particularly, it may mean excellence in relation to certain things that a consumer wants in a particular product. There are a number of different types of reasons why product may have unsatisfactory quality in this popular sense. There may be certain characteristics desired by a consumer (for example, strength, durability, appearance, performance of some sort) that were not designed into the product because the manufacturer did not intend to do so. Or the characteristics may not have been achieved by the product designer even though they were intended by the manufacturer. Or they may have been designed into the product but the design specifications may not have been carried out when the product was manufactured. Because this popular concept of quality applies to design specifications as well as to inspection specifications, it may be difficult to use numbers to express quality in this sense.

In contrast, if one is concerned solely with inspection specifications, it is common practice to attach numbers to the concept of quality. In the sense of quality of conformance, all product is either good or bad. Nondefective (good) product conforms to specifications; defective (bad) product does not conform. The per cent rejected is a numerical measure of quality of conformance.

The Common Condition of a "Twilight Zone" near the Specification Limits

Part Two of this book deals with a variety of plans that involve the use of sampling in acceptance inspection. In general, such plans are based on the concept of quality of conformance; each unit of product is classed as either good or defective.

Nevertheless, matters are seldom quite so straightforward as this simple classification seems to imply. As pointed out in Chap. 1, it is fairly common for design specifications to contain some margin of safety. That is, they are more severe than the designer really thinks is necessary for the functioning of the product under ordinary circumstances. Where this is the case, product slightly outside specification limits falls in a twilight zone that will actually be good enough for most purposes. The formal allowance for some percentage of rejects that is a necessary part of any acceptance sampling plan may be based in part on the assumption that such a twilight zone exists.

When a designer makes a conscious decision to incorporate a margin of safety into one or more tolerance limits, in effect, that decision is an economic decision. The extent of the margin of safety that is appropriate depends on certain cost factors and requires consideration of the acceptance procedures that are to be used. From a broad viewpoint, the design specification and the inspection specification may be thought of as two different aspects of a problem in engineering economy. A brief discussion of the economic analysis of this type of problem is given in Chap. 19, following the explanation of various schemes for acceptance sampling.

Why Designers Should Indicate the Relative Importance of Various Specifications

The quotation from W. B. Rice at the start of this chapter described a condition in which process inspectors, under pressure from production personnel, tended to ease up a bit on the enforcement of specifications. Such easing up is likely to be defended by production and inspection personnel on the grounds that product a bit outside of specifications is within the twilight zone of product that is good enough for practical purposes. As Rice points out, one of several objections to this practice is that the easing up on enforcement may occur in the wrong places because supervisors and process inspectors may have poor judgment as to which specifications are the critical ones.

In certain industries the practice has grown up of having a "material review board" or "plant salvage committee" that decides whether parts that do not conform to specifications may be approved for use in an assembled product. Here again, the approval of nonconforming parts may imply that it is believed that there is an out-of-tolerance twilight zone from which some parts are acceptable. Such a board or committee usually includes a representative of the design department who has a veto power in any decisions. A representative of design can therefore make an *ex post facto* judgment as to which specifications are the important ones.

In general, the basis for decisions on acceptance will be improved if designers stipulate *in advance* which of the numerous specifications are the most important ones from the viewpoint of the satisfactory functioning of completed product. This topic is discussed further after three short examples that illustrate certain points made in the last few pages.

Example 10-5 Failure of a successful control-chart application *Facts of the case* A certain small plant not only manufactured its own main product but also made precision parts for several larger companies. The chief inspector of the small plant attended a statistical quality control course. On returning to the plant, a control chart for $\bar{X}$ and R was started on a dimension (which we may call dimension A) on which a substantial percentage of the parts were being produced outside specified close tolerances. Dimension A proved to be badly out of control. By working a few hours on each shift of the several shifts for some weeks the sources of trouble were finally diagnosed and after much effort corrective action was secured. Dimension A was brought into control and brought within specified tolerances.

However, the purchaser who had rejected some lots of this part in the past continued to reject as many lots as ever. Investigation disclosed that dimension A was one which, even though specified by the purchaser to very close tolerances, was really of minor importance. The purchaser could actually accept parts far outside specified tolerances on dimension A without causing any trouble; for this reason the dimension was subject only to a very perfunctory check by the receiving inspection of the purchasing company and actually had not been the cause for past rejection of lots.

The real trouble had been dimension B on which *no* departures from specified tolerances could be permitted. Although the vendor's quality level on dimension B was good, it was not perfect; a single out-of-tolerance part in a sample was cause for rejection of a lot. As the chief inspector had not realized this fact, control charts had not been applied to dimension B.

The chief inspector was very discouraged. From the viewpoint of the owner of the plant and of the supervisors and machine operators who had cooperated in the trouble-shooting activity, the lack of this tangible success tended to discredit the use of statistical quality control. As a result no further use of the control chart was made; the technique was not applied to dimension B or to other quality characteristics on which it might have been used to advantage.

Example 10-6 A case of a designer's error† *Facts of the case* A homemaker purchased a high-priced electric stove made by the X Company, a well-known large manufacturer. This stove had two ovens. Normally, only the smaller oven was used. However, some months after the purchase of the stove, the large oven was needed to cook a turkey. The pan containing the turkey rested on a grating supported by projections on the two walls of the oven. The purchaser was extremely unhappy when the grating, turkey, and pan fell

---

† Examples 10-6 and 10-7 are adapted from E. L. GRANT and L. F. BELL, Some Economic Aspects of Quality Standards, *ASQC Convention Transactions* 1960, pp. 231–236, American Society for Quality Control, Milwaukee, 1960.

to the floor of the oven because the inner wall of the oven was not stiff enough to support its side of the loaded grating.

When a complaint was made to the retailer who had sold the oven, it was explained that the X Company had discovered this weakness in this particular model of stove and had provided a kit to be installed without charge. The retailer's service technician installed this kit. However, several months later when another attempt was made to cook a turkey, it was found that the kit had not been effective; the turkey, pan, and grating again fell to the bottom of the oven.

This time the retailer explained that the guarantee period had expired and that an alteration of the stove could not be made without charge, but that the company had now discovered the change that was needed to increase the stiffness of the inner wall of the large oven. When the service technician came to make the estimate of the cost of this alteration (about $50), the owner of the stove spoke quite unfavorably of the X Company. "Well," said the technician, "the X Company is usually pretty good but it sure pulled a boo-boo when it designed the oven for this stove!"

Example 10-7 A case of an imperfect design specification and a satisfactory product *Facts of the case* In a fairly complex electrical product for household use, there were many company-designed parts that the Y Company purchased from outside vendors. For one such part purchased from vendor A, the Y Company's designer specified an aimed-at value of a certain mechanical quality characteristic with tolerances of plus or minus 10%. Perhaps because special apparatus was needed to test this quality characteristic, no tests of this characteristic were made by the Y Company's receiving department. The parts purchased from vendor A were installed in the complex product and functioned satisfactorily.

After this state of affairs had continued for several years, a few of these parts were tested as one of the operations in a quality audit. When none of these parts fell within specification limits, the parts in stock and the incoming lots were tested. The group making the audit finally reached the opinion that it was likely not one of the many components purchased from vendor A over a period of years had even fallen within the specification limits. Moreover, the quality audit indicated that the finished product would have functioned less satisfactorily if vendor A actually had made this part in accordance with the designer's specifications.

Some Comments on Examples 10-5, 10-6, and 10-7

Comment on certain interesting cost matters and organizational matters illustrated by these examples will be put off until Chap. 19. The following comments deal only with topics covered in this chapter.

Example 10-5 illustrates how a particular specification that was recognized as being too tight was not enforced by the receiving department of the purchaser. It also illustrates the kind of adverse consequences that may occur if a purchaser gives no information to the vendors about the relative importance of different design specifications.

Even if all the stoves of the particular model discussed in Example 10-6 had shown perfect quality of conformance to specifications, the stoves would not have satisfied their purchasers. The "boo-boo" made by the designer caused their quality of design to be unsatisfactory as judged by any reasonable standard. (Incidentally, the purchaser did not pay the $50 demanded by the retailer to correct the designer's error. In effect, the support for the grating in the large oven was redesigned by using four empty cans to hold it up at its four corners.)

In contrast to Example 10-6, the components of the complex product made by vendor A in Example 10-7 were 100% defective in the sense of showing a complete lack of conformance to specifications. Moreover, the quality of design was somewhat poorer than might resonably have been expected. Nevertheless, in the sense in which *quality* ordinarily is used in everyday speech, the quality of the finished product was satisfactory. Surprisingly, the failure to check on quality of conformance offset the inadequacies in quality of design.

These three examples have been inserted at this point to ensure that any readers who are unfamiliar with manufacturing will not conclude from this discussion of specifications and tolerances that the whole story about quality is necessarily told by a division of product into two categories, namely, conforming and nonconforming to design specifications.

The Use of a Formal Classification of Characteristics (or Classification of Defects)

Modern acceptance procedures often divide the various possible defects of a product (in the sense of nonconformity to specifications) into three or four classes, depending on the seriousness of the different defects. Feigenbaum describes a fourfold classification as follows:†

> A critical characteristic is one which threatens loss of life or property or makes the product nonfunctional if it was outside prescribed limits.
> A major characteristic is one which makes the product fail to accomplish its intended function if outside prescribed limits.
> A minor characteristic is one which makes the product fall short of its intended function if outside prescribed limits.
> An incidental characteristic is one such as a small scratch on a painted surface.

Formal classifications of defects such as this are discussed in greater detail in Chap. 14.

---

† A. V. FEIGENBAUM, "Total Quality Control," p. 138, McGraw-Hill Book Company, Inc., New York, 1961.

PROBLEMS

10-1 Suppose it is desired to establish the relationship between nominal dimensions of extensions and sockets on hand tools in a situation similar to Example 10-3 but involving another size. Assume that a study of consumer requirements indicated a desirable minimum clearance of 0.005 in and a maximum clearance of 0.018 in. Assume a study of past production showed an average dimension of extensions of 0.7510 with a standard deviation of 0.0018 and an average dimension of sockets of 0.7650 with a standard deviation of 0.0011. Both distributions are statistically controlled and approximately normal.

Compute the respective probabilities of a smaller clearance than the desired minimum and a larger clearance than the desired maximum for average clearances of 0.015, 0.014, 0.013, 0.012, 0.011, and 0.010. Would you recommend any change in the existing average clearance? Explain your reasoning.

10-2 Two mating parts, A and B, have dimensions specified as 2.610 in and 2.615 in, respectively. Control-chart analysis indicates the standard deviations of A and B to be 0.0012 in and 0.0015 in, respectively. If the distributions of A and B are normal and centered about the specified dimensions, and if parts are assembled at random, find the probability of interference between the two distributions. Solve, using Fig. 10-3.

Answer: About 0.005.

10-3 Using the data of Problem 10-2, make use of Table A to compute the probability of a greater clearance than 0.010 in.

Answer: 0.0047.

10-4 Control-chart analysis indicates that the standard deviations of the distributions of dimensions of two mating parts, C and D, are 0.0008 in and 0.0020 in, respectively. It is desired that the probability of a smaller clearance than 0.002 in should be 0.005. What distance between the average dimensions of C and D should be specified by the designer? Assume normal distributions and random assembly, and solve using Fig. 10-3. With this distance specified, what is the probability that two parts assembled at random will have a greater clearance than 0.012 in?

Answer: 0.0076 in; 0.02.

10-5 Ten parties of students in a course in elementary surveying each made two measurements of the length in feet of a given line, with the following results:

Party	Measurement a	Measurement b	Discrepancy	Average value
A	421.59	421.37	0.22	421.48
B	421.73	421.65	0.08	421.69
C	421.70	422.28	0.58	421.99
D	421.79	421.72	0.07	421.76
E	421.64	421.67	0.03	421.66
F	421.58	421.56	0.02	421.57
G	421.53	421.69	0.16	421.61
H	421.52	421.66	0.14	421.59
I	421.69	421.68	0.01	421.68
J	421.76	421.69	0.07	421.72

The taping methods used by these elementary students called for alignment by eye and estimation of difference of elevation by eye. These methods tend to give a measured distance that is slightly longer than the true distance. An advanced surveying class, using better methods for alignment and finding difference of elevation, made several measurements of this same line; the average of these measurements was 421.58.

What conclusions, if any, can you draw regarding the precision, the reproducibility, and the accuracy of the measurements made by the elementary class?

10-6 Table 2-6 gives the distribution of markings of chips in Shewhart's bowl. Assume these represent the excess over 0.0800 in of the thicknesses of metal washers measured to the nearest 0.0001 in; for example, 30 corresponds to a thickness of 0.0830.

The standard deviation σ' of this distribution is approximately 0.0010. Table 2-7, in which chips (that is, washers) are drawn in groups of 4, illustrates the distribution that might be expected if washers were assembled at random in groups of 4. The sum of the four figures in each group, added to 0.3200, gives the thickness of one assembly.

Table 2-8 gives a frequency distribution that can be adapted to find the frequency distribution of the thickness of the 100 assemblies if appropriate changes are made in the cell boundaries. Find the standard deviation of the frequency distribution of assembly thicknesses as adapted from Table 2-8. How does this standard deviation check with the one that would be anticipated by the use of the theorem for the sum of 4 independent variables?

10-7 Control charts for $\bar{X}$ and R have been used to monitor a process for a long time. The process is sampled in subgroups of 4 items at intervals of about two hours. Control limits have been based on an aimed-at mean of 3.750 and an $\bar{R}$ of 0.1647.

(a) Estimate σ' from this control chart data.

(b) If the standard deviation of error of measurement is known to be 0.020, what is the actual standard deviation of the process?

(c) Assuming the process output to be normally distributed, what actual percentage of product will not meet specifications of 3.810 ± 0.240?

(d) In order to minimize scrap loss, it is decided to adjust the process centering to exactly $3\sigma'$ above the lower specification limit. Where should the process be centered?

10-8 A certain mass-produced electrical product contains a circuit in which the resistance is the sum of the resistances of three components, F, G, and H. The average resistances of F, G, and H are 60, 120, and 200 ohms, respectively; the estimated σ' values are 3, 6, and 10 ohms, respectively.

(a) If the three components are assembled at random, what would you expect to be the average resistance of the circuit? How would your answer change if the assembly were not done at random?

(b) If the three components are assembled at random, what would you expect to be the σ' of the resistance of the circuit? How would your answer change if the assembly were not at random?

(c) It is apparent that components F, G, and H are alike in having a σ' value that is 5 per cent of the average resistance. If assemblies are at random, will the σ' value of the resistance of the circuit also be 5 per cent of the average resistance of the circuit? Explain.

10-9 The standard deviation of the measured values of a quality characteristic is 40.0 units. However, the standard deviation of the error of measurement of this characteristic has been determined to be 10.0 units.

(a) Estimate the value of the true σ' of this quality characteristic.

(b) How much improvement in the measuring technique would be required to reduce the overall standard deviation to within 2% of the true standard deviation?

10-10 Two parts, A and B, are received in an assembly operation where each part is permanently attached to the other. When the combined width of the parts does not meet the required specification of 10.000 ± 0.020 inches, the assembled product must be scrapped. The width of part A is normally distributed with $\bar{X}'$ equal to 3.000 inches and a σ' of 0.004 inches. The width of part B is also normally distributed with $\bar{X}'$ equal to 7.00 inches and a σ' of 0.006 inches. Assembly is at random. Determine the percentage of the assembled product that will have to be scrapped.

10-11 The average clearance specified between two mating parts, A and B, is 0.0075 inches. The distributions of A and B are considered to be normal and, from control charting of the two parts, their respective standard deviations have been determined to be 0.0015 and 0.0035. Assembly is at random.

(a) Using Fig. 10-3, determine the probability of interference between the two parts.

(b) Perform the necessary calculations to determine this probability analytically and comment on your results.

10-12 Two mating parts E and F have normal distributions and are assembled at random. The standard deviations of the dimensions of E and F are 0.0025 and 0.0045, respectively.

(a) Using Fig. 10-3, determine what the average clearance should be in order that the probability of interference between these two parts is 0.002.

(b) Make the necessary mathematical calculations to determine this clearance. Comment on your results.

10-13 Manufacturer A produces a metal piece the dimension of which is normally distributed with an $\bar{X}'$ of 8.500 inches and an $\bar{R}$ of 0.004 inches based on a subgroup size of four. Manufacturer B produces a second metal piece with a dimension that is also normally distributed with $\bar{X}'$ equal to 6.500 inches and an $\bar{R}$ value of 0.005 inches based on a subgroup size of nine. Company C purchases these two parts and assembles them together to obtain a combined dimension of 15.00 inches. What per cent of the combined assemblies would you expect to have a dimension in excess of 15.006 inches?

10-14 It has been suggested that, when extremely high performance of certain missile components is required, a boundary on the stress requirement be set at 6 standard deviations of the stress requirement above the average stress. The average strength requirement of the article would then be set at 5 standard deviations of the strength of the component above this boundary.

A certain critical electronic component must operate in salt air environment at an average temperature stress of 30° Celsius. The standard deviation of this operating temperature is believed to be 5°C.

(a) What must be the minimum acceptable average strength, in terms of average failing temperature, of this component? Assume that the standard deviation of strength in this case is 3°C.

(b) How much of a safety margin does the requirement provide in multiples of the standard deviation of the combined strength-stress characteristic?

10-15 A certain automatic filling operation fills metal containers with a sticky plastic compound. Each container is supposed to contain 6 lb of compound (96 oz). Once a container is filled, it is impracticable to empty it to find the exact weight of its contents because some of the compound adheres to the sides and bottom of the container. For this reason, indirect methods of analyzing filling weights were used in the following study. The purpose of the study was to find out whether more overfill than necessary was being used to satisfy the weight specification or there was not enough overfill.

One part of the study dealt with the weights of the containers themselves. A random sample of 100 was taken from the most recent shipment of containers (purchased from an outside vendor). Each container was weighed, and the following frequency distribution was obtained:

Weight, oz	Frequency	Weight, oz	Frequency
22.0	1	20.25	16
21.75	1	20.0	15
21.5	2	19.75	12
21.25	5	19.5	8
21.0	7	19.25	3
20.75	13	19.0	2
20.5	15		

In the second part of the study, a random sample of 8 filled containers was taken from each day's production for a 12-day period. The filled containers were weighed, and the following control-chart data were obtained. (The figures given are the excess in ounces above 110 oz. Thus, the first figure, 6.2, means 116.2 oz. The 110 figure has been restored in showing the values of $\bar{X}$.) No changes in the setting of the filling machine were made during the 12-day period.

Day	Weights								$\bar{X}$	R	σ
1	6.2	8.9	9.9	5.8	8.1	9.3	6.4	8.6	117.90	4.1	1.46
2	7.0	7.6	8.3	7.5	8.0	6.6	6.5	7.9	117.42	1.8	0.62
3	6.6	6.7	8.9	6.4	8.4	6.7	6.9	7.4	117.25	2.5	0.86
4	8.5	8.9	6.9	6.3	6.8	7.0	9.1	7.4	117.61	2.8	0.96
5	6.8	8.2	8.9	7.9	8.1	9.7	7.5	7.3	118.05	2.9	0.86
6	8.0	6.8	5.6	5.0	7.8	6.0	8.5	7.4	116.89	3.5	1.17
7	6.3	7.5	6.7	7.0	6.8	7.5	6.5	6.4	116.84	1.2	0.44
8	5.2	7.7	8.1	8.3	7.4	7.5	8.4	7.6	117.52	3.2	0.95
9	8.1	5.7	7.9	7.0	8.1	8.2	8.4	7.7	117.64	2.7	0.83
10	8.3	5.4	7.0	8.4	5.6	8.9	7.4	7.4	117.30	3.5	1.19
11	7.6	6.3	7.6	7.0	6.7	9.2	5.7	7.2	117.16	3.5	0.98
12	7.4	6.9	7.7	8.9	8.7	7.1	7.7	7.2	117.70	2.0	0.69

$$\bar{\bar{X}} = 117.44 \text{ oz}$$
$$\bar{R} = 2.81 \text{ oz}$$
$$\bar{\sigma} = 0.918 \text{ oz}$$

(a) Compute the average and standard deviation of the weights of the containers shown in the frequency distribution.

(b) Make the necessary calculations to judge whether or not the weights of the filled containers exhibit statistical control. It is not necessary to plot control charts.

(c) What can you say about the inherent variability of the filling operation itself? For example, can you estimate the standard deviation of the weights of the *contents* of the containers (as distinct from the weights of the filled containers)? If so, what is your estimate of this figure?

(d) Overfill is defined as the excess of the contents of the containers above 96 oz. What is your estimate of the average overfill?

(e) If the distribution of the weights of contents of containers is normal and can be maintained in statistical control, what is your estimate of the percentage of containers having contents less than 96 oz?

(f) If the manufacturer is willing for 5% of the containers to have slightly less than 96 oz of contents, on the basis of the limited information available to you what would you recommend as the aimed-at value for average overfill?

SOME ASPECTS OF THE RELATIONSHIP BETWEEN CONTROL CHARTS AND CERTAIN OTHER STATISTICAL TECHNIQUES

I often say that when you can measure what you are speaking about, and express it in numbers, you know something about it; but when you cannot measure it, when you cannot express it in numbers, your knowledge is of a meagre and unsatisfactory kind; it may be the beginning of knowledge, but you have scarcely, in your thoughts, advanced to the stage of Science, whatever the matter may be.—Lord Kelvin

Purposes of This Chapter

This book deals chiefly with two types of statistical tools that have been found to be broadly useful in controlling the quality of manufactured product. These two tools, control charts, and acceptance sampling procedures, have many different aspects. We have already observed a variety of possible control charts and a considerable diversity of possible objectives for such charts. We shall discover a similar variety of methods and objectives when we examine the subject of acceptance sampling. Nevertheless, these are only two of a large number of types of statistical techniques that are useful in the physical, biological, and social sciences as well as in manufacturing.

Many of the persons who read this book will already have read one or more general treatises on statistical inference. Doubtless most of the other readers will eventually read such a book.

This chapter aims to help the reader to bridge the gap between the general literature of probability and statistical inference and the literature of control charts and acceptance sampling. More specifically, the objectives of this chapter are as follows:

1. To emphasize certain basic differences between the usual purposes of control charts and of some other common statistical techniques.

2. To introduce certain general terminology of the literature of statistical inference.
3. To relate certain symbols and formulas commonly used in connection with control charts to certain corresponding symbols and formulas that are common in the literature of statistical inference.

A Classification of the Problems of the Statistician

Enoch B. Ferrell of Bell Telephone Laboratories, writing in *Industrial Quality Control,* makes an interesting distinction among four classes of statistical problems.† We have paraphrased his classification as follows:

1. *Descriptive statistics* involves the summarizing of a set of numbers by means of relatively few numbers, for example, by a measure of central tendency and a measure of dispersion.
2. *Probability* a priori involves prediction of the characteristics of samples drawn at random from a known universe. It is as if there were a bowl full of known numbers and it is proposed to draw samples from this known bowl.
3. *Statistical inference* involves estimating the parameters of a universe on the basis of a sample drawn from that universe. It is as if there were a bowl full of unknown numbers and it is desired to draw conclusions about these unknown numbers on the basis of a sample or samples drawn from the bowl.
4. Although a quality controller often is confronted with the three foregoing types of problems, one of the basic statistical problems is quite different. It is *to determine the presence or absence of statistical control.* The controller has certain observed numbers and needs to know whether it is reasonable to treat them as a sample from one universe or whether they should be treated as coming from two or more universes. In other words, was there just one bowl or were there several bowls from which these numbers were drawn?

Explanation of Certain Words and Phrases Used in the Literature of Statistical Inference

This chapter contains explanations of a number of terms and concepts used in the literature of estimation and statistical inference. Many of the concepts associated with the terms have been introduced in earlier chapters even though the following discussion constitutes the first mention in this book of the term itself.

---

† E. B. FERRELL, Control Charts Using Midranges and Medians, *Industrial Quality Control,* vol. 9, no. 5, p. 30, March, 1953.

Random Variables

Wadsworth and Bryan give the following clear explanation of this important concept.†

On an abstract level, ordinary mathematics is concerned with independent variables, the values of which may be chosen arbitrarily, and dependent variables, which are determined by the values assigned to the former. In the concrete domain, science aims at the discovery of laws whereby natural phenomena are interrelated, and the value of a particular variable can be determined when pertinent conditions are prescribed. Nevertheless, there exist enormous areas of objective reality characterized by changes which do not seem to follow any definite pattern or have any connection with recognizable antecedents. We do not mean to suggest an absence of causality. However, from the viewpoint of an observer who cannot look behind the scenes, a variable produced by the interplay of a complex system of causes exhibits irregular (though not necessarily discontinuous) variations which are, to all intents and purposes, random. Broadly speaking, a variable which eludes predictability in assuming its different possible values is called a random variable, or synonymously a variate. More precisely, a random variable must have a specific range or set of possible values and a definable probability associated with each value.

The reader will note that the stipulation that a random variable requires a definable probability for each value implies the existence of some single " bowl" as a source of the variable mentioned in Ferrell's cases 2 and 3.

The reader who recalls the discussion in Chap. 2 of sampling from a statistically controlled process will recognize that a great many different random variables may be generated by a single universe, or "bowl." For example, we illustrated not only the behavior of individual drawings from Shewhart's normal bowl but also the behavior of $\bar{X}$ values, σ values, and R values from samples of 2, 4, 8, etc. All these $\bar{X}$, σ, and R values were random variables.

Point Estimates and Estimators

In Ferrell's case 3, it is desired to use various statistics of a sample (or of a number of samples) to estimate various parameters that help to describe a universe. A single value used as an estimate of a given parameter is called a *point estimate*. The sample statistic used in making the estimate is called an *estimator*.

For instance, it might be desired to estimate the arithmetic mean of an unknown universe on the basis of a sample taken from the universe. Some possible estimators would be the sample arithmetic mean, the sample median, and the sample midrange. In judging the merits of proposed estimators, it is desirable to consider whether they are *unbiased* and whether they are *efficient*.

† G. P. WADSWORTH and J. G. BRYAN, "Applications of Probability and Random Variables," pp. 40, McGraw-Hill Book Company, New York, 1974.

Unbiased and Biased Estimates

A statistic provides an unbiased estimate of a universe parameter if the arithmetic mean of the sampling distribution of the statistic is equal to the value of the universe parameter. The arithmetic mean of a sample gives an unbiased estimate of the arithmetic mean of the universe.

In contrast to the arithmetic mean, we noted in Table 3-3 that the RMS deviations of samples from Shewhart's normal bowl tended to give a decidedly biased estimate of the standard deviation in the bowl. The amount of the bias evidently decreased as the sample size increased. To correct for this bias when the $\bar{\sigma}$ of a set of samples or the σ of one sample is used to estimate the σ' of a normal universe, the reader will recall that it is necessary to divide $\bar{\sigma}$ or σ by the c_2 factor given in Table B of App. 3. This c_2 factor, which is only 0.5642 for a sample size of 2, is 0.9925 for a sample size of 100 and approaches unity as the sample size is increased. It will be recalled that the c_2 factors are based on the assumption that the universe is normal.

Efficiency of an Estimate

Consider the arithmetic mean, the median, and the midrange of a sample as possible estimators for the arithmetic mean of a normal universe. All these happen to be unbiased. However, if a great many samples of, say, size 5 were taken from a given normal universe, the dispersions of the medians and midranges would be greater than the dispersion of the arithmetic means. (We already know that the standard deviation of the arithmetic mean, $\sigma_{\bar{x}}$, would be $\sigma'/\sqrt{5}$ or approximately $0.45\sigma'$. It can be shown that the respective standard deviations of medians and midranges are approximately $0.54\sigma'$ and $0.51\sigma'$ when samples of 5 are taken from a normal universe.)

Mathematical statisticians define the most *efficient* estimator of a parameter as the estimator that has the minimum variance. (It will be recalled that the variance is the square of the standard deviation.) The *efficiency* of any other unbiased estimator is defined as the ratio of the variance of the sampling distribution of the efficient estimator to the variance of the sampling distribution of the other estimator. When the arithmetic mean of a normal distribution is estimated from samples of 5, the efficiency of the median is 0.697 and the efficiency of the midrange is 0.767. Dixon and Massey give efficiencies of these estimators for sample sizes from 2 to 20.[†]

The efficiency of a particular estimator depends on the form of the universe. For example, the midrange of a sample is more efficient than the arithmetic mean of the sample as an estimator of the arithmetic mean of a rectangular universe.

The reader should note that the variances of the sampling distributions, rather than the standard deviations of these distributions, are used by mathematical

---

[†] W. J. Dixon and F. J. Massey, Jr., "Introduction to Statistical Analysis," 3d ed., McGraw-Hill Book Company, New York, 1969.

statisticians in defining the efficiency of an estimator. Therefore, the ratio of standard deviations of the respective sampling distributions is the square root of the efficiency. For instance, the ratio of $\sigma_{\bar{x}}$ to the standard deviation of midranges in samples of 5 from a normal distribution is $\sqrt{0.767} = 0.88$.

The Problem of Selecting a Parameter to Describe Universe Dispersion and of Choosing an Estimator for that Parameter

A source of possible confusion to readers of books on statistics is that two different parameters, namely, standard deviation and variance, may be used to describe the dispersion of a universe. At first glance, this does not appear to be a source of trouble. The standard deviation of a universe is defined as the root-mean-square deviation from the arithmetic mean of the universe; the variance of the universe is defined as the square of its standard deviation. Because universe variance is readily computed from universe standard deviation and vice versa, it might appear to be immaterial which parameter is preferred. Nevertheless, because the choice of the parameter is related to the choice of the estimator, it really makes a difference which parameter is to be estimated.

When values of $(X - \bar{X})^2$ from samples are used to estimate universe dispersion, a source of difficulty is that the $\bar{X}'$ of the universe is unknown; the deviations that are squared must be measured from the $\bar{X}$ of each sample. Except in the occasional case where the $\bar{X}$ of a sample happens to be identical with the unknown $\bar{X}'$, $\Sigma(X - \bar{X})^2$ will be less than $\Sigma(X - \bar{X}')^2$. Some method of compensation for this bias is therefore needed in any statistic based on $\Sigma(X - \bar{X})^2$ if the statistic is to be used to estimate the universe standard deviation σ' or the universe variance $(\sigma')^2$.

In our explanation of control charts for variables in Chap. 2 and thereafter, we generally used the sample range R as a measure of sample (or subgroup) dispersion and we used $\bar{R}/d_2$ as an estimate of σ'. However, $\bar{\sigma}/c_2$ was presented as another estimate of σ'; σ was referred to as the sample RMS deviation or sample standard deviation and was defined as follows:

$$\sigma = \sqrt{\frac{\Sigma(X - \bar{X})^2}{n}}$$

When σ or $\bar{\sigma}$ is used to estimate σ', the c_2 factor given in Table B is used to compensate for the bias created by measuring deviations from $\bar{X}$ rather than from $\bar{X}'$. If sampling is from a normal universe, the statistic σ/c_2 for a single sample gives an unbiased estimate of σ' and the statistic $\bar{\sigma}/c_2$ for a set of samples of equal size also gives an unbiased estimate of σ'.

However, many of the derivations in mathematical statistics make use of the universe variance $(\sigma')^2$ rather than the universe standard deviation σ'. An unbiased estimate of $(\sigma')^2$ may be obtained from the sample statistic s^2 defined as follows:

$$s^2 = \frac{(X_1 - \bar{X})^2 + (X_2 - \bar{X})^2 + \cdots + (X_n - \bar{X})^2}{n - 1} = \frac{\Sigma(X - \bar{X})^2}{n - 1}$$

The foregoing statement is true for a random sample from any universe and does not depend on the universe being normal. The use of $n - 1$ rather than n in the denominator has an effect similar to the use of the c_2 factor; it tends to compensate for the bias created by measuring deviations from the sample average $\bar{X}$ rather than from the unknown universe average $\bar{X}'$. Writers on statistics generally refer to s^2 as the *sample variance*.

Many of these writers also refer to s (the square root of s^2) as the *sample standard deviation*. Although s^2 gives an unbiased estimate of universe variance, s gives a biased estimate of universe standard deviation. The bias involved in the use of s may be fairly substantial where n is small (the usual condition in control charts for variables).

Conflicting Expressions for the Standard Deviation of a Set of Numbers

Persons who read two or more books on statistics often are puzzled because writers appear to use two different expressions for what they call the standard deviation of a set of numbers, namely:

$$s = \sqrt{\frac{\Sigma(X - \bar{X})^2}{n - 1}} \quad \text{and} \quad \sigma = \sqrt{\frac{\Sigma(X - \bar{X})^2}{n}}$$

Readers should not regard this difference merely as a matter of terminology or symbols; symbols other than s and σ may be used for the same quantities. The difference exists because some expressions use $n - 1$ and others use n in the denominator under the radical. The matter is complicated by the fact that some writers give both expressions, using each where it is deemed to be appropriate, whereas other writers give only one of the expressions and do not mention the other.

In the preceding chapters of this book, we have used only the expression with the n in the denominator under the radical. We have consistently used the symbol σ but have used the terms *RMS deviation* and *standard deviation* interchangeably.

The definition of the standard deviation of a set of numbers as the root-mean-square deviation from the arithmetic mean is in the classical tradition of writings on mathematical statistics.[†] When the techniques and terminology of statistical quality control were being developed in the 1920s, it was natural that the current definition for standard deviation should be used. Moreover, because an estimate of σ' is so important in judging process capability, and because s and σ both give biased estimates of σ', s has no advantage over σ as an estimator for this purpose.

In the original (1951) version of ASQC Standard A 1, "Definitions and Symbols for Control Charts," *standard deviation* (σ) was defined as "*the root-mean-square (r.m.s.) deviation of the numbers from their average.*" In the first revision of this standard (1968), *sample standard deviation* was defined as s with the $(n - 1)$ in

---

[†] For example, see H. L. RIETZ (ed.), "Handbook of Mathematical Statistics," p. 5, Houghton Mifflin Company, Boston, 1924.

the denominator under the radical. The definition of s was followed by the definition of σ as the root-mean-square deviation, also referred to as "*another measure sometimes used as the sample standard deviation.*"

Correcting the Bias of s as an Estimator of σ' for a Normal Universe

Table 11-1 uses the 400 drawings from Shewhart's normal bowl to illustrate certain aspects of the difference between the use of s and σ as measures of the dispersion of samples from a normal universe. The drawings are divided into 100 subgroups of four just as they were in Table 2-7. The values of s^2, s, and σ have been computed for each subgroup, and the average value for each of these statistics for the 100 samples has been calculated. (For obvious reasons, the average value of s will not be the square root of the average value of s^2.)

It happens that we know that the true universe standard deviation σ' is 9.954 and the true universe variance $(\sigma')^2$ is 99.08. The average value of s^2 is 102.97; this is an unbiased estimate of $(\sigma')^2$. But the average values of s and σ both give us biased estimates of σ'.

To correct the bias of $\bar{\sigma}$, we know that we divide by c_2. (The values of c_2 for subgroup sizes from 2 to 100 are given in Table B, App. 3.) In this case, our estimate of σ' is $\bar{\sigma}/c_2 = 8.078/0.7979 = 10.12$. This estimate is fairly close to the known true value of 9.95. (It will be recalled from Chap. 2 that $\bar{R}/d_2$ was 10.08, also a close estimate of σ'.)

Table 11-1 Calculations illustrating the bias or lack of bias in certain methods of estimating the universe variance and universe standard deviation of Shewhart's normal bowl

(The first 400 drawings are divided into 100 samples of 4 just as in Table 2-7; values computed from drawings 21 to 380 have been included in totals but are not shown in this table)

Numbers of drawings	$\Sigma(X - \bar{X})^2$	$s^2 = \dfrac{\Sigma(X - \bar{X})^2}{3}$	$s = \sqrt{\dfrac{\Sigma(X - \bar{X})^2}{3}}$	$\sigma = \sqrt{\dfrac{\Sigma(X - \bar{X})^2}{4}}$
1–4	153.00	51.00	7.1	6.2
5–8	1.00	0.33	0.6	0.5
9–12	6.75	2.25	1.5	1.3
13–16	666.00	222.00	14.9	12.9
17–20	174.00	58.00	7.6	6.6
. . . .	. . . .	. . . .	. . . . . .	. . . .
381–384	1,258.00	419.33	20.5	17.7
385–388	243.00	81.00	9.0	7.8
389–392	370.00	123.33	11.1	9.6
393–396	153.75	51.25	7.2	6.2
397–400	112.75	37.58	6.1	5.3
Totals for 100 samples		10,297.41	932.8	807.8
Averages		102.97	9.328	8.078

Each value of s is $\sqrt{n/(n-1)}$ times the corresponding value of σ. It follows that $\bar{s}$ must be $\sqrt{n/(n-1)}\,\bar{\sigma}$. The same c_2 correction factor that was used with $\bar{\sigma}$ can be used with $\bar{s}$ as follows:

$$\text{Estimated } \sigma' = \left(\frac{1}{c_2}\right)\frac{1}{\sqrt{\dfrac{n}{n-1}}}\,\bar{s}$$

As applied to the data of Table 11-1:

$$\text{Estimated } \sigma' = \left(\frac{1}{0.7979}\right)\left(\frac{1}{\sqrt{\frac{4}{3}}}\right)(9.328) = 10.12$$

For obvious reasons, $\bar{s}$ and $\bar{\sigma}$ give identical estimates of σ'; it makes no difference at all which of these two estimators is used. For convenience, the 1968 version of the ASQC Standard A 1 (ANSI Std. Z1.5-1971) designated $c_2\sqrt{n/(n-1)}$ as c_4 and tabulated values of c_4 for values of n from 2 to 25.

If s is used as the measure of subgroup dispersion in control charts for variables, the analyst should always divide $\bar{s}$ by $c_2\sqrt{n/(n-1)}$ (or by c_4) whenever estimating σ' in a study of process capability. Without this correction, the inherent bias in the use of s tends to give a too favorable view of the natural capabilities of a manufacturing process.

Control Charts for s

Chapters 2 and 3 explained why R is preferable to σ as a measure of subgroup dispersion in most control charts for variables. The same reasons that make R preferable to σ also make R preferable to s. If R is to be used as the measure of subgroup dispersion, the problem does not arise of choosing between a chart for σ and a chart for s.

However, certain types of acceptance sampling procedures that will be discussed in Chap. 17 require the calculation of s for purposes that have nothing to do with control charts. Where values of s are already available from such calculations, it is likely to be advantageous to maintain control charts for $\bar{X}$ and s.

In locations where special pocket or desk calculators that automatically calculate s are in general use, it may also be desirable to use the control chart for s. Care must be taken, however, to ensure that an s statistic is not plotted on a control chart for σ and *vice versa*.

A control chart for s is a magnified image of the control chart for σ for the same data. Each value on the s chart will be $\sqrt{n/(n-1)}$ times the corresponding value on a σ chart. The central line at $\bar{s}$ will be at $\sqrt{n/(n-1)}$ times the corresponding figure for the central line at $\bar{\sigma}$. And the spread from the central line to 3-sigma control limits on an s chart will be $\sqrt{n/(n-1)}$ times the spread on a corresponding σ chart. The s chart and the σ chart will give identical conclusions about the presence or absence of statistical control.

If $\bar{s}$ is used to calculate 3-sigma control limits on an $\bar{X}$ chart, the A_1 factor from Table D may be employed, modified as follows:

$$UCL_{\bar{X}} = \bar{\bar{X}} + \sqrt{\frac{n-1}{n}} A_1 \bar{s}$$

$$LCL_{\bar{X}} = \bar{\bar{X}} - \sqrt{\frac{n-1}{n}} A_1 \bar{s}$$

The 1968 version of ASQC Standard A 1 (ANSI Std. Z1.5-1971) used the symbol A_3 for

$$\sqrt{\frac{n-1}{n}} A_1$$

Values of A_3 were tabulated for values of n from 2 to 25.

The B_3 and B_4 factors from Table D may be used directly in computing 3-sigma limits on a chart for s, as follows:

$$UCL_s = B_4 \bar{s}$$

$$LCL_s = B_3 \bar{s}$$

Using σ or s^2 from a Large Sample to Estimate σ' and $(\sigma')^2$

Suppose that the first 400 drawings from Shewhart's normal bowl (Table 2-7) were available only as a frequency distribution and that there were no basis for dividing these 400 numbers into rational subgroups. The σ of the 400 numbers is 10.19. (Calculations are not shown here.) From such a large sample, σ may be used as a direct estimate of σ'. Although, in principle, σ should be divided by c_2 in making this estimate, c_2 is so close to unity that this correction for bias may be omitted. (Table B gives c_2 as 0.9925 when n is 100 and does not give values of c_2 when n is over 100.) The same point applies to the use of s.

For such a large sample, it makes no practical difference whether σ^2 or s^2 is used to estimate $(\sigma')^2$. It is obvious that s^2 is always $[n/(n-1)]\sigma^2$; with an n of 400, $s^2 = 1.00251\sigma^2$.

Of course, any estimate of the standard deviation or variance of a universe assumes that there is really only one universe—one bowl as in Ferrell's case 3 rather than several bowls as in his case 4. If a set of numbers is given with no basis for dividing the numbers into rational subgroups, there is no satisfactory way to test the hypothesis that all the numbers constitute a sample from a single universe.

PROBLEMS

11-1 In the discussion of Table 11-1, the following statement appears: "For obvious reasons, the average value of s will not be the square root of the average value of s^2." Compute the average value of s and the square root of the average value of s^2 for the first five subgroups (drawings 1 to 20) of Table

11-1. Each of these figures might conceivably be proposed as an estimate of the σ' of Shewhart's normal bowl. Explain why these two figures are not the same.

11-2 Make the same calculation and explanation asked for in Problem 11-1 with respect to the final 5 subgroups (drawings 381–400) of Table 11-1.

11-3 In order to ensure that wood pulp quality remains at a desired level, a paper manufacturer monitors a particular quality characteristic of the wood pulp and the results are plotted on $\bar{X}$ and s control charts. Based on 75 subgroups of size four, the average ($\bar{\bar{X}}$) of the quality characteristic is 35.6 and the average sample standard deviation ($\bar{s}$) is 4.65. Determine the 3σ control limits for the $\bar{X}$ and s charts for monitoring this characteristic.

    Answer: 43.17, 28.02; 10.56, 0.

11-4 The true universe variance $(\sigma')^2$ of a certain characteristic is known to be 100.0. If the characteristic is monitored in subgroups of four, evaluate the corresponding values of σ', $\bar{\sigma}$, $\bar{s}$, and s.

    Answer: 10.0, 7.98, 9.18, 11.5.

11-5 Plot control charts for $\bar{X}$ and s for the data of Problem 2-10.

11-6 Plot control charts for $\bar{X}$ and s for the data of Problem 2-19.

11-7 Use the factors in Table B to determine the values of the factors c_4 and A_3 for subgroup sizes from 2 to 10.

11-8 Use the factors in Table B to determine the values of the factors c_4 and A_3 for subgroup sizes from 11 to 20.

11-9 Solve Problems 3-27 and 3-28 using control charts for $\bar{X}$ and s. Assume that $\Sigma s = 1.946$. What would be the difference between the appearance of the s chart required here and the σ chart called for in Problem 3-27? Which of the dispersion charts would be more sensitive to shifts in σ'?

11-10 Solve Problems 3-31 and 3-32 using control charts for $\bar{X}$ and s. Assume that $\Sigma s = 196.7$ grams. What would be the difference between the appearance of the s chart required here and the σ chart called for in Problem 3-31? Which dispersion chart would be more sensitive to shifts in σ'?

PART

TWO

ACCEPTANCE SAMPLING

TWELVE

SOME FUNDAMENTAL CONCEPTS IN ACCEPTANCE SAMPLING

You can't inspect quality into a product.—Anon.

Importance of Sampling for Acceptance Purposes

Inspection for acceptance purposes is carried out at many stages in manufacturing. There may be inspection of incoming materials and parts, process inspection at various points in the manufacturing operations, final inspection by a manufacturer of his own product, and—ultimately—inspection of the finished product by one or more purchasers.

Much of this acceptance inspection is necessarily on a sampling basis. All acceptance tests that are destructive of the item tested must inevitably be done by sampling. In many other instances sampling inspection is used because the cost of 100% inspection is prohibitive. As pointed out in Chap. 1, where there are a great many similar items of product to be inspected, sampling inspection is likely to be better done than 100% inspection because of the influence of inspection fatigue in 100% inspection. An important advantage of modern acceptance sampling systems such as those discussed in Chaps. 13 to 17 is that they exert more effective pressure for quality improvement than is possible with 100% inspection.

Pressure for Quality Improvement Exerted by Rejection of Entire Lots

Inspection, in the sense of sorting product that conforms to specifications from nonconforming product, cannot be relied on to ensure that all accepted product really conforms. Inspection fatigue on repetitive inspection operations often will limit the effectiveness of 100% inspection. Obviously, no *sampling* procedure can eliminate all nonconforming product. It follows that the best way to be sure that accepted product conforms to specifications is to have the product made right in the first place.

Where a producer does not make product right in the first place and, in effect, relies on the consumer to do screening inspection, it often happens that striking quality improvements can be caused by the outright rejection of entire lots of product on the basis of the numbers of nonconforming items found in samples. The rejection of entire lots brings much stronger pressure for quality improvement than the rejection of individual articles. Example 12-1 describes a case where such pressure was exerted in an effective manner.

Example 12-1 Substitution of occasional lot rejections for acceptance of an unsatisfactory process average *Facts of the case* A public utility company purchased many measuring devices of a certain type from three competing manufacturers. The specified tolerances for a certain quality characteristic of these devices were fairly tight. (These specifications had been established by the state regulatory commission with the concurrence of the utility company.) However, for many years both the manufacturers of the devices and the utility buying them had acted as if it were believed to be impossible for the manufacturers to make substantially all the devices within the specified tolerances. It was not uncommon for shipments to be accepted containing 5 to 10% of the devices that were defective in the sense of failing to meet these specifications. The invariable procedure was for the utility company to test all the purchased devices in its laboratory. Out-of-tolerance devices usually were adjusted or rebuilt by the utility rather than returned to the manufacturers.

Finally, the management of the utility concluded that it was doing work that it had already paid the manufacturers to do. It seemed unlikely that any improvement in submitted quality would take place either as a result of complaints to the manufacturers or as a result of returning to the manufacturers only the individual out-of-tolerance devices.

The utility therefore notified the three manufacturers that in the future acceptance inspection would be conducted under Military Standard 105B (an earlier version of the standard discussed in Chap. 14).† At the time of this example, this military standard and its predecessors had the prestige of many years of use by government and industry. The utility chose a sampling scheme based on a stated "acceptable quality level" that seemed reasonable in relation to the manufacturers' claims for their product. For the time being, lots accepted under this scheme continued to receive 100% testing with adjustment or rebuilding of out-of-tolerance devices.

The long record of quality history from its past testing program made it possible for the management of the utility to predict that at the start a moderate percentage of lots would be rejected by the new sampling scheme. These lot rejections occurred very much as predicted. As anticipated, the manufac-

---

† Military Standard 105B involved acceptance or rejection of entire lots on the basis of the results of tests on a random sample selected from each lot.

turers initially took the view that they were being treated unjustly by the rejection of the good articles contained in the rejected lots. Somewhat illogically (because the actions of the utility were reasonable without reference to any published sampling procedures), the prestige of the military standard was successfully used to justify the actions of the utility. As time went on, the manufacturers were able to diagnose the reasons for their difficulties with this quality characteristic and the quality of the product submitted to the utility was greatly improved.

Some Weaknesses of Certain Traditional Practices in Acceptance Sampling

Before the widespread use in industry of modern acceptance sampling systems, inspectors often used a working rule that is still recognized as based on a correct principle. This rule was to permit an inspector's current decisions on acceptance to be influenced by his knowledge of the past quality history of the product being sampled. For instance, where the same part or article was purchased from two or more sources, an inspector might check only one or two items in a lot from a source that he considered reliable but might give critical examination to a lot from a source that he considered to be unreliable.

Although this rule is sound as far as it goes, such an informal system for determining size and frequency of sample and basis of acceptance has obvious limitations. Inspectors' memories of past quality history sometimes may be short and inaccurate. The inspector who tries to remember the quality history of a number of products may die or resign or be transferred to another job. Or the inspector's confidence in past quality may lead to the neglect of current inspection and therefore to failure to discover when quality has changed for the worse.

These limitations suggest the need of definite working rules regarding size and frequency of sample and basis for acceptance or rejection. But it is not sufficient that such rules merely be *definite*. Many of the definite rules that at one time were common in industry were bad because they seemed to give a promise of quality protection that they could not fulfill. Formal schemes such as the once-popular one analyzed in Example 1-3 often gave less quality protection than the informal scheme of letting the inspector use personal judgment.

Purpose of This Chapter

The real problem in most acceptance sampling is to design a satisfactory acceptance sampling *system* or, more commonly, to select such a system from a number of possible systems already developed by someone else. Although Example 12-1 necessarily gave the reader an oversimplified view of such systems, it made the essential point that an important aspect of any such system is its influence on the quality of submitted product. To judge the suitability of any proposed acceptance sampling system in a particular case, it is desirable to have an understanding of the strategy and tactics built into the various available types of systems.

This chapter is intended to lay the groundwork for more detailed discussion in Chaps. 13 through 17 of a number of widely used modern acceptance sampling systems. As a prerequisite for an understanding of such systems, the reader needs to know certain terminology, concepts, and probability calculations involved in acceptance sampling. This chapter uses lot-by-lot acceptance sampling by attributes to develop the terminology and concepts and to illustrate some types of probability calculations. Discussion of acceptance sampling from a continuous stream of product is deferred until Chap. 16. Discussion of acceptance sampling by variables is deferred until Chap. 17.

Use of the Words *Defective* and *Defect* in Part Two of This Book

It was pointed out in Chap. 1 that when these words are used in their technical senses dealing with lack of conformity to specifications, they do not necessarily mean *defective* and *defect* in the popular sense. It is common for specifications to contain a margin of safety; therefore, some product that does not meet specifications can be satisfactory for its intended use. The difference between the technical and popular meanings has been a source of confusion and misunderstanding in lawsuits involving product liability.

In the interest of clarity in writing and speaking about topics related to quality of manufactured product, it would be desirable if everyone concerned with quality matters would abandon the use of *defective* and *defect* in the restricted technical sense. In Part One of this edition of *Statistical Quality Control*, with a few exceptions that generally involve quotations, the authors have been able to substitute appropriate words or phrases where previous editions have used one of these words. For example, we have referred to *nonconforming* product, percent *rejected*, and numbers of *nonconformities*.

Unfortunately, it does not seem reasonable to continue such substitutions throughout Part Two. The acceptance sampling systems that we examine in the following chapters all make considerable use of the words *defective* and *defect*. Therefore the words should be used in explaining the systems. Nevertheless, the reader should understand that in the coming pages these words are used in their restricted technical senses. A defective item is one that does not conform to specifications in some respect; a defect is a nonconformity to some specification.

Some Symbols and Terms Used in Relation to Acceptance Sampling Plans

The probability principles presented in Chap. 6, and the explanation of control charts for fraction rejected and for numbers of nonconformities given in Chaps. 7 and 8, provide a background for a discussion of the evaluation of acceptance plans involving sampling by attributes. In discussing such plans, the following symbols are used:†

> N = number of pieces in a given lot or batch.
>
> n = number of pieces in a sample.
>
> M = number of defective pieces (i.e., pieces not conforming to specifications) in a given lot of size N.
>
> m = number of defective pieces (i.e., pieces not conforming to specifications) in a given sample of size n.
>
> c = acceptance number, the maximum allowable number of defective pieces in a sample of size n.‡ (Also denoted by A_c in some cases.)
>
> p = fraction defective. In a given submitted lot, this is M/N; in a given sample, it is m/n.
>
> p' = true process average fraction defective of a product submitted for inspection.
>
> $\bar{p}$ = average fraction defective in observed samples.
>
> P_a = probability of acceptance.
>
> β = Consumer's Risk, the probability of accepting product of some stated undesirable quality. It is the value of P_a at that stated quality.
>
> α = Producer's Risk, the probability of rejecting product of some stated desirable quality. $\alpha = 1 - P_a$ at that stated quality.

$p_{0.95}$, $p_{0.50}$,
$p_{0.10}$, etc. = fraction defective having a probability of acceptance of 0.95, 0.50, 0.10, etc., under any given acceptance criteria.

Lot-By-Lot Acceptance, Using Single Sampling by Attributes

In acceptance inspection a defective article is defined as one that fails to conform to specifications in one or more quality characteristics. A common procedure in acceptance sampling is to consider each submitted lot of product separately and to base the decision on acceptance or rejection of the lot on the evidence of one or more samples chosen at random from the lot. When the decision is always made on the evidence of only one sample, the acceptance plan is described as a *single sampling* plan.

Any systematic plan for single sampling requires that three numbers be specified. One is the number of articles N in the lot from which the sample is to be drawn. The second is the number of articles n in the random sample drawn from the lot. The third is the acceptance number c.

---

† Where applicable, the notation used in this text follows that recommended by the American Society for Quality Control in "ASQC Standard A2, Definitions and Symbols for Acceptance Sampling by Attributes," 1971 (ANSI Std. Z1.6-1971).

‡ See footnote on p. 64 in Chap. 2 for the justification for the use of the symbol c in a different meaning from those previously employed.

This acceptance number is the maximum allowable number of defective articles in the sample. More than c defectives will cause the rejection of the lot. In sampling plans developed without benefit of statistical analysis, c often is specified as zero under the illusion that if the sample is perfect, the lot will be perfect.

In the discussion that follows, sampling acceptance plans of this type are described by these three numbers. For instance, the sampling plan of Example 1-3

is specified in this way as
$$\begin{cases} N = 50 \\ n = 5. \\ c = 0 \end{cases}$$
These three numbers may be interpreted as

saying: "Take a random sample of 5 from a lot of 50. If the sample contains more than 0 defectives, reject the lot; otherwise, accept the lot."

Example 1-3 examined this plan critically under a particular assumption, namely, that the plan was used for acceptance of product that on the average was 4% defective. The distribution of defectives among the lots was assumed to follow the laws of chance. (This amounted to an assumption either that the production process was statistically controlled or that the product was well mixed before being divided into lots.) Under this assumption, the lots accepted by the plan proved to be 3.6% defective; this modest improvement in product quality was accomplished at the cost of rejecting 18.5% of the submitted lots. After the defective articles found in the rejected lots were eliminated, the average quality of the remainder of the rejected lots was not appreciably worse than the average of the accepted lots. It was evident that this sampling acceptance plan was not a satisfactory one under the assumed conditions.

The Operating Characteristic (OC) Curve of an Acceptance Sampling Plan Shows the Ability of the Plan to Distinguish between Good and Bad Lots

In judging various acceptance sampling plans it is desirable to compare their performance over a range of possible quality levels of submitted product. An excellent picture of this performance is given by the *operating characteristic curve*, first mentioned in Chap. 1.† Such curves are commonly referred to as OC curves.

For any given fraction defective p in a submitted lot, the OC curve shows the probability P_a that such a lot will be accepted by the given sampling plan. Or, stated a little differently, the OC curve shows the long-run percentage of submitted lots that would be accepted if a great many lots of any stated quality were

---

† Most of the terminology of acceptance sampling originated in the Bell Telephone Laboratories in the 1920s, where such curves were called "probability of acceptance curves." The phrase "operating characteristic curve," however, originated in the Ballistic Research Laboratories at Aberdeen Proving Ground, Maryland, just before World War II. It was first suggested by a nonstatistician, Col. H. H. Zornig, when he was director of that laboratory and was used by Gen. (then Major) Leslie E. Simon in his writings on quality control at that time. A number of years later, the phrase was incorporated into the general language of statistical inference and is now used in connection with many kinds of statistical tests of hypotheses.

submitted for inspection. Figures 12-1 to 12-3 give the OC curves of a number of single sampling plans.

As explained later in this chapter, in most cases OC curves may also be thought of as showing the probability of accepting lots from a stream of product having a fraction defective p.

Sampling Acceptance Plans with Same Per Cent Samples Give Very Different Quality Protection

Before the widespread use of modern acceptance sampling systems, a common practice in industry was to specify that the sample inspected should be some fixed percentage of the lot, such as 5, 10, or 20%. This specification was generally based on the mistaken idea that the protection given by sampling schemes is constant if the ratio of sample size to lot size is constant. Such specifications were often associated with an acceptance number of zero.

Figure 12-1 illustrates just how wrong this idea really is. This figure compares the OC curves of four sampling acceptance plans, all of which involve a 10% sample and an acceptance number of zero. The differences in the quality protections provided by these plans are obvious and impressive. They may be emphasized by statements of fact that can be read from the OC curves.

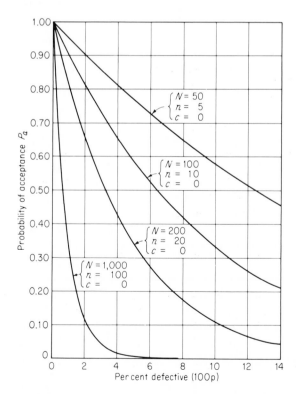

Figure 12-1 Comparison of operating characteristic curves for four sampling plans involving 10% samples

For example, the curves show that lots which are 4% defective will be accepted 81% of the time using a 10% sample from a lot of 50, 65% of the time using a 10% sample from a lot of 100, 42% of the time using a 10% sample from a lot of 200, and less than 2% of the time (actually 1.35%) by a 10% sample from a lot of 1,000, assuming an acceptance number of zero in all cases. Obviously, a producer making product 4% defective would have a strong motive for trying to have his product inspected in lots of 50 rather than in lots of 1,000.

Or, considered in a slightly different way, the curves show the quality of lot that will be passed 50% of the time by each plan. $\begin{cases} N = 50 \\ n = 5 \\ c = 0 \end{cases}$ will pass a 12%

defective lot half the time, $\begin{cases} N = 100 \\ n = 10 \\ c = 0 \end{cases}$ a 6% defective lot, $\begin{cases} N = 200 \\ n = 20 \\ c = 0 \end{cases}$ a 3% defective

lot, and $\begin{cases} N = 1,000 \\ n = 100 \\ c = 0 \end{cases}$ a 0.65% defective lot.

These curves are based on computations such as those illustrated in Chap. 6.

Fixed Sample Size Tends toward Constant Quality Protection

From the standpoint of quality protection, the absolute size of a random sample is much more important than its relative size compared to the size of the lot. This fact is illustrated by Fig. 12-2. This figure shows the OC curves of four different sampling plans all having the same sample size 20 but having lot sizes of 50, 100, 200, and 1,000, respectively.

The three upper curves, in which the sample size varies from 20% to 2% of the lot, show close agreement. This agreement is in sharp contrast to the great difference among the curves in Fig. 12-1. These two figures together emphasize the point that it is the absolute size of the sample rather than its relative size that determines the quality protection given by an acceptance sampling plan. The story told by these two figures is particularly striking because it contradicts many preconceived notions on the subject of sampling.

The upper curve corresponding to a lot size of 1,000 is practically identical with the OC curve that would be obtained for an infinite lot size. For example, the probability of acceptance of a 5% defective lot when $N = 1,000$ is 0.355. When $N = \infty$, the corresponding probability is 0.358. For a 10% defective lot, the respective probabilities of acceptance are 0.119 and 0.122. (These figures are obtained using hypergeometric probabilities for the lot of 1,000 and using the binomial for the infinite lot.) For a given lot fraction defective, the probability of acceptance computed for a finite lot is always less than that computed for an infinite lot because of the recognition of the partial exhaustion of the lot by the sample.

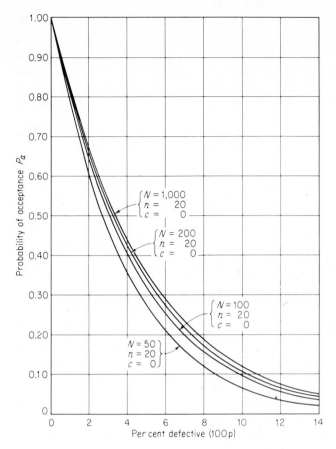

Figure 12-2 Comparisons of OC curves for four sampling plans involving samples of 20, each with acceptance number of 0.

It is evident that unless a sample is a large proportion of the lot, such as the 10%, 20%, and 40% samples in the three lower OC curves of Fig. 12-2, it will usually be good enough for practical purposes to compute OC curves as if lot sizes were infinite. Moreover, if the OC curve is viewed as giving probabilities of acceptance of lots from a statistically controlled product having a fraction defective, p, the OC curve computed in this way is correct in principle.

No Sampling Plan Can Give Complete Protection against the Acceptance of Defective Product

A practical difficulty in devising an ideal sampling plan is that it is not possible to change the laws of chance.

All lot-by-lot sampling plans are certain to pass some of the lots containing

defective product if such product exists in many of the lots submitted for acceptance. This fact needs to be faced by all who specify and use acceptance sampling.

It follows that the selection of an acceptance sampling plan requires a decision
on the risks that the user of the plan is willing to face, all things considered. This is
an economic decision that depends on a number of matters discussed in Chap. 19.
In lot-by-lot sampling by attributes, the risks of acceptance of submitted lots
containing any stated percentage of defectives are given by the OC curve of the
particular sampling plan. It is therefore appropriate to give careful consideration
to the OC curve in the selection of a sampling plan. As pointed out in the
following discussion of acceptance sampling, the users of sampling plans often find
it convenient to concentrate attention on one or two points on the OC curve
rather than on the whole curve.

OC Curve of an Ideal Sampling Plan

Suppose that it is decided that 2.2% is the maximum tolerable proportion defective in any submitted lots. Once this decision has been made, it might seem that an
ideal lot-by-lot sampling scheme would be one that rejected all lots that were
worse than 2.2% defective and accepted all lots 2.2% defective or better. The OC
curve of such an ideal scheme would be a vertical line at $p = 0.022$. Of course, no
such scheme can exist short of 100% inspection.

It is, however, possible to select a sampling plan in which a 2.2% defective lot
has some desired probability of acceptance. If it should be decided that the consumer can take 1 chance in 10 that if a 2.2% defective lot is submitted the lot will
be accepted, the OC curve of the selected plan should pass through the point
$P_a = 0.10$, $p = 0.022$ (or $100p = 2.2\%$).

Figure 12-1 shows that the OC curve of the plan $\begin{cases} N = 1{,}000 \\ n = \quad 100 \\ c = \quad\;\; 0 \end{cases}$ passes through

this point. If the product is to be submitted for acceptance in lots of 1,000 articles,
this plan is a possible one to give the consumer his desired quality protection
against accepting 2.2% defective lots.

Conflicting Interests of Consumer and Producer in the
Selection of Sampling Plans

There are always two parties to an acceptance procedure, the party submitting the
product for acceptance and the party for whom the decision is made regarding
acceptance or rejection. In all discussions of acceptance procedures in this book,
these parties are concisely referred to as the *producer* and *consumer*. It should be
recognized that for many inspection operations the producer and consumer may
be part of the same organization; for instance, the producer might be the machine
shop and the consumer the assembly department. In a manufacturer's final inspection of his own product, the sales department may be thought of as the consumer. In

acceptance inspection of some purchased product, the producer—in the sense used here—may actually be a dealer who had no connection with the original production.

At first impression, it might seem that the producer and consumer should have completely opposite viewpoints toward the selection of sampling plans. The consumer requires protection against the acceptance of too much defective product. The producer, on the other hand, needs to be protected against the rejection of too much product that conforms to specifications.

As an example, assume that a consumer selects the plan $\begin{cases} N = 1{,}000 \\ n = 100 \\ c = 0 \end{cases}$ in order

to fairly well be protected against accepting lots more than 2.2% defective. As already pointed out, if a lot exactly 2.2% defective should be submitted, there is only 1 chance in 10 of its acceptance. The consumer will have even greater protection if lots of poorer quality are submitted.

This plan, however, gives unsatisfactory protection to the producer who submits product considerably better than 2.2% defective. For instance, the OC curve of Fig. 12-3 shows that if the producer submits lots 1% defective, 65% of them will be rejected. (The curve says 35% will be accepted; this is subtracted from 100% to get the percentage rejected.) If lots 0.5% defective are submitted, 41% will be rejected. If lots 0.2% defective are submitted, 19% will be rejected. It is evident that the consumer's protection against accepting product 2.2% defective is obtained only by rejecting a large proportion of any submitted lots that are of much better quality.

A more critical consideration will show that, where there is a continuing relationship between producer and consumer, such substantial rejections of acceptable product in the effort to exclude product not conforming to specifications are not necessarily in the consumer's interest. The consumer is interested in quality, but also in cost. In the long run the costs incident to the rejection of acceptable product tend to be passed on by the producer to the consumer. The consumer may also be interested in having the product now. Any acceptable product rejected by the consumer is not available for immediate use.

It seems clear that, even from the consumer's viewpoint, it is not sufficient to ask that a sampling plan protect the consumer against the acceptance of lots having a higher percentage of defectives than some maximum tolerable figure.

The Acceptance Number Need Not Be Zero

Figures 12-1 and 12-2 emphasized the fact that a perfect sample does not ensure a perfect lot. Once this fact is recognized, the objections sometimes raised to permitting some defectives in a sample may be shown to have no logical foundation.

The users of modern acceptance sampling procedures recognize certain psychological advantages of allowing at least one defective in a sample. Moreover, the operating characteristics of plans with acceptance numbers greater than zero are

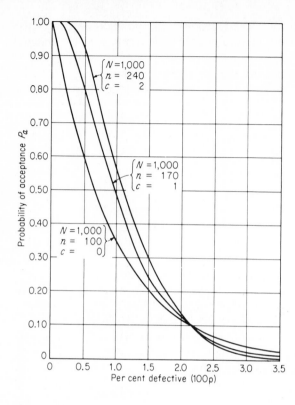

Figure 12-3 OC curves for three sampling plans having a 0.10 probability of acceptance of a 2.2% defective lot.

superior to those of comparable plans with acceptance number of zero. For a desired protection against accepting lots containing some stated percentage of defectives, larger acceptance numbers involve larger sample sizes. Plans having larger sample sizes have greater ability to discriminate between satisfactory and unsatisfactory lots.

For example, consider our consumer who wants protection against accepting lots of 2.2% defective or worse and insists that any 2.2% defective lots submitted shall have only a 0.10 probability of acceptance. Assume that product is submitted in lots of 1,000. This consumer's requirement will be met by using $n = 100$ and $c = 0$, or by using $n = 170$ and $c = 1$, or by using $n = 240$ and $c = 2$, or by various other possible plans.

The OC curves for these three plans are shown in Fig. 12-3. It will be noted that although all three plans give the consumer equal protection against the acceptance of a 2.2% defective lot, the plans with acceptance numbers of 1 and 2 give the producer much better protection against the rejection of lots that are satisfactory in the sense of being greatly superior to 2.2% defective lots. A few figures read from the three curves serve to emphasize this point.

	$N = 1,000$ $n = 100$ $c = 0$	$N = 1,000$ $n = 170$ $c = 1$	$N = 1,000$ $n = 240$ $c = 2$
Lots 1% defective rejected......	65%	51%	44%
Lots 0.5% defective rejected....	41%	20%	8%
Lots 0.2% defective rejected....	19%	3%	0%

The plans with the higher acceptance numbers and better OC curves have higher sample sizes for a given lot size. This means more inspection and hence more inspection cost. If, however, as is often the case, the rejection of a lot by sampling inspection means that the lot is to be 100% inspected, the total amount of resulting inspection may actually be less with the higher sample size and acceptance number.

Generally Speaking, the Larger the Sample Size, the Steeper the Slope of the OC Curve

It is of interest to compare several plans having different sample sizes and having the same ratio of acceptance number to sample size. Consider the plans

$$\begin{vmatrix} n = 75 \\ c = 1 \end{vmatrix} \quad \begin{vmatrix} n = 150 \\ c = 2 \end{vmatrix} \quad \text{and} \quad \begin{vmatrix} n = 750 \\ c = 10 \end{vmatrix}$$

Assume a lot size N of 10,000. This lot size is large enough so that even the largest of these samples is a relatively small fraction of the lot. The OC curves of these three plans are shown in Fig. 12-4.

Although these three plans each permit 1.33% (that is, $\frac{1}{75}$) of the sample to be defective, it is evident that they have quite different OC curves. The larger the sample size, the greater the ability of a sampling plan to discriminate between lots of different qualities. For example, a 3% defective lot, if submitted, has more than 1 chance in 3 of acceptance if $n = 75$ and $c = 1$ but is practically certain to be rejected if $n = 750$ and $c = 10$. The larger sample, which protects the consumer against the acceptance of relatively bad lots, also gives the producer better protection against the rejection of relatively good ones. Thus a 0.7% defective lot has 1 chance in 10 of rejection if $n = 75$ and only 2 chances in 100 of rejection if $n = 750$.

Type A and Type B OC Curves

Dodge and Romig make the helpful distinction between two types of OC curves.[†] Type A curves give the probabilities of acceptance for various fractions defective

---

† H. F. DODGE and H. G. ROMIG, "Sampling Inspection Tables—Single and Double Sampling," 2d ed., pp. 56–59, John Wiley & Sons, Inc., New York, 1959.

as a function of the *lot* quality of finite lots. In principle, such curves should be computed by hypergeometric probabilities; the binomial or Poisson distributions often give satisfactory approximations. In principle, also, such curves are discontinuous. For example, a lot of 200 items may be 0.5 or 1.0% defective but not 0.8%. In practice, it is common to draw Type *A* curves as continuous.

Type *B* curves give the probabilities of acceptance of a lot as a function of *product* quality. Such curves are calculated as if the lot size were infinite. For Type *B* curves the binomial is exact and the Poisson often gives a satisfactory approximation. Such curves are correctly viewed as continuous.

In the discussion of Fig. 12-2, which gave Type *A* OC curves for several plans that had an *n* of 20, a *c* of 0, and various lot sizes, it was pointed out that there was no practical difference between the OC curve for $N = 1,000$ and $N = \infty$. In general, where the sample size *n* is not more than one-tenth of the lot size *N*, Type *A* and Type *B* curves may be considered as identical for most practical purposes.

In judging the appropriateness of using Type *B* curves where *n* is more than one-tenth of *N*, certain assumptions underlying such uses should be recognized. Assume that a statistically controlled process exists that has some fraction defective p'. The lots of size *N* that come from this process are, in a statistical sense, random samples from the process. Each random sample of size *n* selected from some lot of *N* items may therefore be viewed as a random sample from the process that has the fraction defective p'. It follows that the Type *B* curve gives the expected results of a given sampling plan over the entire range of possible values of process fraction defective.

In examining a Producer's Risk, it usually is appropriate to adopt the viewpoint of the Type *B* OC curve. That is, it is reasonable for a producer to want to know what percentage of his lots will be rejected by a proposed sampling plan for any given level of process quality.

In contrast, the viewpoint of the Type *A* curve may be desirable in evaluating a Consumer's Risk with respect to individual lots. That is, a consumer reasonably may want to know the risk he takes of accepting a relatively bad *lot* if it is submitted. As pointed out in the discussion of Fig. 12-2, the Type *A* curve always falls *below* the Type *B*; it follows that the use of Type *B* curves tends to give a figure for Consumer's Risk that is somewhat too high.

Use of Table *G* for Approximate Calculation of Type *B* OC Curves of Sampling Plans

Although the binomial distribution is correct in principle for computing Type *B* OC curves, it is usually satisfactory and convenient to compute approximate probabilities of acceptance by use of a Poisson distribution table such as Table *G*, App. 3.

Table 12-1 illustrates the use of Table *G* in computing the three OC curves shown in Fig. 12-4. The probabilities of acceptance are read directly from Table *G* (or interpolated where necessary) as the figures corresponding to *c* (that is, "*c* or

Table 12-1 Calculation of approximate type B OC curves for three sampling plans

Fraction defective in lot p'	Expected average number of defectives, np', in sample			Probability of acceptance, P_a		
	$n = 75$	$n = 150$	$n = 750$	$\begin{cases} n = 75 \\ c = 1 \end{cases}$	$\begin{cases} n = 150 \\ c = 2 \end{cases}$	$\begin{cases} n = 750 \\ c = 10 \end{cases}$
0.002	0.15	0.30	1.5	0.990	0.996	1.000
0.004	0.30	0.60	3.0	0.963	0.977	1.000
0.006	0.45	0.90	4.5	0.925	0.937	0.993
0.008	0.60	1.20	6.0	0.878	0.879	0.957
0.010	0.75	1.50	7.5	0.827	0.809	0.862
0.012	0.90	1.80	9.0	0.772	0.731	0.706
0.014	1.05	2.10	10.5	0.718	0.650	0.521
0.016	1.20	2.40	12.0	0.663	0.570	0.347
0.018	1.35	2.70	13.5	0.610	0.494	0.211
0.020	1.50	3.00	15.0	0.558	0.423	0.118
0.025	1.875	3.75	18.75	0.441	0.278	0.021
0.030	2.25	4.50	22.5	0.343	0.174	0.003
0.035	2.625	5.25	26.25	0.262	0.106	0.000
0.040	3.00	6.00	.....	0.199	0.062	
0.050	3.75	7.50	.....	0.112	0.020	
0.060	4.50	9.00	.....	0.061	0.006	
0.070	5.25	10.50	.....	0.033	0.002	
0.080	6.00	12.00	.....	0.017	0.001	
0.090	6.75	13.50	.....	0.009	0.000	
0.100	7.50	.....	.....	0.004		

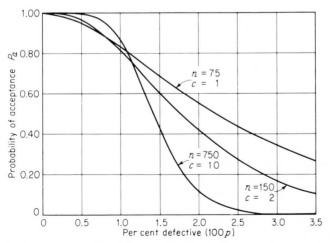

Figure 12-4 Comparison of OC curves with different sample sizes, all permitting the same fraction of the sample to be defective.

less") occurrences of the event with an average np'. Table 12-1 gives all probabilities to three decimal places in order to permit readers to check their use of Table G. Nevertheless, it should be recognized that because of the approximate method used, three decimal places are not really justified.†

The Indexing of Acceptance Plans by a Single Point on the OC Curve

Chapters 13 through 17 include descriptions of a number of different tables of acceptance sampling plans. Certain tables classify acceptance plans in accordance with a single point on the OC curve. Three points on the OC curve have been given particular importance in the design of systems of sampling plans, namely:

1. The lot (or process) quality for which $P_a = 0.95$. In this book, this quality is referred to as $p_{0.95}$.‡

2. The lot (or process) quality for which $P_a = 0.50$. In this book, this is referred to as $p_{0.50}$.§

3. The lot (or process) quality for which $P_a = 0.10$. To be consistent with the preceding symbols, this is referred to as $p_{0.10}$. In the literature of acceptance sampling, this quality is most frequently referred to as the lot tolerance fraction defective; $100p_{0.10}$ is described as the lot tolerance per cent defective (LTPD).¶

The same acceptance plan may therefore be referred to by several different product quality values, depending on the point of indexing. There are legitimate reasons for this variability in indexing sampling plans. Nevertheless, this has naturally proved to be a source of confusion to some users of acceptance sampling tables. Further comment on this topic is made in the next three chapters.

---

† The approximation of the Poisson to the binomial is, of course, best for the smallest values of p. Hence the OC curves computed using Table G (or other Poisson tables or diagrams) are more accurate at the upper end than at the lower end. As an example, consider the plan $N = \infty$, $n = 75$, $c = 1$ as applied to product 1% and 5% defective. The correct probabilities of acceptance computed by the binomial are 0.827 and 0.106, respectively. Table 12-1, computed by the Poisson, shows the approximate values to be 0.827 and 0.112, respectively.

‡ In the tables developed by the Columbia Statistical Research Group, discussed in Chap. 14, this quality is referred to as the AQL (acceptable quality level).

§ This has been referred to by some writers as the "point of control" and by others as the "indifference quality."

¶ More properly, in its original usage by Dodge and Romig, the notion of a tolerance per cent defective may be associated with any Consumer's Risk. For example, the lot quality having a P_a of 0.05 could be described as the lot tolerance per cent defective associated with a Consumer's Risk of 0.05. However, because the widely used Dodge-Romig tables (described in Chap. 13) all assume a Consumer's Risk of 0.10, the term LTPD sometimes is incorrectly used without qualification to mean $100p_{0.10}$.

Double Sampling

Single sampling calls for decision on acceptance or rejection of a lot on the basis of the evidence of *one* sample from that lot.

Double sampling involves the possibility of putting off the decision on the lot until a second sample has been taken. A lot may be accepted at once if the first sample is good enough or rejected at once if the first sample is bad enough. If the first sample is neither good enough nor bad enough, the decision is based on the evidence of the first and second samples combined. In general, double sampling schemes will involve less total inspection than single sampling for any given quality protection. They also have certain psychological advantages based on the idea of giving a second chance to doubtful lots.

The additional symbols used in connection with double sampling are as follows:

n_1 = number of pieces in the first sample.
c_1 = acceptance number for first sample, the maximum number of defectives that will permit the acceptance of the lot on the basis of the first sample.
n_2 = number of pieces in the second sample.
$n_1 + n_2$ = number of pieces in the two samples combined.
c_2 = acceptance number for the two samples combined, the maximum number of defectives that will permit the acceptance of the lot on the basis of the two samples.

An example of the use of these symbols to describe a double sampling plan is

$$\begin{cases} N = 1{,}000 \\ n_1 = \quad 36 \\ c_1 = \quad 0. \\ n_2 = \quad 59 \\ c_2 = \quad 3 \end{cases}$$

This may be interpreted as follows:

1. Inspect a first sample of 36 from a lot of 1,000.
2. Accept the lot on the basis of the first sample if the sample contains 0 defectives.
3. Reject the lot on the basis of the first sample if the sample contains more than 3 defectives.
4. Inspect a second sample of 59 if the first sample contains 1, 2, or 3 defectives.
5. Accept the lot on the basis of the combined sample of 95 if the combined sample contains 3 or less defectives.
6. Reject the lot on the basis of the combined sample if the combined sample contains more than 3 defectives.

Analysis of a Double Sampling Plan

Figure 12-5 shows three Type *A* OC curves involved in the analysis of this double sampling plan.

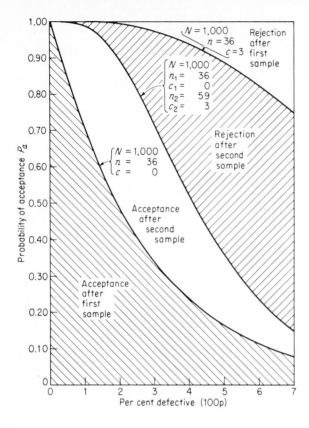

Figure 12-5 Characteristics of a double sampling plan.

There are four possibilities for acceptance or rejection of a lot submitted for double sampling, namely,

1. Acceptance after the first sample
2. Rejection after the first sample
3. Acceptance after the second sample
4. Rejection after the second sample

The lowest of the three OC curves in Fig. 12-5 shows the probability of (1) acceptance after the first sample. This is simply the curve for $\begin{cases} N = 1,000 \\ n = \quad 36 \\ c = \quad 0 \end{cases}$ The highest of the three OC curves shows the probability that the lot will not be rejected after the first sample. It is the curve for $\begin{cases} N = 1,000 \\ n = \quad 36 \\ c = \quad 3 \end{cases}$ Both of these limiting curves may be calculated in the manner already illustrated for the calculation of curves for all single sampling plans. For any given value of per cent defective, the distance between these two curves corresponds to the probability that for a lot of that per cent defective a second sample will be required.

The middle curve of Fig. 12-5 is the actual OC curve of the double sampling plan. To compute points for this curve it is necessary to find the probability that if a second sample is taken, the lot will be accepted. The necessary calculations may be illustrated for a single point on the curve corresponding to $p' = 0.010$.

The lot may be accepted in the following ways:

0 defectives in the first sample
1 defective in first sample followed by 0, 1, or 2 defectives in second sample
2 defectives in first sample followed by 0 or 1 defectives in second sample
3 defectives in first sample followed by 0 defectives in second sample

The probability of accepting the lot is the sum of the probabilities of these different ways in which it may be accepted. To compute these, it is first necessary to find the probabilities of 0, 1, 2, and 3 defectives in the first sample of 36.

$$M = p'N = (0.010)(1,000) = 10$$

$$P_0 = \frac{C_n^{N-M} C_0^M}{C_n^N} = \frac{C_{36}^{990} C_0^{10}}{C_{36}^{1,000}} = \frac{990!\,36!\,964!}{954!\,36!\,1,000!} = 0.692$$

$$P_1 = \frac{C_{n-1}^{N-M} C_1^M}{C_n^N} = \frac{C_{35}^{990} C_1^{10}}{C_{36}^{1,000}} = \frac{990!\,36!\,964!\,(10)}{955!\,35!\,1,000!} = 0.261$$

$$P_2 = \frac{C_{n-2}^{N-M} C_2^M}{C_n^N} = \frac{C_{34}^{990} C_2^{10}}{C_{36}^{1,000}} = \frac{990!\,36!\,964!\,(45)}{956!\,34!\,1,000!} = 0.043$$

$$P_3 = \frac{C_{n-3}^{N-M} C_3^M}{C_n^N} = \frac{C_{33}^{990} C_3^{10}}{C_{36}^{1,000}} = \frac{990!\,36!\,964!\,(120)}{957!\,33!\,1,000!} = 0.004$$

The calculations involving the factorials may be made with the aid of Table H and a table of 4-place logarithms, as illustrated in Chap. 6.

Assume that exactly one defective is found in the first sample. The taking of the second sample may, for purposes of calculation, be thought of as a new single sampling plan for the remainder of the lot. It calls for the selection of a sample of 59 (a new n) from the 964 (a new N) articles in the remaining portion of the lot. This remaining portion of the lot contains 9 (a new M) defectives. The new acceptance number, $c_1 = 2$.

$$P_0 = \frac{C_{59}^{955} C_0^9}{C_{59}^{964}} = \frac{955!\,59!\,905!}{896!\,59!\,964!} = 0.565$$

$$P_1 = \frac{C_{58}^{955} C_1^9}{C_{59}^{964}} = \frac{955!\,59!\,905!\,(9)}{897!\,58!\,964!} = 0.335$$

$$P_2 = \frac{C_{57}^{955} C_2^9}{C_{59}^{964}} = \frac{955!\,59!\,905!\,(36)}{898!\,57!\,964!} = 0.086$$

$$\underline{}$$

Total   0.986

If exactly two defectives are found in the first sample, the probabilities that the second sample will contain zero or one defectives are as follows:

$$P_0 = \frac{C_{59}^{956} C_0^8}{C_{59}^{964}} = \frac{956!\,59!\,905!}{897!\,59!\,964!} = 0.602$$

$$P_1 = \frac{C_{58}^{956} C_1^8}{C_{59}^{964}} = \frac{956!\,59!\,905!\,(8)}{898!\,58!\,964!} = 0.316$$

$$\text{Total} \quad 0.918$$

If exactly three defectives are found in the first sample, the probability that the second sample will contain zero defectives is

$$P_0 = \frac{C_{59}^{957} C_0^7}{C_{59}^{964}} = \frac{957!\,59!\,905!}{898!\,59!\,964!} = 0.642$$

The probability of acceptance may now be computed, using the theorem of conditional probabilities

0 defectives in first	$= 0.692$
1 defectives in first, with 0, 1, or 2 in second	$= (0.261)(0.986) = 0.257$
2 defectives in first, with 0 or 1 in second	$= (0.043)(0.918) = 0.039$
3 defectives in first, with 0 in second	$= (0.004)(0.642) = 0.003$

$$\text{Probability of acceptance of a lot } 1.0\% \text{ defective} \quad 0.991$$

The foregoing time-consuming calculations may be shortened greatly by an approximation. If it is assumed that the binomial is applicable to this sampling problem (in other words, that samples are drawn from an infinite lot or that a Type B curve is desired) and that the Poisson is a satisfactory approximation to the binomial, Table G may be used.

In using Table G to compute the respective probabilities of results of the first sample, $np' = 36(0.010) = 0.36$. Interpolating in Table G between the values for np' of 0.35 and 0.40, we find

$$P_0 = 0.698$$

$$P_{1 \text{ or less}} = 0.948$$

$$P_1 = 0.948 - 0.698 = 0.250$$

$$P_{2 \text{ or less}} = 0.994$$

$$P_2 = 0.994 - 0.948 = 0.046$$

$$P_{3 \text{ or less}} = 1.000$$

$$P_3 = 1.000 - 0.994 = 0.006$$

If there is one defective on the first sample, calculations regarding the second sample should be based on $np' = (59)(9/964) = 0.55$. Table G gives directly

$$P_{2 \text{ or less}} = 0.982$$

If there are two defectives on the first sample, $np' = (59)(8/964) = 0.49$. Table G gives

$$P_{1 \text{ or less}} = 0.913$$

and if there are three defectives on the first sample,

$$P_0 = 0.648$$

These probabilities may be used to estimate the probability of acceptance, as follows:

0 defectives in first	$= 0.698$
1 defective in first, with 0, 1, or 2 in second	$= (0.250)(0.982) = 0.246$
2 defectives in first, with 0 or 1 in second	$= (0.046)(0.913) = 0.042$
3 defectives in first, with 0 in second	$= (0.006)(0.648) = 0.004$

Probability of acceptance of a lot 1.0% defective   0.990

In this case the difference was negligible between the result of theoretically correct calculations and the result obtained by the approximate method using the Poisson and Table G. Although the check between exact and approximate calculations will not usually be so good as this, the OC curve obtained by the use of the Poisson will ordinarily be close enough for practical purposes.

Multiple and Sequential Sampling

Just as double sampling plans may defer the decision on acceptance or rejection until a second sample has been taken, other plans may permit any number of samples before a decision is reached. The phrase *multiple sampling* is generally used when three or more samples of a stated size are permitted and when the decision on acceptance or rejection must be reached after a stated number of samples. The phrase *sequential sampling* is generally used when a decision is possible after each item has been inspected and when there is no specified limit on the total number of units to be inspected. However, some writers use the two phrases interchangeably. For this reason, plans involving the possibility of decision after each item are referred to in this book as item-by-item sequential plans. The design of an item-by-item plan is illustrated in Chap. 15.

Usually multiple or item-by-item sequential plans can be designed to give OC curves closely similar to the OC curve of any given single or double sampling plan. The following single, double, and multiple plans illustrate a set of matched plans having nearly identical OC curves.

Type of plan	Sample number	Individual sample size	Combined sample size	Acceptance number	Rejection number
Single	1	75	75	2	3
Double	1	50	50	1	4
	2	100	150	3	4
Multiple	1	20	20	*	2
	2	20	40	0	3
	3	20	60	1	3
	4	20	80	2	4
	5	20	100	2	4
	6	20	120	2	4
	7	20	140	3	4

* Acceptance not permitted on first multiple sample.

The foregoing method of describing acceptance sampling plans differs slightly from the one used earlier in this chapter for single and double sampling. It is generally not convenient to use n and c numbers to describe a multiple plan.

Figure 12-6 shows the OC curves for these three attributes plans together with the OC curve for a matched plan using variables criteria. The calculation of the OC curve for the multiple plan follows the same pattern already explained for

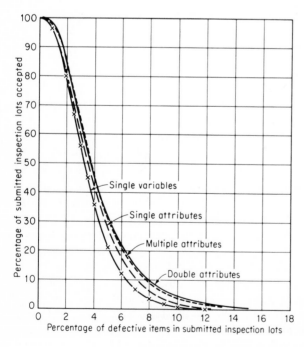

Figure 12-6 OC curve for the single sampling attributes plan $n = 75$, $c = 2$, and OC curves for three matching sampling plans.

double sampling. The following calculations apply to a single point on the curve, namely, the probability of acceptance of a 2% defective lot. To simplify the calculation, it is assumed that the lot size is large enough so that the unsampled portion of the lot will still be substantially 2% defective regardless of the results of past samples. Under this assumption, it is not necessary to recalculate np' based on the number of defectives found in the first sample as was done in the previous article. Each multiple sample consists of 20 articles. To use Table G, it should be noted that $np' = (20)(0.02) = 0.4$. Table G then gives the following useful figures applicable to any sample:

$$P_0 = 0.670$$

$$P_1 = 0.938 - 0.670 = 0.268$$

$$P_2 = 0.992 - 0.938 = 0.054$$

$$P_3 \text{ or more} = 1.000 - 0.992 = 0.008$$

These may be combined by the theorem of conditional probabilities to obtain the following probabilities of acceptance or rejection on each sample:

Sample number	Probability of	
	Acceptance	Rejection
1	0.000	0.062
2	0.449	0.022
3	0.241	0.058
4	0.113	0.010
5	0.000	0.015
6	0.000	0.010
7	0.013	0.007
	0.816	0.184

It will be noted that for 2% defective lots, this particular multiple sampling plan will arrive at a decision with one or two samples (not more than 40 items inspected) more than half the time and will nearly always reach a decision within four samples (with not more than 80 items inspected.)

Calculations are along the same general lines as those illustrated in connection with finding Type B OC curves in double sampling. For the first three samples, the actual calculations are as follows:

Sample 1
$P_0 = 0.670$ (Continue sampling, entering sample 2 with 0 defectives.)
$P_1 = 0.268$ (Continue sampling, entering sample 2 with 1 defective.)
$P_{2 \text{ or more}} = 0.054 + 0.008 = 0.062$ (Reject.)

Note: The probability of continuing sampling is $0.670 + 0.268 = 0.938$. The sum of the computed probabilities of the different possible results in Sample 2 must be equal to this figure.

Sample 2

$P_{0-0} = (0.670)(0.670) = 0.449$ (Accept.)

$P_{0-1} = (0.670)(0.268) = 0.1795$
$P_{1-0} = (0.268)(0.670) = 0.1795$

$\overline{0.359}$ (Continue sampling, entering sample 3 with 1 defective.)

$P_{0-2} = (0.670)(0.054) = 0.036$
$P_{1-1} = (0.268)(0.268) = 0.072$

$\overline{0.108}$ (Continue sampling, entering sample 3 with 2 defectives.)

$P_{0-3 \text{ or more}} = (0.670)(0.008) = 0.005$
$P_{1-2 \text{ or more}} = (0.268)(0.062) = 0.017$

$\overline{0.022}$ (Reject.)

Check: $0.449 + 0.359 + 0.108 + 0.022 = 0.938$

Note: The probability of continuing sampling is $0.359 + 0.108 = 0.467$. The sum of the computed probabilities of the different possible results in sample 3 must be equal to this figure.

Sample 3

$P_{1-0} = (0.359)(0.670) = 0.241$ (Accept.)

$P_{1-1} = (0.359)(0.268) = 0.096$
$P_{2-0} = (0.108)(0.670) = 0.072$

$\overline{0.168}$ (Continue sampling, entering sample 4 with 2 defectives.)

$P_{1-2 \text{ or more}} = (0.359)(0.062) = 0.022$
$P_{2-1 \text{ or more}} = (0.108)(0.330) = 0.036$

$\overline{0.058}$ (Reject.)

Check: $0.241 + 0.168 + 0.058 = 0.467$

The topic of the difference in average amount of sampling inspection under single, double, and multiple sampling is discussed in Chap. 14, which also considers other relative advantages and disadvantages of these competing types of sampling.

An explanation of the calculation of the OC curve of the matching variables plan shown in Fig. 12-6 is deferred until Chap. 17.

Rejection Number for First Sample in Double Sampling

The reader will observe that in the double sampling plans discussed in this chapter and in Chap. 13, the rejection number is the same for the first sample as for the combined samples. This is in contrast to the multiple sampling plan just explained, which had rejection numbers of 2, 3, or 4, depending on the sample number. We shall see that in nearly all multiple sampling plans, two or more rejection numbers are used.

Administrative simplicity is gained by the policy of having only one rejection number for any given double sampling plan. Before 1963, this policy was adopted for the various tables of double sampling plans that were in popular use.

At some sacrifice of administrative simplicity, the average amount of sampling inspection in double sampling can often be reduced for a given quality protection by making the rejection number for the first sample less than the rejection number for the combined samples. Two such rejection numbers are used in most of the double sampling plans in ABC-STD-105, an international standard for acceptance sampling by attributes adopted in 1963. This ABC standard is discussed in Chap. 14.

Randomness in Acceptance Sampling

The probability calculations used to compute OC curves assume that samples are drawn at random. That is, each item in the lot is assumed to have an equal chance to be selected in the sample. If the items in a lot have been thoroughly mixed, a sample chosen anywhere in the lot meets the requirement of randomness. However, a common condition is that there is no reason to believe that the items have had a thorough mixing. Moreover, it may be impracticable to carry out a thorough mixing because of physical difficulties or excessive costs incident to mixing or for other reasons. Sometimes the best that can be done in drawing a sample is to avoid any obvious type of bias. For instance, if items are packed in layers, it clearly is not sensible to draw the entire sample from the top layers.

If it is practicable to assign a different number to each item in a lot and to draw an item from any place in the lot, a formal scheme for drawing a random sample may be adopted. Such a scheme may use a table of random numbers or some mechanical device for generating random numbers as needed.

Use of Random Numbers to Select a Sample

Random digits can be generated in any way that gives each digit from 0 to 9 an equal chance to be selected. Extensive tables of random digits can be generated rapidly by modern electronic computers. Table Z in App. 3 contains 2,500 random digits reproduced by permission from an extensive table prepared by the RAND Corporation.†

Let us illustrate the use of a table of random digits by a numerical example based on Table Z. Assume that it is desired to select a sample of 15 from a lot of 750 items. Each item in the lot is identified by a number from 1 to 750. Therefore it is necessary to select 15 random three-digit numbers from 001 to 750.

† The RAND Corporation, "A Million Random Digits with 100,000 Normal Deviates," Glencoe Free Press Division of The Macmillan Company, New York, 1955.

First it is necessary to determine a starting point in the table. Table Z contains 50 rows and 50 columns of digits. Assume that a pencil point is placed at random in the table and the first two-digit number to the right from 1 to 50 determines the row to be selected. The procedure is repeated to determine the starting column. Assume that the 8th row and the 39th column are chosen. Assume that the decision was made in advance that the starting digit chosen will be the first digit of a three-digit number read to the right and that succeeding numbers will be read down the table. The following numbers are obtained. (Numbers that are not between 001 and 750 must be discarded; these are shown in parentheses. A number that has already occurred must also be discarded; there are no such numbers in this example.)

471, 098, 443, 335, 015, 106, (932), 682, (864), 531, 379, (909), 225, 233, 404, (812), 392, (820), (934), 183, (929), 592.

The selection of the sample is simplified if the 15 numbers between 001 and 750 are rearranged in order of increasing size as follows:

015, 098, 106, 183, 225, 233, 335, 379, 392, 404, 443, 471, 531, 592, 682.

If samplers wish to generate their own random numbers, a convenient method is to use a set of Japanese random dice. Each die is a regular icosahedron. Each digit from 0 to 9 is engraved on two faces so that the 10 digits occur with equal probability. The dice come in sets of three colors. When the dice are used to generate three-digit random numbers, one color may be assigned to each digit.

In cases where it is deemed to be imperative to use a formal scheme to ensure a random sample, there may be a psychological advantage in having the person who selects the sample use random dice or some other mechanical device. The use of a device that obviously involves the laws of chance may add interest to the job of selecting the sample. Because of this interest, there may be less tendency for the sampler to disregard a stipulated formal set of rules for randomization.

Tables of Random Permutations

In the use of conventional tables of random numbers such as Table Z or of Japanese random dice, an additional operation is caused in identifying and discarding numbers that occur more than once. This operation is eliminated by the use of a table of random permutations. (Such tables are also useful in design of experiments and in other matters unrelated to acceptance sampling.) An extensive set of such tables has been prepared by Moses and Oakford.†

Stratified Sampling

In large lots, the difficulties of random selection may be so great that is advisable to adopt stratified (proportional) sampling. In the volume " Sampling Inspection "

---

† L. E. MOSES and R. V. OAKFORD, " Tables of Random Permutations," Stanford University Press, Stanford, Calif., 1963. This 233-page volume contains many random permutations of 9, 16, 20, 30, 50, 100, 200, 500, and 1,000 integers.

the Statistical Research Group of Columbia University made the following suggestions for this type of sampling[†]

1. Draw proportional samples. According to this rule, inspection lots should, wherever possible, be divided into sublots on the basis of factors that are likely to lead to variation in the quality of the product. ... From each sublot into which the inspection lot is divided a subsample should be selected. The size of the subsample from each sublot should be proportional to the size of that sublot.
2. Draw sample items from all parts of each sublot of the inspection lot.
3. Draw sample items blind.

Such a stratified sample is, of course, different from a random sample. In taking many such stratified samples from a given lot, the average number of defectives will be the same as if samples were drawn at random, but the variation in number of defectives from sample to sample will be less. The result is that the OC curve for any given acceptance criteria will be steeper under stratified sampling than under random sampling. Lots substantially better than those at $p_{0.50}$ will have a somewhat greater chance of acceptance than indicated by the OC curve for random sampling; lots substantially worse than those at $p_{0.50}$ will have a somewhat smaller chance of acceptance. OC curves under stratified sampling cannot be calculated without making an assumption as to the variation of quality from sublot to sublot. Investigations by the Statistical Research Group indicate that for practical situations likely to arise in industrial sampling, the use of stratified samples will seldom make much change from the OC curve computed for random sampling.

Estimating the Lot Quality from the Sample Quality

In lot-by-lot acceptance sampling, the immediate practical question is what to do with the lot. A decision must be made to accept a lot or reject it or perhaps to screen it. Definite criteria are established to settle such decisions. Usually, the estimation of lot quality from sample quality is viewed merely as an academic question. In some instances, however, particularly in dealing with isolated lots and in borderline cases, it may be desired to have an idea of the probabilities of various possible values of quality of a sampled lot.

If it is desired to estimate from a given sample by attributes the probability that the true lot quality is within given limits, such an estimate requires the use of Bayes' theorem. A solution of this problem was made by General Simon, who has presented this solution in compact form in his I_Q charts.[‡] These charts are based

---

[†] H. A. FREEMAN, MILTON FRIEDMAN, FREDERICK MOSTELLER, and W. A. WALLIS (eds.), "Sampling Inspection," pp. 48–52, McGraw-Hill Book Company, New York, 1948.

[‡] These charts, $5\frac{1}{2}$ by $7\frac{1}{2}$ in, are inserted in a pocket in the back of "An Engineers' Manual of Statistical Methods." However, if any considerable use of these charts is to be made, it is desirable to purchase them enlarged to $7\frac{1}{2}$ by 11 in. L. E. SIMON, "Enlarged I_Q Charts," John Wiley & Sons, Inc., New York, 1941.

on the assumption that prior to sampling, all fractions defective were equally likely. The five charts apply to probabilities of 0.995, 0.9, 0.5, 0.1, and 0.005. For instance, with any given sample size (up to 500) from an infinite or very large lot and with any given number of observed defectives in the sample, the probability is 0.995 that the true fraction defective in the lot is less than a value that may be read from the 0.995 chart.

An illustration of the numerical information given by these charts may help the reader to decide whether they will be useful in dealing with his particular problems. Assume a sample of 240 from a very large lot contains exactly 2 defectives. The charts give the probability as 0.995 that the true fraction defective is below 0.038, and as 0.005 that it is less than 0.0014. In other words, it is a fairly safe estimate (with a 0.99 probability) that the true fraction defective of the lot is between 0.038 and 0.0014. The charts give the probability as 0.9 that the true fraction defective is less than 0.022 and as 0.1 that it is less than 0.0046. In other words, there are four chances out of five that the true fraction defective is between 0.022 and 0.0046. The 0.5 chart gives the estimated lot fraction defective as 0.011. This contrasts with the sample fraction defective of $\frac{2}{240} = 0.0083$.

A contrast is afforded by the probabilities for a sample half as big with half as many defectives. Assume a sample of 120 has exactly 1 defective. The probability is 0.99 that the true fraction defective is between 0.06 and 0.0009, and 0.8 that it is between 0.032 and 0.0043. The estimated lot fraction defective is 0.014. All these probabilities depend on the assumption underlying the charts, namely, that prior to sampling, one fraction defective is as likely as another.

PROBLEMS

12-1 A single sampling plan uses a sample size of 15, and an acceptance number of 1. Using hypergeometric probabilities, compute the respective probabilities of acceptance of lots of 50 articles 2%, 6%, 10%, and 20% defective.
Answer: 1.000; 0.789; 0.524; 0.121.

12-2 The single sampling plan of Problem 12-1 is used with a relatively large lot. Use Table G to compute the approximate probabilities of acceptance of lots 2%, 6%, 10%, and 20% defective.
Answer: 0.963; 0.772; 0.558; 0.199.

12-3 A single sampling plan has $n = 110$ and $c = 3$. The lot size is large in comparison with sample size. Use Table G to compute the approximate probabilities of acceptance of lots 0.5%, 1%, 2%, 3%, 4%, 5%, 6%, and 8% defective.
Answer: 0.998; 0.974; 0.819; 0.580; 0.359; 0.202; 0.105; 0.025.

12-4 Plot the OC curve for the sampling plan of Problem 12-3. What are the approximate values of lot per cent defective for which probabilities of acceptance are 0.95, 0.50, and 0.10, respectively?
Answer: 1.2%; 3.3%; 6.1%.

12-5 A double sampling plan is as follows:

(a) Select a sample of 2 from a lot of 20. If both articles inspected are good, accept the lot. If both are defective, reject the lot. If 1 is good and 1 defective, take a second sample of one article.

(b) If the article in the second sample is good, accept the lot. If it is defective, reject the lot.

If a lot 25% defective is submitted, what is the probability of acceptance? Compute this by the method that is theoretically correct rather than by an approximate method.
Answer: 0.860.

12-6 A multiple sampling plan is as follows:

Sample number	Individual sample size	Combined sample size	Acceptance number	Rejection number
1	5	5	*	2
2	5	10	0	2
3	5	15	0	3
4	5	20	1	3
5	5	25	2	3

* Acceptance not permitted on first sample.

Assuming that lot size is large enough for Table G to be applicable, compute the probability of acceptance of a 10% defective lot.

Answer: 0.586.

12-7 A double sampling plan is $n_1 = 25$, $c_1 = 1$, $n_2 = 50$, $c_2 = 3$. Compute the probability of acceptance of a 4.0% defective lot. Assume lot size is large in comparison with sample size.

Answer: 0.819.

12-8 A double sampling plan is $n_1 = 150$, $c_1 = 2$, $n_2 = 300$, $c_2 = 4$. Compute the probability of acceptance of a 1.5% defective lot. Assume lot size is large in comparison with sample size.

Answer: 0.623.

12-9 The following multiple sampling plan involves a maximum of 7 samples of 40 each:

Sample number	Combined sample size	Acceptance number	Rejection number
1	40	*	2
2	80	*	2
3	120	0	2
4	160	0	3
5	200	1	3
6	240	2	4
7	280	4	5

* Acceptance not permitted on first or second sample.

Compute the probability of acceptance of a 1.0% defective lot. Assume lot size is large in comparison with sample size.

Answer: 0.582.

12-10 A single sampling plan uses a sample size of 8 and an acceptance number of zero. Using the correct hypergeometric probabilities, compute the probabilities of acceptance of lots of 50 articles 2%, 6%, 10%, and 20% defective, respectively.

12-11 The single sampling plan of Problem 12-10 is used with relatively large lots. Use Table G to compute the approximate probabilities of acceptance of lots 2%, 6%, 10%, and 20% defective, respectively.

12-12 A single sampling plan has $n = 100$ and $c = 2$. The lot size is 500 items. Using hypergeometric probabilities, compute the respective probabilities of acceptance of lots 0.5%, 2%, 4%, and 6% defective, respectively.

12-13 The single sampling plan of Problem 12-12 is used with relatively large lots. Use Table G to compute the approximate probabilities of acceptance of lots 0.5%, 2%, 4%, and 6% defective, respectively.

12-14 For the single sampling plan $n = 150$, $c = 2$, what are the values of $p_{0.95}$, $p_{.50}$, and $p_{0.10}$? See Table 12-1 for probabilities of acceptance and interpolate to obtain the values of p.

12-15 For the single sampling plan $n = 75$, $c = 1$, what are the values of $p_{0.95}$, $p_{0.50}$, and $p_{.10}$? See Table 12-1 for probabilities of acceptance and interpolate to obtain the values of p.

12-16 Consider the single sampling plan $n = 75$, $c = 1$. Table 12-1 gives the probability of acceptance of a 2% defective lot as 0.558. This computation assumes a very large lot. Using the correct hypergeometric formula, compute the probability of acceptance of a 2% defective lot when $N = 300$.

12-17 In a double sampling plan, $N = 40$, $n_1 = 5$, $c_1 = 0$, $n_2 = 5$, $c_2 = 1$. Using the correct hypergeometric formula, compute the probability that a lot exactly 7.5% defective will be accepted by this plan.

12-18 The double sampling plan in Problem 12-17 is used for relatively large lots. Use Table G to compute the approximate probability of acceptance of lots exactly 7.5% defective.

12-19 Consider the double sampling plan $n_1 = 100$, $c_1 = 1$, $n_2 = 200$, $c_2 = 3$. Use Table G to compute the probability of acceptance of 2.5% defective lots assuming the lot size is large in comparison to the sample size.

12-20 A random sample of 10 is to be selected from a lot of 500 articles. Each article in the lot has been assigned a number. Table Z of App. 3 is to be used to select 10 three-digit numbers between 001 and 500; these numbers will determine the articles to be chosen as the sample. A random choice from Table Z results in a first number of 288 taken from the 13th, 14th, and 15th digits on line 13. The rule established is to read down the table directly below these digits. Select the required 10 three-digit numbers (of course eliminating all numbers above 500) and arrange them in order of increasing magnitude.

12-21 An electrical manufacturer receives components from three different suppliers. At present, the user accepts lots based on his own sampling plan. The policy is to draw a random sample equal to 10% of the lot size with a lot being rejected if one or more defective components are found. Suppliers A, B, and C submit components in lots of 100, 250, and 1,000, respectively.

(a) Use Table G to determine for each supplier the lot fractions defective for which 95%, 50%, and 10% of the lots will be accepted.

(b) Do you consider the user's sampling plan fair? Why or why not?

12-22 A double sampling plan calls for a first sample of 25 items to be inspected. If no defectives are found, the lot is accepted; if three or more defectives are found, it is rejected. Otherwise, a second sample of 50 items is drawn and the lot is accepted if the combined number of defectives found does not exceed four. Assuming the lot size is large in comparison to the sample size, use Table G to find the following:

(a) the Producer's Risk (α) at a fraction defective of 0.02.

(b) the Consumer's Risk (β) at a fraction defective of 0.12.

12-23 A multiple sampling plan is as follows:

Sample number	Individual sample size	Combined sample size	Acceptance number	Rejection number
1	50	50	*	3
2	50	100	1	3
3	50	150	2	4
4	50	200	3	5
5	50	250	5	6

* Acceptance not permitted on first sample.

Use Table *G* to calculate the approximate probability of acceptance of 3% defective lots. Assume the lot size is large in comparison to the combined sample size.

12-24 In the sampling plan described in Problem 12-23, compute the probabilities of acceptance and rejection on the first two samples and the probability of taking the third sample.

12-25 In the sampling plan described in Problem 12-23, compute the probabilities of acceptance and rejection on the first three samples and the probability of taking the fourth sample.

12-26 In the sampling plan described in Problem 12-23, compute the probability of acceptance on the first four samples and the probability of taking the fifth sample.

THIRTEEN

THE DODGE-ROMIG SYSTEM FOR LOT-BY-LOT ACCEPTANCE SAMPLING BY ATTRIBUTES

The question is sometimes asked as to why it is necessary to have so many tables. ... In industry, acceptable quality levels vary and the necessary risks of wrong decisions vary. For each combination of acceptable quality level and risk, a different plan is required; hence the need for many tables. Series of tables that cover nearly all ordinary requirements have been computed and published.—A. C. Richmond†

An Attributes Sampling Procedure Involving Consideration of the Effects of Screening Rejected Product

The great bulk of acceptance inspection is carried out on an attributes basis, with articles classified into those conforming to specifications and those failing to conform. Attributes inspection is well adapted to the establishment of standard sampling procedures.

The decision to accept a lot, based on the outcome of one or more samples drawn from the lot, leads to rather obvious results. The decision to reject, however, leads to another series of actions and decisions, usually well stipulated in contractual agreements or standard operating procedures, but nevertheless more complex than the actions required by a decision to accept.

Frequently the result of a decision to reject a lot is 100% inspection of that particular lot. Such action is referred to as *screening inspection*, or sometimes as *detailing*. Responsibility for screening inspection may rest with either the producer or the consumer.

---

† A. C. RICHMOND, Acceptance Inspection, *Paper* No. 8, Fourth National Convention of American Society for Quality Control, June, 1950.

Selecting an Acceptance Inspection Scheme

The choice among various possible types of procedure for acceptance of manufactured product is essentially an economic one. In making a decision regarding acceptance inspection for any particular product, it may be desirable to consider not only various possible schemes of acceptance sampling by attributes but also the alternatives of (1) no inspection at all, (2) 100% inspection, and (3) possibilities of acceptance sampling by variables. It also is true that a satisfactory evaluation of all the pertinent economic factors is often quite difficult. For this reason, the choice of an acceptance plan is commonly made on an intuitive basis.

An important element in the selection of an acceptance inspection scheme should be the probable contribution of the scheme to quality improvement. The acceptance sampling schemes described in this and the following chapters have often been strikingly successful in leading to such improvement.

Two Useful Volumes of Standard Tables

Anyone responsible for the choice of an acceptance sampling procedure by attributes should have two volumes available for consultation. One of these is the volume "Sampling Inspection Tables" by Dodge and Romig.† The other is "Sampling Inspection" prepared by the Statistical Research Group (SRG) of Columbia University.‡ Both of these volumes not only contain extensive tables of acceptance sampling plans for attributes inspection but also contain much useful material on the theory and practice of acceptance sampling.

The Dodge-Romig tables were originally prepared for use within the Bell Telephone System. They were designed primarily to minimize the total amount of inspection, considering both sampling inspection and screening inspection of rejected lots.

Some Further Comments on Indexing of Sampling Systems

It was pointed out in Chap. 12 that three points on the OC curve have been used as methods of indexing sets of sampling plans. These, and other statistical measures, provide the logical basis for combining sets of plans into a sampling system. For example, the Philips Standard Sampling System described in Chap. 15 employs the *point-of-control*, or *indifference quality*, $p_{0.50}$, as the index base to the sampling system. The Dodge-Romig system employs the $p_{0.10}$ point as the index to two sets of tables in the system. The point $100p_{0.10}$ is termed the *Lot Tolerance Per Cent Defective (LTPD)*, that per cent defective which has a probability of

† H. F. DODGE and H. G. ROMIG, "Sampling Inspection Tables—Single and Double Sampling," 2d ed., John Wiley & Sons, Inc., New York, 1959.

‡ H. A. FREEMAN, MILTON FRIEDMAN, FREDERICK MOSTELLER, and W. A. WALLIS (eds.), "Sampling Inspection," McGraw-Hill Book Company, New York, 1948.

acceptance of 0.10.† Thus the two sets of tables are indexed on Consumer's Risk, β, where β equals 0.10.

Selected points on the OC curve need not be the only indexes of sampling plans. Another such index is the *Average Outgoing Quality Limit*, abbreviated *AOQL*. In the Dodge-Romig system of plans described in this chapter, two of the four sets of tables are indexed on the AOQL. All of the sampling plans in the Dodge-Romig tables aim at minimizing the *Average Total Inspection* (ATI) considering both sampling inspection and screening inspection of rejected lots.

The Average Outgoing Quality Limit

In many instances, the rejection of a lot on the basis of sampling inspection results in 100% inspection of that particular lot. Particularly in the British literature of

---

† The Dodge-Romig tables refer to this point as p_t rather than $100p_{0.10}$ as used in this text. In order to maintain consistency in this text, all references to p_t have been changed to $100p_{0.10}$ in the tables and discussions. See the footnote on page 374 for a further discussion of the meaning of LTPD.

Table 13-1 Average outgoing quality from $\begin{cases} n = 75 \\ c = 1 \end{cases}$

when used as an acceptance/rectification plan

Per cent defective in submitted lots, $100p'$	Probability of acceptance, P_a	Average per cent defective in accepted product, AOQ
0.2	0.990	0.198
0.4	0.963	0.385
0.6	0.925	0.555
0.8	0.878	0.702
1.0	0.827	0.827
1.2	0.772	0.926
1.4	0.718	1.005
1.6	0.663	1.061
1.8	0.610	1.098
2.0	0.558	1.116
2.1	0.533	1.119
2.2	0.509	1.120
2.3	0.486	1.118
2.4	0.463	1.111
2.5	0.441	1.102
3.0	0.343	1.029
3.5	0.262	0.917
4.0	0.199	0.796
4.5	0.150	0.675
5.0	0.112	0.560

the subject this is sometimes described as an *acceptance/rectification* scheme. The accepted lots will contain approximately the per cent defective submitted although they will be slightly improved by the elimination of any defectives found in the samples whenever c is one or more. The rejected lots, after screening, will presumably contain no defectives. For any plan, it is possible to compute the maximum possible value of the average per cent defective in the outgoing product. This maximum figure is referred to as the *average outgoing quality limit*, the AOQL.

A common type of approximate calculation to determine the AOQL is illustrated in Table 13-1. This table refers to the plan $\begin{vmatrix} n = 75 \\ c = \quad 1 \end{vmatrix}$, when N is large in comparison with n. The probabilities of acceptance were computed in Table 12-1. The right-hand column gives *average outgoing quality* (AOQ) for each assumed per cent defective in submitted lots. The maximum value of the AOQ is 1.12%, occurring when submitted lots are 2.2% defective. This maximum value is the AOQL. Figure 13-1 illustrates the variation of AOQ with incoming quality.

The assumptions underlying Table 13-1 may be explained by examining one particular calculation. Consider that incoming lots come from a process that is 0.6% defective. The probability (Type B) that such lots will be accepted on the basis of the sample is 0.925 or $\frac{37}{40}$. In the long run, therefore, only 3 lots out of 40 will be screened. For 40 such lots, 37 will be passed containing, on the average, 0.6% of defectives and 3 will contain no defectives after screening. The AOQ expressed in per cent defective will therefore be

$$(P_a)(100p') = (0.925)(0.6\%) = 0.555\%$$

Several simplifying assumptions in the foregoing calculation are as follows:

1. The lot size N is constant. Thus the 3 screened lots may be assumed to be the same size as the 37 unscreened ones.
2. The screening inspection finds all the defectives in the screened lots, and these defectives are removed.

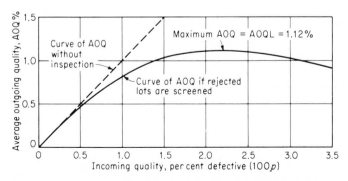

Figure 13-1 Average outgoing quality for acceptance/rectification plan $n = 75$, and $c = 1$.

3. The defective articles removed from the screened lots are replaced with good articles. Thus each screened lot contributes N good articles to the final stream of product.

It should be emphasized that any calculation of average outgoing quality gives the expected quality *in the long run*. As its name implies, the AOQ is an *average*. Over a short period, the outgoing quality may be better or worse than the long-run average. Subject to the limitations of the three simplifying assumptions just stated, any acceptance/rectification plan guarantees that, regardless of the incoming quality submitted, the outgoing quality in the long run will not be worse than the plan's AOQL. This guarantee, however, does not apply to short periods.

Some Comments on the Significance of the AOQL

Sampling schemes based on stated AOQL values have gained widespread use in industry. They are used particularly in a manufacturer's inspection of his own product, both in process inspection and in final inspection. They have also been used advantageously in the inspection of lots of purchased product. If the purchaser's sampling inspection takes place in the vendor's plant, the vendor may do the screening of rejected lots and submit a certification of the screening work done. If the purchaser's sampling inspection takes place elsewhere, the purchaser may carry out the screening, where necessary, and by agreement charge the cost thereof to the vendor.

AOQL plans have also proved well adapted to many circumstances outside manufacturing, particularly to the checking of clerical work. Such "nonproduct" applications are discussed briefly in Chap. 21.

At various points in our discussion of lot-by-lot acceptance sampling, we shall have occasion to note that the continued use of a sampling scheme tends to be confined to circumstances where most of the time the quality is good enough for nearly all lots to be accepted on the basis of a sample. AOQL plans are no exception to this rule.

Where nearly all the lots are accepted on the basis of the sample, the average outgoing quality will be only slightly better than the average quality in these accepted lots. If submitted lots are badly out of statistical control, so that the screened lots are generally much worse than the unscreened lots, the screening may effect an important improvement in quality. If the submitted product is in good statistical control and few lots are screened, the outgoing quality will not differ greatly from incoming quality. In any event, the AOQ will nearly always be considerably better than the AOQL.

Even though the simplifying assumptions used in the calculation of AOQL's may depart somewhat from actual facts, it follows that this departure is not a matter of great practical importance. Only rarely will the users of schemes based on the AOQL have need to cash in on the guarantee that outgoing quality will not be worse than the computed AOQL.

Choosing a Sampling Plan to Minimize Average Total Inspection

The question of minimum total inspection depends on the number of rejected lots that must be detailed (that is, 100% inspected). This, in turn, depends on the quality level of the product submitted. In analyzing and evaluating various sampling plans it is convenient to state the problem in terms of the ATI, *Average Total Inspection*, and the AFI, *Average Fraction Inspected*. For single sampling plans the ATI and AFI may be found from:

$$\text{ATI} = nP_a + N(1 - P_a)$$
$$= n + (N - n)(1 - P_a)$$

and

$$\text{AFI} = \text{ATI}/N$$

Use of these formulas to choose among sampling plans may be illustrated using the three plans of Fig. 12-3 under different assumptions as to the quality level of incoming lots. Assume that a large number of lots which are 0.5% defective are submitted for acceptance by each plan. The required values are:

N	1,000	1,000	1,000
n	100	170	240
c	0	1	2
P_a	0.59	0.80	0.92
nP_a	59.0	136.0	220.8
$N(1 - P_a)$	410.0	200.0	80.0
ATI	460.0	336.0	300.8
AFI	0.460	0.336	0.301

With the quality level submitted for inspection 0.5% defective, it is evident that the plan $\begin{cases} N = 1,000 \\ n = \quad 240 \\ c = \quad 2 \end{cases}$ requires the least total inspection. However, if the quality level submitted should be 0.2% defective rather than 0.5% defective, the minimum total inspection will be required using $\begin{cases} N = 1,000 \\ n = \quad 170 \\ c = \quad 1 \end{cases}$. This is shown in the following calculation:

N	1,000	1,000	1,000
n	100	170	240
c	0	1	2
P_a	0.81	0.97	1.00
nP_a	81.0	164.9	240.0
$N(1 - P_a)$	190.0	30.0	0.0
ATI	271.0	194.9	240.0
AFI	0.271	0.195	0.240

It should be noted that the amount of sampling inspection always increases with increasing n. The minimization of AFI results from a trade-off between increased sampling inspection and decreased risk of detailing. In those cases where the purchaser charges detailing costs back to the vendor, there may be strong pressure to minimize the sample size rather than the AFI. In the long run such action will prove to be uneconomical.

For a double sampling plan, the formula for *Average Total Inspection* is:

$$\text{ATI} = n_1 P_a(n_1) + (n_1 + n_2)P_a(n_2) + N(1 - P_a)$$

where $P_a(n_1)$ = probability of acceptance on the first sample.

$\quad\quad P_a(n_2)$ = probability of acceptance on the second sample.

$\quad\quad P_a = P_a(n_1) + P_a(n_2)$.

Referring to the double sampling plan of Fig. 12-5 ($N = 1,000$, $n_1 = 36$, $c_1 = 0$, $n_2 = 59$, $c_2 = 3$), if incoming lots are 1.0% defective, the AFI is found from (see p. 379 for probabilities of acceptance):

$$\text{ATI} = 36(0.698) + 95(0.292) + 1,000(1 - 0.990) = 62.87$$

$$\text{AFI} = 62.87/1,000 = 0.063$$

The mathematical relationship between the AFI and the AOQ is:

$$\text{AOQ} = p(1 - \text{AFI})$$

Frequently, when very complex sampling plans are to be analyzed, this formula is used rather than direct solution for the AOQ. For the previous double sampling plan, we could solve for AOQ as follows:

$$\text{AOQ} = 0.01(1 - 0.063) = 0.00937$$

By varying the value of p for lots entering inspection from 0 to 1, the value of P_a will range from 1 to 0 in accordance with the OC curve for the individual plan. Thus the AFI will range from a minimum of n/N to a maximum of 1. Analysis of AFI values of alternative sampling plans at specific values of p permits the analyst to choose that plan with minimum AFI. Such calculations were used as the basis for specifying the plans contained in the Dodge-Romig tables.

The Dodge-Romig Tables

The Dodge-Romig volume contains four sets of tables, as follows:

  I. Single Sampling Lot Tolerance Tables
 II. Double Sampling Lot Tolerance Tables
III. Single Sampling AOQL Tables
IV. Double Sampling AOQL Tables

Sets I and II apply to the following lot tolerance per cent defectives (assuming Consumer's Risk = 0.10):

0.5%	3.0%	7.0%
1.0%	4.0%	10.0%
2.0%	5.0%	

Sets III and IV apply to the following values of AOQL:

0.1%	1.5%	4.0%
0.25%	2.0%	5.0%
0.5%	2.5%	7.0%
0.75%	3.0%	10.0%
1.0%		

Single Sampling Lot Tolerance Tables

Table 13-2 is representative of Dodge-Romig Set I.

All the sampling plans in this table have the same lot tolerance per cent defective (LTPD), namely, 5.0%. However, the plans have different values of AOQL. The table gives the AOQL figure for each plan.

The table contains six columns, each for a different value of process average per cent defective. The purpose of these different columns is to indicate the plan that involves the minimum total inspection, considering both the inspection of samples and the 100% inspection of rejected lots.

For example, consider the inspection plans indicated in the table for the lot size range from 501 to 600. Six different plans, namely, $\begin{cases} n = 45 \\ c = 0 \end{cases}$ $\begin{cases} n = 75 \\ c = 1 \end{cases}$ $\begin{cases} n = 100 \\ c = 2 \end{cases}$ $\begin{cases} n = 125 \\ c = 3 \end{cases}$ $\begin{cases} n = 150 \\ c = 4 \end{cases}$ and $\begin{cases} n = 175 \\ c = 5 \end{cases}$ all have a lot tolerance fraction defective of 0.05. But, as previously explained, if rejected lots are to be detailed, the total amount of inspection of samples and rejected lots under these plans will depend on the quality level of the product submitted for inspection. Table 13-2 simply says that this total inspection will be a minimum for $\begin{cases} n = 45 \\ c = 0 \end{cases}$ if the process average is 0–0.05% defective, that it will be a minimum for $\begin{cases} n = 75 \\ c = 1 \end{cases}$ if the process average is 0.06–0.50%, and so forth.

If there is no basis for estimating the process average, the sampling plan should be selected from the right-hand column of the table. This gives the desired quality protection and gives satisfactory lots a better chance of acceptance. Moreover, it collects data more rapidly to permit reliable estimates of the process average.

Table 13-2 Example of Dodge-Romig single sampling lot tolerance tables

Lot tolerance per cent defective = 5.0%

Consumer's risk = 0.10

(Reprinted by permission from H. F. Dodge and H. G. Romig, "Sampling Inspection Tables—Single and Double Sampling," 2d ed., John Wiley & Sons, Inc., New York, 1959)

Process Average %	0–.05			.06–.50			.51–1.00			1.01–1.50			1.51–2.00			2.01–2.50		
Lot Size	n	c	AOQL %	n	c	AOQL %	n	c	AOQL %	n	c	AOQL %	n	c	AOQL %	n	c	AOQL %
1–30	All	0	0	All	0	0	All	0	0	All	0	0	All	0	0	All	0	0
31–50	30	0	.49	30	0	.49	30	0	.49	30	0	.49	30	0	.49	30	0	.49
51–100	37	0	.63	37	0	.63	37	0	.63	37	0	.63	37	0	.63	37	0	.63
101–200	40	0	.74	40	0	.74	40	0	.74	40	0	.74	40	0	.74	40	0	.74
201–300	43	0	.74	43	0	.74	70	1	.92	70	1	.92	95	2	.99	95	2	.99
301–400	44	0	.74	44	0	.74	70	1	.99	100	2	1.0	120	3	1.1	145	4	1.1
401–500	45	0	.75	75	1	.95	100	2	1.1	100	2	1.1	125	3	1.2	150	4	1.2
501–600	45	0	.76	75	1	.98	100	2	1.1	125	3	1.2	150	4	1.3	175	5	1.3
601–800	45	0	.77	75	1	1.0	100	2	1.2	130	3	1.2	175	5	1.4	200	6	1.4
801–1000	45	0	.78	75	1	1.0	105	2	1.2	155	4	1.4	180	5	1.4	225	7	1.5
1001–2000	45	0	.80	75	1	1.0	130	3	1.4	180	5	1.6	230	7	1.7	280	9	1.8
2001–3000	75	1	1.1	105	2	1.3	135	3	1.4	210	6	1.7	280	9	1.9	370	13	2.1
3001–4000	75	1	1.1	105	2	1.3	160	4	1.5	210	6	1.7	305	10	2.0	420	15	2.2
4001–5000	75	1	1.1	105	2	1.3	160	4	1.5	235	7	1.8	330	11	2.0	440	16	2.2
5001–7000	75	1	1.1	105	2	1.3	185	5	1.7	260	8	1.9	350	12	2.2	490	18	2.4
7001–10,000	75	1	1.1	105	2	1.3	185	5	1.7	260	8	1.9	380	13	2.2	535	20	2.5
10,001–20,000	75	1	1.1	135	3	1.4	210	6	1.8	285	9	2.0	425	15	2.3	610	23	2.6
20,001–50,000	75	1	1.1	135	3	1.4	235	7	1.9	305	10	2.1	470	17	2.4	700	27	2.7
50,001–100,000	75	1	1.1	160	4	1.6	235	7	1.9	355	12	2.2	515	19	2.5	770	30	2.8

In the use of these lot tolerance tables, it should be understood that the tables contemplate the screening of rejected lots. However, the tables give the consumer the stated quality protection regardless of any provision for screening. Even though rejected lots are merely returned by the consumer to the producer with no formal provision for screening by anyone, it is reasonable to suppose that the producer will screen these lots. Under such circumstances, the consumer's use of the process average to determine his acceptance criteria may be thought of as aimed at minimizing the total inspection done by industry as a whole, considering both the consumer's sampling inspection and the screening presumably done by the producer.

Double Sampling Lot Tolerance Tables

Table 13-3 is representative of Dodge-Romig Set II.

Some differences between single and double sampling plans are evident from a

Table 13-3 Example of Dodge-Romig double sampling lot tolerance tables

Lot tolerance per cent defective = 5.0%

Consumer's risk = 0.10

(Reprinted by permission from H. F. Dodge and H. G. Romig, "Sampling Inspection Tables—Single and Double Sampling," 2d ed., John Wiley & Sons, Inc., New York, 1959)

Lot Size	n_1	c_1	n_2	n_1+n_2	c_2	AOQL %	n_1	c_1	n_2	n_1+n_2	c_2	AOQL %	n_1	c_1	n_2	n_1+n_2	c_2	AOQL %	n_1	c_1	n_2	n_1+n_2	c_2	AOQL %	n_1	c_1	n_2	n_1+n_2	c_2	AOQL %	n_1	c_1	n_2	n_1+n_2	c_2	AOQL %
Process Average %	**0–.05**						**.06–.50**						**.51–1.00**						**1.01–1.50**						**1.51–2.00**						**2.01–2.50**					
1–30	All 30	0	—	—	—	0	All 30	0	—	—	—	0	All 30	0	—	—	—	0	All 30	0	—	—	—	0	All 30	0	—	—	—	0	All 30	0	—	—	—	0
31–50	30	0	—	—	—	.49	30	0	—	—	—	.49	30	0	—	—	—	.49	30	0	—	—	—	.49	30	0	—	—	—	.49	30	0	—	—	—	.49
51–75	38	0	—	—	—	.59	38	0	—	—	—	.59	38	0	—	—	—	.59	38	0	—	—	—	.59	38	0	—	—	—	.59	38	0	—	—	—	.59
76–100	44	0	21	65	1	.64	44	0	21	65	1	.64	44	0	21	65	1	.64	44	0	21	65	1	.64	44	0	21	65	1	.64	44	0	21	65	1	.64
101–200	49	0	26	75	1	.84	49	0	26	75	1	.84	49	0	26	75	1	.84	49	0	51	100	2	.84	49	0	51	100	2	.91	49	0	51	100	2	.91
201–300	50	0	30	80	1	.91	50	0	30	80	1	.91	50	0	55	105	2	1.0	50	0	55	105	2	1.0	50	0	80	130	3	1.1	50	0	100	150	4	1.1
301–400	55	0	30	85	1	.92	55	0	55	110	2	1.1	55	0	55	110	2	1.1	55	0	80	135	3	1.1	55	0	100	155	4	1.2	85	1	105	190	6	1.3
401–500	55	0	30	85	1	.93	55	0	55	110	2	1.1	55	0	80	135	2	1.2	55	0	105	160	4	1.3	55	0	150	205	5	1.4	85	1	140	225	7	1.4
501–600	55	0	30	85	1	.94	55	0	60	115	2	1.1	55	0	85	140	3	1.2	55	0	110	165	4	1.3	85	1	145	230	7	1.5	85	1	165	250	8	1.5
601–900	55	0	35	90	1	.95	55	0	65	120	2	1.1	55	0	85	140	3	1.3	90	1	125	215	6	1.3	90	1	170	260	8	1.6	120	2	185	305	10	1.6
801–1000	55	0	35	90	1	.96	55	0	65	120	2	1.1	55	0	115	170	4	1.4	90	1	150	240	7	1.5	90	1	200	290	9	1.7	120	2	210	330	11	1.7
1001–2000	55	0	35	90	1	.98	55	0	95	150	3	1.3	55	0	120	175	4	1.4	90	1	185	275	8	1.7	120	2	225	345	11	1.9	175	4	260	435	15	2.0
2001–3000	55	0	65	120	2	1.2	55	0	95	150	3	1.3	55	0	150	205	5	1.5	120	2	180	300	9	1.9	150	3	270	420	14	2.1	205	5	375	580	21	2.3
3001–4000	55	0	65	120	2	1.2	55	0	95	150	3	1.3	90	1	140	230	6	1.6	120	2	210	330	10	2.0	150	3	295	445	15	2.3	230	6	420	650	24	2.4
4001–5000	55	0	65	120	2	1.2	55	0	95	150	3	1.4	90	1	165	255	7	1.8	120	2	255	375	12	2.1	150	3	345	495	17	2.3	255	7	445	700	26	2.5
5001–7000	55	0	65	120	2	1.2	55	0	95	150	3	1.4	90	1	165	255	7	1.8	120	2	260	380	13	2.1	150	3	370	520	18	2.3	255	7	495	750	28	2.6
7001–10,000	55	0	65	120	2	1.2	55	0	120	175	4	1.5	90	1	190	280	8	1.9	120	2	285	405	13	2.1	175	4	370	545	19	2.4	280	8	540	820	31	2.7
10,001–20,000	55	0	65	120	2	1.2	55	0	120	175	4	1.5	90	1	190	280	8	1.9	120	2	310	430	14	2.2	175	4	420	595	21	2.4	280	8	660	940	36	2.8
20,001–50,000	55	0	65	120	2	1.2	55	0	150	205	5	1.7	90	1	215	305	9	2.0	120	2	335	455	15	2.2	205	5	485	690	25	2.5	305	9	745	1050	41	2.9
50,001–100,000	55	0	65	120	2	1.2	55	0	150	205	5	1.7	90	1	240	330	10	2.1	120	2	360	480	16	2.3	205	5	555	760	28	2.6	330	10	810	1140	45	3.0

comparison of Tables 13-2 and 13-3. These differences may be brought out to best advantage by comparing any single sampling plan with a double sampling plan for the same lot size and process average that gives the same lot quality protection. For example, consider the plans from Tables 13-2 and 13-3 for a lot size of 801–1,000 and a process average of 0.51–1.00% defective:

Single sampling   Double sampling

$n = 105$ $n_1 = 55$ $n_2 = 115$

$c = 2$ $c_1 = 0$ $n_1 + n_2 = 170$

$c_2 = 4$

The first sample in double sampling is smaller than the one sample in single sampling; in this case it is 55 instead of 105. On the other hand, the combined sample in double sampling is larger—170 compared to 105. The relative number of articles inspected in the samples in the two plans evidently depends on the quality of submitted product. If the product sampled is good enough that very few second samples have to be taken, the inspection will be substantially less with the double sampling plan. If many second samples need to be taken, the single sampling will require less sampling inspection. Dodge and Romig give a diagram that compares the inspection under single and double sampling for various lot sizes and ratios of process average to lot tolerance fraction defectives.† They state that over the portion of the tables most useful in practice, the saving in inspection due to double sampling is usually over 10% and may be as much as 50%.

One characteristic of all the Dodge-Romig double sampling plans is that c_2 is always 1 or more. This means that no lot is ever rejected as a result of only 1 defective.

Single Sampling AOQL Tables

Table 13-4 is representative of Dodge-Romig Set III.

In contrast to Table 13-2 in which all the single sampling plans had the same lot tolerance per cent defective, all the plans in Table 13-4 have the same AOQL, namely, 2%. The table gives the lot tolerance per cent defective for each plan. It is of interest to note that the larger the sample size and acceptance number for a given AOQL, the lower the lot tolerance per cent defective.

Like all the Dodge-Romig tables, columns are given for various process averages; the plan in each column is the one which gives the minimum total inspection for the process average at the head of the column. Thus all the plans on any line of the table are alike in quality protection (as measured by the AOQL) and differ only in total amount of inspection required. As remarked in the discussion of Table 13-2, if there is no basis for estimating the process average, the sampling plan should be chosen from the right-hand column of the table.

---

† DODGE and ROMIG, *op. cit.*, Fig. 2-5, p. 31.

Table 13-4 Example of Dodge-Romig single sampling AOQL tables

Note: Average outgoing quality limit = 2.0%
(Reprinted by permission from "Sampling Inspection Tables" by Dodge & Romig, John Wiley & Sons, Inc.)

Process Average % Lot Size	0–.04 n	c	$100p_{0.10}$	.05–.40 n	c	$100p_{0.10}$	.41–.80 n	c	$100p_{0.10}$	.81–1.20 n	c	$100p_{0.10}$	1.21–1.60 n	c	$100p_{0.10}$	1.61–2.00 n	c	$100p_{0.10}$
1–15	All	0	—	All	0	—	All	0	—	All	0	—	All	0	—	All	0	—
16–50	14	0	13.6	14	0	13.6	14	0	13.6	14	0	13.6	14	0	13.6	14	0	13.6
51–100	16	0	12.4	16	0	12.4	16	0	12.4	16	0	12.4	16	0	12.4	16	0	12.4
101–200	17	0	12.2	17	0	12.2	17	0	12.2	17	0	12.2	35	1	10.5	35	1	10.5
201–300	17	0	12.3	17	0	12.3	17	0	12.3	37	1	10.2	37	1	10.2	37	1	10.2
301–400	18	0	11.8	18	0	11.8	38	1	10.0	38	1	10.0	38	1	10.0	60	2	8.5
401–500	18	0	11.9	18	0	11.9	39	1	9.8	39	1	9.8	60	2	8.6	60	2	8.6
501–600	18	0	11.9	18	0	11.9	39	1	9.8	39	1	9.8	60	2	8.6	60	2	8.6
601–800	18	0	11.9	40	1	9.6	40	1	9.6	65	2	8.0	65	2	8.0	85	3	7.5
801–1000	18	0	12.0	40	1	9.6	40	1	9.6	65	2	8.1	65	2	8.1	90	3	7.4
1001–2000	18	0	12.0	41	1	9.4	65	2	8.2	65	2	8.2	95	3	7.0	120	4	6.5
2001–3000	18	0	12.0	41	1	9.4	65	2	8.2	95	3	7.0	120	4	6.5	180	6	5.8
3001–4000	18	0	12.0	42	1	9.3	65	2	8.2	95	3	7.0	155	5	6.0	210	7	5.5
4001–5000	18	0	12.0	42	1	9.3	70	2	7.5	125	4	6.4	155	5	6.0	245	8	5.3
5001–7000	18	0	12.0	42	1	9.3	95	3	7.0	125	4	6.4	185	6	5.6	280	9	5.1
7001–10,000	42	1	9.3	70	2	7.5	95	3	7.0	155	5	6.0	220	7	5.4	350	11	4.8
10,001–20,000	42	1	9.3	70	2	7.6	95	3	7.0	190	6	5.6	290	9	4.9	460	14	4.4
20,001–50,000	42	1	9.3	70	2	7.6	125	4	6.4	220	7	5.4	395	12	4.5	720	21	3.9
50,001–100,000	42	1	9.3	95	3	7.0	160	5	5.9	290	9	4.9	505	15	4.2	955	27	3.7

Double Sampling AOQL Tables

Table 13-5 is representative of Dodge-Romig Set IV.

Dodge and Romig point out that the lot tolerance concept was first developed and applied in the Bell Telephone System in 1923. The concept of the AOQL was developed and applied in 1927. Thus tables involving both concepts, and involving single and double sampling, have been available within the Bell System for application to all types of inspection for many years. It is significant that Dodge and Romig state that the double sampling AOQL tables, of which Table 13-5 is an example, have proved the most useful of all the tables.

Relationship between the Process Average Used in Selecting a Dodge-Romig Sampling Plan and the OC Curve of the Plan Selected

Tables 13-2 to 13-5 all have six columns, each corresponding to a stated process average. In general, the greater the process average used in entering any Dodge-Romig table, the larger will be the sample size for any stated lot size. The plans having larger sample sizes have steeper OC curves with resulting better discrimination between lots superior to the quality standard and lots worse than the quality standard. This point is illustrated by Figs. 13-2 and 13-3.

Figure 13-2 shows the OC curves for the six double sampling plans given in Table 13-3 (LTPD = 5%) for the lot size 4,001–5,000. All these curves naturally show that the probability of acceptance of a 5% defective lot is 0.10. At all other points, however, the OC curves differ considerably. The differences are particularly striking at about half the 5% LTPD. Thus a 2.5% defective lot is almost certain to be accepted under the plan corresponding to the process average 2.01–2.50% (curve 6) but has only about a 0.50 probability of acceptance under the plans corresponding to the process averages 0–0.05% and 0.06–0.50% (curves 1 and 2). In general, where submitted lots are as good as the process average used in entering the tables, they are almost certain to be accepted.

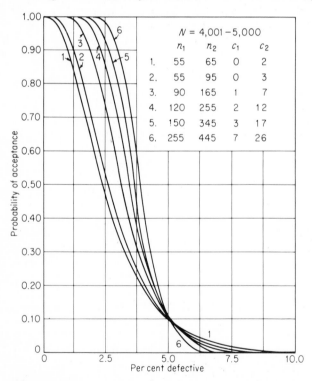

Figure 13-2 OC curves for the six Dodge-Romig double sampling plans for LTPD of 5% and lot size 4,001–5,000. (*Reproduced from H. F. Dodge, "Administration of a Sampling Inspection Plan," Industrial Quality Control, vol. 4, no. 3, pp. 12–19, November, 1948.*)

Table 13-5 Example of Dodge-Romig double sampling AOQL tables

Note: Average outgoing quality limit = 2.0%

(Reprinted by permission from "Sampling Inspection Tables" by Dodge & Romig, John Wiley & Sons, Inc.)

Lot Size	0–.04						.05–.40						.41–.80						.81–1.20						1.21–1.60						1.61–2.00					
	Trial 1		Trial 2			$100p_{0.10}$	Trial 1		Trial 2			$100p_{0.10}$	Trial 1		Trial 2			$100p_{0.10}$	Trial 1		Trial 2			$100p_{0.10}$	Trial 1		Trial 2			$100p_{0.10}$	Trial 1		Trial 2			$100p_{0.10}$
	n_1	c_1	n_2	n_1+n_2	c_2		n_1	c_1	n_2	n_1+n_2	c_2		n_1	c_1	n_2	n_1+n_4	c_2		n_1	c_1	n_2	n_1+n_2	c_2		n_1	c_1	n_2	n_1+n_2	c_2		n_1	c_1	n_2	n_1+n_2	c_2	
1–15	All	0	—	—	—	—	All	0	—	—	—	—	All	0	—	—	—	—	All	0	—	—	—	—	All	0	—	—	—	—	All	0	—	—	—	—
16–50	14	0	—	—	—	13.6	14	0	—	—	—	13.6	14	0	—	—	—	13.6	14	0	—	—	—	13.6	14	0	—	—	—	13.6	14	0	—	—	—	13.6
51–100	21	0	12	33	1	11.7	21	0	12	33	1	11.7	21	0	12	33	1	11.7	21	0	12	33	1	11.7	21	0	12	33	1	11.7	23	0	23	46	2	10.9
101–200	24	0	13	37	1	11.0	24	0	13	37	1	11.0	24	0	13	37	1	11.0	27	0	28	55	2	9.6	27	0	28	55	2	9.6	27	0	28	55	2	9.6
201–300	26	0	15	41	1	10.4	26	0	15	41	1	10.4	29	0	31	60	2	9.1	29	0	31	60	2	9.1	32	0	48	80	3	8.4	32	0	48	80	3	8.4
301–400	26	0	16	42	1	10.3	26	0	16	42	1	10.3	30	0	35	65	2	9.0	33	0	52	85	3	8.2	33	0	52	85	3	8.2	36	0	69	105	4	7.6
401–500	27	0	16	43	1	10.3	30	0	35	65	2	9.0	30	0	35	65	2	9.0	34	0	56	90	3	7.9	36	0	74	110	4	7.5	60	1	90	150	6	7.0
501–600	27	0	16	43	1	10.3	31	0	34	65	2	8.9	35	0	55	90	3	7.9	35	0	55	90	3	7.9	37	0	78	115	4	7.4	65	1	95	160	6	6.8
601–800	27	0	17	44	1	10.2	31	0	39	70	2	8.8	35	0	60	95	3	7.7	38	0	82	120	4	7.3	38	0	82	120	4	7.3	70	1	120	190	7	6.4
801–1000	27	0	17	44	1	10.2	32	0	38	70	2	8.7	36	0	59	95	3	7.6	38	0	87	125	4	7.2	70	1	100	170	6	6.5	70	1	145	215	8	6.2
1001–2000	33	0	37	70	2	8.5	33	0	37	70	2	8.5	37	0	63	100	3	7.5	43	0	112	155	5	6.5	80	1	160	240	8	5.8	110	2	205	315	11	5.5
2001–3000	34	0	41	75	2	8.2	34	0	41	75	2	8.2	41	0	84	125	4	7.0	75	1	115	190	6	6.1	115	2	195	310	10	5.3	160	3	310	470	15	4.7
3001–4000	34	0	41	75	2	8.2	38	0	62	100	3	7.3	41	0	89	130	4	6.9	80	1	140	220	7	5.8	120	2	255	375	12	5.0	235	5	415	650	20	4.3
4001–5000	34	0	41	75	2	8.2	38	0	62	100	3	7.3	42	0	88	130	4	6.9	80	1	175	255	8	5.5	125	2	285	410	13	4.9	275	6	475	750	23	4.2
5001–7000	35	0	40	75	2	8.1	38	0	62	100	3	7.3	44	0	116	160	5	6.4	85	1	205	290	9	5.3	125	2	320	445	14	4.8	280	6	575	855	26	4.1
7001–10,000	35	0	40	75	2	8.1	38	0	62	100	3	7.3	45	0	115	160	5	6.3	85	1	210	295	9	5.2	165	3	335	500	15	4.5	320	7	645	965	29	4.0
10,001–20,000	35	0	40	75	2	8.1	39	0	66	105	3	7.2	45	0	115	160	5	6.3	90	1	260	350	11	5.1	170	3	425	595	18	4.4	395	9	835	1230	37	3.9
20,001–50,000	35	0	40	75	2	8.1	43	0	92	135	4	6.6	47	0	148	195	6	6.0	130	2	300	430	13	4.7	205	4	515	720	22	4.3	480	11	1090	1570	46	3.7
50,001–100,000	35	0	45	80	2	8.0	43	0	92	135	4	6.6	85	1	185	270	8	5.2	135	2	345	480	14	4.5	250	5	615	865	26	4.1	580	13	1460	2040	58	3.5

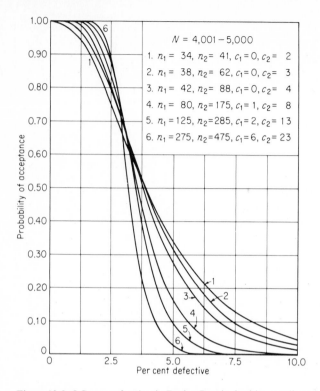

Figure 13-3 shows the OC curves for the six double sampling plans given in Table 13-5 (AOQL = 2%). A comparison with Fig. 13-2 may be helpful in emphasizing certain similarities and certain differences between using the LTPD and the AOQL as the quality standard. Just as in the LTPD tables, any lots at the assumed process average or better are almost certain of acceptance. The probability of acceptance of lots at exactly the AOQL value varies from about 0.84 (curve 1) to 0.99 (curve 6). The differences in the right-hand sections of the OC curves reflect different degrees of protection against accepting lots considerably worse than the stated AOQL; these differences are also brought out in Table 15-4 by the LTPD values given for each sampling plan.

Determining the Process Average in Dodge-Romig Inspection

The minimizing of total inspection depends on making a correct estimate of the process average as a basis for the selection of the sampling plan. It follows that in all Dodge-Romig inspection, it is advantageous to make systematic use of the results of sampling inspection to determine the process average.

Two forms that may be used to record this information are illustrated in an article by Keeling and Cisne describing the AOQL double sampling methods used at Western Electric Company.[†] This article has been reproduced as Chap. III in the Dodge-Romig volume. One form (page 48 of Dodge and Romig) records the numbers inspected and numbers of defectives in lot-by-lot samples for a given inspection operation for a week, separating the results of first samples and second samples in double sampling. Columns are provided to show the number of defects of each type observed in first samples.

Another form (page 50 of Dodge and Romig) contains a weekly summary of the inspection results. One side of the form consists of a control chart for p on which are plotted the weekly percentages of defectives in first samples. Two-sigma limits are used on this chart.

Whenever double sampling is used, the process average should be estimated from first samples only. Otherwise the estimate would be too heavily weighted by the samples from the poorer lots.

Relationship between Lot Size and Sample Size in Dodge-Romig Tables

The Dodge-Romig tables apply to lot sizes from 1 to 100,000 and may be used for any lots that happen to be submitted for acceptance. Where practicable, however, it may be advantageous to establish the size of lots to be submitted for acceptance rather than to take lots as they come. The tables help in making a decision on lot size by showing clearly the disadvantage of small lots as compared with large ones from the viewpoint of the amount of sampling necessary for a given quality protection. For example, the first column of Table 13-2 calls for a sample size of "All" (that is, 100%) of a lot of 30 or less, a sample size of 37 (that is, 37%) of a lot of 100, and a sample size of 45 (that is, 2.25%) of a lot of 2,000 all for the same quality protection.[‡] This emphasizes again the point made in Chap. 12 that it is the absolute size of the sample, much more than its size relative to the lot, that governs the quality protection.

It is evident that wherever possible it is desirable to avoid the very small lot sizes. At the same time it is apparent that the great saving in inspection for a given quality protection consists in taking lots of the order of magnitude of 1,000 rather than the conventional lots of 50 or 100. For example, in Table 13-2 a reduction from a 37% sample from lots of 100 to a 4.5% sample from lots of 1,000 is a reduction in inspection of 32.5% of the total number of articles submitted in the lots. In contrast, a reduction from a 4.5% sample from lots of 1,000 to a 2.25% sample from lots of 2,000 is a reduction of only 2.25%.

[†] D. B. KEELING, and L. E. CISNE, Using Double Sampling in a Manufacturing Plant, *Bell System Technical Journal*, vol. 21, pp. 37–50, June, 1942.

[‡] The only reason the sample size jumps to 75 for lots of 2,001 to 100,000 is that $n = 75$ and $c = 1$ gives less total inspection of samples and rejected lots than $n = 45$ and $c = 0$. Even for a lot size of 100,000, the sampling plan $n = 45$ and $c = 0$ gives a 0.10 probability of acceptance for a 5% defective lot.

There are several possible practical objections to very large lot sizes such as those from 10,000 to 100,000. One objection is that there are often practical difficulties in bringing such large lots together for inspection purposes; the cost of doing this may more than offset the inspection savings. Another objection is that it is frequently much harder to get a random sample out of a lot of 10,000 than out of a lot of 1,000. Moreover, the adverse effect on producer-consumer relationships of the rejection of very large lots is sometimes serious.

Making Dodge-Romig AOQL Procedures Contribute to Quality Improvement

The record of sampling inspection may contribute in various ways to the improvement of quality. The control chart maintained as part of this record will indicate out-of-control situations and will show quality trends. This gives guidance as to when to hunt for trouble and helps to concentrate executive pressure for improvement in those places where it will be most effective. The lot-by-lot record listing defects in first samples is helpful to anyone engaged in the actual hunting for the sources of trouble.

Moreover, the contribution of the sampling procedure is not limited to the supplying of useful information. The costs of carrying out screening inspection of rejected lots may be used to provide an effective financial incentive to quality improvement. Where producer and consumer are two departments of the same organization, the producer may be required to do all such screening. Or, where this is not practicable, the cost of any screening inspection may be charged against the budget of the producing department. Example 13-1 describes a case in which both of these types of pressure were used.

When a vendor and purchaser are involved, an agreement can be made that whenever lots fail to pass the purchaser's sampling inspection, a stipulated deduction from the price will be made to cover the purchaser's screening costs. Under such circumstances, the AOQL to be used is a matter for prior agreement between vendor and purchaser.

Example 13-1 Use of AOQL inspection to produce quality improvement
Facts of the case In a large manufacturing plant, the practice for many years had been for the inspection department to carry out 100% inspection on numerous parts and products. On many of these items, the average percentages of defectives had been much worse than any reasonable AOQL, and it appeared that no sampling scheme would be as economical as 100% inspection.

It was decided that any required 100% inspection was properly an operating department expense and that inspection should bear only the cost of sampling inspection with sampling criteria based on reasonable quality standards. AOQL inspection was instituted with AOQL figures set at values considered to be satisfactory objectives. Many lots were rejected, and the cost of screening was charged to the operating departments. These charges caused greatly increased attention to quality among operating personnel. In a surprisingly short time, quality was brought to the desired level for the great majority of items.

This new quality consciousness in the operating departments was accompanied by a new viewpoint on the relative responsibilities of operations and inspection. Product costs were considerably reduced. Once the program reached the point where nearly all items were at qualities better than the AOQL figures adopted for them, the responsibility for carrying out all needed screening inspection was transferred to the operating departments. This transfer of responsibility applied both to the 100% inspection of any lots rejected under sampling inspection and to 100% inspection prior to sampling inspection of those few items where it was not possible to produce at an average quality equal to or better than the desired AOQL.

Selecting an AOQL Value as a Quality Standard

Two figures may properly be considered in any decision on the AOQL. One is the maximum percentage of defectives that is tolerable in the outgoing product after inspection. The other is the capability of the production process, expressed as the percentage of defectives, that will be expected in most of the submitted lots. It is evident that 100% inspection by *someone* is necessary whenever the submitted quality is appreciably worse than the tolerable percentage of defectives. As illustrated in Example 13-1, the chief purpose of adopting sampling inspection in this case may be to use frequent lot rejections to force the producer either to improve his quality or to carry out an adequate screening inspection.

Various considerations may enter into the decision on the maximum tolerable percentage of defectives. If the design specification for a quality characteristic contains a margin of safety, some articles that are technically classified as defectives may really be satisfactory for the purpose intended. Sometimes there may be a good chance that any defectives in the outgoing product from this inspection will be eliminated in a later manufacturing or inspection operation; in other cases this inspection may be the last chance to eliminate them. It is obviously necessary to consider the number of quality characteristics involved in the particular inspection and their importance in the functioning of the product being inspected. Comments on some economic aspects of this decision are made in Chap. 19.

It is likely to be easier to estimate the capabilities of a production process than to decide on the maximum tolerable percentage of defectives. If nearly all of the submitted lots are to be accepted on the basis of the sample, the quality of these accepted lots needs to be somewhat better than the selected AOQL. An approximate rule for guidance is that, as things work out in practice, the net result of using an AOQL scheme will usually be an average outgoing per cent defective not worse than half to two-thirds of the AOQL value.† This rule may be viewed in reverse to judge the implications regarding process capability when a particular AOQL value is selected. For instance, suppose a 1.5% AOQL value is selected; this implies that it is believed that—except, perhaps, for occasional out-of-control bad lots—the process can ultimately be made capable of submitting lots that are not worse than about 1.0% defective.

PROBLEMS

For all of the problems in this chapter assume that nonconforming items in screened lots and in samples from accepted lots are removed and replaced.

13-1 What single sampling plan should be used for a lot size of 1,500 and an LTPD of 5.0% with a Consumer's Risk of 0.10 if the process average is estimated as 0.6% defective?

Answer: $n = 130, c = 3$.

13-2 What double sampling plan should be used for the conditions described in Problem 13-1?

Answer: $n_1 = 55, c_1 = 0; n_2 = 120, c_2 = 4$.

13-3 What single sampling plan should be used for a lot size of 900 and an AOQL of 2.0% if the process average is estimated as 0.9% nonconforming?

Answer: $n = 65, c = 2$.

13-4 What double sampling plan should be used for the conditions described in Problem 13-3?

Answer: $n_1 = 38, c_1 = 0; n_2 = 87, c_2 = 4$.

13-5 Determine from Table 13-4 the single sampling plans for an AOQL of 2%, an estimated process average of 1%, and lot sizes of 200, 1,000, and 5,000, respectively. What percentage of the product will be subject to sampling inspection with each lot size?

Answer: 8.5%, 6.5%, 2.5%.

13-6 A consumer receives lots of 2,000 items and uses a single sampling plan to accept or reject the lots. The plan calls for 200 items to be inspected and for the lot to be accepted if two or less nonconforming units are found. All rejected lots are screened by the consumer and the resultant cost is billed to the producer. Compute the Average Outgoing Quality (AOQ) if 0.8% nonconforming lots are submitted for inspection.

Answer: 0.564%.

13-7 In a single sampling plan, $N = 10,000, n = 300$, and $c = 1$. This is used with the stipulation that all rejected lots are to be screened. Compute the AOQ if all lots submitted are 0.5% nonconforming.

Answer: 0.279%.

13-8 In a double sampling plan, $N = 5,000, n_1 = 100, c_1 = 0, n_2 = 100$, and $c_2 = 1$.

(*a*) Use Table G to compute the probability of acceptance of a 1% nonconforming lot.

(*b*) Assume that a lot rejected by this sampling plan will be 100% inspected. What will be the AOQ if the submitted product is 1% nonconforming?

(*c*) Considering both the inspection of samples and inspection of rejected lots, what will be the average number of articles inspected per lot if the submitted product is 1% nonconforming?

Answer: (*a*) 0.503; (*b*) 0.503%; (*c*) 2,549.

---

† H. F. DODGE, "Administration of a Sampling Inspection Plan," *Industrial Quality Control*, vol. 5, no. 3, pp. 12–19, November, 1948, and reprinted in *Journal of Quality Technology*, vol. 9, no. 3, July, 1977. This article contains excellent concise advice regarding the development of sampling inspection procedures in a manufacturing plant.

13-9 Prepare an AOQ curve for the single sampling plan $n = 100$, $c = 0$. What is the AOQL?
Answer: 0.37%.

13-10 The lot size N is 2,000 in a certain AOQL inspection procedure. The desired AOQL of 2.0% can be obtained with any one of three single sampling plans. These are $n = 65$, $c = 2$; $n = 41$, $c = 1$; and $n = 18$, $c = 0$. If a large number of lots 0.3% nonconforming are submitted for acceptance, what will be the average number of units inspected per lot under each of these three sampling plans?
Answer: 67; 55; 121.

13-11 (a) Determine the single sampling plan to be used for a lot size of 250 items and an LTPD of 5% with a Consumer's Risk of 10% if the process average is estimated at 1.1%.
(b) What percentage of the product will be subject to sampling inspection with this sampling plan?
(c) What is the probability of acceptance of a lot 4.0% nonconforming under this plan?
(d) Compute the average total inspection (ATI) at 4.0% and at 1.1% assuming that rejected lots are screened.
Answer: (a) $n = 70$, $c = 1$; (b) 28%; (c) 0.231; (d) 208.4, 102.4.

13-12 In Problem 13-5, out of 100 submitted lots 1% nonconforming, how many would you expect to be subject to screening inspection for each lot size?
Answer: 16, 3, 1.

13-13 Using the answers in Problems 13-5 and 13-12, what will be the total percentage of inspection for each of the three lot sizes, considering both sampling inspection and screening inspection of rejected lots?
Answer: 23%, 9%, 3.5%.

13-14 What single sampling plan should be used for a lot size of 2,500 and an LTPD of 5% with a Consumer's Risk of 0.10 if the process average is estimated as 1.2%?
Answer: $n = 210$, $c = 6$.

13-15 Find the Dodge-Romig 2% AOQL double sampling plan for a lot size of 300 items and a process average p' of 0.015.

13-16 For the plan found in Problem 13-15, compute the following quantities assuming incoming lots contain 4% nonconforming items:
(a) The approximate probability of acceptance on the first sample using Table G;
(b) The approximate total probability of acceptance using Table G;
(c) The AOQ;
(d) The average fraction inspected (AFI).

13-17 A manufacturer has specified sampling in accordance with the Dodge-Romig AOQL system. A 2% AOQL plan is to be used for a lot size of 3,500 items and a process average of 1.0 per cent.
(a) Find the proper double sampling plan and identify its LTPD point.
(b) Find the corresponding single sampling plan.
(c) Use Table G to compute the approximate probability of acceptance under the plan found in (b) assuming that incoming lots contain 2% nonconforming units.

13-18 (a) Compute the AOQ for the single sampling plan found in part (b) of Problem 13-17.
(b) Compute the ATI for this plan.

13-19 A Dodge-Romig single sampling 2% AOQL plan is to be used to sample from lots of 26,000 items.
(a) Find the appropriate plan for a process average of 1.95%.
(b) Find the corresponding double sampling plan.

13-20 (a) Find the single sampling 5% LTPD plan for a process average of 1.0% and a lot size of 500 units.
(b) Find the corresponding double sampling plan.
(c) What are the respective AOQL's for these plans?

13-21 (a) For the single sampling plan found in Problem 13-20, use Table G to compute the approximate probability of acceptance if incoming lots contain 2% nonconforming units.

(b) Compute the AOQ.

(c) Compute the AFI.

13-22 Compute the average number of items sampled for the double sampling plan found in Problem 13-20 assuming incoming lots contain 2% nonconforming items. How does this average value compare with the single sample size found in part (a) of Problem 13-20?

13-23 (a) Find the Dodge-Romig 2% AOQL single sampling plan for a lot size of 300 units and a process average of 1.5%.

(b) Find the corresponding double sampling plan.

13-24 (a) For the double sampling plan found in Problem 13-23, compute the approximate probability of acceptance on the first sample if incoming lots contain 4% nonconforming units. Use Table G.

(b) Compute the total probability of acceptance.

(c) Compute the AOQ.

(d) Compute the AFI.

13-25 (a) Find the Dodge-Romig 5% LTPD single sampling plan for a lot size of 1,250 units and a process average of 2.1%.

(b) What proportion of the product will be subject to sampling inspection with this sampling plan?

(c) Compute the ATI at the process average.

13-26 (a) For the plan found in Problem 13-25, use Table G to compute the approximate probability of acceptance of lots containing 4.0% nonconforming units.

(b) Compute the ATI.

(c) Compute the AOQ.

13-27 (a) Find the Dodge-Romig 5% LTPD double sampling plan for a lot size of 3,500 units and a process average of 1.25%. What is the AOQL of this plan?

(b) Find the 2% AOQL double sampling plan for the same lot size and process average. What is the LTPD of this plan?

13-28 The lot size is 2,000 units in a certain Dodge-Romig AOQL inspection procedure. The desired AOQL of 2.0% can be obtained with any one of three single sampling plans. These plans are: $n = 65$, $c = 2$; $n = 41$, $c = 1$; and $n = 18$, $c = 0$. Answer the following questions under the assumption that incoming lots contain 0.8% nonconforming items.

(a) Use Table G to compute the approximate probabilities of acceptance for each plan.

(b) Compute the ATI for each plan.

(c) Compute the AOQ for each plan.

(d) Taking all three of these measures of effectiveness into account, which plan would you recommend in this case? Explain.

13-29 The Dodge-Romig 5% LTPD Table specifies the following single sampling plans for a lot size of 501 to 600 items: (1) $n = 100$, $c = 2$ for a process average of 0.51 to 1.00 per cent; and (2) $n = 175$, $c = 5$ for an unknown process average or one in the range 2.01 to 2.50 per cent nonconforming.

(a) What is the probability of acceptance under each plan if lots containing 2 per cent nonconforming product are inspected under each plan?

(b) Assuming a lot size of 550 items, what is the AFI under each plan?

(c) What is the AOQ under each plan?

13-30 A company receives lots of 500 items from a certain manufacturer. It uses the following double sampling plan for receiving inspection: $n_1 = 30$, $c_1 = 0$; $n_2 = 40$, $c_2 = 2$. Incoming lots contain 5% nonconforming items. Use Table G to compute the approximate probabilities necessary to answer the following questions:

(a) What is the probability of acceptance on the first sample?

(b) What is the probability of taking the second sample?

(c) What is the total probability of acceptance?

(d) Calculate the AOQ.

13-31 A single sampling plan for lots of 300 items has $n = 25$ and $c = 2$. Incoming lots contain 8% nonconforming items.

(a) Use Table G to find the approximate probability of acceptance.

(b) Compute the ATI assuming that rejected lots are screened. What is the AFI?

(c) Compute the AOQ.

13-32 (a) Find the Dodge-Romig single sampling 2% AOQL plan for a lot size of 550 items and a process average of 1.4% nonconforming items.

(b) What is the LTPD of this plan?

13-33 (a) For the AOQL sampling plan found in Problem 13-32, find the probability of acceptance when incoming lots contain 3% nonconforming units.

(b) Compute the AOQ under this circumstance.

(c) Compute the ATI and the AFI for these lots.

13-34 (a) Find the Dodge-Romig 5% LTPD double sampling plan for a lot size of 250 items and a process average of 1.8%.

(b) What is the AOQL of this plan? Under what special circumstance is it meaningful?

(c) What is the corresponding 5% LTPD single sampling plan?

13-35 (a) For the single sampling plan found in Problem 13-34, use Table G to find the fraction nonconforming that has a probability of acceptance of 90%.

(b) What is the ATI for each of the plans assuming incoming lots contain 3% nonconforming items and rejected lots are screened?

(c) What is the AOQ for each of the plans under the assumptions in part (b)?

13-36 A single sampling AOQL plan calls for $n = 200$, and $c = 3$ for a lot size of 6,000 items.

(a) What is the probability of acceptance if incoming lots contain 2.5% nonconforming items?

(b) Compute the ATI for this plan at 2.5%. What is the AFI?

(c) Compute the AOQ at 2.5%.

CHAPTER

FOURTEEN

AN AQL SYSTEM FOR LOT-BY-LOT ACCEPTANCE SAMPLING BY ATTRIBUTES (ABC-STD-105)

One trouble with 100% inspection, where it is practicable, is that the inspector merely cleans up the faults of others, sorting the good from the bad, and the production man takes it as a matter of course if just individual articles are returned to him for repair. But if a whole lot is returned to him, as when lot sampling is used, and he is required to undertake the entire corrective action, the steady outward flow of product is interrupted. If there are many lot rejections, he must get busy to find the cause and eliminate it in order to avoid further lot rejections. This is an indirect power of sampling—it forces correction of the process, where the fault lies.—H. F. Dodge†

Some Reasons for Not Basing a Quality Standard on a Provision for Screening Inspection

The acceptance procedures described in the preceding chapter all gave consideration to the effect of a formal provision for screening inspection whenever the results of sampling inspection were sufficiently unfavorable. In the AOQL plans, the stated quality standard (i.e., the AOQL) was dependent, in part, on this provision for screening inspection.

Where the producer and consumer are different organizations, dealing at arm's length, there may be good reasons why the consumer is unwilling for the stated quality standard to be based on the assumption that such screening inspection will occur. It may be considered impracticable or inadvisable for the consumer to carry out this screening himself in all cases, and he may be unwilling to rely on any such screening carried out by the producer.

---

† H. F. Dodge, Administration of a Sampling Inspection Plan, *Industrial Quality Control*, vol. 5, no. 3, pp. 12–19, November, 1948, and reprinted in *Journal of Quality Technology*, vol. 9, no. 3, July, 1977.

Screening inspection by the consumer (either of all the product or of rejected lots) may be impracticable because it is unduly costly or because of lack of sufficient inspection facilities or personnel or for other reasons. Even though practicable, it may be deemed inadvisable. As a consequence of the consumer carrying out screening inspection of all product, it may be found that inspection that should have been done by the producer is being executed by the consumer. Moreover, the pressure for quality improvement exerted by outright rejection of one or more entire lots is much stronger than the pressure exerted by the rejection of individual articles classified as defective by a consumer's 100% inspection. These points were illustrated in Example 12-1 and emphasized in Dodge's quotation at the start of this chapter.

A Historical Note Regarding Acceptance Sampling Systems Based on the AQL Concept

The AQL (Acceptable Quality Level) concept was first devised in connection with the development of statistical acceptance sampling for the Ordnance Department of the U.S. Army. The Ordnance tables and procedures were developed in 1942 by a group under the direction of distinguished engineers from the Bell Telephone Laboratories. With some changes and extensions, these became the Army Service Forces tables developed by the same group.† These tables permitted single and double sampling, with double sampling preferred wherever practicable. Several of the Army Service Forces tables were included in the first edition of this book.

Statistical sampling tables and procedures developed for the Navy by the Statistical Research Group of Columbia University were first issued in 1945. The general pattern of these tables and procedures was similar to that used by the Army Service Forces. However, multiple sampling schemes were made available, and there were other important points of difference. After the unification of the armed services, these Navy tables were adopted by the Department of Defense early in 1949 as JAN (Joint Army Navy) Standard 105. The tables were made available for public use through the publication of the SRG's volume "Sampling Inspection," mentioned in Chaps. 12 and 13.

MIL-STD-105A superseded JAN-STD-105 in 1950. Although the underlying pattern was similar to the preceding standards, there were again many important changes in detail.‡ The second edition of this book included the master tables from MIL-STD-105A. Only minor changes from 105A were involved in MIL-STD-105B, adopted by the U.S. Department of Defense in 1958, and in MIL-STD-105C, adopted in 1961.

---

† G. D. EDWARDS, then Director of Quality Assurance of Bell Telephone Laboratories, H. F. DODGE, H. G. ROMIG, and G. R. GAUSE, then of Army Ordnance, all played an important part in developing these tables.

‡ For a statement of the main points of difference among the earlier military acceptance procedures, see S. J. LORBER and E. L. GRANT, A Comparison of Military Standard 105A with the 1944 Army Service Forces Sampling Procedures and Tables and with JAN-Standard 105, *Industrial Quality Control*, vol. 8, no. 1, pp. 27–29, July, 1951.

During the years 1960 to 1962, a committee, known as the ABC† Working Group, from the military agencies of the United States of America, Great Britain, and Canada, was engaged in developing a common standard for acceptance sampling by attributes to be used by the three countries.‡ The committee worked with the assistance and cooperation of the American and European organizations for quality control. Because this standard may be viewed as somewhat of an evolution from the earlier systems based on the AQL concept, it is used in this chapter to illustrate various aspects of such systems. Tables K to W in App. 3 are taken from this standard. In the United States, this standard was adopted in 1963 and was designated as MIL-STD-105D. In order to stress the international character of this standard, it is referred to throughout this chapter as the ABC standard (from the name of the working group that prepared it). The international designation of MIL-STD-105D is ABC-STD-105.

It is not merely the use of AQL systems in purchases by governmental organizations that makes such systems important. Systems based on the AQL have been widely adopted by private industry for acceptance sampling of all kinds of products. In most cases, these systems were adapted from one of the military systems.

Some Decisions Made in the Original Establishment of the AQL as a Quality Standard

The persons who developed the original Army Ordnance procedures made a number of decisions that have remained practically unchanged in the many later systems based on the AQL concept. Some of these decisions were as follows:

1. In order to establish acceptance criteria for any particular quality characteristics of a product, it first is necessary to decide on a per cent defective that is considered acceptable as a process average. This "acceptable quality level" usually has been abbreviated to AQL.§
2. In the absence of unsatisfactory quality history or other reasons for misgivings about the quality of submitted product, the acceptance criteria should be selected with the objective of protecting the producer against the rejection of submitted lots from a process that is at the AQL value or better.
3. Such acceptance criteria generally give the consumer unsatisfactory protection against accepting lots that are moderately worse (sometimes considerably worse) than the AQL. For this reason, more severe acceptance criteria designed to protect the consumer must be used whenever the quality history is unsatisfactory or when there are other good reasons for being suspicious about qual-

---

† For America, Britain, Canada.

‡ The members of the ABC Working Group were G. J. Keefe, chairman, Omberto Cocca, I. D. Hill, Paul Martel, W. G. Milne, and William Pabst, Jr.

§ The similarity between the initials AQL and AOQL sometimes is a source of confusion. The reader should note that only the Q in these sets of initials stands for the same word, namely, *quality*. In AQL, A means *acceptable* and L means *level*. In AOQL, A means *average* and L means *limit*.

ity. This concept of *tightened inspection* as an alternative to *normal inspection* is at the heart of all acceptance sampling systems based on the AQL. It is an essential part of any acceptance/rejection procedures where the acceptance criteria are chosen to protect the producer under "normal" conditions.

4. The acceptance criteria for serious defects should be more severe than for trivial defects. In other words, relatively low AQL values should be used for those types of defects that would have serious consequences and relatively high AQL values for those defects that are of little importance. The provision for a *classification of defects* is an essential feature of systems based on the AQL.

5. Economies for the consumer can be realized by permitting *reduced inspection* when the quality history is good enough. This permits the concentration of attention of inspectors on those products where attention seems to be needed most.

6. In establishing the relationship between lot size and sample size, weight should be given to the greater difficulty of obtaining random samples from large lots and the more serious consequences of a wrong decision on acceptance or rejection of a large lot. For this reason, the relationship between lot size and sample size is based more on empirical grounds than on considerations arising from the mathematics of probability.

Early Difficulties in the Way of a Formalized Allowance for a Percentage of Defectives

H. R. Bellinson has made the following interesting comments about the difficulties of introducing the AQL concept in 1942:†

> [A] unique feature in the Army Sampling Tables ... was the concept of acceptable quality level. It was a concept that had to be introduced because the policy of the Ordnance Department, the policy of all the government purchasing agencies at that time, was that here was a contract; here were drawings and specifications; the contractor agrees to manufacture that way; we pay if it is that way and if it is not that way we don't buy it; the material must be perfect. Unfortunately, you can't develop a sampling plan for attributes on the basis of accepting only perfect material. You just can't ensure perfect material with attributes and sampling. We had to say that we will accept a certain fraction defective; make that as small as you please, but there had to be a fraction. That may sound as though we proposed to degrade quality, but the fact was that the proportion defective being accepted under the methods of inspection then in use was much larger than anything we proposed.
>
> There were difficulties selling that concept, obviously, and difficulties of different types, depending on whom you talked to. The engineering department, for example, was concerned about accepting any defects whatever. The engineers were convinced on the theory that these defects, and they were largely dimensional, followed a distribution law which was presumably the well-known single-peaked affair. Therefore, if the per cent defective was small enough, that is, if

† "Acceptance Sampling—A Symposium," American Statistical Association, Washington, D.C., 1950. Bellinson's quoted remarks are on pages 46 and 47. They were part of a prepared discussion of two papers on "Acceptance Sampling by Attributes" by Paul Peach and E. G. Olds. The symposium was held at the first postwar meeting of the American Statistical Association at Cleveland, Ohio, Jan. 27, 1946.

the area on the tail outside our drawing limit was very small, then the tail couldn't go very far out, and the actual degree of defectiveness in accepted material would be extremely small.

That is a sound engineering argument because every engineer puts a factor of safety in his designs. If the degree of defectiveness is small, the engineer is quite willing to permit it. I am not quite sure that the theory is correct. I suspect that under the conditions which we met, that is, where material is presented for acceptance after inspection by the contractor, the distribution is not a monotonic† function. However, we never got into trouble on that score.

The fiscal department had a different point of view. The fiscal department's point of view was that the government had a contract to pay for 100% perfect material and they simply didn't like the idea of paying the contractor for that one per cent of material which was not perfect. However, after we had gotten together and written an explanation of acceptable quality in which we were able to prove that the proposed inspection plan was much more economical to the government than the former methods of inspection, they gave us their blessing.

The legal department had still another point of view. The legal department was not concerned with the fact we were going to accept a few bad ones; the legal department was concerned with the fact we were going to reject a lot of good ones. Because, you see, if we put in acceptance and rejection plans, we would accept lots one per cent defective; but if we find that a lot is 2% defective, we reject that, even though that lot is 98% perfect. The legal department said that we had no right to reject any individual piece which was without defects. That argument was settled by changing specifications.

Some Aspects of the Master Tables Reproduced from the ABC Standard

Tables L to T in App. 3 give sample sizes and acceptance and rejection numbers. To enter any one of these tables, it is necessary to know the AQL and sample size code letter. To determine which table should be used, it is necessary to know whether single, double, or multiple sampling is to be used and to know whether normal, tightened, or reduced inspection is to be used.

The AQL values in the standard may be interpreted either as per cent defective or as defects per hundred units depending on whether acceptance criteria are to be based on the number of *defectives* observed in a sample or on the number of *defects*. However, AQL values above 10.0 are interpreted as applying to defects per hundred units. Most of our discussion of the standard will assume the more common acceptance criteria based on numbers of defectives with AQL specified as a per cent defective.

All the AQL values are multiples of the numbers 1, 1.5, 2.5, 4.0, and 6.5. These numbers are roughly in a geometrical progression and correspond to systems of "preferred numbers" in common use for other industrial purposes.

Determining the Sample Size Code Letter

Table K, reproduced from the ABC standard, gives the relationship between lot or batch‡ size and the code letter that determines the sample size. The "general inspection levels" on the right-hand side of the table are the ones to use in most

---

† A monotonic frequency curve is one in which the frequencies decline continuously on both sides of the mode.

‡ *Lot* is the usual word in North America; *batch* is the usual word in Great Britain.

cases. The standard states: "unless otherwise specified, Inspection Level II will be used. However, Inspection Level I may be specified when less discrimination is needed, or Level III may be specified for greater discrimination."

The four special levels, S-1 to S-4 at the left-hand side of the table, are included for the special case where relatively small sample sizes are necessary and large sampling risks can or must be tolerated.

Selecting a Sampling Plan for Normal Inspection

Assume that an AQL of 1.5% has been specified for a certain class of defects. Assume normal inspection with a lot size of 1,000 and inspection level II. Table *K* indicates that the sample size code letter is J.

Table *L* gives acceptance criteria with normal inspection, single sampling. It tells us that for code letter J and a 1.5% AQL, sample size is 80 and the acceptance number is 3. The rejection number is stated as 4. In all these single sampling plans, the rejection number is one more than the acceptance number.

Table *O* gives acceptance criteria with normal inspection, double sampling. Table *R* gives criteria with normal inspection, multiple sampling. For code letter J and an AQL of 1.5%, these are:

Sample number	Sample size	Cumulative sample size	Acceptance number	Rejection number
Double:				
First..............	50	50	1	4
Second............	50	100	4	5
Multiple:				
First..............	20	20	*	3
Second............	20	40	0	3
Third.............	20	60	1	4
Fourth	20	80	2	5
Fifth.............	20	100	3	6
Sixth.............	20	120	4	6
Seventh..........	20	140	6	7

* Acceptance not permitted at this sample size.

The standard gives OC curves for all single sampling plans for normal and tightened inspection. It is stated that "curves for double and multiple sampling are matched as closely as practicable." The various issues involved in choosing among single, double, and multiple sampling are discussed later in this chapter. For our discussion of a number of aspects of the standard, we shall concentrate our attention on single sampling.

Definitions of AQL in the Various Military Standards

AQL is defined as follows in the ABC standard: "The AQL is the maximum per cent defective (or the maximum number of defects per hundred units) that, for purposes of sampling inspection, can be considered satisfactory as a process average."

With the addition of the reference to defects per hundred units, this is consistent with the definition given in the original Army Ordnance tables in 1942. It also is identical with the definition used in the standards of the American Society for Quality Control.†

However, other definitions of AQL have also been used. JAN-STD-105 defined AQL as: "Percentage of defective items in an inspection lot such that the sampling plan will result in the acceptance of 95% of submitted inspection lots containing that percentage of defective items." Substantially the same definition was used in the SRG volume "Sampling Inspection."

MIL-STD-105A and 105B contained the following definition: "The acceptable quality level (AQL) is a nominal value expressed in terms of per cent defective or defects per hundred units whichever is applicable, specified for a given group of defects of a product."

A similar but slightly different definition appeared in MIL-STD-105C.

The original definition, readopted for the ABC standard, is superior because it does the best job of making clear what is implied when an AQL value is selected in any AQL system.

Probabilities of Acceptance of Lots Having AQL Per Cent Defective

In all AQL systems, the acceptance criteria under normal inspection have been chosen to protect the producer against rejection of lots meeting the quality standard. However, in most AQL systems the Producer's Risk that such lots will be rejected is not the same for all sampling plans.

Figure 14-1 shows a portion of the OC curves for four single sampling plans from the ABC standard all having an AQL of 1%. It is evident that the smaller the sample size, the greater the risk the producer takes that a lot will be rejected when it is exactly 1% defective.

Of course, the Consumer's Risk of accepting a lot much worse than the AQL is also much greater with a small sample size. For example, Fig. 14-1 shows that a 5% defective lot has more than a 0.5 probability of acceptance with $n = 13$ and $c = 0$. In contrast, such a lot is practically certain to be rejected with $n = 500$ and $c = 10$. We have already noted that, when the acceptance number is zero, the OC curve has no point of inflection; it is concave upward through its entire length. If a plan with $c = 0$ were selected to reduce the Producer's Risk of rejection of a 1% defective lot to, say, 0.05, the consumer would have even less protection against

---

† "ASQC Standard A2–1971: Definitions and Symbols for Acceptance Sampling by Attributes," (ANSI Std. Z1.6-1971), American Society for Quality Control, Milwaukee, Wisconsin.

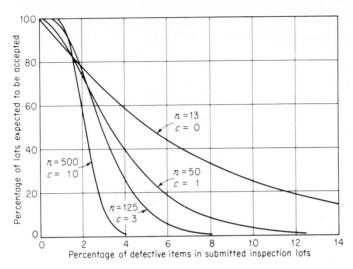

Figure 14-1 OC curves for four single sampling plans from the ABC standard, all with an AQL of 1%.

accepting bad product than he has with $n = 13$ and $c = 0$. (A P_a of 0.95 for 1% defective product with $c = 0$ would require $n = 5$. With this n, even a 12% defective lot would have a better than even chance of being accepted.)

In designing an AQL system, it is reasonable to give some weight to the entire OC curve of each of the sampling plans in the system rather than merely to a point near one end of the OC curve, namely, the P_a at the AQL value. In the ABC system, the probability of acceptance at the AQL value in normal inspection varies from about 0.88 for plans with the smaller sample sizes where $c = 0$ to about 0.99 for the large sample sizes and acceptance numbers.

H. F. Dodge† has proposed an AQL system, discussed briefly in Chap. 15, which eliminates the use of $c = 0$ in single sampling under normal inspection (although $c = 0$ is used in tightened inspection). This elimination makes practicable a standardized aimed-at P_a of 0.95 at the AQL value under normal inspection.

The Relationship between Lot Size and Sample Size in the Military AQL Systems

The discussion on page 417 illustrated the use of Table K, App. 3, to determine the sample size code letter from the lot size and inspection level in the ABC standard. A similar system of inspection levels and code letters was used in JAN-STD-105 and MIL-STD-105A, 105B, and 105C. The code letter then determines the sample

---

† H. F. DODGE, "A General Procedure for Sampling Inspection by Attributes—Based on the AQL Concept," Technical Report No. 10, The Statistics Center, Rutgers the State University, New Brunswick, N.J., 1959.

size as shown in Tables L to T. (The original Army Ordnance system, like the Philips System discussed in Chap. 15, specified definite sample sizes for each lot size.)

All the military AQL systems have used a somewhat empirical relationship between lot size and sample size. It is true, of course, that unless a sample is a substantial fraction of its lot, the OC curve of the sampling plan is practically independent of lot size, depending almost entirely on sample size and acceptance number. Nevertheless, computed OC curves always assume random sampling. The use of larger samples for larger lots recognizes that it is relatively difficult to get a small random sample from a very large lot. Moreover, large samples with their steeper OC curves give better discrimination between good and bad lots; the larger the lot size, the more important this discrimination is likely to be.[†]

It should be emphasized that, although the absolute sample size increases with lot size in the military AQL systems, the relative sample size decreases. Consider the following lot sizes under inspection level II applicable to the four plans shown in Fig. 14-1 from the ABC standard:

N	n	c
51–90	13	0
281–500	50	1
1,201–3,200	125	3
35,001–150,000	500	10

The sample of 13 is 20% of a lot of 65; the sample of 50 is 10% of a lot of 500; the sample of 500 is only 1% of a lot of 50,000.

In Table K, the sample size code letter depends only on the lot size and inspection level and is not influenced by the AQL. The military standards have not provided an automatic decrease in sample size with a relaxation of the quality standard such as is illustrated in the Philips Standard Sampling System, discussed in Chap. 15.

Nevertheless, an inspection of Tables L to T indicates that the AQL as well as the code letter may determine the sample size. For example, consider Table L, applicable to normal inspection and single sampling. For code letter E, the stated sample size is 13. However, because of the vertical arrows in the table, all the small AQL's require larger sample sizes than 13 when code letter E is specified. Thus n must be 1,250 when the AQL is 0.010%; n must be 200 when the AQL is 0.065%.

[†] For an extended comment on the relationship between lot size and sample size, see H. A. FREEMAN, MILTON FRIEDMAN, FREDERICK MOSTELLER, and W. A. WALLIS (eds.), "Sampling Inspection," pp. 171–177, McGraw-Hill Book Company, New York, 1948.

Criteria for Shifting to Tightened Inspection and Requalification for Normal Inspection

In acceptance/rejection systems that make use of normal and tightened inspection, it is customary for normal inspection to be used for the first lots submitted.† In effect, the producer is given the benefit of the doubt; if his product meets the stated quality standard for process average, there is relatively little chance that his lots will be rejected.

Because normal inspection will accept nearly all lots submitted that are at the AQL value or better, it will also accept a high percentage of any submitted lots that are moderately worse than the AQL. (The exact protection against such lots is, of course, given by the OC curve, the steepness of which is greatly influenced by sample size.) The consumer's protection against continuing to accept such lots if they are submitted depends on having rules requiring a shift to more severe acceptance criteria whenever there is good evidence that the process quality is worse than the AQL.

The ABC standard states:‡ "When normal inspection is in effect, tightened inspection shall be instituted when 2 out of 5 consecutive lots or batches have been rejected on original inspection (i.e., ignoring resubmitted lots or batches for this procedure)."

The statement regarding requalification for normal inspection is as follows: "When tightened inspection is in effect, normal inspection shall be instituted when 5 consecutive lots or batches have been considered acceptable on original inspection."

The preceding military standards based the rules for shifting between normal and tightened inspection on a process average estimated from the samples from some number (frequently 10) of the most recent lots. (Only first samples were used in estimating process average under double or multiple sampling.) Unless the estimated process average exceeded the AQL by some stipulated amount, normal inspection was continued. Usually the stipulated amount corresponded roughly to an upper 3-sigma limit on a p chart using p' as the AQL and n as the total number of sample units used in estimating the process average. Once tightened inspection had been started, requalification for normal inspection required an estimated process average equal to or less than the AQL.

Acceptance Criteria under Tightened Inspection

In all the military AQL systems using sample size code letters, the code letter in tightened inspection is determined just as in normal inspection. The acceptance criteria under tightened inspection in the ABC standard are shown in Tables M, P,

---

† The ABC standard states: "Normal inspection will be used at the start of inspection unless otherwise directed by the responsible authority."

‡ These are based on the rules for shifts between normal and tightened inspection that were suggested in 1959 by H. F. DODGE, *op. cit.*

and S. The relationship between criteria under normal and tightened inspection may be illustrated with reference to the normal plans for a 1% AQL that were shown in Fig. 14-1.

Code letter	Normal		Tightened	
	n	c	n	c
E	13	0	20	0
H	50	1	80	1
K	125	3	125	2
N	500	10	500	8

In the first three cases the criteria under tightened inspection for a 1% AQL are the same as the criteria under normal inspection for the stated code letter for the next lower AQL, namely, 0.65%. In most cases in the ABC standard, the tightened criteria are identical with the normal criteria for the next lower AQL class, although there are a number of exceptions.

Later in this chapter there is an illustration of the difference between the OC curves in normal and tightened inspection. The various AQL systems have differed considerably in this respect.

Criteria for Qualification and Loss of Qualification for Reduced Inspection

Generally speaking, eligibility for reduced inspection should be based on recent quality history indicating average quality considerably better than the AQL. Moreover, it should seem likely that the product to be inspected under reduced inspection will be produced under the same conditions that gave rise to the recent good quality history.

The ABC standard states the following conditions for a shift from normal to reduced inspection:

> *a.* The preceding 10 lots or batches (or more, as indicated by the note to Table VIII)† have been on normal inspection and none has been rejected on original inspection; and
> *b.* The total number of defectives (or defects) in the samples from the preceding 10 lots or batches (or such other number as was used for condition *a* above) is equal to or less than the applicable number given in Table VIII. If double or multiple sampling is in use, all samples inspected should be included, not "first" samples only; and
> *c.* Production is at a steady rate; and
> *d.* Reduced inspection is considered desirable by the responsible authority.

† Table VIII of the standard is reproduced in this book as Table W of App. 3.

Normal inspection must be reinstated whenever "a lot or batch is rejected" or "production becomes irregular or delayed, or other conditions warrant that normal inspection shall be instituted." A further condition requiring that normal inspection be reinstated is discussed in the next article.

Acceptance Criteria under Reduced Inspection

In all the military AQL systems using sample size code letters, the code letter in reduced inspection has been determined just as in normal inspection. The acceptance criteria under reduced inspection in the ABC standard are shown in Tables N, Q, and T. The relationship between the criteria under normal and reduced inspection may be illustrated with reference to the single sampling normal plans for a 1% AQL that were shown in Fig. 14-1.

Code letter	Normal			Reduced		
	n	Accept	Reject	n	Accept	Reject
E	13	0	1	5	0	1
H	50	1	2	20	0	2
K	125	3	4	50	1	4
N	500	10	11	200	5	8

The reader will observe that the acceptance criteria shown for code letters H, K, and N under reduced inspection all have an area of indecision in which the lot is neither accepted nor rejected. The standard states that, whenever the number of defectives falls in this indecision region (for example, if there should be exactly one defective in the sample of 20 with code letter H), the lot in question shall be accepted but reduced inspection shall be discontinued and normal inspection reinstated.

General Comments on Reduced Inspection in Acceptance/Rejection Plans

A provision for reduced inspection is not a necessary part of an acceptance/rejection plan. Nevertheless, such a provision is based on a principle that is economically sound. This principle is to concentrate inspection attention on those products and quality characteristics where the quality history is doubtful and to give less attention where the quality history is very good.

The consumer's savings in inspection costs under reduced inspection are apparent. The producer's advantages are not quite so obvious. However, because the acceptance criteria in reduced inspection are not so stringent, the producer receives added protection against lot rejection. The producer may also have a real sense of accomplishment in having qualified for reduced inspection. Hence, from

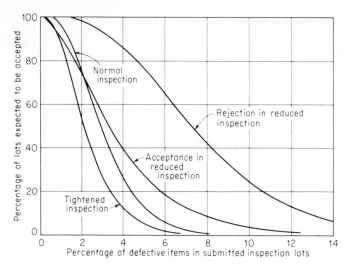

Figure 14-2 OC curves under normal, tightened, and reduced inspection; single sampling code letter K, 1% AQL, ABC standard.

the consumer's viewpoint, the provisions for reduced inspection in any acceptance program may provide a useful nonfinancial incentive to the producer to improve quality. This point is illustrated in Example 16-1 with reference to reduced inspection in multilevel continuous sampling.

OC Curves under Normal, Tightened, and Reduced Inspection

Figure 14-2 compares the OC curves for the various single sampling plans for code letter K, 1% AQL, in the ABC standard. The reader will note that two OC curves are necessary for reduced inspection. The left-hand curve ($n = 50, c = 1$) gives the probabilities of lot acceptance accompanied by continuation of reduced inspection for the next lot. The right-hand curve ($n = 50, c = 3$) gives the probabilities of failure to reject; in effect, the difference between the two P_a values for any p' tells us the probability that a lot at that p' will be accepted but normal inspection will be reinstated.

It is evident that the left-hand reduced inspection curve shows almost as good consumer protection as the OC curve for normal inspection with code letter K. (In fact, this reduced plan for code letter K happens to be the normal plan for code letter H.) Therefore, reduced inspection will not be continued for long unless the process quality is good enough for its lots to have passed normal inspection if normal inspection had been in effect. On the other hand, the right-hand curve shows that any particular lot under reduced inspection has a much greater chance of not being rejected than the same lot would have had under normal inspection.

An examination of the OC curve under tightened inspection makes it clear that lots appreciably worse than the AQL still have a fair chance of acceptance.

For example, the indifference quality $p_{0.50}$ for this 1% AQL tightened plan is about 2.2% defective. It may be desirable to supplement the tightened inspection criteria by less formal pressures based on a current estimate of the process average.

Calculation of Estimated Process Average

Most AQL systems have required a formal estimate of the most recent process average (often from the samples from the past 10 lots) to guide the decisions about shifts back and forth among tightened, normal, and reduced inspection. The ABC standard has simplified the administrative rules regarding such shifts and does not make it imperative that an estimated process average be calculated.

Nevertheless, it is a good idea to require calculation of an estimated process average at regular intervals. It is desirable for both producer and consumer to know whether quality is, on the average, better or worse than the AQL and to know whether quality seems to be improving or deteriorating.

The calculated process average from any series of samples is merely the total number of defective units found divided by the total number of sample units inspected. If single sampling is used, it is customary to inspect the entire sample in all cases even though sometimes enough defectives may be found to cause rejection of a lot before all the sample units have been examined. Otherwise, samples from rejected lots will not be given sufficient weight in computing the process average. For the same reason, it is customary to inspect the entire first sample in double and multiple sampling.

In double and multiple sampling, it has been customary to use only the results from first samples in estimating process average. Otherwise, lots requiring more than one sample tend to be given undue weight in the calculation.

The lot-by-lot data used to calculate the process average may also be used to plot a p chart (or an np chart where appropriate) to supply a basis for judgment as to whether or not the process seems to be in statistical control.

Single, Double, and Multiple Sampling Plans in AQL Systems

In the AQL systems making use of code letters, the attempt has been made to match OC curves as closely as practicable among the single, double, and multiple sampling plans for any stated code letter and AQL. It follows that the choice of one of these three types of sampling usually should be made on other grounds than the difference in OC curves.

We have already illustrated the use of Tables O and R to select double and multiple plans applicable to normal inspection in the ABC standard. Tables P and S may be used in a similar way for tightened inspection, and Tables Q and T for reduced inspection.

In the double sampling plans in the ABC standard, the second sample is the same size as the first sample. This is a point of difference from all the earlier military AQL systems, in which the second sample in double sampling was invariably twice as large as the first sample. It should be noted that the purpose of a fixed ratio between first and second sample size in double sampling is to achieve administrative simplicity. The reader will recall that in the Dodge-Romig tables, designed to minimize total inspection, there was no fixed ratio of sizes of the two samples in double sampling.

Another aspect of the double sampling plans in the ABC standard is that the rejection number for the first sample is usually less than the rejection number for both samples combined. In all the double sampling plans discussed in Chaps. 12 and 13 and in all the earlier military AQL standards, the rejection number for the first sample was the same as for the two samples combined. In this respect, the ABC standard reduces the amount of inspection under double sampling at some sacrifice of administrative simplicity.

The multiple sampling plans in the ABC standard all provide for seven samples. In all of the military AQL standards, all of the individual samples in any multiple sampling plan have been the same size.

For any given code letter in the ABC standard, a sample in double sampling is approximately $\frac{5}{8}$ of the corresponding single sample size; each sample in multiple is $\frac{1}{4}$ of the corresponding single sample size. There are a few slight exceptions to the foregoing ratios that are caused by the need to have integral values of sample sizes.

Curtailment of Sampling Inspection in Double and Multiple Sampling

For reasons already mentioned in our discussion of the calculation of the process average, it is customary to inspect the entire first sample in double and multiple sampling.

When the rejection number is reached in the second sample in double sampling, it is customary to discontinue inspection. For example, assume the following plan applicable to normal inspection, 1.5% AQL, code letter L, in the ABC standard:

Sample size	Cumulative sample size	Acceptance number	Rejection number
125	125	3	7
125	250	8	9

On the first sample, 6 defectives are found. This requires a second sample. Suppose that 3 more defectives are found by the time 15 items from the second sample have been inspected. Since the rejection number of 9 has been reached, no further inspection is needed. In this instance, curtailment saves inspecting 110 items that would have been examined if the full second sample of 125 had been inspected.

In a similar way it is common to curtail multiple inspection whenever a rejection number is reached on any sample after the first. The advantage of curtailment in double and multiple sampling occurs particularly when product is bad enough to cause a fair percentage of lot rejections.

Comparing the Amount of Sampling Inspection in Single, Double, and Multiple Sampling in the ABC Standard

Figure 14-3, taken from the ABC standard, shows the approximate values of *Average Sample Number* (ASN) for double and multiple sampling relative to the sample size in single sampling.

Each of the 15 sets of curves applies to a set of plans characterized by a particular value of c in single sampling. The horizontal scale in each diagram is the product of single sample size and fraction defective. The ABC standard contains the following statement about these curves:

> The curves assume no curtailment of inspection and are approximate to the extent that they are based upon the Poisson distribution, and that the sample sizes for double and multiple sampling are assumed to be $0.631n$ and $0.25n$ respectively, where n is the equivalent single sample size.

A reader who inspects the 15 diagrams in Fig. 14-3 might gain the impression that the average amount of inspection in multiple sampling in the ABC standard is much less than in double sampling. As applied to the portion of the standard that ordinarily will have the greatest use, this is an incorrect impression for the following reasons:

1. The plans from the standard that are likely to be used the most are those corresponding to the relatively low c numbers in single sampling, particularly numbers from 0 to 5. Upon examining Table L, the reader will observe that the higher values of c apply to the relatively high AQL values or to the relatively large sample sizes (or both).
2. It is the left-hand portion of the ASN curve—particularly to the left of the AQL value for normal inspection (shown by vertical arrows in Fig. 14-3)—that is of the most interest from a practical point of view. No AQL acceptance sampling plan is likely to be continued for any very long time if the quality of submitted product is consistently much worse than the AQL.

Consider the portions of the ASN curves to the left of the AQL arrows where c is 1, 2, 3, and 5 in single sampling. (Figure 14-3 does not contain a diagram for $c = 0$ because the standard does not have matching double and multiple plans for this value of c.) Where c is 1, double sampling involves less inspection than multiple sampling because all the multiple sampling plans corresponding to this c value will not accept until the third sample. Where c is 2, 3, or 5, the ASN values in multiple sampling are generally from 80 to 85% of those in double sampling; for these plans, acceptance is possible on the second multiple sample.

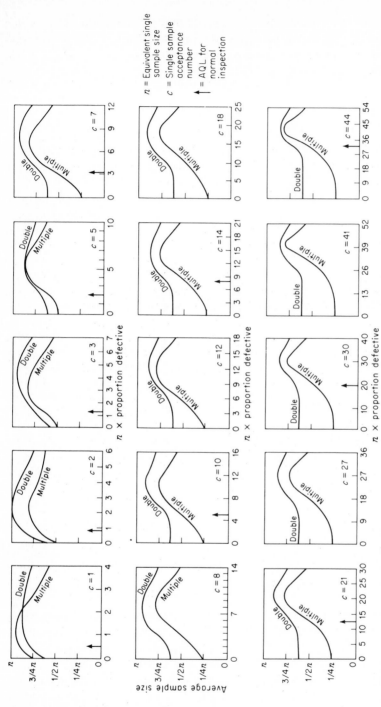

Figure 14-3 Table IX of MIL-STD-105D (ABC standard) showing ratio of average sample size in double and multiple sampling to single sample size (normal and tightened inspection) assuming no curtailment.

It is chiefly where c in single sampling is 7 or more that the multiple sampling plans involve large savings in amount of inspection as compared with the double sampling plans. As previously stated, this advantage occurs chiefly where AQL values are relatively high or sample sizes are relatively large. For example, with an n of 32 in single sampling (code letter G), the AQL is 10% for a c of 7 in normal inspection. For an AQL of 1% and a c of 7 in normal inspection, n is 315 (code letter M).

The average sample numbers in double sampling in the ABC standard are somewhat lower than in corresponding double sampling plans in earlier AQL systems. In part, this is due to the fact that the second sample size is equal to the first sample size rather than twice the first sample size as in the earlier standards. In part, it is because the rejection number for the first sample usually is less than for the two samples combined.

The reader should note that the average sample number (ASN) is related to but not the same as the average total inspection (ATI) discussed in Chap. 13. As generally used, ASN refers to comparisons between average numbers of items inspected in sampling where other characteristics of the plans, such as their OC curves, are nearly identical. ATI applies only to cases where rejected lots are subjected to 100% inspection. This usage is adhered to consistently in this book. Such is not always the case in general literature of acceptance sampling.

Computing Average Sample Numbers in Double and Multiple Sampling

The following numerical examples are intended to illustrate how to calculate a point on an ASN curve. They also aim to show why each of the 15 graphs in Fig. 14-3 is applicable to the entire family of plans in the ABC standard that corresponds to a particular value of c in single sampling.

Consider the following plans for normal inspection from the ABC standard:

	Code letter J, 0.65% AQL		Code letter P, 0.065% AQL		
Cumulative sample size	Acceptance number	Rejection number	Cumulative sample size	Acceptance number	Rejection number
Single:					
80	1	2	800	1	2
Double:					
50	0	2	500	0	2
100	1	2	1,000	1	2
Multiple:					
20	*	2	200	*	2
40	*	2	400	*	2
60	0	2	600	0	2
80	0	3	800	0	3
100	1	3	1,000	1	3
120	1	3	1,200	1	3
140	2	3	1,400	2	3

* Acceptance not permitted at this sample size.

Assume that product 1% defective is being submitted to the double sampling plan shown for code letter J and an AQL of 0.65%. To compute the average sample number it is first necessary to find the respective probabilities that a decision will be reached on each sample. (It was explained in Chap. 12 that such probabilities are computed in finding each point on an OC curve in double and multiple sampling.)

Assume that calculations will be based on the Poisson approximation. Then np' for each sample of 50 is $50(0.01) = 0.5$. Table G gives P_0 as 0.607, P_1 as 0.303, and $P_{2 \text{ or more}}$ as 0.090. The probability of a decision on the first sample is the P_a of 0.607 plus the P_r of $0.090 = 0.697$. In double sampling, the probability of a decision on the second sample is identical with the probability that a second sample will be taken, in this case 0.303. If there is no curtailment of inspection, 0.697 of the lots will require a sample of 50 and 0.303 will require a sample of 100. It follows that

$$\text{ASN} = 0.697(50) + 0.303(100) = 65.2$$

Calculations regarding the ASN in multiple sampling follow the same lines, although they require considerably more arithmetic. In the multiple sampling scheme for code letter J and an AQL of 0.65%, each sample is 20. With a p' of 0.01, the np' for each sample is 0.2. Table G gives $P_0 = 0.819$, $P_1 = 0.163$, $P_2 = 0.017$, $P_3 = 0.001$. These figures may be used to compute probabilities of acceptance and rejection on each sample. These probabilities are as follows:

Sample	P_a	P_r	$P_a + P_r$
1st	0.000	0.018	0.018
2nd	0.000	0.045	0.045
3rd	0.549	0.060	0.609
4th	0.000	0.006	0.006
5th	0.220	0.015	0.235
6th	0.000	0.016	0.016
7th	0.058	0.013	0.071
Totals........	0.827	0.173	1.000

If it is assumed that there is no curtailment of inspection, the probabilities of a decision (that is, $P_a + P_r$) on each sample may be used to compute the ASN value as follows:

$$\text{ASN} = 20(0.018) + 40(0.045) + 60(0.609) + 80(0.006) + 100(0.235)$$
$$+ 120(0.016) + 140(0.071) = 74.5$$

Now, let us compare the single, double, and multiple sampling plans shown for code letter P and an AQL of 0.065% with the corresponding plans shown for code letter J and an AQL of 0.65%. It is evident that the acceptance and rejection numbers are identical and that all sample sizes in the plans for code letter P are 10 times those for code letter J. If we assume a p' of 0.001, one-tenth of the p' value used in our calculations for the plan from code letter J, the np' values for the sample sizes of 500 and 200 with code letter P will be the same as those with samples of 50 and 20 with J. It follows that, if the Poisson approximation is used, the values of P_a and P_r for each sample will be identical with those calculated for a p' of 0.01 with code letter J. The ASN values will be 652 with double sampling and 745 with multiple sampling, exactly 10 times the values calculated for code letter J.

In Fig. 14-3, one ASN curve for double sampling and another for multiple sampling applied to the plans we have analyzed for code letters J and P and to all other plans corresponding to a c of 1 in single sampling. The use of one ASN curve to represent many different plans is possible, in part, because of the generalized scales used in plotting the curves in Fig. 14-3, and, in part, because of certain unique aspects of the ABC standard.

One relevant aspect of the ABC standard is that there is only one set of acceptance and rejection numbers in double and multiple sampling corresponding to each value of c in single sampling. Another aspect is that the ratio of double and multiple sample size to single sample size is approximately constant for all corresponding plans.

Moreover, the product of single sample size and AQL value in normal inspection is approximately constant for all plans having the same value of c in single sampling. For this reason, it is possible to show arrows indicating AQL values in normal inspection on the graphs in Fig. 14-3. (The graphs without AQL arrows apply to plans used only in tightened inspection.)

Effect of Curtailment on Amount of Sampling Inspection

The curves in Fig. 14-3 assume no curtailment of inspection when the rejection number is reached in the second sample in double sampling or in the second or subsequent samples in multiple sampling. (This assumption simplified the calculation of average sample numbers and made possible the plotting of one set of curves for each value of c.) However, such curtailment is a desirable practice and is commonly used. Economies due to curtailment occur particularly where quality is sufficiently worse than the AQL for a fair percentage of lots to be rejected.

The larger the sample sizes, the greater the possible savings due to curtailment. For this reason, in a comparison of corresponding double and multiple sampling plans, curtailment will cause greater economies in double sampling than in multiple sampling. It follows that, where curtailment is to be used, Fig. 14-3 exaggerates the differences in average amount of inspection between double and multiple sampling, particularly in the right-hand portion of the curves.

Choosing Among Single, Double, and Multiple Sampling

It sometimes happens that double and multiple sampling are impracticable. There may be physical reasons why only one sample can be drawn from a lot, or it may not be feasible to provide for the variable inspection load associated with double and multiple sampling. Under such circumstances, it is necessary to use single sampling. More often however, there is opportunity for choice. In deciding among these three types of sampling, consideration should be given to a number of factors in addition to the expected differences in average amount of inspection. Some of these factors are as follows:

1. *The psychological advantages of double sampling.* Two such advantages have played an important part in decisions to adopt double sampling. One is that borderline lots are given a "second chance" to be accepted. The other is that no lot is rejected because of a single defective article.

   There is no doubt that the idea of giving a lot a second chance has a definite appeal to practical inspectors. It seems more convincing to say that a lot was rejected after *two* samples than to say that it was rejected on the evidence of a single sample.

   Where lots are large, there is often a strong objection by the producer to the rejection of an entire lot on the basis of a single defective article found in a sample. None of the double sampling plans will reject on a single defective.

   These psychological advantages of double sampling apply also to multiple sampling. However, it is questionable whether the appeal of the third, fourth, or fifth chance adds anything to the appeal of the second chance.

2. *The expected differences in costs of administration.* These costs tend to be highest for multiple sampling and lowest for single sampling. The more complicated the acceptance plan, the greater the attention required from inspection supervisors. Moreover, the variability of inspection load in multiple sampling and double sampling introduces extra difficulites into the scheduling of inspectors' time. In those cases where double and multiple sampling can make relatively small savings in average amount of inspection, the more complicated plans may actually increase total inspection cost.

3. *The difficulty of training inspectors to use multiple sampling correctly.* This difficulty seems to vary with the quality of the inspectors and perhaps with other matters. In some plants where inspectors have made frequent bad errors in interpreting instructions, quality control engineers refuse to specify anything but single sampling. In other plants, no serious troubles are reported in securing correct use of sampling procedures as complicated as item-by-item sequential plans (discussed in Chap. 15).

   Sometimes special devices are designed to make it easier for inspectors to use the more complicated schemes correctly. J. W. Enell, writing in "Quality Control Handbook,"† illustrates a storage board designed to simplify multiple sampling. A board similar to Enell's is shown in Fig. 14-4. In the figure, a circle represents a good article and a cross represents a bad article. The sample shown in Fig. 14-4 resulted in a lot rejection when a total of 8 defectives was

---

† J. M. JURAN (ed.), "Quality Control Handbook," First Ed., p. 435, McGraw-Hill Book Company, New York, 1951.

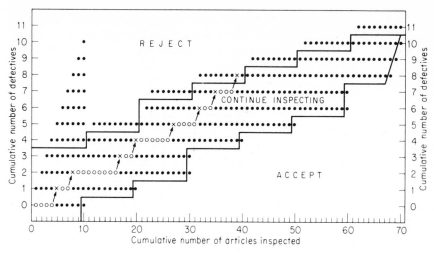

Figure 14-4 Storage board for multiple sampling.

found in the first 39 articles inspected. The sampling plan (from MIL-STD-105A) for which the board was designed is as follows:

Cumulative sample size	Acceptance number	Rejection number
10	0	4
20	1	5
30	3	7
40	4	8
50	5	9
60	7	10
70	10	11

4. *The need for quick and reliable estimates of process average for various purposes including decision among normal, tightened, and reduced inspection.* In the various types of AQL systems prior to the ABC standard, the shifts among these three types of inspection depended on the estimated process average, often estimated from the samples from the most recent 10 lots. The process average was estimated from full single samples or from first samples in double and multiple sampling. The sampling error in an estimate of the recent process average is smallest with the relatively large sample size in single sampling and largest with the relatively small sample size in multiple sampling. For this reason, it may be sensible to use single sampling in the early stages of a contract even though a change to double or multiple sampling is made after there is satisfactory evidence regarding the process average.

Even in systems (such as the ABC standard) where the process average is not formally required, it is helpful to have as good information as possible about the process average and the presence or absence of statistical control. Single sampling does the best job of providing such information.

5. *The availability of inspection personnel and facilities.* This should properly be an important factor in the choice of the type of sampling in a number of instances.

One extreme example of this influence may be cited from the experience of the inspection department of a certain government agency. The inspectors employed by this agency typically did sampling inspection in the plants of several different producers during the course of a week, using public transportation to go to and from each plant. The length of the visit to each plant was controlled by bus schedules and train schedules. With multiple sampling, an inspector generally finished his work some time before it was necessary to leave a plant. Under single sampling, his time at a plant was more likely to be fully occupied. It was therefore decided to change from multiple to single sampling. This change did not increase cost, and, because of the larger single sample size, it gave much better current information regarding process quality.

Similar cases may exist in industrial plants where it is desired to keep an inspection force intact throughout a temporary period of reduced inspection activity.

The opposite extreme exists when the need for inspection personnel and facilities is rapidly increasing. Such a period would seem to be an appropriate one in which to introduce double or multiple sampling, particularly in those spots where such plans seem likely to make large reductions in the average inspection per lot. The alternative to reducing average inspection per lot is the hiring and training of new inspectors (presumably less competent than the old ones) and the making of investments in additional inspection facilities.

Classification of Defects

In AQL systems for acceptance sampling by attributes, it is common for one AQL to apply to a group of possible defects rather than to have a separate AQL value for each possible way in which product may fail to conform to specifications. Unless trivial defects are to be given the same weight as serious ones, it is essential to have a classification of defects or classification of characteristics. (These two phrases seem to be used interchangeably.) Such classifications were mentioned at the end of Chap. 10.

The ABC standard calls for defects to be classified as critical, major, and minor. The defintions of these are as follows:

Critical Defect. A critical defect is a defect that judgment and experience indicate is likely to result in hazardous or unsafe conditions for individuals using, maintaining, or depending upon the product; or a defect that judgment and experience indicate is likely to prevent performance of the tactical function of a major end item such as a ship, aircraft, tank, missile or space vehicle.

Major Defect. A major defect is a defect, other than critical, that is likely to result in failure, or to reduce materially the usability of the unit of product for its intended purpose.

Minor Defect. A minor defect is a defect that is not likely to reduce materially the usability of the unit of product for its intended purpose, or is a departure from established standards having little bearing on the effective use or operation of the unit.

Product usually is subject to 100% inspection for critical defects. But there are many types of product with no defects classed as critical; all are either major or minor. It is fairly common to divide minor defects into two groups depending on their relative importance. The more important minors may be designated Minor *A*; the less important ones, Minor *B*. (In the original Army Ordnance and Army Service Forces tables, the more descriptive adjective "incidental" was used for the relatively unimportant defects of the type later classified as "Minor *B*.")

An Illustration of the Use of a Classification of Defects in Acceptance Sampling

Assume that the classification of defects for certain bolts includes 5 defects classified as Major, 11 classified Minor *A*, and 8 classified as Minor *B*. Bolts are to be inspected in lots of 10,000 under the ABC standard. Double sampling and inspection level II are to be used. The AQL is 1.0% for Majors, 4.0% for Minor *A*, and 6.5% for Minor *B*.

The sample size code letter L is determined by the lot size and inspection level. In this case, the acceptance criteria are:

Cumulative sample size	Major		Minor *A*		Minor *B*	
	Accept	Reject	Accept	Reject	Accept	Reject
125	2	5	7	11	11	16
250	6	7	18	19	26	27

A first sample of 125 will be drawn from the lot. This sample is inspected separately for each class of defects. The numbers of defective articles found in each class are as follows:

Major—2
Minor *A*—10
Minor *B*—7

Therefore the lot is passed for Major and Minor *B* defects on the basis of the first sample. A second sample of 125 must be drawn and inspected only for Minor *A* defects. If not more than 8 additional bolts containing such defects are found, the lot is passed. If 9 or more are found, the lot is rejected for Minor *A* defects.

In general, it is economical and convenient to inspect the same sample for all classes of defects. However, the acceptance criteria are applied separately for each class. A lot is rejected if it fails to meet the acceptance criteria for one or more classes.

The Formation of Inspection Lots†

In sampling acceptance inspection, an inspection lot is a group of articles accepted or rejected on the basis of one or more samples. An inspection lot is not necessarily identical with a production lot, a purchase lot, or a lot for other purposes.

Many practical matters such as rate of production and availability of storage space necessarily influence the formation of inspection lots. From the point of view of getting the best results from acceptance sampling, two rules should govern decisions on this matter, namely:

1. Within each lot, the factors that seem likely to cause marked variability in product quality should be as nearly constant as practicable. This may include such matters as sources of raw materials, machines, operators, and time of production.
2. Subject to the limitation of the foregoing rule, inspection lots should be as large as possible.

The desire to have each lot come from a homogeneous source obviously conflicts with the desire to have large lots. Practical decisions usually call for a compromise between these two objectives.

The reason for the requirement of homogeneity should be evident. If most lots are relatively good and a few are relatively bad, sampling inspection can discriminate among lots and the quality of the product accepted can be much better than the average quality submitted. On the other hand, if there is a good deal of mixing of product from various sources, the percentage of defectives may not vary greatly from lot to lot; in this case the average quality of lots accepted will not be appreciably better than the average quality submitted. Where lot formation is close to production, both in time and place, there is a minimum of opportunity for mixing of product among inspection lots.

The reason for the requirement of making lots as large as possible should also be clear. It is the absolute size of the sample that governs its ability to discriminate between good and bad lots. Large lots permit larger samples than do small lots. Moreover, inspection cost will be less with large lots because samples are a smaller fraction of the lot.

Problems Arising out of Resubmission of Rejected Lots

Whenever rejected lots are returned to the producer, the resubmission of these lots for another sampling inspection creates certain problems.

Obviously, it is not in the consumer's interest for lots to be submitted unchanged. This point can be illustrated by a simple probability calculation.

---

† For a more complete discussion of this important topic, see FREEMAN, FRIEDMAN, MOSTELLER, and WALLIS, *op. cit.*, pp. 40–43, 87–90.

Assume the probability of acceptance of a lot of given quality is 0.80. This will not only be the probability of its acceptance on the first submission but also on any subsequent submission. The probability of acceptance with a maximum of two resubmissions is as follows:

Probability of acceptance on first submission	= 0.80
Probability of rejection on first submission followed by acceptance on second submission = (0.20)(0.80)	= 0.16
Probability of rejection on first and second submission followed by acceptance on third submission = (0.20)(0.20)(0.80)	= 0.03
Probability of acceptance with not more than three submissions	= 0.99

Of course, the normal action by a reputable producer is to screen a rejected lot before resubmitting it. The ABC standard contains the following reasonable stipulation: "Lots or batches found unacceptable shall be resubmitted for reinspection only after all units are reexamined or retested and all defective units are removed or defects corrected."

Resubmitted lots that have received 100% inspection by the producer after rejection presumably are considerably better on their second submission than they were on their first submission. Therefore, the results from sampling inspection of resubmitted lots should not be viewed as representative of the process average. Criteria for determining whether normal, tightened, or reduced inspection is to be used should be based solely on the results of original inspection, and the results from any resubmitted lots should be ignored.

Acceptance Based on Numbers of Defects

A defective article is an article containing one or more defects. In our discussion up to this point, acceptance decisions have been based on the numbers of defectives contained in a sample. Decisions on lot acceptance or rejection have not been influenced by the number of defects observed in each defective article. The sampled article with eight defects has had the same influence on lot acceptance as the sampled article with only one defect; each has counted as a single defective.

Under certain conditions, it may be more reasonable to base acceptance decisions on defects rather than on defectives. For instance, some defects might be tolerable in a bolt of cloth, but it might be desired to limit the average defects per bolt in a shipment of bolts of cloth. In general, the field of application of acceptance based on defects is similar to the field for the c chart discussed in Chap. 8. With acceptance based on defects, AQL values, OC curves, etc., are interpreted in terms of defects per hundred units rather than as per cent defective.

The entire ABC standard may be used for inspection based on defects as well as for inspection based on defectives. In general, the only changes necessary are to substitute the word *defects* wherever *defectives* is used and to interpret AQL's as defects per hundred units. Of course, the highest AQL values in the standard may be interpreted only as defects per hundred units. For example, it would be meaningless to have an AQL of 150% defective but entirely reasonable to have an AQL of 150 defects per hundred units in sampling inspection of, say, bolts of cloth (that is, 1.5 defects per bolt). Normal, tightened, and reduced inspection can be used in inspection based on defects just as in inspection based on defectives.

The binomial distribution is correct in principle for Type *B* OC curves based on defectives; in the ABC standard, the binomial is used for OC curves for AQL's of 10.0 or less. The Poisson distribution is correct in principle for OC curves based on defects; in the ABC standard, the Poisson is used for AQL's of 15.0 or more.

The Army Service Forces tables contained separate tables for inspection based on defects per unit. In addition to limiting the number of defects in a sample, the acceptance criteria in these tables also included a *spottiness limit*, which was specified for each AQL. Any inspected unit having more defects than this limit was called a *spotty* unit. For smaller sample sizes, one spotty unit would cause lot rejection regardless of the quality of the rest of the sample. For the large sample sizes, not more than one spotty unit was permitted. This spottiness concept was not included in the later military standards.

A Systematic Record of Quality History is an Important Aspect of Statistical Acceptance Procedures

As pointed out at the start of Chap. 12, when acceptance procedures are on an informal basis, it frequently is recognized that a common-sense principle is to base the severity of acceptance criteria on the quality history of the product being sampled. An AQL system involving normal, tightened, and reduced inspection substitutes a systematic way of doing this for an informal and unsystematic way. In this systematic procedure, a written record of quality history takes the place of the inspector's memory.

It is helpful if the written record not only gives data on the current quality level but also tells whether the process is in control. Figure 14-5 illustrates a possible form for use with double sampling.† The scale for the control chart shown on the right can readily be adapted to any quality level by changing the value of a division on the chart.

Such quality records of sampling inspection are useful even though the acceptance criteria are not affected by past performance (as, for instance, in the Philips System described in the next chapter). They often bring out differences between the quality levels of different vendors that had not been recognized before a formal record was kept. In this way they may bring about a decision not to do business with a vendor submitting product with an unsatisfactory process average; such a

---

† See H. F. DODGE and H. G. ROMIG, "Sampling Inspection Tables," 2d ed., pp. 48–50, John Wiley & Sons, Inc., New York, 1959, for two forms used by the Western Electric Company for a record of sampling inspection. Many forms used by other manufacturers have been adapted from these Western Electric forms.

CONTROL CHART AND DATA SHEET FOR SAMPLING ACCEPTANCE INSPECTION

| Vendor | | | | | | | Article purchased | | | | | | | | | |

| Inspection procedure | | | | | | | Acceptable quality level | | | | | | | | | |

Remarks

Date	Lot size	First sample		Percent defective in first sample	Second sample		Action on lot	Control chart for first samples									
		Number insp'd	Defectives		Number insp'd	Defectives											

Figure 14-5 Form that combines record of sampling inspection with control chart for per cent rejected.

decision has an effect similar to the adoption of tightened acceptance criteria that reject a majority of his lots.

In the use of acceptance plans having large samples and an acceptance number greater than 0, some inspectors are reluctant to call the defect that requires the taking of a second sample or the rejection of a lot. Where this type of flinching exists, the situation should be evident from the written quality record. A record showing that nearly all lot acceptances have been based on the maximum number of defectives permissible suggests that inspectors have acted in this way.

Selecting an Acceptance Plan for an Isolated Lot

The teeth in any AQL system are in the provision for tightened inspection whenever the recent quality record is bad enough. An AQL is enforced through the overall system, not through the lot-by-lot acceptance criteria used in normal inspection. As has been explained, such criteria are chosen to protect the producer by making sure that nearly all lots will be accepted as long as the process average is at the AQL value or better. Therefore, if individual lots considerably worse than the AQL are submitted, such lots have a good chance to be accepted.

Where lots are isolated or infrequent, an overall acceptance sampling system cannot be used to develop pressure for the submission of good quality. The consumer dealing with an isolated lot needs to take a good look at the OC curve of the proposed sampling plan to judge whether it gives adequate protection. If it

Table 14-1 ABC-STD-105 Limiting quality tables for which $P_a = 10\%$. Normal inspection, single sampling

(Reproduced from MIL-STD-105D, pp. 24–25)

In per cent defective ($100p_{0.10}$)

Code letter	Sample size	Acceptable quality level															
		0.010	0.015	0.025	0.040	0.065	0.10	0.15	0.25	0.40	0.65	1.0	1.5	2.5	4.0	6.5	10
A	2																
B	3																58
C	5										11	16	25	37	54	68	
D	8															41	54
E	13														27	36	44
F	20							2.8	4.5	6.9				18	25	30	42
G	32												12	16	20	27	34
H	50											7.6	10	13	18	22	29
J	80					1.2	1.8				4.8	6.5	8.2	11	14	19	24
K	125									3.1	4.3	5.4	7.4	9.4	12	16	23
L	200								2.0	2.7	3.3	4.6	5.9	7.7	10	14	
M	315			0.46	0.73			1.2	1.7	2.1	2.9	3.7	4.9	6.4	9.0		
N	500						0.78	1.1	1.3	1.9	2.4	3.1	4.0	5.6			
P	800				0.31	0.49	0.67	0.84	1.2	1.5	1.9	2.5	3.5				
Q	1,250		0.29			0.43	0.53	0.74	0.94	1.2	1.6	2.3					
R	2,000	0.18		0.20	0.27	0.33	0.46	0.59	0.77	1.0	1.4						

440

Table 14-1 ABC-STD-105 Limiting quality tables for which $P_a = 10\%$. Normal inspection, single sampling. (*Continued*)

(Reproduced from MIL-STD-105D, pp. 24–25)

In defects per hundred units

Acceptable quality level

Code letter	Sample size	0.010	0.015	0.025	0.040	0.065	0.10	0.15	0.25	0.40	0.65	1.0	1.5	2.5	4.0	6.5	10	15	25	40	65	100	150	250	400	650	1000
A	2															120			200	270	330	460	590	770	1000	1400	1900
B	3														77			130	180	220	310	390	510	670	940	1300	1800
C	5													46			78	110	130	190	240	310	400	560	770	1100	
D	8												29			49	67	84	120	150	190	250	350	480	670		
E	13											18			30	41	51	71	91	120	160	220	300	410			
F	20										12			20	27	33	46	59	77	100	140						
G	32									7.2			12	17	21	29	37	48	63	88							
H	50								4.6			7.8	11	13	19	24	31	40	56								
J	80							2.9			4.9	6.7	8.4	12	15	19	25	35									
K	125						1.8			3.1	4.3	5.4	7.4	9.4	12	16	23										
L	200					1.2			2.0	2.7	3.3	4.6	5.9	7.7	10	14											
M	315				0.73			1.2	1.7	2.1	2.9	3.7	4.9	6.4	9.0												
N	500			0.46			0.78	1.1	1.3	1.9	2.4	3.1	4.0	5.6													
P	800		0.29			0.49	0.67	0.84	1.2	1.5	1.9	2.5	3.5														
Q	1,250	0.18			0.31	0.43	0.53	0.74	0.94	1.2	1.6	2.3															
R	2,000			0.20	0.27	0.33	0.46	0.59	0.77	1.0	1.4																

is required to be protected against product worse than, say, 1% defective, one should not select a sampling plan indexed under an AQL of 1% in any of the various AQL tables. Such a plan will not give the required protection.

At the start of this chapter and thereafter, we noted that one of the serious objections to regular 100% inspection by the consumer is that such inspection does not exert enough pressure on a producer to improve the process. Of course, this objection applies only when there is a continuing relationship between producer and consumer; it is not valid when there is only one lot. In general, the consumer should be willing to screen an isolated lot whenever high quality is deemed essential and when such screening is practicable (as in the case of nondestructive tests). A possible compromise between the interests of producer and consumer might be to use an acceptance plan for isolated lots based on a stated quality standard at $p_{0.50}$, the indifference quality, with the consumer screening any *accepted* lot.

The ABC standard stipulates that, when a lot or batch is of an isolated nature, sampling plans should be chosen based on the identification of a Consumer's Risk point associated with the designated AQL. Tables for Consumer's Risks of 5 and 10%, called the *Limiting Quality* (LQ) tables, are contained in the standard. Table 14-1 reproduces the LQ table for a 10% Consumer's Risk. The term LQ, in this instance, is synonymous with the LTPD discussed in Chap. 13.

The user enters the table by the designated AQL and searches the column until an acceptable value of LQ ($100p_{0.10}$) is found. The sample size code letter is then read from the left-hand side. In using this table, the choice of a sampling plan is based, in effect, on the choice of two points on the OC curve, a Producer's Risk point (AQL) and a Consumer's Risk point ($100p_{0.10}$).

Importance of AOQL Values in Sampling Plans Based on the AQL

Tables U and V in App. 3 are reproduced from the ABC standard. They give AOQL factors for normal and tightened inspection, respectively, for the single sampling plans in the standard. With the exception of those plans where $c = 0$, the AOQL values in tightened inspection are fairly close to the stipulated AQL values. The AOQL value is significant in an AQL plan because it is reasonable to expect that a reputable producer will screen lots that have been rejected under the sampling plan.

Some persons object to the policy of placing reliance on the quality protection promised by a computed AOQL value on the grounds that one cannot be *certain* that errors will not be made by the inspectors who screen the rejected lots. To be consistent, such persons also should object to all OC curves for sampling inspection plans because such curves assume that the inspector discovers the defective items in a sample. They also should object to *all* use of 100% inspection.

In general, there is no reason to be more concerned with the possibility of inspectors' errors in screening rejected lots than with the possibility of such errors made in other inspection activities. In fact, it usually is reasonable to expect that more care will be exercised in screening rejected lots than when 100% inspection is used in the first place.

PROBLEMS

14-1 In acceptance sampling under the ABC standard, single sampling is to be used with inspection level II, an AQL of 4%, and a lot size of 2,500. What are the acceptance criteria under
  (a) normal and
  (b) tightened inspection?
  Answer: (a) $n = 125, c = 10$; (b) $n = 125, c = 8$.

14-2 In Problem 14-1, use Table G to compute the approximate probabilities of acceptance of 4% nonconforming product under normal and tightened inspection.
  Answer: 0.986, 0.932.

14-3 Assume that normal inspection is being used for the conditions stated in Problem 14-1. A series of lots 8% nonconforming are submitted for acceptance. What is the approximate value of the probability that a shift to tightened inspection will be required after the first two such lots? Assume that no rejections have occurred in the preceding 4 lots.
  Answer: 0.17.

14-4 Assume that tightened inspection is being used for the conditions stated in Problem 14-1. After the rejection of one lot, the product quality improves to the point where lots are now only 4% nonconforming. What is the approximate probability that normal inspection will be reinstated after the next 5 such lots?
  Answer: 0.70.

14-5 What are the acceptance criteria under reduced inspection for the conditions stated in Problem 14-1?
  Answer: $n = 50$, acceptance number $= 5$; rejection number $= 8$.

14-6 Assume that an 8% nonconforming lot is submitted under the reduced inspection plan of Problem 14-5. Use Table G to compute the approximate probabilities that
  (a) the lot will be accepted and reduced inspection continued,
  (b) the lot will be accepted but normal inspection will be reinstated, and
  (c) the lot will be rejected.
  Answer: (a) 0.785; (b) 0.164 (c) 0.051.

14-7 In acceptance sampling under the ABC standard, double sampling is to be used with inspection level II, an AQL of 1%, and a lot size of 750. What are the acceptance criteria under
  (a) normal and
  (b) tightened inspection?
  Answer: (a) $n_1 = 50$, acceptance number $= 0$, rejection number $= 3$; $n_2 = 50$, acceptance number $= 3$, rejection number $= 4$; (b) $n_1 = 50$, acceptance number $= 0$, rejection number $= 2$; $n_2 = 50$, acceptance number $= 1$, rejection number $= 2$.

14-8 In Problem 14-7, use Table G to compute the approximate Type B probabilities of accepting lots from 1.5% nonconforming product under
  (a) normal and
  (b) tightened inspection.
  Answer: (a) 0.922; (b) 0.640.

14-9 What are the acceptance criteria under reduced inspection for the conditions of Problem 14-7?
  Answer: $n_1 = 20$, acceptance number $= 0$, rejection number $= 3$; $n_2 = 20$, acceptance number $= 0$, rejection number $= 4$.

14-10 Assume that a lot from 2% nonconforming product is submitted under the reduced inspection plan of Problem 14-9. Use Table G to compute the approximate probabilities that
  (a) the lot will be accepted and reduced inspection continued,
  (b) the lot will be accepted but normal inspection will be reinstated, and
  (c) the lot will be rejected.
  Answer: (a) 0.670; (b) 0.316; (c) 0.014.

14-11 Assume that the double sampling plan of Problem 14-7 for normal inspection is being used where process averages are, respectively, 0.5, 3, and 6% nonconforming. Assuming no curtailment, compute the ASN value for each process average. Use the Poisson approximation to the binomial in your calculation. Express the respective ASN values as a percentage of the single sample size corresponding to this double sampling plan in the ABC standard.

Answer: 61.0, 79.3, 68.6; 76%, 99%, 86%.

14-12 In acceptance sampling under reduced inspection in the ABC standard, double sampling is used with code letter J and an AQL of 2.5%. Assume that a lot from product 5% nonconforming is submitted. Use Table G to compute the approximate probabilities that

(a) the lot will be accepted and reduced inspection will be continued

(b) the lot will be accepted but normal inspection will be reinstated

(c) the lot will be rejected.

Answer: (a) 0.864; (b) 0.107; (c) 0.029.

14-13 In acceptance sampling under the ABC standard, single sampling is to be used with inspection level II, an AQL of 0.40%, and a lot size of 1,500.

(a) What plan is called for under normal inspection?

(b) What plan is called for under tightened inspection?

14-14 For the plans called for in Problem 14-13, assume that the inspection process has been operating on normal inspection and that the last 5 lots have been accepted. Suddenly the lot quality shifts to 1.6% nonconforming.

(a) Use Table G to calculate the approximate probability that the next lot sampled will be accepted.

(b) What is the probability that a shift from normal to tightened inspection will be required within the next 5 lots inspected?

14-15 In the situation described in Problems 14-13 and 14-14, tightened inspection is now in force. Corrective action has been taken on the process and the process average has been reduced to 0.40% nonconforming product, the AQL value. The last lot inspected was rejected.

(a) Using Table G, compute the approximate probability that the next lot inspected will be accepted.

(b) What is the probability of a shift from tightened to normal inspection within the next 5 lots inspected?

14-16 (a) Find the ABC standard normal inspection plan for inspection level II, an AQL of 1.5%, and a lot size of 1,000 units.

(b) Assuming no curtailment of inspection, compute the ASN values for process averages of 2.9, 4.5, and 8.0%.

(c) Sketch a curve of ASN as a function of process average over the range 2.0 to 8.0%.

14-17 A plan for inspecting isolated lots of 1,500 items is to be selected from the ABC standard based on a 10% probability of acceptance Limiting Quality of 4.5% nonconforming product.

(a) Find the most appropriate single sampling plan if the AQL is 1.0%.

(b) If the Limiting Quality (LQ) were not specified in this case, which normal inspection single sampling plan would be used under inspection level II?

14-18 In acceptance sampling under the ABC standard, single sampling is to be used with inspection level II, an AQL of 1.5%, and a lot size of 5,000 units.

(a) What plans are called for under normal, tightened, and reduced inspection?

(b) Use Table G to find the approximate probability that lots with a p' of 0.03 will be accepted when normal inspection is in force.

(c) Use the results of (b) to find the probability that a shift to tightened inspection will be required after 5 such lots have been inspected on normal inspection.

14-19 Assume that rectifying inspection is to be used in the inspection process for the plans found in Problem 14-18.

(a) What is the AOQL of the normal inspection plan?

(b) Use the results of part (b) of Problem 14-18 to compute the AFI of the plan when p' is 0.03.

(c) Calculate the AOQ at a p' of 0.03.

14-20 In acceptance sampling under the ABC standard, single sampling is to be used with inspection level II, an AQL of 0.25%, and a lot size of 2,000 items.

(a) What are the single sampling plans under normal, tightened, and reduced inspection?

(b) Assuming that rectifying inspection is to be used, find the AOQL for the normal inspection plan.

(c) Use Table G to compute the approximate probability of acceptance under normal inspection for lots with a p' of 0.01.

(d) What is the probability of shifting to tightened inspection within the first 5 lots inspected for the lots described in part (c)?

14-21 In acceptance sampling under the ABC standard, double sampling is to be used with inspection level II, an AQL of 2.5%, and a lot size of 1,000 items.

(a) What plans are called for under normal and tightened inspection?

(b) Assuming no curtailment, use Table G to compute the ASN values under normal inspection for lot quality p' values of 0.02, 0.05, and 0.15.

(c) Compare the sample size for the single sampling normal inspection plan with these values of ASN and comment on the relative efficiency of the double sampling plan.

14-22 A manufacturer ships a certain product in lots of 400 items which are subject to receiving inspection under the ABC standard, inspection level I, and an AQL of 1.5%.

(a) Find the appropriate double sampling plans for normal, tightened, and reduced inspection.

(b) Use Table G to find the approximate probability of acceptance for the normal inspection plan if incoming lots have a p' of 0.04.

(c) Use the results of part (b) to compute the ASN at a p' of 0.04. How does this value compare with the sample size of the corresponding single sample plan?

14-23 In acceptance sampling under the ABC standard for receiving inspection of lots of 3,000 items, a manufacturer uses inspection level II and and a 1.0% AQL.

(a) What is the normal inspection double sampling plan?

(b) Use Table G to compute the approximate probability of acceptance of lots for which p' is 0.015.

(c) Rejection of a lot requires that the remainder of the lot be screened. Cost of screening the remaining items is charged to the vendor along with the cost of returning rejected items for replacement. What is the average number of items inspected on sampling inspection (ASN) and the average number of items screened (ATI-ASN) when p' is 0.015?

14-24 In acceptance sampling under the ABC standard, single sampling is used with inspection level II, an AQL of 1.0%, and a lot size of 1,000.

(a) What plans are called for under normal, tightened, and reduced inspection?

(b) Assuming that rectifying inspection is to be used, what are the AOQL values under normal and tightened inspection?

14-25 (a) For the acceptance sampling plans found in Problem 14-24, use Table G to compute the probabilities of acceptance under normal and tightened inspection for lots with a p' of 0.02.

(b) Compute the values of the AOQ under normal and tightened inspection for lots with a p' of 0.02.

(c) What is the probability of switching to tightened inspection within the first 5 lots inspected on normal inspection for these lots?

14-26 In acceptance sampling under the ABC standard, double sampling is used with inspection level III, an AQL of 2.5%, and a lot size of 1,500 items.

(a) What plans are called for under normal, tightened, and reduced inspection?

(b) For the reduced sampling plan, use Table G to compute the approximate probabilities of accepting a lot and continuing on reduced inspection and of accepting a lot but switching back to normal inspection if incoming lots have a p' of 0.05.

(c) Use Table G to compute the ASN under normal inspection if the p' of incoming lots equals the AQL. How does this value compare with the sample size of the corresponding normal inspection single sampling plan?

14-27 In a double sampling plan, $n_1 = 100$, $c_1 = 1$, $n_2 = 100$, $c_2 = 3$ for a lot size of 8,000 items. Use Table G to compute the approximate probabilities needed for the following questions.

(a) Compute the probabilities of acceptance on the first sample, rejection of the first sample, acceptance on the second sample, and acceptance overall when incoming lots have a p' of 0.02.

(b) Rectifying inspection is to be employed with this plan. Compute the AOQ when incoming lots have a p' of 0.02.

(c) Compute the average number of items inspected on sampling (ASN) for the lots described in part (b).

(d) Compute the ATI for the lots described in part (b). What impact does the screening requirement have on inspection personnel requirements in this case?

14-28 In acceptance sampling under the ABC standard, single sampling is used with inspection level II, an AQL of 1.0%, and a lot size of 5,000 items.

(a) What plan is called for under normal inspection?

(b) Use Table G to find the approximate probability of acceptance of lots with a p' of 0.04.

(c) Rectifying inspection is to be employed with this plan. Compute the ATI for the lots described in part (b).

(d) Determine the AOQ for the lots described in part (b).

14-29 The ABC standard is to be used for receiving inspection of a certain product. The specification calls for inspection level II, an AQL of 2.5%, and a lot size of 350 items.

(a) What single sampling plans are called for under normal, tightened, and reduced inspection?

(b) If incoming lots have a p' of 0.05, what is the probability that tightened inspection will be invoked after 5 lots have been inspected on normal inspection?

(c) If incoming lots have a p' of 0.05, what is the probability of shifting from tightened to normal inspection after 5 lots have been inspected on tightened inspection?

(d) If incoming lots have a p' of 0.02, what is the probability of shifting from tightened to normal inspection after 5 lots have been inspected on tightened inspection?

14-30 The ABC-STD-105 specifies $n = 200$ and $c = 5$ under Code Letter L, a 1.0% AQL, and a lot size of 5,000 units.

(a) Use Table G to compute the approximate probability of acceptance if incoming lots contain 3% nonconforming units.

(b) Rectifying inspection is used in which all nonconforming units in rejected lots and in samples from accepted lots are removed and replaced. Compute the AFI for the lots described in part (a).

(c) Compute the AOQ for these lots.

14-31 (a) Find the ABC standard single sampling plans under inspection level II, and AQL of 1.0%, and a lot size of 100 items for normal, tightened, and reduced inspection.

(b) Use Table G to compute the approximate probabilities of acceptance for each plan assuming that incoming lots contain 5% nonconforming items.

(c) What is the probability of shifting from normal to tightened inspection after 5 of these lots have been inspected?

14-32 (a) Find the ABC standard single sampling plan for inspection level II, a 1.5% AQL, and a lot size of 400 items for normal inspection.

(b) An np chart is to be used to plot the results of inspection of incoming lots. Assuming that the AQL value is to be used as the aimed at mean value of p_0', find 3σ control limits for the chart.

(c) What fraction of nonconforming units does the UCL represent?

(d) Use Table G to calculate the approximate probability that a point will fall outside the UCL when incoming lots are at the AQL.

FIFTEEN

CERTAIN OTHER PLANS FOR LOT-BY-LOT ACCEPTANCE SAMPLING BY ATTRIBUTES

The fundamental difference between engineering with and without statistics boils down to the difference between the use of a scientific method based upon the concept of laws of nature that do not allow for chance or uncertainty and a scientific method based upon the concept of laws of probability as an attribute of nature.—W. A. Shewhart†

Topics Covered in This Chapter

Where acceptance sampling is to be adopted, the first decision usually should be on the acceptance sampling *system* to be chosen. The two preceding chapters have described two types of widely used systems.

Even where all that is needed is a particular sampling plan that involves certain stated risks, the publications describing existing systems are useful. Such publications generally give the OC curves for each of the many sampling plans included; usually a plan can be found that comes fairly close to giving a desired OC curve. Moreover, as brought out in Example 12-1, there may be tactical and other advantages in using a plan chosen from a system that has the prestige associated with being well-known and well-established.

However, it also is a fairly simple matter to design certain types of attributes plans that have a stipulated value of the risk of accepting product containing some stated percentage of defectives. The first part of this chapter discusses the design of single sampling plans having a stated value of the "indifference quality," $p_{0.50}$. It also discusses the design of single sampling plans and item-by-item sequential plans for which both Producer's Risk and Consumer's Risk are stipulated.

---

† W. A. SHEWHART, Contribution of Statistics to the Science of Engineering, included in "University of Pennsylvania Bicentennial Conference. Volume on Fluid Mechanics and Statistical Methods," pp. 97–124, University of Pennsylvania Press, Philadelphia, 1941.

The second part of this chapter gives brief descriptions of three systems of lot-by-lot acceptance sampling by attributes that are less complex than the ones explained in Chap. 13 and 14. The first of these is the Philips Standard Sampling System, which uses $p_{0.50}$ as the basis for referencing all its sampling plans. The second is a simplified AQL-type system proposed by Harold Dodge. The third, also developed by Dodge, is devised for the special case where sample sizes must be so small that the only practicable acceptance number is zero.

I. DESIGNING LOT-BY-LOT ACCEPTANCE SAMPLING PLANS FOR CERTAIN STATED RISKS

Designing Single Sampling Attributes Plans Having a Stated Value of $p_{0.50}$

The quality $p_{0.50}$, for any lot-by-lot acceptance sampling plan, is the lot or process quality that has a probability of acceptance of 0.50. In the Philips Standard Sampling System, discussed later in this chapter, $p_{0.50}$ is called the *point of control*. In some other statistical literature it is called the *indifference quality*.

It is easy to devise homemade single sampling acceptance criteria for any desired $p_{0.50}$, using the following approximate formula.†

$$n = \frac{c + 0.67}{p_{0.50}}$$

Suppose that lots 2.5% defective or better are considered to be acceptable but that it is desired to reject lots that are any worse. With this quality standard, we wish to find a set of single sampling plans for which a lot 2.5% defective will have a P_a of 0.50. Assume values of the acceptance number c from 0 up to any desired number, and solve the foregoing formula for sample size n, using $p_{0.50}$ as 0.025. The resulting family of acceptance plans is as follows:

c	n	c	n	c	n
0	27	4	187	8	347
1	67	5	227	9	387
2	107	6	267	10	427
3	147	7	307	11	467

† This relationship was first pointed out by G. A. Campbell writing in the *Bell System Technical Journal* in 1923. It assumes that the Poisson distribution gives a satisfactory approximation to the OC curve.

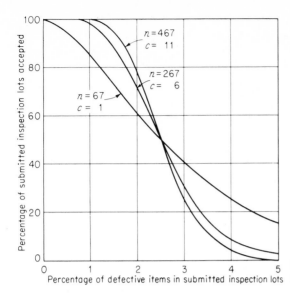

Figure 15-1 OC curves for three single sampling plans having a $p_{0.50}$ of 2.5%.

Although the OC curves of these 12 single sampling plans all pass fairly closely through the one point $P_a = 0.50$, $p = 0.025$, the plans having the larger sample size give better discrimination between lots that are somewhat better than 2.5% defective and lots that are somewhat worse. This point is illustrated by Fig. 15-1, which compares the plans with sample sizes of 67, 267, and 467, which have acceptance numbers of 1, 6, and 11, respectively. A choice among the various plans requires balancing the extra inspection costs of larger samples against the advantage of better assurance that a lot meeting the quality standard will be accepted and one failing to meet it will be rejected.

Comment on the Relationship between Acceptance Number, Sample Size, and $p_{0.50}$

A view commonly held by producers is that if the consumer is willing to tolerate a stated percentage of defectives in the lot, there should be willingness to tolerate the same percentage in the sample. For instance, if willing to accept lots 2.5% defective, the consumer should be satisfied with acceptance criteria no more severe than $n = 40$ and $c = 1$, or $n = 80$ and $c = 2$, or in general $n = 40c$. This view is expressed particularly with regard to acceptance criteria for isolated lots or for tightened inspection in schemes involving normal and tightened inspection such as were described in Chap. 14.

The difficulty with this view is that it concentrates attention on the *acceptance* number to the exclusion of the *rejection* number. If $n = 40$ and $c = 1$, lots are accepted if the sample is 2.5% defective but cannot be rejected unless the sample is at least 5% defective. Of course the larger the sample, the smaller the disparity between the acceptance percentage and the rejection percentage.

The value of $p_{0.50}$ for $n = 40$ and $c = 1$ may be calculated as follows:

$$p_{0.50} = \frac{c + 0.67}{n} = \frac{1.67}{40} = 0.0418, \text{ or } 4.18\%$$

We have already noted that with $c = 1$, n should be 67 for $p_{0.50}$ to be 2.5%.

Generally speaking, where samples are relatively small and percentages of defectives are relatively low, samples tend to give a too favorable impression of a lot somewhat more often than an impression that is too unfavorable. For example, consider the following distribution of probabilities of various numbers of defectives in drawing samples of 40 from a large lot 2.5% defective, as estimated from Table G:

Number of defectives in sample	Percentage of defectives in sample	Probability of occurrence
0	0.0	0.368
1	2.5	0.368
2	5.0	0.184
3	7.5	0.061
4	10.0	0.015
5	12.5	0.003
6	15.0	0.001

The average number of defectives in a great many samples of 40 from lots 2.5% defective will of course be 1, that is, 2.5% of defectives. For this to be the average, however, 0 defectives must occur once for every time there are 2 defectives, twice for every time there are 3, three times for every time there are 4, and so on. Thus the probability of 0 defectives is 0.368, whereas the probability of 2 or more is only 0.264.

Designing Single Sampling Plans for Stipulated Producer's and Consumer's Risks

The topic of the choice of a sampling plan based on the assessment of both Consumer and Producer Risks was discussed near the end of Chap. 14. The reader will remember that the definition of AQL, the basis of the ABC standard, related to a high quality (low value of p') considered acceptable as a process average. Once such a value of the AQL is fixed, a definite point on the upper end of the OC curve may be established. The coordinates of this point are $(p_1, 1 - \alpha)$, where p_1 is the value of the AQL and α is the Producer's Risk. In the ABC standard system, α ranges from 0.01 to 0.12 with the highest values occurring for those plans where c equals 0.

In the discussion of the LQ tables, it was pointed out that, in instances where isolated lots of product are to be inspected using a sampling plan, equal attention should be directed to the Consumer's Risk. The LQ tables gave values of p' with probabilities of acceptance, that is, Consumer's Risks (β), of 5 and 10%. The tables were organized in such a manner that the user searched the AQL column until an acceptable Consumer's Risk point (p_2, β) was found. Thus the consumer's interest may be most closely associated with the lower end of the OC curve. While this duality in the relationship between the interests of the producer and consumer may be strongest in those cases where judgment must be passed on isolated lots of product, a strong argument could be made that the appropriate balancing of consumer and producer interests in the operating characteristics of a sampling plan is basic to the selection of a good plan.

Mathematically, the selection of two points on an operating characteristic curve uniquely defines a single sampling plan through those points. In practice, this means that the appropriate balancing of consumer and producer interests, as exemplified by the choice of a Producer's Risk point (p_1, $1 - \alpha$) and a Consumer's Risk point (p_2, β) leads to a unique single sampling plan. For simplicity, this fact is demonstrated using the Poisson distribution.

Since the producer wishes product with the stipulated quality, p_1, accepted with probability $1 - \alpha$, the Poisson formula for probability of acceptance describing the stipulated preference is:

$$P_a \ (producer) = \sum_{m=0}^{c} \frac{(np_1)^m}{m!} e^{-np_1} = 1 - \alpha$$

The corresponding formula describing the Consumer's Risk preference is:

$$P_a \ (consumer) = \sum_{m=0}^{c} \frac{(np_2)^m}{m!} e^{-np_2} = \beta$$

Since p_1, p_2, $1 - \alpha$, and β are known, the two unknowns in these equations are n, the sample size, and c, the acceptance number. These two equations in two unknowns may be solved simultaneously for unique values of n and c.

It is not the intent here to present a mathematical solution to this problem but rather to introduce some work by J. M. Cameron[†] which simplifies the procedure of deriving sampling plans based on stipulated Producer's and Consumer's Risks. Two features of the derivation of plans are worth pointing out here. Both of these features are exemplified in the sample calculations given in the following paragraphs. First, if α and β are small and the *difference* between p_1 and p_2 is small, the resulting sample size, n, is likely to be very large.

Second, because of the requirement for integer values for n and c, it is virtually impossible to derive a sampling plan that passes exactly through the two points

---

[†] J. M. CAMERON, Tables for Constructing and for Computing the Operating Characteristics of Single-sampling Plans, *Industrial Quality Control*, vol. 9, pp. 37–39, July, 1952.

$(p_1, 1 - \alpha)$ and (p_2, β). Some compromise in the vicinity of one point or the other is almost always required.

Table 15-1, based on the Poisson distribution and adapted from two more extensive tables in the article by Cameron, can be used to design sampling plans with stated Producer's and Consumer's Risk points.

In the following numerical examples, we shall deal particularly with two columns of this table. The column headed $np_{0.95}$ enables us to compute a family of single sampling plans that have a common value of $P_a = 0.95$ for any stated "good" quality (expressed as a fraction defective). The Producer's Risk, α, is 0.05. The column headed $np_{0.10}$ enables us to compute a family of plans for which the Consumer's Risk is 0.10 for any stated "bad" quality.

Assume that a family of plans is desired having a Producer's Risk of 0.05 that product 0.65% defective will be rejected if submitted to sampling inspection. That is, 0.65% defective is viewed as "good" quality; it is desired to protect the producer by having only 1 chance in 20 that product of such quality be rejected. Assume that it is desired to know for each plan the percentage defective for which the Consumer's Risk is 0.10. The following family of plans may be computed from factors given in Table 15-1.

c	n	$100p_{0.10}$, %	c	n	$100p_{0.10}$, %	c	n	$100p_{0.10}$, %
0	8	28.8	4	303	2.6	8	722	1.80
1	55	7.1	5	402	2.3	9	835	1.70
2	126	4.2	6	506	2.1	10	949	1.62
3	210	3.2	7	612	1.9	11	1,065	1.56

The required calculations may be illustrated for the case where $c = 3$:

$$n = \frac{np_{0.95}}{p_{0.95}} = \frac{1.366}{0.0065} = 210.15 \approx 210$$

$$p_{0.10} = \frac{np_{0.10}}{n} = \frac{6.681}{210} = 0.032 \text{ or } 3.2\%$$

Now assume that a family of plans is desired having a Consumer's Risk of 0.10 that product 1.0% defective will be accepted if submitted to sampling inspection. That is, 1.0% defective is viewed as "bad" quality; it is desired to protect the consumer by having only 1 chance in 10 that product of such quality will be accepted. Assume also that it is desired to know for each plan the percentage defective for which the Producer's Risk is 0.05. The following family of plans may be computed from factors given in Table 15-1. The calculations are similar to those illustrated in connection with the stipulated Producer's Risk.

Table 15-1 Generalized table of single sampling plans that have certain specified Producer's and Consumer's Risks

(This table, based on the Poisson distribution, is adapted by permission from J. M. Cameron, Tables for Constructing and for Computing the Operating Characteristics of Single-sampling Plans, *Industrial Quality Control*, vol. 9, p. 39, July, 1952)

c	$np_{0.99}$	$np_{0.95}$	$np_{0.90}$	$np_{0.50}$	$np_{0.10}$	$np_{0.05}$	$np_{0.01}$	$\dfrac{p_{0.10}}{p_{0.95}}$
0	0.010	0.051	0.105	0.693	2.303	2.996	4.605	44.890
1	0.149	0.355	0.532	1.678	3.890	4.744	6.638	10.946
2	0.436	0.818	1.102	2.674	5.322	6.296	8.406	6.509
3	0.823	1.366	1.745	3.672	6.681	7.754	10.045	4.890
4	1.279	1.970	2.433	4.671	7.994	9.154	11.605	4.057
5	1.785	2.613	3.152	5.670	9.275	10.513	13.108	3.549
6	2.330	3.286	3.895	6.670	10.532	11.842	14.571	3.206
7	2.906	3.981	4.656	7.669	11.771	13.148	16.000	2.957
8	3.507	4.695	5.432	8.669	12.995	14.434	17.403	2.768
9	4.130	5.426	6.221	9.669	14.206	15.705	18.783	2.618
10	4.771	6.169	7.021	10.668	15.407	16.962	20.145	2.497
11	5.428	6.924	7.829	11.668	16.598	18.208	21.490	2.397
12	6.099	7.690	8.646	12.668	17.782	19.442	22.821	2.312
13	6.782	8.464	9.470	13.668	18.958	20.668	24.139	2.240
14	7.477	9.246	10.300	14.668	20.128	21.886	25.446	2.177
15	8.181	10.035	11.135	15.668	21.292	23.098	26.743	2.122
16	8.895	10.831	11.976	16.668	22.452	24.302	28.031	2.073
17	9.616	11.633	12.822	17.668	23.606	25.500	29.310	2.029
18	10.346	12.442	13.672	18.668	24.756	26.692	30.581	1.990
19	11.082	13.254	14.525	19.668	25.902	27.879	31.845	1.954
20	11.825	14.072	15.383	20.668	27.045	29.062	33.103	1.922
21	12.574	14.894	16.244	21.668	28.184	30.241	34.355	1.892
22	13.329	15.719	17.108	22.668	29.320	31.416	35.601	1.865
23	14.088	16.548	17.975	23.668	30.453	32.586	36.841	1.840
24	14.853	17.382	18.844	24.668	31.584	33.752	38.077	1.817
25	15.623	18.218	19.717	25.667	32.711	34.916	39.308	1.795
30	19.532	22.444	24.113	30.667	38.315	40.690	45.401	1.707
35	23.525	26.731	28.556	35.667	43.872	46.404	51.409	1.641
40	27.587	31.066	33.038	40.667	49.390	52.069	57.347	1.590
45	31.704	35.441	37.550	45.667	54.878	57.695	63.231	1.548
50	35.867	39.849	42.089	50.667	60.339	63.287	69.066	1.515

c	n	$100p_{0.95}$, %	c	n	$100p_{0.95}$, %	c	n	$100p_{0.95}$, %
0	230	0.02	4	799	0.25	8	1,300	0.36
1	389	0.09	5	928	0.28	9	1,421	0.38
2	532	0.15	6	1,053	0.31	10	1,541	0.40
3	668	0.20	7	1,177	0.34	11	1,660	0.42

Now, assume that both stipulations are made, namely, that the Producer's Risk shall be 0.05 of rejection of product 0.65% defective and that the Consumer's Risk shall be 0.10 of acceptance of product 1.0% defective. It is evident that these two stipulations will not be met by any plan in either of these two tabulated families of plans. Even the tabulated plans with sample sizes above 1,000 do not come close to meeting both these stipulations. (In fact, the sample size must be approximately 5,600 for a single sampling plan to meet these two stipulations.)

The difficulty here is that the two stipulated values of product quality, 0.65 and 1.0% defective, are too close together for the stipulated values of Producer's Risk and Consumer's Risk. That is, they are so close together that the stipulations cannot be met without a sample size that is too large to be practicable in most circumstances that arise in industry.

The final column of Table 15-1 gives for each value of c the ratio of $p_{0.10}$ to $p_{0.95}$. Assume that it is desired to have a Producer's Risk of 0.05 of rejection of a lot 0.40% defective and a Consumer's Risk of 0.10 of acceptance of a lot 1.50% defective. The ratio $p_{0.10}/p_{0.95}$ is 0.015/0.004 or 3.75. The final column of Table 15-1 tells us that a ratio of 4.057 is obtained when c is 4 and 3.549 is obtained when c is 5. Because neither of these values is exactly 3.75, it is not possible to have a single sampling plan that has an OC curve passing *exactly* through the two stipulated points. A choice might be made of one of the following four plans that can be computed from Table 15-1; the OC curve of each plan passes through one of the specified points and provides a near miss to the other point.

c	n	$100p_{0.95}$, %	$100p_{0.10}$, %
4	492	0.40	1.62
5	653	0.40	1.42
4	533	0.37	1.50
5	618	0.42	1.50

The Importance of the Acceptance Number c in Determining the Shape of the OC Curve

Consider our tabulated family of plans that had a Consumer's Risk of 0.10 of accepting product 1% defective. If the requirement had been for a family of plans with a Consumer's Risk of 0.10 of accepting product 5% defective, all values of n

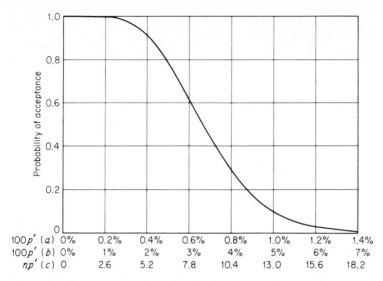

Figure 15-2 Depending on units used for the horizontal scale, this is the approximate OC curve for (*a*) $n = 1,300$, $c = 8$; (*b*) $n = 260$, $c = 8$; or (*c*) all plans for which $c = 8$.

would have been $\frac{1}{5}$ of the figure shown in our table and all values of $100p_{0.95}$ would have been 5 times the figure shown. For example, the plan with $c = 8$ would have an n of 260 rather than 1,300 and a value of $100p_{0.95}$ of 1.8 rather than 0.36%.

Figure 15-2 illustrates the point that the same OC curve can be used for (1) $n = 1,300$, $c = 8$, and (2) $n = 260$, $c = 8$, provided the units on the horizontal scale are changed by a factor of 5. Moreover, the OC curve in Fig. 15-2 applies to all single sampling plans for which $c = 8$ if the horizontal scale is in units of np' as in scale c of the figure. Such a generalized OC curve for all plans with a particular c assumes that the Poisson distribution is deemed to give a close enough approximation for the intended purpose.

This relationship between the acceptance number and the OC curve made possible the classification by acceptance number of the ASN curves contained in ABC-STD-105.

Design of a Sequential Plan Having an OC Curve Passing through Two Designated Points

A certain product is subject to lot-by-lot acceptance or rejection on the basis of a destructive test applied to a sample. The conditions of the test are considerably more severe than it is expected will be encountered in practice. All items tested are damaged to the point where they are of no further use. In order to keep the number of items tested to a minimum consistent with the desired quality protection, it is decided to design an item-by-item sequential plan.

Such a plan may be designed so that the OC curve passes through any two points desired. In this instance, the desired points are $P_a = 0.95$, $p_1 = 0.10$; and

$P_a = 0.20$, $p_2 = 0.30$. Because of the margin of safety in the test procedure, it is believed that lots are satisfactory when not more than 10% of the items would fail if subjected to this test; with a P_a of 0.95, the producer takes only 1 chance in 20 that such lots will be rejected. From the consumer's viewpoint, there is to be one chance in five of acceptance of a lot in which 30% of the items would fail this test. In the symbols commonly used in the mathematics of sequential sampling, these desired points on the OC curve are represented by ($p_1 = 0.10$, $\alpha = 0.05$) and ($p_2 = 0.30$, $\beta = 0.20$).

Item-by-item sequential sampling was developed from the Wald sequential probability ratio test (SPRT).† The mathematical form that the probability ratio takes is:

$$\frac{p_1^d(1 - p_1)^{n-d}}{p_2^d(1 - p_2)^{n-d}}$$

If the actual fraction defective of the lot, p', is at the level p_1, the lot should be accepted. Thus the P_a associated with the numerator of the equation is $1 - \alpha$ and that associated with the denominator is β. When the value of the probability ratio exceeds the ratio of $B = (1 - \alpha)/\beta$, the lot is accepted. Conversely, if p' is at the level p_2, the probabilities of rejection are α and $1 - \beta$, respectively, for the numerator and denominator of the probability ratio. Thus if the value of the ratio falls below $A = \alpha/(1 - \beta)$, the lot is rejected. B and A are associated with the acceptance and rejection lines, respectively. The solution, in terms of d and n, is found with the use of logarithms.

Figure 15-3 gives a graphical representation of an item-by-item sequential plan. The plan is fully defined by the equation of the rejection line, $d_2 = sn + h_2$,

---

† For a complete development of the SPRT and many of its uses, see ABRAHAM WALD, "Sequential Analysis," John Wiley & Sons, New York, 1947.

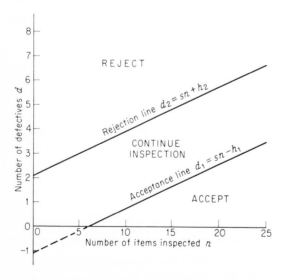

Figure 15-3 Graphical representation of an item-by-item sequential plan.

and the acceptance line, $d_1 = sn - h_1$. To compute s, the slope of these lines, and h_1 and h_2, the intercepts, certain auxiliary symbols, g_1, g_2, a, and b, are used. The necessary computations are as follows:

$$g_1 = \log \frac{p_2}{p_1} = \log \frac{0.30}{0.10} = 0.4771$$

$$g_2 = \log \frac{1 - p_1}{1 - p_2} = \log \frac{0.90}{0.70} = 0.1091$$

$$a = \log \frac{1 - \beta}{\alpha} = \log \frac{0.80}{0.05} = 1.2041$$

$$b = \log \frac{1 - \alpha}{\beta} = \log \frac{0.95}{0.20} = 0.6767$$

$$h_1 = \frac{b}{g_1 + g_2} = \frac{0.6767}{0.5862} = 1.154$$

$$h_2 = \frac{a}{g_1 + g_2} = \frac{1.2041}{0.5862} = 2.054$$

$$s = \frac{g_2}{g_1 + g_2} = \frac{0.1091}{0.5862} = 0.186$$

This gives the following equations:

Rejection line: $d_2 = 0.186n + 2.054$

Acceptance line: $d_1 = 0.186n - 1.154$

For practical use, these lines should be converted into an item-by-item table of acceptance and rejection numbers. Computed values of d_1 and d_2 are generally not whole numbers. In the following tabulation of acceptance and rejection numbers up to $n = 24$, the rejection number is the next whole number above d_2, and the acceptance number is the next whole number below d_1.

n	Acceptance number	Rejection number	n	Acceptance number	Rejection number	n	Acceptance number	Rejection number
1	*	†	9	0	4	17	2	6
2	*	†	10	0	4	18	2	6
3	*	3	11	0	5	19	2	6
4	*	3	12	1	5	20	2	6
5	*	3	13	1	5	21	2	6
6	*	4	14	1	5	22	2	7
7	0	4	15	1	5	23	3	7
8	0	4	16	1	6	24	3	7

* Acceptance requires a sample of at least 7 items.
† Rejection requires a sample of at least 3 items.

The purpose of adopting such an item-by-item scheme is to reduce the average amount of inspection below the amount that would obtain with a multiple scheme giving about the same quality protection. However, it is usually advisable to fix some upper limit to the size of n; otherwise, an occasional borderline lot might conceivably require the indefinite continuation of sampling.

It should be recognized that a maximum value for n changes the OC curve from that contemplated in the calculations to design an item-by-item sequential plan. In order to avoid a substantial effect, some writers recommend truncation at a value of n about three times that for a single sampling plan passing through the same two designated points on the OC curve. In the example calculations given here, the recommendation would suggest truncation at a value of n of about 80. In many cases, the user can derive a corresponding single sampling plan rather quickly with the aid of Table 15-1 from which an appropriate terminating value for n may be decided. Some users of item-by-item sequential plans accept all lots that have not been rejected at this maximum sample size; others reject all that have not been accepted.

Five points on the OC curve of an item-by-item sequential plan can be found without difficulty. Two of these are the points used in designing the plan. Two more points are established by the knowledge that when $p = 0$, $P_a = 1.00$ and when $p = 1$, $P_a = 0$. A fifth point is fixed by the relationship that when $p = s$, $P_a = h_2/(h_1 + h_2)$.

As previously mentioned, the objective in using item-by-item sequential sampling is usually to minimize the amount of sampling inspection necessary to reach a decision. The ASN function is therefore an important characteristic of the plan. Sufficiently good OC curves and ASN functions often can be sketched from the five points as follows:

Value of p'	OC Curve (P_a)	ASN
0.0	1.0	$\dfrac{h_1}{s}$
p_1	$1 - \alpha$	$\dfrac{(1 - \alpha)h_1 - \alpha h_2}{s - p_1}$
s	$\dfrac{h_2}{h_1 + h_2}$	$\dfrac{h_1 h_2}{s(1 - s)}$
p_2	β	$\dfrac{(1 - \beta)h_2 - \beta h_1}{p_2 - s}$
1.0	0	$\dfrac{h_2}{1 - s}$

For the sequential plan just computed, the values would be as follows:

Value of p'	OC Curve (P_a)	ASN
0.0	1.0	6.20
0.10	0.95	11.55
0.186	0.64	15.65
0.30	0.20	12.39
1.0	0.0	2.52

An explanation of the more complicated calculations of additional points on the OC curve and ASN function is contained in the basic source material on sequential analysis.†

II. SOME SIMPLIFIED SYSTEMS FOR LOT-BY-LOT ACCEPTANCE SAMPLING

The Philips Standard Sampling System

Table 15-2 reproduces an attributes sampling system developed by Dr. H. C. Hamaker and his associates of N. V. Philips' Gloeilampenfabrieken, Eindhoven, Holland.‡ The system uses $p_{0.50}$, the point of control or indifference quality, as the basis for referencing all its sampling plans. This type of system has had considerable use in Europe but apparently only limited use in North America.

Figure 15-4 shows the OC curves of all the plans in the Philips Standard Sampling System. It is desirable for the reader to note certain features of the Philips system as follows:

1. All plans are classified by a particular point on the OC curve, the product quality for which the probability of acceptance is 0.50.
2. Producer and consumer, in effect, share equally in the risk of a "wrong" decision by any sampling plan included in the system. Thus, if a 2% plan is

---

† A. WALD, "Sequential Analysis," *op. cit.*

Statistical Research Group, Columbia University, "Sequential Analysis of Statistical Data: Applications," Columbia University Press, New York, 1945.

‡ H. C. HAMAKER, Lot Inspection by Sampling, *Philips Technical Review*, vol. 11, pp. 176–182, December, 1949.

H. C. HAMAKER, The Theory of Sampling Inspection Plans, *Philips Technical Review*, vol. 11, pp. 260–270, March, 1950.

H. C. HAMAKER, J. J. M. TAUDIN CHABOT, and F. G. WILLEMZE, The Practical Application of Sampling Inspection Plans and Tables, *Philips Technical Review*, vol. 11, pp. 362–370, June, 1950.

W. FUIJT and F. G. WILLEMZE, "Directions on the Use of the Philips Standard Sampling System," N. V. Philips' Gloeilampenfabrieken, Eindhoven, Holland, 1955.

See also A. H. SCHAAFSMA and F. G. WILLEMZE, "Modern kwaliteitsbeleid," N. V. Uitgeversmij. Centrex, Eindhoven, Holland. This is the title of the original edition in the Dutch language. Titles of French, German, and Spanish language editions are respectively: "Gestion moderne de la qualité," "Moderne Qualitätskontrolle," and "Gestion moderna de la calidad."

Table 15-2 Philips Standard Sampling System

A means inspect entire lot. For second sample, $n_2 = 2n_1$

		Point of control																						
		0.25%			0.5%			1%			2%			3%			5%			7%			10%		
Lot size		n/n_1	c/c_1	c_2	n/n_1	c/c_1	c_2	n/n_1	c/c_1	c_2	n/n_1	c/c_1	c_2	n/n_1	c/c_1	c_2	n/n_1	c/c_1	c_2	n/n_1	c/c_1	c_2	n/n_1	c/c_1	c_2
Single sampling	20–50	A	—		A	—		A	—		30	0		20	0		13	0		10	0		7	0	
	51–100	A	—		A	—		60	0		30	0		20	0		13	0		10	0		7	0	
	101–200	A	—		100	0		60	0		35	0		55	1		35	1		25	1		17	1	
	201–500	175	0		100	0		135	1		75	1		55	1		35	1		40	2		25	2	
	501–1,000	225	0		225	1		150	1		85	1		85	2		55	2		55	3		35	3	
Double sampling	1,001–2,000	330	0	1	150	0	1	110	0	2	55	0	2	45	0	3	25	0	3	30	1	5	22	1	5
	2,001–5,000	425	0	2	200	0	2	135	0	3	70	0	3	70	1	5	45	1	5	55	2	10	40	2	10
	5,001–10,000	525	0	3	260	0	3	220	1	5	110	1	5	125	2	10	75	2	10	75	3	15	55	3	15
	10,001–20,000	875	1	5	440	1	5	380	2	10	190	2	10	180	3	15	110	3	15	100	4	20	70	4	20
	20,001–50,000	1,500	2	10	750	2	10	540	3	15	270	3	15	240	4	20	140	4	20	120	5	25	85	5	25
	50,001 and over	2,200	3	15	1,100	3	15	700	4	20	350	4	20	290	5	25	175	5	25	145	6	30	105	6	30

460

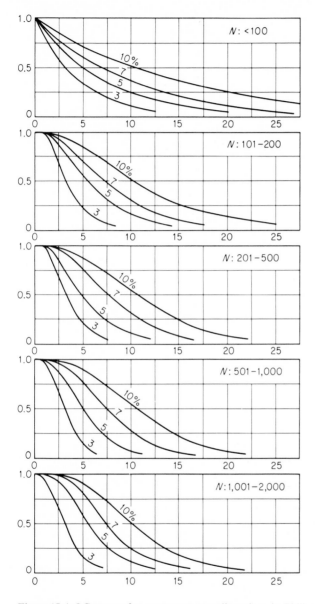

Figure 15-4 OC curves for acceptance sampling plans in Philips Standard Sampling System. *(Reproduced by permission from N. V. Philips' Gloeilampenfabrieken, Eindhoven, Holland.)*

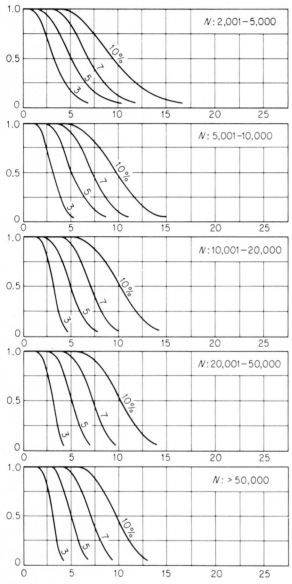

Fig. 15-4 (*Continued*)

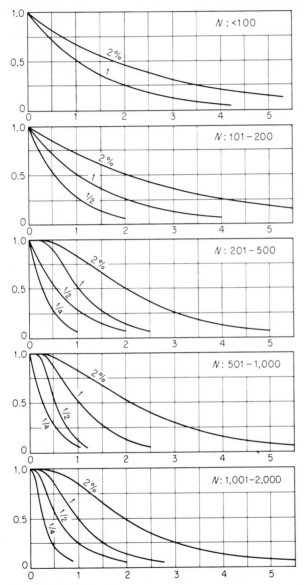

Fig. 15-4   (*Continued*)

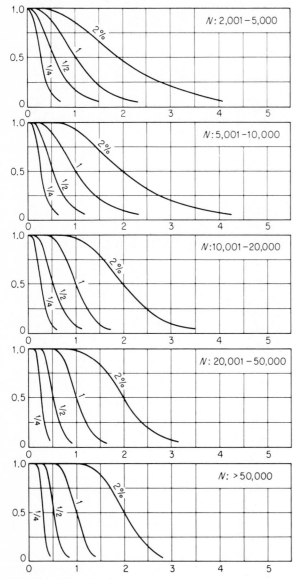

Fig. 15-4 *(Continued)*

used, product exactly 2% defective is as likely to be accepted as it is to be rejected.

3. As nearly as practicable, all the sampling plans in the system have the same ratio of the slope of the OC curve at $p_{0.50}$ to the value of the quality standard $p_{0.50}$. In other words, the relative discrimination between good and bad product is approximately constant at the indifference quality or point of control.

4. A consequence of item 3 is that the Producer's Risk of rejection of product at some stated amount moderately better than the quality standard is roughly comparable to the Consumer's Risk of acceptance of product at the same amount worse than the standard. For instance, consider the 2% plan ($n = 85$, $c = 1$) applicable to a lot of 1,000. The Producer's Risk of rejection of a 1% defective lot is approximately 0.21; the Consumer's Risk of acceptance of a 3% defective lot is approximately 0.28.

5. Another consequence of item 3 is that the sample size is relatively large for plans designed for maximum consumer protection and decreases as the quality standard is relaxed. For instance, the sample size for a lot of 501 to 1,000 is 225 when the point of control is 0.25% defective and decreases to 35 when the point of control is 10% defective.

6. Single sampling is stipulated whenever the lot is 1,000 or less. Double sampling is stipulated whenever the lot is greater than 1,000, with n_2 always equal to $2n_1$.

A Simple AQL System Proposed by Dodge

The earliest AQL tables—Army Ordnance and Army Service Forces—were relatively simple. The Philips Standard Sampling System also is quite simple. However, all the military standards starting with JAN-STD-105 have involved fairly extensive and complex sets of tables. The Dodge-Romig tables discussed in Chap. 13 also are quite extensive. The complex tables make it possible to provide many different alternative sampling plans adapted for use under many different circumstances. Nevertheless, there are often real advantages in having a system that is simple.

In a brilliant monograph written in 1959, H. F. Dodge made a number of proposals regarding the design of sampling systems based on the AQL concept.† One aspect of his proposals was that they made possible the design of an AQL system that could be presented on a simple one-page table. Three such systems, designated Plan 1, Plan 2, and Plan 3, are presented in the monograph. One of these, Plan 1, is reproduced here as Table 15-3.

---

† H. F. DODGE, "A General Procedure for Sampling Inspection by Attributes—Based on the AQL Concept," Technical Report No. 10, The Statistics Center, Rutgers the State University, Dec. 15, 1959. In January, 1960, the material in this monograph was presented to the ABC Working Group and also in a public lecture at the Navy Building, Washington, D.C., sponsored by the Assistant Chief for Production and Quality Control, Bureau of Naval Weapons. The reader will note that a number of the features proposed by Dodge were incorporated into the ABC standard.

This paper, in substance, was later presented under the same title at the 1963 convention of the American Society for Quality Control. See "Annual Convention Transactions, Seventeenth Annual Convention," pp. 7–19, American Society for Quality Control, Milwaukee, Wis., 1963.

Table 15-3 Composite single sampling table for Plan 1 of Dodge's proposed AQL system for acceptance sampling by attributes

(Adapted by permission from H. F. Dodge, A General Procedure for Sampling Inspection by Attributes—Based on the AQL Concept, The Statistics Center, Rutgers the State University, *Technical Report* No. 10, Dec. 15, 1959)

Lot size, inspection level II†	Sample size n	Acceptance number in normal inspection, c_N* AQL; %										
		0.10	0.15	0.25	0.40	0.65	1.0	1.5	2.5	4.0	6.5	10.0
3–15	3									↓	↓	↓
16–22	4										↓	1
23–40	6										1	↓
41–70	10								↓	1	↓	2
71–120	15							↓	1	↓	2	3
121–210	25						↓	1	↓	2	3	5
211–400	40	↓	↓			↓	1	↓	2	3	5	7
401–700	65	↓	↓		↓	1	↓	2	3	5	7	10
701–1,300	100	↓	↓		1	↓	2	3	5	7	10	15
1,301–3,200	150	↓	↓	1	↓	2	3	5	7	10	15	22
3,201–15,000	250	↓	1	↓	2	3	5	7	10	15	22	↑
15,001–80,000	400	1	↓	2	3	5	7	10	15	22	↑	
Over 80,000	650	↑	2	3	5	7	10	15	22	↑		

* For tightened inspection, acceptance number $c_T = c_N - 1$.

† For inspection level I, use plan with next smaller sample size. For inspection level III, use plan with next larger sample size.

Some of Dodge's proposals, illustrated with respect to single sampling in Table 15-3, were as follows:

1. The *same* series of preferred numbers (numbers approximating a geometric progression) is used for AQL values and sample sizes. Thus in Table 15-3, AQL values include 1.0, 1.5, 2.5, 4.0, 6.5, and 10.0%; sample sizes include 10, 15, 25, 40, 65, and 100. This gives a systematic diagonal pattern of acceptance numbers.† One consequence of this pattern is that when $100p' = $ AQL, np' is

---

† This diagonal pattern of acceptance numbers can also be observed in the ABC standard. It did not exist in the previous military standards. Although, starting with MIL-STD-105A, these standards used preferred numbers for AQL values, they did not use them for sample sizes. The numbers 1.0, 1.5, 2.5, 4.0, 6.5, and 10.0 involve rounding of the values obtained when the first number is 1.0, and each succeeding number is found by multiplying the preceding number by $\sqrt[5]{10} = 1.585$. In the ABC standard, a similar "5-series" set of preferred numbers is used for single sample sizes with the first number as 2.0.

almost constant along any diagonal line of the table. (If the preferred number series used were an exact geometric progression, as would be the case if there were no rounding of numbers for more convenient use, np' would be exactly constant along a diagonal.) It follows that the probability of acceptance at AQL value is almost constant along any diagonal. (This statement assumes a Type B OC curve and the use of the Poisson approximation.)

2. The smallest acceptance number available in normal inspection is 1. (In a number of places in this book we have noted that, when $c = 0$, the shape of the OC curve is unsatisfactory and there is generally poor discrimination between good and bad lots.)

3. The table is designed for a probability of acceptance at the AQL value of approximately 0.95. The systematic pattern mentioned in 1 and the elimination of any plan with $c = 0$ mentioned in 2 both simplify the design of a set of plans that have a single aimed-at value of P_a at the AQL value.

4. In tightened inspection, the sample size is always the same as in normal inspection and the acceptance number is one less than in normal inspection. (This simple rule obviously would be impossible if there were any plans stipulating $c = 0$ in normal inspection.) It turns out that this rule gives an AOQL in tightened inspection that is approximately equal to the $100p_{0.95}$ in normal inspection. It follows that, if rejected lots in tightened inspection are given 100% inspection that is really effective, and if such lots are then resubmitted and accepted, the average outgoing quality will be no worse than the AQL, the per cent defective that originally was deemed to be satisfactory as a process average.†

5. No code letters are used. The lot sizes that correspond to each sampling plan under ordinary circumstances are given in the table. These values given in the table are designated as applying to inspection level II. Where necessary, smaller sample sizes for a given lot size can be used by shifting to the next smaller sample size in the table (inspection level I); larger sample sizes can be used by shifting to the next larger sample size (inspection level III).

A number of other features of AQL systems, not illustrated in Table 15-3, were also proposed by Dodge. One important proposal was that a shift from normal to tightened inspection be required if 2 of the last 5 (or less) lots under normal inspection were rejected. (The reader will recall that this was the rule adopted for the ABC standard.) Normal inspection was to be reinstated when 5 successive lots were accepted under tightened inspection. Dodge commented regarding these proposed rules as follows:

> The criteria given for shifting from normal to tightened inspection and from tightened back to normal inspection are very simple and easy to apply. Simple criteria have been made possible by holding to a reasonably constant probability pattern for normal inspection and a reasonably

† In the original Army Ordance and Army Service Forces tables, the aimed-at AOQL in tightened inspection was the stated AQL value. This feature was lost in the subsequent military standards.

constant AOQL pattern for tightened. The rule[†] for shifting to tightened inspection "if 2 of the last 5 lots were rejected" seems appropriate as a general rule only so long as all plans under normal inspection have about the same probability of acceptance for AQL quality.

To be effective and to be used, the rules for shifting from normal to tightened inspection must be reasonable, and must appear to be reasonable to inspection personnel. It is the author's observations that the penalty of shifting from normal to tightened inspection has been sufficiently drastic in certain areas of existing sampling tables and procedures based on the AQL concept, that there has been a strong tendency to avoid using tightened inspection at all. This constitutes a basic misuse of the procedures; it undermines and relegates to a position of secondary importance, the consumer's protection against product running at a substandard level of quality. The magnitude of the change in going from normal to tightened inspection in the proposed system is relatively small, and intentionally so, yet it is adequate for the intended purpose here.

The two factors, ease of application, and less drastic shifts, should be conducive to a more willing acceptance and a better following of the rules and hence a better realization of a major objective—maintenance of quality equal to or better than the AQL.

As indicated ..., the maintenance of a control chart showing graphically the results of lot-by-lot inspections, while not required, is highly recommended. Such charts have been found invaluable as an aid to an understanding of the operations of the inspection system, especially when quality difficulties are encountered and shifts in inspection plans are necessary.

Dodge's Chain Sampling Inspection Plan

Special problems exist in cases where there is continuing production of lots or batches but where very small sample sizes are selected for each lot or batch because tests are destructive or costly. For small samples such as 4, 5, 6, or even 10, the only practicable acceptance number is 0. It has been pointed out that an acceptance number of 0 gives an unsatisfactory shape of OC curve (concave upward throughout) with poor discrimination between good and bad lots. With such small samples, the producer can be given better protection against chance rejection of lots from a satisfactory process without serious loss in consumer protection if acceptance decisions on each lot can be influenced by the results of samples from the most recent preceding lots. In presenting his Chain Sampling Plan (designated as ChSP-1), H. F. Dodge discusses certain aspects of this type of case as follows:[‡]

> Suppose we consider such a situation with a continuing supply of some processed material, such as a particular type of copper-alloy rod or sheet. Say that a single sampling plan $n = 5, c = 0$ is being used for tensile strength. For each lot, five standard specimens are prepared and subjected to a standard test. If all five tests meet specification, the lot is accepted. If one of the five specimen tests fails to meet specification (i.e., one defect is observed), then the lot is considered nonconforming under the sampling plan and is subject to rejection or other disposition.
>
> At this point certain questions arise. If the immediately preceding lot, or one of the most recently submitted lots, was also found nonconforming, then it would be reasonable to consider

[†] Dodge includes the following footnote here: "H. C. Hamaker mentions a comparable rule in a Philips specification for radio valves; Undated memo M. S. 3203, 'Attributes Sampling in Practice, Part I, General Principles,' handed to the author in Sept. 1959."

[‡] H. F. DODGE, Chain Sampling Inspection Plan, *Industrial Quality Control*, vol. 11, no. 4, pp. 10–13, January, 1955 and reprinted in *Journal of Quality Technology*, vol. 9, no. 3, July, 1977.

the current lot and perhaps the whole run of recent product to be of doubtful quality and hence probably subject to rejection. On the other hand, if no tensile test failures had been observed in the samples for quite a number of preceding lots, one might reason as follows: "We can't expect perfection. A small percentage of marginal failures to meet specification is reasonable for most such products. And if some small per cent defective is reasonable, this one defect that we have just observed is probably that occasional one that we must expect every now and then." Now if the current defect were in fact the occasional defect, the lot should be accepted. To be able to act as though the observed defect is merely the occasional one requires several things:

(*a*) the lot should be one of a series in a continuing supply as mentioned above,
(*b*) lots should normally be expected to be of essentially the same quality,
(*c*) the consumer should have no reason for believing that this particular lot is poorer than the immediately preceding ones, and
(*d*) the consumer must have confidence in the supplier, confidence that the supplier would not take advantage of a good record to slip in a bad lot now and then when it would have the best chance of acceptance.

Dodge describes the plan ChSP-1 as follows:

1. Conditions for Application
    (*a*) Interest centers on an individual quality characteristic that involves destructive or costly tests, such that normally only a small number of tests per lot can be justified.
    (*b*) The product to be inspected comprises a series of successive lots (of material or of individual units) produced by an essentially continuing process.
    (*c*) Under normal conditions the lots are expected to be of essentially the same quality (expressed in per cent defective).
    (*d*) The product comes from a source in which the consumer has confidence.
2. Procedure
    (*a*) For each lot, select a sample of n units (or specimens) and test each unit for conformance to the specified requirement.
    (*b*) Acceptance number of defects, $c = 0$; except $c = 1$ if no defects are found in the immediately preceding i samples of n. $(i = 1, 2, 3, ...)$

OC curves for plans with sample sizes of 4, 5, 6, and 10 are shown in Fig. 15-5. These curves show what is expected to happen over a series of lots for any stated process average $100p'$. Dodge comments further as follows:

> Curves for individual ChSP-1 plans can be compared with the OC curves for basic $c = 0$ plans of single sampling. It is seen that adding the provision for using cumulative results for i preceding samples has the same effect on the characteristic curve as taking a second sample. It increases the chance of acceptance in the region of principal interest—where the product per cent defective is very small. Since in addition it calls for rejection provided only that two defects are fairly close together, it modifies the basically undesirable features of the $c = 0$ single sampling plans.
>
> It is believed that values of $i = 3$ or more, say three to five, will be found most helpful in practical applications. The curve for $i = 1$ is shown dotted, merely to suggest that this is not a preferred choice. Theoretically, any value of i can be used. ...
>
> With the use of this plan for measurable characteristics, for example, tensile strength and elongation of a material, it will normally be useful to keep a running chart of the measured values to provide supplementary information on the distribution of quality. Among other things, a continuing time-plot or control chart of measured values helps to identify wild points and is of assistance in problems of determining whether troubles are measurement troubles or product troubles.

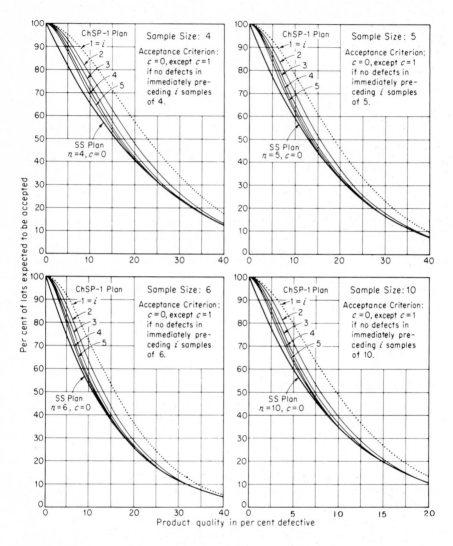

Figure 15-5 OC curves for ChSP-1 plans with values of *i* from 1 to 5. For comparison, single sampling plans (*n* = 4, 5, 6, and 10, with *c* = 0) are shown. *(Reproduced from H. F. Dodge, "Chain Sampling Inspection Plan," Industrial Quality Control, vol. 11, no. 4, pp. 10–13, January 1955, and reprinted in "Journal of Quality Technology," 9(3), July, 1977.)*

The probability of acceptance in ChSP-1 is the probability of 0 defectives in a given sample plus the probability that the given sample will have exactly 1 defective and be preceded by i samples that had 0 defectives. For example, for $n = 4$, $i = 3$, and $p' = 0.02$:

$$P_a = (0.98)^4 + 4(0.98)^3(0.02)(0.98)^4(0.98)^4(0.98)^4$$

$$= 0.9224 + 0.0591 = 0.9815\dagger$$

PROBLEMS

15-1 For a $p_{0.50}$ of 0.025 what should be the single sample sizes corresponding to acceptance numbers of 0, 1, 3, 5, and 7, respectively?

15-2 Use Table G to determine the approximate OC curves of the plans in Problem 15-1 that have acceptance numbers of 0, 3, and 7.

15-3 A producer and consumer agree that a single sampling plan will be used to accept and reject lots. The single sampling plan specified will pass through the indifference quality point at 3% defective.

(a) Use Table G to define operating characteristic curves for sampling plans with acceptance numbers of 0, 1, 2, and 3.

(b) Disregarding inspection costs, which plan do you feel will provide the consumer with the best protection against poor quality?

(c) If 200 lots of 3% nonconforming product are shipped to the consumer, how many items do you anticipate will be inspected if all rejected lots of 1,000 items are screened, based on the plan with an acceptance number of 2?

15-4 For an indifference quality $(p_{0.50})$ of 0.01, develop single sampling plans corresponding to acceptance numbers of 0, 1, 2, 3, and 4.

15-5 It is desired that the Producer's Risk of rejecting product 0.5% nonconforming shall be 0.10. Use Table 15-1 to find the respective sample sizes for single sampling plans that meet this requirement and have acceptance numbers of 1, 2, and 3. For each of these plans, find the percentage nonconforming corresponding to a Consumer's Risk of 0.05.

   Answer: $n = 106$, $c = 1$, $100p_{0.05} = 4.5\%$; $n = 220$, $c = 2$, $100p_{0.05} = 2.9\%$; $n = 349$, $c = 3$, $100p_{0.05} = 2.2\%$.

15-6 It is desired that the Consumer's Risk of accepting product 1.2% nonconforming shall be 0.01. Use Table 15-1 to find the respective sample sizes for single sampling plans that meet this requirement and have acceptance numbers of 1, 2, and 3. For each of these plans find the percentage nonconforming corresponding to a Producer's Risk of 0.01.

   Answer: $n = 553$, $c = 1$, $100p_{0.99} = 0.027\%$; $n = 700$, $c = 2$, $100p_{0.99} = 0.062\%$; $n = 837$, $c = 3$, $100p_{0.99} = 0.098\%$.

15-7 It is desired to have a single sampling plan for which the Producer's Risk of rejection of a 1% nonconforming lot is 0.05 and the Consumer's Risk of accepting a 3% nonconforming lot is 0.10. Using Table 15-1, find the plan that exactly meets the stipulation on Producer's Risk and comes as close as possible on Consumer's Risk. For this plan, what percentage nonconforming has a Consumer's Risk of 0.10%?

   Answer: $n = 398$; $c = 7$; $100p_{0.10} = 2.96\%$.

---

† The following important paper should be studied by any readers interested in the special problems arising where small samples are necessary or desirable for one reason or another:

A. F. CONE and H. F. DODGE, A Cumulative-results Plan for Small-sample Inspection, *Industrial Quality Control*, vol. 21, pp. 4–9, July, 1964.

15-8 It is desired that a single sampling plan for attributes data satisfy a Producer's Risk of rejection of 1.5% nonconforming lots of 0.05 and a Consumer's Risk of acceptance of 6.0% nonconforming lots of 0.10.

(a) Use Table 15-1 to find the plan that fits the Consumer's Risk and is as close as possible to the Producer's Risk.

(b) What is the percentage nonconforming that has a probability of rejection of 0.05?

15-9 A single sampling plan is to be developed to inspect large lots of a certain product based on a Producer's Risk of 0.05 of rejecting lots containing 1.6% nonconforming items. The Consumer's Risk of accepting lots containing 6% nonconforming items is to be as close as possible to 0.10.

(a) Use Table 15-1 to find the two plans which fit the Producer's Risk point and most nearly fit the Consumer's Risk point.

(b) What per cent nonconforming has a 10% chance of acceptance under each plan?

15-10 A single sampling plan is to be developed based on a Producer's Risk of 0.05 of rejecting lots which contain 0.435% nonconforming items. The Consumer's Risk of accepting lots containing 3.30% nonconforming items should be as close as possible to 0.05. Use Table 15-1 to determine the plan. (*Hint:* The right-hand column in Table 15-1 contains the ratio $np_{0.10}/np_{0.95}$. You will need the ratio $np_{0.05}/np_{0.95}$.)

15-11 It is proposed that a system of single sampling acceptance sampling plans for attributes data be developed, all using an acceptance number of zero. Each plan in the system is to be designed such that the probability of acceptance at a certain unacceptable quality level is 0.10 (a specified Consumer's Risk point).

(a) Use Table 15-1 to compute the values of n for unacceptable quality levels of 0.01, 0.02, 0.05, 0.10, and 0.15.

(b) What undesirable characteristic of the OC Curve is contained in the stipulation of an acceptance number of zero?

(c) In the application of this system of plans, it is found that all lot sizes are between 100 and 250 items. What assumptions made in the use of Table 15-1 to develop the plans do not hold? Explain your answer and give the correct formula for the OC Curve.

15-12 It is proposed to develop a single sampling plan for attributes that satisfies a Producer's Risk of 0.05 of accepting lots containing 1.5% nonconforming units. The plan is to come as close as possible to satisfying a Consumer's Risk of 0.05 of accepting lots containing 18% nonconforming units.

(a) Use Table 15-1 to find the appropriate plan. (*Hint:* The right-hand column in Table 15-1 gives the ratio $p_{0.10}/p_{0.95}$. In this case, you will need the ratio $p_{0.05}/p_{0.95}$.)

(b) What is the true value of $p_{0.05}$ for this plan?

15-13 It is proposed to have a set of single sampling plans in which the percentage nonconforming corresponding to a Consumer's Risk of 0.10 is, as nearly as practicable, 2.5 times the percentage nonconforming corresponding to a Producer's Risk of 0.05. Use Table 15-1 to find the plan for which $100p_{0.10}$ is 1.0% and $100p_{0.95}$ is 0.4% and for which $100p_{0.10}$ is 10% and $100p_{0.95}$ is 4%. Does it seem to you that it is a good idea to stipulate that $p_{0.10}$ shall always be 2.5 times $p_{0.95}$? Why or why not?

15-14 It is desired to have a system of single sampling plans, all of which have a sample size of 150. Use Table 15-1 to find the respective values of $np_{0.99}$, $np_{0.50}$, and $np_{0.01}$ for a system of plans having acceptance numbers of 0, 2, 4, 6, and 10. Sketch the OC curves of these plans.

15-15 Determine the equations of the rejection and acceptance lines for an item-by-item sequential plan in which $p_{0.90} = 0.05$ and $p_{0.20} = 0.15$.

Answer: $d_2 = 0.092n + 1.719$; $d_1 = 0.092n - 1.243$.

15-16 Plot an approximate OC curve for the sequential plan of Problem 15-15. Prepare an item-by-item table of acceptance and rejection numbers for values of n from 1 to 50. In this table, make the rejection number the next whole number above d_2 and the acceptance number the next whole number below d_1.

15-17 (a) Determine the acceptance and rejection lines for an item-by-item sequential sampling plan in which $p_{0.95} = 0.015$ and $p_{0.10} = 0.059$.

(b) Prepare a table of values of n for acceptance numbers from zero through four.

(c) What are the corresponding values of the rejection numbers in this range of n?

15-18 Use Table 15-1 to compute the single sampling plan corresponding to the item-by-item sequential sampling plan found in Problem 15-17.

15-19 (a) Determine the equations of the acceptance and rejection lines for an item-by-item sequential sampling plan in which $p_{0.95} = 0.04$ and $p_{0.10} = 0.15$.

(b) Sketch an ASN curve for this plan and indicate the maximum point on the curve.

(c) Use Table 15-1 to develop a single sampling plan satisfying the operating characteristics prescribed in part (a).

(d) Compare the value of n found in part (c) with the ASN values found in part (b).

15-20 (a) Determine the equations of the acceptance and rejection lines for an item-by-item sequential sampling plan in which $p_{0.95} = 0.015$ and $p_{0.10} = 0.10$.

(b) Sketch an ASN curve for this plan and indicate the maximum point on this curve.

(c) On the assumption that $p_{0.95}$ is a reasonable AQL value, find the ABC standard single sampling plan for Code Letter H under normal inspection.

(d) Compare the value of n found in part (c) with the ASN values found in part (b).

15-21 Determine the equations of the rejection and acceptance lines for an item-by-item sequential plan in which $p_{0.95} = 0.02$ and $p_{0.10} = 0.10$. Compute the respective acceptance and rejection numbers where n is 20, 40, 60, 80, and 100. In this calculation make the rejection number the next whole number above d_2 and the acceptance number the next whole number below d_1.

15-22 Plot the approximate ASN curve for the sequential plan of Problem 15-21. What are the values of the ASN at the Producer's and Consumer's Risk points? What is the maximum ASN and at approximately what value of p does it occur?

15-23 Select from Table 15-2 the sampling plan for a point of control of 1% and a lot size of 1,000. Under what AQL value is this plan listed in Table 15-3?

Answer: $n = 150$, $c = 1$; 0.25%.

15-24 Compute

(a) the value of $100p_{0.10}$ and

(b) the AOQL for the sampling plan of Problem 15-23. Make your calculations using Table G.

Answer: (a) 2.6%; (b) 0.6%.

15-25 (a) Select from Table 15-2 the sampling plan for a lot size 400 and a point of control of 2%.

(b) Use Table G to calculate the per cents of nonconforming product for which the probability of acceptance is 0.95 and 0.10.

15-26 (a) Find the appropriate Philips Standard Sampling System plan for a point of control of 2% and a lot size of 1,500 items.

(b) Use Table G to compute the approximate probability of acceptance of lots containing 4% nonconforming product.

(c) Compute the ASN for these lots.

(d) Compute the AFI on the assumption that rectifying inspection is to be used.

15-27 (a) Using the Philips Standard Sampling System, determine the acceptance criteria if the lot size is 800 and the point of control is 5.0%.

(b) What is the probability of rejection of a lot that is 4% defective for the plan found in (a)?

(c) Find a double sampling plan from the Philips Standard Sampling System for a lot size of 1,200 and a point of control of 5%.

(d) What is the probability of rejection of a 4% defective lot using the plan found in (c)?

(e) Compare the ASN values under the two plans if incoming lots are 4% defective.

15-28 A consumer has the choice of using an ABC standard single sampling plan or a Philips Standard single sampling plan. The ABC standard would be used with an inspection level II, an AQL of 1.0%, and a lot size of 500. The Philips plan would be used with a point of control of 3%.

(a) Find the acceptance criteria under both plans.

(b) If the consumer's primary concern is the assurance that lots 5% nonconforming are rejected, which plan would give him the best protection? Explain.

15-29 In Dodge's proposed system shown in Table 15-3, what are the acceptance criteria in normal and tightened inspection for inspection level I, 1.5% AQL, and a lot size of 1,000? What are the respective probabilities of acceptance under normal and tightened inspection when the process average is at the AQL value? What is the AOQL under tightened inspection?

15-30 A vendor inspects his own product before shipment using the Philips Standard Sampling System, screening all rejected lots before shipment. The lot size is 2,500, and the point of control is 2%. The purchaser inspects the same lots under the Dodge system shown in Table 15-3. He uses inspection level II, normal inspection, and an AQL of 1.0%.

Use Table G to obtain approximate answers to the following questions:

(a) What is the probability that a 2.5% nonconforming lot will pass both the vendor's and purchaser's sampling inspection?

(b) What is the probability that a 2.5% nonconforming lot will pass the vendor's sampling inspection and be rejected by the purchaser's?

15-31 For inspection level III, an AQL of 2.5%, and a lot size of 80, what are the acceptance plans under normal and tightened inspection using the Dodge simplified AQL system given in Table 15-3? Use Table G to plot the OC curves of these two plans.

15-32 (a) Using Dodge's simplified AQL system shown in Table 15-3, determine the acceptance criteria under normal and tightened inspection for inspection level III, 2.5% AQL, and a lot size of 500.

(b) What is the probability of acceptance of lots 5.0% nonconforming under both plans?

(c) Compute the AOQL under tightened inspection for the plan derived in (a) assuming rejected lots are screened and nonconforming items replaced, and also that nonconforming items found in the samples from accepted lots are replaced with good items.

15-33 A manufacturer inspects all of his product before shipment using Dodge's single sampling system shown in Table 15-3. Inspection level II for normal inspection is used. Lots are shipped in quantities of 1,500 under an AQL requirement of 2.5%. On receiving lots, the customer also inspects the material using a plan from the Dodge system. However, the customer uses inspection level III and tightened inspection with the same AQL.

(a) Find the acceptance criteria for both plans.

(b) Compute the probability that a lot with 3.5% nonconforming will be accepted by both plans consecutively.

15-34 A purchaser of steel rods uses a chain sampling acceptance plan, ChSP-1, since only a limited amount of inspection is possible. The plan in use requires that five rods from each lot be inspected. If no defective rods are found, the lot is accepted. If one defective is found, the lot is accepted only if the four previous lot samples inspected contained no defectives. Otherwise, the lot is rejected. If the lots received are 6% defective, determine the probability of accepting any given lot.

15-35 A Chain Sampling Plan (ChSP-1) is used by a vendor to approve material for shipment. The plan in use requires that three items be inspected from each lot to be shipped. If no defectives are found in a lot, then that lot is approved. If one is found, the lot is approved only if no defectives were found in the previous five lots. Otherwise, the lot is rejected. Determine the OC curve for this plan using product qualities of 0.1%, 1.0%, 3.0%, 5.0%, 10.0%, and 25.0% defective material. Is this a Type A or Type B OC curve?

SIXTEEN

ACCEPTANCE INSPECTION FOR CONTINUOUS PRODUCTION

Multi-level continuous sampling plans ... offer some important advantages. The fact that it is not necessary to accumulate a lot before making a decision is highly advantageous for large and expensive items. The production organization can deliver products more rapidly. Less storage space is required and, as long as the quality is good, both the producer and the consumer save on the inspection cost. On the other hand, as soon as the quality gets worse than the AOQL, the rate of inspection increases rapidly. Thus, there is a better chance of detecting causes of defects soon after they occur than if the product were accumulated for lot-by-lot acceptance provided corrective action is initiated as soon as the inspection rate increases. The quality control function can be of more assistance to the production organization by keeping it informed currently regarding the status of the product and by assisting it in corrective action to eliminate causes of defects. (Many of the above points are true for all types of continuous sampling plans.)†

Dodge's AOQL Plan for Continuous Production—CSP–1

The earliest acceptance/rectification plan for application to continuous production was one described by Dodge in 1943. Where production is continuous, the formation of inspection lots for lot-by-lot acceptance is somewhat artificial. Moreover, where conveyor lines are used, it may be impracticable or unduly costly to form inspection lots. Dodge explained his procedure (subsequently referred to as CSP-1) as follows:‡

---

† " Multi-level Continuous Sampling Procedures and Tables for Inspection by Attributes," Inspection and Quality Control Handbook (Interim) H 106, Office of the Assistant Secretary of Defense (Supply and Logistics), Washington, D.C., 1958.

‡ H. F. DODGE, A Sampling Inspection Plan for Continuous Production, *The Annals of Mathematical Statistics*, vol. 14, no. 3, pp. 264–279, September, 1943. H. F. DODGE, Sampling Plans for Continuous Production, *Industrial Quality Control*, vol. 4, no. 3, pp. 5–9, November, 1947. Both of these articles have been reprinted in *Journal of Quality Technology*, vol. 9, no. 3, July, 1977.

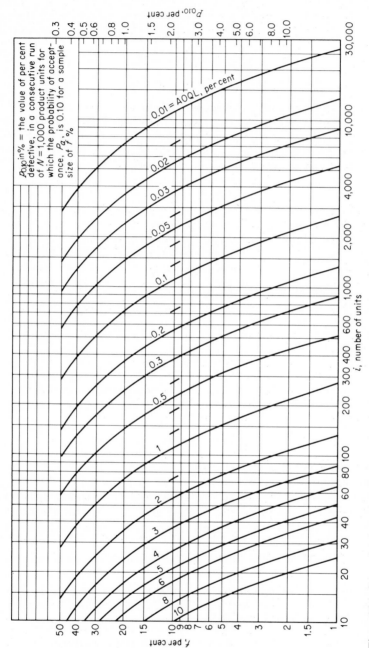

Figure 16-1 Curves for determining values of f and i for a given value of AOQL in Dodge's plan for continuous production CSP-1. *(Reproduced by permission from H. F. Dodge, A Sampling Inspection Plan for Continuous Production,"The Annals of Mathematical Statistics," vol. 14, pp. 264–729, September, 1943.)*

Within the figure:

$p_{0.10}$% = the value of per cent defective, in a consecutive run of $N = 1,000$ product units for which the probability of acceptance, P_a, is 0.10 for a sample size of f %

$p_{0.10}$, per cent

0.01 = AOQL, per cent

i, number of units

f, per cent

(a) At the outset, inspect 100% of the units consecutively as produced and continue such inspection until *i* units in succession are found clear of defects.

(b) When *i* units in succession are found clear of defects, discontinue 100% inspection, and inspect only a fraction *f* of the units, selecting individual sample units one at a time from the flow of product, in such a manner as to assure an unbiased sample.

(c) If a sample unit is found defective, revert immediately to a 100% inspection of succeeding units and continue until again *i* units in succession are found clear of defects, as in paragraph (a).

(d) Correct or replace, with good units, all defective units found.

Figure 16-1 gives the necessary information for the selection of such a plan for any desired AOQL. As an example, suppose the desired AOQL is 2%, and it is desired to establish a plan that calls for inspection of 1 piece out of every 20 pieces from the conveyor belt. Then *f*, the fraction inspected, is $\frac{1}{20}$ or 0.05 or 5%. In Fig. 16-1, find the value of *i* corresponding to an *f* of 5% on the curve for an AOQL of 2%. This *i* = 76. The acceptance plan is then as follows:

1. Inspect all the units consecutively as produced until 76 units in succession are free from defects.
2. As soon as 76 successive units are free from defects, inspect a sample consisting of only one unit out of every twenty. Accept all the product as long as the sample is free from defects.
3. Whenever one of these sample units is found defective, resume 100% inspection until 76 units in succession have again been found free from defects. Then resume sampling inspection.

The Dodge-Torrey Modifications of Continuous Sampling Plan 1

H. F. Dodge and Miss M. N. Torrey have developed two modifications of CSP-1. These are referred to as CSP-2 and CSP-3, respectively.† They describe CSP-2 as follows:

> Plan CSP-2 differs from Plan CSP-1 in that, once sampling inspection is started, 100% inspection is not invoked when each defect is found but is invoked only if a second defect occurs in the next k or less sample units. In other words, if two defects observed during sampling are separated by k or less good inspected units, 100% inspection is invoked. Otherwise sampling is continued.

Although the factor k might conceivably be assigned any value, the only CSP-2 plans prepared for use have been those in which k = *i*. Table 16-1 gives

---

† H. F. DODGE and M. N. TORREY, Additional Continuous Sampling Inspection Plans, *Industrial Quality Control*, vol. 7, no. 5, pp. 7–12, March, 1951 and reprinted in *Journal of Quality Technology*, vol. 9, no. 3, July, 1977. Plans CSP-1 and CSP-2 were adopted for procurement purposes by the Department of Defense and published in "Single Level Continuous Inspection Procedures and Quality Control Handbook Tables for Inspection by Attributes," Inspection and Quality Control Handbook (Interim) H 107, Office of the Assistant Secretary of Defense (Supply and Logistics), Washington, D.C., 1959.

Table 16-1 Comparison of value of i for various AOQL's in CSP-1 and CSP-2 for 5% and 10% sampling inspection (assuming $i = k$ in CSP-2)

AOQL, %	$f = 5\%$		$f = 10\%$	
	i in CSP-1	$i\ (= k)$ in CSP-2	i in CSP-1	$i\ (= k)$ in CSP-2
0.3	510	650	370	490
0.5	305	390	220	290
1	150	195	108	147
2	76	96	55	72
3	49	64	36	48
4	37	48	27	36
5	29	38	21	29
6	24	31	17	23
8	18	23	13	17
10	14	18	10	14

values of i in CSP-1 and CSP-2 using 5% and 10% samples and various AOQL values. These values for CSP-2 were obtained from a graph similar to Fig. 16-1 given in the Dodge-Torrey article.

Consider the application of CSP-2 when f is 5% and the AOQL is 2%. Table 16-1 gives $i = 96$. The acceptance plan is then as follows:

1. Inspect all the units consecutively as produced until 96 units in succession are free from defects.
2. As soon as 96 successive units are free from defects, inspect a sample consisting of only 1 out of every 20. Accept all the product as long as the sample is free from defects.
3. If one defective is found in this sampling, continue sampling inspection for the time being. However, if a second sample defective is found within the next 96 samples, resume 100% inspection immediately. Continue 100% inspection until 96 units in succession have been found free from defects. Then resume sampling under the foregoing rules.

Plan CSP-3 is a refinement of CSP-2 to provide greater protection against a sudden run of bad quality. When one sample defective is found, the next four units from the production line are inspected. If none of these are defective, the sampling procedure is continued as in CSP-2. If one of the four units is defective, 100% inspection is resumed at once and continued under the rules of CSP-2. In CSP-3, the value of i used for a given f and AOQL is the same as in CSP-2. Figure 16-2 shows an abbreviated flow process chart of the operation of the CSP-1, CSP-2, and CSP-3 plans.

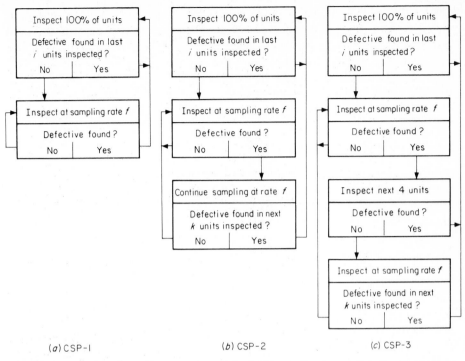

(*a*) CSP-I   (*b*) CSP-2   (*c*) CSP-3

Figure 16-2 Flow Process Chart for Dodge and Dodge-Torrey Continuous Sampling Plans CSP-1, CSP-2, and CSP-3.

Multilevel Continuous Sampling Plans

Sometimes it is desired to start any sampling inspection with a relatively large fraction sampled, such as $\frac{2}{3}$, $\frac{1}{2}$, or $\frac{1}{3}$. In such cases, economies can be obtained by permitting a subsequent change to a smaller sampling fraction whenever the quality observed on the initial sampling inspection turns out to be good enough. To secure these economies and to obtain certain other advantages, multilevel continuous sampling schemes have been developed that stipulate two or more different sampling fractions and give rules for shifting back and forth among the stipulated fractions.

One particular type of multilevel plan was developed and analyzed by Lieberman and Solomon.† Just as in the CSP plans described, the Lieberman-Solomon plans start with 100% inspection which continues until i nondefective units have been found in succession. Then sampling inspection is initiated with a fraction f inspected. If i nondefective units in succession are found under this sampling inspection, subsequent inspection is at the fraction f^2. Another i nondefectives in a

† G. J. LIEBERMAN and HERBERT SOLOMON, Multi-level Continuous Sampling Plans, *The Annals of Mathematical Statistics*, vol. 26, pp. 686–704, 1955.

row qualify for inspection at f^3, and so on. When a defective is found, inspection is shifted back to the next lower level. Any number of levels may be provided from two to an infinite number. The Lieberman-Solomon article provides a graph similar to Fig. 16-1 for two-level plans and gives approximate formulas for the relationship among f, i, and AOQL for plans with more than two levels. Bowker and Lieberman[†] give graphs similar to Fig. 16-1 for two-level, three-level, four-level, and infinite-level plans.

A Convenient Source for Multilevel Plans

In 1956, under a contract with the U.S. Air Force, Stanford University's Department of Industrial Engineering developed a proposed AMC Manual 74 entitled "Multi-level Continuous Sampling Acceptance Plans for Attributes." With minor additions and deletions of certain plans, this set of plans was adopted by the Air Force and later published by the U.S. Department of Defense as "Inspection and Quality Control Handbook (Interim) H 106, Multi-level Continuous Sampling Procedures and Tables for Inspection by Attributes." Table 16-2 combines the plans given in these two pamphlets. (H 106 added plans for AOQL values of 0.35, 0.15, and 0.10% and deleted those for 20 and 4%; plans for $f = \frac{2}{3}$ were shown in the proposed AMC Manual but not in H 106.)

The plans in these two pamphlets are based on the Lieberman-Solomon type of procedure combined with the special feature of the Dodge-Torrey plan CSP-3, namely, the inspection of the next four units whenever a defective is found. Figure 16-3, reproduced from H 106, illustrates the general features of all these plans by giving specific instructions for the operation of a three-level plan using an f of $\frac{1}{2}$.

Selection and Operation of a Multilevel Continuous Sampling Plan

Three decisions must be made in choosing a plan from Table 16-2. The AOQL and f must be selected, and it must be decided how many levels will be permitted. Assume that a three-level plan is desired with an AOQL of 2.0% and an f of $\frac{1}{2}$. Table 16-2 gives $i = 40$ for such a plan.

We may use Fig. 16-3 to see how this plan will operate. There will first be 100% inspection until 40 consecutive nondefective units are found. Then sampling inspection will start with half the units inspected. If all goes well and the next 40 sample units are nondefective, sampling will then be applied to $\frac{1}{4}$ of the units. If another 40 consecutive nondefective sample units occur, sampling inspection will be applied to $\frac{1}{8}$ of the units. Inspection of $\frac{1}{8}$ will continue indefinitely until a defective is found.

Figure 16-3 also shows the operating rules whenever a defective unit is found under sampling inspection. One hundred per cent inspection is applied to the next 4 units, with the state described as $1R$, $2R$, or $3R$ depending on the sampling rate

---

† A. H. BOWKER and G. J. LIEBERMAN, "Engineering Statistics," 2 ed., pp. 553–555, Prentice-Hall, Inc., Englewood Cliffs, N.J., 1972.

Table 16-2 Values of i for multilevel continuous sampling plans

[These values are taken in part from U.S. Department of Defense's "Inspection and Quality Control Handbook (Interim) H 106 (31 October 1958)" and in part from the Stanford University Department of Industrial Engineering's "Proposed AMC Manual 74 (15 June 1956)"]

AOQL, % defective	For f = 1/2					For f = 1/3					For f = 2/3		
	k = 1	k = 2	k = 3	k = 4	k = 5	k = 1	k = 2	k = 3	k = 4	k = 5	k = 1	k = 2	k = 3
20.0	*	*	*	*	*	*	*	4	5	6	*	*	*
15.0	*	*	*	4	5	*	4	6	7	8	*	*	*
10.0	*	4	6	8	9	*	7	10	12	13	*	*	*
7.5	*	6	9	11	13	6	11	14	16	18	*	*	*
5.0	5	11	15	18	20	10	18	22	25	27	*	5	8
4.0	7	14	19	22	25	14	23	29	32	34	*	7	11
3.0	11	20	26	31	34	19	32	39	43	46	5	11	16
2.0	18	31	40	47	51	31	48	59	66	71	9	18	25
1.5	25	43	55	63	69	42	66	80	89	95	13	25	34
1.0	39	65	83	95	104	64	100	120	134	142	21	39	52
0.75	54	88	112	128	140	87	134	161	179	191	30	53	71
0.50	82	132	168	193	210	133	202	243	269	287	46	80	107
0.35	119	197	241	275	302	190	290	349	386	408	96	164	217
0.25	167	269	337	386	422	269	406	488	540	576			
0.15	218	446	564	636	706	450	680	815	903	960			
0.10	421	675	847	969	1,059	677	1,022	1,224	1,354	1,443			

* Sampling plans not available for values of i less than 4.

481

FLOW PROCESS CHART FOR MULTILEVEL CONTINUOUS SAMPLING PLANS

$$f = 1/2 \quad k = 3$$

100% level

| Inspect 100% of the units in the order produced. |

If i consecutive units are found to be free of defectives, shift to Level No.1.

If a defective is found among the 4 inspected units, shift to 100% inspection.

| Sampling rate Level No.1 |
| Inspect at rate $f = 1/2$ |

If a defective is found while sampling at rate $f = 1/2$, shift to State 1R.

| **State 1R** |
| Inspect next 4 units following the defective found. |

| **State 1*** |
| Resume inspection at rate $f = 1/2$ |

If the 4 inspected units are found to be free of defectives, shift to State 1*.

If a defective is found after resuming inspection at rate $f = 1/2$, shift to 100% inspection.

If i inspected units are found to be free of defectives, shift to Level No. 2.

If $i-4$ inspected units are found to be free of defectives, shift to Level No. 2.

If a defective is found among the 4 inspected units, shift to State 1R.

| Sampling rate Level No.2 |
| Inspect at rate $f^2 = 1/4$ |

If a defective is found while sampling at rate $f^2 = 1/4$, shift to State 2R.

| **State 2R** |
| Inspect next 4 units following the defective found. |

| **State 2*** |
| Resume inspection at rate $f^2 = 1/4$ |

If the 4 inspected units are found to be free of defectives, shift to State 2*.

If a defective is found after resuming inspection at rate $f^2 = 1/4$, shift to State 1R.

If i inspected units are found to be free of defectives, shift to Level No. 3.

If $i-4$ inspected units are found to be free of defectives, shift to Level No.3.

If a defective is found among the 4 inspected units, shift to State 2R.

| Sampling rate Level No.3 |
| Inspect at rate $f^3 = 1/8$ |

If a defective is found while sampling at rate $f^3 = 1/8$, shift to State 3R.

| **State 3R** |
| Inspect next 4 units following the defective found. |

| **State 3*** |
| Resume inspection at rate $f^3 = 1/8$ |

If the 4 inspected units are found to be free of defectives, shift to State 3*.

If a defective is found after resuming inspection at rate $f^3 = 1/8$, shift to State 2R.

If $i-4$ inspected units are found to be free of defectives, shift to Level No. 3.

Figure 16-3 Example of rules for operating the multilevel continuous sampling plans of Table 16-2, assuming a three-level plan with $f = \frac{1}{2}$. (*Reproduced from "Multi-level Continuous Sampling Procedures and Tables for Inspection by Attributes," Inspection and Quality Control Handbook (Interim) H 106, Office of the Assistant Secretary of Defense (Supply and Logistics), Washington, D.C., 1958.*)

that has been in effect. If there are no defectives in these four units, sampling inspection continues at the previous rate, $\frac{1}{2}, \frac{1}{4},$ or $\frac{1}{8}$ as the case may be. If a defective is found in the 4 units, there is a shift to 100% inspection if sampling has been at rate $\frac{1}{2}$ or to 4-unit inspection with state $1R$ or $2R$, respectively, if sampling has been at the rate $\frac{1}{4}$ or $\frac{1}{8}$.

Incentives for Quality Improvement under Continuous Sampling Plans

Example 13-1 described how lot-by-lot AOQL plans were used to stimulate quality improvement in a particular case. Similar types of incentive may be incorporated into continuous sampling AOQL plans. Dodge comments on this point as follows:†

> These plans have been used rather extensively and found most effective when administered in such a way as to provide an incentive to clear faults in process promptly. Such an incentive may be provided, for example, by requiring the production department to perform the necessary 100% inspections when defects are found. To this end, the following administrative procedure has met with good success. A regularly assigned process inspector performs all sampling inspections required; if additional assistance is needed when it becomes necessary to revert to 100% inspection or in performing the initial 100% inspections required, the process inspector notifies the foreman in charge of the production line; the foreman must then immediately assign temporary inspectors who are acceptable to the process inspector and who work under the jurisdiction and supervision of the senior process inspector on the line; when sampling inspection is reinstated the temporary inspectors return to their regular assignments.

There may be special incentive aspects of multilevel schemes owing to the fact that some producers gain satisfaction by qualifying for inspection at one of the reduced levels. This point is illustrated in Example 16-1.

Example 16-1 Quality improvement resulting from nonfinancial incentives created by a multilevel continuous sampling plan *Facts of the case under* 100% *inspection* A manufacturer was the sole producer of a certain complex product for which there was only one customer. A few of these products were completed each working day. The contract for the manufacture of this product continued throughout several years.

At many points in the production operation, the manufacturer conducted acceptance inspection of components and subassemblies. The manufacturer's final inspection consisted of a performance test involving a check on many of the specified quality characteristics. This test was carried out on 100% of the product. In a number of cases, this test disclosed the need for adjustment of the product or replacement of certain components. After such adjustments or replacements were made, the product was given another performance test.

As soon as a product passed the manufacturer's final performance test, it

† In his 1947 article in *Industrial Quality Control, op. cit.*

was delivered to the customer. Immediately after this delivery, the customer carried out a performance test that was almost the same as the one made by the manufacturer. Although most of the products passed the customer's test, there were occasional failures that were returned to the manufacturer. The performance test was a fairly complicated and costly matter.

Occasional items of this complex product developed certain serious difficulties in their early weeks of use by the customer. It seemed evident that the difficulties were due to failure to conform to certain design specifications; the 200% final inspection had not been fully effective in removing all defects.

Consequences of adoption of a multilevel continuous sampling plan For his acceptance testing, the customer initiated a three-level sampling plan with an f of $\frac{1}{2}$. The plan was similar to the one illustrated in Fig. 16-3. Apparently the customer adopted this plan chiefly because of the high cost of the 100% inspection; it was thought that, if the manufacturer could qualify for sampling inspection, this considerable cost could be reduced. Initially, the manufacturing company made no changes in any of its production or inspection procedures.

After a short time the manufacturer qualified for customer testing of only half of the product. This event, reflecting favorably on the quality of the product, was noted with approval by the top management of the manufacturing company. When, somewhat later, the customer reverted to 100% testing because of two successive failures of product on the customer's test, the top management personnel were extremely unhappy.

The consequence of this unhappiness was a great tightening up of the manufacturer's inspection procedures on components and subassemblies, accompanied by the application of somewhat more care in the manufacturer's final performance test. Strong efforts were made to diagnose and correct certain production troubles that seemed to be causing quality variation. Soon the manufacturer qualified again for customer testing of half the product. After a while, the good record on the customer's test led to qualification for testing of one-fourth. Before the end of the contract, testing was on only one-eighth, the smallest fraction permissible under the three-level scheme.

Varying reactions to the multilevel plan The different reactions of some of the personnel in the customer's and manufacturer's organizations were interesting to outside observers of this application of multilevel continuous sampling. The persons who were most pleased seemed to be the users of the complex product in the customer's organization. There was no question that these users ultimately received better product under the sampling scheme because of the improvement in the quality of the product submitted by the manufacturer.

In contrast, some of the inspection executives in the manufacturer's organization privately expressed their displeasure over the customer's use of the multilevel plan. As far as outsiders could judge, this displeasure was due to the top management pressure on the company's inspection executives not to permit a reversion to 100% inspection or to a lower level of sampling inspection than the one in current operation. (The inspection executives felt, justifiably, that the pressure should have been directed as much to the production departments as to the inspection department.)

A simple but ingenious mechanical device had been built to randomize the customer's choice of the items to be tested under sampling inspection. The customer's personnel who conducted the testing were greatly intrigued by the operation of this device. Their jobs seemed to have been made more interesting to them by this simple example of the laws of chance operating to control certain aspects of their daily activities. Moreover, it was evident that they did somewhat more thorough and careful testing under the sampling inspection than they had done under 100% inspection.

The general opinion in the manufacturer's organization seemed to be that the manufacturer's total cost on the contract had been increased a bit as a result of the customer's change from 100% inspection to multilevel sampling. However, the company's top management seemed to feel that this adverse effect on cost was more than offset by the better reputation of the manufacturer's product with the ultimate users in the customer's organization. The top management personnel seemed to feel that this better reputation put the manufacturing company in a more favorable position to receive future contracts from this customer and others.

From the viewpoint of the customer's top management, the effects of having introduced the multilevel scheme were entirely good because testing costs were reduced and incoming quality was improved. The quality improvement was somewhat of an unexpected dividend to the customer; the sole objective in introducing the scheme had been to reduce testing costs.

The MIL-STD-1235 System for Sampling from Continuous Production

In 1959, just less than a year after publication of Handbook H 106 for multilevel continuous sampling, Handbook H 107 was published consisting of three single-level continuous sampling plans.† The set included Dodge's CSP-1 and CSP-2 and a plan developed for the U.S. Navy designated CSP-A. Most of the operating procedures of CSP-1 and CSP-2 were identical with those previously discussed with the single exception of a provision for terminating acceptance altogether when 100% (screening) inspection continues for too great a period of time. In 1962 the Handbooks H 106 and H 107 were amalgamated into a single document designated MIL-STD-1235(ORD).‡ The main procedural features of these plans have already been presented. The multilevel continuous sampling plans from H 106 were given the code designation CSP-M.

---

† "Single-Level Continuous Sampling Procedures and Tables for Inspection by Attributes," Inspection and Quality Control Handbook (Interim) H 107, Office of the Assistant Secretary of Defense (Supply and Logistics), Washington, D.C., April, 1959.

‡ "Single- and Multi-Level Continuous Sampling Procedures and Tables for Inspection by Attributes," MIL-STD-1235(ORD), Department of the Army, Washington, D.C., July, 1962.

Administrative Procedures of MIL-STD-1235(ORD)

Application of this standard is restricted to product flowing in assembly-line fashion, although there is no requirement that it actually be flowing on a conveyor system. Since inspection alternates between screening and sampling, ample physical facilities and personnel must be available to permit rapid 100% inspection when necessary.

In addition, very stringent homogeneity requirements are placed on the production system. All product units must be made in accordance with the same specifications and drawings under stable conditions of production that might be realized by a process in statistical control. Any unusual interruption in the production process, such as the change of material source or change of tooling or any discontinuance of manufacture beyond that resulting from the end of a shift, day, or week, is assumed to terminate a production run under homogeneous conditions. All schemes except CSP-A may operate continuously within the limitations defined as homogeneity. The CSP-A plans begin at the start and terminate at the end of a *production interval,* usually a shift or day.

The basic measure of effectiveness of CSP's is usually the AOQ function with indexing of sets of plans based on the AOQL. However, in order to make administration of the system consistent with the much-used ABC-STD-105, the CSP-1, CSP-2, and CSP-A plans were cross-referenced in terms of AQL. The plans in MIL-STD-1235(ORD) are therefore indexed by both AQL and AOQL.†

A system of code letters is specified for the selection of sampling plans. Code letter designation is set by the estimated number of units in a production interval. Thus the matrix format by AQL and number of units originated in MIL-STD-105 is carried over intact to MIL-STD-1235(ORD).

Inspection Requirements

Another feature of the military standard is the specification of three classes of inspection: screening inspection; sampling inspection; and verification inspection. Screening and sampling inspection are employed in the general operation of all of the sampling plans. This military standard permits both screening and sampling inspection to be done by the producer, subject to the consent of the consumer.

Verification inspection, which is performed at the option of the consumer, is intended as a double-check on the effectiveness of both screening crews and sampling inspectors. It may be performed by either the producer or consumer and proceeds at some sampling rate f of the items actually inspected under screening or sampling. The sampling rate f may be that designated by the particular sampling plan in use or some other rate acceptable to the consumer. All acceptance of

† For a more complete discussion of the evolution of the plans and their indexing as contained in MIL-STD-1235(ORD), see R. A. BANZHOF and R. M. BRUGGER, "Reviews of Standards and Specifications—MIL-STD-1235(ORD), Single- and Multi-Level Continuous Sampling Procedures and Tables for Inspection by Attributes," *Journal of Quality Technology,* vol. 2, no. 1, January, 1970.

product is terminated, until an improvement in product quality and inspection effectiveness is demonstrated, if one critical defect is found, or two major or minor defects are found separated by fifty or less good units, while screening inspection is in force. If sampling inspection is in force and verification inspection results in finding the defects listed, inspection reverts to screening. Other rules for the termination of acceptance are discussed in the next article.

Since the plans assume sampling from a continuous flow of product from a statistically controlled process, maintenance of the order of production is vital. If acceptance of the product is terminated, all units in process must be screened by the producer prior to resubmittal for acceptance. Resubmitted lots of product are inspected separately from the flow of original product and are usually inspected in accordance with a lot-by-lot acceptance plan.

Inspection for critical defects is restricted to CSP-1 and CSP-A.

MIL-STD-1235(ORD) Continuous Sampling Schemes

Since the basic operational procedures of three of the four plans have been presented, it is only necessary to present those features that are unique to the military standard.

Since inspection under each plan begins with 100% inspection, it is quite conceivable that it would never switch to sampling if the process average fraction defective is sufficiently high. In order to force adjustment of the process to an acceptable level, each sampling scheme is provided with a table of inspection limit values. If, while on 100% inspection, a total of L or more units are inspected without having switched to sampling inspection, acceptance of the product is suspended until the producer corrects the cause of the high rate of defectives. A separate table of values of L is provided for each sampling scheme.

CSP-A, not here reproduced, is procedurally identical to CSP-1 with two exceptions. First, a selected plan must begin with 100% inspection at the start of each production interval, usually a day or shift. Thus the scheme holds a tighter constraint on the homogeneity requirements previously discussed than do the other schemes. Second, in addition to specifying values for i and f, a third criterion specifies that no more than a total defects or defective units may be accumulated during the production interval. If $a + 1$ are found, acceptance of product is suspended until the cause of the high rate of defectives is corrected. Values of i and a are tabulated for each plan.

CSP-1 and CSP-A are the only schemes that may be used to inspect for critical defects. The identification of a critical defect during sampling inspection requires switching to 100% inspection effective with the last good unit inspected prior to finding the defective unit. In all other cases, the switch to 100% inspection is effective with the next unit in order of production after the defective unit.

CSP-A is the only scheme that provides for switching to tightened or reduced inspection. Switching to tightened inspection may be required at the discretion of the consumer if two consecutive production intervals had at least one inspection termination each. Usually switching to tightened inspection requires the use of a sampling plan whose AQL or AOQL is one step smaller than that required under normal inspection. If the plan is being used to inspect for critical defects, the tightened inspection plan calls for a value of i twice that used for normal inspection. Resumption of normal inspection is at the discretion of the consumer.

Inspection may switch to a reduced level by changing to a sampling frequency, f, one-fifth that of the normal inspection plan at the discretion of the consumer if:

(a) *The preceding ten full production intervals have been under normal inspection and without any inspection suspensions.*
(b) *The estimated process average (usually the total number of defectives found divided by the total number of items inspected accumulated over both screening and sampling) is less than*

$$AQL - 3 \sqrt{\frac{AQL(1 - AQL)}{number\ inspected}}$$

where AQL is expressed as a fraction defective rather than as a percentage.
(c) *Production is at a steady rate.*

Sampling reverts back to normal inspection if:

(a) *Inspection is suspended.*
(b) *The estimated process average rises above the AQL.*
(c) *The customer deems that normal inspection frequency should be reinstated.*

Reduced inspection may not be instituted for sampling of critical defects. These rules for reduced inspection correspond with those employed in MIL-STD-105 prior to Revision D.

AOQ Functions for Continuous Sampling Schemes

The primary measure of effectiveness of continuous sampling schemes is the AOQ function, or, more specifically, the AOQL. The bulk of MIL-STD-1235(ORD) is composed of characteristic curves, plots of per cent of product accepted on a sampling basis versus per cent defective of submitted product, for CSP-1, CSP-2, and CSP-A, and AOQ functions for CSP-1, CSP-2, and CSP-M.

Rather than attempt to reproduce all or part of these functions, approximate general formulas for the AOQ function are given for CSP-1, CSP-2, and CSP-M. Since CSP-A is procedurally very close to CSP-1, the formula for CSP-1 may be used to calculate values of AOQ for CSP-A. Given an estimate of the process average, p', the following formulas may be used to determine the approximate average outgoing quality of product:†

$$\text{CSP-1: AOQ} = \frac{p(1-f)q^{i-1}}{f+(1-f)q^{i-1}}$$

where p = fraction defective
$\quad q = (1-p)$

$$\text{CSP-2:} \quad \text{AOQ} = \frac{p(1-f)(2q^i - q^{2i})}{fq + (1-f)(2q^i - q^{2i})}$$

$$\text{CSP-M:} \quad \text{AOQ} = p \frac{\displaystyle\sum_{j=1}^{k}\left(\frac{1}{f_j}-1\right)\left(\frac{q^i}{1-q^i}\right)^j}{\displaystyle\sum_{j=0}^{k}\left(\frac{1}{f_j}\right)\left(\frac{q^i}{1-q^i}\right)^j}$$

where j = indexes over the number of inspection levels in the plan
$\quad k$ = maximum number of inspection levels in the plan

Further Comment on Continuous Sampling Plans

Various other types of continuous sampling AOQL plans may be developed. Some plans start with sampling inspection rather than with 100% inspection.‡ These plans, in effect, give a process credit for such good quality as has been shown in past samples and base the decision regarding the shift from sampling inspection to 100% inspection on cumulative evidence from past samples.

As in all acceptance/rectification schemes, a necessary condition for the successful use of continuous sampling schemes is that the submitted quality should be good enough for most product to be passed without screening. The sampling is intended to give protection against runs of bad quality. If the protection against short runs of bad quality (so-called "spotty" quality) is to be satisfactory, the sample percentage f should not be too low. The relative weakness of small values of f in this respect is brought out by the scale on the right-hand side of Fig. 16-1 showing values of $p_{0.10}$.

Mention should be made of one practical difference between lot-by-lot acceptance/rectification schemes and most continuous sampling schemes. In lot-

---

† R. A. BANZHOF and R. M. BRUGGER, "MIL-STD-1235(ORD), Single- and Multi-Level Continuous Sampling Procedures and Tables for Inspection by Attributes," Reviews of Standards and Specifications department in *Journal of Quality Technology*, vol. 2, no. 1, January, 1970.

‡ M. A. GIRSHICK, "A Sequential Inspection Plan for Quality Control." This was issued by the Applied Mathematics and Statistics Laboratory, Stanford University, Stanford, Calif., as Technical Report No. 16, 1954.

ABRAHAM WALD and J. WOLFOWITZ, Sampling Inspection Plans for Continuous Production Which Insure a Prescribed Limit on the Outgoing Quality, *The Annals of Mathematical Statistics*, vol. 16, pp. 30–49, 1945.

by-lot schemes, an unfavorable sample from a lot results in the screening inspection of that particular lot. In continuous sampling, a bad sample calls for the screening of *subsequent* production. In effect, the sample is considered as representative of the production process, and 100% inspection is applied to later articles from the same process. In some instances, where the physical conditions of production permit, a modification of continuous sampling procedures is made to require screening inspection applied to a specified number of units immediately preceding a defective sample. Such is the case with CSP-A in MIL-STD-1235.

PROBLEMS

16-1 In Dodge's CSP-1 it is desired to apply sampling inspection to 1 piece out of every 15 and to maintain an AOQL of 2%. What should be the value of i?

Answer: 68.

16-2 In the Dodge-Torrey CSP-2 it is desired to apply sampling inspection to 1 piece out of every 10 and to maintain an AOQL of 3%. What should be the value of i? Assume that $i = k$.

Answer: 48.

16-3 In Dodge's CSP-1 it is desired to apply sampling inspection to 1 piece out of every 8 and to maintain an AOQL of 1%. What should be the value of i?

16-4 In the Dodge-Torrey CSP-3 it is desired to apply sampling inspection to 1 piece out of every 10 and to maintain an AOQL of 4%. Prepare a flow chart of the operation of this plan.

16-5 In Dodge's CSP-1, it is desired to apply sampling inspection to 1 piece out of every 50 and to maintain an AOQL of 5%. What should be the value of i? Prepare a flow chart of the operation of this plan.

16-6 In Dodge's CSP-1, it is desired to apply sampling inspection to 15% of the product and to maintain an AOQL of 0.2%. Find the value of i to be used. Prepare a flow chart of the operation of this plan.

16-7 It is desired to apply continuous sampling inspection to 1 piece out of every 10 and to maintain a AOQL of 2%.

    (*a*) Find the value of i for applying Dodge's CSP-1.

    (*b*) Find the values of i and k for applying Dodge's CSP-2.

    (*c*) Prepare flow charts of the operation of these plans.

16-8 Select from Table 16-2 a four-level continuous sampling plan for an AOQL of 1.5% and an f of $\frac{1}{3}$. If a defective is found shortly after the third level is reached, describe how the plan would operate.

16-9 Select from Table 16-2 a three-level continuous sampling plan for an AOQL of 2.0% and an f of $\frac{1}{2}$. Prepare a flow chart of the operation of this plan.

16-10 Consider the question of the use of the plan selected in Problem 16-9 after the first defective has been found on the second inspection level.

    (*a*) What action is taken if the next two consecutive units inspected are both defective?

    (*b*) What action is taken if the next consecutive unit is defective and the following 4 consecutive units are all good?

    (*c*) What action is taken if the next 4 consecutive units are all good?

16-11 Select from Table 16-2 a two-level continuous sampling plan for an AOQL of 1.5% and an f of $\frac{2}{3}$. Give detailed rules for the operation of this plan up to the time when the first defective unit is found. Assume that the first defective is found shortly after the second level has been reached.

16-12 Answer questions (*a*), (*b*), and (*c*) of Problem 16-10 for the plan selected in Problem 16-11.

16-13 A certain manufacturing group decides to use a Dodge-Torrey CSP-2 sampling inspection plan on a line of small motors. It is decided to inspect 10% of the units when sampling and to maintain a desired AOQL of 1.0%.

(a) Find the appropriate values of i and k.

(b) Prepare a flow chart of the detailed operation of this plan.

16-14 Select from Table 16-1 a Dodge-Torrey CSP-3 plan for an AOQL of 2% and a 10% sampling rate. Determine the value of i and prepare a flow chart of the detailed operation of the plan.

16-15 In Dodge's CSP-1, it is desired to apply sampling to 1 item out of every 25 and maintain a 2% AOQL. What should be the value of i? Prepare a flow chart of the operation of this plan.

16-16 In Dodge's CSP-1, it is desired to apply sampling to 1 item out of every 5 and maintain a 2% AOQL. What should be the value of i? Comment on the differences between this 2% AOQL plan and that found in Problem 16-15.

16-17 Assume that the process in Problems 16-15 and 16-16 is generating 3% nonconforming product. What is the actual AOQ under each of these plans?

16-18 Sketch the AOQ curve for the plan found in Problem 16-3. Use values of p of 0, 0.005, 0.01, 0.015, and 0.02.

16-19 For the plan found in Problem 16-7, compute the AOQ when the process is generating 3% nonconforming product.

16-20 For the plan found in Problem 16-9, compute the AOQ when the process is generating 4% nonconforming product.

SEVENTEEN

ACCEPTANCE SAMPLING BY VARIABLES

I have never yet seen an inspection problem which would not benefit from the point of view that the product to be inspected was a frequency distribution.—G. D. Edwards

Some Advantages and Limitations of Acceptance Sampling by Variables

Most acceptance sampling is by attributes and will doubtless continue to be so. Nevertheless, the growth of knowledge of statistical quality control techniques has led to a considerable increase in the industrial use of acceptance sampling by variables. It seems likely that this tendency will continue.

One obvious limitation on the use of variables criteria in acceptance sampling is the fact that many quality characteristics are observable only as attributes. Where this is true, sampling by variables is out of the question. Nevertheless, it often turns out to be possible to devise methods of measurement in cases where at first glance it seems that inspection must be by attributes.

For those quality characteristics that can be measured, it is usually true that the cost of inspection per item is less by attributes than by variables. Often this is due to the greater economy of inspection methods using the go—not-go principle. Moreover, clerical costs are usually less with attributes inspection; it is less expensive to record merely the conformance or nonconformance to specifications than to record an actual measured value and to make computations using that value.

Perhaps the most serious limitation on the use of sampling by variables is the fact that acceptance criteria must be applied separately to each quality characteristic. This tends to increase the cost of acceptance inspection. For example, if 20 quality characteristics of a product are to be examined at a given inspection station, a single set of attributes sampling criteria can be applied to the acceptance decision. In contrast, if each characteristic is subject to variables inspection, 20 different sets of variables criteria must be used.

An additional limitation on certain types of variables criteria exists in that the computed protection against various percentages of defectives depends on an assumption regarding the form of the underlying frequency distribution of the quality characteristic. This limitation is discussed near the end of this chapter.

In spite of the foregoing limitations, acceptance sampling by variables is often preferable to acceptance sampling by attributes, particularly for those quality characteristics that are the source of troubles. Possibly only 2 of the 20 characteristics mentioned in the preceding paragraph may turn out to be troublesome. If so, it may be that variables criteria can be applied profitably to these even though attributes criteria are used for the remaining 18.

The great advantage of the use of acceptance sampling by variables is that more information is obtained about the quality characteristic in question. This may lead to a number of desirable results, as follows:

1. For a given sample size, better quality protection may usually be obtained with variables criteria than with attributes. Or, stated a little differently, for a given quality protection against various possible percentages of defectives (as reflected in the OC curve) smaller samples may be used with variables than with attributes.
2. The extent of conformance or nonconformance to the desired value of a quality characteristic is given weight where variables criteria are used. This may be important wherever there is a margin of safety in the design specifications or a twilight zone of values of the quality characteristic between clearly satisfactory and clearly unsatisfactory.
3. Variables information usually gives a better basis for guidance toward quality improvement.
4. Variables information may provide a better basis for giving weight to quality history in acceptance decisions.
5. Errors of measurement are more likely to be disclosed with variables information.

Some Different Types of Acceptance Criteria Involving Variables

There are many different ways in which the actual measured values of quality characteristics in a sample can be used to influence decisions on acceptance of submitted product. The following general classification of types of variables criteria is intended to provide a convenient basis for discussion of the subject:

1. Criteria in which the decision depends in some way on the frequency distribution of the sample. The Shainin Lot Plot is an example of this type of plan.
2. Criteria using a control chart for variables to divide a series of consecutive inspection lots into "grand lots" with acceptance criteria applied to each grand lot.
3. Criteria in which the decision on acceptance or rejection of a lot is based on the sample average alone. Plans using such criteria may be referred to as *known-sigma* plans or plans with *variability known*.

4. Criteria in which the decision is based on the sample average in combination with a measure of sample dispersion. Such plans may be referred to as *unknown-sigma* or as having *variability unknown.*

Sometimes there are legal or other reasons why variables criteria should not be used for lot rejection even though such criteria are appropriate for lot acceptance. This condition may lead to some combination of variables and attributes criteria. This topic is examined following the discussion of known-sigma and unknown-sigma plans.

Using Plotted Frequency Distributions in Acceptance Sampling

In the technical language of inspection, an article is *defective* if it fails to conform to specifications. A slight departure beyond specification limits makes the article defective; so, also, does a large departure beyond the limits. This definition of a defective gives no weight to the extent of the nonconformity to specifications.

Nevertheless, the extent of nonconformity may be a matter of great practical importance. Consider any measurable quality characteristic on which the designer has specified upper and lower limits. There frequently is a twilight zone of values just outside one or both specification limits within which it is satisfactory to accept a moderate percentage of "defective" articles.

In many manufacturing plants, it is common for some purchased lots to be rejected initially under the regular acceptance procedures and then finally to be accepted under some sort of material-review procedure. Sometimes there is a highly formalized procedure involving a material-review board; in other cases material review may be quite an informal matter, involving a decision by some one individual. In any event, the extent of nonconformity to specifications is usually given consideration in material-review decisions. Extra costs may be avoided and interruptions of production may be prevented by using material-review procedures to accept a product that is good enough for the purpose at hand, even though it is technically nonconforming to specifications.

Where sample frequency distributions for certain quality characteristics are plotted as part of the regular acceptance procedures, one objective usually is the provision of a more rational basis for material review. The frequency distribution is a great aid to judgment on the question of the extent of nonconformity to specifications.

Moreover, the frequency distribution has the advantage that it may disclose certain common types of departure from normality, such as skewed distributions, bimodal distributions, distributions with cutoff points, and distributions containing strays at some distance from the main distribution. The larger the sample, the better the chance to recognize such nonnormal distributions when they occur, and the less the danger that a sample really taken from a normal distribution will give a false indication of nonnormality.

Example 17-1 illustrates a common type of use of a frequency distribution on an informal basis with a good deal of judgment permitted in the acceptance decision.

Example 17-1 Acceptance decisions based on plotted frequency distributions

Facts of the case An electrical manufacturer purchased mica insulators from a number of different vendors. Shipments generally consisted of lots of 8,000 to 10,000 pieces. All vendors seemed to have some difficulty in meeting the dimensional specification on thickness.

The acceptance procedure involved measuring the thicknesses of a sample of 200 from each lot and plotting the frequency distribution on a tally sheet similar to the one shown in Fig. 2-1. The decision on acceptance or rejection was made by the quality control engineer after examining this tally sheet. No formal written criteria were established to govern this decision. Weight was given to the form of the frequency distribution, the number of items outside of specification limits, and the extent to which the nonconforming items failed to meet specifications. Consideration in the acceptance decision was also given to the number of items of this product in stock at the particular moment and the hazard that returning a lot to the vendor might interfere with production schedules.

The Shainin Lot Plot Method

This is a more formalized method of using a frequency distribution in receiving inspection to guide decisions on acceptance or rejection. This plan, also known as the Hamilton Standard Lot Plot Method, was developed by Dorian Shainin when he was Chief Inspector, Hamilton Standard, now a Division of United Technologies. A full description was given in an article in the July, 1950, issue of *Industrial Quality Control*.† Some later refinements were explained in a series of articles in the March, 1952, issue of the same journal.‡ The following brief discussion explains the general characteristics of the method but does not aim to reproduce the full directions for its use that are given in Shainin's 1950 article. (Reproduction of the entire 1950 article would require about 50 book-sized pages.)

In the Lot Plot method, the sample size always is 50. In the Hamilton Standard usage, random numbers were used in drawing the sample to ensure randomness in its selection. Figure 17-1 shows one version of the Lot Plot form. A check on the cell width used in the left-hand column of the form is obtained from the first 5 articles measured; if possible, twice the range of this set of 5 values should be from 7 to 16 cells.

---

† DORIAN SHAININ, The Hamilton Standard Lot Plot Method of Acceptance Sampling by Variables, *Industrial Quality Control*, vol. 7, no. 1, pp. 15–34, July, 1950. Copyright 1950, American Society for Quality Control, Inc.

‡ DORIAN SHAININ, Recent Lot Plot Experiences around the Country, *Industrial Quality Control*, vol. 8, no. 5, pp. 20–29, March, 1952.

R. L. ASHLEY, Modification of the Lot Plot Method of Acceptance Sampling, *Industrial Quality Control*, vol. 8, no. 5, pp. 30–31, March, 1952.

RICHARD WILSON, A Convenient Short Cut in the Use of Lot Plot, *Industrial Quality Control*, vol. 8, no. 5, pp. 32–33, March, 1952. Copyright 1952, American Society for Quality Control, Inc.

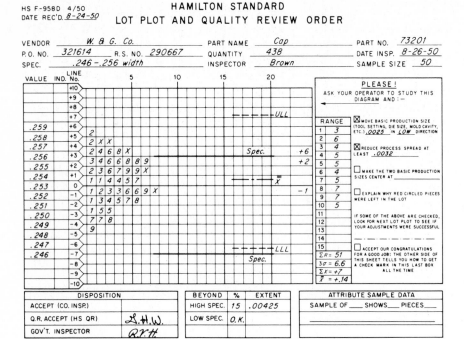

Figure 17-1 Example of Lot Plot form. (*Reproduced from Dorian Shainin, The Iron Age, October 12, 1950.*)

The sample is divided into 10 groups of 5 articles each for the purpose of recording the measured values in the Lot Plot form. For each article in the first group, the figure 1 is entered in the appropriate cell. For example, Fig. 17-1 indicates that the 5 measured values in the first group fell in the cells 254–253, 254–253, 253–252, 252–251, and 251–250. For each article in the second group, the figure 2 is entered in the appropriate cell, and so on. As each group of 5 is entered, the range of the group in cell units is entered in the "Range" column near the right-hand side of the form.

When the 50 measured values have been recorded, the next step is to compute the $\bar{X}$ of the sample and to estimate the 3σ value of the lot from the $\bar{R}$ of the 10 groups of 5 in the sample. In his 1952 article, Shainin explains the short-cut method used for computing $\bar{X}$ as follows:

"(a) Cut out the column of plus and minus line values from a blank Lot Plot form.
(b) Place this column to cover the line values of the Lot Plot so that the zero cell falls opposite the mode or longest horizontal row of entries.
(c) Note whether the +1 or −1 cell contains the most readings.
(d) Compare the quantities in these two cells by moving the cut column of paper horizontally to the right until the smaller of the two compared rows is just covered.

(e) Count the remaining uncovered squares in the partially covered cell row, multiply this count by the cell sign and value, and enter the result at the extreme right side of the grid in that cell row.

(f) Repeat using the +2 and −2 cells, and continue until only the zero cell remains.

(g) Total the results algebraically and enter the answer opposite "Totals" in the lower right-hand section of the Plot.

(h) Multiply this answer by 2 and point off 2 decimal places to the left.

(i) Enter this result in the ($\bar{\bar{X}} =$) space.

(j) Point off from the middle of the mode or peak cell row the portion of a cell found by step i, in the direction corresponding to the sign of the i value, and draw a horizontal line labeled $\bar{\bar{X}}$."

The 3σ value needed to estimate the position of the lot limits is computed as $1.3\bar{R}$. (Actually $3\bar{R}/d_2 = 1.29\bar{R}$ when n is 5; the 1.3 factor is used for ease of calculation.) As there are 10 values of R, it is merely necessary to add the R's and point over one decimal place to find $\bar{R}$; 0.3 of $\bar{R}$ is then added to find 3σ.

In Fig. 17-1, $\bar{\bar{X}}$ (in cell units) is 0.14, and 3σ (also in cell units) is 6.6. The lot limits, designated ULL and LLL, are drawn at a distance of 3σ on either side of $\bar{\bar{X}}$. In Fig. 17-1 it is evident that the spread of the process is somewhat greater than the spread of the specifications, and that the process is not centered midway between the specification limits.

The key figures to guide the quality review are those contained in the box in the center near the bottom of the Lot Plot form. This box gives an estimate of the extent to which the extreme values of the lot fall beyond the specification limits. The computed 3-sigma lot limits supply the basis for this estimate. The box also contains an estimate of the percentage of the lot beyond each specification limit. This latter estimate is made from a diagram based on a normal-curve-area table (such as Table A, App. 3).

Shainin has classified typical Lot Plots into eleven types, as shown in Fig. 17-2. The frequency distribution in Fig. 17-1 gives no grounds for suspicion of non-normality and is therefore treated as if the lot were normal. The rules for interpretation of nonnormal appearing Lot Plots are not reproduced here. Much of Shainin's 1950 article deals with detailed instructions for handling the various types of nonnormal Lot Plots. For a number of the types, special rules are required for estimating lot limits; examples of this are skewed Lot Plots (for example, type 5), Lot Plots indicating screening or cutoff points (for example, type 6), and bimodal Lot Plots (for example, type 7). Where lot limits fall outside of specification limits, the rules for action are influenced by the type of Lot Plot. In certain instances, doubtful Lot Plots lead to the use of AOQL attributes inspection. Special rules are given for the treatment of lots in which the Plots indicate strays (type 11).

The plotted frequency distributions in the Lot Plot method often provide a good diagnosis for quality troubles and thus lead to quality improvement. A copy of the Lot Plot form is always sent to the vendor. It will be noted that the

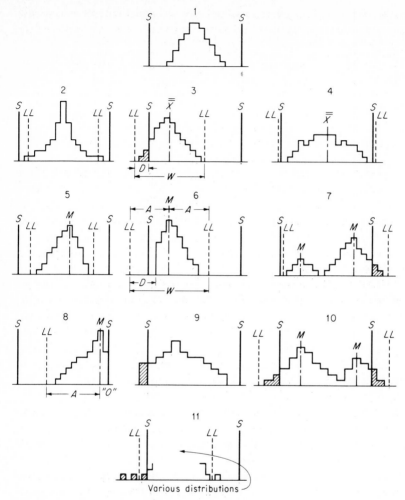

Figure 17-2 Eleven different types of lot plots. *(Reproduced from Dorian Shainin, "The Hamilton Standard Lot Plot Method of Acceptance Sampling by Variables," Industrial Quality Control, vol. 7, no. 1, pp. 15–34, July, 1950.)*

right-hand side of the form permits the inspector to check one of several types of comments regarding quality, filling in the necessary blanks when there are quality troubles. The reverse side of the Lot Plot form contains concise directions for a Sum and Range chart.

In his 1950 article Shainin made the following comment on this topic of vendor's quality improvement:

The initial use of Lot Plots will probably reveal only a few specifications running as well as the Type 1 situation—a normal shaped distribution included well within the specification limit. If such is the case and it is surprising to your organization, you should realize that by the use of proper cell widths, of a really representative or random sample, and by the elimination of flinching on the part of the inspector, you now have a picture of the condition of the lot that corresponds to the revelations brought to your eye by a microscope of the surface of an object.

The correct use by the supplier of Shewhart type control charts, of course, will bring specification after specification into line to give the inspector Type 1 Lot Plots. It is our experience, and that of several other concerns, that sending a copy of each Lot Plot to the supplier of the material also often results in an increasing frequency of Type 1 situations. By far the majority of our Plots are now of this type.

Some Comments on the Use of Plotted Distributions in Receiving Inspection

Example 17-1 described an informal use of frequency distributions in the inspection of purchased material. The original development of the Lot Plot technique was also aimed at receiving inspection. A common condition in such inspection is that the buyer does not know whether all the items in a lot were produced under the same essential conditions. Often, the items in an inspection lot come from two or more universes that have different values of $\bar{X}'$ or σ' or both. Such a mixing of universes may be due to a mixing of items from different production sources or to a mixing of articles made at different times by a single production source that has not been in statistical control. Moreover, the lot may have been given screening inspection by the vendor, and this inspection may have been effective or ineffective.

For these and other reasons, a quality characteristic of items in a purchased lot may have many different types of frequency distribution. As indicated in Fig. 17-2, some lots are bimodal, some are skewed, some are truncated with no strays, some are truncated with strays, and so on.

Under these common circumstances in receiving inspection, there are two possible major advantages from the use of plotted frequency distributions of important quality characteristics of samples, as follows:

1. The information gained from the frequency distributions may be fed back to vendors in a way that will cause substantial quality improvements and thus lead to the submission of lots that are satisfactory. The right-hand portion of Fig. 17-1 illustrated such a feedback; this point also was mentioned in the quotation from Shainin's 1950 article. Example 17-2 describes a case in which conditions were favorable to this type of vendor quality improvement.
2. There is better guidance to informal decisions regarding marginal lots—particularly decisions made in connection with material-review procedures. (In the original Lot Plot usage, unless a lot was accepted on the basis of the Lot Plot, it was submitted for a material-review decision. Often this decision gave weight not only to the plot for the lot under review but also to any evidence available in preceding plots from the same vendor.)

The most serious objections to the use of frequency distributions in acceptance inspection are related to the point that it is difficult to be sure about the form of the frequency distribution in a lot from inspecting a plotted frequency distribution from a moderate sized random sample, such as 50.† There often are false indications of the form of the distribution in the lot. The cell interval chosen may have a considerable influence on the appearance of a frequency distribution of a sample as small as 50. Moreover, in the Lot Plot technique it is necessary for the user to decide which one of the 11 types of plot (Fig. 17-2) is applicable; this decision involves personal judgment. A particular plot may be classified in several different ways by different persons. It follows that the quality protection given by the Lot Plot or any similar procedure cannot be stated in probability terms; any computation of an OC curve must assume that the form of the frequency distribution in the lot is known.

In many of the cases where manufacturers state that they are using the Lot Plot, the actual procedures adopted differ in a number of ways from those stipulated in Shainin's articles. These manufacturers have, generally speaking, employed Shainin's basic concepts, usually with the same objectives as the original Lot Plot, even though the details of their procedures have not followed Shainin's specific rules. One interesting variation uses special templates to help in the identification of different forms of frequency distribution.‡ Example 17-2 describes an orthodox application of the Lot Plot technique; Example 17-3 describes an unorthodox application.

Example 17-2 Successful use of advice based in part on lot plots to improve quality of product submitted by vendors *Facts of the case* One of the products of the *W* Company was a certain complex mechanism. Initially, all the precision parts for this mechanism were made in the *W* Company's own plant. However, when the major purchaser of this mechanism contracted for a greatly increased production, it was necessary to subcontract with a number of vendors for the production of many of the precision parts. Most of these vendors were several hundred miles from *W* Company's factory.

Lot Plots were used in receiving inspection for many important dimensions and other quality characteristics of these precision parts. Interpretation of the plots with reference to the methods used in production was helped by the fact that all these parts had previously been made by the *W* Company.

---

† For an elaboration of this point and for criticism of Shainin's rules for nonnormal plots, see the following reports issued by the Applied Mathematics and Statistics Laboratory, Stanford University, Stanford, Calif., in connection with a contract with the Office of Naval Research:

L. E. MOSES, "Some Theoretical Aspects of the Lot Plot Sampling Inspection Plan," Technical Report No. 18, 1954.

W. G. IRESON, "Some Practical Aspects of the Lot Plot Sampling Inspection Plan," Technical Report No. 19, 1954.

‡ D. A. HILL, The Lot Template Method of Inspection by Variables, *Proceedings of the Aircraft Quality Control Conference*, November, 1953, p. 24, American Society for Quality Control, Milwaukee, 1953.

E. W. ELLIS, The Mechanical Lot Plot Templet, *Industrial Quality Control*, vol. 14, no. 9, pp. 15–18, March, 1958.

Whenever a plot indicated that a vendor was having trouble in meeting a particular quality specification, the suggestions for corrective action (on the right-hand side of the Lot Plot) were written by someone who had been familiar with the particular manufacturing operation when the part had been made by the *W* Company. In this way, the advice to the vendors could combine the *W* Company's prior knowledge gained by trouble shooting on the various operations with the knowledge gained by inspection of the Lot Plots. In most cases, this advice was successful in securing vendors' quality improvement. Many vendors were astonished by the fact that someone who had never visited their plants could make a correct diagnosis of the reasons for their quality troubles.

Example 17-3 Use of frequency distributions of samples for final inspection following a production operation *Facts of the case* Among other products, a manufacturer made socket screws of all sizes, both standard and special. About 180 so-called Lot Plots were made daily for different production lots. Outside pitch diameter was the quality characteristic plotted. Other quality characteristics of the screws were checked using sampling inspection by attributes.

Each plot was made on a form similar in appearance to Fig. 17-1. Just as in Fig. 17-1, the end product of the analysis consisted of four sets of numbers to be inserted in the box in the center of the bottom of the form, namely, numbers indicating the estimated per cent and extent beyond the high and low specification limits. However, the sampling, recording, and calculation all were different from the orthodox Lot Plot.

Fifty screws were taken by the inspector as a grab sample from a tote box containing a batch of screws. (It was felt that the screws had received so much mixing prior to inspection that it was not necessary to use random numbers to select the samples.) Typical quantities in the batch sampled varied from several hundred to several thousand. On the table by the inspector was a sheet of cardboard (or plywood) ruled into squares. The squares were marked in units from the nominal dimension. (Usually, the value of a unit was 0.0001 in.) The dial gage that showed the pitch diameter was set to show the nominal dimension as zero. When each screw was measured, it was put in the appropriate square. After 50 screws had been measured, the inspector filled in the Lot Plot form by making a check mark in the corresponding square of the form. Each square represented one item in a cell of the frequency distribution. There was no division of the 50 measurements into subgroups of 5 each as in the conventional Lot Plot form; vertical lines were drawn on the boundaries of the appropriate squares on the form so that, in effect, the completed form showed a histogram for the sample of 50. The inspector could carry out the measurements and the filling out of the form very rapidly.

The calculation, performed by office workers rather than the inspectors, was a conventional one for mean and standard deviation of a frequency distribution. Certain auxiliary tables and graphs simplified the calculation of per cent and extent outside specification limits assuming a normal distribution.†

No attempt was made to identify the 11 types of Lot Plots given in Fig. 17-2. All plots on which the computed total percentage outside specification limits exceeded 2% were to be brought to the Chief Inspector's attention. So also were all plots having frequency distributions that looked peculiar. (Just as in Example 2-1, these latter were viewed as indicating that an inspection error might have been made; for this reason, the Chief Inspector usually required a new plot for these lots.) All other lots were accepted.

Under these instructions, an average of 15 plots per day out of the 180 were set aside for the Chief Inspector's attention. In effect, he constituted a one-man material-review board. His decision could be to accept, to scrap, or to screen (or to require the inspection of a new sample of 50 where inspection errors were suspected). Cost considerations usually governed the choice between scrapping and screening.

A special advantage of variables inspection for pitch diameter was the avoidance of the troubles due to gage wear that are common in attributes inspection for this quality characteristic.

Use of Control Charts to Identify Grand Lots

In a brilliant paper,‡ Gen. Leslie E. Simon suggests a concept of a lot which is useful for many practical purposes. His definition is "a lot is an aggregation of articles which are essentially alike." He defines "essentially alike" as meaning "that small subgroups of sample items taken from the lot in arbitrary order will respond to the Shewhart criterion of control."

Example 17-4 illustrates the application of this concept to acceptance. The control chart in Fig. 17-3 makes it evident that there were two different grand lots. The average for the first grand lot fell within the specifications; the average for the second grand lot fell outside. Each grand lot should properly have had a single acceptance/rejection decision applicable to the entire grand lot.

Where this concept is used, it is necessary to put off the decision on acceptance or rejection of a sub-lot until the entire grand lot has been identified. This postponement of an acceptance decision is sometimes referred to as *deferred sentencing.*

Example 17-4 Grand lots are identified by control charts for $\bar{X}$ and R *Facts of the case* General Simon gives an excellent example of the way in which a

---

† See WILSON, *op. cit.*, for examples of the tracing overlays and one of the auxiliary tables.

‡ L. E. SIMON, The Industrial Lot and Its Sampling Implications, *Journal of the Franklin Institute*, vol. 237, pp. 359–370, May, 1944.

Table 17-1 Averages and ranges of muzzle velocity for samples of 5 taken from 25 consecutive lots of ammunition

Lot	Average muzzle velocity, ft/s	Range, ft/s
1*	1710	42
2*	1711	40
3*	1713	39
4	1718	26
5	1735	10
6	1739	25
7	1723	14
8	1741	15
9	1738	11
10	1725	31
11	1731	25
12	1721	19
13	1719	43
14	1735	39
15	1741	17
16	1783	51
17	1777	9
18*	1794	15
19	1773	37
20*	1789	54
21*	1798	15
22*	1789	29
23*	1788	39
24*	1799	30
25*	1807	44

control chart may show the existence of grand lots, and how the neglect of grand lots in acceptance criteria may lead to accepting and rejecting the wrong lots. Table 17-1 and Fig. 17-3 are taken from his paper.†

Muzzle velocities were determined for samples of 5 from 25 consecutive lots from a manufacturer of complete rounds of ammunition. Table 17-1 gives the average $\bar{X}$ and the range R from these samples. The specifications for lot acceptance or rejection were based on the values of average and range (rather than on individual values). $\bar{X}_{max}$ was 1,785 ft/s, $\bar{X}_{min}$ was 1,715; the maximum allowable sample range was 70. The lots rejected by this specification are marked with an asterisk (*).

---

† *Ibid.* General Simon states that the data in Table 17-1 have been altered in scale only, so as to reveal no actual military information.

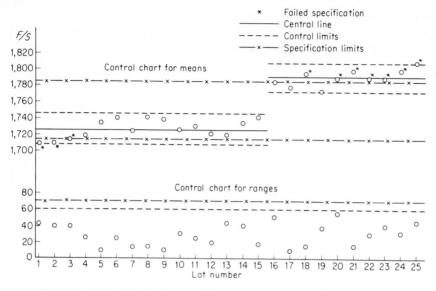

Figure 17-3 Control chart illustrating two different grand lots (data of Table 17-1). *(Reproduced from L. E. Simon, "The Industrial Lot and Its Sampling Implications," Journal of the Franklin Institute, vol. 237, pp. 359–370, May, 1944.)*

Figure 17-3 shows $\bar{X}$ and R control charts for these data. General Simon's comments on the conclusions from these charts are as follows:

"It is quite evident that the first 15 lots are of essentially the same quality, and none should have been rejected. Those which were rejected (or retested until they passed) represent merely so much economic loss. However, near or between Lots 15 and 16 a change occurred. If the specification criteria are really important, all the Lots 16 through 25 (not just part of them) should have been rejected. Thus, it is all too evident that Lots 1 through 15 constitute the real lot (called the grand lot) in the sense that they are *an aggregation of articles which are essentially alike.* In a like manner Lots 16 through 25 constitute another real lot, but a lot which should not pass the specification."

Computing the OC Curve for a Known-Sigma Variables Sampling Plan Based on the Assumption of a Normal Distribution

Many specifications are one-sided. That is, the specification merely states a lower limit L or an upper limit U to apply to individual articles. Perhaps the simplest variables test is one sometimes used with this type of specification in cases where it is believed that the standard deviation of submitted lots will remain fairly constant, that the average $\bar{X}'$ is likely to shift up and down, and that the distribution of the variable is normal.

This test requires taking a sample of size n and measuring the value of the specified quality characteristic for each item of the sample. The item values are averaged to find the $\bar{X}$ of the sample. If this $\bar{X}$ exceeds the lower specification limit L by $k'\sigma'$, the lot is accepted; otherwise it is rejected. (If the limit is an upper one U, $\bar{X}$ must be not more than $U - k'\sigma'$.) The figure for σ' must be estimated from past experience, possibly from a control chart that shows process dispersion to have been in statistical control. The factor k' depends on n and on the desired quality protection; the larger the value of k' for any given n, the more severe the acceptance criteria.

In the literature of variables inspection, such acceptance schemes are described as *known-sigma* plans or plans with *variability known*. In illustrating the necessary calculations for the OC curves of such plans, it may be helpful to use a numerical example. Assume that the specification for a certain product calls for a minimum tensile strength of 20,000 lb/in^2 (pounds per square inch). $\bar{X}$ and R charts have been maintained on the test results of past samples. All points have fallen within control limits on the R chart; the estimated value of σ' is 1,000 lb/in^2. The $\bar{X}$ chart has shown lack of control.

Assume that it is desired to use a variables plan giving quality protection against defectives resulting from a shift in process average comparable with the protection obtainable from the attributes plan $\begin{vmatrix} n = 75 \\ c = 2 \end{vmatrix}$ and from the equivalent double and multiple plans shown in Fig. 12-6. In their volume on variables acceptance inspection,[†] Bowker and Goode give values of n and k' for known-sigma variables plans that have OC curves corresponding fairly well to many different attributes plans. To match the attributes plan of $\begin{vmatrix} n = 75 \\ c = 2 \end{vmatrix}$ n is given as 16 and k' 1.846. In our particular example, this means that the average tensile strength of a sample of 16 test specimens should be at least

$$20,000 + 1.846(1,000) = 21,846 \text{ lb/in}^2$$

It is not possible to compute an OC curve for such an acceptance plan without making some assumption about the frequency distribution of the quality characteristic in question. The OC curve for this plan that was shown in Fig. 12-6 is based on the assumption of a normal distribution. Figure 17-4 illustrates the calculation of the probability of acceptance of 2% defective product. It shows the frequency distribution of individual values and the frequency distribution of averages of samples of 16 when 2% of the product falls below the lower specification limit. In this calculation, two questions must be answered. (In the following explanation, $\bar{X}'$ refers to product average and $\bar{X}$ to the average of a sample of size n).

1. *What is $\bar{X}'$ for the particular per cent defective?* Consult Table A, App. 3, to find the value of $(\bar{X}_i - \bar{X}')/\sigma'$ corresponding to an area of 0.0200. Interpolation in

† A. H. BOWKER and H. P. GOODE, "Sampling Inspection by Variables," McGraw-Hill Book Company, New York, 1952.

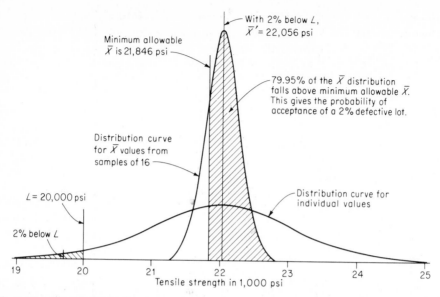

Figure 17-4 Diagram illustrating the calculation of the probability of accepting 2% defective product under the known-sigma plan $n = 16$, $k' = 1.846$.

this table shows that 2% of a normal distribution falls below the value $\bar{X}' - 2.056\sigma'$. If 2% of the product falls below the lower specification limit L, then $\bar{X}'$ must be $L + 2.056\sigma'$. Hence as L is 20,000 lb/in² and σ' is 1,000 lb/in², $\bar{X}' = 22,056$ lb/in².

2. *With $\bar{X}'$ at this figure, what proportion of the $\bar{X}$ distribution will fall above the minimum allowable value of $\bar{X}$?* The difference between $\bar{X}'$ and the minimum $\bar{X}$ must be computed. This is $22,056 - 21,846 = 210$ lb/in². The standard deviation of $\bar{X}$ must be computed. In this case

$$\sigma_{\bar{X}} = \frac{\sigma'}{\sqrt{n}} = \frac{1,000}{\sqrt{16}} = 250 \text{ lb/in}^2$$

The value 210 lb/in² is $0.84\sigma_{\bar{X}}$. Table A shows that 0.7995 of a normal distribution is above the value $\bar{X}' - 0.84\sigma$. It follows that the probability of acceptance is 0.7995 or approximately 0.80.

Although the preceding calculation used numerical values of L and σ' for purposes of illustration, the computed probability of acceptance is, of course, independent of these values and depends only on n and k'.

One advantage of variables sampling is the use of smaller sample sizes to obtain the same quality protection against a particular type of trouble. In the preceding example, the variables sample was 16 whereas the attributes single sample was 75.

Some Aspects of Unknown-Sigma Variables Sampling Plans Based on the Assumption of a Normal Distribution

The known-sigma plan illustrated in Fig. 17-4 specified a minimum allowable $\bar{X}$ of 21,846 lb/in² for a sample of 16. This minimum $\bar{X}$ was computed by adding 1.846σ' to the L of 20,000 lb/in² using an estimate that σ' was 1,000 lb/in². If it had been estimated that σ' was only, say, 100 lb/in², the same OC curve would have been obtained by specifying a minimum $\bar{X}$ of only 20,184.6 lb/in² for a sample of 16. The smaller the estimate of σ', the closer $\bar{X}$ could be to L. The general relationship among the centering of a process (or lot), its dispersion, a single specification limit, and the fraction defective were first discussed in Chap. 4 and illustrated in Figs. 4-4 to 4-6.

Assume that it is desired to design a variables acceptance plan for a stipulated sample size n and a specified L of 20,000 lb/in². Assume that nothing is known about the σ' of the product sampled. Obviously it is necessary to use some measure of sample dispersion to estimate σ'. Conceivably this measure might be the s, σ, or R of the sample, or if the sample is to be divided into two or more subsamples, $\bar{R}$ may be used. Because σ' is unknown, it is not possible to specify any single minimum value of the sample $\bar{X}$ such as 21,846 or 20,184.6 lb/in². In effect, the specification has to be that $\bar{X}$ must exceed L by a stated multiple of some chosen measure of the sample dispersion.

Bowker and Goode's "Sampling Inspection by Variables," already mentioned, is the pioneer treatise on variables sampling plans in which computed OC curves are based on the assumption of a normal distribution. This volume contains a large number of known-sigma and unknown-sigma plans having OC curves matched to those of the attributes plans given in the Columbia Statistical Research Group's volume "Sampling Inspection," mentioned in Chaps. 13 and 14. Bowker and Goode give OC curves for all their unknown-sigma plans based on one-sided specifications. Table X in App. 3 gives a representative group of plans from the Bowker-Goode volume.

The unknown-sigma plans in Bowker and Goode use s as the measure of sample dispersion. The reader will recall that s is the square root of an unbiased estimate of the universe variance and that it is defined as follows:

$$s = \sqrt{\frac{\sum (X - \bar{X})^2}{n - 1}}$$

The acceptance criterion for a lower limit is

$$\bar{X} \geq L + ks$$

and for an upper limit, it is

$$\bar{X} \leq U - ks$$

MIL-STD-414, discussed later in this chapter, also uses s as one of the possible measures of sample dispersion. In addition, this standard permits the use of $\bar{R}$ (or, in some cases, R) as the measure of sample dispersion.

Our chapter follows Bowker and Goode in using k as the symbol for the multiplier of s in unknown-sigma plans and using k' as the multiplier for the estimated σ' in known-sigma plans.

Where σ' may have only one value (such as the 1,000 lb/in² in Fig. 17-4), there is only one value of $\bar{X}'$ that will correspond to any particular per cent defective in the case of a one-sided specification (such as the 2% defective in Fig. 17-4). In contrast, if σ' may have any value, there are an infinite number of values of $\bar{X}'$ that will correspond to, say, 2% defective; each σ' will have a different $\bar{X}'$ for 2% defective. It follows that the mathematics of computing OC curves for unknown-sigma plans is more complicated than for known-sigma plans. To compute an OC curve for an unknown-sigma plan, it is necessary to use certain probability distributions not discussed in this book. A simple explanation of the computation of such curves along the lines of Fig. 17-4 is not possible for unknown-sigma plans.† Nevertheless, anyone who understands the explanation of Fig. 17-4 can doubtless also see the general reasoning that must underlie the calculation of an OC curve for an unknown-sigma plan even though he may not be able to compute such an OC curve himself.

Known-Sigma and Unknown-Sigma Plans for Two-Sided Specifications

Where both an upper limit U and a lower limit L are specified for the quality characteristic and the distribution is normal, the ability of a process to make product meeting specifications depends on the relationship between $(U - L)$ and the spread of the process, often assumed as $6\sigma'$. It also depends on the centering of the process. This point was brought out by Figs. 4-1 to 4-3 and in the accompanying discussion.

In the situation illustrated in Fig. 4-1, where $(U - L)$ is substantially greater than the spread of the process—say $7.5\sigma'$ or more—and the distribution in a lot is normal, both specification limits will not be exceeded in a single lot. It follows that where a known-sigma plan is used with such relatively loose tolerances, the OC curve of the plan can be computed as if the specification were one-sided in the way illustrated in our discussion of Fig. 17-4. The only difference in the acceptance criterion from the case of the one-sided specification is that there are now two limits on the permissible value of the sample average; $\bar{X}$ may not exceed $U - k'\sigma'$ and may not fall below $L + k'\sigma'$.

The matter is more complicated in the cases illustrated in Figs. 4-2 and 4-3, where the tolerances are tight in relation to the process capability. Here some defectives are sure to be produced. For instance, with a normal distribution there will be 0.27% defective even when $(U - L) = 6\sigma'$. The minimum percentage of defectives will occur when the process is centered midway between U and L. With

---

† Some sources that explain the mathematical basis of computing such OC curves are: BOWKER and GOODE, *op. cit.* A. H. BOWKER and G. J. LIEBERMAN, "Engineering Statistics," 2d ed., Prentice-Hall, Inc., Englewood Cliffs, N.J., 1972. "Mathematical and Statistical Principles Underlying Military Standard 414," Superintendent of Documents, Government Printing Office, Washington, D.C., 1958.

this centering and such tight tolerances, some defectives will be produced above the upper specification limit and others below the lower limit. It follows that in calculating the OC curve for a known-sigma variables acceptance plan for a two-sided specification with tight tolerances, it is necessary to compute percentages of defectives in both tails of the frequency distribution. Except for this need of considering both tails of the distribution, such calculations follow the lines explained in our discussion of Fig. 17-4.

Bowker and Goode give values of n and a coefficient designated as k'^* for known-sigma variables plans for two-sided specifications assuming a normal distribution. These plans are to be used where the tolerances are tight in reference to process capability. With these plans, $\bar{X}$ may not exceed $U - k'^*\sigma'$ or fall below $L + k'^*\sigma'$. Like the other types of variables plans in the Bowker-Goode volume, a plan is provided to match the OC curve of each of the attributes plans in "Sampling Inspection." Some of these values of n and k'^* are reproduced in Table X, App. 3.

Whenever unknown-sigma plans are used for two-sided specifications, the uncertainty regarding σ' *always* makes it necessary to consider the possibility of defectives in both tails of the distribution. Procedures in connection with such plans are discussed briefly in our explanation of MIL-STD-414.

Use of the Estimated Lot Percentage Defective in Acceptance Sampling by Variables

If one *knew* the $\bar{X}'$ and σ' of a lot and also *knew* that the frequency distribution in the lot was normal, he could compute the exact percentage of the lot outside any specification limits. Similarly, if the $\bar{X}'$ of the lot is estimated from the $\bar{X}$ of the sample, and if it is assumed that the σ' of the lot is known, or if σ' is estimated from some measure of sample dispersion, and if the lot is assumed to be normal, it is possible to make an estimate of lot percentage defective. Of course, any such estimate is subject to sampling errors.

We have discussed acceptance criteria in known-sigma and unknown-sigma variables plans that are expressed in terms of the relationship between the sample average and the specification limits. If a normal distribution in the lot is assumed, any such criteria may be converted into criteria expressed in terms of the maximum permissible estimated percentage defective in a lot.

Example 17-3 described a case in which variables criteria were used and all lots were accepted for which the estimated percentage defective was not more than 2%. This somewhat unorthodox adaptation of the Lot Plot technique was, in effect, a special type of unknown-sigma variables plan for a two-sided specification. The more orthodox Lot Plot illustrated in Fig. 17-1 also made use of estimates of percentages outside specification limits, although these estimates were to be used chiefly in an informal way in connection with material-review decisions.

The use of a variables sample to estimate the percentage defective in a lot is an important feature of MIL-STD-414, "Sampling Procedures and Tables for Inspection by Variables for Percent Defective," adopted by the U.S. Department of Defense in 1957.

Some General Aspects of Military Standard 414

In many respects this variables standard was similar to the series of successive military standards that had been used for many years for attributes sampling. Some points of similarity were that the procedures and tables were based on the concept of the AQL; that they assumed lot-by-lot acceptance inspection; that they provided for normal, tightened, or reduced inspection depending on circumstances; that sample size was greatly influenced by lot size; that several inspection levels were made available; and that all plans were identified by sample size code letter.

This variables standard was also like the attributes standards in stipulating sampling plans under normal inspection that were designed to protect the producer by making the probability of rejection of a lot having AQL per cent defective relatively small. Just as in the military standards for attributes, the protection to the consumer depended largely on the use of tightened inspection whenever the process average appeared to be unsatisfactory or there were other reasons to be suspicious of the process.

The plans in this standard were like those in the Bowker-Goode volume in that the OC curves given for all the plans assumed a normal distribution of any variable to which the acceptance procedures were to be applied. Tables included in the standard supplied a source for estimates of the fraction defective in each inspected lot; these estimates also assumed a normal distribution of the variable.

Different Procedures Available in MIL-STD-414

The standard could be applied either with a single specification limit, L or U, or with two specification limits. Known-sigma plans included in the standard were designated as having "variability known." Unknown-sigma plans were designated as having "variability unknown." In the latter type plans it was possible to use either the "standard deviation method" or the "range method" in estimating the lot variability.

Two types of computational forms were made available. In "Form 2" the decision on acceptance or rejection required the use of an auxiliary table that provided an estimate of the lot percentage defective based on a "quality index" computed from certain statistics of the sample. In "Form 1," available only for one-sided specifications, this auxiliary table was not needed. The differences between the two forms applied only to the computational procedure; the two forms gave identical results as far as acceptance and rejection were concerned.

Exposition of MIL-STD-414

Because this standard is a relatively long one (110 pages 8 by 10 in, with many of the pages using very fine print), it is not practicable to reproduce all its tables in this book. (Moreover, the standard itself can be purchased for a nominal price from The Naval Publications and Forms Center, 5801 Tabor Avenue, Philadelphia, PA 19120.) The tables that we have reproduced here deal chiefly with the code letter H, and all our discussions and problems relate to that code letter. Any reader who understands the use of the tables and procedures for one code letter should have no difficulty with their use for any other code letter.

Determining the Sample Size Code Letter

To use MIL-STD-414 it is necessary to stipulate an AQL applicable to the quality characteristic being sampled. The standard contains an AQL conversion table (A-1), not reproduced here, that must be used whenever the stipulated AQL falls between two of the AQL values used in the standard.

The standard also contains a table (A-2) similar to Table K of App. 3. This table gives the sample size code letter for any lot size. In contrast to the most recent military standards for attributes, which have had three general inspection levels, the variables standard provides for five such levels. Lot sizes calling for the use of code letter H are as follows:

Inspection level	Lot size
I	8,001–22,000
II	1,301–3,200
III	501–800
IV	181–300
V	66–110

It is evident from the foregoing tabulation that the decision on inspection level has an important influence on sample size. This point is perhaps shown even more strikingly in the following tabulation which shows the sample sizes under "variability unknown—standard deviation method" for lot sizes 181–300 and an AQL of 2.5%.

Inspection level	Sample size code letter	Sample size in normal and tightened inspection
I	B	3
II	D	5
III	F	10
IV	H	20
V	J	30

The standard states that "unless otherwise specified, inspection level IV shall be used." The lower inspection levels evidently are provided particularly for those cases where the cost of testing per unit is relatively high.

Table 17-2 Constants required to determine acceptance criteria in normal, tightened, and reduced inspection when variability is unknown—standard deviation method—code letter H of MIL-STD-414

AQL normal and reduced inspection	AQL tightened inspection	Constants in normal and tightened inspection				Constants in reduced inspection			
		Single specification limit, Form 1		Single limit, Form 2, and double limit		Single specification limit, Form 1		Single limit, Form 2, and double limit	
		n	k	n	M	n	k	n	M
0.04	0.065	20	2.69	20	0.135	15	2.53	15	0.186
0.065	0.10	20	2.58	20	0.228	15	2.42	15	0.312
0.10	0.15	20	2.47	20	0.365	10	2.24	10	0.349
0.15	0.25	20	2.36	20	0.544	7	2.00	7	0.422
0.25	0.40	20	2.24	20	0.846	7	1.88	7	1.06
0.40	0.65	20	2.11	20	1.29	7	1.75	7	2.14
0.65	1.00	20	1.96	20	2.05	7	1.62	7	3.55
1.00	1.50	20	1.82	20	2.95	7	1.50	7	5.35
1.50	2.50	20	1.69	20	4.09	7	1.33	7	8.40
2.50	4.00	20	1.51	20	6.17	7	1.15	7	12.20
4.00	6.50	20	1.33	20	8.92	7	0.955	7	17.35
6.50	10.00	20	1.12	20	12.99	7	0.755	7	23.29
10.00	15.00	20	0.917	20	18.03	7	0.536	7	30.50
15.00	. . . . . .	20	0.695	20	24.53				

Tables Reproduced from MIL-STD-414

This chapter includes five tables dealing with code letter H.

Table 17-2 gives acceptance criteria in normal, tightened, and reduced inspection for all AQL values for plans based on variability unknown, standard deviation method. This table contains factors taken from Tables B-1 to B-4 of the standard. Table 17-5 contains corresponding criteria for plans based on variability unknown, range method; its factors come from Tables C-1 to C-4 of the standard. Table 17-6 has corresponding factors for plans based on known variability; these are taken from Tables D-1 to D-4 of the standard.

Table 17-4 provides a source of estimates of lot percentage defective as a function of the "quality index." This incorporates information from Tables B-5, C-5, and D-5 of the standard.

Table 17-7 contains certain criteria for deciding whether to use tightened or reduced inspection rather than normal inspection for the case of variability unknown, standard deviation method. It includes factors taken from Tables B-6 and B-7 of the standard.

Numerical Data to Illustrate Normal Inspection under MIL-STD-414

Assume a one-sided specification for which $L = 20,000$ lb/in^2, the AQL is 2.50%, and normal inspection is to be used with code letter H. Tables 17-2, 17-5, and 17-6 indicate respective sample sizes of 20, 25, and 9.

The largest sample size, 25, is the one required for unknown variability, range method. To use the range method this sample must be divided into subsamples of 5, with ranges computed for each subsample. Assume that the respective tensile strengths in pounds per square inch and the computed ranges are as follows:

Subsample number						Range
1	22,030	21,800	20,980	20,750	21,480	1,280
2	20,570	21,110	20,270	18,970	22,110	3,140
3	22,740	21,220	21,300	21,920	21,050	1,690
4	21,780	21,800	21,580	20,990	21,740	810
5	21,170	20,390	21,300	20,760	21,440	1,050
					Sum of ranges	7,970

Assume that the first 20 of the foregoing figures are the tensile strengths obtained for the required sample under the standard deviation method with variability unknown. Assume that the first 9 of the figures are the ones obtained for the required sample with variability known.

Calculations with Variability Unknown—Standard Deviation Method—Form 1

From Table 17-2, it may be determined that an AQL of 2.50% with code letter H calls for an n of 20 and a k of 1.51. In effect, these criteria say that the $\bar{X}$ of a sample of 20 must exceed the L of 20,000 lb/in^2 by at least $1.51s$, where s is computed from the sample.

The calculation form suggested in MIL-STD-414 is illustrated in the upper part of Table 17-3. The reader will note that the recommended computational procedure for s makes use of the identity

$$\sum (X - \bar{X})^2 = \sum X^2 - n\bar{X}^2$$

The correction factor in line 4 is, of course, equal to $n\bar{X}^2$. Obviously the method of calculation shown in Table 17-3 is designed for use on a calculating machine, where there is no loss of significant figures in multiplication or division.

The form refers to s as the "estimate of lot standard deviation."

$$L + ks = 20,000 + 1.51(804.9) = 21,215 \text{ lb/in}^2$$

Table 17-3 Illustration of calculation forms using MIL-STD-414—variability unknown—standard deviation method

Single specification limit—Form 1

Line	Information needed	Value obtained	Explanation
1	Sample Size: n	20	
2	Sum of Measurements: ΣX	426,190	
3	Sum of Squared Measurements: ΣX^2	9,094,204,500	
4	Correction Factor (CF): $\dfrac{(\Sigma X)^2}{n}$	9,081,895,805	$(426,190)^2/20$
5	Corrected Sum of Squares (SS): $\Sigma X^2 - CF$	12,308,695	$\begin{cases} 9,094,204,500 \\ -9,081,895,805 \end{cases}$
6	Variance (V): $SS/(n-1)$	647,826	12,308,695/19
7	Estimate of Lot Standard Deviation s: $\sqrt{V}$	804.9	$\sqrt{647,826}$
8	Sample Mean $\bar{X}$: $\Sigma X/n$	21,309.5	426,190/20
9	Specification Limit (Lower): L	20,000	
10	The quantity: $(\bar{X} - L)/s$	1.63	$\dfrac{(21,309.5 - 20,000)}{804.9}$
11	Acceptability Constant: k	1.51	See Table 17-2
12	Acceptability Criterion: Compare $(\bar{X} - L)/s$ with k	1.63 > 1.51	

The lot meets the acceptability criterion, since $(\bar{X} - L)/s$ is greater than k

Single specification limit—Form 2

Lines 1 to 9 are the same as in Form 1

10	Quality index: $Q_L = \dfrac{(\bar{X} - L)}{s}$	1.63	$\dfrac{(21,309.5 - 20,000)}{804.9}$
11	Estimate of lot per cent defective: P_L	4.75%	See Table 17-4
12	Maximum allowable per cent defective: M	6.17%	See Table 17-2
13	Acceptability criterion: Compare P_L with M	4.75% < 6.17%	

The lot meets the acceptability criterion, since P_L is less than M

Since the sample $\bar{X}$ of 21,309.5 lb/in² is not less than this figure, the lot is acceptable.

However, this minimum acceptable value for $\bar{X}$ of 21,215 lb/in² is not actually used in the computational procedure illustrated in Table 17-3. Instead of comparing $\bar{X}$ with $L + ks$, the same result is obtained by comparing $(\bar{X} - L)/s$ with k. In Table 17-3, $(\bar{X} - L)/s$ equals 1.63. Since 1.63 is not less than the stipulated k of 1.51, the lot is accepted.

Calculations with Variability Unknown— Standard Deviation Method—Form 2

As indicated in Table 17-3, the first 9 lines are identical in Forms 1 and 2. In effect, the 10th line is also the same except that, in Form 2, $(\bar{X} - L)/s$ is designated as Q_L, the "quality index."

In Form 2, the quality index is used with an auxiliary table (B-5) to estimate the lot percentage defective. Table 17-4 reproduces part of this auxiliary table. The Q_L of 1.63 gives us the estimate that the lot is 4.75% defective. Since Table 17-2 states that M, the "maximum allowable per cent defective," is 6.17%, the lot is accepted.

As previously stated, the k values used in the Form 1 procedure are consistent with the M values used in the Form 2 scheme; therefore the decision on acceptance or rejection is not influenced by the choice between Form 1 and Form 2.

Whether or not the Form 2 procedure is used to determine the acceptance decision, it is essential to use the quality index to estimate the percentage defective in each lot. These estimates are needed to compute an estimated process average and to determine whether normal, tightened, or reduced inspection should be used. This is true with the range method and with known variability as well as with the standard deviation method.

Calculations with Variability Unknown—Range Method

Assume normal inspection as before with an AQL of 2.5% and code letter H. Table 17-5 gives the sample size as 25. Using the Form 1 procedure, k is 0.647. For the Form 2 procedure, d_2^* is 2.358 and M is 5.98%. The following discussion illustrates the two types of computational procedure but does not include a reproduction of the types of computational forms given in the standard (such as Table 17-3 for the standard deviation method).

The sum of the 25 tensile strengths is 531,250. The sum of the five ranges is 7,970. In both procedures, $\bar{X}$ and $\bar{R}$ must be computed.

$$\bar{X} = \frac{\sum X}{25} = \frac{531,250}{25} = 21,250 \text{ lb/in}^2$$

$$\bar{R} = \frac{\sum R}{5} = \frac{7,970}{5} = 1,594 \text{ lb/in}^2$$

Using the Form 1 procedure, $(\bar{X} - L)/\bar{R}$ is computed; if this computed value is equal to or greater than k, the lot is accepted; otherwise, it is rejected. In this case, $(\bar{X} - L)/\bar{R} = (21,250 - 20,000)/1,594 = 0.784$. Since this figure exceeds the stipulated k of 0.647, the lot is accepted. In effect, the $\bar{X}$ of the sample is required to be at least

$$L + k\bar{R} = 20,000 + 0.647(1,594) = 21,031$$

Table 17-4 Estimates of lot percentage defective for various values of quality index as defined in MIL-STD-414

Q_U or Q_L	Variability unknown—standard deviation method				Variability unknown—range method				Variability known
	$n = 7$	$n = 10$	$n = 15$	$n = 20$	$n = 7$	$n = 10$	$n = 15$	$n = 25$	Any n
0.00	50.00	50.00	50.00	50.00	50.00	50.00	50.00	50.00	50.000
0.10	46.26	46.16	46.10	46.08	46.29	46.20	46.13	46.08	46.017
0.20	42.54	42.35	42.24	42.19	42.60	42.42	42.29	42.19	42.074
0.30	38.87	38.60	38.44	38.37	38.95	38.70	38.51	38.38	38.209
0.35	37.06	36.75	36.57	36.49	37.15	36.87	36.65	36.50	36.317
0.40	35.26	34.93	34.73	34.65	35.36	35.05	34.82	34.66	34.458
0.45	33.49	33.13	32.92	32.84	33.60	33.27	33.02	32.85	32.636
0.50	31.74	31.37	31.15	31.06	31.85	31.51	31.25	31.07	30.854
0.55	30.01	29.64	29.41	29.32	30.13	29.78	29.52	29.33	29.116
0.60	28.32	27.94	27.72	27.63	28.44	28.08	27.82	27.64	27.425
0.65	26.66	26.28	26.07	25.98	26.78	26.42	26.17	25.99	25.785
0.70	25.03	24.67	24.46	24.38	25.14	24.80	24.56	24.39	24.196
0.75	23.44	23.10	22.90	22.83	23.55	23.22	22.99	22.84	22.663
0.80	21.88	21.57	21.40	21.33	21.98	21.69	21.48	21.34	21.186
0.85	20.37	20.10	19.94	19.89	20.46	20.20	20.01	19.89	19.766
0.90	18.90	18.67	18.54	18.50	18.98	18.75	18.60	18.50	18.406
0.95	17.48	17.29	17.20	17.17	17.54	17.36	17.24	17.17	17.106
1.00	16.10	15.97	15.91	15.89	16.14	16.02	15.94	15.89	15.866
1.05	14.77	14.71	14.68	14.67	14.79	14.73	14.69	14.67	14.686
1.10	13.49	13.50	13.51	13.52	13.50	13.49	13.50	13.52	13.567
1.15	12.27	12.34	12.39	12.42	12.25	12.31	12.37	12.42	12.507
1.20	11.10	11.24	11.34	11.38	11.05	11.19	11.29	11.38	11.507
1.25	9.98	10.21	10.34	10.40	9.91	10.12	10.27	10.39	10.565
1.30	8.93	9.22	9.40	9.48	8.83	9.11	9.32	9.47	9.680
1.35	7.92	8.30	8.52	8.61	7.80	8.16	8.41	8.60	8.851
1.40	6.98	7.44	7.69	7.80	6.83	7.27	7.57	7.79	8.076
1.45	6.10	6.63	6.92	7.04	5.93	6.44	6.78	7.03	7.353
1.50	5.28	5.87	6.20	6.34	5.08	5.66	6.05	6.33	6.681
1.55	4.52	5.18	5.54	5.69	4.30	4.94	5.37	5.68	6.057
1.60	3.83	4.54	4.92	5.09	3.58	4.28	4.74	5.08	5.480
1.65	3.19	3.95	4.36	4.53	2.93	3.68	4.17	4.52	4.947
1.70	2.62	3.41	3.84	4.02	2.35	3.13	3.64	4.00	4.457
1.75	2.11	2.93	3.37	3.56	1.83	2.63	3.16	3.54	4.006
1.80	1.65	2.49	2.94	3.13	1.38	2.19	2.73	3.11	3.593
1.85	1.26	2.09	2.56	2.75	0.99	1.79	2.34	2.73	3.216
1.90	0.93	1.75	2.21	2.40	0.67	1.45	1.99	2.38	2.872
1.95	0.65	1.44	1.90	2.09	0.42	1.15	1.68	2.07	2.559
2.00	0.43	1.17	1.62	1.81	0.23	0.89	1.41	1.79	2.275

Table 17-4 Estimates of lot percentage defective for various values of quality index as defined in MIL-STD-414. (*Continued*)

Q_U or Q_L	Variability unknown—standard deviation method				Variability unknown—range method				Variability known
	$n = 7$	$n = 10$	$n = 15$	$n = 20$	$n = 7$	$n = 10$	$n = 15$	$n = 25$	Any n
2.05	0.26	0.94	1.37	1.56	0.10	0.67	1.17	1.54	2.018
2.10	0.14	0.74	1.16	1.34	0.02	0.49	0.96	1.32	1.786
2.15	0.06	0.58	0.97	1.14	0.00	0.35	0.78	1.13	1.578
2.20	0.015	0.437	0.803	0.968	0.000	0.236	0.625	0.954	1.390
2.25	0.001	0.324	0.660	0.816	0.000	0.150	0.495	0.802	1.222
2.30	0.000	0.233	0.538	0.685	0.000	0.089	0.386	0.672	1.072
2.35	0.000	0.163	0.435	0.571	0.000	0.047	0.296	0.558	0.939
2.40	0.000	0.109	0.348	0.473	0.000	0.021	0.223	0.461	0.820
2.45	0.000	0.069	0.275	0.389	0.000	0.007	0.165	0.378	0.714
2.50	0.000	0.041	0.214	0.317	0.000	0.001	0.118	0.307	0.621
2.55	0.000	0.023	0.165	0.257	0.000	0.000	0.083	0.247	0.539
2.60	0.000	0.011	0.125	0.207	0.000	0.000	0.056	0.198	0.466
2.65	0.000	0.005	0.094	0.165	0.000	0.000	0.037	0.157	0.402
2.70	0.000	0.001	0.069	0.130	0.000	0.000	0.023	0.123	0.347
2.75	0.000	0.000	0.049	0.102	0.000	0.000	0.014	0.096	0.298
2.80	0.000	0.000	0.035	0.079	0.000	0.000	0.007	0.074	0.256
2.85	0.000	0.000	0.024	0.060	0.000	0.000	0.004	0.055	0.219
2.90	0.000	0.000	0.016	0.046	0.000	0.000	0.002	0.042	0.187
2.95	0.000	0.000	0.010	0.034	0.000	0.000	0.001	0.031	0.159
3.00	0.000	0.000	0.006	0.025	0.000	0.000	0.000	0.022	0.135
3.10	0.000	0.000	0.002	0.013	0.000	0.000	0.000	0.011	0.097
3.20	0.000	0.000	0.001	0.006	0.000	0.000	0.000	0.005	0.069
3.30	0.000	0.000	0.000	0.003	0.000	0.000	0.000	0.003	0.048
3.40	0.000	0.000	0.000	0.001	0.000	0.000	0.000	0.001	0.034
3.50	0.000	0.000	0.000	0.000	0.000	0.000	0.000	0.000	0.023
3.60	0.000	0.000	0.000	0.000	0.000	0.000	0.000	0.000	0.016
3.70	0.000	0.000	0.000	0.000	0.000	0.000	0.000	0.000	0.011
3.80	0.000	0.000	0.000	0.000	0.000	0.000	0.000	0.000	0.007
3.90	0.000	0.000	0.000	0.000	0.000	0.000	0.000	0.000	0.005
4.00	0.000	0.000	0.000	0.000	0.000	0.000	0.000	0.000	0.003

Table 17-5 Constants required to determine acceptance criteria in normal, tightened, and reduced inspection when variability is unknown—standard deviation method—code letter H of MIL-STD-414

AQL, normal and reduced inspection	AQL, tightened inspection	Constants in normal and tightened inspection					Constants in reduced inspection				
		Single specification limit, Form 1		Single limit, Form 2, and double limit			Single specification limit, Form 1		Single limit, Form 2, and double limit		
		n	k	d_2^*	n	M	n	k	d_2^*	n	M
0.04	0.065	25	1.14	2.358	25	0.125	15	1.04	2.379	15	0.136
0.065	0.10	25	1.10	2.358	25	0.214	15	0.999	2.379	15	0.253
0.10	0.15	25	1.05	2.358	25	0.336	10	0.916	2.405	10	0.23
0.15	0.25	25	1.01	2.358	25	0.506	7	0.702	2.830	7	0.28
0.25	0.40	25	0.951	2.358	25	0.827	7	0.659	2.830	7	0.89
0.40	0.65	25	0.896	2.358	25	1.27	7	0.613	2.830	7	1.99
0.65	1.00	25	0.835	2.358	25	1.95	7	0.569	2.830	7	3.46
1.00	1.50	25	0.779	2.358	25	3.82	7	0.525	2.830	7	5.32
1.50	2.50	25	0.723	2.358	25	3.96	7	0.465	2.830	7	8.47
2.50	4.00	25	0.647	2.358	25	5.98	7	0.405	2.830	7	12.35
4.00	6.50	25	0.571	2.358	25	8.65	7	0.336	2.830	7	17.54
6.50	10.00	25	0.484	2.358	25	12.59	7	0.266	2.830	7	23.50
10.00	15.00	25	0.398	2.358	25	17.48	7	0.189	2.830	7	30.66
15.00	. . . . . .	25	0.305	2.358	25	23.79					

NOTE: In order to agree with symbols used in the discussion of Table 3-4 of this book as well as in other quality control literature, the symbol d_2^* is used here for the factor shown in the first column under "Single limit, Form 2, and double limit." The military standard uses the symbol c for this factor.

Under the Form 2 procedure, it is necessary to compute the quality index Q_L, now defined as $[(\bar{X} - L)d_2^*]/\bar{R}$. In this case,

$$Q_L = \frac{(21{,}250 - 20{,}000)(2.358)}{1{,}594} = 1.85$$

For this Q_L, Table 17-4 gives an estimated lot percentage defective of 2.73%. Because 2.73% is not greater than the stipulated M of 5.98%, this lot is accepted.

Calculation with Known Variability

Now assume normal inspection with an AQL of 2.5%, code letter H, and an estimated σ' of 1,000 lb/in². (In fact, our sample of values for tensile strengths was taken from a table of normal random deviates, assuming that $\bar{X}' = 21{,}000$ lb/in² and $\sigma' = 1{,}000$ lb/in².) Table 17-6 gives the sample size as 9. Using the Form 1

Table 17-6 Constants required to determine acceptance criteria in normal, tightened, and reduced inspection when variability is known—code letter H of MIL-STD-414

AQL, normal and reduced inspection	AQL, tightened inspection	Constants in normal and tightened inspection						Constants in reduced inspection				
		Single specification limit, Form 1		Single limit, Form 2, and double limit				Single specification limit, Form 1		Single limit, Form 2, and double limit		
		n	k'	n	M	v		n	k'	n	M	v
0.04	0.065	4	2.65	4	0.111	1.115		3	2.49	3	0.114	1.225
0.065	0.10	4	2.55	4	0.161	1.115		4	2.39	4	0.290	1.155
0.10	0.15	5	2.46	5	0.296	1.118		3	2.19	3	0.369	1.225
0.15	0.25	5	2.34	5	0.445	1.118		2	1.94	2	0.310	1.414
0.25	0.40	6	2.23	6	0.721	1.095		2	1.81	2	0.510	1.414
0.40	0.65	6	2.08	6	1.14	1.095		3	1.69	3	1.94	1.225
0.65	1.00	7	1.95	7	1.75	1.080		3	1.56	3	2.76	1.225
1.00	1.50	7	1.80	7	2.62	1.080		3	1.44	3	3.85	1.225
1.50	2.50	8	1.68	8	3.68	1.069		4	1.28	4	6.99	1.155
2.50	4.00	9	1.49	9	5.68	1.061		4	1.11	4	9.97	1.155
4.00	6.50	10	1.31	10	8.43	1.054		5	0.919	5	15.21	1.118
6.50	10.00	12	1.11	12	12.35	1.045		5	0.728	5	20.80	1.118
10.00	15.00	14	0.906	14	17.36	1.038		6	0.515	6	28.64	1.095
15.00		16	0.685	16	23.96	1.033						

NOTE: In order to agree with symbols used elsewhere in this book, the symbol k' is used to represent the acceptability constant in a known-sigma plan. The military standard uses k for this constant.

procedure, $k' = 1.49$. For the Form 2 procedure, M is 5.68% and v is 1.061. The following discussion illustrates the two types of computation procedures but does not reproduce the forms given in the standard.

The sum of the nine measurements is 187,960. (These are the values shown on page 513 as subsample 1 and the first 4 values in subsample 2.) Both Form 1 and Form 2 procedures call for computing the sample average.

$$\bar{X} = \frac{\sum X}{9} = \frac{187,960}{9} = 20,884 \text{ lb/in}^2$$

Under the Form 1 procedure, $(\bar{X} - L)/\sigma'$ is computed. For our sample, this is $(20,884 - 20,000)/1,000 = 0.884$. If this computed value is equal to or greater than the stipulated k', the lot is accepted; otherwise it is rejected. Since k' is stipulated as 1.49 and 0.884 is less than 1.49, this lot is rejected. In effect, this procedure stipulates a minimum value for the $\bar{X}$ of the sample of $L + k'\sigma'$. In our example, the minimum $\bar{X}$ for acceptance is 21,490 lb/in².

Under the Form 2 procedure applicable to a single specification limit, a quality index is computed. This index Q_L is now defined as

$$\frac{[(\bar{X} - L)v]}{\sigma'}$$

where v (tabulated in the standard and in our Table 17-6 for various values of n) is $\sqrt{n/(n-1)}$. For the observed sample of 9,

$$Q_L = \frac{(20,884 - 20,000)(1.061)}{1,000} = 0.94$$

This quality index is used to enter a table (our Table 17-4) to determine the estimated percentage defective in the lot. In this case, Table 17-4 indicates 17.4% defective for a Q_L of 0.94. If the estimated lot percentage defective is equal to or less than the stipulated maximum M, the lot is accepted; otherwise it is rejected. Since M is 5.68% in this instance, the lot is rejected.

Tightened Inspection in MIL-STD-414

The standard specifies that the estimated process average at any time "is the arithmetic mean of the estimated lot per cent defectives computed from the sampling inspection results of the preceding 10 lots or as may be otherwise designated." The process average is needed to determine when shifts shall be made between normal and tightened inspection and between normal and reduced inspection. Tightened inspection is required when the estimated process average is greater than the AQL with more than a certain number T of the lots used to compute the process average that have estimates of percentage defective exceeding the AQL.

The standard gives values of T assuming that the process average has been computed using the preceding 5, 10, and 15 lots, respectively. The stipulated T depends on the sample size code letter and the AQL. Table 17-7 gives values of T for code letter H, assuming variability unknown and the standard deviation method. (Most T values are the same for the range method and for known standard deviation, although there are a few slight differences.)

The use of Table 17-7 may be illustrated with reference to an AQL of 2.50%, assuming that normal inspection has been in force and that the preceding 10 lots have given the following estimates of process average:

$$†4.01\% \quad 2.02\% \quad †4.46\% \quad †3.22\% \quad 2.27\%$$
$$†2.56\% \quad 1.79\% \quad †3.59\% \quad 1.58\% \quad †2.87\%$$

The estimated process average is the arithmetic mean of these 10 figures, namely, 2.84%. Thus one condition for the shift to tightened inspection is met; the estimated process average is greater than the AQL of 2.50%. However, the second condition is not met; only six of the lots (the ones marked with a dagger) had an estimated percentage defective of more than 2.50, whereas the standard (Table

Table 17-7 Criteria relating to establishment and discontinuance of tightened and reduced inspection when variability is unknown—standard deviation method—code letter H of MIL-STD-414

AQL	Values of T for tightened inspection			Limits of estimated lot per cent defective for reduced inspection		
	Number of lots			Number of lots		
	5	10	15	5	10	15
0.04	3	5	6	0.000	0.004	0.013
0.065	3	5	7	0.000	0.010	0.029
0.10	3	5	7	0.002	0.023	0.058
0.15	3	6	8	0.005	0.048	0.105
0.25	4	6	8	0.017	0.111	0.215
0.40	4	6	9	0.048	0.225	0.396
0.65	4	7	9	0.123	0.445	0.65
1.00	4	7	9	0.266	0.785	1.00
1.50	4	7	10	0.521	1.31	1.50
2.50	4	7	10	1.14	2.40	2.50
4.00	4	8	11	2.24	4.00	4.00
6.50	4	8	11	4.29	6.50	6.50
10.00	4	8	11	7.40	10.00	10.00
15.00	4	8	11			

17-7) stipulates that tightened inspection is not required unless more than seven out of the ten lots have values of estimated percentage defective above the AQL. Therefore, normal inspection would be continued for the time being.

The acceptance criteria under tightened inspection are shown in Tables 17-2, 17-5, and 17-6 for code letter H. In all instances, these are the criteria under normal inspection for the next smaller AQL class. Once tightened inspection has been initiated, normal inspection is not reinstated until the estimated process average of the lots under tightened inspection is equal to or less than the AQL.

Reduced Inspection in MIL-STD-414

To initiate reduced inspection, all the preceding 10 lots (or other designated number) must have been accepted and the estimated percentage defective for *each* of these preceding lots must have been less than a stated lower limit. Moreover, production must be "at a steady rate." For 10 lots with code letter H, unknown variability, the standard deviation method, and an AQL of 2.50%, Table 17-7 shows this lower limit to be 2.40%.

The acceptance criteria for code letter H under reduced inspection are given in Tables 17-2, 17-5, and 17-6. For an AQL of 2.50% with unknown variability and the standard deviation method, n is 7 and k is 1.15; for the Form 2 procedure, M is 12.20%. Just as in the military standards for acceptance sampling by attributes, if a bad lot is submitted, it has a better chance of acceptance under reduced inspection than under normal inspection.

Reduced inspection must be discontinued and normal inspection reinstated whenever a lot is rejected, whenever the estimated process average exceeds the AQL, whenever "production becomes irregular or delayed" or "other conditions" exist that "may warrant that normal inspection should be reinstated."

An Upper Specification Limit in MIL-STD-414

The foregoing numerical examples all have assumed a one-sided specification with a lower limit L. The only difference when there is a single upper limit U is that it is necessary to measure down from U rather than up from L; $U - \bar{X}$ replaces $\bar{X} - L$ in the analysis. This point may be illustrated by noting the definitions of the quality indexes Q_L and Q_U for the various procedures.

For unknown variability, standard deviation method, these are

$$Q_L = \frac{\bar{X} - L}{s} \qquad Q_U = \frac{U - \bar{X}}{s}$$

For unknown variability, range method, they are

$$Q_L = \frac{(\bar{X} - L)d_2^*}{\bar{R}} \qquad Q_U = \frac{(U - \bar{X})d_2^*}{\bar{R}}$$

For known variability, they are

$$Q_L = \frac{(\bar{X} - L)v}{\sigma'} \qquad Q_U = \frac{(U - \bar{X})v}{\sigma'}$$

The foregoing definitions of Q_L and Q_U also apply to the case of two-sided specifications.

Two-Sided Specifications in MIL-STD-414

Only the Form 2 procedure is applicable with a double specification limit. Two types of condition are recognized. In one type, an AQL is assigned to both limits combined. In the other type, different AQL's are assigned to each specification limit.

In both types, sample size code letters are obtained just as for one-sided specifications. Moreover, in both types the same tables used for Form 2 with a single limit are used to find n, M, and—where applicable—d_2^* or v. Q_L and Q_U are computed just as for single limits, and the percentage of defectives outside each limit is estimated from a table such as our Table 17-4. These percentages are designated p_L and p_U. The estimated lot percentage defective p is defined as $p_L + p_U$.

Where one AQL has been assigned to both limits combined, if " p is equal to or less than the stipulated maximum allowable per cent defective M, the lot meets the acceptability criterion; if p is greater than M or if either Q_U or Q_L or both are negative, then the lot does not meet the acceptability criterion."

Where different AQL values have been assigned to L and U, the rules are somewhat more complicated. For example, assume code letter H, normal inspection, with unknown variability and the standard deviation method. Assume an AQL of 2.5% for the lower specification limit and 1.0% for the upper limit.

Table 17-2 tells us that n is 20 for both AQL's and that M is 6.17% for the lower limit and 2.95% for the upper. These values are designated as M_L and M_U, respectively.

Now assume that the sample of 20 has been inspected and that Q_L and Q_U have been computed following the procedure illustrated in Table 17-3. Assume that Q_L is 1.60 and Q_U is 2.10. We may enter Table 17-4 to find $p_L = 5.09\%$ and $p_U = 1.34\%$.

For the lot to be accepted:

1. p_U must be equal to or less than M_U. Since 1.34% is less than 2.95%, this condition is met.
2. p_L must be equal to or less than M_L. Since 5.09% is less than 6.17%, this condition also is met.
3. p must be equal to or less than the larger of M_L and M_U. Here

$$p = 1.34\% + 5.09\% = 6.43\%$$

Since 6.43% is greater than 6.17%, this condition is not met and the lot is rejected.

The general rules regarding tightened and reduced inspection are the same for two-sided and one-sided specifications.

MIL-STD-414 contains two auxiliary tables (B-8 and C-8) not reproduced here. These tables provide an aid in judging whether the dispersion of a quality characteristic is too great to meet a stated quality standard even under the most favorable conditions of centering between U and L.

The Relationship among Sample Sizes under the Standard Deviation Method, the Range Method, and the Procedures Assuming Known Variability

There is no code letter A in MIL-STD-414. For code letters B to G with variability unknown, the standard deviation method and the range method have identical sample sizes under normal inspection, namely, 3, 4, 5, 7, 10, and 15, respectively. For code letter H and beyond, sample sizes in normal inspection are from about 12 to 20% smaller in the standard deviation method than in the range method.

For code letters of H and beyond, the choice of the standard deviation method over the range method will cause some saving in inspection cost; choice of the range method presumably will cause some saving in the cost of calculations to apply the acceptance criteria. The relative importance of these cost differences will depend chiefly on the costs per item associated with inspection. Where tests are destructive or otherwise costly, it will usually be more economical to use the standard deviation method.

For any given AQL and code letter, the OC curves for the standard deviation method and the range method are matched as closely as practicable. For this reason, the question of quality protection to the consumer should be viewed primarily as a matter of choosing the desired AQL and inspection level rather than as a matter of choice between the standard deviation method and the range method.

In the range method, all sample sizes of 10 or more are multiples of 5 and the sample must be divided into subsamples of 5 each to compute $\bar{R}$. For sample sizes of 3, 4, 5, and 7, the R of the entire sample is used as the measure of sample dispersion and no calculation of $\bar{R}$ is required.

The standard deviation method and the range method in MIL-STD-414 are alike in the feature that the sample size under normal inspection depends only on the code letter and is not influenced by the AQL. For example, Tables S and T for code letter H show sample sizes of 20 and 25, respectively, for all AQL values under normal inspection. In contrast, the sample size for a given code letter with known variability changes greatly with the AQL. For this reason, no simple statement applicable to all AQL values can be made about the relationship between sample sizes with known and unknown variability.

For example, Table 17-6 for code letter H shows sample sizes under normal inspection varying from 4 for an AQL of 0.04% to 16 for an AQL of 15%. This is a variation of from 20 to 80% of the required sample size with the standard deviation method, variability unknown. The paradox that sample size increases with the relaxation of the quality standard arises because the known-sigma plans in the standard were designed to match the OC curves obtained for the unknown-sigma plans.

For the popular AQL value of 1.00% and between code letters D and Q, the sample size under normal inspection for known-sigma plans varies from 40 to 32.5% of that required for unknown-sigma plans using the standard deviation method.

Some Comments on Table 17-4

This table has been condensed in various ways from Tables B-5, C-5, and D-5 of the standard. Thus the quality index varies by steps of 0.05 in Table 17-4 whereas it varies by steps of 0.01 in the standard. The only values of n given in Table 17-4 for the case of variability unknown are those required for normal, tightened, and reduced inspection with code letter H; the standard, of course, gives all values of n required by any code letter.

The user of Table 17-4 needs to remember that the quality index is defined differently for each of the three parts of the standard. He should also be aware that, given the respective definitions of quality index, Table 17-4 and Tables B-5, C-5, and D-5 of the standard are sources of unbiased minimum variance estimates of lot percentage defective based on the assumption of normality. These tables may therefore be used for other purposes than the application of the acceptance criteria of MIL-STD-414.

For all three parts of the standard, Table 17-4 starts with an estimate that the lot is 50% defective when the quality index is zero. Of course, a zero quality index occurs when the sample average is the same as the specification limit in question, either L or U. Whenever the sample $\bar{X}$ falls below L or above U, the quality index is negative, implying that more than 50% of the lot is defective. All lots that have negative quality indexes should be rejected without further calculation.

The final column of Table 17-4, applicable to all values of n with variability known, is, in effect, merely a normal curve area table such as our Table A.†

The Choice between Unknown-Sigma and Known-Sigma Plans

In starting to use MIL-STD-414, the Bowker-Goode tables, or other comparable variables procedures for acceptance inspection of a new product, there may be no basis for estimating σ'. Where this is true, it is necessary to start with unknown-sigma procedures.

Nevertheless, if many lots are expected from the same production source, it always is a good idea to start gathering data to provide a basis for judgment on the question of whether or not there is statistical control of the dispersion of the quality characteristic being measured. Usually this calls for a control chart for s or R. (The reader should refer to the discussion in Chap. 11 of the differences between control charts for s and σ.) If such a chart indicates that the lots are coming from a process that is in statistical control with respect to its dispersion, it makes sense to switch from the unknown-sigma procedure to a known-sigma one. In the initial stages of a switch to known-sigma, it will be conservative to estimate σ' a little on the high side. Often the estimated σ' may be reduced as more evidence is accumulated.

Usually an incidental advantage of the switch to known-sigma will be a reduction in sample size. In the common case where sample size is small, a more important advantage is that a much better estimate of σ' is obtained from a series of samples that exhibit statistical control of dispersion than can be had from a single small sample. Even where there is not full statistical control, a conservatively chosen σ' may be better than unknown-sigma if it is imperative to use a very small sample size. The reader may get a feeling for the unreliability of any estimate of σ' from a small sample by examining the variation of any measure of dispersion, such as R, σ, s, or s^2, in successive samples from a statistically controlled process.

---

† For a discussion of the mathematics underlying the estimates of lot percentage defective with both known and unknown variability, see G. J. LIEBERMAN and G. J. RESNIKOFF, Sampling Plans for Inspection by Variables, *Journal of the American Statistical Association*, vol. 50, pp. 457–516, June, 1955.

For instance, in our first page of drawings from Shewhart's normal bowl (page 57) R varied from 1 to 42 for samples of 4 and σ varied from 0.5 to 16.6.

Of course, whenever a known-sigma plan is used, a control chart should be maintained on some measure of dispersion, R, σ, or s. Such a chart will serve to check the assumption that σ' is in statistical control, and, as time goes on, may provide a basis for a better estimate of the "known" value of σ' that should be used.

Some Sources of OC Curves for Variables Plans Based on the Assumption of Normality

MIL-STD-414 contains OC curves for all code letters and all AQL values for its plans using the standard deviation method for normal inspection. These curves may be viewed as approximations to the corresponding plans based on the range method and on known variability. The standard contains such a wide variety of OC curves that it may be viewed as a convenient source from which it usually is possible to find a plan that gives an approximation to any desired OC curve.†

The OC curves shown in MIL-STD-414 apply to the case of a one-sided specification. A plan applicable to a two-sided specification does not have a unique OC curve because the probability of acceptance depends on the way the total percentage defective is divided into percentages above U and below L. Nevertheless, for any given plan in the military standard, the group of OC curves applicable to two-sided specifications is contained within a fairly narrow band. The particular OC curve applicable to a one-sided specification is used as an approximation to all the curves in this narrow band.

The Bowker-Goode volume constitutes another convenient source of variables plans having desired OC curves. Some representative plans from Bowker and Goode are given in Table X, App. 3.

Table Y in App. 3 gives values of $100p_{0.95}$, $100p_{0.50}$, and $100p_{0.10}$ for many unknown-sigma plans for one-sided specifications having values of n from 5 to 50 and values of k from 0.6 to 3.0. These three points on each OC curve permit the user to make a rough plotting of the entire OC curve of any desired plan. If, for a given sample size n, a value of k is to be selected corresponding to certain stipulated quality protection, it is advantageous to use the values from Table Y to plot curves that show how $p_{0.95}$, $p_{0.50}$, and $p_{0.10}$ vary with k. These curves may then be read to determine the approximate k value for any desired $p_{0.95}$, $p_{0.50}$, or $p_{0.10}$.‡

---

† All the OC curves and sampling plans for MIL-STD-414 can also be found in Bowker and Lieberman, *op. cit.*

‡ Table Y is taken by permission from more extensive tables in W. G. Ireson, "Sampling Tables for Inspection by Variables." This was issued by the Applied Mathematics and Statistics Laboratory, Stanford University, Stanford, Calif., as Technical Report No. 7, 1952.

Comment on the Assumption of a Normal Distribution in Known-Sigma and Unknown-Sigma Plans

The frequency distribution of many industrial quality characteristics is roughly normal. This is particularly so where the product comes from a single source and is produced within a short period of time. For this reason, the assumption of a normal distribution is good enough for practical purposes in many instances. This assumption is most likely to be a reasonable one where inspection lots are formed close to the point of production, so that the chance for the mixing of product having different frequency distributions is held to a minimum.

Nevertheless, even though inspection lots have been produced under apparently homogeneous conditions, it is always well to view the assumption of normality with a somewhat critical eye, investigating to see whether conditions exist that are likely to cause serious departure from a normal distribution. Sometimes the underlying frequency distribution is skewed, or it may be symmetrical but either peaked or flat-topped. The percentages in the extreme tails of such distributions may differ considerably from those obtaining under a normal distribution, and the protection against stated percentages of defectives given by variables acceptance criteria may be either greater or less than the protection indicated by OC curves computed on the assumption of normality. The tighter the quality standard (for example, the smaller the AQL), the less reasonable it is to use acceptance criteria based on the assumption of normality.

One important departure from normality exists when a producer has given 100% screening inspection by attributes to a lot prior to its variables sampling inspection by the consumer. In such a case the frequency distribution in the screened lot may be truncated; one or both of the tails of the distribution may have been removed. With such truncated distributions, the variables criteria based on the assumption of normality may indicate that a lot should be rejected even though the actual nonnormal distribution in the lot may contain no defectives.

Acceptance/Rejection Plans May be Devised to Accept on Variables Criteria but to Reject Only on Attributes Criteria

Two objections are sometimes raised to the use of either known-sigma or unknown-sigma plans for lot rejection. One objection relates to the point just mentioned that, for certain nonnormal distributions, the variables criteria may occasionally lead to the rejection of a lot containing no defectives.

The other objection relates to the obvious legal and psychological difficulties incident to rejecting a lot on the basis of a sample even though no defectives have been found in the sample. Consider, for example, the known-sigma plan of Fig. 17-4 in which the design specification stated that the minimum tensile strength of an individual item must be 20,000 lb/in^2, whereas the acceptance specification stated that the minimum $\bar{X}$ for a sample of 16 must be 21,846 lb/in^2.

It is quite possible for a sample to fail this acceptance specification without any of the individual tensile strengths falling below 20,000 lb/in^2.†

These objections are sometimes met by devising double sampling plans in which variables criteria are applied to a first sample. When these criteria do not lead to acceptance, a second larger sample is taken and the final decision on acceptance or rejection is based on attributes criteria. A number of acceptance plans of this type are described in the Bowker-Goode volume.‡

Some Statistical Aspects of Proof Testing

Where, because testing is destructive, only a small sample can be tested, a possible alternative is the application of some load short of destruction to 100% of the product. Some advantages and limitations of such proof tests are brought out in the following comments by J. J. Taylor relative to routine tests of ceramic insulators:§

> Ceramic parts may be inspected visually, sometimes with the aid of penetrating fluids; or aurally by " ringing out " methods. Attention has been given also to X-Ray examination and to non-destructive tests involving supersonic response. Many tests are, however, potentially destructive and would produce failure if increased sufficiently in severity. Dielectric soundness is checked by high frequency or 60 cycle flashover on ceramic parts and assembled units. For certain specialized types of insulators, impulse tests are routine procedure. Routine mechanical tests of assemblies are made at a load level about half the rated ultimate strength and are followed by a dielectric test.
>
> Since routine tests for both dielectric and mechanical strength are potentially destructive, some compromise is necessary between tests too mild to eliminate defectives and those severe enough to damage an appreciable portion of specimens near the minimum end of the distribution pattern.
>
> Mechanical tests at half the rated strength are not intended to cut off the minimum end of the distribution curve. They are used to give assurance against defectives with potential characteristics far below the minimum level of expectancy.
>
> It cannot safely be assumed that high levels of routine test guarantee quality. Such tests may be particularly undesirable on a product manufactured with good factory control but with no great margin in average strength. In Figure [17-5], two distribution curves are shown that have the same probability of failure at or below the specified minimum level. If both groups of product are proof-tested to eliminate units lying below the minimum line, and if the test is harmful to units only slightly stronger than the proof load, then it is likely that such testing will be detrimental to design (a) and beneficial to design (b). In the first case it damages more units than it eliminates and in the other cases it eliminates more units than it damages.

---

† A possible way to avoid this particular type of objection is to incorporate the acceptance specification as an additional requirement in the design specification. Thus two separate requirements may be made, one that individual values should be at least 20,000, and the other that averages of samples of 16 should be at least 21,846.

‡ See also GEOFFREY GREGORY and G. J. RESNIKOFF, " Some Notes on Mixed Variables and Attributes Sampling Plans." This was issued by the Applied Mathematics and Statistics Laboratory, Stanford University, Stanford, California, as Technical Report No. 10, 1955.

§ J. J. TAYLOR, Statistical Methods Applied to Insulator Development and Manufacture, *Transactions American Institute of Electrical Engineers*, vol. 64, pp. 495–499, July, 1945.

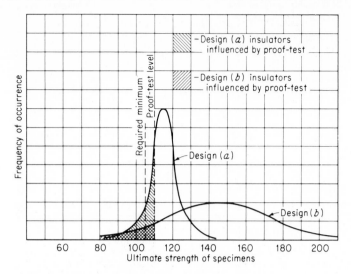

Figure 17-5 Proof testing in relation to strength distribution.

It is probable that no amount of proof testing, however drastic, can select from carelessly manufactured material a finished batch as dependable as one made in the first instance with good technical control and given routine tests at reasonable levels. This view implies, in specifications, emphasis on consistency of tested characteristics; a carefully drawn sampling plan; a cumulative record of test history so that past experience can be of real value in interpreting the results of samples under immediate review.

It should be noted also that some product characteristics cannot be given routine tests that will check them. Line and station insulators are designed and design-tested to withstand electrical surges of great severity, but so far it has not been practical to surge test at these extreme levels in routine fashion. Even if it were possible it might be proved an undesirable practice because of the damaging nature of the tests. In such instances reliance must be placed on methods of quality control which give high-probability assurance that the required characteristic is present.

PROBLEMS

17-1 The specification on a certain dimension of a manufactured part is 1.7030 ± 0.0030 in. In a Lot Plot for this dimension, the first 3 digits of the measured values for all 50 items are 1.70. The final 2 digits are those given in Table 2-7 (pages 57–58) for drawings 101 to 150 from the Shewhart bowl, in the order stated. Prepare the Lot Plot, assuming cell boundaries of 32.5, 36.5, 40.5, etc. Compute the upper and lower lot limits by the method described in the explanation of the Lot Plot plan. Draw these limits on your Lot Plot.

17-2 Follow the directions for Problem 17-1, using the Shewhart bowl drawings 301–350 as shown on page 59.

17-3 A sample of 50 cans of tomatoes is taken from a large lot. The drained weights of contents of these cans are to be shown on a Lot Plot. Assume that these 50 weights are the second 50 figures (samples 11 through 20) in Table 2-1 (page 35), in the order given. Prepare a Lot Plot, assuming the cell boundaries as 20.25, 20.75, 21.25, etc. Compute lot limits and draw them on your Lot Plot.

17-4 Follow the directions for Problem 17-3, using the third 50 measured weights (sample numbers 21 through 30) in Table 2-1.

17-5 A sample of 50 thermostatic control devices is taken from a large lot. The temperature at which each device turns " on " is to be shown in a Lot Plot. Assume that these 50 temperatures are the first 50 figures (subgroup numbers 1 through 10) in Problem 2-1 (page 69). Prepare a Lot Plot and plot the lot limits on your Lot Plot.

17-6 A known-sigma variables plan for a one-sided specification uses $n = 9$ and $k' = 1.466$. Assuming a normal distribution and a correct estimate of σ', what is the probability of acceptance of a 3.75% defective lot?

   Answer: 0.827.

17-7 A known-sigma variables acceptance plan for a one-sided specification uses $n = 25$ and $k' = 1.97$. Compute the probability of acceptance of a 3% defective lot assuming that the frequency distribution in the lot is normal and σ' is estimated correctly.

   Answer: 0.326.

17-8 Assume normal inspection, MIL-STD-414, range method, variability unknown, code letter H, 1.50% AQL, single specification limit $L = 14.5$. Assume that the measured values in the sample are the first 25 drawings from Shewhart's normal bowl (Table 2-7, page 57). Use the procedures of MIL-STD-414 to estimate the lot percentage defective.

17-9 Answer the questions in Problem 17-8 changing the AQL to 1.0%.

17-10 Answer the questions in Problem 17-8 using the third 25 drawings (i.e., drawings 51–75) from Shewhart's normal bowl (Table 2-7). (Note that it is necessary to arrange these drawings in subgroups of 5 rather than in the subgroups of 4 shown in Table 2-7.) Will the lot be accepted or rejected? What is the actual percentage below 14.5 in Shewhart's normal bowl? (See Table 2-6, page 55.)

17-11 Assume normal inspection, MIL-STD-414, variability unknown, standard deviation method, code letter H, 1.00% AQL, single specification limit $L = 14.5$. Assume that the measured values in the sample are the first 20 drawings from Shewhart's normal bowl. Prepare a calculation using the Form 1 portion of Table 17-3 as a model. What is the value computed on line 10? Will the lot be accepted or rejected?

   Answer: 2.21; accepted.

17-12 Change the instructions in Problem 17-11 to call for a Form 2 calculation. What is the estimate of the lot percentage defective? Will the lot be accepted or rejected?

   Answer: 0.94%; accepted.

17-13 From your solutions to Problems 17-11 and 17-12 and from inspection of Table 17-2, determine the smallest AQL for which this lot would be accepted under normal inspection and under tightened inspection, respectively.

   Answer: 0.40%; 0.65%.

17-14 The single specification limit L for tensile strength of certain wire is 215 lb. MIL-STD-414 is used with normal inspection, code letter H, and an AQL of 1.0%. Variability is unknown, and the range method is to be used. A computation using the Form 2 criterion is to be made. The required sample of 25 is measured with the following results:

   Subgroup 1   231, 238, 228, 231, 235
   Subgroup 2   224, 245, 263, 231, 245
   Subgroup 3   224, 228, 235, 238, 235
   Subgroup 4   221, 242, 242, 235, 224
   Subgroup 5   224, 224, 242, 252, 252

Make the necessary calculations to determine whether or not the lot should be accepted.

17-15 Assume that the same lot in Problem 17-14 is to be inspected with variability unknown and the standard deviation method. Assume that a sample of 20 is observed and that the measured values are the ones shown in subgroups 1, 2, 3, and 4 of Problem 17-14. Prepare a calculation using Form 2 to determine whether or not the lot will be accepted. Use Table 17-3 as a model.

   (*Hint:* The computations will be simplified if 200 is subtracted from each measurement before starting your calculations.)

17-16 Assume normal inspection, MIL-STD-414, variability known, code letter H, 1.50% AQL, single specification limit $L = 60{,}000$ lb/in² (tensile strength). The assumed value of σ' is 2,000 lb/in². The required sample of 8 is tested with the following tensile strengths: 65,060; 66,260; 65,240; 61,550; 65,760; 64,850; 63,880; 60,830. Use the Form 2 procedures of MIL-STD-414 to estimate the lot percentage defective. Will the lot be accepted or rejected?

Answer: 1.29%; accepted.

17-17 Assume normal inspection, MIL-STD-414, variability known, code letter H, 2.50% AQL, single specification limit. Compute the probability of acceptance of a normally distributed lot containing 5% of defective product if the σ' of the lot is estimated correctly.

Answer: 0.68.

17-18 Figure 17-4 was used to illustrate the calculation of the probability of acceptance of a 2% defective lot under a certain known-sigma acceptance plan. For the same plan, compute the probability of acceptance of a lot that is 8% defective. Continue to assume normality and a correct estimate of σ'.

Answer: 0.04.

17-19 The single specification limit U for the elongation of a certain yarn fiber is 6.86 mm per gram weight applied. MIL-STD-414 is used with normal inspection, code letter H, and an AQL of 2.5%. Variability is unknown, and the standard deviation method is used. The required sample measurements to apply the Form 2 procedure are as follows:

$$6.73, 7.24, 6.10, 6.05, 6.40$$
$$6.32, 6.40, 6.88, 5.82, 6.38$$
$$6.91, 6.73, 6.32, 6.38, 6.91$$
$$6.63, 6.91, 6.81, 6.32, 6.45$$

Make the necessary calculations to determine whether or not the lot should be accepted.

17-20 A MIL-STD-414 variables acceptance sampling plan uses code letter H and an AQL of 1.5%. Variability is unknown and there is a single upper specification of 6.850.

(*a*) What are the required critical numbers using the Range method for tightened inspection under both the Form 1 and Form 2 procedures?

(*b*) What are the critical numbers using the standard deviation method for normal inspection under both the Form 1 and Form 2 procedures?

(*c*) Assuming $s = 0.125$ for a sample (and is the best estimate of σ'), compute the location of the process mean for incoming lots with a p' of 0.04.

(*d*) Sketch the distribution of product with respect to U, the distribution of $\bar{X}$ with respect to the acceptance criterion, and compute the probability of acceptance for the lots described in (*c*). Assume the normal distribution applies.

17-21 The single lower specification limit, L, for tensile strength for a certain wire is 62 lb. MIL-STD-414 is used with normal inspection, code letter H, and an AQL of 1.0%. Variability is unknown, and the range method and Form 2 procedure are to be used.

(*a*) What critical numbers are required for the plan?

(*b*) A sample from a lot yields $\sum X = 1,681$ and $\sum R = 32$. Make the necessary calculations to determine whether or not the lot should be accepted.

17-22 The single lower specification limit on a certain item is 14.5 units. MIL-STD-414 is used with normal inspection, code letter H, and an AQL of 1.5%. Variability is unknown and the range method and Form 2 procedure are to be used.

(*a*) What factors from the standard are required to estimate the lot percentage nonconforming and to decide whether or not to accept a lot?

(*b*) The required sample of 25 is measured with the following results:

Subgroup 1	45, 26, 37, 33, 12
Subgroup 2	29, 43, 25, 22, 37
Subgroup 3	33, 29, 32, 30, 13
Subgroup 4	40, 18, 30, 11, 21
Subgroup 5	18, 36, 34, 26, 35

Make the necessary calculations to determine whether or not the lot should be accepted.

(c) What is the probability of acceptance of lots having the proportion of nonconforming product found in (b)? Use $\bar{R}/d_2^*$ to estimate σ' and the value of k listed for the Form 1 procedure to find P_a.

17-23 An ABC standard single sampling plan calls for $n = 50$ and $c = 2$ for code letter H, an AQL of 1.5%, and normal inspection.

(a) What Form 1 MIL-STD-414 variables sampling plan corresponds to this ABC standard attributes plan? Assume σ' is known and that there is a single specification limit for this characteristic.

(b) Find the probability of acceptance of a lot containing 10% nonconforming items under the plan found in (a).

17-24 The minimum temperature of operation for a certain device is specified as 180°. A known-sigma variables acceptance plan with a sample size of 9 is to be used. The desired value of $100p_{0.10}$ is 4.0%. From Table X, find k'. If the assumed value of σ' is 6°, will a lot be accepted when the sample items have operating temperatures of 197, 188, 184, 205, 201, 190, 195, 193, and 199°?

17-25 From Table X find the n and k of the unknown-sigma plan having its OC curve agreeing most closely with that of the known-sigma plan selected in Problem 17-24.

17-26 In the absence of adequate information on σ', the unknown-sigma plan of Problem 17-25 is to be used for acceptance of the product mentioned in Problem 17-24. Will a lot be accepted when the sample items have operating temperatures of 202, 195, 191, 198, 178, 185, 194, 191, 192, 188, 203, 197, 197, 190, 189, and 182°?

17-27 In order to gain an impression of the way in which sample size influences the OC curves of unknown-sigma variables plans for a given value of k, use Table Y to plot approximate OC curves of four plans all having a k of 1.4 and having values of n of 5, 10, 25, and 50, respectively. What general comment can you make about the effect of increased sample size?

17-28 It is desired to have an unknown-sigma variables plan having a value of $100p_{0.95}$ of approximately 2.50%. Table Y gives plans of $n = 15, k = 1.4; n = 35, k = 1.6$; and $n = 50, k = 1.6$ that are close to meeting this requirement. Sketch the approximate OC curves of these three plans. Comment on the effect of increasing the sample size in this instance.

17-29 A known-sigma variables acceptance sampling plan has $n = 5$ and $k = 1.522$. When measured against a single upper specification of 950, incoming lots contain 5% nonconforming items. Distribution of product is approximately normal with a σ' of 100.

(a) At approximately what level is this process centered?

(b) What is the probability of acceptance for these incoming lots?

17-30 The plan described in Problem 17-29 has a Producer's Risk of 0.05 of rejecting lots with a p' of 0.012 and a Consumer's Risk of 0.10 of accepting lots with a p' of 0.172.

(a) What plan is recommended in MIL-STD-414 for code letter H, an AQL of 1.0%, and normal inspection using the Form 1 procedure when σ' is known?

(b) What is the probability of acceptance of lots containing 5% nonconforming items under this plan?

(c) What percentage of nonconforming items has a 10% probability of acceptance (Consumer's Risk point) under this plan? Comment on the reasons for the difference between this value and that stated for the plan described in Problem 17-29.

17-31 The $\bar{X}$ control chart reject limits discussed on pages 306 to 308 constitute a special case of known-sigma variables acceptance criteria. Table 9-7 gives a V factor of 2.25 for an n of 16. Assume that these values of V and n are being used for an $\bar{X}$ chart that shows only reject limits. Assume that the process is centered so that 2% of the product is outside one specification limit and no product is outside the other specification limit. What is the probability that the first $\bar{X}$ value from a process so centered will fall within the reject limits? Assume a normal distribution and a correct estimate of σ'.

Answer: 0.22

17-32 Specifications require that a certain quality characteristic of a manufactured product have a minimum value of 200 units. This quality characteristic can be tested only by a destructive test. The product is made in batches of several thousand. The past practice regarding acceptance inspection has been to test four articles from each batch. If all four articles met the quality specification of 200, the batch was accepted. If two or more failed, the batch was rejected. If one failed, a second sample of four was taken; with no failures on the second sample, the batch was accepted; otherwise it was rejected.

(a) What is the probability that a batch containing 6% of defectives will be accepted by this procedure?

(b) Control charts for $\bar{X}$ and R have been plotted from the first samples. These charts indicate that the range stays in statistical control even though the average shifts from batch to batch. The standard deviation of a batch appears to be 10 units. The suggestion is made that the acceptance decision be based on the average value computed from a single sample of four, with the batch accepted if the average is 210 or more. Assuming that the standard deviation continues to be at 10 units and assuming a normal distribution of the quality characteristic within a batch, what is the probability of acceptance of a 6% defective lot?

17-33 A mixed variables-attributes sampling plan stipulates the following procedures. (1) Draw a sample of 20 items from the lot and calculate the average of the sample: if $(\bar{X} - L)/\sigma' \geq 2.0$, accept the lot, otherwise (2) draw a second sample of 100 items: if the number of nonconforming items in this sample does not exceed 2, accept the lot, otherwise, reject the lot. Assume the lot size is 3,000, σ' is 100, the lower specification limit (L) is 1,000, and that incoming lots contain 3% nonconforming items.

(a) Assuming that this process is approximately normally distributed, what is the centering of the process from which these lots are formed?

(b) Find the probability of acceptance on the first sample.

(c) Find the total probability of acceptance under this plan.

(d) Control charts for $\bar{X}$ and σ are to be maintained on the data from first samples. Find the values of the central lines and control limits assuming 3% nonconforming items.

17-34 A company uses a combined variables-attributes sampling plan to inspect large batches of incoming items. Items are tested against a single upper specification limit of 3.00 units on a certain characteristic. On receiving a new lot, a random sample of 9 items is selected. If the average of the measurements of this characteristic is 2.90 or less, the lot is accepted. Otherwise, a new random sample of 25 items is selected. If no item in this sample exceeds 3.00 when tested, the lot is accepted. Otherwise the lot is rejected. In answering the following questions, assume a normal distribution underlies this characteristic and that σ' is 0.20 units.

(a) What is the probability of acceptance on the first sample for a lot containing 10% nonconforming items?

(b) What is the probability of taking the second sample?

(c) What is the total probability of acceptance of this lot?

EIGHTEEN

SOME ASPECTS OF LIFE TESTING AND RELIABILITY

A word is not a crystal, transparent and unchanged; it is the skin of a living thought, and may vary greatly in color and content according to the circumstances and the time in which it is used.—Justice Oliver Wendell Holmes[†]

Purpose of This Chapter

For a number of types of manufactured products, both components and complex systems, life may be one of the quality characteristics specified by the designer. Acceptance sampling relative to life testing has many elements in common with acceptance sampling for the testing of other quality characteristics. Nevertheless, there are certain important points of difference. The objective of this chapter is to help the reader to recognize these similarities and differences.

The subject can be explained to best advantage with reference to certain common sampling plans based on a relatively simple assumption, namely, that throughout the period of time of interest to the life tester, the probability of failure on a life test is constant. Certain limitations of this simple assumption and some possible alternative assumptions that are more complex are discussed briefly near the end of the chapter.

A Conventional Model of the Probability of Equipment Failure

Figure 18-1, reproduced from the AGREE Report[‡] (named from the initials of the committee that prepared it), shows a common set of assumptions that seem to give a fairly accurate description of the pattern of failures of certain types of electronic components as well as certain kinds of complex systems. Because of its shape, a

---

[†] In *Towne v. Eisner*, 245 U.S. 418 at 425 (1918).

[‡] "Reliability of Military Electronic Equipment," p. 120, Report by Advisory Group on Reliability of Electronic Equipment, Office of the Assistant Secretary of Defense (Research and Engineering), Superintendent of Documents, Government Printing Office, Washington, D.C., 1957.

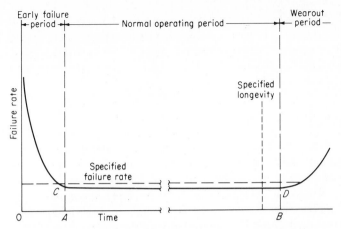

Figure 18-1 A common set of assumptions about equipment failure rate as a function of time under constant environmental operating conditions. *(Reproduced from " Reliability of Military Electronic Equipment," p. 120, Report by Advisory Group on Reliability of Electronic Equipment, Office of the Assistant Secretary of Defense (Research an Engineering), Superintendent of Documents, Government Printing Office, Washington, D.C., 1957.)*

failure-rate curve of the type shown in Fig. 18-1 has been called a " bathtub" curve. The initial early failure period OA is sometimes called the *infant-mortality* or the *burn-in* or the *debugging* period. The AGREE Report (page 121) describes this failure-rate curve, in part, as follows:

> The early failure period ... begins at the first point during manufacture that total equipment operation is possible and continues for such a period of time as permits (through maintenance and repair) the elimination of marginal parts, initially defective though not inoperative, and unrecognizable as such until premature failure. Upon replacement of all such prematurely failing items, the failure rate will have reached a lower value (point C) which will remain fairly constant and which defines the beginning of the normal operating period. Because customary curve smoothing techniques, necessary to develop an average from random data points, markedly reduce the accuracy with which a point of inflection can be located, it is probable that some difficulty may generally be encountered in determining the abscissa (time) location of point C....
>
> The normal operating period (A to B) is that period in terms of equipment operating time in which the average failure rate is and remains essentially constant.

Consider the fairly common cases where it is believed that Fig. 18-1 gives a satisfactory picture of the failure pattern of the component or system in question and where acceptance sampling plans are based on the assumption that the failure rate is constant throughout life. In effect, the use of sampling plans based on a constant failure rate implies that only the region from A to B on Fig. 18-1 needs to be considered. Presumably, acceptance sampling will not start until all the early failures in region OA have occurred. Conceivably, the early failures in this region could be eliminated by a 100% "burn-in" (for components) or by an initial "debugging" (of a complex system). Therefore, the "life" subject to test by acceptance sampling is viewed as starting either from point A of Fig. 18-1 or from some point to the right of A. Presumably, also, service will terminate before the start of the "wearout period"; it therefore is good enough for practical purposes to interpret acceptance criteria on the basis of an assumption that some unknown constant failure rate will continue indefinitely for any particular lot of items subject to acceptance sampling.

Some Modern Definitions of Reliability

Starting in the early 1950s, the word *reliability* acquired a highly specialized technical meaning in relation to the control of quality of manufactured product.†
Many formal definitions have been proposed that are similar in their general intent but differ a bit in their exact phrasing. Three of these are as follows:

"Reliability is the probability of a device performing its purpose adequately for the period of time intended under the operating conditions encountered."‡

"The reliability of a (system, device, etc.) is the probability that it will give satisfactory performance for a specified period of time under specified operating conditions."§

"(a) Failure: the inability of an equipment to perform its required function.

(b) Reliability: the probability of no failure throughout a prescribed operating period."¶

One obvious point in common among these definitions is that reliability is defined as a probability. Another important point is that all the definitions imply the need for an exact statement of what constitutes failure (i.e., inadequate or unsatisfactory performance).

Bazovsky states the modern concept of reliability in popular language as follows:‖ "Stated simply, reliability is the capability of an equipment not to break

---

† As nearly as the authors can determine, the first use of the word *reliability* in its "modern" technical sense was by Maj. Gen. Leslie E. Simon when he was Director of Ordnance Research and Development and Assistant Chief of Ordnance of the United States Army; this use was in connection with the Nike missile program. The following three articles are suggested to those readers who are interested in the semantic and organizational problems of reliability:

E. L. Grant and L. F. Bell, Some Comments on the Semantics of Quality and Reliability, *Industrial Quality Control*, vol. 17, no. 11, pp. 14–17, May, 1961.

E. G. D. Paterson, Quality Control vs. Quality Assurance vs. Reliability, *Industrial Quality Control*, vol. 19, no. 4, pp. 5–9, October, 1962.

Simon, L. E., The Relationship of Engineering to Very High Reliability, *Proceedings—Tenth National Symposium on Reliability and Quality Control*, pp. 226–232, Institute of Electrical and Electronic Engineers, New York, 1964.

‡ This is the official definition of the Electronics Industries Association (EIA), quoted by S. R. Calabro in his "Reliability Principles and Practices," p. 1, McGraw-Hill Book Company, New York, 1962.

§ The Bureau of Naval Weapons, U.S. Department of the Navy, "Reliability—Fundamental Concepts," Part I, A Brochure of the Material Presented in Film MN 8770a, p. 3, Government Printing Office, Washington, D.C., 1962.

¶ AGREE Report, *op. cit.*, p. 30.

‖ Igor Bazovsky, "Reliability Theory and Practice," p. 3, Prentice-Hall, Inc., Englewood Cliffs, N.J., 1961.

down in operation. When an equipment works well, and works whenever called upon to do the job for which it was designed, such equipment is said to be reliable."

The Interpretation of a "Failure" with Reference to Life Testing

In studies of human mortality, there is no question of the moment of death of an individual. Similarly, in the types of mortality studies of physical property made in connection with the requirements of depreciation accounting, the moment of retirement of, say, a telephone pole would be evident to anyone who observed the pole being removed from service.†

In contrast, where the "life" of a manufactured product is tested for purposes of acceptance inspection, the moment of termination of life may not be evident to a superficial observer. Elaborate test apparatus may be required to find the exact moment at which the performance ceases to be satisfactory. Moreover, specifications on what constitutes satisfactory performance naturally depend on the use to which the product is to be put. For example, a particular electron tube might have a short life under one set of specifications and a long life under another set.

Although there are exceptions, when a simple product fails (in the sense that its performance no longer conforms to specifications), the product usually cannot be restored to its original condition of giving satisfactory performance. Generally speaking, the failure of a component is viewed as terminating its life.

When a complex manufactured device fails, it often may be possible to restore the device to its original satisfactory performance, possibly by the replacement of one or more components. Even though "life" may be renewed in this way, a relevant question regarding any such complex device is how long a time may be expected to elapse between successive failures.

Possible Confusion between Technical and Popular Meanings of the Word Failure

In Chap. 1 we pointed out that when the words *defective* and *defect* were used in their technical senses they dealt with nonconformity to specifications. Because of the common practice of incorporating a margin of safety into specifications a product that is defective in the technical meaning of the word is not necessarily defective when the word is used in its popular meaning. This difference in meanings has been a source of confusion in litigation about product liability. To avoid the bad effects of such confusion, Arthur Bender, Jr., and others have pointed out that it is desirable for industry to abandon the use of *defective* and *defect* in their technical senses. The reader will doubtless recall that the authors tried to follow

---

† For an explanation of the methods used in mortality studies for depreciable fixed assets, see E. L. GRANT and P. T. NORTON, JR., "Depreciation," chap. 5, The Ronald Press Division of John Wiley & Sons, Inc., New York, 1955.

this good advice through Part One of this book, substituting such words or phrases as nonconformities, nonconforming product, and percent rejected in places where earlier editions had mentioned defects, defectives, and percent defective.

The word *failure* is like *defective* and *defect* in having a technical meaning that often differs from its popular meaning. The event that denotes a failure in the sense of nonconformity to specifications may not be the same as the event that would be recognized as a failure in the intended use of a product. For example, some quality characteristic may deteriorate with the amount of use of a product; a failure for test purposes may be defined as taking place when the value of this quality characteristic falls below some stipulated figure. Moreover, the test conditions used in accelerated life testing often are more severe than the conditions that will occur in the actual use of a product.

Using the word *failure* in its technical meaning may lead to confusion in product liability litigation similar to the confusion caused when *defective* and *defect* are used in their technical meanings. It follows that it would be desirable to substitute other words or phrases where the word *failure* has been used in connection with life testing and reliability. For example, persons engaged in life testing might refer to the *test life* of a component rather than to its *time to failure*.

Unfortunately, authors who write about published acceptance procedures and tables need to adopt the language of the published documents. For this reason, even though it was possible to avoid saying *defective* and *defect* in discussing control charts and related matters in Part One of this book, the authors have made frequent use of these words in their discussion of acceptance sampling in Part Two. In Chap. 12, the reader was warned that these words should be interpreted in their technical senses as referring to nonconformity to specifications.

For the same reason, our discussion in the present chapter needs to use the word *failure*. Here, also, it is necessary to warn the reader that here is a word being used in its restricted technical meaning.

The Relationship between a Constant Failure Rate and Mean Life or Mean Time between Failures

Assume that the probability of a failure of a component or complex device is constant per unit of time. That is, the failure rate is independent of the number of hours the component or device has been operated. This is the case in region AB of Fig. 18-1. As explained earlier in this chapter, in those cases where the failure pattern of Fig. 18-1 is believed to apply, the assumption of a constant failure rate implies that the measurement of life will not start before time A. This assumption also implies that the uniform failure rate will continue for a longer time than the intended period of use; for this reason, the final wearout period can be disregarded in the design and interpretation of acceptance sampling plans.

Consider that, say, 100 components are being tested with a new component being substituted whenever one fails. Even though the probability of a failure is constant for any stated time interval, the actual numbers of failures in successive equal time intervals will be subject to chance fluctuations. When we use the mathematics of probability to compute OC curves for acceptance sampling plans used in life testing, we are recognizing the inevitability of these chance fluctuations.

Two related quantities that we shall use in computing OC curves are as follows:†

λ' = failure rate, i.e., the probability of a failure in a stated unit of time. Conceivably, any unit of time could be adopted. However, for consistency throughout this chapter, we shall arbitrarily select 1 hour as the time unit in all instances.

θ' = the arithmetic mean or average of the lives (of components), usually referred to in the literature of realiability as the *mean life*, or *mean time to failure* (MTTF). As applied to complex devices, θ' is interpreted as the *mean time between failures* (sometimes designated as mtbf or MTBF). θ' should be expressed in the same time units that are used for λ'.

For our special case of the constant failure rate: $\theta' = 1/\lambda'$. (It is pointed out later in this chapter that this reciprocal relationship between θ' and λ' depends on the use of a time unit that is a relatively small fraction of the mean life.)

Although our discussion in this chapter is based on failure rates and mean lives expressed in units of time, it should be mentioned that other units than time may be used in certain instances. For example, the number of operating cycles of certain switching devices is a more appropriate unit for measuring life than the number of operating hours.

Computing an OC Curve for an Acceptance Sampling Plan Based on a Stipulated Maximum Number of Test Hours

Consider the following lot-by-lot acceptance sampling plan (taken from "Handbook H 108," Example 2C-4‡):

Select 22 items at random from a lot. Place these items on test. Whenever an item fails, replace it with another item selected at random from the lot. If the test continues for 500 h with not more than 2 failures, accept the lot. If 3 failures occur before the 500 h of testing, reject the lot and terminate the test.

---

† There is considerable variability in the symbols chosen by different writers on the mathematics of reliability. The symbols λ and θ adopted here are used by some writers. For the purpose of our discussion here, they have the advantage that they are not used elsewhere in this book with some other meaning. λ is the lowercase form of the Greek letter *lambda* and is read as "lambda." θ is the lowercase form of the Greek letter *theta* and is read as "theta." The prime (') notation for a universe parameter has been adopted here to be consistent with the method of identifying such parameters elsewhere in this book.

‡ The full name of this handbook is "Quality Control and Reliability Handbook (Interim) H 108—Sampling Procedures and Tables for Life and Reliability Testing (Based on Exponential Distribution)," Office of the Assistant Secretary of Defense (Supply and Logistics), Government Printing Office, Washington, D.C., 1960. In subsequent references in this chapter, the name of this document is abbreviated to "H 108."

Table 18-1 Calculation of OC curve for acceptance sampling plan requiring 11,000 item hours of life testing with an acceptance number of 2

(Calculation assumes that the failure rate λ' is independent of the age of the item tested)

Failure rate per hour, λ'	Mean life h, $\theta' = 1/\lambda'$	Expected average number of failures in 11,000 test hours $(11{,}000\ \lambda')$	Probability of acceptance (probability of 2 or less failures, read from Table G)
0.00002	50,000	0.22	0.999
0.00005	20,000	0.55	0.982
0.00006	16,667	0.66	0.971
0.00008	12,500	0.88	0.939
0.00010	10,000	1.1	0.900
0.000125	8,000	1.375	0.839
0.00015	6,667	1.65	0.770
0.00020	5,000	2.2	0.623
0.00025	4,000	2.75	0.480
0.00030	3,333	3.3	0.360
0.00040	2,500	4.4	0.185
0.00050	2,000	5.5	0.088
0.00060	1,667	6.6	0.040
0.00080	1,250	8.8	0.007

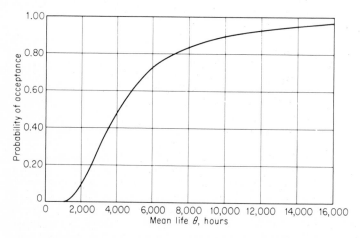

Figure 18-2 OC curve for a test of 11,000 item hours with an acceptance number of 2 (based on assumption of a constant failure rate).

Acceptance under this plan requires 22(500) = 11,000 item hours of test with an acceptance number of 2. Under the assumption that the probability of a failure is the same for every item hour, the calculation of the OC curve is the same as if we had an ordinary single sampling attributes plan with an n of 11,000 and a c of 2. Table 18-1 illustrates the use of Table G to calculate the OC curve of this plan. The method of calculation is identical with the method first illustrated in Table 12-1. However, the failure rate λ' takes the place of the fraction defective p'. Moreover, because it is customary to plot OC curves of life testing plans in terms of mean life rather than in terms of failure rate, Table 18-1 shows the value of θ' corresponding to each value of λ'. Figure 18-2 shows the OC curve plotted in the usual manner for such curves.

Table 18-1 and the OC curve of Fig. 18-2 are valid for all plans requiring 11,000 item hours for acceptance and having an acceptance number of 2. They apply to the stated plan from H 108 that called for 22 items to be tested for 500 h with replacement of any items failing during the test. They also apply if 44 items are to be tested with replacement for 250 h or if 110 items are to be tested with replacement for 100 h, provided an acceptance number of 2 is used. Or, with this acceptance number, they apply to any other set of specified items and hours that have a product of 11,000. Under the assumption that the probability that an item will fail is independent of the number of hours the item has been tested, one OC curve applies to all plans that have the same stipulated item hours for acceptance and the same acceptance number. OC curves for life testing plans are frequently plotted as a function of θ/θ_0, rather than as a function of θ, where θ_0 is the *acceptable value* of mean life for the component or system.

Discontinuance of Life Testing when the Rejection Number is Reached

Our sampling plan from H 108 stipulated a maximum of 500 h of testing for the 22 items. However, it stipulated that testing should end when the rejection number of 3 was reached. If the third failure occurs after, say, 140 h, no more testing takes place; the decision on the lot is reached with only 3,080 item hours of test rather than with the stipulated maximum of 11,000 item hours.

In the Dodge-Romig systems described in Chap. 13 and in some of the military standards referred to in Chap. 14, it has been customary to inspect an entire single sample regardless of the number of defects found; such inspection gives a better basis for the required estimate of process average. In such systems, curtailment of inspection ordinarily occurs only in double and multiple sampling. However, there is nothing inherent in single sampling that prevents curtailing inspection as soon as a rejection decision is reached. In the usual nondestructive acceptance sampling by attributes, there may be only a small incremental cost of inspecting the remainder of a single sample after a rejection decision; the value of the information gained may be deemed to be considerably greater than this small cost. In life testing, this incremental cost usually is fairly high and it is customary to curtail single sampling.

Producer's Risks and Consumer's Risks in Acceptance Sampling Plans Used in Life Testing

OC curves for life testing plans, like OC curves for other types of acceptance sampling plans, may be interpreted in terms of stated Producer's and Consumer's Risks. The plan for which the OC curve was computed in Table 18-1 was stipulated in H 108 for a Producer's Risk of 0.10 of rejecting a lot that has a mean life of 10,000 h and a stipulated approximate value of 0.10 for the Consumer's Risk of accepting a lot that has a mean life of 2,000 h. (In Table 18-1, the Consumer's Risk for a 2,000-h mean life was computed to be 0.088.) Several of the tables in H 108 deal with the case in which both Producer's and Consumer's Risks are stipulated.

In our discussion (on pages 450 to 455) of the design of ordinary single sampling attributes plans where both Producer's and Consumer's Risks are stipulated, we noted the very high sample sizes needed where the lot qualities associated with the two risks were close together. As might be expected, the same difficulty arises in the design of life testing plans for both risks. This difficulty can be illustrated by the following plans from H 108, all requiring 500 h of testing with replacement to accept a lot and all involving values of 0.10 for both Producer's and Consumer's Risks.

Mean life for Producer's Risk, h	Mean life for Consumer's Risk, h	Items tested	Acceptance number	Item hours required for acceptance
10,000	1,000	10	1	5,000
10,000	2,000	22	2	11,000
10,000	3,333	63	5	31,500
10,000	5,000	205	14	102,500
10,000	6,667	660	40	330,000

It is evident that, if one starts with the premise that the producer should be protected against chance rejections of lots having mean lives of 10,000 h or more, it is going to be quite expensive to protect the consumer against chance acceptance of lots with mean lives of, say, 5,000 h or less.

An Experiment to Illustrate Certain Aspects of a Constant Failure Rate

In Chap. 2, we used the first 400 drawings from Shewhart's normal bowl as an aid in the explanation of certain principles. There were a number of advantages gained by such use of data from bowl drawings rather than data from some industrial process. With bowl drawings, we knew the shape of the universe and its parameters. Moreover, we knew that, because the same bowl had been used throughout and because the chips had been stirred thoroughly between drawings, it was reasonable to assume that a constant system of chance causes had been operating.

In a similar way, it should be helpful to have a set of numbers of trials to failure (i.e., lives) generated by a series of experiments in which the failure rate is known and is kept constant. We might generate such numbers in various ways, such as by drawing chips from a bowl (see Problem 18-11), by throwing dice, or by the use of tables of random numbers or of random permutations.

Assume that we are interested in a failure rate of 0.02 and want to generate our data by throwing two icosohedral Japanese random dice. (These were described in Chap. 12.) A failure could be designated as a throw of, say, either 00 or 99. Successive throws could be made until either 00 or 99 occurred. The number of successive throws made to obtain a failure could be counted and recorded. This number might be viewed as the time to failure (i.e., life) of one item in a sample. The experiment might be repeated as often as desired to obtain a distribution of times to failure.

The same sort of experiment might be made using a table of random numbers such as Table Z, App. 3 (see Problem 18-12). Or it might be done using a set of tables of random permutations of the integers 1 to 50.

Table 18-2 was generated from the Moses-Oakford tables.[†] These tables include 400 different permutations of the integers 1 to 50. For each of the 120 experiments recorded in Table 18-2, two integers from 1 to 50 were picked from a table of random numbers. The first integer determined the position to be examined in each random permutation; the appearance of the second integer in this position constituted a failure.

Consider an industrial sampling situation in which 5 items are selected at random from each lot and are tested to determine the number of hours to failure. The averages and ranges in Table 18-2 show the considerable variation that might occur from sample to sample even though all the 24 lots had identical values of 0.02 for the failure rate λ'.

The 120 lives of Table 18-2 have been rearranged in order of increasing magnitude in Table 18-3. Much of our subsequent discussion will deal with this latter table. The lives in this table are listed in the order in which they would have been observed if the 120 life tests had all started at the same moment. The arrangement of the data in this table is useful in bringing out certain aspects of acceptance sampling procedures often used in life testing.

The reader should note that Table 18-3 is similar to a tabulation of the results of a life test carried out without replacement of an item that fails. It will be recalled that our OC curve of Fig. 18-1 dealt with a life test carried out with replacement. We shall see that acceptance sampling plans involving life testing may be designed either with or without replacement.

Estimating Mean Life at Various Stages in a Life Test

Assume the existence in a lot or process of an unknown constant failure rate per item hour λ'. We wish to estimate this probability of failure in an item hour. On

---

† L. E. Moses and R. V. Oakford, "Tables of Random Permutations," Stanford University Press, Stanford, Calif., 1963.

Table 18-2 Length of life, measured in numbers of successive trials to failure, obtained when 120 sets of observations were made with a constant probability of failure of 0.02

Sets of observations	Length of life					Average of 5 values	Range of 5 values
1–5	115	105	34	120	30	80.8	90
6–10	23	14	59	10	18	24.8	49
11–15	4	28	55	11	95	38.6	91
16–20	15	54	45	5	17	27.2	49
21–25	13	50	165	5	40	54.6	160
26–30	4	46	27	30	52	31.8	48
31–35	17	20	7	67	9	24.0	60
36–40	114	132	18	39	37	68.0	114
41–45	147	3	5	23	5	36.6	144
46–50	44	140	125	11	119	87.8	129
51–55	53	86	32	148	1	64.0	147
56–60	78	8	16	14	54	34.0	70
61–65	25	118	10	9	62	44.8	109
66–70	75	2	64	171	17	65.8	169
71–75	2	1	101	26	35	33.0	100
76–80	140	93	11	148	31	84.6	137
81–85	34	52	1	33	36	31.2	51
86–90	105	56	2	5	21	37.8	103
91–95	19	1	111	28	140	59.8	139
96–100	37	98	63	73	43	62.8	61
101–105	43	17	108	35	147	70.0	130
106–110	31	14	94	5	39	36.6	89
111–115	72	127	25	25	22	54.2	105
116–120	4	33	68	20	23	29.6	64
Totals...						1,182.4	2,408

the basis of all the information from life tests from the lot or process available at any moment, our best estimate obviously is

$$\text{Estimated } \lambda' = \frac{\text{number of failures observed}}{\text{number of item hours of test}}$$

This equation simply applies the frequency definition of probability and assumes that all trials of the event in question (i.e., failure) are made "under the same essential conditions." If the probability of a failure does not depend on the age of the item tested, each item hour of test should be viewed as providing the same amount of information as any other item hour. For example, 1,000 item hours obtained from testing 1,000 items each for 1 h give just as good a basis for estimating λ' as if only 10 items were tested (with replacement) for 100 h each.

Table 18-3 Data of Table 18-2 rearranged in order of increasing magnitude

(This may be viewed as representing a distribution of lives in hours that might have been found if simultaneous tests to failure had been made of a random sample of 120 items from a universe that had a constant failure rate of 0.02 per hour)

1	4	9	15	20	27	34	43	54	73	105	132
1	5	10	16	21	28	34	43	55	75	108	140
1	5	10	17	22	28	35	44	56	78	111	140
1	5	11	17	23	30	35	45	59	86	114	140
2	5	11	17	23	30	36	46	62	93	115	147
2	5	11	17	23	31	37	50	63	94	118	147
2	5	13	18	25	31	37	52	64	95	119	148
3	7	14	18	25	32	39	52	67	98	120	148
4	8	14	19	25	33	39	53	68	101	125	165
4	9	14	20	26	33	40	54	72	105	127	171

Total.. | 5,912

The greater the number of item hours, the more confidence it is reasonable to have in the resulting estimate of λ'. However, in this connection, the reader should recall the point brought out in the discussion of Table 6-1 that a small number of trials may occasionally, by chance, give an estimate closer to the true probability than will be obtained from a larger number of trials.

Because mean life is the reciprocal of failure rate, an estimate of θ' in hours may be made at any time during a life test as follows:

$$\text{Estimated } \theta' = \frac{\text{number of item hours of test up to the time of estimate}}{\text{number of failures up to the time of estimate}}$$

Table 18-4 shows a series of estimates of mean life such as might have been

Table 18-4 Some estimates of mean life that might have been made from the data of Table 18-3

Hours of test at moment of estimate	Failures up to moment of estimate	Item hours of test up to moment of estimate	Estimate of mean life, h
4	11	461	41.9
5	17	570	33.5
6	17	673	39.7
8	19	878	46.2
10	23	1,078	46.9
15	31	1,556	50.2
20	41	1,970	48.0
30	55	2,696	49.0
171	120	5,912	49.3

made at various times during a life test that had the results shown in Table 18-3. It should be noted that, in such a test made without replacement, the number of item hours of test at any time can be computed by adding the lives in hours, t_i, of the items that have failed (m in all) up to the moment of estimate to the number of item hours of life observed, t, for the items that have not yet failed ($n - m$). For example, the estimate after 4 h could be computed as follows:
Estimated

$$\theta'_m = \frac{\sum\limits_{i=1}^{m} t_i + t(n - m)}{m}$$

$$= \frac{1 + 1 + 1 + 1 + 2 + 2 + 2 + 3 + 4 + 4 + 4 + 4(120 - 11)}{11}$$

$$= \frac{25 + 436}{11} = \frac{461}{11} = 41.9 \text{ h}$$

In examining the successive estimates of mean life shown in Table 18-4, the reader should keep in mind that the data were generated using a failure rate of 0.02 per hour. This failure rate corresponds to a "true" mean life of 50 h.

Some Economic Considerations in Designing Acceptance Sampling Procedures under the Assumption of a Constant Failure Rate

If we were conducting a simultaneous life test on the 120 items that had the distribution of lives shown in Table 18-3, there are good reasons why we might want to stop the test before the end of the 171st hour when the 120th item had failed. If a decision to accept or reject a lot depended on the results of the test, there would be costs of storage of the lot that would be increased by a delay in reaching a decision. If the conclusions from the test were to be fed back to designers or production people to influence design or production methods on future lots, it would be desirable to have this feedback take place as soon as some dependable conclusions could be obtained. Moreover, if the probability of failure really is independent of age, every item not destroyed by the test may be assumed to end the test as good as new. A substantial part of the cost of a life test may be the cost of the items destroyed; the sooner a life test is terminated, the less will be this element of cost.

Generally speaking, the longer the lives of the items to be tested, the greater is the economic advantage in using an acceptance sampling plan that will reach a decision with a maximum test period considerably shorter than the mean life. To illustrate this point, let us assume that the failure rate of 0.02 used in generating Tables 18-2 and 18-3 is interpreted as a rate per 100 h rather than per hour. (The reader will recognize that our choice of a time unit of 1 h was purely arbitrary.)

The mean life would then be 5,000 h rather than 50 h; it would have taken 17,100 h before the failure of the 120th item. In such a case, there would doubtless be compelling reasons for terminating the test in a period not to exceed, say, 1,000 h.

Economic considerations therefore dictate that many acceptance sampling plans that involve life testing call for terminating a test at a time considerably short of the mean life. It therefore becomes important to estimate mean life by the methods illustrated in Table 18-4 at a time when most of the items tested are still surviving.

In choosing among alternative possible acceptance sampling plans involving life testing, the item hours of test to give the desired protection may be obtained by testing a relatively few items for a long time or more items for a shorter time. Under the assumption that the failure rate is independent of the age of the items tested, it has been pointed out that all plans with the same item hours and acceptance numbers involve identical OC curves. Therefore, the choice of a plan may involve balancing the extra costs associated with a long delay in reaching a decision against the extra costs associated with placing a larger number of items on test.

Use of Acceptance Criteria Based on Estimated Mean Life

In Table 18-1, we showed the calculation of the OC curve of a plan requiring 11,000 item hours of life testing with not more than 2 failures permitted. The acceptance criterion for this plan could have been expressed in terms of minimum allowable mean life rather than maximum allowable number of failures.

Suppose the 3d failure—the one causing rejection—took place at the last possible moment, namely, at the 11,000th item hour. The estimated θ' would then have been $11,000/3 = 3,667$ h. Any earlier occurrence of the 3d failure would have given an estimate of less than 3,667 h. Therefore, the same acceptance decision would have been reached if it had been stipulated that the estimated mean life should exceed 3,667 h.

(Incidentally, it is of interest to note that, if there had been 2 failures at the end of 11,000 item hours of test, the estimated mean life would have been $11,000/2 = 5,500$ h. With this particular plan of testing, there can be no estimated mean life between 3,667 and 5,500 h.)

It may be impracticable or inconvenient to carry out a life test with replacement in the way illustrated by the acceptance plan that was the subject of Table 18-1. One possible alternative is to require a test of a stipulated number of items for a stipulated number of hours without replacement; in plans of this type, the acceptance criterion usually is stated in terms of minimum acceptable estimated mean life. Other plans involve testing a stipulated number of items until a stipulated number of failures has occurred; these plans also base the acceptance decision on the estimated mean life. In all such plans that involve a uniform failure rate, mean lives are estimated in the way that was illustrated in Table 18-4.

Acceptance Sampling Plans Involving the Combination of Samples from a Series of Lots

Consider the case of, say, an electronic component to be used in a service where it is desired to have a failure rate of not more than 0.00001 per hour. (Sometimes it is desired to avoid the use of very small decimal fractions; if so, a rate of 0.00001 per hour might be stated as 1% per 1,000 h.) Such a specification tells us that the mean life must be at least 100,000 h.

The need to combine the evidence of the samples from a series of successive lots is particularly great when one is dealing with a requirement for such an extremely low failure rate. Otherwise, if the decision on each lot is to be made solely on the evidence of the sample from the lot itself the required item hours of test from each lot may be extremely high and the test may be extremely costly.

The following plan illustrates one possible method of combining the results of samples from successive lots. The plan is one of a set that has been suggested for use in acceptance sampling for certain long-lived electronic components. The sample sizes and acceptance numbers in this particular plan are related to a desired mean life of at least 100,000 h.

1. The plan starts with a qualification sample requiring 418,000 item hours of test (say 936 items tested for 500 h). Not more than 3 failures are allowed in this sample. The sample size and acceptance number are chosen to give a Consumer's Risk of 0.40 of accepting product having a mean life of 100,000 h. (In some of the literature of reliability, such a Consumer's Risk is referred to as a "confidence level" of 0.60.)
2. After qualification has been obtained, a sample of 44 items from each lot is tested for 250 h, a total of 11,000 item hours. Not more than 1 failure is allowable to pass the lot.
3. The item hours and failures of the samples from each set of 10 successive lots are to be cumulated. The total item hours from the 10 lots will be 10(11,000) = 110,000. If a total of more than 2 failures is found at any time during the 110,000 item hours, reduced inspection is discontinued and a new qualification sample is required. If lots are held and accepted or rejected in sets of 10, these criteria give a Producer's Risk of 0.10 of rejecting product that has a mean life of 100,000 h.
4. Item hours and failures from successive samples are cumulated until 418,000 item hours, the number used in the qualification test, have been observed. If a total of more than 3 failures is found, reduced inspection is discontinued and a new qualification sample is required.

The reader will note that three different OC curves are relevant in judging how a scheme of this type affects the producer and consumer (see Problems 18-14 to 18-19). Nevertheless, because the criteria of paragraph (1) are also applied cumulatively in (4), the OC curve of the qualification sample is the one of greatest interest to the producer. Unless he can make product that has a mean life considerably longer than 100,000 h, he takes a substantial risk that he cannot qualify in the first place. (He has 6 chances out of 10 that he will not qualify if his λ' is exactly 0.00001.) He also takes the same risk that, if he qualifies, he will be disqualified before one cycle of procedure (paragraph 4) has run its course.

Although the OC curve of the acceptance plan in paragraph 1 measures the consumer's protection relative to qualification, he needs to look at the OC curve of the plan in (2) to evaluate the worst condition that he faces in the short run (i.e., his protection against accepting an individual lot after a producer achieves qualification). All things considered, it is evident that the consumer takes substantial risks of accepting product that has a failure rate much worse than the desired 0.00001.

The foregoing type of acceptance procedure has been included in this chapter to emphasize the difficulties that inevitably arise in devising acceptance sampling schemes when tolerable failure rates are extremely low. In meeting these difficulties, it is desirable that all parties concerned recognize the need for quite large sample sizes and for a substantial sharing of risks between producer and consumer.

The "Exponential" Reliability Function that Results from the Assumption of a Constant Failure Rate

In generating Tables 18-1 and 18-3, we made successive trials of an event that had a constant probability 0.02 that a failure would occur on any single trial. The probability that any one trial will not result in a failure is $1 - 0.02 = 0.98$. If trials are to be continued until a failure occurs, we can apply the theorem of conditional probabilities to determine the probability of survival (i.e., of no failure) after any stipulated number of trials. For example, the probability of survival after 10 trials is $0.98^{10} = 0.817$. In general, if λ' represents a constant probability of failure per hour, the probability of an item surviving for H hours is $(1 - \lambda')^H$.

Early in this chapter, several formal definitions of reliability were quoted. Although the phrasing differed slightly, all the definitions viewed reliability as being the probability of no failure throughout some specified period of time. In this sense, the third column of Table 18-5 gives reliability values corresponding to a λ' of 0.02 and to the various possible "specified periods of time" from 2 to 200 h that are given in the first column of the table. In examining Table 18-5, it is of interest to note the fairly close agreement between the computed probabilities of survival 0.98^H given in the third column and the observed fractions surviving given in the fifth column based on the experiment recorded in Table 18-3.

Nevertheless, although our experiment employed a constant failure rate of 0.02 per trial, it failed in one minor respect to simulate the results that would occur in an actual life test where the failure rate was constant. A constraint in our test was that we could obtain only integral values of lives; no fractional values were possible. That is, we could find a life of 5 h (5 trials with each trial interpreted as an hour) or 6 h but not, say, 5.37 h. Of course, in an actual life test, failure may occur at any moment, not merely at the end of an hour. This point bears on the

Table 18-5 An illustration of the validity of the negative exponential formula to estimate reliability (i.e., probability of survival) under the assumption of a constant failure rate

(The assumed failure rate λ' is 0.02 per hour, the rate that was used in generating Tables 18-2 and 18-3. The values of the negative exponential can be read from Table G, Appendix 3, using the column headed $c = 0$)

Age, h H	Ratio of age to mean life $H/\theta' = H\lambda'$	Probability of survival		Actual fraction surviving among the 120 items of Table 18-3
		By theorem of conditional probabilities $(1 - \lambda')^H$	By negative exponential $e^{-H\lambda'}$	
2	0.04	0.960	0.961	0.94
4	0.08	0.922	0.923	0.91
6	0.12	0.886	0.887	0.86
8	0.16	0.851	0.852	0.84
10	0.20	0.817	0.819	0.81
15	0.30	0.739	0.741	0.74
20	0.40	0.668	0.670	0.66
30	0.60	0.546	0.549	0.54
40	0.80	0.446	0.449	0.42
50	1.00	0.364	0.368	0.37
60	1.2	0.298	0.301	0.30
70	1.4	0.243	0.247	0.26
80	1.6	0.199	0.202	0.23
90	1.8	0.162	0.165	0.22
100	2.0	0.133	0.135	0.18
120	2.4	0.089	0.091	0.10
140	2.8	0.059	0.061	0.05
160	3.2	0.039	0.041	0.02
180	3.6	0.026	0.027	0.00
200	4.0	0.018	0.018	0.00

relative merits of the methods of computing probability of survival illustrated in the third and fourth columns of Table 18-5.

The fourth column of Table 18-5 gives values of $e^{-H\lambda'}$ for our λ' of 0.02. The reader will recall from the discussion of the binomial and Poisson distributions in Chap. 6 that $e^{-np'}$ is a limit of $(1 - p')^n$ as n increased and p' decreased with the product np' held constant. Or, stated a little differently, $e^{-np'}$ gives a satisfactory approximation to $(1 - p')^n$ provided p' is small enough and n is large enough. Of course, the symbols that we employ are purely arbitrary; it is equally appropriate to view $e^{-H\lambda'}$ as an approximation to $(1 - \lambda')^H$. By comparing the values in the third and fourth columns of Table 18-5, we can see that this approximation is fairly close with a λ' of 0.02. For smaller values of λ', the approximation would be even better.

The theorem of conditional probabilities used in the manner illustrated in Table 18-5 is correct in principle for an artificial experiment in which lives can be only integers. However, the concept of a constant failure rate applied to actual lives presumably means a constant instantaneous failure rate; for such a rate the negative exponential formula for probability of survival is correct in principle.

Although the expression $e^{-H\lambda'}$ is more precisely described as negative exponential, the literature of life testing and reliability usually refers to it simply as "exponential." With one exception (the discussion of a graph reproduced from a source that uses "negative exponential"), the word *exponential* is the one used throughout the remainder of this chapter.

The Relationship between the Reliability Function and the Probability Density Function in the Case of a Constant Failure Rate

Consider any desired unit of time t (which might be, say, 10, 500, 1,000 h, etc.). Assume that there is a constant probability of 0.9 that a unit entering a time interval of length t will survive to the end of the interval. The probability of failure during the interval will, of course, be $1 - 0.9 = 0.1$. The second column of Table 18-6 gives the respective probabilities that a unit starting at time zero will survive for 1, 2, 3, 4, 5, and 6 time intervals. Of course, each figure in this column is obtained by multiplying the preceding figure by 0.9. A mathematical function

Table 18-6 Illustration of the distinction between a reliability function and a probability density function

(The constant probability that an item will survive a time interval is 0.9)

Number of time intervals from time zero	Probability of survival (reliability)	Probability of item failing during time interval (probability density)
0	1.000000	
		0.100000
1	0.900000	
		0.090000
2	0.810000	
		0.081000
3	0.729000	
		0.072900
4	0.656100	
		0.065610
5	0.590490	
		0.059049
6	0.531441	

(such as the exponential) that gives probability of survival is called a reliability function.

Each figure for probability density in the third column of Table 18-6 might have been computed in either of two ways. The probability of failure during each time interval (0.1) might have been multiplied by the probability that the item would have survived until the start of the time interval. Or the probability of survival to the end of the time interval could have been subtracted from the probability of survival to the beginning of the interval. These two mathematical operations obviously must give identical results.

The reader will note that the probability densities in column 3 of Table 18-6 are proportional to the reliabilities in column 2. The use of a constant failure rate causes this relationship. In general, if the reliability function is exponential, the probability density function must also be exponential. However, it is important that the student of reliability understand that the reliability curve (survivor curve) and the probability density curve will not have the same shape except in the special case where probability of failure is independent of age (i.e., where there is a constant failure rate).

Some Aspects of the Exponential Reliability Function

The numbers in the fourth column of Table 18-5 were read or interpolated from the column headed $c = 0$ in Table G, App. 3. This column for the probability of 0 occurrences in a family of Poisson distributions gives the value of $e^{-np'}$. (See the original discussion of the Poisson in Chap. 6.) Because this one column of Table G gives values of e with various negative exponents, it happens to describe the shape of all exponential reliability functions regardless of the value of λ'. That is, we can observe from this column of Table G that, with a constant failure rate, approximately 60.7% of the items in a group will survive to half the average life of the group, approximately 36.8% will survive to the average life, approximately 13.5% will survive to twice the average life, and so on.

The figures in the fifth column of Table 18-5 give the actual fractions surviving after various numbers of trials in our experiment in which we made 120 series of trials with a known constant probability of failure of 0.02. All such observed values naturally are subject to sampling fluctuations and therefore will not agree exactly with the probabilities of survival computed from a known constant failure rate. (The observed values in the fifth column of Table 18-5 are all well within 3-sigma limits based on the known rate, using n as 120 in all cases and p' in each case as the computed probability of survival shown in the same line of the third column of the table.)

Actual life testing differs from our experiment in that we never can *know* that we have a constant failure rate. If it is proposed to base engineering designs and acceptance sampling plans on the assumption that certain failure rates are constant, and if failure data are available, it is appropriate to apply various statistical tests to judge whether the data are consistent with the hypothesis of a constant failure rate. A number of such tests were summarized in a paper by Benjamin Epstein that appeared (in two parts) in the February and May, 1960, issues of *Technometrics*. Dr. Epstein's useful paper was reprinted as a U.S. Department of Defense Technical Report.†

Some Limitations on the Use of the Reciprocal Relationship between Failure Rate and Mean Life

When the useful formula $\theta' = 1/\lambda'$ was introduced earlier in this chapter for the special cases of the constant failure rate, it was mentioned that the validity of this formula depended on the use of a time unit that is a relatively small fraction of the average life. We are now in a position to explain that statement.

Consider our experiment of 120 sets of trials to failure that was summarized in Tables 18-2 and 18-3. The reciprocal relationship between θ' and λ' is exact for the conditions of this experiment. Our distribution of failures was not a continuous one; we could have a failure on trial 22 or trial 23 but not on, say, trial 22.57. Our probability of failure applied to a trial that was an identifiable single operation rather than to an arbitrarily chosen interval of time throughout which there was a continuing chance for failure.

Now imagine that we are making life tests of a type of item for which the probability of failure *sometime* within any hour is 0.02. An experiment testing 120 such items would result in the same type of variability observed in Tables 18-2 and 18-3. However, if the moment of failure should be recorded to the nearest 0.01 h, three failures during the 23d hour would not be recorded as 23, 23, and 23 but rather as numbers such as 22.15, 22.57, and 22.89. It is intuitively evident that a continuous failure rate that would cause the probability of failure during an hour to be 0.02 would result in a slightly shorter mean life than would occur if the probability were 0.02 that a failure would occur only at the *end* of an hour.

The true mean life is approximately 99% of the life given by the reciprocal formula in the case of a continuous failure rate that results in a probability of failure of 0.02 during a chosen time period. Therefore, the reciprocal formula usually may be accepted as good enough for practical purposes in the common case where the chosen time period is short enough for the failure rate per unit time interval to be 2% or less.‡

The most important practical limitation of the reciprocal formula that always should be kept in mind is the assumption that there really is a λ', a failure rate that is independent of the age of an item. Where the assumption of a constant failure rate is used for purposes of acceptance sampling and the bathtub curve (Fig. 18-1) is believed to describe the expected failure rate pattern, two further limitations of the reciprocal formula should be kept in mind:

---

† "Tests for the Validity of the Assumption that the Underlying Distribution of Life Is Exponential," Superintendent of Documents, Government Printing Office, Washington, D.C. 20402, 1960.

‡ If h represents the chosen unit time period in hours and f' is the probability of failure during period h, the exponential reliability function yields the following formula for mean life in hours:

$$\theta' = \frac{h \log e}{\log(1 - f')}$$

1. Time zero from which life is being measured is assumed to start after the infant mortality period has ended.
2. The wearing-out period is disregarded. It is obvious that, if the wearing-out period is considered, the mean life will be less than the figure given by the reciprocal formula.

Some of the acceptance sampling plans in H 108 (the U.S. Department of Defense handbook mentioned earlier in this chapter) are based on what is called a "two-parameter" exponential. These plans assume a zero failure rate for some initial period of time, followed by a constant failure rate thereafter. (The second parameter is the duration of the failure-free period.) Because the reciprocal formula $\theta' = 1/\lambda'$ assumes that the failure rate starts with time zero, it is necessary to add the assumed length of the failure-free period to the θ' computed from the formula in order to find the mean life for this two-parameter exponential.

Principal U.S. Government Documents that Treat Life Testing under the Assumption of a Constant Failure Rate

Three principal documents have been issued by the U.S. Department of Defense dealing with sampling plans and procedures for life testing in those cases where the constant failure rate assumption is appropriate. They are H 108, which has been discussed in part in earlier articles of this chapter, MIL-STD-690B, and MIL-STD-781C.

Handbook H 108, the earliest of the three, contains three sets of plans. The first is a set of life test plans that terminate upon the occurrence of a preassigned number of failures. In the second set, termination occurs at a preassigned time, H, or when r (the rejection number) failures have been detected, whichever occurs first. The third set contains plans for sequential life testing, based on Wald's sequential probability ratio test, in which both the acceptance/rejection numbers and total unit time on test vary. All three sets stipulate procedures for life testing either with replacement or without replacement of failed units. In addition, the choice of individual plans may be made based upon the selection of a range of stipulated Producer's Risk points (θ_0, α), and Consumer's Risk points (θ_1, β).

Handbook H 108 and the Military Standards 690 and 781, along with many other standards and specifications, resulted directly from the 1957 AGREE report. Whereas H 108, first published in 1960, emphasized the use of standard tables of life test plans, the military standards emphasize the procedural aspects of analysis of design and production results. MIL-STD-690B, "Failure Rate Sampling Plans and Procedures,"† establishes detailed procedures for demonstration

---

† "Failure Rate Sampling Plans and Procedures," MIL-STD-690, was first published in 1963. Revision A followed in 1965 and Revision B, which is discussed in this book, was published in April, 1968. A discussion of the history of its development along with the changes that have taken place since first publication may be found in S. GRUBMAN, C. A. MARTIN, and W. R. PABST, JR., "MIL-STD-690B, Failure Rate Sampling Plans and Procedures," *Journal of Quality Technology*, vol. 1, no. 3, July, 1969, pp. 205–216.

(qualification) testing and for production run tests, failure rate test records and quality history requirements, as well as providing guidance to specification writers.

Following several military directives in the early 1960s it was determined that procedures were needed whereby manufacturers could qualify their product against established standards. Such standard data on basic electronic components were necessary in the development of military hardware systems design as well as in the prediction of reliability of these systems. MIL-STD-690B provides four inspection procedures as follows:

I. Qualification testing at an initial failure rate.
II. Extension of qualification to a lower failure rate level.
III. Maintenance of failure rate level qualification.
IV. Lot conformance failure rate inspection.

Specific requirements for certain of these procedures are discussed later in this chapter.

MIL-STD-781C,† while equally applicable to component parts testing, is particularly useful for testing assemblies and systems. A number of the test plans included in the standard employ the principles of sequential sampling based on Wald's sequential probability ratio test. The standard emphasizes requirements for preproduction reliability qualification tests, production reliability acceptance tests employing both sampling and all-units testing, and combined environmental test conditions.

Test Procedures under MIL-STD-690B

The sets of plans contained in MIL-STD-690B, which are similar in operation to those in H 108, provide for failure rate (FR) qualification at six designated levels ranging from a FR level in excess of 1% per 1,000 hours operation, designated code letter L, to 0.0001% per 1,000 hours operation, designated code letter T. Intermediate FR levels beginning with code letter M (1.0% per 1,000 hours) decrease in decade units for code letters P, R, S, and T. The special failure rate code letter, L, is provided for new-design items for which there is no clear manufacturing precedence, so-called state-of-the-art items. The producer and consumer jointly stipulate the FR for items to be qualified under this code letter. Test times are derived by dividing the FR value stipulated for L into the times stipulated under code letter M.

Qualification testing plans are provided for each FR level at 60% and 90% confidence levels. That is, qualification may be achieved at either a 60% or 90%

---

† MIL-STD-781C, "Reliability Design Qualification and Production Acceptance Tests. Exponential Distribution," U.S. Department of Defense, Washington, D.C., 21 October 1977. Revision C is substantially a complete revision, including change in title, of MIL-STD-781B dated 15 November 1967.

**Table 18-7 MIL-STD-690B qualification failure rate sampling plans based on 60%
confidence level (FRSP-60) and 90% confidence level (FRSP-90)**

FRSP-60 (Consumer's Risk 40% at FR level)

FR level symbol	Qualified FR level, %/1,000 h	Cumulative unit hours in millions (c = number of failures permitted)					
		c = 0	c = 1	c = 2	c = 3	c = 4	c = 5
L	*	("M" row divided by "L")					
M	1.0	0.0916	0.202	0.311	0.418	0.524	0.629
P	0.1	0.916	2.02	3.11	4.18	5.24	6.29
R	0.01	9.16	20.2	31.1	41.8	52.4	62.9
S	0.001	91.6	202	311	418	524	629
T	0.0001	916	2,020	3,110	4,180	5,240	6,290

FRSP-90 (Consumer's Risk 10% at FR level)

FR level symbol	Qualified FR level, %/1,000 h	Cumulative unit hours in millions (c = number of failures permitted)					
		c = 0	c = 1	c = 2	c = 3	c = 4	c = 5
L	*	("M" row divided by "L")					
M	1.0	0.230	0.389	0.532	0.668	0.799	0.927
P	0.1	2.30	3.89	5.32	6.68	7.99	9.27
R	0.01	23.0	38.9	53.2	66.8	79.9	92.7
S	0.001	230	389	532	668	799	927
T	0.0001	2,300	3,890	5,320	6,680	7,990	9,270

* Where a FR level greater than 1.0 per cent is required, level "L" shall be specified and the
cumulative unit hours computed as shown.

confidence level where entering product at exactly the code letter FR level has a
40% or 10% chance of qualifying, respectively. The failure rate—confidence level
combination therefore represents a Consumer's Risk point.

The test procedures of MIL-STD-690B are reproduced in Table 18-7 as
FRSP-60 and FRSP-90 for values of the acceptable number of failures, c, equal to
zero through five. The values in the tables for any qualification level (code letter
and confidence level) are in millions of unit hours of test. Thus if an item, say a
resistor, is to be qualified at code letter P, a failure rate of 0.1% per 1,000 hours
operation, under an acceptance number of 1, a total of 2,020,000 unit hours test
are required at the 60% confidence level. At the 90% confidence level, a total of
3,890,000 unit hours test would be required with no more than one failure.

Once the product has been qualified, periodic tests at the 10% confidence
level are prescribed by the standard. Table 18-8 reproduces these plans. The tests
are intended to maintain the level of qualification of the producer in the published
Qualified Products List distributed periodically to federal procurement agencies.

Table 18-8 MIL-STD-690B maintenance of qualification failure rate sampling plans based on 10% confidence level

FRSP-10 (Producer's Risk 10% at FR level)

FR level symbol	Qualified FR level, %/1,000 h	Qualification maintenance period			Cumulative unit hours in millions (c = number of failures permitted)				
		Period A	Period B	Period C	$c = 1$	$c = 2$	$c = 3$	$c = 4$	$c = 5$
L	*	3 mo.	6 mo.	Each lot	("M" row divided by "L")				
M	1.0	3 mo.	6 mo.	Each lot	0.0532	0.110	0.175	0.243	0.315
P	0.1	6 mo.	9 mo.	6 mo.	0.532	1.10	1.75	2.43	3.15
R	0.01	9 mo.	12 mo.	24 mo.	5.32	11.0	17.5	24.3	31.5
S	0.001	12 mo.	15 mo.	....	53.2	110	175	243	315
T	0.0001	......	......	....	532	1,100	1,750	2,430	3,150

* Where a FR level greater than 1.0 per cent is required, level "L" shall be specified and the cumulative unit hours computed as shown.

Rules and procedures are included in the standard for re-qualification at reduced FR levels and increased confidence levels, for maintenance of qualification, and for periodic checking of lot conformance.†

Comparison of Plans Stipulated in MIL-STD-690B

In this book, we shall not attempt to describe all the procedures contained in MIL-STD-690B. It is worthwhile, however, to consider the general form which the set of plans takes under FR qualification and maintenance of FR qualification.

Figure 18-3 shows the operating characteristic (OC) curves for several plans stipulated under code letter M, 1.0% FR per 1,000 hours. The reader will immediately recognize that these OC curves are shaped similar to those for standard acceptance sampling plans. This shape results from the fact that the horizontal axis (abscissa) of the graph measures failure rate rather than mean life as shown in Fig. 18-2. Also, the vertical scale (ordinate) measures probability of qualification, rather than probability of acceptance, because the end result of the acceptance/rejection decision is either qualification of the producer to code his product at the designated level or denial of the privilege to do so.

† Readers with particular interests in these requirements should refer to the military standard and to the specifications and standards referenced therein. MIL-STD-790C, "Reliability Assurance Program for Electronic Parts Specification," 18 April 1968, is heavily referenced as a basic document as are many others. Most of these documents are unclassified and may be purchased from the Naval Publications and Forms Center, 5801 Tabor Avenue, Philadelphia, Pennsylvania.

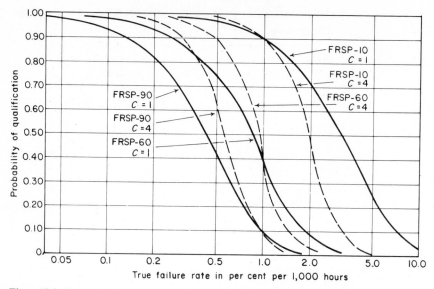

Figure 18-3 Comparison of OC curves of MIL-STD-690B Failure Rate Sampling Plans. Code letter *M* (1.0% FR per 1,000 h).

Material qualified at code letter M qualifies the product to be marketed at an assumed failure rate no greater than 1.0% per 1,000 hours operation. Under the FRSP-90 (Failure Rate Sampling Plan—90% Confidence Level) plans, the various plans for a given code letter will all pass through the 10% probability of qualification point at the failure rate designated by the code letter. The differences between the various plans is reflected in the acceptance number (c) and the total unit hours on test (H). A comparison of these test requirements may be shown as follows:

Accept. no.	Total unit hours on test		
	FRSP-90	FRSP-60	FRSP-10
1	389,000	202,000	53,200
4	799,000	524,000	243,000

FRSP-60 and FRSP-90 are designated for qualification tests while FRSP-10 is designated as a periodic test to assure continued maintenance of the quality level. It is obvious from the reduced testing required by FRSP-10 that it constitutes a reduced inspection plan.

In order for a producer to qualify under FRSP-90, code letter M, with probability in excess of 90%, the true failure rate of the product must be 0.13% per 1,000 hours or better using the plan $c = 1$, $H = 389,000$ hours. However, if he can afford to test according to the plan $c = 4$, $H = 799,000$ hours, the true process average FR with 90% probability of qualification increases to 0.3% per 1,000 hours. Therefore, under assumed stable production conditions, the longer the producer chooses to test, by choosing a plan with a higher acceptance number, the closer the actual failure rate may approach the FR designated by the code letter. This statement only holds true if the constant failure rate assumption is valid.

Once qualified at a failure rate level, all FRSP-10 plans provide a 90% probability of qualification, that is, continuation of qualification, at the qualification FR level. This can be seen in Fig. 18-3 from the FRSP-10 curves for $c = 1$ and $c = 4$. The OC curves of both plans, which are based on a qualification FR level of 1.0% per 1,000 hours, intersect the 1.0% FR line at 90% probability of qualification.

Test Procedures under MIL-STD-781C

Important features of MIL-STD-781C include extensive discussion of environmental and physical stress test requirements and detailed instructions on procedural and documentation requirements. The statistical test plans are contained in App. C of the standard. They include twelve fixed test time length acceptance sampling plans and eight variable time length plans based on Wald's sequential probability ratio test (SPRT). These eight plans are called the PRST (Probability Ratio Sequential Test) plans. A final test plan, with variations indicated, is specified for all-units inspection. Designated PRST XVIIIC, it also is based on the Wald SPRT.

In the discussion of life testing based on the exponential distribution so far we have introduced tests which terminate on a given number of failures and those which terminate at a fixed test time length. Rather than present all of the test plans contained in MIL-STD-781C, we will discuss those based on the Wald SPRT and illustrate two of the eight contained in the standard.

Application of the Wald SPRT to Life Testing

As pointed out in earlier discussions of the Wald SPRT, the primary advantages of sequential sampling are that a decision is likely to be reached within a minimum average number of failures and a minimum average waiting time. Sequential analysis, therefore, lends itself particularly well to life tests of complex systems where the complexity of the test procedure is much less important than savings in average time on test and average observed failures.

In the formulation of the problem, unit hours on test replaces the number of items inspected and number of observed failures replaces number of defectives found. Assuming a constant failure rate, the total unit hours on test, $V(t)$, at any point in time during the test is nt, if failed units are immediately replaced, where n

is the number of units or assemblies being tested and t is the elapsed time. If the test is performed without replacing failed units, $V(t)$ becomes somewhat more complicated because it is necessary to accumulate the times of the failed units individually. For the nonreplacement case, therefore,

$$V(t) = \sum_{i=1}^{m} t_i + (n - m)t$$

where t_i = elapsed test time of the ith failed unit, m in all
$\quad\quad t$ = elapsed time of the test

Individually, the t_i's will be less than or equal to t.

The mathematical form of the probability ratio is very similar to that shown in Chap. 15 except for the fact that the negative exponential distribution replaces the binomial. As usual, the function in the numerator is based on an *acceptable value* of the mean life (or MTBF), θ_0, and the denominator is based on an *unacceptable value* of mean life, θ_1. The probability ratio is:

$$\frac{(1/\theta_0)^m \exp\{(-1/\theta_0)V(t)\}}{(1/\theta_1)^m \exp\{(-1/\theta_1)V(t)\}}$$

This ratio may be simplified to the following form:

$$\left(\frac{\theta_1}{\theta_0}\right)^m \exp\left\{-\left(\frac{1}{\theta_0} - \frac{1}{\theta_1}\right)V(t)\right\}$$

As previously described in Chap. 15, this formula, often referred to as a continuation rule, is bounded from below by $A = \alpha/(1 - \beta)$ for rejection and from above by $B = (1 - \alpha)/\beta$ for acceptance. Solution of the complete formulation yields two sloping boundary lines: an upper boundary line called the rejection boundary, and a lower boundary line called the acceptance boundary line. The cumulative number of failures, m, is plotted on the vertical axis (ordinate). $V(t)$, the total time on test, is plotted along the horizontal axis (abscissa). The value of $V(t)$ is calculated according to the formulas given previously depending upon whether or not failed units are replaced.†

The formulas for the acceptance and rejection lines are:

$$\text{Acceptance line} \quad m_0 = sV(t) - h_0$$

$$\text{Rejection line} \quad m_1 = sV(t) + h_1$$

where s is the slope of the line from the abscissa and h_0 and h_1 are the intercepts of the ordinate axis on the scale of number of failures. Auxiliary symbols will be used to find the values of s, h_0, and h_1 for the example problem. In this case, θ_0, the acceptable MTBF, is 1,500 hours, and θ_1, the unacceptable MTBF is 300 hours and the desired Producer's and Consumer's Risks are 5% and 10%, respectively.

---

† Handbook H 108 and some texts on reliability use just the opposite form of the plot. Failures are plotted along the horizontal axis and unit test time on the vertical axis. The formulation used in this book is consistent with MIL-STD-781C plans discussed in subsequent paragraphs.

We shall let:

$$g_1 = \log \frac{\theta_0}{\theta_1} = \log \frac{1,500}{300} = 0.6990$$

$$g_2\dagger = 0.4343\left(\frac{1}{\theta_1} - \frac{1}{\theta_0}\right) = 0.4343\left(\frac{1}{300} - \frac{1}{1,500}\right) = 0.001158$$

$$a = \log \frac{1-\beta}{\alpha} = \log \frac{0.90}{0.05} = 1.2553$$

$$b = \log \frac{1-\alpha}{\beta} = \log \frac{0.95}{0.10} = 0.9777$$

$$h_0 = \frac{b}{g_1} = \frac{0.9777}{0.6990} = 1.399$$

$$h_1 = \frac{a}{g_1} = \frac{1.2553}{0.6990} = 1.796$$

$$s = \frac{g_2}{g_1} = \frac{0.001158}{0.6990} = 0.00166$$

The resulting test plan calls for:

Acceptance line $m_0 = 0.00166V(t) - 1.399$

Rejection line $m_1 = 0.00166V(t) + 1.796$

The reader will note that n, the number of items on test, appears nowhere in the formulation. The values plotted are m, the number of failures, vs. $V(t)$, the total time on test.

Significant points on the OC curve for sequential life testing plans and approximate average total unit hours of test, $E_\theta(t)$, may be found from the following formulas:

Value of θ	OC curve point $L(\theta)$	Average hours on test $E_\theta(t)$
θ_1	β	$\dfrac{(1-\beta)h_1 - \beta h_0}{1/\theta_1 - s}$
$1/s$	$\dfrac{h_1}{h_0 + h_1}$	$\dfrac{h_0 h_1}{s}$
θ_0	$1 - \alpha$	$\dfrac{(1-\alpha)h_0 - \alpha h_1}{s - 1/\theta_0}$
∞	1	h_0/s

† The constant 0.4343 in the factor g_2 is required when a base 10 log table, such as Table J in this book, is used. If a table of natural (or napierian) logarithms is used, this constant must be dropped, i.e., changed to 1.0.

T, the total time on test, is a random variable with expected values as given. An estimate of the maximum average time can be obtained by recognizing that $E_\theta(t)$ will be maximum at θ equal to $1/s$ and, in the replacement case, this value will equal *nt*, the number of units on test multiplied by the number of hours all units are on test. Conversely, the number of test units required to complete testing within a maximum *average* time may be estimated by dividing $E_s(t)$ by some stipulated time period. Again, it should be emphasized that this figure is only an *average*. If θ is equal to $1/s$, the actual time on test may greatly exceed $E_s(t)$.

In the case of the example problem, $E_s(t)$ is 1513.4 hours. Thus the maximum average time to complete the test with replacement of failed units and ten units on test would be 151.3 hours.

Sequential Life Testing Plans from MIL-STD-781C

While the sequential life test plans in Handbook H 108 provide for truncation at some reasonable point in time, the plots of expected waiting time and the OC curves are based on no truncation and therefore are not completely accurate. Most of the sequential plans of MIL-STD-781C, however, provide explicitly for truncation, in some cases at an early time in relation to the acceptable MTBF of the equipment under test, and provide exact OC curves and expected waiting time curves for the plans.

A sample of two of the eight sequential life test plans contained in the standard are illustrated in abbreviated form in Figs. 18-4 and 18-5. The general operation and design of these plans is as described in the previous article except for the

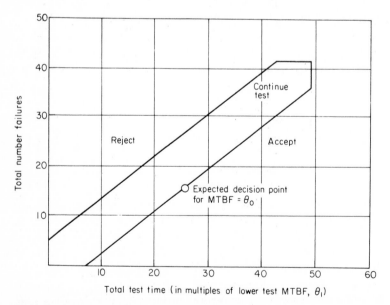

Figure 18-4 MIL-STD-781C Probability Ratio Sequential Test Plan IC.

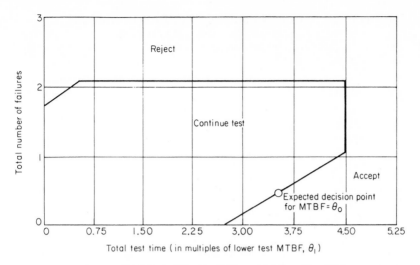

Figure 18-5 MIL-STD-781C Probability Ratio Sequential Test Plan VIC.

truncation provisions. Cumulative failures are plotted against the vertical axis and $V(t)$, the total test time expressed in multiples of the unacceptable MTBF, θ_1, is plotted against the horizontal axis.

Plan IC in the standard is illustrated in Fig. 18-4. This plan provides a rather steep OC curve by specifying a small discrimination ratio ($\theta_0/\theta_1 = 1.5$) and Producer's and Consumer's Risks of only 10%. Truncation does not occur until 50 times the unacceptable MTBF.

Plan VIC of the standard, illustrated in Fig. 18-5, has a larger discrimination ratio, $\theta_0/\theta_1 = 3.0$, with higher Producer's and Consumer's Risks of 20% each and is truncated at 4.5 times the unacceptable MTBF. The allowances for considerable risk and the rapid truncation make possible much shorter test times than is the case with Plan IC.

In the standard, θ_1 is defined as follows: "Lower test MTBF (θ_1) is that value which is unacceptable and the standard test plans will reject, with high probability, equipment with a true MTBF that approaches θ_1." θ_0 is defined as "Upper test MTBF (θ_0) is an acceptable value of MTBF equal to the discrimination ratio times the lower test MTBF (θ_1). The standard plans will accept, with high probability, equipment with a true MTBF that approaches θ_0."

Procedures are given in the standard for estimating the true MTBF from the test data and setting 40, 60, and 80 per cent confidence limits around these estimates. Such estimates always assume a constant system of chance causes was in operation during sampling. Thus, when these estimates are to be made, the techniques and procedures of process control should be in force.

The reader should surmise from this very brief exposition of the types of sequential life testing plans contained in MIL-STD-781C that a large variety of plans are available. With the aid of the OC curves and expected waiting time curves, a wide variety of test and operating conditions can be satisfied.

The Broad General Usefulness of Sampling and Testing Standards

During the last several chapters, many documents and standards published by the United States Government have been discussed in varying degrees of depth. In part, the discussion has been directed at particular statistical methodologies and in part it has been directed at familiarizing the reader with the wealth of developed material available. In a book such as this, which is devoted to the statistical aspects of quality control, it is natural that methodology should take precedence. Nevertheless, the reader should not lose sight of a point that we have emphasized at various places in our exposition of acceptance sampling. This point is that the improvement of the quality of product submitted for inspection often is the most important consequence of the adoption and use of an acceptance sampling system.

The authors of a review of the previous MIL-STD-781B, published in the *Journal of Quality Technology*, in 1969, made some significant observations about the impact of such documents.† They pointed out that these standards make possible a better framework of communication among designers and manufacturers. A primary consequence of the use of the standards ought to be an improvement in quality. The plans contained in such standards should not be viewed merely as the source for decisions on acceptance or rejection of product. Any discussion that emphasizes only the statistical aspects of the standards tends to neglect the more important effects that generally occur because of their use.

The reader should note here that the techniques of process control presented in Part One of this book play a major role in accomplishing the objectives resulting from the imposition of acceptance sampling or product qualification procedures. Virtually all acceptance procedures begin with the assumption of process control. To the extent that control exists, and analysis for corrective action is performed, product quality will be improved. Nothing could be more true than the quotation at the beginning of Chap. 12: "You can't inspect quality into a product."

A Variety of Survivor Curves

In connection with the requirements of depreciation accounting and engineering valuation and for other purposes, mortality studies of industrial assets have been made for many years. Doubtless the most extensive experience with such studies has been in the Bell Telephone System. Figure 18-6,‡ reproduced by permission from the 1977 edition of a Bell System publication, reflects this extensive experience. The publication explains this figure in part as follows:

---

† R. D. NEATHAMMER, W. R. PABST, JR., and C. G. WIGGINTON, "MIL-STD-781B, Reliability Tests: Exponential Distribution," Reviews of Standards and Specifications department, *Journal of Quality Technology*, vol. 1, no. 1, January, 1969, p. 59.

‡ "*Engineering Economy—A Manager's Guide to Economic Decision Making*," 3d ed, 1977, pp. 349–51, American Telephone & Telegraph Co., Construction Plans Department, published by McGraw-Hill Book Co., New York.

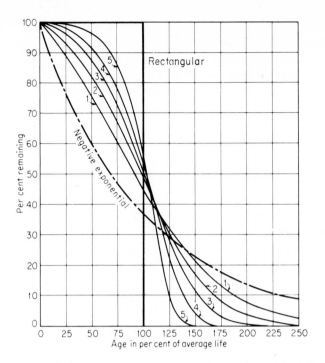

Figure 18-6 Seven typical survivor curves for fixed assets. *(Reproduced from " Engineering Economy; A Manager's Guide to Economic Decision Making," 3d ed., American Telephone & Telegraph Co., 1977, Construction Plans Department. Published by McGraw-Hill Book Company, New York.)*

The Bell System has gathered vast amounts of data based on years of actuarial analysis of the characteristics of telephone plant life.....

Figure [18-6] illustrates seven survivor curves. Curves numbered 1 to 5 plus the negative exponential are typical of those used with telephone plant. These curves show varying degrees of dispersion. Since the vertical change in a survivor curve during a year represents the retirements in that year, the steeper the initial slope of the survivor curve, the greater the rate of retirements at an early age. So, the negative exponential has the greatest dispersion, and curve No. 5 has the least except for the rectangular curve shown in Fig. [18-6]. This rectangular curve would not normally be representative of the life characteristics of a large mass of plant, because it assumes that all retirements occur at one point in time. The rectangular survivor curve is usually assumed in an economy study when a single unit of plant is involved, or whenever dispersion is not significant.

Survivor curve No. 5 shows that most of the vintage is retired in a relatively short period of time, which is centered near the average life. Such experience would be typical of motor vehicles, for example. A few might be retired early because of accidents or other reasons, but most would be retired within a short time of each other as they reached an age when replacement would be appropriate. In such a pattern, age appears to be the predominant reason for retirement. By contrast, the negative exponential curve is assumed typical of the life of the station connection account. In that account, age plays little part in the retirement, because a customer may decide to move at any time after taking service, thus retiring a telephone connection.

From the viewpoint of someone interested in mathematical models in reliability, the foregoing quotation brings out the point that, at least in the field of mortality of industrial assets, the negative exponential is somewhat of a maverick among survivor curves. (This is true for industrial assets in general, not merely for telephone plant.) Although life experience with industrial assets is a different matter from life experience with electronic and mechanical components, Fig. 18-6 suggests the sound conclusion that one should not assume without investigation that the negative exponential is applicable to any particular case.

Is it Desirable to have the Probability of Survival Follow the Exponential Curve?

We have seen certain advantages of the constant failure rate in the design of acceptance sampling plans involving life testing. The determination of the OC curve of a sampling plan is a fairly simple matter because only one parameter is involved, namely, the failure rate (or its reciprocal, the mean life).

Of even greater importance is the economic advantage gained because, for purposes of life testing and acceptance sampling, item hours in the early portion of life are interchangeable with item hours in the later portion of life. This interchangeability of item hours makes it possible to shorten the time needed to reach acceptance or rejection decisions merely by testing more items. As we have already noted, a consequence of the constant failure rate is that items that survive the test period have not lost any of their life expectancy.

If one looked only at the foregoing aspects of the matter, one might conclude that it always is desirable to have survivor curves for manufactured product that look like the negative exponential of Fig. 18-6. But if one looks at the broader question of achieving high reliability without excessive cost, there are some obvious advantages of survivor curves that are closer to No. 5 of Fig. 18-6.

With an exponential distribution, one must have a relatively long mean life in order to have a high reliability for a relatively short service. For instance, if one desires a reliability of 0.99 for a 500-h service, one needs to use product that has a mean life of approximately 50,000 h. This ratio of 100 to 1 exists with the exponential because approximately 1% of the items will fail in the first 1% of the mean life. In contrast, if the survival curve is of the form of No. 5 of Fig. 18-6, approximately one-third of the mean life will have expired before 1% of the product has failed. Thus a mean life of 1,500 h with curve 5 would provide the same reliability at 500 h as a mean life of 50,000 h with the exponential.

The Weibull Distribution

Acceptance sampling procedures based on the exponential distribution assume that the *shape* of the survivor curve is known; the only unknown is some number—such as failure rate or mean life—that determines the actual values associated with the curve. Similarly, if one could assume that the survivor curve had some other shape that was known, it would be possible to devise acceptance procedures deemed appropriate for that shape.

In 1951, W. Weibull proposed the use of a mathematical function that, by changing the values of its three parameters, could fit many different shapes of survivor curves.† A number of published sets of acceptance sampling plans for use in life testing have been based on this distribution.

The Weibull reliability function may be written in various ways. The following method of expressing the Weibull distribution may be helpful in relating our brief discussion of this distribution to our discussion of the exponential:

Probability of survival after H time units from time zero $= e^{-(H-\gamma/\eta)^{\beta}}$

In the above equation:

β (the lowercase form of the Greek letter beta) is called the *shape* parameter.
η (the lowercase form of the Greek letter eta) is called the true *scale* parameter or the characteristic life.
γ (the lowercase form of the Greek letter gamma) is called the *location* parameter.

The location parameter is zero if failures can start at time zero. Otherwise it is the time elapsing between time zero and the first moment when the probability of failure is greater than zero. It has the same significance as the second parameter of the "two-parameter" exponential that was briefly mentioned in connection with certain acceptance sampling plans of H 108. Ordinarily, the location parameter is assumed to be zero and the Weibull formula becomes:

Probability of survival $= e^{-(H/\eta)^{\beta}}$

When we approached the exponential distribution from the viewpoint of failure rate λ', we stated the probability of survival with that distribution to be $e^{-H\lambda'}$. If we had approached the matter from the viewpoint of mean life θ', we might have expressed the exponential as $e^{-H/\theta'}$. In a general way, the scale parameter in the Weibull corresponds to this use of θ' in the exponential. If we are interested in observing the influence of the *shape* parameter, we may arbitrarily assume the *scale* parameter $\eta = 1$. This assumption has been made in Fig. 18-7.‡

It should be pointed out that the curves in Fig. 18-7 are probability density functions and not survivor curves (reliability functions). (See the discussion of Table 18-6 for the distinction between probability density and reliability.) In the special case where $\beta = 1$, the Weibull distribution becomes the exponential distribution. Nevertheless, Fig. 18-7 makes it evident that a wide variety of failure patterns—some of them very unlike the exponential—are encompassed within the Weibull formula.

---

† WALLODI WEIBULL, A Statistical Distribution Function of Wide Applicability, *Journal of Applied Mechanics*, vol. 18, no. 3, pp. 293–297, September, 1951.

‡ The United States government publication shown as the source of Fig. 18-7 was prepared by Profs. Henry P. Goode and John H. K. Kao of Cornell University. Prior to its appearance in the government's TR 3, Fig. 18-7 appeared in Goode and Kao's "Sampling Plans Based on the Weibull Distribution," Technical Report No. 1, Department of Industrial and Engineering Administration, Cornell University, Ithaca, N.Y., 1961.

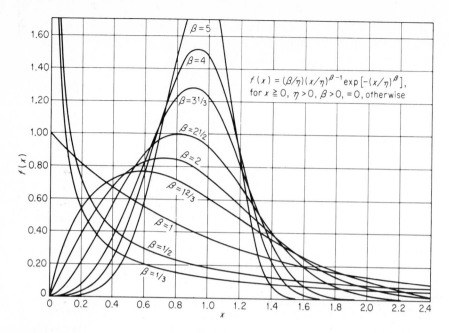

$$f(x) = (\beta/\eta)(x/\eta)^{\beta-1}\exp\left[-(x/\eta)^{\beta}\right],$$
$$\text{for } x \geq 0, \ \eta > 0, \ \beta > 0, \ = 0, \text{ otherwise}$$

Figure 18-7 Plot of the Weibull probability density function for various values of the shape parameter β. *(Reproduced from Quality Control and Reliability Technical Report TR-3, Sampling Procedures and Tables for Life and Reliability Testing Based on the Weibull Distribution (Mean Life Criterion), Government Printing Office, Washington, D.C., 1961.)*

It follows that, if acceptance sampling plans are to be based on the Weibull distribution, it is of critical importance to have a good estimate of the shape parameter β. Weibull's original 1951 paper indicated a method of estimating Weibull parameters by eye using a double logarithmic transformation. "Weibull probability paper" has been developed by H. P. Goode and J. H. K. Kao, and by others, to simplify graphical procedures for estimating these parameters.†

Two pamphlets of acceptance sampling tables based on the Weibull distribution have been issued by the U.S. Department of Defense, Office of the Assistant Secretary of Defense (Installations and Logistics). The titles of these pamphlets are:

"Quality Control and Reliability Technical Report TR 3. Sampling Procedures and Tables for Life and Reliability Testing Based on the Weibull Distribution (Mean Life Criterion)."

---

† See Appendix *B* of the report TR 3 mentioned in the text. See also:

J. H. K. Kao, A Graphical Estimation of Mixed Weibull Parameters in Life Testing of Electron Tubes, *Technometrics*, vol. 1, no. 4, pp. 389–407, November, 1959.

R. K. Ruzicka, Weibull Distribution Analysis—Short Method, *Journal of the Electronics Division, American Society for Quality Control*, vol. 1, no. 1, pp. 38–54, November, 1962.

"Quality Control and Reliability Technical Report TR 4. Sampling Procedures and Tables for Life and Reliability Testing Based on the Weibull Distribution (Hazard Rate Criterion)."

The pamphlets were prepared by Profs. Henry P. Goode and John H. K. Kao of Cornell University through the cooperation of the Office of Naval Research.

The acceptance sampling plans in these technical reports assume that the shape parameter β is known. Both pamphlets contain tables to aid in the selection of plans for values of β of $\frac{1}{3}$, $\frac{1}{2}$, 1, $1\frac{2}{3}$, 2, $2\frac{1}{2}$, $3\frac{1}{3}$, 4, and 5. TR 4 also includes values of β of $\frac{2}{3}$ and $1\frac{1}{3}$.

In TR 3 product quality is expressed in terms of mean life. (The reader will recall that our OC curve in Fig. 18-2 plotted probability of acceptance as a function of mean life.) In TR 4, product quality is expressed in terms of the probability of failure (i.e., the "hazard rate") at some specified age in hours. Of course, hazard rate varies with age except in the special case where $\beta = 1$ (i.e., where the Weibull is the same as the exponential). If the shape parameter is greater than 1, the hazard rate increases with age; if it is less than 1, the hazard rate decreases with age.

Some Aspects of Reliability of Complex Systems

In general, the reason one is concerned with the reliability of components of electrical and mechanical systems is to ensure that the systems will be reasonably free from failure. In our discussion of the constant failure rate we have already noted one matter related to systems: whereas θ' is interpreted as mean life of components, it is interpreted as mean time between failures of a system.

Incidentally, the "bathtub curve" of Fig. 18-1 seems more reasonable for many complex electrical and mechanical devices than for some of the components of such devices. Between the initial "debugging" period and the final wearout period, there may well be an extended time during which the probability of a breakdown is relatively constant.

An interesting and somewhat controversial question in connection with complex systems is the extent to which the multiplication theorem ought to be used in estimating system reliability. As phrased on page 183, the multiplication theorem is: "If a compound event be made up of a number of separate and independent subevents, and the occurrence of the compound event be the result of each of these subevents happening, the probability of occurrence of the compound event is the product of the probabilities that each of the subevents will happen." In relation to the estimation of system reliability, the key word in the foregoing definition is *independent*.

Suppose a system consists of three mechanical devices A, B, and C that operate in series in such a way that a failure in any one device causes a failure in the system. Assume that the probability that A will operate without failure for 100 h is estimated to be 0.95 and that corresponding probabilities for B and C are 0.90 and 0.80, respectively. If failures in A, B, and C are completely independent, the probability that the system will operate without failure for 100 h should be estimated to be $(0.95)(0.90)(0.80) = 0.684$.

However, the multiplication theorem has sometimes been misused to obtain unrealistically low estimates of system reliability. Consider an electronic system with 2,000 components, each with an estimated probability of 0.999 of operating without failure for 500 h. "Failure" is defined as taking place when certain electrical characteristics of the various components fall outside their respective specification limits. An application of the multiplication theorem would appear to show that the system had an estimated probability of only $(0.999)^{2000} = 0.135$ of operating without failure for 500 h. In the common cases where such component failures are not independent or where the system does not necessarily fail when a component falls outside its specification limits, such a use of the multiplication theorem is invalid.†

Some Comments on the Limited Scope of This Chapter

The introduction of the word *reliability* in its modern technical sense in the early 1950s was followed by a rapid growth in the number of persons in manufacturing and government who were assigned staff duties that were designated as dealing somehow with reliability. There naturally has been much diversity in such assignments of duties. However, one important duty often has been to give certain kinds of advice to designers. In giving this advice, reliability personnel often are feeding back to designers their interpretations of the results of acceptance tests and field trials of components and systems. Often the need for a formal arrangement for this type of advice arises, at least in part, from the newness and the complexity of product that is being designed.

A fair part of the extensive literature of reliability deals with matters of organization structure related to such assignments. Such matters are clearly outside the scope of this book and are not discussed here.

The chief aim of the present chapter is to give the reader an introduction to the subject of acceptance sampling in life testing. In this connection, it is desirable to mention certain topics that have been omitted even though they are related to this subject. These are:

1. The relationship between the environmental conditions in life testing and the expected environmental conditions in operation.
2. The use of acceptance specifications involving accelerated tests and tests of increased severity in order to reach acceptance decisions more rapidly.

---

† It is easier to say what *not* to do in estimating system reliability than to give good advice on what *to* do. For a comprehensive bibliography of this subject accompanied by a brief survey of the literature, see H. E. BLANTON and R. M. JACOBS, A Survey of Techniques for Analysis and Prediction of Equipment Reliability, *Industrial Quality Control*, vol. 19, no. 6, pp. 18–25, December, 1962, and no. 7, pp. 13–18, January, 1963.

3. The relationship of the reliability of complex devices to redundancy in design or provision for parallel operation.
4. The relationship between reliability, maintainability, and availability.

PROBLEMS

18-1 In one of the plans quoted from H 108 (page 542), 10 items were to be tested for 500 h with replacement and with an acceptance number of 1. Using values of λ' that seem to you to be appropriate, make a calculation similar to Table 18-1 to find enough points to define the OC curve of this plan. Plot your OC curve showing probability of acceptance as a function of mean life.

18-2 The acceptance sampling plan of Problem 18-1 was stipulated for an approximate value of 0.10 for the Producer's Risk of rejection of a lot having a mean life of 10,000 h and for an approximate value of 0.10 for the Consumer's Risk of acceptance of a lot having a mean life of 1,000 h. Use Table G to compute the respective values of these two risks.

   Answer: Producer's, 0.09; Consumer's, 0.04.

18-3 In one of the plans quoted from H 108 (page 542), 63 items were to be tested for 500 h with replacement and with an acceptance number of 5. Using values of λ' that seem to you to be appropriate, make a calculation similar to Table 18-1 to find enough points to define the OC curve of this plan. Plot your OC curve showing probability of acceptance as a function of mean life.

18-4 The acceptance sampling plan of Problem 18-3 was stipulated for an approximate value of 0.10 for the Producer's Risk of rejection of a lot having a mean life of 10,000 h and for an approximate value of 0.10 for the Consumer's Risk of acceptance of a lot having a mean life of 3,333 h. Use Table G to compute the respective values of these two risks.

   Answer: Producer's, 0.10; Consumer's, 0.092.

18-5 The following table indicates the time a lot of electronic parts operated until failure. The times are presented in the order in which the trials were measured and includes 30 measurements made with a constant failure rate of 0.0005 per h.

   (a) Rearrange the data values in order of increasing magnitude in the manner illustrated in Table 18-3.

   (b) Compute the respective estimates of mean life in hours that would have been appropriate after 1,000, 3,000, 5,000, and 7,713 hours of testing.

Set of observations	Time until failure (hours)				
	1	2	3	4	5
1	2,737	1,281	1,855	1,472	2,638
2	2,147	4,522	428	3,727	7,713
3	961	617	6,715	714	3,303
4	714	4,025	5,618	1,474	1,567
5	1,285	3,132	501	1,661	2,148
6	456	3,913	1,846	2,114	2,713

18-6 For the rearranged data of Problem 18-5, compute to the nearest two decimal places the fractions surviving after 500, 1,000, 1,500, 2,000, 3,000, 4,000, 5,000, and 7,000 hours, respectively. Compare these observed values with the appropriate values for probability of survival that you obtain from the column in Table G headed $c = 0$.

18-7 The following lengths of lives, measured in numbers of successive trials to failure, were obtained when 60 sets of observations were made with a constant probability of failure of 0.01.

Sets of observations	Lengths of lives				
1–5	45	431	16	388	34
6–10	59	27	107	233	88
11–15	276	84	7	40	13
16–20	1	106	121	24	223
21–25	277	156	261	35	81
26–30	2	24	42	56	131
31–35	31	47	6	179	2
36–40	36	128	20	78	112
41–45	301	22	4	121	20
46–50	44	7	163	245	74
51–55	51	23	107	3	10
56–60	31	62	142	296	101

Rearrange the foregoing 60 numbers in order of increasing magnitude in the manner illustrated by the rearrangement of the numbers of Table 18-2 into the numbers of Table 18-3.

18-8 Your rearranged table in Problem 18-7 may be viewed as representing a distribution of lives in hours that might have been found if simultaneous tests to failure had been made of a random sample of 60 items from a universe that had a constant failure rate of 0.01 per hour. Compute the respective estimates of mean life in hours that would have been appropriate after the following numbers of hours of test:

(a) 30   (b) 60   (c) 80   (d) 100   (e) 431.

  Answer: (a) 82.8   (b) 81.4   (c) 90.5   (d) 95.9   (e) 97.6.

18-9 Rearrange the first 60 numbers of Table 18-2 in order of increasing magnitude. Assume that your rearranged table represents the lives in hours found when simultaneous tests to failure were made of a sample of 60 items out of a large lot. Compute the respective estimates of mean life in hours that would have been appropriate after the following numbers of hours of test:

(a) 4   (b) 5   (c) 10   (d) 15   (e) 20   (f) 165.

18-10 An acceptance sampling plan for life testing requires that a sample of 40 items be tested with replacement for 500 hours. If no more than five of these items fail, the lot is accepted. Otherwise it is rejected.

(a) Assuming that the failure rate is constant, compute the mean life for which the Producer's Risk of lot rejection is 0.05.

(b) Compute the mean life for which the Consumer's Risk of lot acceptance is 0.10.

18-11 Assume that a failure is designated as the drawing of a chip marked 0 to 9, inclusive, from Shewhart's normal bowl. Examine the 400 drawings given in Table 2-7 to determine values of the number of trials to failure. (Eight such values can be obtained from the first 384 drawings.) Assume that the observed number of trials to failure correspond to the lives in hours of a sample of 8 electronic components subject to life tests.

(a) What is λ' (see Table 2-6)?

(b) What is θ'?

(c) What estimate of mean life would be obtained from the test to failure of the sample of 8 components?

(*d*) What estimate of mean life would have been obtained after the first 10 h of test, assuming that the 8 tests were carried out concurrently?

(*e*) After the first 20 h?

Answer: (*a*) $\frac{20}{998}$; (*b*) 49.9 h; (*c*) 48 h; (*d*) 38.5 h; (*e*) 31.8 h.

18-12 Assume that a failure is designated as the occurrence of 00 or 99 in one of the pairs of random numbers shown in Table Z, App. 3. Start counting in the upper left-hand corner of the table, and count downward in the left-hand column of pairs of numbers. From the bottom of the left-hand column, go to the top of the second column from the left, and so on. Record the numbers of successive trials to failure in tabular form in the manner illustrated in Table 18-2. (Your first 4 numbers should be 4, 11, 17 and 100.) Continue until 20 values have been obtained. Rearrange these values in order of increasing magnitude in the manner illustrated in Table 18-3. (Your first 4 numbers should be 3, 4, 6, and 11.)

18-13 Assume that the values in your second table of Problem 18-12 represent the hours to failure obtained when a sample of 20 electronic components is being tested until each component fails. Compute the respective estimates of mean life in hours that would have been appropriate after the following numbers of hours of test:

(*a*) 10,   (*b*) 20   (*c*) 30   (*d*) 184.

Answer: (*a*) 61.0, (*b*) 55.5, (*c*) 50.8, (*d*) 57.4.

18-14 In the qualification test (1) mentioned on page 548, 418,000 item hours of test are required with an acceptance number of 3.

(*a*) Approximately what mean life in hours corresponds to a Producer's Risk of 0.05?

(*b*) To a Consumer's Risk of 0.10?

Answer: (*a*) 307,000; (*b*) 62,600.

18-15 Plot the OC curve of the qualification test (1) mentioned in Problem 18-14. Show the probability of qualification as a function of θ'.

18-16 In the acceptance test (2) for individual lots mentioned on page 548, 11,000 item hours of test are required with an acceptance number of 1.

(*a*) Approximately what mean life in hours corresponds to a Producer's Risk of 0.05?

(*b*) To a Consumer's Risk of 0.10?

Answer: (*a*) 31,250; (*b*) 2,820.

18-17 Plot the OC curve of the lot acceptance test (2) mentioned in Problem 18-16. Show the probability of acceptance as a function of θ'.

18-18 In the test for continued qualification (3) applied to a series of 10 lots (page 548), 110,000 item hours of test are required with an acceptance number of 2.

(*a*) Approximately what mean life in hours corresponds to a Producer's Risk of 0.05?

(*b*) To a Consumer's Risk of 0.10?

Answer: (*a*) 134,000; (*b*) 20,600.

18-19 Plot the OC curve of the test for continued qualification mentioned in Problem 18-18. Show the probability of acceptance as a function of θ'.

18-20 On pages 548 to 549, there was given an illustration of a proposed type of acceptance procedure to be used in life testing where the tolerable failure rates are extremely low. With reference to the qualification criteria illustrated in (1) and applied again in (4), it has been suggested that the principle of the indifference quality should be used. In other words, the Consumer's Risk (and Producer's Risk) associated with some stipulated failure rate should be 0.50.

The specific numerical example of a qualification test given on page 548 called for a test of 418,000 item hours with an acceptance number of 3. This gives a probability of qualification of 0.40 of product having a mean life of 100,000 hours.

(*a*) If the probability of qualification for such product is to be 0.50 and the acceptance number is 3, how many item hours should be tested to qualify?

Answer: 367,000.

(b) With your revised qualification criteria, approximately what mean life in hours corresponds to a Producer's Risk of 0.05?

Answer: 270,000.

(c) With your revised qualification criteria, approximately what mean life in hours corresponds to a Consumer's Risk of 0.10?

Answer: 55,000.

18-21 In connection with the matters discussed in Problem 18-20, it has also been suggested that the qualification criteria are too lenient from the point of view of the consumer. Answer questions (a), (b), and (c), changing the probability of qualification to 0.10 for product having a mean life of 100,000 h.

Answer: (a) 668,000 item hours; (b) 490,000 h; (c) 100,000 h.

18-22 For your rearranged data of Problem 18-7, compute to the nearest two decimal places the fractions surviving after 10, 20, 40, 60, 80, 100, 150, 200, 300, and 400 h, respectively. Compare these observed values from this sample of 60 items with the appropriate values for probability of survival that you obtain from the column in Table G headed $c = 0$.

18-23 A certain type of electronic component has a uniform failure rate of 0.00001 per hour. What is its reliability for a specified period of service of 10,000 h? Of 2,000 h?

Answer: 0.905; 0.980.

18-24 Although an acceptance procedure is being used to ensure the failure rate of not more than 0.00001 mentioned in Problem 18-23, it happens that a producer qualifies who has a λ' of 0.0000125. What now will be the respective values of reliability for services of 10,000 and 2,000 h?

18-25 Given a θ' of 5,000 h and a uniform failure rate, what is the reliability associated with a specified service period of 200 h?

Answer: 0.961.

18-26 Two hundred solid state electronic devices were tested to determine the failure rate of these units. Testing was conducted for 1,000 hours with four units failing after 425, 575, 650, 920 hours, respectively.

(a) Assuming a constant failure rate, calculate the total unit hours on test, $V(t)$, where failed units are immediately replaced;

(b) where failed units are not replaced.

(c) What is the probability that one of these units will survive for a required 500 hours of operation?

18-27 After an initial burn-in period of 50 h, one hundred electrical units are placed on test for 500 h. Three units failed at 230, 300, and 420 h, respectively.

(a) Estimate the mean life, θ', for this unit, where failed units are not replaced, assuming a constant failure rate.

(b) What is the probability that one of these units will survive for a required 200, 300, and 400 h of operation?

18-28 An item has a mean life, θ', of 15,000 h. Assuming a uniform failure rate, what is the probability that one of these units will survive for a required 1,000 h of operation?

18-29 An item is required to have a failure rate no greater than 0.10% per 1,000 h of operation.

(a) Assuming a constant failure rate, what is the probability that one of these units will survive for a required 2,000 h of service.

(b) Determine the minimum acceptable failure rate where the probability of survival for a required 2,000 h of operation is 0.999.

(c) Find the MIL-STD-690B FRSP-90 qualification sampling plan that meets this requirement.

18-30 A company wishes to qualify a solid state device under MIL-STD-690B FR level symbol M.

(a) Assuming a choice of $c = 0$, $c = 2$, or $c = 4$, determine how many items must be placed on test if the test must be completed within 2 months using FRSP-60.

(b) Sketch the OC curves of these three plans and discuss the advantages of using the longer tests with higher acceptance numbers.

18-31 Determine the acceptance and rejection lines for a sequential life testing plan where the acceptable mean life (θ_0) is 50,000 h and the unacceptable mean life (θ_1) is 35,000 h. The desired Producer's and Consumer's Risks are 10%. How do your results compare graphically with the MIL-STD-781C PRST Plan IC?

18-32 For the sequential life testing plan found in Problem 18-31, calculate the significant points on the OC curve and sketch the OC curve and average hours on test curve.

18-33 Determine the acceptance and rejection lines for a sequential life testing plan where the acceptable mean life (θ_0) is 50,000 hours and the unacceptable mean life (θ_1) is 20,000 h. The desired Producer's and Consumer's Risks are 10%.

18-34 For the sequential life testing plan found in Problem 18-33, calculate the significant points on the OC curve and sketch the OC curve and average hours on test curve.

18-35 Compare the results of Problem 18-32 with those of Problem 18-34 and comment on the effect of changing the discrimination ratio (θ_0/θ_1) has on these important measures.

SOME RELATED TOPICS

NINETEEN

SOME ECONOMIC ASPECTS OF QUALITY DECISIONS

Finding the correct balance between cost of quality and value of quality is not so easy, since the facts are widely scattered throughout the various company departments, the distribution chain, the customers, the vendors, and still other locations. . . . The balance to be struck (between cost and value) is not as to quality generally; it applies to each quality characteristic.—J. M. Juran and F. M. Gryna, Jr.†

Problems of Business Alternatives are Problems in Economy

Decisions of many sorts are always being called for in the management of any productive enterprise. All decisions are between alternatives—either express or implied. In business enterprises operated for profit, the real basis of a choice between alternatives is the prospective effect of each alternative on the costs and revenues of the business. Where technical considerations are involved in the alternatives, a study comparing specific money estimates of the differences between the alternatives as well as other estimated differences not readily expressible in money terms is called an *engineering economy study.*

Engineering economy studies dealing with quality matters are often more difficult than studies dealing with such matters as proposed investments in industrial assets. This is primarily because of the difficulty of expressing in money terms the probable effect of particular quality decisions. In some manufacturing plants, this difficulty may be due in part to the fact that the accounts of the enterprise do not identify certain types of costs, such as costs of spoilage and rework, in any satisfactory way. Nevertheless, to a large extent the difficulty is an inherent one in quality decisions; certain elements in such decisions are extremely hard to measure in money terms.

---

† J. M. JURAN and F. M. GRYNA, JR., "Quality Planning and Analysis," p. 38, McGraw-Hill Book Company, New York, 1970.

Perhaps for this reason, many quality decisions seem to be made on an intuitive basis without any conscious attempt to evaluate the elements of each decision in the only units that can make all the elements commensurable, namely, in money units. Intuition may be a good enough guide in many circumstances, but it may occasionally prove to be a very costly one. Moreover, it is common to find that different individuals in an organization will reach opposite conclusions on quality matters whenever the basis for such decisions depends entirely on intuition.

The brief discussion in the remainder of this chapter is intended to suggest the controlling elements in certain types of quality decisions. A recognition of these elements should be helpful in improving the rational basis for quality decisions even in the numerous cases where a money evaluation of all of the elements in a particular decision turns out to be impracticable.

Some Basic Concepts in Engineering Economy

The authors of this book, in collaboration with W. G. Ireson, have suggested the following conceptual framework for economy studies:†

1. Decisions are among alternatives; it is desirable that alternatives be clearly defined and that the merits of all appropriate alternatives be evaluated.
2. Decisions should be based on the expected consequences of the various alternatives.
3. Before establishing procedures for project formulation and project evaluation, it is essential to decide whose viewpoint is to be adopted.
4. In comparing alternatives, it is desirable to make consequences commensurable with one another insofar as practicable. That is, consequences should be expressed in numbers and the same units should apply to all the numbers. In economic decisions, money units are the only units that meet the foregoing specification.
5. Only the differences among alternatives are relevant in their comparison.
6. Insofar as practicable, separable decisions should be made separately.
7. It is desirable to have a criterion for decision making, or possibly several criteria.
8. The primary criterion to be applied in a choice among alternative proposed investments in physical assets should be selected with the objective of making the best use of limited resources.
9. Even the most careful estimates of the monetary consequences of choosing different alternatives may turn out to be incorrect. It often is helpful to a decision maker to make use of secondary criteria that reflect in some way the lack of certainty associated with all estimates of the future.

---

† E. L. GRANT, W. G. IRESON, and R. S. LEAVENWORTH, "Principles of Engineering Economy," 6th ed., chaps. 1 and 2, The Ronald Press Division of John Wiley & Sons, Inc., New York, 1976.

10. Decisions among investment alternatives should give weight to any expected differences in consequences that have not been reduced to money terms as well as to the consequences that have been expressed in terms of money.
11. Often there are side effects that tend to be disregarded when individual decisions are made. To consider such side effects adequately, it may be necessary to examine the interrelationships among a number of decisions before any of the individual decisions can be made.

Even though the remainder of this chapter does not refer specifically to the foregoing concepts, the discussion and the examples illustrate the application of many of them. For instance, Example 19-4 illustrates the desirability of defining the appropriate alternatives and basing a decision on their expected consequences expressed in terms of money; Example 19-5 illustrates the need to decide whose viewpoint is to be adopted and the need to recognize that only the prospective differences among alternatives are relevant in their comparison.

A Comment on the Semantics of Quality

In using the word *quality*, it is helpful to recognize the distinction between *quality of design* and *quality of conformance*. In the sense that a Lincoln is considered to be a better quality automobile than a Ford, or a Cadillac a better quality one than a Chevrolet, the word is used in the sense of quality of design. The designers of the higher priced automobiles have included certain more costly features aimed to secure greater comfort, better appearance, better performance, etc.

When we discussed specifications and tolerances in Chap. 10, we noted that, with respect to specific quality characteristics, the designer's specifications do not always seem to be consistent with the design objectives. Some instances where this occurred were cited in Examples 10-5, 10-6, and 10-7.

In the sense used in this chapter, quality of conformance relates to whether or not the quality characteristics of a product correspond to those really needed to secure the results intended by the designer. Used in this sense, margins of safety written into design specifications are often aimed chiefly at securing quality of conformance. Where such margins of safety are used with this objective, design specifications and acceptance specifications are properly viewed as interrelated matters.

Three General Classes of Consequences that Should be Recognized in Making Certain Quality Decisions

Economy studies involving quality of conformance may relate to the amount and type of inspection, to production methods and objectives, and to margins of safety used in design specifications. In studies to guide decisions on these matters, it is helpful to divide the expected economic consequences of the decisions into three general classes. These consequences may be somewhat loosely referred to as (1) production costs, (2) acceptance costs, and (3) unsatisfactory-product costs.

In this usage, the expression *production costs* is intended to refer to those costs involved in the production of the article under consideration. Different design specifications may require different materials, different labor skills, different amounts of labor time, and different machines. For example, increased strength requirements for a part may change the material to be used; closer required tolerances on dimensions may call for the use of newer or different machines. This general class of costs properly includes *spoilage costs*, i.e., the production expenses on all product discarded as not meeting specifications minus any receipts from the disposal of this discarded product. It also includes *rework costs* necessary to make product acceptable and screening costs, if any, on rejected lots.

The *acceptance costs* include not only testing and inspection costs but also the costs of administering the acceptance program.

The expression *unsatisfactory-product costs* is intended to refer to those costs resulting from the acceptance of product that turns out to be unsatisfactory for the purpose intended. In this sense the word *cost* should be interpreted as including a reduction in revenue as well as an increase in expense. It should be recognized that some or all of the product that is technically defective in the sense of failing to meet design specifications is not necessarily unsatisfactory for the purpose intended whenever the common practice is followed of including a margin of safety in the specifications. This distinction between product that is really unsatisfactory and product that is satisfactory even though nonconforming to specifications is an important one in any discussion of the economics of quality decisions.

Of these three classes of costs affected by quality decisions, unsatisfactory-product costs are inherently the most difficult to evaluate. Doubtless the greatest difficulty occurs in the consumer's goods industries, where the product goes to a great many different customers who make no formal acceptance tests. It is hard to predict the consequences to the manufacturer of consumers' goods when some stated percentage of his product fails to give satisfactory service to its purchasers, and it is even more difficult to place a money value on these consequences. Where the consumers' product carries a guarantee, past customer service costs can be used as a guide to judgment and changes in these costs can be carefully watched and related to changes in design specifications and in inspection and acceptance procedures.

The most favorable circumstances exist for securing reliable information on unsatisfactory-product costs when all of the product goes to one user. This user may be another department in the producer's organization, or it may be a single purchaser who is responsible for the design specification.

Reasons for Margins of Safety in Design Specifications

In specifying a quality characteristic such as a dimension, strength, resistance, etc., there will often be a twilight zone of uncertainty within which the product will be satisfactory under most conditions of use but not under all conceivable conditions. Design specifications may be drawn in a way that classifies as defective all articles falling in this twilight zone. Moreover, designers often seem to believe that they cannot secure the quality characteristics that are really needed without re-quiring a margin of safety. This common practice has not been changed by the advent of statistical quality control techniques in industry. Some reasons for continuing to require a margin of safety are clearly stated by Wyatt H. Lewis, as follows:†

1. Acceptance sampling plans, although they may guarantee a long range average quality level of no worse than say 2% defective, may accept occasional lots with as much as 8% defective. Such a high per cent defective may cause dislocation of manufacturing operations at consider-able cost due to lost time, excessive rework, special handling to make up for delays, etc.
2. Even a control chart using actual measurements may not detect slight shifts in the $\bar{X}$ or σ values for a matter of several samples and you might be in trouble before you realized it.
3. The vendor may have a process operating in control but there are times when causes arise to disturb the state of control. In such cases the margin of safety is very handy for acceptance of material on the basis of deviation from the specification in order to keep assembly lines going and to avoid sending operators home and cancelling orders. The cost of the latter cannot be ignored.
4. Laboratory instruments and inspection gages, although given periodic checks, sometimes drift and such drift is not detected until the next periodic check.
5. There is also the human element to consider: lack of experience, acceptance of borderline cases, etc.

In many industrial plants, it is a fairly common experience for parts first to be rejected by the inspection department because they fail to conform to specifications and later to be accepted by a plant salvage committee or material-review board primarily on the grounds that their lack of conformity falls within the margin of safety included in the specifications.

Some Economic Aspects of Decisions on the Amount and Type of Inspection

Sometimes it is economical to do no inspection at all, sometimes 100% inspection is the most economical, and sometimes sampling inspection of one type or another is better than either. The objective should be to select that amount and type of inspection that will minimize the sum of the production costs, acceptance costs, and unsatisfactory-product costs influenced by the decision regarding inspection. Once this viewpoint has been adopted, certain conditions are evident that are favorable, respectively, to no inspection, to 100% inspection, and to sampling inspection.

Where submitted product is consistently satisfactory for the purpose in-tended, it is likely to be most economical to have no inspection whatever. In this case, there are no unsatisfactory-product costs to be reduced by inspection. Neither do there appear to be production costs such as spoilage and rework to be reduced through diagnosis by control charts or through the pressure for process

---

† W. H. LEWIS, Discussion of E. L. Grant, The Economic Relationship between Design and Acceptance Specifications, *Special Technical Publication* No. 103, Symposium on Application of Statistics, American Society for Testing and Materials, Philadelphia, Pa., 1950.

improvement exerted when product is rejected. Sometimes, however, as in the case of overfill of containers, concealed opportunities may exist for reducing production costs; such opportunities might be disclosed by variables sampling inspection using control charts.

Low unsatisfactory-product costs per unit of such product may also make it economical to do no inspection whatever. For example, where unsatisfactory product is readily discovered and eliminated in a subsequent production operation, it may be cheaper to tolerate a moderate percentage of such product than to eliminate it by inspection.

Where submitted product is consistent in quality but nearly always contains a substantial percentage of unsatisfactory product, 100% inspection may be the most economical alternative. Here the choice is likely to be between 100% inspection and no inspection for acceptance purposes; with a statistically controlled product, sampling inspection cannot be expected to separate the relatively good lots from the relatively bad ones. The higher the percentage of unsatisfactory product submitted and the higher the unsatisfactory-product cost per unit of such product, the more favorable the conditions for 100% inspection as compared with no inspection. The higher the unit cost of inspection and the less the effectiveness of 100% inspection in eliminating unsatisfactory product, the more favorable the conditions for no inspection.

In making economy studies regarding the amount and type of inspection, it should be recognized that sampling inspection schemes may possibly reduce unsatisfactory-product costs in two ways. One way is by the rejection or rectification of the relatively bad lots of product, thereby making the proportion of unsatisfactory product approved less than the proportion submitted. The other way is by reducing the proportion of unsatisfactory product submitted; sampling inspection may improve product quality through diagnosis of causes of quality troubles and through the exertion of effective pressure for process improvement. This improvement of product quality may also reduce production costs, particularly costs of spoilage and rework.

If this possible contribution of sampling inspection to the improvement of product quality is neglected, the following general statement may be made: The economic field for sampling inspection is where submitted product is usually good enough for no inspection to be more economical than 100% inspection and where submitted product is occasionally bad enough for 100% inspection to be more economical than no inspection.

A set of generalizations about economy studies regarding acceptance inspection that is somewhat more complete and realistic is as follows:

1. No economic comparison of alternative plans for acceptance inspection is possible without making assumptions regarding the quality of the product submitted for acceptance. The conclusions of any economy study will depend on these assumptions.
2. In general, as the level of submitted quality is improved and as its consistency is improved, it becomes economical to use acceptance schemes involving less inspection. This is one of the reasons for keeping a record of quality history and

for making periodic reviews of acceptance procedures in the light of that history.

3. In any proposal for a change in acceptance procedures, it is insufficient to consider merely the expected change in acceptance costs. Attention should also be given to the probable influence of the proposed change on production costs and on unsatisfactory-product costs.

4. The most important point favorable to certain acceptance sampling schemes is their prospective contribution to the improvement of submitted quality in some cases through diagnosis of quality troubles and in others through effective pressure for quality improvement. This improvement of quality decreases production costs by reducing the cost of spoilage and rework. It also tends to decrease unsatisfactory-product costs. In the long run it permits a reduction in acceptance costs.

Will it Pay to Use a Control Chart for Variables?

The greatest opportunities for cost reduction from statistical quality control often arise out of applications of the Shewhart control chart for variables. These savings are sometimes spectacular. They come from many sources—from reduction in cost of spoilage and rework, from reduction in inspection cost, from better control over the quality of purchased product, from the use of more economical materials or methods due to their greater reliability under statistical control, from better decisions on proposed investments in plant and machinery.

On the other hand, each control chart for variables involves some costs. The measurements of the variable must be made and recorded. Clerical labor is required for plotting the charts and computing the averages and limits. The time of people who have good technical ability is required for interpreting charts as a basis for action. Troubleshooting based on the evidence of the charts may sometimes be a costly matter.

Each set of $\bar{X}$ and R charts may be thought of as a gamble that the resulting savings will be greater than the cost of keeping the charts. In the introduction of the control chart for variables in any mass-production industry, experience indicates that from the overall viewpoint this gamble almost amounts to betting on a sure thing; there are certain to be *some* opportunities for substantial cost savings. However, there are bound to be many quality characteristics for which $\bar{X}$ and R charts will not pay their way.

Before applying $\bar{X}$ and R charts to any given quality characteristic, it is seldom possible to be *certain* that the resulting cost savings will more than pay for the charts. It is, however, often possible to eliminate many quality characteristics from consideration by observing that sufficient opportunities for cost savings do not seem to exist, and to observe that for other quality characteristics there seem to be excellent opportunities for savings. This calls for an examination of costs that might be reduced, such as spoilage, rework, and inspection costs, and for a consideration of the possibilities of using the control-chart information as a basis for changes in design, specifications, or manufacturing methods.

Sometimes the question of whether it is a good gamble to use $\bar{X}$ and R charts for a given quality characteristic cannot be answered without the evidence of the charts themselves. Fortunately this is not a serious obstacle, as the cost of maintaining charts for a short period usually is small. It is always possible to discontinue control charts whenever it is clear that they are no longer justified.

Example 19-1 deals with the question of whether prospective savings in spoilage and rework will justify the expense of a control chart. Example 19-2 illustrates possible economies in the control of product weight when a control chart is used. Example 19-3 deals with a decision as to whether it is likely to be worth while to use a control chart for this purpose.

Example 19-1 Analysis of spoilage reports *Facts of the case* In the introduction of statistical quality control in one manufacturing plant, many p charts were initiated. In most cases, these charts made use of inspection records that already were maintained for 100% inspection by attributes. The p charts indicated the quality level of various parts and products, and the presence or absence of statistical control. In this way, they suggested possible places for the use of $\bar{X}$ and R charts to diagnose the causes of trouble.

The chances of reducing costs by reducing the amount of spoilage and rework on any given part or product depend on the percentage defective, on the subdivision of defectives into spoilage and rework, on the unit cost of a spoiled part or product and on the average rework cost, and on the prospective future production of the part or product.

From the standpoint of possible $\bar{X}$ and R chart applications, it was evidently necessary to break down the defectives by reasons for rejection and to note particularly those defectives which resulted from failure to meet specifications on some quality characteristic that might readily be measured (such as dimension, weight, resistance, tensile strength, etc.). For rejections due to each such characteristic, defective work reports or other cost records should be examined to estimate the average net cost of a spoiled unit (usually the manufacturing costs up to the point of spoilage minus scrap value of the unit) and average rework cost.

In manufacturing operations on a job that has a definite forseeable termination and that is unlikely to be repeated, the possible saving from elimination of spoilage and rework is limited by the total amount still to be produced. For instance, assume 20,000 units are still to be produced on a given job. Past spoilage due to failure to meet specifications on a certain dimension has averaged 2%; rework has averaged 4%. The net cost of a spoiled unit is $5, and the average rework cost is $0.30. The total possible saving from the complete elimination of spoilage and rework from all remaining product is therefore

Spoilage	20,000($5)(0.02)	= $2,000
Rework	20,000($0.30)(0.04) =	240
Total		$2,240

This estimate neglects the fact that anything learned in troubleshooting on this particular job may also prove helpful in reducing spoilage and rework on other similar operations.

Where manufacturing operations on the given product are expected to continue for an indefinite period, it is desirable to estimate expected annual production. The maximum possible annual saving from complete elimination of spoilage and rework may then be estimated.

Such estimates guide the selection of quality characteristics for the application of $\bar{X}$ and R charts so that each chart has definite possibilities for substantial cost savings.

Example 19-2 Control of product weight *Facts of the case* Figure 19-1, taken from an article by O. P. Beckwith,† illustrates the effect of successive changes in a textile manufacturing operation. The purchase specification for this fabric stated that the average weight in ounces per square yard of a sample of five from a lot of material should not be less than a stated value. As time went on, it proved possible to work closer and closer to this specification limit with safety.

The first section of the chart shows a few points close to the specification minimum, even though there was a relatively high average value. At this time the operation was not in statistical control. Moreover, trouble was experienced with yarn strength. Beckwith explains the successive changes as follows:

"In the first change the weight of the yarn was increased, which, under the particular conditions of manufacture, made a more uniform yarn. At the same time the yarn-weight increase was compensated for by a decrease in fabric picks per inch. Meanwhile considerable investigation of the spinning process

---

† O. P. BECKWITH, A Fresh Approach to Quality Control, *Textile World,* vol. 94, pp. 79–81, January, 1944.

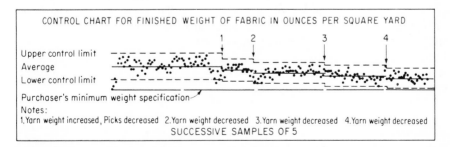

Figure 19-1 $\bar{X}$ chart illustrating the effect of successive changes working closer to a minimum specification limit on weight—Example 19-2. (*Reproduced from O. P. Beckwith, "A Fresh Approach to Quality Control," Textile World, vol. 94, pp. 79–81, January, 1944.*)

showed how yarn could be spun at required strength and uniformity, but at reduced weight. The yarn weights were therefore lowered progressively, as is reflected by the third, fourth, and fifth changes in limits."

Because the specification applied to *averages* of samples of five rather than to individual values, it was appropriate to show the specification limit on this $\bar{X}$ chart.

Example 19-3 Possible reduction in overfill of containers *Facts of the case* In the packaging of a cereal product in 10-lb sacks, it was suggested that a study be made to determine the advisability of using $\bar{X}$ and R charts.

It was possible to make preliminary guesses as to possible savings prior to the use of $\bar{X}$ and R charts for an experimental period. The value of the material being sacked per operator per hour was $500. Thus it was evident that a 2% overfill would cost $10 per h. This estimate showed that if there were really an overfill and if it could be reduced without falling below specifications, there was a chance for a good saving.

A trial period of control-chart operation was required to provide a basis for judgment as to the average amount of overfill and the possibility of improvement. This showed that the filling process was not in statistical control. If the process could be brought into control, it was evident that the average overfill could be substantially reduced. An estimate indicated that the annual cost of overfill on this particular item was nearly forty thousand dollars. Although it was apparent that all overfill could not be eliminated, it was clear that even a small reduction would more than pay the cost of a control-chart program.

Some Economic Aspects of the Margin of Safety in Design Specifications†

Designers have not commonly thought of the margin of safety to be included in specified tolerance limits as a problem in economy. Nevertheless, because such margins are aimed at quality of conformance, they should properly be viewed in the same way as the selection of acceptance criteria.

Serious adverse consequences of accepting unsatisfactory product and high unit costs of inspection are two conditions favorable to the economic use of large margins of safety in design specifications.

---

† For additional comment on this topic, see E. L. GRANT, The Economic Relationship between Design and Acceptance Specifications, *Special Technical Publication* No. 103, Symposium on Application of Statistics, American Society for Testing and Materials, Philadelphia, Pa., 1950. See also E. L. GRANT, Some Possible Contributions of Statistical Quality Control to Engineering Economy, Paper no. 1, Fourth National Convention ASQC, American Society for Quality Control, New York, 1950.

On the other hand, an uncritical use of large margins of safety under all conditions may turn out to be very costly. Generally speaking, the design specification determines the production method to be employed. Unnecessary margins of safety may require more costly materials, more precise machines, and more expensive workmanship than really needed to secure satisfactory product. Conditions favorable to small margins of safety in the design specification are as follows:

1. Evidence that the manufacturing process can be kept in good statistical control with an average and dispersion that result in product that is satisfactory for the purpose intended with very little margin of safety.
2. Evidence that a costly change in the manufacturing process will be required in order to increase this margin.
3. Either low unsatisfactory-product cost per unit of such product or relatively low cost of applying acceptance criteria to give adequate protection.

Quality Decisions in Choosing a Production Method

The choice of a production method is influenced by the quality objective. The quality objective, in turn, is influenced by the design and acceptance criteria. Where acceptance criteria are such that lots with moderate percentages of defectives have only a small probability of rejection, it may be more economical to have an occasional lot rejected than to increase production costs in order to prevent any rejections. This seems particularly likely to happen where the producer has some degree of statistical sophistication and where he believes that the design specifications contain enough margin of safety so that moderately defective lots are really good enough for the purpose intended.

In some instances it may be economical to adopt production methods in which a certain amount of rework or spoilage seems inevitable. This point is illustrated in Example 19-4.

Example 19-4 Reducing a high percentage of defectives will not necessarily reduce costs *Facts of the case* In the manufacture of a certain type of pressure gage, many different types of defects were responsible for rejection at final inspection. The defects causing each rejection were shown on the inspection record. More than half the rejections were shown to be made for one reason, associated with the zero registration of the gage. On the average, about 20% of the gages produced had this defect. A *p* chart plotted for this type of defect indicated that the process was in control at this level; the day-to-day fluctuations above and below 20% defective were such as might be attributable to chance. This defect was always correctible by a rework operation which, for most gages, was relatively simple.

Analysis and action An engineering study indicated that this type of defect could be almost completely eliminated by an extra operation on one of the parts of the gage. The costs of doing this for 100% of the gages were compared with the costs of carrying out the rework operation on 20% of the gages. This cost comparison showed it to be more economical to rework 20% of the gages than to carry out the extra operation on 100% of them. Consequently it was decided that, until a less costly method of eliminating this defect was discovered, the 20% level for this defect would be accepted as normal.

Some Special Difficulties of Estimating Indirect Costs in Economy Studies

Cost accounting systems recognize three classes of manufacturing costs, namely, direct material cost, direct labor cost, and indirect manufacturing expense, often called *burden* or *overhead*. The classification *indirect manufacturing expense* includes a great variety of costs, such as supervision, inspection, factory transportation, janitors, repairs and maintenance on machines and buildings, heat, light, and power, manufacturing supplies, factory clerical expense, accident compensation, tools and dies, factory insurance and taxes, and depreciation on buildings and machinery. Defective work and spoilage are sometimes charged directly to a job or process, and sometimes included as part of overhead. Indirect manufacturing expense is apportioned among cost centers and applied to each job or process in proportion to something directly measurable such as direct labor cost, direct labor hours, or machine hours. The most common basis is direct labor cost. If, for example, the machine shop carried a burden rate of 150% of direct labor cost, this would mean that for every dollar of direct labor cost charged against a job in the machine shop, there would also be charged $1.50 of indirect manufacturing expense. This charge would be, in effect, an apportionment against the job of the many different indirect expenses, i.e., supervision, janitors, heat, light, and power, factory taxes, etc.

Although such an apportionment serves many useful purposes, such as valuation of inventories of goods in process and finished goods, determination of cost of goods sold, and sometimes determination of selling price, it does not follow that the saving of a dollar of direct labor in the machine shop will save $1.50 of disbursements for indirect manufacturing expense. Neither does it follow that an increase of a dollar of direct labor cost in the machine shop increases disbursements for indirect manufacturing expense by $1.50. From the standpoint of an economy study, the real question is what receipts and disbursements are likely to be influenced by the choice between alternatives.†

---

† For a more extended presentation of this point of view, see E. L. GRANT, W. G. IRESON, and R. S. LEAVENWORTH, *op. cit.*, particularly chap. 15.

See also E. L. GRANT and P. T. NORTON, JR., "Depreciation," chap. 16, The Ronald Press Company, New York, 1955; B. E. GOETZ, "Management Planning and Control," McGraw-Hill Book Company, New York, 1959; E. L. GRANT and L. F. BELL, "Basic Accounting and Cost Accounting," 2d ed., chap. 21, McGraw-Hill Book Company, New York, 1964; and JOEL DEAN, Managerial Economics, in W. G. IRESON and E. L. GRANT, eds., "Handbook of Industrial Engineering and Management," 2d ed., Prentice-Hall, Inc., Englewood Cliffs, New Jersey, 1971.

It is a general principle of all economy studies that indirect costs should not be included in cost comparisons simply by the uncritical application of burden rates. The relevant question regarding indirect expenses is always the probable effect of the choice between the given alternatives on each separate indirect expense. If no disbursements for indirect expense seem likely to be influenced by the choice, there is no need to consider indirect expenses in the economy study. In many economy studies relative to quality control, it may be good enough for practical purposes to limit the estimates to the direct costs involved in the alternatives being compared.

Did It Pay to Use Statistical Quality Control?

Up to this point the discussion in this chapter has dealt with *prospective* uses of statistical quality control techniques. *Each* use of these techniques should be based on a favorable prospect that the particular use in question will more than pay its costs.

It sometimes happens that when statistical quality control has been newly introduced into an organization and has been used for a few months, a continuation of the *overall* use of the techniques requires evidence satisfactory to management that their use has paid on the whole. Management is inclined to look to the financial accounts and cost accounts for this evidence, and often wants before-and-after figures for comparison. Although in some cases a fairly satisfactory picture of the effect of statistical quality control may be had by examining costs before the use of the techniques and comparing them with costs after the techniques have been used for some time, this point of view has definite limitations that should be understood.

Where there have been reductions in the amount of spoilage and rework over a short period and these reductions are clearly due to statistical quality control, there is a good measure of cost saving. Also, where the amount of destructive testing has been reduced due to the use of the control chart for variables as a basis for acceptance, it is possible to arrive at a definite figure for the saving.

But in most cases the situation is sufficiently complicated that a fair before-and-after picture cannot be obtained solely from accounting figures. It is seldom as simple as being able to say, for example, that the charges to account 317-B-1 were $1,427 in January before statistical quality control, and $955 in May after statistical quality control. (Logically, of course, such a comparison is never appropriate. The correct comparison is between the actual costs in May with statistical quality control and the costs in May as they would have been without statistical quality control; the practical difficulty is that there is no way to be certain of the latter figure.) Too many changes are constantly taking place to make it reasonable to ascribe all cost changes over a period of time to a single influence. Any before-and-after study needs to combine all the relevant evidence; the figures in the accounts constitute only one part of this evidence.

For example, the use of the control chart may reduce the number of machine shutdowns for readjustment by 75% and thus increase productive machine time and reduce costs. In any given period, this saving might be neutralized by other causes which were responsible for idle machine time.

Or an improvement in the outgoing quality from the forge shop might reduce the number of defective forgings transmitted to the machine shop. This, in turn, might reduce excessive machining costs and tool breakage in the machine shop. These savings, however, would be only two of many possible influences on machine-shop costs. If the unit costs in the machine shop actually decreased, this improvement might be attributed by the machine-shop superintendent to causes within the machine shop, even though better forgings were really responsible for most of the savings.

Or an improvement in the quality of purchased parts might reduce the delays due to defective parts on an assembly line. But there might be enough other variations in assembly costs that the effect of this improvement could not be isolated in the accounts.

Or improvement in the quality level of final product might tend to reduce the number of customer complaints. But the time lag between production and complaints might be such that this would only be evident after a long period of time.

Moreover, it should be recognized that the chances for before-and-after studies showing spectacular cost savings come chiefly in the early days of statistical quality control. As time goes on, the function of statistical quality control becomes more and more one of holding the line of better quality and improved quality assurance, and there is no " before " figure from a few months ago that can be contrasted with current performance.

Sometimes a misinterpretation of accounting figures may lead to an unsound conclusion regarding the merits of past changes. Example 19-5 is a case in point.

Example 19-5 A misinterpretation of the ratio of indirect manufacturing expense to direct labor cost *Facts of the case* One of the important raw materials in a certain manufacturing operation was subject to considerable inherent variability. For this reason, it had always been assumed that satisfactory product was not possible without 100% inspection following the manufacturing operation. The percentage of spoilage disclosed by this inspection was always fairly high. Nearly half of the direct labor cost charged on this operation was for this 100% inspection, which was carried out by production personnel. All the different sizes and designs of the plant's basic product required this manufacturing operation.

The plant quality control director introduced $\bar{X}$ and R charts on this operation. As often happens, it proved possible to diagnose the causes of a number of the quality troubles and to eliminate them. For most of the sizes and designs of the product, it was possible to bring the fraction defective to a low enough figure so that an AOQL sampling plan could be substituted for the mandatory 100% inspection.

In the cost accounts of this company, factory burden (i.e., indirect manufacturing expense) was apportioned to product in each department in proportion to direct labor cost. In effect, the burden rate was a fraction in which the numerator was departmental indirect manufacturing expense and the denominator was departmental direct labor cost.

The effect of the quality improvement was to make a large increase in this fraction for the particular department affected. The elimination of the direct labor for screening inspection on most of the product cut the denominator to some 60% of its previous figure. The AOQL sampling inspection was carried out by inspection personnel rather than production personnel and was therefore classified as an indirect manufacturing expense; it increased the value of the numerator of the fraction. This increase in the numerator and decrease in the denominator nearly doubled the burden rate.

The controller of this company was located at company headquarters several hundred miles from this manufacturing plant. He viewed the ratio of indirect manufacturing expense to direct labor cost as a figure that should be kept as low as possible in every department. When this ratio was greatly increased as a result of the activities of the plant quality control director, the controller was extremely critical of both the director and the head of the manufacturing department, and in fact proposed to top management that the previous inspection scheme should be reinstated and that the plant quality control director's responsibilities should be severely curtailed. Fortunately, after a review of the matter, top management did not accept the controller's suggestions.

Comment on the case Of course, the changes brought about by these quality control activities had really caused a substantial decrease in *total* manufacturing costs. There had been a substantial decrease in spoilage. (The accounts in this company had never isolated the costs of spoilage.) The costs incident to the sampling inspection were much less than the cost of the previous 100% inspection.

It seems hardly conceivable that this controller, trained in accounting, could have been so unaware of the limitations of conclusions that may be drawn from an uncritical examination of ratios taken from the accounts. However, the controller had become preoccupied with the need to control all costs that were classified as indirect manufacturing expense and, moreover, had come to accept the ratio of such indirect expense to direct labor cost as the best measure of success in controlling indirect expense. These attitudes seemed to blind the controller to the realities of the situation and to lead to the making of recommendations that were adverse to the company's best interests.

Who Should Get Credit for Savings from Quality Improvement?

It is futile to argue the question, "Who was responsible for making this saving?" Any quality improvements made on the basis of a diagnosis of troubles by the control chart are necessarily based on teamwork. Inspection personnel, production personnel, methods engineers, tool engineers, design engineers, and others may all participate.

From the standpoint of managerial decisions, the important question is not, "Who gets the credit?" but rather, "What methods and policies shall we adopt?" In judging whether or not to use statistical quality control techniques, the question for management is, "What savings will be made with these techniques that will not be made without them?" All such savings are relevant in the decision whether to use statistical quality control, even though the statistical techniques are only one of the necessary links in the chain by means of which the savings are accomplished.

Some Problems Connected with Budgetary Control

The reduction of costs and the prevention of cost increases call for the continuous exercise of executive pressure. In modern manufacturing plants, this pressure is exerted by the use of budgets. A principle of budgetary control is that each comparison between actual performance and the budgeted figure must follow the lines of individual responsibility. Pressure, to be effective, must be exerted on individuals—on works managers, department heads, supervisors, and operators.

Because department heads and supervisors are judged by their superiors in terms of conformance to their own budgets, they are sometimes inclined to view all decisions and proposed actions solely in terms of the effect on those budgets. This point of view often is adverse to the best interests of the business enterprise as a whole. It frequently happens that a small increase in expenditure in one department will bring about a much larger saving in another department. Or a decrease in cost in one department may cause a much larger increase in cost elsewhere.

This concentration of attention on individual budgets may, in some organizations, constitute a serious obstacle to the effective use of statistical quality control. Control charts may cause increases in inspection costs (at least temporarily) even though they may result in much larger decreases in production costs. Quality improvements in the manufacture of parts may require increased fabrication costs, even though they result in much larger decreases in assembly costs, and so forth. Nearly every application of statistical quality control, and, for that matter, nearly all policies related to product quality, will cross the lines of departmental responsibility.

For this reason, many decisions related to quality ought to be made at a management level higher than that of the supervisors who seem to be immediately concerned.

The Increasing Importance of Costs Related to Product Liability

The 1960s and 1970s were decades in which there was an extraordinary increase in the number of lawsuits involving product liability. A distinguished authority on this subject, Professor John Mihalasky, estimated in 1977 that the annual number of product liability lawsuits in the United States had increased to more than 500,000 from a figure of less than 5,000 some ten to fifteen years earlier. The dollar amount of representative settlements of such suits had also increased very rapidly.†

The increased litigation about product liability resulted in part from drastic changes in court-made law and in part from specific legislation and the establishment of new government regulatory agencies. There was, in effect, a shift from the older legal doctrine that has been described as "Let the buyer beware" to a newer doctrine that might be called "Let the manufacturer beware." The legal basis for increased product liability litigation naturally varied from one country to another, and, in the United States, from one state to another. The U.S.A. had certain special aspects of its legal system that contributed to its rapid increase in the volume and costs of such litigation, as follows:‡

(a) The amount of the award in the United States has not been limited to the actual damages claimed to have been sustained; in addition it has been possible to award so-called exemplary or punitive damages.

(b) Such cases may be tried by juries. Experience has indicated that decisions by juries in cases of this type seem to be capricious and unpredictable. The extremely high awards that sometimes occur have encouraged manufacturers and their insurance companies to make an out-of-court settlement in many instances rather than to let a case go to trial. (Of course such out-of-court settlements also eliminate the defendant's expenses incident to the actual trial of a case.)

(c) Lawyers in the United States have been permitted to take suits for damages with the payment of any fee by the client contingent on the success of the case. If the case is lost, the client owes nothing. If the case is won, the sum awarded for damages is split between the lawyer and the client according to some agreed-on percentage (possibly 50% to each). The chance for good out-of-court settlements of many cases has made such contingency-fee agreements attractive to a number of lawyers.

(d) It sometimes has been possible to hold a manufacturer liable for damages resulting from the use of that manufacturer's product regardless of the number of years that may have elapsed between the date of the purchase of the product new and the date of the use of the product that is alleged to have caused the injuries or other damages in question.

Product liability litigation is only one of many types of litigation that has been influenced by the foregoing differences between the United States and other

---

† JOHN MIHALASKY, The Status of Product Liability in the U.S.A., *Reports, First European Seminar on Product Liability*, vol. 1, pp. 119–130, April 28/29, 1977. This seminar was held jointly by the European Organization for Quality Control and Associazione Italiana Controllo Qualità. The two volumes of reports on the seminar include papers on the status of product liability in a dozen or so countries. These reports are copyrighted by the European Organization for Quality Control, P.O. Box 2613—CH 3001, Bern, Switzerland.

‡ See J. G. COWELL, Products Liability—European Insurance Perspectives, *Reports, First European Seminar on Product Liability*, op. cit., vol. 2, pp. 25–30. Our list is adapted from a similar one in the Cowell paper that explains some of the differences between Europe and the United States in this matter.

countries. For example, during the same years when product liability litigation was increasing so rapidly, there was also a great increase in the number of malpractice suits against physicians and hospitals and in the size of the monetary awards in such suits.

Statistical Quality Control Techniques in Relation to Certain Economic Aspects of Product Liability

Where a manufacturer carries insurance against product liability, the cost of this insurance is one element of product liability cost. Other elements include legal expenses and other expenses in connection with the defense of lawsuits, judgments for damages in suits that go to trial and are lost, and payments in suits that are settled out of court rather than going to trial, to the extent that all of these are not covered by insurance. It needs to be recognized that although current insurance costs may give a good enough estimate of a major part of product liability costs for the immediate future, the long-run costs of insurance will be greatly influenced by a manufacturer's experience in having to pay damages and in making out-of-court settlements. In our classification of three general classes of costs that need to be recognized in decisions about quality, product liability costs clearly should be classified as unsatisfactory-product costs.

We started this chapter with a quotation from Juran and Gryna. This stated a general principle, namely, that the economic balance to be struck between the cost of quality and the value of quality applies to each quality characteristic. This principle applies both to decisions on quality of design (such as a choice among alternate possible materials) and to decisions on quality of conformance (such as the classification of a particular nonconformity as critical, major, or minor, or the choice of a LTPD or AOQL). Rarely, if ever, is it possible to make a satisfactory estimate of the product liability cost associated with each alternative that is being considered either in decision making about quality of design or about quality of conformance.

One would not expect to find the phrases "quality of design" and "quality of conformance" used in legal actions involving product liability. Nevertheless, it is the authors' impression that a large proportion of the alleged deficiencies in manufactured product that give rise to such actions are really deficiencies in quality of design. Such deficiencies cannot be eliminated by the better use of the techniques of statistical quality control. What is needed is a careful design review of materials, methods, and specifications dealing with quality characteristics that seem likely to be the source of lawsuits involving product liability.

To the extent that awards in product liability suits depend on alleged unsatisfactory quality of conformance to specifications, the use of statistical quality control techniques ought to help. That is, the techniques may help wherever it is possible to identify those quality characteristics for which nonconformity to specifications seems to be a likely source of such litigation.

The techniques of statistical quality control may be useful here both in process control and in manufacturers' inspection of parts and of outgoing product. Control charts may help to diagnose and eliminate certain causes of failure to meet specifications. If a classification of quality characteristics (a so-called classification of defects) is used in a factory's inspection of its own product, characteristics should be classed as critical if nonconformities are likely to cause product liability suits. If acceptance sampling is used for such quality characteristics, the quality standard (AOQL, LTPD, or indifference quality) should be tight.

A Comment on Certain Social Aspects of Product Liability Costs

Although such costs initially are costs to particular manufacturers, a large part (in many cases, nearly all) of such costs tend to be passed on to the consumers of manufactured products. To the extent that such costs are industry-wide in any industry in which prices are determined by competition, the influence of product liability costs on prices is the same as the influence of all other costs associated with the manufacturing operation. Therefore it is in the public interest as well as in the interest of manufacturers that product liability costs not be excessive.

One possible way to reduce the social costs of product liability would be to eliminate some of the awards of damages that are not justified by the facts but are made because juries do not understand the difference between the technical meaning of the word *defective* (nonconforming to specifications) and its popular meaning (unsatisfactory for the intended use). Other descriptive words, such as *nonconforming* and *nonconformity*, could replace *defective* and *defect* when the words are intended to be interpreted in their technical senses. If this change could be made throughout the manufacturing industries, it seems reasonable to expect that the change would reduce or eliminate one possible source of misunderstanding in product liability litigation. The reader will recall that this change was made in our discussion of process control in Part One of this book.

But we did not feel that it was possible to eliminate the words *defective* and *defect* in our explanation of acceptance sampling in Part Two. The difficulty was that these words are generally used in the various acceptance sampling systems that we discuss. We hope the language of these systems eventually will be changed in the interest of clarity. Also, for reasons explained in our discussion of reliability in Chap. 18, clarity would be promoted by replacing the phrase *time to failure* with *test life* or some similar phrase.

PROBLEMS

19-1 As an assistant to a consulting quality control engineer, you encounter the following situation in the plant of one of his clients:

A certain operation involves the packaging of a dry cereal product in 10-lb bags of heavy paper. The bags are filled by an automatic weighing and filling machine which cuts off the flow of the product when the weight of the bag and its contents has reached a certain predetermined setting. After the flow has been stopped by this automatic cutoff, there is a small amount of the cereal product which has already passed the cutoff point and which therefore goes into the bag. When operating without interruption, the machine fills 110 bags per hour. The practice of the operator appears to have been to aim at an overfill of 3 oz. (This value presumably was determined on the basis of past experience that any less overfill caused trouble with the government inspector.) The weight of an empty bag has been assumed to be 7 oz. This has given an aimed-at weight of 170 oz (160 + 3 + 7) for the filled package. Every hour or so the operator has weighed a single filled package on a spring scales which weighs to the nearest half ounce. If this measured weight is above 170 oz, the operator changes the machine setting to cut off at a lower weight; if the measured weight is below 170 oz, the operator changes the machine setting to cut off at a higher weight.

The government inspector at this plant has the job of checking weights and other quality characteristics that are controlled by legislation and government regulations in the interests of the ultimate consumer. The inspector's time is kept fully occupied as the job carries the responsibility for checking many products. The inspector's practice in checking weights on this particular product has been to select 5 bags at random from each day's production. (Daily production has averaged about 1,500 bags from two 8-h shifts.) Each bag has been emptied and the contents weighed on a small platform scales weighing to 0.1 oz. If the contents of each of the 5 bags weigh 160 oz or more, the inspector approves the day's output as to weight. If 2 or more of the bags have contents weighing less than 160 oz, the entire day's output is required to be stamped "Substandard Weight." If just 1 of the bags has contents below 160 oz, an additional 5 bags is taken for inspection. If all of this second sample is satisfactory, the day's production is considered to be satisfactory. If 1 or more of the second sample are below 160 oz, the day's output is considered to be all substandard weight. This particular acceptance procedure is not specified in any written instructions that have been given to the government inspector but appears to have been the traditional one at this plant. At least the present government inspector, who has worked on this job for the past 2 years, is simply following the acceptance procedure explained to him by his predecessor.

You talk with the government inspector and find a conscientious and cooperative person, anxious to carry out the functions of protecting the general public and at the same time having no desire to make unreasonable demands on the manufacturer. You obtain from the inspector the record of the measurements of weights of contents of bags for the past 50 days. (No earlier records are available.) You plot $\bar{X}$ and R charts from the first samples of 5 for these days. $\bar{X}$ is 164.1; $\bar{R}$ is 3.9. The $\bar{X}$ chart shows definite evidence of lack of statistical control with 5 points above the upper control limit and 3 points below the lower control limit. Two points are slightly above the upper control limit on the R chart; a recomputed $\bar{R}$ with these two points eliminated is 3.6. On 5 of the 50 days a second sample of 5 was taken because one of the weights in the first sample fell below 160 oz. Two of the days requiring second samples were days on which $\bar{X}$ was below the lower control limit; on the other 3 days $\bar{X}$ was within limits. Two of the 5 second samples contained one sack with contents below 160 oz. The entire day's product for these 2 days was stamped "Substandard Weight." Packages so stamped are accepted by the trade only at a 5% reduction from the regular factory price of $11.70 for a 10-lb bag.

(a) Write a general discussion analyzing the statistical aspects and other related aspects of this situation. In preparing this discussion, assume that the reader is familiar with the facts as given in the preceding statement and is familiar with the terminology and general principles of statistical quality control. This discussion might be one such as you would prepare for your chief or for a colleague in your own organization.

(b) Make a proposed draft for a letter to the plant superintendent making specific proposals for any action that you recommend should be taken. Explain in as definite terms as possible the advantages that you expect will be gained by following out your proposals. Insofar as possible, this letter should not assume that the plant superintendent is familiar with the terminology and concepts of statistical quality control.

(c) Assume that it is the government bureau carrying out the inspection that is your client rather than the manufacturer. Draft a report to the bureau chief discussing the problems involved in setting and enforcing specifications on filling weights with a view to consumer protection. Illustrate any general statements you make by reference to this specific case. Assume that the bureau chief (or his subordinate who reads the report) is familiar with the terminology and concepts of statistical quality control; for example, he will understand the meaning of an OC curve if one is included in your report.

TWENTY

DEMONSTRATING THE OPERATION
OF SYSTEMS OF CHANCE CAUSES

The most powerful mathematical tools are sometimes less important to the engineer than some of the simpler or less powerful tools. But often, for lack of information about either, neither is used.—C. M. Ryerson[†]

Use of Group Experiments in Introducing the Subjects
of Control Charts and Acceptance Sampling Procedures

In presenting an introductory course or seminar in statistical quality control (or, for that matter, in almost any other subject involving the operation of the laws of chance), it is helpful if 2 or 3 h are devoted to experiments that illustrate the operation of systems of chance causes. Such experiments are desirable in courses for college students as well as in their more usual setting of seminars given to supervisors, inspectors, and designers in industrial plants. The best time for such experiments is near the start of the course or seminar.

In part, such experiments give the group a better feeling for the way in which systems of chance causes really operate. In part, also, they provide a kind of assurance of the reasonableness of certain important formulas and relationships. This is useful even to groups that do not have to take the formulas and relationships on faith. Many of us, doubtless somewhat illogically, find experimental demonstration somewhat more satisfying than mathematical proof. Wherever practicable, the entire group should participate in each experiment (or at least enough of the group to make it obvious that the results are not being manipulated by the instructor).

[†] In the Foreword to D. M. Chorafas, "Statistical Processes and Reliability Engineering," p. v, D. Van Nostrand Company, Inc., Princeton, N.J., 1960.

Demonstrating Frequency Distributions and Control Charts for Variables

It is important for everyone dealing with variability of industrial product to have a feeling for the manner in which variation can occur even when a constant system of chance causes is operating. An experiment involving the drawing of chips, somewhat in the manner illustrated in our discussion of the Shewhart bowl, can help the members of a group to develop this feeling. Such an experiment can also illustrate the construction of $\bar{X}$ and R control charts and the estimation of universe parameters from relatively small samples (such as 5) and from relatively large samples (such as 125 or 150).

In their classes, the authors have used a cookie can containing several thousand chips, each with a number written on it. First, the instructor draws a sample of five; the number on each chip is recorded on the blackboard or on an overhead projector slide, and $\bar{X}$ and R are calculated and recorded for the subgroup. The chips are replaced, the can is closed and shaken, and one of the class now draws five chips. This drawing is repeated with a different member of the class selecting the subgroup until 25 subgroups have been obtained. (If there are enough chips in the universe, the timesaving practice of making replacement after each five chips rather than after each chip is good enough for practical purposes.) If matters are properly organized, a 50-min period is sufficient to conduct the sampling, compute $\bar{X}$ and R values as each subgroup is recorded on the blackboard, compute the control limits, draw the control charts on the blackboard or slide, and compute the estimated value of σ'. Near the end of the period, the students are given a sheet containing the frequency distribution in the cookie can and its values of $\bar{X}'$ and σ'.

Control charts and frequency distributions can also be demonstrated by the use of a *quincunx*, illustrated in Fig. 20-1. Such an apparatus was first developed by Sir Francis Galton in the 1890s. It might be thought of as an ancestor of the modern pinball machine. Beads drop through an arrangement of pins, eventually falling into any one of twenty-five parallel slots at the bottom of the inclined plane into which the pins are driven. The quincunx provides a visual demonstration of the effect of chance in producing variation within small subgroups, by holding samples of five beads above a slide located near the top of the slots, and the variation in a large frequency distribution. With the funnel located in the central position, it tends to give a distribution approximately normal (actually a binomial with $p' = \frac{1}{2}$). By shifting the funnel to various positions, assignable causes may be introduced into the sampling procedure giving rise to changed process averages and to skewed distributions. (The particular quincunx shown in Fig. 20-1 was made by the Lightning Calculator Company, St. Petersburg Beach, Florida.)

Figure 20-2 shows a control chart simulator useful in illustrating the operation of chance causes.† When used in conjunction with a quincunx, or some similar device, the control chart gives an immediate and clear illustration of the effect of shifts in process average, as well as the effect on the generation of a frequency histogram (lower portion of the quincunx).

---

† The complete device, manufactured by the Lightning Calculator Company, St. Petersburg Beach, Florida, 33736, contains a distribution shift simulator as well as the control chart simulator.

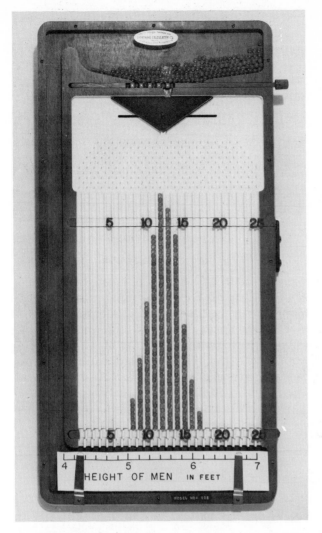

Figure 20-1 Quality control chart demonstrator (quincunx). *(Photo courtesy Lightning Calculator Co., St. Petersburg Beach, Florida.)*

Demonstrating Acceptance Sampling by Attributes

It is advantageous to have at least one experiment devoted to variables and at least one devoted to attributes. The attributes experiment can be planned to serve several purposes. If designed to illustrate the operation of an acceptance sampling plan, it may also illustrate certain matters about *p* charts (or *np* charts) and the laws of probability.

A good way to demonstrate sampling by attributes is to use a sampling tray to scoop 50 wooden beads out of a box containing a mixture of white and colored beads. Such a device, designed by Holbrook Working, is illustrated in Fig. 20-3.

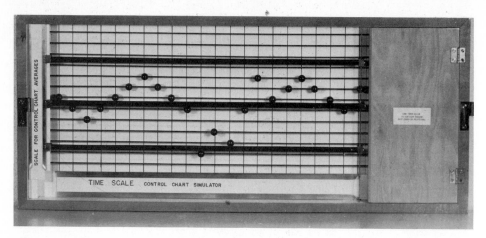

Figure 20-2 Quality control chart simulator. (*Photo courtesy Lightning Calculator Co., St. Petersburg Beach, Florida.*)

Other devices are available that operate on an open box basis as shown in Fig. 20-3 and on a closed box basis wherein the beads cannot escape from the device. White beads are frequently designated as good articles; colored beads, as defective ones. The fraction of colored beads in the box represents the p' of a production process. The fraction of colored beads in the tray after each scooping operation represents the fraction defective in a lot of 50 from that process.

This type of tray is particularly well adapted for use in a classroom experiment analyzing the acceptance plan $N = 50$, $n = 5$, $c = 0$ that was discussed in Example 1-3. (The authors have observed that many people who ought to know

Figure 20-3 Sampling scoop used to select 50 beads from a bulk of mixed white and colored beads.

better are not aware of the serious weakness of this particular plan; this statement applies to persons of such different backgrounds as chief inspectors and Ph.D.'s in mathematical statistics.) A box may be filled with, say, 1,880 white beads and 120 colored ones. The fact that the "process" actually is 6% defective should not be disclosed to the class until the end of the experiment. When a member of the class scoops 50 beads out of the box, he has an inspection lot. The number of defectives in each lot may be observed by the class and recorded on the blackboard. (For a process 6% defective, inspection lots of 50 typically will vary from 0 defectives to 7 or 8 defectives.) It should be emphasized that the class, which can observe the quality of the entire lot, has knowledge that would not be available to an inspector who would test only 5 of the 50 articles in the lot.

The beads from each inspection lot should be replaced in the box, and the beads in the box should be thoroughly mixed before the sampling tray is used to select the next lot. For convenience in carrying out the experiment rapidly, it is desirable that the sample be selected by choosing some one of the 10 vertical columns of 5 beads on the sampling tray. Each column on the tray may be marked with one of the 10 digits. If a 20-sided Japanese random die is available, it can be thrown to select the sample from each inspection lot. Otherwise, a table of random numbers may be used. If the experiment is properly organized, a 50-min period is sufficient to arrive at acceptance or rejection decisions on 40 or 50 inspection lots, to tabulate the observations on the blackboard (somewhat along the lines of Table 1-3), to make the appropriate calculations, and to discuss conclusions.

Like the experiment involving drawing chips, this sampling tray experiment is a good one to use near the start of a course or seminar—considerably before any assignments dealing with acceptance sampling systems. It is helpful for the instructor to be able to make reference to such an experiment in initial discussions of various aspects of probability. Moreover, two class experiments—one involving variables and the other attributes—serve to dramatize the important difference between inspection by variables and inspection by attributes.

Even though, at the time of this class experiment, the group seems merely to be analyzing the plan $N = 50$, $n = 5$, $c = 0$, the results of the experiment may be used later to bring out a variety of other matters. For instance, the successive trays of 50 beads may be viewed as random samples from a process 6% defective and the numbers of defectives observed on successive trays may be plotted on an np chart, or the successive trays may be viewed as single samples with $n = 50$ from a lot or process 6% defective and the data from the experiment may be used to estimate the position of one point on each of the respective OC curves with acceptance numbers c of 0, 1, 2, 3, etc.

Demonstrating Statistical Aspects of Tolerances

R. E. Wagenhals describes a device to demonstrate the addition of tolerances when assemblies of parts are at random.†

---

† R. E. WAGENHALS, Mechanical Aids for Presenting the Quality Control Story, "Quality Control Conference Papers 1951," pp. 383–389, American Society for Quality Control, Milwaukee, 1951. This article also describes other types of demonstration equipment.

A number of parts painted in 5 colors—red, blue, yellow, green, and brown—are used. A pile consisting of one piece of each color represents an assembly. Each group of one color represents a controlled process in that the frequency distribution closely follows the normal curve.

The parts illustrated in the Wagenhals article are cylindrical metal pieces. (A similar demonstration apparatus of this type was made by W. G. Ireson using wooden dowel rods.) A backboard is prepared against which an assembly may be stacked. Solid horizontal lines are drawn on this board to show the extreme possible values, the upper line showing the total height with the largest piece of each color and the lower line showing the total height with the smallest piece of each color. Within these solid lines, there are drawn dotted lines that show the 3-sigma limits for total height based on the theorem for the standard deviation of the sum of independent variables (Chap. 10). It may be shown that, when pieces are assembled at random, the chance of an assembly outside the dotted lines is very small.

TWENTY-ONE

THE WIDESPREAD USEFULNESS
OF CONTROL CHARTS AND
ACCEPTANCE SAMPLING PROCEDURES

There are two fairly widespread but nevertheless erroneous notions about control charts that have impeded their application in some areas. These are:

1. *That "our product is different" and so control charts are not applicable.*
2. *That our process must be more-or-less in control and the product rather homogeneous before we can use control charts to advantage.*

Actually, if we can make satisfactory measurements on our product, its nature has no bearing on the applicability of control charts; and control charts can be very useful in getting a process into control, as well as keeping it there.—J. B. Pringle†

Nonproduct Applications of $\bar{X}$ and R Charts

It is worth while to consider the possibility of using a control chart for variables whenever the centering, dispersion, and stability of some variable are matters of interest. It often happens in nonproduct applications that information is desired that corresponds in a general way to a knowledge of process capability in manufacturing; it is desired to know a value of $\bar{X}'$ and σ' that could be achieved under the operation of a constant system of chance causes. Of course, the issue of the stability of the variable in question is at the heart of the use of most control charts. If there is reason to believe that assignable causes of variation exist and that desirable results can be achieved by identifying and eliminating these assignable causes, there is a good case for initiating $\bar{X}$ and R charts. In this respect, nonproduct applications do not differ greatly from conventional applications to manufactured product.

---

† J. B. PRINGLE, S. Q. C. Methods in Telephone Transmission Maintenance, *Annual Convention Transactions* 1961, pp. 151–158, American Society for Quality Control, Milwaukee, Wis., 1961.

However, two differences should be mentioned between many nonproduct applications and the usual applications in manufacturing. Whereas there are usually definite tolerance limits that apply to quality characteristics of product, there may be no such limits in nonproduct applications. Moreover, considerably more imagination may be required to select the appropriate variable in the non-product case.

In one successful nonproduct application, the variable was the difference between estimated performance time and actual performance time for the many component operations in several projects being carried out under a system of critical path scheduling. In a nonproduct application described by J. B. Pringle of the Bell Telephone Company of Canada,† the variable was the deviation of the measured transmission loss in decibels on certain toll telephone trunks from the design loss for the same trunks. Although this latter problem had been analyzed for years by conventional statistical methods and substantial improvements obtained, the use of $\bar{X}$ and R charts was responsible for still further improvements. On this point, Mr. Pringle comments as follows:

> By this procedure, it was possible to bring the standard deviation of the distribution of trunk net loss deviations down from about 1.35 dB to 0.93 dB within the trial period. This was within the bogey of 1.0 dB and hence a matter of some satisfaction. But to me, probably the most satisfaction came about the third quarter of the trial, when reviewing the results with the foreman responsible for carrying out the trial. I asked him to estimate the amount of effort being expended on the trial compared to the amount expended previously when it seemed impossible to improve on $\sigma = 1.35$. After some thought, he said:—"Even including the time it took us to learn about the control chart method, I think we are spending only about 80% of the time we spent previously." This is the meaning of the quotation "Better Quality at Lower Cost."
>
> The essence of the process is that action is taken only when it is highly probable that assignable causes are present and can be found. This directs effort into constructive channels, and reduces effort expended in pursuing minor causes, difficult to find, and which do not contribute much to total variability. Only after major contributing causes are found and removed, is there much to be gained from going after minor things. But the Control Chart, by itself, only points out where action can be taken with profit. It is the action taken that improves things. If we don't act to discover and remove causes, we won't get improvement.

Nonproduct Applications of p, np, c, or u Charts

Charts for per cent rejected or for numbers of nonconformities sometimes are applied with advantage to the control of clerical errors. The following discussion is not based on one specific case but is a composite of observations based on a number of reported cases.

In many clerical operations, a certain number of errors seem to be inevitable. Just as in manufacturing, the skill, training, and fatigue of the individual will play an important part in the proportion of errors made. However, differences among individuals tend to be particularly important when one is dealing with clerical errors. The variability in materials and in machines that often is so important in

† *Ibid.*

manufacturing tends to be absent or of minor importance in many clerical operations. It follows that rational subgrouping for control charts for clerical operations ought to separate the work of different individuals whenever practicable.

In the discussion of p charts in Chap. 7 and c charts in Chap. 8, it was explained that these charts often are applied to the results of 100% inspection. Conceivably, control charts might also be applied to 100% verification of clerical work. Nevertheless, the usual condition is that 100% verification of clerical work is deemed to be unduly costly. Many types of clerical errors tend to be discovered, if at all, as a result of subsequent operations; the discovery of such errors is comparable to defective manufactured parts being discovered in the assembly department or defective final product being discovered by customers.

If it is desired to reduce the frequency of clerical errors in work not subject to 100% verification, a first step is to use sample verification to estimate how many such errors are being made on the average. A second step is to secure a basis for judgment on whether the differences in proportion of errors from individual to individual, from day to day, etc. (i.e., the variations among rational subgroups), are so great that they cannot be attributed to chance causes. A control chart is useful in both steps; just as in manufacturing, the chart provides an estimate of the process average and provides evidence about the presence or absence of statistical control.

For instance, consider a case where a complex type of form is being filled out in a certain department with many places on the form where an error might be made. Although some one person is responsible for filling out each particular form, a number of different people are involved in filling out the type of form. Assume that it is decided to select three forms each day from each person's output, using random numbers to determine the particular forms to be selected. Each form selected is given a careful verification by a well-qualified person, and the number of errors is noted.

A c chart similar to Fig. 8-1 is plotted; c is the total number of errors found on the three forms inspected for each individual's daily output. Where the chart is to be available only to management, each individual may be identified by a different symbol. (Such an identification of different shifts was illustrated in Fig. 8-2.) Before long, evidence will be available on the quality level expressed in average number of errors per form. The control chart will also show whether certain persons or certain days have more errors than would be expected because of chance fluctuations from the process average.

The evidence about the quality level may turn out to be favorable or unfavorable. Perhaps it will be found that the error rate is so low that no action is required; if so, the sample verification and the related control chart can be discontinued. On the other hand, the error rate may turn out to be much higher than management had expected—possibly much higher than considered to be tolerable. (Similar cases in manufacturing were described in the quotation at the start of Chap. 7.)

If so, and if there are a number of out-of-control high points on the chart, a first action should be to try to bring the process into statistical control. If certain individuals are responsible for most of the high points, these persons may need to be retrained or perhaps shifted to other duties. If eliminating such high points does not improve the quality level enough, action may be called for comparable to a fundamental change in a manufacturing process.

In Part One of this book, we noted that the mere introduction of a control chart in manufacturing sometimes is accompanied by an appreciable process improvement that is unrelated to any managerial use of the data charted. Such an improvement also can occur in nonproduct applications, particularly where each posted chart applies to the work of a group of persons and where pride of workmanship causes the group to want to improve its showing.

Nonproduct Use of the Demerits-per-Unit Concept

In Chap. 8, a brief reference was made to a variant of the c chart in which demerits per unit are plotted rather than nonconformities per unit. Manufacturing applications of charts for demerits per unit included quality rating of manufacturing departments, quality rating of vendors, and manufacturers' quality audit of their own finished products. The techniques of computing and charting demerits per unit may also be applied in nonproduct situations.

The usefulness of this technique can be illustrated by describing an application that was made to a fairly complex servicing operation being carried out by teams of workers in widely separated locations. There were many ways in which the actual carrying out of the operation could differ from what was considered to be ideal. Some of the differences were much more serious than others.

Management suspected that the quality of these servicing operations was much better at some locations than at others but had not taken action because of the lack of a suitable way to measure this quality. To provide a basis for such measurement, a demerit rating scheme was drawn up, listing various possible deviations from ideal performance and assigning demerits to each deviation. This rating scheme was given a trial run in one location and modified in a way that made it possible for it to be applied by a pair of trained observers at any location. When applied to a random sample of servicing operations at each location, the resulting control chart, as was anticipated, showed great lack of statistical control. It was then possible to continue control charts for demerits per unit for a period of time at each of the poorer locations until an adequate improvement had been made in the quality of servicing.

Nonproduct Applications of Acceptance Sampling

Many nonproduct applications of sampling are somewhat comparable to acceptance inspection of isolated lots of manufactured product. In such cases, relevant concepts may include OC curves, indifference qualities, Producer's Risks associated with rejection of some " good " quality, and Consumer's Risks associated with acceptance of some " bad " quality. However, in such isolated lot applications there is no chance to use the concepts of strategy and tactics that have evolved in connection with acceptance sampling systems.

Nevertheless, such concepts can be applied to advantage in those nonproduct cases where many acceptance/rectification decisions must be made. AOQL systems are of particular value in such cases.

In nonproduct activities such as clerical work, it often happens that great differences exist between the quality of work of the best individuals or teams and the quality of work of the poorest individuals or teams. It may be felt to be essential to apply 100% verification to the poorest individuals or teams, and it may be clear that it is uneconomical to apply such verification to the best ones. Example 21-1 describes a case in which it was possible to use AOQL sampling to distinguish between good and bad teams.

Example 21-1 Application of a double sampling AOQL plan to the checking of an annual merchandise inventory for a department store† *Facts of the case* The top management of a large department store considered it necessary that the annual merchandise inventory be as accurate as possible. The need for accuracy existed not only because of the use of the inventory figure for accounting purposes but also because departmental inventory figures were used to provide certain useful information to management. The inventory count was in two parts. The count of reserve (warehouse) stock presented no unusual problems. However, the count of forward (on-the-floor) stock was complicated by the requirement that no merchandise ready for sale should be tied up more than a few hours.

The forward inventory count was carried out by dividing each department of the store into sections and assigning a two-person team to each section. One member of the team called information about the stock from the shelves, tables, bins, etc., and the other entered the items on the inventory sheet. The stock was listed by price, description, quantity, classification within the store, and season letter. This count was carried out under considerable time pressure. In the past, a 100% check had always been made of all work performed in the forward inventory, as it was believed that such a check was necessary for reliable results. This 100% check nearly doubled the cost of the inventory and also nearly doubled the time required.

Effective use of a double sampling AOQL scheme The management of this store assigned to one individual the job of reviewing various store activities from the point of view of possible economic applications of the techniques of statistical quality control. A likely application seemed to be the substitution of

---

† When this example appeared in the second edition of this book, it was based on an unpublished paper by C. S. Brinegar. For Mr. Brinegar's own later more detailed story of this case, see his paper, Department Store Uses of Statistical Quality Control, *Industrial Quality Control*, vol. 12, no. 2, pp. 3–5, August, 1955.

an acceptance/rectification sampling scheme for 100% verfication in the checking of forward inventory.

The errors that were presumably corrected in the 100% verification were those within the control of the inventory teams. These were primarily the errors caused by improper calling of the price, quantity, classification, or season letter of the item or by the improper listing of these items by the inventory writer. Fortunately, information about the types, frequency, and severity of errors that had been discovered by the check inventory teams in past years could be obtained by examining the old inventory sheets. No corrections to inventory sheets had ever been permitted by erasure; every correction required calling the inventory supervisor, crossing out the improper entry, and making the corrected entry at the bottom of the sheet. By examining the handwriting of corrected entries, it was possible to tell whether the correction had been made by the original team or by the checking team.

Some 3,000 inventory sheets from the previous year were analyzed. The analysis indicated that a few teams were usually responsible for most of the errors made in any department. A large majority of the teams produced work of quite respectable accuracy. Large errors in price or quantity were infrequent, the most common errors being over or under one unit in physical count, one dollar off in price, or listing the wrong season letter. Different types of goods seemed to differ greatly in their liability to inventory error.

As a result of this analysis, an inventory sampling plan was inaugurated for the forthcoming annual inventory. (The 100% double check was maintained in a very few spots, particularly on lines of merchandise where an error in count would prove costly.) The inventory took place during two 4-h periods from 6 to 10 P.M. following regular working days. The work of each inventory team was sampled by a "flying inspection squad." If the sample proved satisfactory, the entire night's output of the team was approved. If the sample contained too many errors, the team was immediately notified of the fact and its procedure was closely observed; all of its previous work was checked 100%; subsequent work was sampled again with the possibility of a further 100% check.

In the sampling procedure, three different Dodge-Romig double sampling AOQL plans were used. The plan to be applied to each department was selected on the basis of the analysis of the previous year's inventory sheets, giving weight to the type and value of merchandise and the probable number of inventory entries. In the use of the sampling tables, one line on the inventory sheet (typically representing 10 to 125 items) corresponded to a single manufactured article subject to inspection; any error on the line caused its classification as a defective. However, a line that was correct except for an error in season letter was counted as only one-half a defective; this error affected, not the count or value of merchandise, but only its estimated age distribution.

Sampling plans were selected having OC curves indicating that not more than 20% of the total work would be rejected and reinspected. This decision was an essential part of the planning of the inventory as it determined the number of reinspection teams to be provided. Actually the work of only 10.4% of the teams was rejected, 48 teams out of 462.

All inventory supervisors were instructed to use idle teams in double checking even though the work checked had been approved by the sample check made by one of the flying squads. As a result of this instruction, a fair amount of approved work was double-checked. An analysis of the inventory sheets from all checked work proved that the sampling procedure had really succeeded in separating the inefficient teams from the efficient teams. In almost every case the double checking of approved teams revealed only a bare minimum of errors, one consistent with the AOQL used. The work of the rejected teams produced additional errors in over 90% of the cases examined.

The auditors and the store executives were well pleased with this application of statistical sampling methods. The scheme was repeated in the inventory of the succeeding year, with minor administrative refinements based on the first year's experience.

APPENDIXES

GLOSSARY OF SYMBOLS

The symbols used in the literature of statistical method are not fully standardized. The same statistical quantity may be represented by different symbols by different writers. Moreover, statistical problems are so numerous and diverse that any given symbol may be used in a number of different meanings, each meaning referring to a particular type of statistical problem. This lack of standardization complicates matters for the reader who consults a number of statistical books and articles.

The principle used in the selection of symbols for this book has been to try to minimize the reader's difficulties of transition to other quality control literature by the adoption for each statistical quantity of that symbol which is most common in the literature of statistical quality control in the United States. In general, where applicable, the symbols used follow the standards of the American Society for Quality Control and also agree with the symbols used in the publications of the American Society for Testing and Materials and the American National Standards Institute.

In the case of a few symbols, this conformance to common practice in the literature of quality control has involved the use of one symbol with two or more meanings. However, in every case the appropriate meaning should be clear from the context. This duplication of meanings for a few symbols seemed less likely to cause confusion than the adoption for this book of symbols that are not in common use in the other literature of the subject.

a = production interval limit number for continuous sampling plan CSP-A of MIL-STD-1235. If $a + 1$ defectives are found during a production interval, acceptance of product is suspended until the cause of the high rate of defectives is corrected.

A, B, C, etc. = in probability, used to designate events that may occur within a probability space.

A^c, etc. = the complement of the event A, etc., is $S - A$, i.e., the occurrence of "not A."

A = a multiplier of σ' to determine the distance from central line to 3-sigma control limits on an $\bar{X}$ chart. It equals $3/\sqrt{n}$ and is given for values of n from 2 to 100 in Table E, App. 3.

A_1 = a multiplier of $\bar{\sigma}$ to determine the distance from central line to 3-sigma control limits on an $\bar{X}$ chart. It equals $3/c_2 \sqrt{n}$ and is given for values of n from 2 to 100 in Table D, App. 3.

A_2 = a multiplier of $\bar{R}$ to determine the distance from central line to 3-sigma control limits on an $\bar{X}$ chart. It equals $3/d_2 \sqrt{n}$ and is given for values of n from 2 to 20 in Table C, App. 3.

A_5 = a multiplier of $m(R)$ to determine the distance from $\tilde{X}$ to 3-sigma control limits on an $\tilde{X}$ chart (control chart for medians). See Table 9-2.

AFI = average fraction inspected. It is the ATI divided by the lot size, N and is generally used in the analysis of rectifying inspection plans.

AOQL = average outgoing quality limit.

AQL = acceptable quality level.

ASN = average sample number. The average number of items sampled in an acceptance sampling plan.

ATI = average total inspection, i.e., average number of items inspected in a given production quantity under a specified acceptance procedure.

B_1 = a multiplier of σ' to determine the 3-sigma lower control limit on a chart for σ. It is given for values of n from 2 to 100 in Table E, App. 3.

B_2 = a multiplier of σ' to determine the 3-sigma upper control limit on a chart for σ. It is given for values of n from 2 to 100 in Table E, App. 3.

B_3 = a multiplier of $\bar{\sigma}$ to determine the 3-sigma lower control limit on a chart for σ. It is given for values of n from 2 to 100 in Table D, App. 3.

B_4 = a multiplier of $\bar{\sigma}$ to determine the 3-sigma upper control limit on a chart for σ. It is given for values of n from 2 to 100 in Table D, App. 3.

$B_{.001}, B_{.005}, B_{.025}, B_{.975}, B_{.995}, B_{.999}$ = factors for computing probability limits for control charts for σ. See Table 9-3.

c = number of nonconformities, usually in a sample of stated size. c may also refer to the number of occurrences of some other chosen event in a sample of stated size.

c = in single sampling acceptance schemes, the acceptance number, i.e., the maximum allowable number of nonconforming pieces in a sample of size n.

$\bar{c}$ = average number of nonconformities per sample in a series of samples of equal size.

c' = universe average number of nonconformities per sample, i.e., parametric value.

c'_o = a standard adopted for control chart purposes for the average number of nonconformities in a sample of stated size.

c_1 = in double sampling acceptance schemes, the acceptance number for the first sample, i.e., the maximum number of nonconforming items that will permit acceptance of the lot on the basis of the first sample.

c_2 = in double sampling acceptance schemes, the acceptance number for the two samples combined, i.e., the maximum number of nonconforming items that will permit acceptance of the lot on the basis of the two samples.

c_2 = a factor used in connection with sampling by variables that is a function of n and expresses the ratio between the expected value of $\bar{\sigma}$ from a long series of samples from a normal universe and the σ' of that universe. Values of c_2 are given in Table B, App. 3.

C_r^n = the number of combinations of n things taken r at a time.

d = deviation in cells from the assumed origin of a frequency distribution.

d_2 = a factor used in connection with sampling by variables that is a function of n and expresses the ratio between the expected value of $\bar{R}$ from a long series of samples from a normal universe and the σ' of that universe. Values of d_2 are given in Table B, App. 3.

d_2^* = a modification of the factor d_2 that gives weight to the number of samples (subgroups) used to compute $\bar{R}$. Where more than 20 subgroups have been used, this factor is almost identical with d_2. See Table 3-4 for values of d_2^* when $n = 5$.

D_1 = a multiplier of σ' to determine the 3-sigma lower control limit on a chart for R. It is given for values of n from 2 to 20 in Table E, App. 3.

D_2 = a multiplier of σ' to determine the 3-sigma upper control limit on a chart for R. It is given for values of n from 2 to 20 in Table E, App. 3.

D_3 = a multiplier of $\bar{R}$ to determine the 3-sigma lower control limit on a chart for R. It is given for values of n from 2 to 20 in Table C, App. 3.

D_4 = a multiplier of $\bar{R}$ to determine the 3-sigma upper control limit on a chart for R. It is given for values of n from 2 to 20 in Table C, App. 3.

$D_{.001}, D_{.005}, D_{.025}, D_{.975}, D_{.995}, D_{.999}$ = factors for computing probability limits for control chart for R. See Table 9-4.

e = napierian or natural base of logarithms, 2.71828 +.

f = frequency; generally, the number of observed values within a cell of a frequency distribution.

f = in continuous sampling plans, the fraction of units that are inspected during the period when sampling is in effect. Used in this sense in Dodge's CSP-1, in Dodge-Torrey CSP-2 and CSP-3, and in MIL-STD-1235. In the multilevel plans, f applies to the first level of sampling. f^2 to the second, f^3 to the third, etc.

i = in continuous sampling plans, the number of successive units that must be found by 100% inspection to be nondefective before acceptance may be carried out by sampling. In the multilevel continuous sampling plans, i also means the number of nondefective units in succession required under one sampling level to justify a shift to the next lower sampling level.

I_Q = incomplete beta function. Gen. L. E. Simon's "An Engineers' Manual of Statistical Method" contains I_Q charts of probability limits for the binomial distribution.

k = number of levels in a multilevel continuous sampling plan.

k = a factor used in connection with unknown-sigma variables acceptance plans. With a one-sided specification, $\bar{X} \geq L + ks$ or $U - ks \geq \bar{X}$.

k' = a factor used in connection with known-sigma variables acceptance plans. With a one-sided specification, $\bar{X} \geq L + k'\sigma'$ or $U - k'\sigma' \geq \bar{X}$.

k'^* = a factor used in connection with known-sigma variables acceptance plans involving two-sided specifications. $\bar{X} \geq L + k'^{*}\sigma'$ and $U - k'^{*}\sigma' \geq \bar{X}$.

L = lower specification limit.

L = 100% inspection limit number for MIL-STD-1235 continuous inspection plans, i.e., the maximum number of items to be detailed before acceptance of the product is terminated until the cause of the high rate of nonconforming items is corrected.

LCL = lower control limit on a control chart. $LCL_{\bar{x}}$ refers to the lower control limit on an $\bar{X}$ chart, LCL_p to lower control limit on a p chart, etc.

LLL = lower lot limit. Used in the Shainin Lot Plot technique, it is $\bar{\bar{X}} - 3\sigma$ of a sample drawn from a lot or batch of product.

$LRL_{\bar{x}}$ = lower reject limit for averages, the lowest possible satisfactory value of the lower control limit on a modified $\bar{X}$ chart.

LTPD = lot tolerance per cent defective.

m = number of nonconforming pieces in a given sample of size n.

$m(R)$ = median of a set of ranges.

M = maximum allowable per cent defective as used in the "Form 2" calculation in MIL-STD-414. See Chap. 17.

M = number of nonconforming pieces in a given lot of size N.

n = the number of pieces or observed values in any given sample or subgroup.

np = number of nonconforming items in a sample of size n.

n_1 = in double sampling, the number of pieces in the first sample.

n_2 = in double sampling, the number of pieces in the second sample.

N = number of pieces in a given lot to be sampled for purposes of acceptance.

$\binom{n}{r}$ = number of combinations of n things taken r at a time.

p = fraction rejected, the ratio of the number of nonconforming items to the total number inspected.

$100p$ = per cent defective.

$\bar{p}$ = average fraction rejected, the ratio of the sum of the number of nonconforming items found in a set of samples to the sum of the number of articles inspected in the same samples.

p' = the probability that a particular event will happen in a single trial. In statistical quality control the event in question is usually the occurrence of a nonconforming article. The parametric value.

p'_0 = a standard adopted for control chart or other purposes for the fraction rejected or for the probability of a nonconforming item.

$p_{0.95}$ = product fraction nonconforming having a probability of acceptance of 0.95 under given acceptance criteria.

$p_{0.50}$ = product fraction nonconforming having a probability of acceptance of 0.50 under given acceptance criteria. In the Philips Standard Sampling System this is referred to as the point of control.

$p_{0.10}$ = product fraction nonconforming having a probability of acceptance of 0.10 under given acceptance criteria.

P_0, P_1, P_2, etc. = probabilities of exactly 0, 1, 2, etc., nonconforming items, respectively.

P_a = probability of accepting any given lot or product.

P_c = Consumer's Risk, i.e., the probability of accepting product of some stated quality under a stipulated acceptance sampling plan; also represented by β.

P_L and P_U = symbols used in MIL-STD-414 to represent estimates of lot percentage defective below a lower specification limit L and above an upper specification limit U, respectively. See Chap. 17.

P_r^n = the number of permutations of n things taken r at a time.

$P(A)$ = the probability of occurrence of an event designated by the letter A.

$P(A|B)$ = the conditional probability of A occurring given that B has already occurred.

$q' = (1 - p')$, the probability that a particular event will not happen in a single trial.

Q_L and Q_U = "quality index" as defined in MIL-STD-414. See Chap. 17.

r = a constant referring to the number of occurrences of some event.

R = the range, the difference between the largest value and the smallest value in any set of numbers.

$\bar{R}$ = the average of a set of ranges.

$s = \sqrt{\dfrac{\sum(X - \bar{X})^2}{n - 1}}$. This is the square root of an unbiased estimate of the variance of an infinite universe as determined from a single sample of size n.

S = the probability space, i.e., the set of all possible outcomes of an experiment.

u = nonconformities per unit, the ratio of the number of nonconformities in a sample to the total number of units in the sample; $u = c/n$.

$\bar{u}$ = average nonconformities per unit; the total number of nonconformities in a set of samples divided by the total number of units in the set.

u' = true universe average number of nonconformities per unit, i.e., the parametric value.

u_0' = the standard value of nonconformities per unit used for purposes of computing control limits on a control chart for u.

U = upper specification limit.

UCL = upper control limit on a control chart. $UCL_{\bar{X}}$ refers to the upper control limit on an $\bar{X}$ chart, UCL_p to the upper control limit on a p chart, etc.

ULL = upper lot limit. Used in the Shainin Lot Plot technique, it is $\bar{X} + 3\sigma$ of a sample drawn from a lot or batch of product.

$URL_{\bar{X}}$ = upper reject limit for averages, the highest possible satisfactory value of the upper control limit on a modified $\bar{X}$ chart.

V = factor for reject limits. It equals $3 - 3/\sqrt{n}$ and is given in Table 9-7.

X = a number representing a value of some variable; in statistical quality control, X is usually the observed value of some quality characteristic for an individual unit. Specific observed values may be designated as $X_1, X_2, X_3, \ldots, X_i, \ldots, X_n$.

$\bar{X}$ = (X bar), the average (arithmetic mean) of two or more X values. The average of n X values is the sum of the X values divided by n.

$\bar{\bar{X}}$ = (X double bar), the average of a set of $\bar{X}$ values, sometimes called the grand average.

X' = (X bar prime), the true universe average, i.e., the parametric value of the arithmetic mean.

$\bar{X}'_o$ = an aimed-at or standard average value of a measurable quality characteristic.

$\tilde{X}$ = median of a subgroup.

$\tilde{\tilde{X}}$ = median of a set of subgroup medians.

α = (alpha), Producer's Risk, i.e., the probability of rejecting product of some stated quality under a stipulated acceptance sampling plan; also represented by $1 - P_a$.

β = (beta), Consumer's Risk, i.e., the probability of accepting product of some stated quality under a stipulated acceptance sampling plan; also represented by P_c.

β = (beta), "shape" parameter in the Weibull distribution. See Chap. 18.

η = (eta), "scale" parameter in the Weibull distribution. See Chap. 18.

λ' = (lambda prime), failure rate, i.e., the probability of a failure in a stated unit of time.

θ' = (theta prime), mean life, the arithmetic mean or average of the lives of a universe of items.

σ = (sigma), the root-mean-square (RMS) deviation of a set of numbers about the average of the set.

$\bar{\sigma}$ = (sigma bar), the average of a set of σ values.

σ' = (sigma prime), the known or estimated true value of universe standard (RMS) deviation, i.e., the parametric value.

σ'_o = a standard value of the universe standard deviation used for control chart purposes.

$\sigma_{\bar{X}}$ = the standard deviation of the expected frequency distribution of the averages $\bar{X}$ of samples of size n. It is equal to $\sigma'/\sqrt{n}$.

$\sigma_c, \sigma_{np}, \sigma_p, \sigma_R, \sigma_u, \sigma_\sigma$ = the standard deviation of the sampling distribution of c, np, p, R, u, and σ, respectively.

$!$ = symbol for factorial. $n!$ is the product of the first n integers.

BIBLIOGRAPHY

The following bibliography is limited to books and pamphlets. Much additional useful material on theory and applications is available in periodical articles.

ABBOTT, W. H.: "Probability Charts," Wendell H. Abbott, St. Petersburg, Fla., 1962.

AMERICAN SOCIETY FOR QUALITY CONTROL: "Annual Convention Transactions." (These papercovered volumes, starting in 1951, typically contain several hundred pages and fifty or more papers.) Published annually by American Society for Quality Control, Inc., Milwaukee, Wis.

"ASTM Manual on Presentation of Data and Control Chart Analysis," Special Technical Pub. 15D, American Society for Testing and Materials, Philadelphia, Pa., 1976.

BAZOWSKY, IGOR: "Reliability: Theory and Practice," Prentice-Hall, Inc., Englewood Cliffs, N.J., 1961.

BLANCHARD, B. S., and E. E. LOWERY: "Maintainability," McGraw-Hill Book Company, New York, 1969.

BOWKER, A. H., and H. P. GOODE: "Sampling Inspection by Variables," McGraw-Hill Book Company, New York, 1952.

——— and G. J. LIEBERMAN: "Engineering Statistics," 2d ed., Prentice-Hall, Inc., Englewood Cliffs, N.J., 1972.

BOX, G. E. P., and N. R. DRAPER: "Evolutionary Operation," John Wiley & Sons, Inc., New York, 1969.

BRADLEY, J. V.: "Distribution-Free Statistical Tests," Prentice-Hall, Inc., Englewood Cliffs, N.J., 1968.

BROWNLEE, K. A., "Statistical Theory and Methodology in Science and Engineering," 2d ed., John Wiley & Sons, Inc., New York, 1965.

BURINGTON, R. S., and D. C. MAY, JR., "Handbook of Probability and Statistics with Tables," 2d ed., McGraw-Hill Book Company, New York, 1970.

BURR, I. W.: "Engineering Statistics and Quality Control," McGraw-Hill Book Company, New York, 1953.

———: "Statistical Quality Control Methods," Marcel Dekker, Inc., New York, 1976.

———: "Applied Statistical Methods," Academic Press, Inc., New York, 1973.

BUTTERBAUGH, G. I.: "A Bibliography of Statistical Quality Control," University of Washington Press, Seattle, 1946.

———: "A Bibliography of Statistical Quality Control—Supplement," University of Washington Press, Seattle, 1951.

CALABRO, S. R.: "Reliability Principles and Practices," McGraw-Hill Book Company, New York, 1962.

CARTER, C. L., JR.: "The Control and Assurance of Quality," C. L. Carter, Jr. & Associates, Dallas, 1968.

CAVÉ, R.: "Le Controle statistique des fabrications," Editions Eyrolles, Paris, 1953.

CHARBONNEAU, H. C., and G. L. WEBSTER: "Industrial Quality Control," Prentice-Hall, Inc., Englewood Cliffs, N.J., 1978.

CHORAFAS, D. N.: "Statistical Processes and Reliability Engineering," D. Van Nostrand Reinhold Company, Inc., Princeton, N.J., 1960.

COCHRAN, W. G.: "Sampling Techniques," 3d ed., John Wiley & Sons, Inc., New York, 1977.

—— and G. M. COX: "Experimental Designs," 2d ed., John Wiley and Sons, Inc., New York, 1957.

"Control Chart Method of Controlling Quality During Production, ANSI Standard Z1.3–1975," American National Standards Institute, New York, 1975.

COWDEN, D. J.: "Statistical Methods in Quality Control," Prentice-Hall, Inc., Englewood Cliffs, N.J., 1957.

DEBRUYN, C. S. V.: "Cumulative Sum Tests: Theory and Practice," Hafner Publishing Company, New York, 1968.

DEMING, W. E.: "Some Theory of Sampling," John Wiley & Sons, Inc., New York, 1966.

DESMOND, DAVID J.: "Quality Control Workbook," Gower Press Limited, London, 1971.

DIXON, W. J., and F. J. MASSEY, JR.: "Introduction to Statistical Analysis," 3d ed., McGraw-Hill Book Company, New York, 1969.

DODGE, H. F.: "A General Procedure for Sampling Inspection by Attributes—Based on the AQL Concept," Technical Report No. 10, The Statistics Center, Rutgers the State University, New Brunswick, N.J., 1959.

—— and H. G. ROMIG: "Sampling Inspection Tables—Single and Double Sampling," 2d ed., John Wiley & Sons, Inc., New York, 1959. (The complete Dodge-Romig tables, with an explanation of how they were derived, the OC curves of all AOQL plans, and an illustration of their use at Western Electric Company. Every inspection department in a mass-production industry should have a copy of this book.)

DRAPER, N. R., and H. SMITH: "Applied Regression Analysis," John Wiley & Sons, Inc., New York, 1966.

DUCKWORTH, W. E.: "Statistical Techniques in Technological Research," Methuen and Company, Ltd., London, 1968.

DUNCAN, A. J.: "Quality Control and Industrial Statistics," 4th ed., Richard D. Irwin, Inc., Homewood, Ill., 1974.

EISENHART, CHURCHILL, M. W. HASTAY, and W. A. WALLIS (eds.): "Techniques of Statistical Analysis," McGraw-Hill Book Company, New York, 1947.

ENRICK, N. L.: "Quality Control and Reliability," 7th ed., The Industrial Press, New York, 1977.

FEIGENBAUM, A. V.: "Total Quality Control—Engineering and Management," McGraw-Hill Book Company, New York, 1961.

FELLER, WILLIAM: "An Introduction to Probability Theory and Its Applications," 3d ed., vol. I, John Wiley & Sons, Inc., New York, 1968.

FREEMAN, H. A.: "Introduction to Statistical Inference," Addison-Wesley Book Company, Reading, Mass., 1963.

FREEMAN, H. A., MILTON FRIEDMAN, FREDERICK MOSTELLER, and W. A. WALLIS (eds.): "Sampling Inspection," McGraw-Hill Book Company, New York, 1948.

FRY, T. C.: "Probability and Its Engineering Uses," D. Van Nostrand Reinhold Company, Inc., Princeton, N.J., 2d ed., 1965.

GENERAL ELECTRIC COMPANY, DEFENSE SYSTEMS DEPARTMENT: "Tables of the Individual and Cumulative Terms of Poisson Distribution," D. Van Nostrand Reinhold Company, Princeton, N.J., 1962.

GIBBONS, J. D.: "Nonparametric Statistical Inference," McGraw-Hill Book Company, New York, 1971.

"Glossary of Terms Used in Quality Control," European Organization for Quality Control, Rotterdam, 1965. (Includes terms in English, French, German, Dutch, and Italian.)

"Guide for Fatigue Testing and Statistical Analysis of Fatigue Data," American Society for Testing and Materials, Philadelphia, 1964.

"Guide for Quality Control and Control Chart Method of Analyzing Data, ANSI Standards Z1.1–1975 and Z1.2–1975," American National Standards Institute, New York, 1975.

GUTTMAN, IRWIN, and S. S. WILKS: "Introductory Engineering Statistics," 2d ed., John Wiley & Sons, Inc., New York, 1971.

HAHN, G. J., and S. S. SHAPIRO: "Statistical Models in Engineering," John Wiley & Sons, Inc., New York, 1967.

HALD, ANDERS: "Statistical Tables and Formulas," John Wiley & Sons, Inc., New York, 1952.

———: "Statistical Theory with Engineering Applications," John Wiley & Sons, Inc., New York, 1952.

HANSEN, B. L.: "Quality Control: Theory and Applications," Prentice-Hall, Inc., Englewood Cliffs, N.J., 1963.

HARRIS, D. H., and F. B. CHANEY: "Human Factors in Quality Assurance," John Wiley & Sons, Inc., New York, 1969.

HARVARD UNIVERSITY: "Tables of the Cumulative Binomial Probability Distribution," Harvard University Press, Cambridge, Mass., 1955.

HAVILAND, R. P., "Engineering Reliability and Long Life Design," Van Nostrand Reinhold Company, Princeton, N.J., 1964.

HAYES, G. E., and H. G. ROMIG: "Modern Quality Control," Bruce Division Benziger, Bruce, and Glencoe, Inc., Encino, California, 1977.

HICKS, C. R.: "Fundamental Concepts in the Design of Experiments," Holt, Rinehart, and Winston, New York, 1964.

"Highway Research Board Special Report 118. Quality Assurance and Acceptance Procedures," Highway Research Board, Washington, D.C., 1971.

HODGES, J. L., JR., and E. L. LEHMANN: "Basic Concepts of Probability and Statistics," 2d ed., Holden-Day, Inc., San Francisco, 1970.

HOEL, P. G.: "Elementary Statistics," 4th ed., John Wiley & Sons, Inc., New York, 1976.

———: "Introduction to Mathematical Statistics," 4th ed., John Wiley & Sons, Inc., 1971.

HOLMAN, J. P.: "Experimental Methods for Engineers," 3rd ed., McGraw-Hill Book Company, New York, 1978.

HOPPER, A. G.: "Statistical Quality Control," McGraw-Hill Book Company, London, 1969.

HUITSON, ALAN, and JOAN KEEN: "Essentials of Quality Control," William Heinemann, Ltd., London, 1965.

INSTITUTE OF ELECTRICAL AND ELECTRONICS ENGINEERS, "Proceedings of National Symposia on Reliability." (These paper-covered volumes, starting in 1955, are typically several hundred pages and contain many papers.) Published annually by The Institute of Electrical and Electronics Engineers, Inc., New York.

IRESON, W. G. (ed.): "Reliability Handbook," McGraw-Hill Book Company, New York, 1966.

IRESON, W. G., and E. L. GRANT (eds.): "Handbook of Industrial Engineering and Management," 2d ed., Prentice-Hall, Inc., Englewood Cliffs, N.J., 1971. (See particularly the section on "Industrial Statistics" by A. H. Bowker and G. J. Lieberman, the section on "Inspection and Quality Control" by T. C. McDermott and D. M. Cound, and the section on "Reliability Methods" by Myron Lipow and D. K. Lloyd.)

JAPANESE STANDARDS ASSOCIATION: "Standardization and Quality Control in Japan," JSA Technical Report No. 1, Japanese Standards Association, Tokyo, Japan, 1963. (This short pamphlet includes a bibliography in English of the numerous books on quality control that have been published in Japanese. It also lists more than 20 Japanese Industrial Standards related to quality control. All these standards have titles in English as well as in Japanese; there are a few with English translations.)

JURAN, J. M.: "Management of Inspection and Quality Control," Harper & Row, Publishers, Incorporated, New York, 1945.

——— (ed.): "Quality Control Handbook," 3d ed., McGraw-Hill Book Company, New York, 1974.

—— and F. M. Gryna, Jr.: "Quality Planning and Analysis," McGraw-Hill Book Company, New York, 1970.

Kirkpatrick, E. G.: "Quality Control for Managers and Engineers," John Wiley & Sons, Inc., New York, 1970.

Knowler, Howell, Gold, Coleman, Moan, and Knowler: "Quality Control by Statistical Methods," McGraw-Hill Book Company, New York, 1969.

Kramer, Amihud, and B. A. Twigg: "Quality Control for the Food Industry: vol. 1, Fundamentals," 3d ed., The AVI Publishing Company, Inc., Westport, Conn., 1970.

—— and ——: "Quality Control for the Food Industry: vol. 2, Applications," The AVI Publishing Company, Inc., Westport, Conn., 1973.

Ku, H. H. (ed.): "Precision Measurement and Calibration," Superintendent of Documents, Government Printing Office, Washington, D.C., 1969.

Lieberman, G. J., and D. B. Owen: "Tables of the Hypergeometric Probability Distribution," Stanford University Press, Stanford, Calif., 1961.

Lindgren, B. W., and G. W. McElrath: "Introduction to Probability and Statistics," 4th ed., The Macmillan Company, New York, 3d ed., 1978.

Lloyd, D. K., and Myron Lipow: "Reliability: Management, Methods, and Mathematics," Prentice-Hall, Inc., Englewood Cliffs, N.J., 1962.

López, D. M., and E. J. González: "Sintesis de un curso de control estadístico de calidad," American Society for Quality Control, Sección Ciudad de Mexico, México, D.F., 1960.

Mendenhall, William: "Introduction to Probability and Statistics," 4th ed., Duxbury Press Division of Wadsworth Pub. Co., N. Scituate, Mass., 1975.

—— and R. L. Scheaffer: "Mathematical Statistics with Applications," Duxbury Press Division of Wadsworth Pub. Co., N. Scituate, Mass., 1973.

Meyer, P. L.: "Introductory Probability and Statistical Applications," 2d ed., Addison-Wesley Publishing Company, Inc., Reading, Mass., 1970.

"Military Standard 105D. Sampling Procedures and Tables for Inspection by Attributes," Superintendent of Documents, Government Printing Office, Washington, D.C., 1963. (The ABC standard.)

"Military Standard 414. Sampling Procedures and Tables for Inspection by Variables for Percent Defective," Superintendent of Documents, Government Printing Office, Washington, D.C., 1957.

"Military Standard 690-B. Failure Rate Sampling Plans and Procedures," Superintendent of Documents, Government Printing Office, Washington, D.C., 1969.

"Military Standard 781-C. Reliability Design Qualification and Production Acceptance Tests, Exponential Distribution," Superintendent of Documents, Government Printing Office, Washington, D.C., 1977.

"Military Standard 1235 (ORD), Single- and Multi-Level Continuous Sampling Procedures and Tables for Inspection by Attributes," Superintendent of Documents, Government Printing Office, Washington, D.C., 1962.

Molina, E. C.: "Poisson's Exponential Binomial Limit," Van Nostrand Reinhold Company, Inc., Princeton, N.J., 1942. (Molina's tables contain individual values and cumulative values of the Poisson, both to six decimal places.) Reprinted in 1973 by Krieger Pub. Co., Huntington, N.Y.

Moroney, M. J.: "Facts from Figures," Penguin Books, Ltd., Harmondsworth, Middlesex, England; and Baltimore, Md., 3d ed., 1956. (Paperback; a good introduction to statistics for the layman.)

Moses, L. E., and R. V. Oakford: "Tables of Random Permutations," Stanford University Press, Stanford, Calif., 1963.

Mosteller, Frederick, R. E. K. Rourke, and C. B. Thomas, Jr.: "Probability with Statistical Applications," 2d ed., Addison-Wesley Publishing Company, Inc., Reading, Mass., 1970.

Myers, B. L., and N. L. Enrick: "Statistical Functions," The Kent State University Press, Kent, Ohio, 1970.

Myers, R. H., K. L. Wong, and H. M. Gordy: "Reliability Engineering for Electronic Systems," John Wiley & Sons, Inc., New York, 1964.

National Bureau of Standards: "Tables of the Binomial Probability Distribution," Applied Mathematics Series, vol. 6, Superintendent of Documents, Government Printing Office, Washington, D.C., 1949.

OTT, ELLIS R.: "Process Quality Control: Trouble-shooting and Interpretation of Data," McGraw-Hill Book Co., New York, 1975.

OWEN, D. B.: "Handbook of Statistical Tables," Addison-Wesley Publishing Company, Inc., Reading, Mass., 1962.

PALAZZI, AURELIO: "Metodi statistici nella ricerca industriale e nel controllo della produzione," Etas Kompass, Milan, 1964.

PARZEN, EMANUEL: "Modern Probability Theory and Its Applications," John Wiley & Sons, Inc., New York, 1960.

PEACH, PAUL: "Quality Control for Management," Prentice-Hall, Inc., Englewood Cliffs, N.J., 1964.

POLOVKO, A. M.: "Fundamentals of Reliability Theory," Academic Press, New York, 1968.

"Proceedings of the International Conference on Quality Control," Union of Japanese Scientists and Engineers, Tokyo, 1969.

"Product Quality Assurance Handbook H-57," Superintendent of Documents, Government Printing Office, Washington, D.C., 1969.

"Quality Control and Reliability Handbook (Interim) H 108. Sampling Procedures for Life and Reliability Testing (Based on Exponential Distribution)," Superintendent of Documents, Government Printing Office, Washington, D.C., 1960.

"Quality Control and Reliability Handbook (Interim) H 109. Statistical Procedures for Determining Validity of Suppliers' Attributes Inspection," Superintendent of Documents, Government Printing Office, Washington, D.C., 1960.

"Quality Control and Reliability Handbook (Interim) H 110. Evaluation of Contractor Quality Control Systems," Superintendent of Documents, Government Printing Office, Washington, D.C., 1960.

"Quality Control and Reliability Technical Report TR 3. Sampling Procedures and Tables for Life and Reliability Testing Based on the Weibull Distribution (Mean Life Criterion)," Superintendent of Documents, Government Printing Office, Washington, D.C., 1961. (This is based on a Cornell University Technical Report prepared by H. P. Goode and J. H. K. Kao.)

"Quality Control and Reliability Technical Report TR 4. Sampling Procedures and Tables for Life and Reliability Testing Based on the Weibull Distribution (Hazard Rate Criterion)," Superintendent of Documents, Government Printing Office, Washington, D.C., 1962. (This is based on a Cornell University Technical Report prepared by H. P. Goode and J. H. K. Kao.)

RAND CORPORATION, "A Million Random Digits with 100,000 Normal Deviates," Glencoe Free Press Division of The Macmillan Company, New York, 1955.

RICKMERS, A. D., and H. N. TODD: "Statistics, An Introduction," McGraw-Hill Book Company, New York, 1967.

ROCHESTER INSTITUTE OF TECHNOLOGY: "Symbols, Definitions and Tables for Industrial Statistics and Quality Control," Rochester Institute of Technology, Rochester, N.Y., 1960.

ROMIG, H. G.: "50-100 Binomial Tables," John Wiley & Sons, Inc., New York, 1953.

SANDLER, G. H.: "System Reliability Engineering," Prentice-Hall, Inc., Englewood Cliffs, N.J., 1963.

SCHAAFSMA, A. H., and F. G. WILLEMZE: "Modern kwaliteitsbeleid," N. V. Uitgeversmij. Centrex, Eindhoven, Holland, 1958. (This is the title of the original edition in the Dutch language. Titles of French, German, and Spanish language editions are respectively: "Gestion moderne de la qualité," "Moderne Qualitätskontrolle," and "Gestion moderna de la calidad.")

SCHEAFFER, R. L., and W. MENDENHALL: "Introduction to Probability; Theory and Applications," Duxbury Press Division of Wadsworth Pub. Co., N. Scituate, Mass., 1975.

SCHINDOWSKI, E., and O. SCHURZ: "Statistische Qualitätskontrolle-Kontrolle," VEB Verlag Technik, Berlin, 1959.

SCHROCK, E. M.: "Quality Control and Statistical Methods," Reinhold Publishing Corporation, New York, 1950.

SHEWHART, W. A.: "Economic Control of Quality of Manufactured Product," Van Nostrand Reinhold Company, Inc., Princeton, N.J., 1931.

SHEWHART, W. A. (edited by W. E. DEMING): "Statistical Method from the Viewpoint of Quality Control," The Graduate School, Department of Agriculture, Washington, D.C., 1939.

SHOOMAN, M. L.: "Probabilistic Reliability: An Engineering Approach," McGraw-Hill Book Company, New York, 1968.

SIMON, L. E.: "An Engineers' Manual of Statistical Methods," John Wiley & Sons, Inc., New York, 1941.

"Special Publication Z–90, Sampling Procedures," Canadian Standards Association, Ottawa, 1967.

STATISTICAL RESEARCH GROUP, COLUMBIA UNIVERSITY: "Sequential Analysis of Statistical Data: Applications," Columbia University Press, New York, 1945.

STOK, T. L., "The Worker and Quality Control," The University of Michigan, Ann Arbor, 1965.

"Supply & Logistics Handbook—Inspection H 105. Administration of Sampling Procedures for Acceptance Inspection," Superintendent of Documents, Government Printing Office, Washington, D.C., 1954.

"Tests for Validity of the Assumption That the Underlying Distribution of Life Is Exponential," Technical Report, Superintendent of Documents, Government Printing Office, Washington, D.C., 1960. (This government pamphlet is a reprint of two articles by Dr. Benjamin Epstein that appeared in *Technometrics* in the issues of February and May, 1960.)

TIPPETT, L. H. C.: "Technological Applications of Statistics," John Wiley & Sons, Inc., New York, 1950.

VOLK, WILLIAM: "Applied Statistics for Engineers," 2d ed., McGraw-Hill Book Company, New York, 1969.

WADE, O. R.: "Tolerance Control in Design and Manufacturing," Industrial Press, Inc., New York, 1967.

WADSWORTH, G. P., and J. G. BRYAN: "Introduction to Probability and Random Variables," 2d ed., McGraw-Hill Book Company, New York, 1974.

WALD, ABRAHAM: "Sequential Analysis," John Wiley & Sons, Inc., New York, 1947. Reprinted in 1973 by Dover Pubns., Inc., New York.

WALLIS, W. A., and H. V. ROBERTS: "Statistics: a New Approach," Glencoe Free Press Division of The Macmillan Company, New York, 1956.

WEIBULL, WALLODI: "Fatigue Testing and Analysis of Results," Pergamon Press, Inc., New York, 1961.

WEINTRAUB, SOL: "Tables of the Cumulative Binomial Probability Distribution for Small Values of p," The Macmillan Company, New York, 1963.

WESTERN ELECTRIC COMPANY: "Statistical Quality Control Handbook," 2d ed., Western Electric Company, Inc., New York, 1958.

WETHERILL, G. B.: "Sampling Inspection and Quality Control," Methuen and Company, Ltd., London, 1969.

WILKS, S. S.: "Mathematical Statistics," 2d ed., John Wiley & Sons, Inc., New York, 1962.

WILLIAMSON, ERIC, and M. H. BRETHERTON: "Tables of the Negative Binomial Probability Distribution," John Wiley & Sons, Inc., New York, 1963.

YOUDEN, W. J., "Statistical Methods for Chemists," John Wiley & Sons, Inc., New York, 1951. Reprinted in 1977 by Krieger Pub. Co., Huntington, NY.

TABLES

Table A Areas under the normal curve

Proportion of total area under the curve that is under the portion of the curve from $-\infty$ to $(X_i - \bar{X}')/\sigma'$. (X_i represents any desired value of the variable X)

$\dfrac{X_i - \bar{X}'}{\sigma'}$	0.09	0.08	0.07	0.06	0.05	0.04	0.03	0.02	0.01	0.00
−3.5	0.00017	0.00017	0.00018	0.00019	0.00019	0.00020	0.00021	0.00022	0.00022	0.00023
−3.4	0.00024	0.00025	0.00026	0.00027	0.00028	0.00029	0.00030	0.00031	0.00033	0.00034
−3.3	0.00035	0.00036	0.00038	0.00039	0.00040	0.00042	0.00043	0.00045	0.00047	0.00048
−3.2	0.00050	0.00052	0.00054	0.00056	0.00058	0.00060	0.00062	0.00064	0.00066	0.00069
−3.1	0.00071	0.00074	0.00076	0.00079	0.00082	0.00085	0.00087	0.00090	0.00094	0.00097
−3.0	0.00100	0.00104	0.00107	0.00111	0.00114	0.00118	0.00122	0.00126	0.00131	0.00135
−2.9	0.0014	0.0014	0.0015	0.0015	0.0016	0.0016	0.0017	0.0017	0.0018	0.0019
−2.8	0.0019	0.0020	0.0021	0.0021	0.0022	0.0023	0.0023	0.0024	0.0025	0.0026
−2.7	0.0026	0.0027	0.0028	0.0029	0.0030	0.0031	0.0032	0.0033	0.0034	0.0035
−2.6	0.0036	0.0037	0.0038	0.0039	0.0040	0.0041	0.0043	0.0044	0.0045	0.0047
−2.5	0.0048	0.0049	0.0051	0.0052	0.0054	0.0055	0.0057	0.0059	0.0060	0.0062
−2.4	0.0064	0.0066	0.0068	0.0069	0.0071	0.0073	0.0075	0.0078	0.0080	0.0082
−2.3	0.0084	0.0087	0.0089	0.0091	0.0094	0.0096	0.0099	0.0102	0.0104	0.0107
−2.2	0.0110	0.0113	0.0116	0.0119	0.0122	0.0125	0.0129	0.0132	0.0136	0.0139
−2.1	0.0143	0.0146	0.0150	0.0154	0.0158	0.0162	0.0166	0.0170	0.0174	0.0179
−2.0	0.0183	0.0188	0.0192	0.0197	0.0202	0.0207	0.0212	0.0217	0.0222	0.0228
−1.9	0.0233	0.0239	0.0244	0.0250	0.0256	0.0262	0.0268	0.0274	0.0281	0.0287
−1.8	0.0294	0.0301	0.0307	0.0314	0.0322	0.0329	0.0336	0.0344	0.0351	0.0359
−1.7	0.0367	0.0375	0.0384	0.0392	0.0401	0.0409	0.0418	0.0427	0.0436	0.0446
−1.6	0.0455	0.0465	0.0475	0.0485	0.0495	0.0505	0.0516	0.0526	0.0537	0.0548
−1.5	0.0559	0.0571	0.0582	0.0594	0.0606	0.0618	0.0630	0.0643	0.0655	0.0668
−1.4	0.0681	0.0694	0.0708	0.0721	0.0735	0.0749	0.0764	0.0778	0.0793	0.0808
−1.3	0.0823	0.0838	0.0853	0.0869	0.0885	0.0901	0.0918	0.0934	0.0951	0.0968
−1.2	0.0985	0.1003	0.1020	0.1038	0.1057	0.1075	0.1093	0.1112	0.1131	0.1151
−1.1	0.1170	0.1190	0.1210	0.1230	0.1251	0.1271	0.1292	0.1314	0.1335	0.1357
−1.0	0.1379	0.1401	0.1423	0.1446	0.1469	0.1492	0.1515	0.1539	0.1562	0.1587
−0.9	0.1611	0.1635	0.1660	0.1685	0.1711	0.1736	0.1762	0.1788	0.1814	0.1841
−0.8	0.1867	0.1894	0.1922	0.1949	0.1977	0.2005	0.2033	0.2061	0.2090	0.2119
−0.7	0.2148	0.2177	0.2207	0.2236	0.2266	0.2297	0.2327	0.2358	0.2389	0.2420
−0.6	0.2451	0.2483	0.2514	0.2546	0.2578	0.2611	0.2643	0.2676	0.2709	0.2743
−0.5	0.2776	0.2810	0.2843	0.2877	0.2912	0.2946	0.2981	0.3015	0.3050	0.3085
−0.4	0.3121	0.3156	0.3192	0.3228	0.3264	0.3300	0.3336	0.3372	0.3409	0.3446
−0.3	0.3483	0.3520	0.3557	0.3594	0.3632	0.3669	0.3707	0.3745	0.3783	0.3821
−0.2	0.3859	0.3897	0.3936	0.3974	0.4013	0.4052	0.4090	0.4129	0.4168	0.4207
−0.1	0.4247	0.4286	0.4325	0.4364	0.4404	0.4443	0.4483	0.4522	0.4562	0.4602
−0.0	0.4641	0.4681	0.4721	0.4761	0.4801	0.4840	0.4880	0.4920	0.4960	0.5000

Table A Areas under the normal curve. (*Continued*)

$\dfrac{X_i-\bar{X}}{\sigma'}$	0.00	0.01	0.02	0.03	0.04	0.05	0.06	0.07	0.08	0.09
+0.0	0.5000	0.5040	0.5080	0.5120	0.5160	0.5199	0.5239	0.5279	0.5319	0.5359
+0.1	0.5398	0.5438	0.5478	0.5517	0.5557	0.5596	0.5636	0.5675	0.5714	0.5753
+0.2	0.5793	0.5832	0.5871	0.5910	0.5948	0.5987	0.6026	0.6064	0.6103	0.6141
+0.3	0.6179	0.6217	0.6255	0.6293	0.6331	0.6368	0.6406	0.6443	0.6480	0.6517
+0.4	0.6554	0.6591	0.6628	0.6664	0.6700	0.6736	0.6772	0.6808	0.6844	0.6879
+0.5	0.6915	0.6950	0.6985	0.7019	0.7054	0.7088	0.7123	0.7157	0.7190	0.7224
+0.6	0.7257	0.7291	0.7324	0.7357	0.7389	0.7422	0.7454	0.7486	0.7517	0.7549
+0.7	0.7580	0.7611	0.7642	0.7673	0.7704	0.7734	0.7764	0.7794	0.7823	0.7852
+0.8	0.7881	0.7910	0.7939	0.7967	0.7995	0.8023	0.8051	0.8079	0.8106	0.8133
+0.9	0.8159	0.8186	0.8212	0.8238	0.8264	0.8289	0.8315	0.8340	0.8365	0.8389
+1.0	0.8413	0.8438	0.8461	0.8485	0.8508	0.8531	0.8554	0.8577	0.8599	0.8621
+1.1	0.8643	0.8665	0.8686	0.8708	0.8729	0.8749	0.8770	0.8790	0.8810	0.8830
+1.2	0.8849	0.8869	0.8888	0.8907	0.8925	0.8944	0.8962	0.8980	0.8997	0.9015
+1.3	0.9032	0.9049	0.9066	0.9082	0.9099	0.9115	0.9131	0.9147	0.9162	0.9177
+1.4	0.9192	0.9207	0.9222	0.9236	0.9251	0.9265	0.9279	0.9292	0.9306	0.9319
+1.5	0.9332	0.9345	0.9357	0.9370	0.9382	0.9394	0.9406	0.9418	0.9429	0.9441
+1.6	0.9452	0.9463	0.9474	0.9484	0.9495	0.9505	0.9515	0.9525	0.9535	0.9545
+1.7	0.9554	0.9564	0.9573	0.9582	0.9591	0.9599	0.9608	0.9616	0.9625	0.9633
+1.8	0.9641	0.9649	0.9656	0.9664	0.9671	0.9678	0.9686	0.9693	0.9699	0.9706
+1.9	0.9713	0.9719	0.9726	0.9732	0.9738	0.9744	0.9750	0.9756	0.9761	0.9767
+2.0	0.9773	0.9778	0.9783	0.9788	0.9793	0.9798	0.9803	0.9808	0.9812	0.9817
+2.1	0.9821	0.9826	0.9830	0.9834	0.9838	0.9842	0.9846	0.9850	0.9854	0.9857
+2.2	0.9861	0.9864	0.9868	0.9871	0.9875	0.9878	0.9881	0.9884	0.9887	0.9890
+2.3	0.9893	0.9896	0.9898	0.9901	0.9904	0.9906	0.9909	0.9911	0.9913	0.9916
+2.4	0.9918	0.9920	0.9922	0.9925	0.9927	0.9929	0.9931	0.9932	0.9934	0.9936
+2.5	0.9938	0.9940	0.9941	0.9943	0.9945	0.9946	0.9948	0.9949	0.9951	0.9952
+2.6	0.9953	0.9955	0.9956	0.9957	0.9959	0.9960	0.9961	0.9962	0.9963	0.9964
+2.7	0.9965	0.9966	0.9967	0.9968	0.9969	0.9970	0.9971	0.9972	0.9973	0.9974
+2.8	0.9974	0.9975	0.9976	0.9977	0.9977	0.9978	0.9979	0.9979	0.9980	0.9981
+2.9	0.9981	0.9982	0.9983	0.9983	0.9984	0.9984	0.9985	0.9985	0.9986	0.9986
+3.0	0.99865	0.99869	0.99874	0.99878	0.99882	0.99886	0.99889	0.99893	0.99896	0.99900
+3.1	0.99903	0.99906	0.99910	0.99913	0.99915	0.99918	0.99921	0.99924	0.99926	0.99929
+3.2	0.99931	0.99934	0.99936	0.99938	0.99940	0.99942	0.99944	0.99946	0.99948	0.99950
+3.3	0.99952	0.99953	0.99955	0.99957	0.99958	0.99960	0.99961	0.99962	0.99964	0.99965
+3.4	0.99966	0.99967	0.99969	0.99970	0.99971	0.99972	0.99973	0.99974	0.99975	0.99976
+3.5	0.99977	0.99978	0.99978	0.99979	0.99980	0.99981	0.99981	0.99982	0.99983	0.99983

Table B Factors for estimating σ' from $\bar{R}$ or $\bar{\sigma}$

Number of observations in subgroup	Factor for estimate from R	Factor for estimate from $\bar{\sigma}$
n	$d_2 = \bar{R}/\sigma'$	$c_2 = \bar{\sigma}/\sigma'$
2	1.128	0.5642
3	1.693	0.7236
4	2.059	0.7979
5	2.326	0.8407
6	2.534	0.8686
7	2.704	0.8882
8	2.847	0.9027
9	2.970	0.9139
10	3.078	0.9227
11	3.173	0.9300
12	3.258	0.9359
13	3.336	0.9410
14	3.407	0.9453
15	3.472	0.9490
16	3.532	0.9523
17	3.588	0.9551
18	3.640	0.9576
19	3.689	0.9599
20	3.735	0.9619
21	3.778	0.9638
22	3.819	0.9655
23	3.858	0.9670
24	3.895	0.9684
25	3.931	0.9696
30	4.086	0.9748
35	4.213	0.9784
40	4.322	0.9811
45	4.415	0.9832
50	4.498	0.9849
55	4.572	0.9863
60	4.639	0.9874
65	4.699	0.9884
70	4.755	0.9892
75	4.806	0.9900
80	4.854	0.9906
85	4.898	0.9912
90	4.939	0.9916
95	4.978	0.9921
100	5.015	0.9925

Estimate of $\sigma' = \bar{R}/d_2$ or $\bar{\sigma}/c_2$.
These factors assume sampling from a normal universe.

Table C   Factors for determining from $\bar{R}$ the 3-sigma control limits for $\bar{X}$ and R charts

Number of observations in subgroup	Factor for $\bar{X}$ chart	Factors for R chart	
		Lower control limit	Upper control limit
n	A_2	D_3	D_4
2	1.88	0	3.27
3	1.02	0	2.57
4	0.73	0	2.28
5	0.58	0	2.11
6	0.48	0	2.00
7	0.42	0.08	1.92
8	0.37	0.14	1.86
9	0.34	0.18	1.82
10	0.31	0.22	1.78
11	0.29	0.26	1.74
12	0.27	0.28	1.72
13	0.25	0.31	1.69
14	0.24	0.33	1.67
15	0.22	0.35	1.65
16	0.21	0.36	1.64
17	0.20	0.38	1.62
18	0.19	0.39	1.61
19	0.19	0.40	1.60
20	0.18	0.41	1.59

Upper Control Limit for $\bar{X} = UCL_{\bar{X}} = \bar{\bar{X}} + A_2\bar{R}$
Lower Control Limit for $\bar{X} = LCL_{\bar{X}} = \bar{\bar{X}} - A_2\bar{R}$

(If aimed-at or standard value $\bar{X}'$ is used rather than $\bar{\bar{X}}$ as the central line on the control chart, $\bar{X}'$ should be substituted for $\bar{\bar{X}}$ in the preceding formulas.)

Upper Control Limit for $R = UCL_R = D_4\bar{R}$
Lower Control Limit for $R = LCL_R = D_3\bar{R}$

All factors in Table C are based on the normal distribution.

Table D Factors for determining from $\bar{\sigma}$ the 3-sigma control limits for $\bar{X}$ and σ charts

Number of observations in subgroup n	Factor for $\bar{X}$ chart A_1	Factors for σ chart	
		Lower control limit B_3	Upper control limit B_4
2	3.76	0	3.27
3	2.39	0	2.57
4	1.88	0	2.27
5	1.60	0	2.09
6	1.41	0.03	1.97
7	1.28	0.12	1.88
8	1.17	0.19	1.81
9	1.09	0.24	1.76
10	1.03	0.28	1.72
11	0.97	0.32	1.68
12	0.93	0.35	1.65
13	0.88	0.38	1.62
14	0.85	0.41	1.59
15	0.82	0.43	1.57
16	0.79	0.45	1.55
17	0.76	0.47	1.53
18	0.74	0.48	1.52
19	0.72	0.50	1.50
20	0.70	0.51	1.49
21	0.68	0.52	1.48
22	0.66	0.53	1.47
23	0.65	0.54	1.46
24	0.63	0.55	1.45
25	0.62	0.56	1.44
30	0.56	0.60	1.40
35	0.52	0.63	1.37
40	0.48	0.66	1.34
45	0.45	0.68	1.32
50	0.43	0.70	1.30
55	0.41	0.71	1.29
60	0.39	0.72	1.28
65	0.38	0.73	1.27
70	0.36	0.74	1.26
75	0.35	0.75	1.25
80	0.34	0.76	1.24
85	0.33	0.77	1.23
90	0.32	0.77	1.23
95	0.31	0.78	1.22
100	0.30	0.79	1.21

$$\text{Upper Control Limit for } \bar{X} = UCL_{\bar{X}} = \bar{X} + A_1\bar{\sigma}$$
$$\text{Lower Control Limit for } \bar{X} = LCL_{\bar{X}} = \bar{X} - A_1\bar{\sigma}$$

(If aimed-at or standard value $\bar{X}'$ is used rather than $\bar{X}$ as the central line on the control chart, $\bar{X}'$ should be substituted for $\bar{X}$ in the preceding formulas.)

$$\text{Upper Control Limit for } \sigma = UCL_\sigma = B_4\bar{\sigma}$$
$$\text{Lower Control Limit for } \sigma = LCL_\sigma = B_3\bar{\sigma}$$

All factors in Table D are based on the normal distribution.

Table E Factors for determining from σ' the 3-sigma control limits for $\bar{X}$, R, and σ charts

Number of observations in subgroup n	Factor for $\bar{X}$ chart A	Factors for R chart		Factors for σ chart	
		Lower control limit D_1	Upper control limit D_2	Lower control limit B_1	Upper control limit B_2
2	2.12	0	3.69	0	1.84
3	1.73	0	4.36	0	1.86
4	1.50	0	4.70	0	1.81
5	1.34	0	4.92	0	1.76
6	1.22	0	5.08	0.03	1.71
7	1.13	0.20	5.20	0.10	1.67
8	1.06	0.39	5.31	0.17	1.64
9	1.00	0.55	5.39	0.22	1.61
10	0.95	0.69	5.47	0.26	1.58
11	0.90	0.81	5.53	0.30	1.56
12	0.87	0.92	5.59	0.33	1.54
13	0.83	1.03	5.65	0.36	1.52
14	0.80	1.12	5.69	0.38	1.51
15	0.77	1.21	5.74	0.41	1.49
16	0.75	1.28	5.78	0.43	1.48
17	0.73	1.36	5.82	0.44	1.47
18	0.71	1.43	5.85	0.46	1.45
19	0.69	1.49	5.89	0.48	1.44
20	0.67	1.55	5.92	0.49	1.43
21	0.65			0.50	1.42
22	0.64			0.52	1.41
23	0.63			0.53	1.41
24	0.61			0.54	1.40
25	0.60			0.55	1.39
30	0.55			0.59	1.36
35	0.51			0.62	1.33
40	0.47			0.65	1.31
45	0.45			0.67	1.30
50	0.42			0.68	1.28
55	0.40			0.70	1.27
60	0.39			0.71	1.26
65	0.37			0.72	1.25
70	0.36			0.74	1.24
75	0.35			0.75	1.23
80	0.34			0.75	1.23
85	0.33			0.76	1.22
90	0.32			0.77	1.22
95	0.31			0.77	1.21
100	0.30			0.78	1.20

$$UCL_{\bar{X}} = \bar{X}' + A\sigma'$$
$$LCL_{\bar{X}} = \bar{X}' - A\sigma'$$

(If actual average is to be used rather than standard or aimed-at average, $\bar{\bar{X}}$ should be substituted for $\bar{X}'$ in the preceding formulas.)

$$\left\{ \begin{array}{l} UCL_R = D_2\sigma' \\ \text{Central line}_R = d_2\sigma' \\ LCL_R = D_1\sigma' \end{array} \right.$$
$$\left\{ \begin{array}{l} UCL_\sigma = B_2\sigma' \\ \text{Central line}_\sigma = c_2\sigma' \\ LCL_\sigma = B_1\sigma' \end{array} \right.$$

Table F 3-sigma control limits for control charts for per cent rejected

Upper control limit

Standard per cent rejected ($100p'$)	Subgroup size																	
	100,000	50,000	20,000	10,000	5,000	4,000	3,000	2,000	1,500	1,000	800	600	500	400	300	200	150	100
0.1	0.13	0.14	0.17	0.19	0.23	0.25	0.27	0.31	0.34	0.40	0.44	0.49	0.52	0.57	0.65	0.77	0.87	1.05
0.2	0.24	0.26	0.29	0.33	0.39	0.41	0.44	0.50	0.55	0.62	0.67	0.75	0.80	0.87	0.97	1.15	1.29	1.54
0.4	0.46	0.48	0.53	0.59	0.67	0.70	0.75	0.82	0.89	1.00	1.07	1.17	1.25	1.35	1.49	1.74	1.95	2.29
0.6	0.67	0.70	0.76	0.83	0.93	0.97	1.02	1.12	1.20	1.33	1.42	1.55	1.64	1.76	1.94	2.24	2.49	2.92
0.8	0.88	0.92	0.99	1.07	1.18	1.22	1.29	1.40	1.49	1.65	1.74	1.89	2.00	2.14	2.34	2.69	2.98	3.47
1.0	1.09	1.13	1.21	1.30	1.42	1.47	1.54	1.67	1.77	1.94	2.06	2.22	2.33	2.49	2.72	3.11	3.44	3.98
1.2	1.30	1.35	1.43	1.53	1.66	1.72	1.80	1.93	2.04	2.23	2.35	2.53	2.66	2.83	3.09	3.51	3.87	4.47
1.4	1.51	1.56	1.65	1.75	1.90	1.96	2.04	2.19	2.31	2.51	2.65	2.84	2.98	3.16	3.43	3.89	4.28	4.92
1.6	1.72	1.77	1.87	1.98	2.13	2.20	2.29	2.44	2.57	2.79	2.93	3.14	3.28	3.48	3.77	4.26	4.67	5.36
1.8	1.93	1.98	2.08	2.20	2.36	2.43	2.53	2.69	2.83	3.06	3.21	3.43	3.58	3.79	4.10	4.62	5.06	5.79
2.0	2.13	2.19	2.30	2.42	2.59	2.66	2.77	2.94	3.08	3.33	3.48	3.71	3.88	4.10	4.42	4.97	5.43	6.20
2.5	2.65	2.71	2.83	2.97	3.16	3.24	3.36	3.55	3.71	3.98	4.16	4.41	4.59	4.84	5.20	5.81	6.32	7.18
3.0	3.16	3.23	3.36	3.51	3.72	3.81	3.93	4.14	4.32	4.62	4.81	5.09	5.29	5.56	5.95	6.62	7.18	8.12
3.5	3.67	3.75	3.89	4.05	4.28	4.37	4.51	4.73	4.92	5.24	5.45	5.75	5.97	6.26	6.68	7.40	8.00	9.01
4.0	4.19	4.26	4.42	4.59	4.83	4.93	5.07	5.31	5.52	5.86	6.08	6.40	6.63	6.94	7.39	8.16	8.80	9.88
5	5.21	5.29	5.46	5.65	5.92	6.03	6.19	6.46	6.69	7.07	7.31	7.67	7.92	8.27	8.77	9.62	10.34	11.54
6	6.23	6.32	6.50	6.71	7.01	7.13	7.30	7.59	7.84	8.25	8.52	8.91	9.19	9.56	10.11	11.04	11.82	13.12
7	7.24	7.34	7.54	7.77	8.08	8.21	8.40	8.71	8.98	9.42	9.71	10.12	10.42	10.83	11.42	12.41	13.25	14.65
8	8.26	8.36	8.58	8.81	9.15	9.29	9.49	9.82	10.10	10.57	10.88	11.32	11.64	12.07	12.70	13.75	14.65	16.14
9	9.27	9.38	9.61	9.86	10.21	10.36	10.57	10.92	11.22	11.71	12.04	12.50	12.84	13.29	13.96	15.07	16.01	17.59
10	10.28	10.40	10.64	10.90	11.27	11.42	11.64	12.01	12.32	12.85	13.18	13.67	14.02	14.50	15.20	16.36	17.35	19.00
12	12.31	12.44	12.69	12.97	13.38	13.54	13.78	14.18	14.52	15.08	15.45	15.98	16.36	16.87	17.63	18.89	19.96	21.75
14	14.33	14.47	14.74	15.04	15.47	15.65	15.90	16.33	16.69	17.29	17.68	18.25	18.66	19.20	20.01	21.36	22.50	24.41
16	16.35	16.49	16.78	17.10	17.56	17.74	18.01	18.46	18.84	19.48	19.89	20.49	20.92	21.50	22.35	23.78	24.98	27.00
18	18.36	18.52	18.81	19.15	19.63	19.82	20.10	20.58	20.97	21.64	22.07	22.71	23.15	23.76	24.65	26.15	27.41	29.53
20	20.38	20.54	20.85	21.20	21.70	21.90	22.19	22.68	23.10	23.79	24.24	24.90	25.37	26.00	26.93	28.49	29.80	32.00
25	25.41	25.58	25.92	26.30	26.84	27.05	27.37	27.90	28.35	29.11	29.59	30.30	30.81	31.50	32.50	34.19	35.61	37.99
30	30.43	30.61	30.97	31.37	31.94	32.17	32.51	33.07	33.55	34.35	34.86	35.61	36.15	36.87	37.94	39.72	41.22	43.75
35	35.45	35.64	36.01	36.43	37.02	37.26	37.60	38.20	38.70	39.52	40.06	40.84	41.40	42.15	43.26	45.12	46.68	49.31
40	40.46	40.66	41.04	41.47	42.08	42.32	42.68	43.29	43.79	44.65	45.20	46.00	46.57	47.35	48.49	50.39	52.00	54.70

Table F 3-sigma control limits for control charts for per cent rejected. (*Continued*)

Lower control limit

Subgroup size

Standard per cent rejected (100p')	100,000	50,000	20,000	10,000	5,000	4,000	3,000	2,000	1,500	1,000	800	600	500	400	300	200	150	100
0.1	0.07	0.06	0.03	0.01	0.00	0.00	0.00	0.00	0.00	0.00	0.00	0.00	0.00	0.00	0.00	0.00	0.00	0.00
0.2	0.16	0.14	0.11	0.07	0.01	0.00	0.00	0.00	0.00	0.00	0.00	0.00	0.00	0.00	0.00	0.00	0.00	0.00
0.4	0.34	0.32	0.27	0.21	0.13	0.10	0.05	0.00	0.00	0.00	0.00	0.00	0.00	0.00	0.00	0.00	0.00	0.00
0.6	0.53	0.50	0.44	0.37	0.27	0.23	0.18	0.08	0.00	0.00	0.00	0.00	0.00	0.00	0.00	0.00	0.00	0.00
0.8	0.72	0.68	0.61	0.53	0.42	0.38	0.31	0.20	0.11	0.00	0.00	0.00	0.00	0.00	0.00	0.00	0.00	0.00
1.0	0.91	0.87	0.79	0.70	0.58	0.53	0.46	0.33	0.23	0.06	0.00	0.00	0.00	0.00	0.00	0.00	0.00	0.00
1.2	1.10	1.05	0.97	0.87	0.74	0.68	0.60	0.47	0.36	0.17	0.05	0.00	0.00	0.00	0.00	0.00	0.00	0.00
1.4	1.29	1.24	1.15	1.05	0.90	0.84	0.76	0.61	0.49	0.29	0.15	0.00	0.00	0.00	0.00	0.00	0.00	0.00
1.6	1.48	1.43	1.33	1.22	1.07	1.00	0.91	0.76	0.63	0.41	0.27	0.06	0.00	0.00	0.00	0.00	0.00	0.00
1.8	1.67	1.62	1.52	1.40	1.24	1.17	1.07	0.91	0.77	0.54	0.39	0.17	0.02	0.00	0.00	0.00	0.00	0.00
2.0	1.87	1.81	1.70	1.58	1.41	1.34	1.23	1.06	0.92	0.67	0.52	0.29	0.12	0.00	0.00	0.00	0.00	0.00
2.5	2.35	2.29	2.17	2.03	1.84	1.76	1.64	1.45	1.29	1.02	0.84	0.59	0.41	0.16	0.00	0.00	0.00	0.00
3.0	2.84	2.77	2.64	2.49	2.28	2.19	2.07	1.86	1.68	1.38	1.19	0.91	0.71	0.44	0.05	0.00	0.00	0.00
3.5	3.33	3.25	3.11	2.95	2.72	2.63	2.49	2.27	2.08	1.76	1.55	1.25	1.03	0.74	0.32	0.00	0.00	0.00
4.0	3.81	3.74	3.58	3.41	3.17	3.07	2.93	2.69	2.48	2.14	1.92	1.60	1.37	1.06	0.61	0.00	0.00	0.00
5	4.79	4.71	4.54	4.35	4.08	3.97	3.81	3.54	3.31	2.93	2.69	2.33	2.08	1.73	1.23	0.38	0.00	0.00
6	5.77	5.68	5.50	5.29	4.99	4.87	4.70	4.41	4.16	3.75	3.48	3.09	2.81	2.44	1.89	0.96	0.18	0.00
7	6.74	6.66	6.46	6.23	5.92	5.79	5.60	5.29	5.02	4.58	4.29	3.88	3.58	3.17	2.58	1.59	0.75	0.00
8	7.74	7.64	7.42	7.19	6.85	6.71	6.51	6.18	5.85	5.43	5.12	4.68	4.36	3.93	3.30	2.25	1.35	0.00
9	8.73	8.62	8.39	8.14	7.79	7.64	7.43	7.08	6.78	6.29	5.96	5.50	5.16	4.71	4.04	2.93	1.99	0.41
10	9.72	9.60	9.36	9.10	8.73	8.58	8.36	7.99	7.68	7.15	6.82	6.33	5.98	5.50	4.80	3.64	2.65	1.00
12	11.69	11.56	11.31	11.03	10.62	10.46	10.22	9.82	9.48	8.92	8.55	8.02	7.64	7.13	6.37	5.11	4.04	2.25
14	13.67	13.53	13.26	12.96	12.53	12.35	12.10	11.67	11.31	10.71	10.32	9.75	9.34	8.80	7.99	6.64	5.50	3.59
16	15.65	15.51	15.22	14.90	14.44	14.26	13.99	13.54	13.16	12.52	12.11	11.51	11.08	10.50	9.65	8.22	7.02	5.00
18	17.64	17.48	17.19	16.85	16.37	16.18	15.90	15.42	15.03	14.36	13.93	13.29	12.85	12.24	11.35	9.85	8.59	6.47
20	19.62	19.46	19.15	18.80	18.30	18.10	17.81	17.32	16.90	16.21	15.76	15.10	14.63	14.00	13.07	11.51	10.20	8.00
25	24.59	24.42	24.08	23.70	23.16	22.95	22.63	22.10	21.65	20.89	20.41	19.70	19.19	18.50	17.50	15.81	14.39	12.01
30	29.57	29.39	29.03	28.63	28.06	27.83	27.49	26.93	26.45	25.65	25.14	24.39	23.85	23.13	22.06	20.28	18.78	16.25
35	34.55	34.36	33.99	33.57	32.98	32.74	32.39	31.80	31.30	30.48	29.94	29.16	28.60	27.85	26.74	24.88	23.32	20.69
40	39.54	39.34	38.96	38.53	37.92	37.68	37.32	36.71	36.21	35.35	34.80	34.00	33.43	32.65	31.51	29.61	28.00	25.30

Table G Summation of terms of Poisson's exponential binomial limit

$1,000 \times$ probability of c or less occurrences of event that has average number of occurrences equal to c' or np'

c c' or np'	0	1	2	3	4	5	6	7	8	9
0.02	980	1,000								
0.04	961	999	1,000							
0.06	942	998	1,000							
0.08	923	997	1,000							
0.10	905	995	1,000							
0.15	861	990	999	1,000						
0.20	819	982	999	1,000						
0.25	779	974	998	1,000						
0.30	741	963	996	1,000						
0.35	705	951	994	1,000						
0.40	670	938	992	999	1,000					
0.45	638	925	989	999	1,000					
0.50	607	910	986	998	1,000					
0.55	577	894	982	998	1,000					
0.60	549	878	977	997	1,000					
0.65	522	861	972	996	999	1,000				
0.70	497	844	966	994	999	1,000				
0.75	472	827	959	993	999	1,000				
0.80	449	809	953	991	999	1,000				
0.85	427	791	945	989	998	1,000				
0.90	407	772	937	987	998	1,000				
0.95	387	754	929	984	997	1,000				
1.00	368	736	920	981	996	999	1,000			
1.1	333	699	900	974	995	999	1,000			
1.2	301	663	879	966	992	998	1,000			
1.3	273	627	857	957	989	998	1,000			
1.4	247	592	833	946	986	997	999	1,000		
1.5	223	558	809	934	981	996	999	1,000		
1.6	202	525	783	921	976	994	999	1,000		
1.7	183	493	757	907	970	992	998	1,000		
1.8	165	463	731	891	964	990	997	999	1,000	
1.9	150	434	704	875	956	987	997	999	1,000	
2.0	135	406	677	857	947	983	995	999	1,000	

Table G Summation of terms of Poisson's exponential binomial limit. (*Continued*)

c' or np'	0	1	2	3	4	5	6	7	8	9
2.2	111	355	623	819	928	975	993	998	1,000	
2.4	091	308	570	779	904	964	988	997	999	1,000
2.6	074	267	518	736	877	951	983	995	999	1,000
2.8	061	231	469	692	848	935	976	992	998	999
3.0	050	199	423	647	815	916	966	988	996	999
3.2	041	171	380	603	781	895	955	983	994	998
3.4	033	147	340	558	744	871	942	977	992	997
3.6	027	126	303	515	706	844	927	969	988	996
3.8	022	107	269	473	668	816	909	960	984	994
4.0	018	092	238	433	629	785	889	949	979	992
4.2	015	078	210	395	590	753	867	936	972	989
4.4	012	066	185	359	551	720	844	921	964	985
4.6	010	056	163	326	513	686	818	905	955	980
4.8	008	048	143	294	476	651	791	887	944	975
5.0	007	040	125	265	440	616	762	867	932	968
5.2	006	034	109	238	406	581	732	845	918	960
5.4	005	029	095	213	373	546	702	822	903	951
5.6	004	024	082	191	342	512	670	797	886	941
5.8	003	021	072	170	313	478	638	771	867	929
6.0	002	017	062	151	285	446	606	744	847	916

c' or np'	10	11	12	13	14	15	16
2.8	1,000						
3.0	1,000						
3.2	1,000						
3.4	999	1,000					
3.6	999	1,000					
3.8	998	999	1,000				
4.0	997	999	1,000				
4.2	996	999	1,000				
4.4	994	998	999	1,000			
4.6	992	997	999	1,000			
4.8	990	996	999	1,000			
5.0	986	995	998	999	1,000		
5.2	982	993	997	999	1,000		
5.4	977	990	996	999	1,000		
5.6	972	988	995	998	999	1,000	
5.8	965	984	993	997	999	1,000	
6.0	957	980	991	996	999	999	1,000

Table G Summation of terms of Poisson's exponential binomial limit. (Continued)

c' or np'	0	1	2	3	4	5	6	7	8	9
6.2	002	015	054	134	259	414	574	716	826	902
6.4	002	012	046	119	235	384	542	687	803	886
6.6	001	010	040	105	213	355	511	658	780	869
6.8	001	009	034	093	192	327	480	628	755	850
7.0	001	007	030	082	173	301	450	599	729	830
7.2	001	006	025	072	156	276	420	569	703	810
7.4	001	005	022	063	140	253	392	539	676	788
7.6	001	004	019	055	125	231	365	510	648	765
7.8	000	004	016	048	112	210	338	481	620	741
8.0	000	003	014	042	100	191	313	453	593	717
8.5	000	002	009	030	074	150	256	386	523	653
9.0	000	001	006	021	055	116	207	324	456	587
9.5	000	001	004	015	040	089	165	269	392	522
10.0	000	000	003	010	029	067	130	220	333	458

	10	11	12	13	14	15	16	17	18	19
6.2	949	975	989	995	998	999	1,000			
6.4	939	969	986	994	997	999	1,000			
6.6	927	963	982	992	997	999	999	1,000		
6.8	915	955	978	990	996	998	999	1,000		
7.0	901	947	973	987	994	998	999	1,000		
7.2	887	937	967	984	993	997	999	999	1,000	
7.4	871	926	961	980	991	996	998	999	1,000	
7.6	854	915	954	976	989	995	998	999	1,000	
7.8	835	902	945	971	986	993	997	999	1,000	
8.0	816	888	936	966	983	992	996	998	999	1,000
8.5	763	849	909	949	973	986	993	997	999	999
9.0	706	803	876	926	959	978	989	995	998	999
9.5	645	752	836	898	940	967	982	991	996	998
10.0	583	697	792	864	917	951	973	986	993	997

	20	21	22
8.5	1,000		
9.0	1,000		
9.5	999	1,000	
10.0	998	999	1,000

Table G Summation of terms of Poisson's exponential binomial limit. (*Continued*)

c' or np'	0	1	2	3	4	5	6	7	8	9
10.5	000	000	002	007	021	050	102	179	279	397
11.0	000	000	001	005	015	038	079	143	232	341
11.5	000	000	001	003	011	028	060	114	191	289
12.0	000	000	001	002	008	020	046	090	155	242
12.5	000	000	000	002	005	015	035	070	125	201
13.0	000	000	000	001	004	011	026	054	100	166
13.5	000	000	000	001	003	008	019	041	079	135
14.0	000	000	000	000	002	006	014	032	062	109
14.5	000	000	000	000	001	004	010	024	048	088
15.0	000	000	000	000	001	003	008	018	037	070

	10	11	12	13	14	15	16	17	18	19
10.5	521	639	742	825	888	932	960	978	988	994
11.0	460	579	689	781	854	907	944	968	982	991
11.5	402	520	633	733	815	878	924	954	974	986
12.0	347	462	576	682	772	844	899	937	963	979
12.5	297	406	519	628	725	806	869	916	948	969
13.0	252	353	463	573	675	764	835	890	930	957
13.5	211	304	409	518	623	718	798	861	908	942
14.0	176	260	358	464	570	669	756	827	883	923
14.5	145	220	311	413	518	619	711	790	853	901
15.0	118	185	268	363	466	568	664	749	819	875

	20	21	22	23	24	25	26	27	28	29
10.5	997	999	999	1,000						
11.0	995	998	999	1,000						
11.5	992	996	998	999	1,000					
12.0	988	994	997	999	999	1,000				
12.5	983	991	995	998	999	999	1,000			
13.0	975	986	992	996	998	999	1,000			
13.5	965	980	989	994	997	998	999	1,000		
14.0	952	971	983	991	995	997	999	999	1,000	
14.5	936	960	976	986	992	996	998	999	999	1,000
15.0	917	947	967	981	989	994	997	998	999	1,000

Table G Summation of terms of Poisson's exponential binomial limit. (*Continued*)

c' or np' \ c	4	5	6	7	8	9	10	11	12	13
16	000	001	004	010	022	043	077	127	193	275
17	000	001	002	005	013	026	049	085	135	201
18	000	000	001	003	007	015	030	055	092	143
19	000	000	001	002	004	009	018	035	061	098
20	000	000	000	001	002	005	011	021	039	066
21	000	000	000	000	001	003	006	013	025	043
22	000	000	000	000	001	002	004	008	015	028
23	000	000	000	000	000	001	002	004	009	017
24	000	000	000	000	000	000	001	003	005	011
25	000	000	000	000	000	000	001	001	003	006

	14	15	16	17	18	19	20	21	22	23
16	368	467	566	659	742	812	868	911	942	963
17	281	371	468	564	655	736	805	861	905	937
18	208	287	375	469	562	651	731	799	855	899
19	150	215	292	378	469	561	647	725	793	849
20	105	157	221	297	381	470	559	644	721	787
21	072	111	163	227	302	384	471	558	640	716
22	048	077	117	169	232	306	387	472	556	637
23	031	052	082	123	175	238	310	389	472	555
24	020	034	056	087	128	180	243	314	392	473
25	012	022	038	060	092	134	185	247	318	394

	24	25	26	27	28	29	30	31	32	33
16	978	987	993	996	998	999	999	1,000		
17	959	975	985	991	995	997	999	999	1,000	
18	932	955	972	983	990	994	997	998	999	1,000
19	893	927	951	969	980	988	993	996	998	999
20	843	888	922	948	966	978	987	992	995	997
21	782	838	883	917	944	963	976	985	991	994
22	712	777	832	877	913	940	959	973	983	989
23	635	708	772	827	873	908	936	956	971	981
24	554	632	704	768	823	868	904	932	953	969
25	473	553	629	700	763	818	863	900	929	950

	34	35	36	37	38	39	40	41	42	43
19	999	1,000								
20	999	999	1,000							
21	997	998	999	999	1,000					
22	994	996	998	999	999	1,000				
23	988	993	996	997	999	999	1,000			
24	979	987	992	995	997	998	999	999	1,000	
25	966	978	985	991	994	997	998	999	999	1,000

Table H Logarithms of factorials

	0	1	2	3	4	5	6	7	8	9
00	0.0000	0.0000	0.3010	0.7782	1.3802	2.0792	2.8573	3.7024	4.6055	5.5598
10	6.5598	7.6012	8.6803	9.7943	10.9404	12.1165	13.3206	14.5511	15.8063	17.0851
20	18.3861	19.7083	21.0508	22.4125	23.7927	25.1906	26.6056	28.0370	29.4841	30.9465
30	32.4237	33.9150	35.4202	36.9387	38.4702	40.0142	41.5705	43.1387	44.7185	46.3096
40	47.9116	49.5244	51.1477	52.7811	54.4246	56.0778	57.7406	59.4127	61.0939	62.7841
50	64.4831	66.1906	67.9066	69.6309	71.3633	73.1037	74.8519	76.6077	78.3712	80.1420
60	81.9202	83.7055	85.4979	87.2972	89.1034	90.9163	92.7359	94.5619	96.3945	98.2333
70	100.0784	101.9297	103.7870	105.6503	107.5196	109.3946	111.2754	113.1619	115.0540	116.9516
80	118.8547	120.7632	122.6770	124.5961	126.5204	128.4498	130.3843	132.3238	134.2683	136.2177
90	138.1719	140.1310	142.0948	144.0632	146.0364	148.0141	149.9964	151.9831	153.9744	155.9700
100	157.9700	159.9743	161.9829	163.9958	166.0128	168.0340	170.0593	172.0887	174.1221	176.1595
110	178.2009	180.2462	182.2955	184.3485	186.4054	188.4661	190.5306	192.5988	194.6707	196.7462
120	198.8254	200.9082	202.9945	205.0844	207.1779	209.2748	211.3751	213.4790	215.5862	217.6967
130	219.8107	221.9280	224.0485	226.1724	228.2995	230.4298	232.5634	234.7001	236.8400	238.9830
140	241.1291	243.2783	245.4306	247.5860	249.7443	251.9057	254.0700	256.2374	258.4076	260.5808
150	262.7569	264.9359	267.1177	269.3024	271.4899	273.6803	275.8734	278.0693	280.2679	282.4693
160	284.6735	286.8803	289.0898	291.3020	293.5168	295.7343	297.9544	300.1771	302.4024	304.6303
170	306.8608	309.0938	311.3293	313.5674	315.8079	318.0509	320.2965	322.5444	324.7948	327.0477
180	329.3030	331.5606	333.8207	336.0832	338.3480	340.6152	342.8847	345.1565	347.4307	349.7071
190	351.9859	354.2669	356.5502	358.8358	361.1236	363.4136	365.7059	368.0003	370.2970	372.5959

Table H Logarithms of factorials. (*Continued*)

	0	1	2	3	4	5	6	7	8	9
200	374.8969	377.2001	379.5054	381.8129	384.1226	386.4343	388.7482	391.0642	393.3822	395.7024
210	398.0246	400.3489	402.6752	405.0036	407.3340	409.6664	412.0009	414.3373	416.6758	419.0162
220	421.3587	423.7031	426.0494	428.3977	430.7480	433.1002	435.4543	437.8103	440.1682	442.5281
230	444.8898	447.2534	449.6189	451.9862	454.3555	456.7265	459.0994	461.4742	463.8508	466.2292
240	468.6094	470.9914	473.3752	475.7608	478.1482	480.5374	482.9283	485.3210	487.7154	490.1116
250	492.5096	494.9093	497.3107	499.7138	502.1186	504.5252	506.9334	509.3433	511.7549	514.1682
260	516.5832	518.9999	521.4182	523.8381	526.2597	528.6830	531.1078	533.5344	535.9625	538.3922
270	540.8236	543.2566	545.6912	548.1273	550.5651	553.0044	555.4453	557.8878	560.3318	562.7774
280	565.2246	567.6733	570.1235	572.5753	575.0287	577.4835	579.9399	582.3977	584.8571	587.3180
290	589.7804	592.2443	594.7097	597.1766	599.6449	602.1147	604.5860	607.0588	609.5530	612.0087
300	614.4858	616.9644	619.4444	621.9258	624.4087	626.8930	629.3787	631.8659	634.3544	636.8444
310	639.3357	641.8285	644.3226	646.8182	649.3151	651.8134	654.3131	656.8142	659.3166	661.8204
320	664.3255	666.8320	669.3399	671.8491	674.3596	676.8715	679.3847	681.8993	684.4152	686.9324
330	689.4509	691.9707	694.4918	697.0143	699.5380	702.0631	704.5894	707.1170	709.6460	712.1762
340	714.7076	717.2404	719.7744	722.3097	724.8463	727.3841	729.9232	732.4635	735.0051	737.5479
350	740.0920	742.6373	745.1838	747.7316	750.2806	752.8308	755.3823	757.9349	760.4888	763.0439
360	765.6002	768.1577	770.7164	773.2764	775.8375	778.3997	780.9632	783.5279	786.0937	788.6608
370	791.2290	793.7983	796.3689	798.9406	801.5135	804.0875	806.6627	809.2390	811.8165	814.3952
380	816.9749	819.5559	822.1379	824.7211	827.3055	829.8909	832.4775	835.0652	837.6540	840.2440
390	842.8351	845.4272	848.0205	850.6149	853.2104	855.8070	858.4047	861.0035	863.6034	866.2044

Table H Logarithms of factorials. (*Continued*)

	0	1	2	3	4	5	6	7	8	9
400	868.8064	871.4096	874.0138	876.6191	879.2255	881.8329	884.4415	887.0510	889.6617	892.2734
410	894.8862	897.5001	900.1150	902.7309	905.3479	907.9660	910.5850	913.2052	915.8264	918.4486
420	921.0718	923.6961	926.3214	928.9478	931.5751	934.2035	936.8329	939.4633	942.0948	944.7272
430	947.3607	949.9952	952.6307	955.2672	957.9047	960.5431	963.1826	965.8231	968.4646	971.1071
440	973.7505	976.3949	979.0404	981.6868	984.3342	986.9825	989.6318	992.2822	994.9334	997.5857
450	1000.2389	1002.8931	1005.5482	1008.2043	1010.8614	1013.5194	1016.1783	1018.8383	1021.4991	1024.1609
460	1026.8237	1029.4874	1032.1520	1034.8176	1037.4841	1040.1516	1042.8200	1045.4893	1048.1595	1050.8307
470	1053.5028	1056.1758	1058.8498	1061.5246	1064.2004	1066.8771	1069.5547	1072.2332	1074.9127	1077.5930
480	1080.2742	1082.9564	1085.6394	1088.3234	1091.0082	1093.6940	1096.3806	1099.0681	1101.7565	1104.4458
490	1107.1360	1109.8271	1112.5191	1115.2119	1117.9057	1120.6003	1123.2958	1125.9921	1128.6893	1131.3874
500	1134.0864	1136.7862	1139.4869	1142.1885	1144.8909	1147.5942	1150.2984	1153.0034	1155.7093	1158.4160
510	1161.1236	1163.8320	1166.5412	1169.2514	1171.9623	1174.6741	1177.3868	1180.1003	1182.8146	1185.5298
520	1188.2458	1190.9626	1193.6803	1196.3988	1199.1181	1201.8383	1204.5593	1207.2811	1210.0037	1212.7272
530	1215.4514	1218.1765	1220.9024	1223.6292	1226.3567	1229.0851	1231.8142	1234.5442	1237.2750	1240.0066
540	1242.7390	1245.4722	1248.2062	1250.9410	1253.6766	1256.4130	1259.1501	1261.8881	1264.6269	1267.3665
550	1270.1069	1272.8480	1275.5899	1278.3327	1281.0762	1283.8205	1286.5655	1289.3114	1292.0580	1294.8054
560	1297.5536	1300.3026	1303.0523	1305.8028	1308.5541	1311.3062	1314.0590	1316.8126	1319.5669	1322.3220
570	1325.0779	1327.8345	1330.5919	1333.3501	1336.1090	1338.8687	1341.6291	1344.3903	1347.1522	1349.9149
580	1352.6783	1355.4425	1358.2074	1360.9731	1363.7395	1366.5066	1369.2745	1372.0432	1374.8126	1377.5827
590	1380.3535	1383.1251	1385.8974	1388.6705	1391.4443	1394.2188	1396.9940	1399.7700	1402.5467	1405.3241

Table H Logarithms of factorials. (*Continued*)

	0	1	2	3	4	5	6	7	8	9
600	1408.1023	1410.8812	1413.6608	1416.4411	1419.2221	1422.0039	1424.7863	1427.5695	1430.3534	1433.1380
610	1435.9234	1438.7094	1441.4962	1444.2836	1447.0718	1449.8607	1452.6503	1455.4405	1458.2315	1461.0232
620	1463.8156	1466.6087	1469.4025	1472.1970	1474.9922	1477.7880	1480.5846	1483.3819	1486.1798	1488.9785
630	1491.7778	1494.5779	1497.3786	1500.1800	1502.9821	1505.7849	1508.5883	1511.3924	1514.1973	1517.0028
640	1519.8090	1522.6158	1525.4233	1528.2316	1531.0404	1533.8500	1536.6602	1539.4711	1542.2827	1545.0950
650	1547.9079	1550.7215	1553.5357	1556.3506	1559.1662	1561.9824	1564.7993	1567.6169	1570.4351	1573.2540
660	1576.0736	1578.8938	1581.7146	1584.5361	1587.3583	1590.1811	1593.0046	1595.8287	1598.6535	1601.4789
670	1604.3050	1607.1317	1609.9591	1612.7871	1615.6158	1618.4451	1621.2750	1624.1056	1626.9368	1629.7687
680	1632.6012	1635.4344	1638.2681	1641.1026	1643.9376	1646.7733	1649.6096	1652.4466	1655.2842	1658.1224
690	1660.9612	1663.8007	1666.6408	1669.4816	1672.3229	1675.1649	1678.0075	1680.8508	1683.6946	1686.5391
700	1689.3842	1692.2299	1695.0762	1697.9232	1700.7708	1703.6190	1706.4678	1709.3172	1712.1672	1715.0179
710	1717.8691	1720.7210	1723.5735	1726.4266	1729.2803	1732.1346	1734.9895	1737.8450	1740.7011	1743.5578
720	1746.4152	1749.2731	1752.1316	1754.9908	1757.8505	1760.7109	1763.5718	1766.4333	1769.2955	1772.1582
730	1775.0215	1777.8854	1780.7499	1783.6150	1786.4807	1789.3470	1792.2139	1795.0814	1797.9494	1800.8181
740	1803.6873	1806.5571	1809.4275	1812.2985	1815.1701	1818.0423	1820.9150	1823.7883	1826.6622	1829.5367
750	1832.4118	1835.2874	1838.1636	1841.0404	1843.9178	1846.7957	1849.6742	1852.5533	1855.4330	1858.3133
760	1861.1941	1864.0755	1866.9574	1869.8399	1872.7230	1875.6067	1878.4909	1881.3757	1884.2611	1887.1470
770	1890.0335	1892.9205	1895.8082	1898.6963	1901.5851	1904.4744	1907.3642	1910.2547	1913.1456	1916.0372
780	1918.9293	1921.8219	1924.7151	1927.6089	1930.5032	1933.3981	1936.2935	1939.1895	1942.0860	1944.9831
790	1947.8807	1950.7789	1953.6776	1956.5769	1959.4767	1962.3771	1965.2780	1968.1794	1971.0814	1973.9840

Table H Logarithms of factorials. (*Continued*)

	0	1	2	3	4	5	6	7	8	9
800	1976.8871	1979.7907	1982.6949	1985.5996	1988.5049	1991.4107	1994.3170	1997.2239	2000.1313	2003.0392
810	2005.9477	2008.8567	2011.7663	2014.6764	2017.5870	2020.4982	2023.4099	2026.3221	2029.2348	2032.1481
820	2035.0619	2037.9763	2040.8911	2043.8065	2046.7225	2049.6389	2052.5559	2055.4734	2058.3914	2061.3100
830	2064.2291	2067.1487	2070.0688	2072.9894	2075.9106	2078.8323	2081.7545	2084.6772	2087.6005	2090.5242
840	2093.4485	2096.3733	2099.2986	2102.2244	2105.1508	2108.0776	2111.0050	2113.9329	2116.8613	2119.7902
850	2122.7196	2125.6495	2128.5800	2131.5109	2134.4424	2137.3744	2140.3068	2143.2398	2146.1733	2149.1073
860	2152.0418	2154.9768	2157.9123	2160.8483	2163.7848	2166.7218	2169.6594	2172.5974	2175.5359	2178.4749
870	2181.4144	2184.3545	2187.2950	2190.2360	2193.1775	2196.1195	2199.0620	2202.0050	2204.9485	2207.8925
880	2210.8370	2213.7820	2216.7274	2219.6734	2222.6198	2225.5668	2228.5142	2231.4621	2234.4106	2237.3595
890	2240.3088	2243.2587	2246.2091	2249.1599	2252.1113	2255.0631	2258.0154	2260.9682	2263.9215	2266.8752
900	2269.8295	2272.7842	2275.7394	2278.6951	2281.6513	2284.6079	2287.5650	2290.5226	2293.4807	2296.4393
910	2299.3983	2302.3579	2305.3179	2308.2783	2311.2393	2314.2007	2317.1626	2320.1250	2323.0878	2326.0511
920	2329.0149	2331.9792	2334.9439	2337.9091	2340.8748	2343.8409	2346.8075	2349.7746	2352.7421	2355.7102
930	2358.6786	2361.6476	2364.6170	2367.5869	2370.5572	2373.5281	2376.4993	2379.4711	2382.4433	2385.4159
940	2388.3891	2391.3627	2394.3367	2397.3112	2400.2862	2403.2616	2406.2375	2409.2139	2412.1907	2415.1679
950	2418.1457	2421.1238	2424.1025	2427.0816	2430.0611	2433.0411	2436.0216	2439.0025	2441.9839	2444.9657
960	2447.9479	2450.9307	2453.9138	2456.8975	2459.8815	2462.8661	2465.8511	2468.8365	2471.8224	2474.8087
970	2477.7954	2480.7827	2483.7703	2486.7584	2489.7470	2492.7360	2495.7255	2498.7154	2501.7057	2504.6965
980	2507.6877	2510.6794	2513.6715	2516.6640	2519.6570	2522.6505	2525.6443	2528.6387	2531.6334	2534.6286
990	2537.6242	2540.6203	2543.6168	2546.6138	2549.6112	2552.6090	2555.6073	2558.6059	2561.6051	2564.6046
1,000	2567.6046	2570.6051	2573.6059	2576.6072	2579.6090	2582.6111	2585.6137	2588.6168	2591.6202	2594.6241

Table J Logarithms of numbers

N	0	1	2	3	4	5	6	7	8	9
10	0000	0043	0086	0128	0170	0212	0253	0294	0334	0374
11	0414	0453	0492	0531	0569	0607	0645	0682	0719	0755
12	0792	0828	0864	0899	0934	0969	1004	1038	1072	1106
13	1139	1173	1206	1239	1271	1303	1335	1367	1399	1430
14	1461	1492	1523	1553	1584	1614	1644	1673	1703	1732
15	1761	1790	1818	1847	1875	1903	1931	1959	1987	2014
16	2041	2068	2095	2122	2148	2175	2201	2227	2253	2279
17	2304	2330	2355	2380	2405	2430	2455	2480	2504	2529
18	2553	2577	2601	2625	2648	2672	2695	2718	2742	2765
19	2788	2810	2833	2856	2878	2900	2923	2945	2967	2989
20	3010	3032	3054	3075	3096	3118	3139	3160	3181	3201
21	3222	3243	3263	3284	3304	3324	3345	3365	3385	3404
22	3424	3444	3464	3483	3502	3522	3541	3560	3579	3598
23	3617	3636	3655	3674	3692	3711	3729	3747	3766	3784
24	3802	3820	3838	3856	3874	3892	3909	3927	3945	3962
25	3979	3997	4014	4031	4048	4065	4082	4099	4116	4133
26	4150	4166	4183	4200	4216	4232	4249	4265	4281	4298
27	4314	4330	4346	4362	4378	4393	4409	4425	4440	4456
28	4472	4487	4502	4518	4533	4548	4564	4579	4594	4609
29	4624	4639	4654	4669	4683	4698	4713	4728	4742	4757
30	4771	4786	4800	4814	4829	4843	4857	4871	4886	4900
31	4914	4928	4942	4955	4969	4983	4997	5011	5024	5038
32	5051	5065	5079	5092	5105	5119	5132	5145	5159	5172
33	5185	5198	5211	5224	5237	5250	5263	5276	5289	5302
34	5315	5328	5340	5353	5366	5378	5391	5403	5416	5428
35	5441	5453	5465	5478	5490	5502	5514	5527	5539	5551
36	5563	5575	5587	5599	5611	5623	5635	5647	5658	5670
37	5682	5694	5705	5717	5729	5740	5752	5763	5775	5786
38	5798	5809	5821	5832	5843	5855	5866	5877	5888	5899
39	5911	5922	5933	5944	5955	5966	5977	5988	5999	6010
40	6021	6031	6042	6053	6064	6075	6085	6096	6107	6117
41	6128	6138	6149	6160	6170	6180	6191	6201	6212	6222
42	6232	6243	6253	6263	6274	6284	6294	6304	6314	6325
43	6335	6345	6355	6365	6375	6385	6395	6405	6415	6425
44	6435	6444	6454	6464	6474	6484	6493	6503	6513	6522
45	6532	6542	6551	6561	6571	6580	6590	6599	6609	6618
46	6628	6637	6646	6656	6665	6675	6684	6693	6702	6712
47	6721	6730	6739	6749	6758	6767	6776	6785	6794	6803
48	6812	6821	6830	6839	6848	6857	6866	6875	6884	6893
49	6902	6911	6920	6928	6937	6946	6955	6964	6972	6981
50	6990	6998	7007	7016	7024	7033	7042	7050	7059	7067
51	7076	7084	7093	7101	7110	7118	7126	7135	7143	7152
52	7160	7168	7177	7185	7193	7202	7210	7218	7226	7235
53	7243	7251	7259	7267	7275	7284	7292	7300	7308	7316
54	7324	7332	7340	7348	7356	7364	7372	7380	7388	7396
N	0	1	2	3	4	5	6	7	8	9

Table J Logarithms of numbers. (*Continued*)

N	0	1	2	3	4	5	6	7	8	9
55	7404	7412	7419	7427	7435	7443	7451	7459	7466	7474
56	7482	7490	7497	7505	7513	7520	7528	7536	7543	7551
57	7559	7566	7574	7582	7589	7597	7604	7612	7619	7627
58	7634	7642	7649	7657	7664	7672	7679	7686	7694	7701
59	7709	7716	7723	7731	7738	7745	7752	7760	7767	7774
60	7782	7789	7796	7803	7810	7818	7825	7832	7839	7846
61	7853	7860	7868	7875	7882	7889	7896	7903	7910	7917
62	7924	7931	7938	7945	7952	7959	7966	7973	7980	7987
63	7993	8000	8007	8014	8021	8028	8035	8041	8048	8055
64	8062	8069	8075	8082	8089	8096	8102	8109	8116	8122
65	8129	8136	8142	8149	8156	8162	8169	8176	8182	8189
66	8195	8202	8209	8215	8222	8228	8235	8241	8248	8254
67	8261	8267	8274	8280	8287	8293	8299	8306	8312	8319
68	8325	8331	8338	8344	8351	8357	8363	8370	8376	8382
69	8388	8395	8401	8407	8414	8420	8426	8432	8439	8445
70	8451	8457	8463	8470	8476	8482	8488	8494	8500	8506
71	8513	8519	8525	8531	8537	8543	8549	8555	8561	8567
72	8573	8579	8585	8591	8597	8603	8609	8615	8621	8627
73	8633	8639	8645	8651	8657	8663	8669	8675	8681	8686
74	8692	8698	8704	8710	8716	8722	8727	8733	8739	8745
75	8751	8756	8762	8768	8774	8779	8785	8791	8797	8802
76	8808	8814	8820	8825	8831	8837	8842	8848	8854	8859
77	8865	8871	8876	8882	8887	8893	8899	8904	8910	8915
78	8921	8927	8932	8938	8943	8949	8954	8960	8965	8971
79	8976	8982	8987	8993	8998	9004	9009	9015	9020	9025
80	9031	9036	9042	9047	9053	9058	9063	9069	9074	9079
81	9085	9090	9096	9101	9106	9112	9117	9122	9128	9133
82	9138	9143	9149	9154	9159	9165	9170	9175	9180	9186
83	9191	9196	9201	9206	9212	9217	9222	9227	9232	9238
84	9243	9248	9253	9258	9263	9269	9274	9279	9284	9289
85	9294	9299	9304	9309	9315	9320	9325	9330	9335	9340
86	9345	9350	9355	9360	9365	9370	9375	9380	9385	9390
87	9395	9400	9405	9410	9415	9420	9425	9430	9435	9440
88	9445	9450	9455	9460	9465	9469	9474	9479	9484	9489
89	9494	9499	9504	9509	9513	9518	9523	9528	9533	9538
90	9542	9547	9552	9557	9562	9566	9571	9576	9581	9586
91	9590	9595	9600	9605	9609	9614	9619	9624	9628	9633
92	9638	9643	9647	9652	9657	9661	9666	9671	9675	9680
93	9685	9689	9694	9699	9703	9708	9713	9717	9722	9727
94	9731	9736	9741	9745	9750	9754	9759	9763	9768	9773
95	9777	9782	9786	9791	9795	9800	9805	9809	9814	9818
96	9823	9827	9832	9836	9841	9845	9850	9854	9859	9863
97	9868	9872	9877	9881	9886	9890	9894	9899	9903	9908
98	9912	9917	9921	9926	9930	9934	9939	9943	9948	9952
99	9956	9961	9965	9969	9974	9978	9983	9987	9991	9996
N	0	1	2	3	4	5	6	7	8	9

Table K Sample size code letters—MIL-STD-105D (ABC Standard)

Lot or batch size	Special inspection levels				General inspection levels		
	S-1	S-2	S-3	S-4	I	II	III
2–8	A	A	A	A	A	A	B
9–15	A	A	A	A	A	B	C
16–25	A	A	B	B	B	C	D
26–50	A	B	B	C	C	D	E
51–90	B	B	C	C	C	E	F
91–150	B	B	C	D	D	F	G
151–280	B	C	D	E	E	G	H
281–500	B	C	D	E	F	H	J
501–1,200	C	C	E	F	G	J	K
1,201–3,200	C	D	E	G	H	K	L
3,201–10,000	C	D	F	G	J	L	M
10,001–35,000	C	D	F	H	K	M	N
35,001–150,000	D	E	G	J	L	N	P
150,001–500,000	D	E	G	J	M	P	Q
500,001 and over	D	E	H	K	N	Q	R

Table L Master table for normal inspection (single sampling)—MIL–STD–105D (ABC Standard)

Acceptable quality levels (normal inspection). Each cell shows **Ac** (acceptance number) and **Re** (rejection number).

Sample size code letter	Sample size	0.010	0.015	0.025	0.040	0.065	0.10	0.15	0.25	0.40	0.65	1.0	1.5	2.5	4.0	6.5	10	15	25	40	65	100	150	250	400	650	1,000
A	2	↓	↓	↓	↓	↓	↓	↓	↓	↓	↓	↓	↓	↓	↓	↓	↓	0 1	1 2	2 3	3 4	5 6	7 8	10 11	14 15	21 22	30 31
B	3	↓	↓	↓	↓	↓	↓	↓	↓	↓	↓	↓	↓	↓	↓	↓	0 1	1 2	2 3	3 4	5 6	7 8	10 11	14 15	21 22	30 31	44 45
C	5	↓	↓	↓	↓	↓	↓	↓	↓	↓	↓	↓	↓	↓	↓	0 1	1 2	2 3	3 4	5 6	7 8	10 11	14 15	21 22	30 31	44 45	↑
D	8	↓	↓	↓	↓	↓	↓	↓	↓	↓	↓	↓	↓	↓	0 1	1 2	2 3	3 4	5 6	7 8	10 11	14 15	21 22	30 31	44 45	↑	↑
E	13	↓	↓	↓	↓	↓	↓	↓	↓	↓	↓	↓	↓	0 1	1 2	2 3	3 4	5 6	7 8	10 11	14 15	21 22	30 31	44 45	↑	↑	↑
F	20	↓	↓	↓	↓	↓	↓	↓	↓	↓	↓	↓	0 1	1 2	2 3	3 4	5 6	7 8	10 11	14 15	21 22	30 31	44 45	↑	↑	↑	↑
G	32	↓	↓	↓	↓	↓	↓	↓	↓	↓	↓	0 1	1 2	2 3	3 4	5 6	7 8	10 11	14 15	21 22	30 31	44 45	↑	↑	↑	↑	↑
H	50	↓	↓	↓	↓	↓	↓	↓	↓	↓	0 1	1 2	2 3	3 4	5 6	7 8	10 11	14 15	21 22	30 31	44 45	↑	↑	↑	↑	↑	↑
J	80	↓	↓	↓	↓	↓	↓	↓	↓	0 1	1 2	2 3	3 4	5 6	7 8	10 11	14 15	21 22	30 31	44 45	↑	↑	↑	↑	↑	↑	↑
K	125	↓	↓	↓	↓	↓	↓	↓	0 1	1 2	2 3	3 4	5 6	7 8	10 11	14 15	21 22	30 31	44 45	↑	↑	↑	↑	↑	↑	↑	↑
L	200	↓	↓	↓	↓	↓	↓	0 1	1 2	2 3	3 4	5 6	7 8	10 11	14 15	21 22	30 31	44 45	↑	↑	↑	↑	↑	↑	↑	↑	↑
M	315	↓	↓	↓	↓	↓	0 1	1 2	2 3	3 4	5 6	7 8	10 11	14 15	21 22	30 31	44 45	↑	↑	↑	↑	↑	↑	↑	↑	↑	↑
N	500	↓	↓	↓	↓	0 1	1 2	2 3	3 4	5 6	7 8	10 11	14 15	21 22	30 31	44 45	↑	↑	↑	↑	↑	↑	↑	↑	↑	↑	↑
P	800	↓	↓	↓	0 1	1 2	2 3	3 4	5 6	7 8	10 11	14 15	21 22	30 31	44 45	↑	↑	↑	↑	↑	↑	↑	↑	↑	↑	↑	↑
Q	1,250	↓	↓	0 1	1 2	2 3	3 4	5 6	7 8	10 11	14 15	21 22	30 31	44 45	↑	↑	↑	↑	↑	↑	↑	↑	↑	↑	↑	↑	↑
R	2,000	↓	0 1	1 2	2 3	3 4	5 6	7 8	10 11	14 15	21 22	30 31	44 45	↑	↑	↑	↑	↑	↑	↑	↑	↑	↑	↑	↑	↑	↑

If sample size equals, or exceeds, lot or batch size, do 100% inspection.

↓ = use first sampling plan below arrow.
↑ = use first sampling plan above arrow.
Ac = acceptance number.
Re = rejection number.

Table M Master table for tightened inspection (single sampling)—MIL-STD-105D (ABC Standard)

Acceptable quality levels (tightened inspection)

Each cell lists the acceptance/rejection pair as "Ac Re".

Sample size code letter	Sample size	0.010	0.015	0.025	0.040	0.065	0.10	0.15	0.25	0.40	0.65	1.0	1.5	2.5	4.0	6.5	10	15	25	40	65	100	150	250	400	650	1,000
A	2	↓	↓	↓	↓	↓	↓	↓	↓	↓	↓	↓	↓	↓	↓	↓	↓	0 1	1 2	2 3	3 4	5 6	8 9	12 13	18 19	27 28	41 42
B	3	↓	↓	↓	↓	↓	↓	↓	↓	↓	↓	↓	↓	↓	↓	↓	0 1	1 2	2 3	3 4	5 6	8 9	12 13	18 19	27 28	41 42	↑
C	5	↓	↓	↓	↓	↓	↓	↓	↓	↓	↓	↓	↓	↓	↓	0 1	1 2	2 3	3 4	5 6	8 9	12 13	18 19	27 28	41 42	↑	↑
D	8	↓	↓	↓	↓	↓	↓	↓	↓	↓	↓	↓	↓	↓	0 1	1 2	2 3	3 4	5 6	8 9	12 13	18 19	27 28	41 42	↑	↑	↑
E	13	↓	↓	↓	↓	↓	↓	↓	↓	↓	↓	↓	↓	0 1	1 2	2 3	3 4	5 6	8 9	12 13	18 19	27 28	41 42	↑	↑	↑	↑
F	20	↓	↓	↓	↓	↓	↓	↓	↓	↓	↓	↓	0 1	1 2	2 3	3 4	5 6	8 9	12 13	18 19	27 28	41 42	↑	↑	↑	↑	↑
G	32	↓	↓	↓	↓	↓	↓	↓	↓	↓	↓	0 1	1 2	2 3	3 4	5 6	8 9	12 13	18 19	27 28	41 42	↑	↑	↑	↑	↑	↑
H	50	↓	↓	↓	↓	↓	↓	↓	↓	↓	0 1	1 2	2 3	3 4	5 6	8 9	12 13	18 19	27 28	41 42	↑	↑	↑	↑	↑	↑	↑
J	80	↓	↓	↓	↓	↓	↓	↓	↓	0 1	1 2	2 3	3 4	5 6	8 9	12 13	18 19	27 28	41 42	↑	↑	↑	↑	↑	↑	↑	↑
K	125	↓	↓	↓	↓	↓	↓	↓	0 1	1 2	2 3	3 4	5 6	8 9	12 13	18 19	27 28	41 42	↑	↑	↑	↑	↑	↑	↑	↑	↑
L	200	↓	↓	↓	↓	↓	↓	0 1	1 2	2 3	3 4	5 6	8 9	12 13	18 19	27 28	41 42	↑	↑	↑	↑	↑	↑	↑	↑	↑	↑
M	315	↓	↓	↓	↓	↓	0 1	1 2	2 3	3 4	5 6	8 9	12 13	18 19	27 28	41 42	↑	↑	↑	↑	↑	↑	↑	↑	↑	↑	↑
N	500	↓	↓	↓	↓	0 1	1 2	2 3	3 4	5 6	8 9	12 13	18 19	27 28	41 42	↑	↑	↑	↑	↑	↑	↑	↑	↑	↑	↑	↑
P	800	↓	↓	↓	0 1	1 2	2 3	3 4	5 6	8 9	12 13	18 19	27 28	41 42	↑	↑	↑	↑	↑	↑	↑	↑	↑	↑	↑	↑	↑
Q	1,250	↓	↓	0 1	1 2	2 3	3 4	5 6	8 9	12 13	18 19	27 28	41 42	↑	↑	↑	↑	↑	↑	↑	↑	↑	↑	↑	↑	↑	↑
R	2,000	↓	0 1	1 2	2 3	3 4	5 6	8 9	12 13	18 19	27 28	41 42	↑	↑	↑	↑	↑	↑	↑	↑	↑	↑	↑	↑	↑	↑	↑
S	3,150	0 1	1 2	2 3	3 4	5 6	8 9	12 13	18 19	27 28	41 42	↑	↑	↑	↑	↑	↑	↑	↑	↑	↑	↑	↑	↑	↑	↑	↑

↓ = use first sampling plan below arrow. If sample size equals or exceeds lot or batch size, do 100 % inspection.
↑ = use first sampling plan above arrow.
Ac = acceptance number.
Re = rejection number.

Table N Master table for reduced inspection (single sampling)—MIL-STD-105D (ABC Standard)

Acceptable quality levels (reduced inspection)†

Sample size code letter	Sample size	0.010 Ac Re	0.015 Ac Re	0.025 Ac Re	0.040 Ac Re	0.065 Ac Re	0.10 Ac Re	0.15 Ac Re	0.25 Ac Re	0.40 Ac Re	0.65 Ac Re	1.0 Ac Re	1.5 Ac Re	2.5 Ac Re	4.0 Ac Re	6.5 Ac Re	10 Ac Re	15 Ac Re	25 Ac Re	40 Ac Re	65 Ac Re	100 Ac Re	150 Ac Re	250 Ac Re	400 Ac Re	650 Ac Re	1,000 Ac Re
A	2													↓		↓	↓	→ 0 1	1 1	2 3	3 4	5 5	6 7	8 10	11 14	15 21	30 31
B	2												↓		↓	0 1	0 1		1 1	2 3	3 5	5 5	6 7	8 10	11 14	15 21	30 31
C	2											↓		↓	0 1	0 1	0 2	1 3	1 4	2 5	3 6	5 6	7 8	10 10	13 14	17 21	24
D	3										↓		↓	0 1	0 1	0 2	1 3	1 4	2 5	3 6	5 6	6 7	8 10	13 14	17 21	21 24	
E	5									↓		↓	0 1		0 2	1 3	1 4	2 5	3 6	5 8	6 7	8 10	10 13	14 17	17 21		
F	8								↓		↓	0 1		0 2	1 3	1 4	2 5	3 6	5 8	6 8	8 10	10 13	13 17	17 21			
G	13							↓		↓	0 1		0 2	1 3	1 4	2 5	3 6	5 8	6 8	8 10	10 13	13 14					
H	20						↓		↓	0 1		0 2	1 3	1 4	2 5	3 6	5 8	7 10	8 10	10 13							
J	32					↓		↓	0 1		0 2	1 3	2 4	3 5	5 6	6 8	8 10	10 13									
K	50				↓		↓	0 1		0 2	1 3	2 4	3 5	5 6	6 8	8 10	10 13										
L	80			↓		↓	0 1		0 2	1 3	2 4	3 5	5 6	7 8	8 10	10 13											
M	125		↓		↓	0 1		0 2	1 3	2 4	3 5	5 6	6 7	8 10	10 13												
N	200	↓		↓	0 1		0 2	1 3	2 5	3 6	5 8	7 10	10 13														
P	315		↓	0 1		0 2	1 3	2 5	3 6	5 8	7 10	10 13															
Q	500	↓	0 1		0 2	1 3	2 5	3 6	5 8	7 10	10 13																
R	800	0 1		0 2	1 3	2 5	3 6	5 8	7 10	10 13																	

↓ = use first sampling plan below arrow. If sample size equals or exceeds lot or batch size, do 100% inspection.

↑ = use first sampling plan above arrow.

Ac = acceptance number.

Re = rejection number.

† If the acceptance number has been exceeded but the rejection number has not been reached, accept the lot but reinstate normal inspection.

Table O Master table for normal inspection (double sampling)—MIL-STD-105D (ABC Standard)

Values are shown as "Ac Re" (acceptance number, rejection number). ↓ = use first sampling plan below arrow; ↑ = use first sampling plan above arrow.

Code	Sample	Sample size	Cum. sample size	0.010	0.015	0.025	0.040	0.065	0.10	0.15	0.25	0.40	0.65	1.0	1.5	2.5	4.0	6.5	10	15	25	40	65	100	150	250	400	650	1,000
A													↓															
B	First	2	2																↓	0 2	0 3	1 4	2 5	3 7	5 9	7 11	11 16	17 22	25 31
B	Second	2	4																	1 2	3 4	4 5	6 7	8 9	12 13	18 19	26 27	37 38	56 57
C	First	3	3															↓	0 2	0 3	1 4	2 5	3 7	5 9	7 11	11 16	17 22	25 31	↑
C	Second	3	6																1 2	3 4	4 5	6 7	8 9	12 13	18 19	26 27	37 38	56 57	
D	First	5	5														↓	0 2	0 3	1 4	2 5	3 7	5 9	7 11	11 16	17 22	25 31	↑	
D	Second	5	10															1 2	3 4	4 5	6 7	8 9	12 13	18 19	26 27	37 38	56 57		
E	First	8	8													↓	0 2	0 3	1 4	2 5	3 7	5 9	7 11	11 16	17 22	25 31	↑		
E	Second	8	16														1 2	3 4	4 5	6 7	8 9	12 13	18 19	26 27	37 38	56 57			
F	First	13	13												↓	0 2	0 3	1 4	2 5	3 7	5 9	7 11	11 16	17 22	25 31	↑			
F	Second	13	26													1 2	3 4	4 5	6 7	8 9	12 13	18 19	26 27	37 38	56 57				
G	First	20	20											↓	0 2	0 3	1 4	2 5	3 7	5 9	7 11	11 16	17 22	25 31	↑				
G	Second	20	40												1 2	3 4	4 5	6 7	8 9	12 13	18 19	26 27	37 38	56 57					
H	First	32	32										↓	0 2	0 3	1 4	2 5	3 7	5 9	7 11	11 16	17 22	25 31	↑					
H	Second	32	64											1 2	3 4	4 5	6 7	8 9	12 13	18 19	26 27	37 38	56 57						
J	First	50	50									↓	0 2	0 3	1 4	2 5	3 7	5 9	7 11	11 16	17 22	25 31	↑						
J	Second	50	100										1 2	3 4	4 5	6 7	8 9	12 13	18 19	26 27	37 38	56 57							
K	First	80	80								↓	0 2	0 3	1 4	2 5	3 7	5 9	7 11	11 16	17 22	25 31	↑							
K	Second	80	160									1 2	3 4	4 5	6 7	8 9	12 13	18 19	26 27	37 38	56 57								
L	First	125	125							↓	0 2	0 3	1 4	2 5	3 7	5 9	7 11	11 16	17 22	25 31	↑								
L	Second	125	250								1 2	3 4	4 5	6 7	8 9	12 13	18 19	26 27	37 38	56 57									
M	First	200	200						↓	0 2	0 3	1 4	2 5	3 7	5 9	7 11	11 16	17 22	25 31	↑									
M	Second	200	400							1 2	3 4	4 5	6 7	8 9	12 13	18 19	26 27	37 38	56 57										
N	First	315	315					↓	0 2	0 3	1 4	2 5	3 7	5 9	7 11	11 16	17 22	25 31	↑										
N	Second	315	630						1 2	3 4	4 5	6 7	8 9	12 13	18 19	26 27	37 38	56 57											
P	First	500	500				↓	0 2	0 3	1 4	2 5	3 7	5 9	7 11	11 16	17 22	25 31	↑											
P	Second	500	1,000					1 2	3 4	4 5	6 7	8 9	12 13	18 19	26 27	37 38	56 57												
Q	First	800	800			↓	0 2	0 3	1 4	2 5	3 7	5 9	7 11	11 16	17 22	25 31	↑												
Q	Second	800	1,600				1 2	3 4	4 5	6 7	8 9	12 13	18 19	26 27	37 38	56 57													
R	First	1,250	1,250		↓	0 2	0 3	1 4	2 5	3 7	5 9	7 11	11 16	17 22	25 31	↑													
R	Second	1,250	2,500			1 2	3 4	4 5	6 7	8 9	12 13	18 19	26 27	37 38	56 57														

Acceptable quality levels (normal inspection)

↓ = use first sampling plan below arrow. If sample size equals or exceeds lot or batch size, do 100% inspection.
↑ = use first sampling plan above arrow.
Ac = acceptance number.
Re = rejection number.
† Use corresponding single sampling plan (or alternatively, use double sampling plan below, where available).

Table P Master table for tightened inspection (doubling sampling)—MIL-STD-105D (ABC Standard)

Acceptance quality levels (tightened inspection)

Sample size code letter	Sample	Sample size	Cumulative sample size	0.010 Ac Re	0.015 Ac Re	0.025 Ac Re	0.040 Ac Re	0.065 Ac Re	0.10 Ac Re	0.15 Ac Re	0.25 Ac Re	0.40 Ac Re	0.65 Ac Re	1.0 Ac Re	1.5 Ac Re	2.5 Ac Re	4.0 Ac Re	6.5 Ac Re	10 Ac Re	15 Ac Re	25 Ac Re	40 Ac Re	65 Ac Re	100 Ac Re	150 Ac Re	250 Ac Re	400 Ac Re	650 Ac Re	1,000 Ac Re
A																												
B	First Second	2 2	2 4																		↑						23 29	52 53
C	First Second	3 3	3 6																			↑				15 20	34 35	23 29	52 53
D	First Second	5 5	5 10																		↑	0 2	2 3		9 14	23 24	15 20	23 29	52 53
E	First Second	8 8	8 16																		0 2	2 3	1 4	4 5	6 10	15 16	9 14	23 24	
F	First Second	13 13	13 26																0 2	2 3	1 4	4 5	2 5	6 7	3 7	11 12	6 10	15 16	
G	First Second	20 20	20 40															0 2	2 3	1 4	4 5	2 5	6 7	3 7	11 12	6 10	15 16	9 14	23 24	
H	First Second	32 32	32 64													0 2	2 3	1 4	4 5	2 5	6 7	3 7	11 12	6 10	15 16	9 14	23 24	
J	First Second	50 50	50 100											0 2	2 3	1 4	4 5	2 5	6 7	3 7	11 12	6 10	15 16	9 14	23 24	
K	First Second	80 80	80 160										0 2	2 3	1 4	4 5	2 5	6 7	3 7	11 12	6 10	15 16	9 14	23 24	
L	First Second	125 125	125 250								0 2	2 3	1 4	4 5	2 5	6 7	3 7	11 12	6 10	15 16	9 14	23 24	
M	First Second	200 200	200 400						0 2	2 3	1 4	4 5	2 5	6 7	3 7	11 12	6 10	15 16	9 14	23 24	
N	First Second	315 315	315 630				0 2	2 3	1 4	4 5	2 5	6 7	3 7	11 12	6 10	15 16	9 14	23 24	
P	First Second	500 500	500 1,000		0 2	2 3	1 4	4 5	2 5	6 7	3 7	11 12	6 10	15 16	9 14	23 24	
Q	First Second	800 800	800 1,600	0 2	2 3	1 4	4 5	2 5	6 7	3 7	11 12	6 10	15 16	9 14	23 24	
R	First Second	1,250 1,250	1,250 2,500	0 2 1 2												
S	First Second	2,000 2,000	2,000 4,000												

↓ = use first sampling plan below arrow.   If sample size equals or exceeds lot or batch size, do 100% inspection.
↑ = use first sampling plan above arrow.
Ac = acceptance number.
Re = rejection number.
† Use corresponding single sampling plan (or, alternatively, use double sampling plan below, where available).

Table Q Master table for reduced inspection (double sampling)—MIL-STD-105D (ABC Standard)

Acceptable quality levels (reduced inspection)†

Legend: ↓ = use first sampling plan below arrow; ↑ = use first sampling plan above arrow; ‡ = use corresponding single sampling plan. Each cell shows **Ac Re** (acceptance number, rejection number).

Code	Sample	n	Σn	0.010	0.015	0.025	0.040	0.065	0.10	0.15	0.25	0.40	0.65	1.0	1.5	2.5	4.0	6.5	10	15	25	40	65	100	150	250	400	650	1,000
A				↓	↓	↓	↓	↓	↓	↓	↓	↓	↓	↓	↓	↓	↓	↓	↓	↓	↓	↓	↓	↓	↓	↓	↓	↓	↓
B				↓	↓	↓	↓	↓	↓	↓	↓	↓	↓	↓	↓	↓	↓	↓	↓	↓	↓	↓	↓	↓	↓	↓	↓	↓	↓
C				↓	↓	↓	↓	↓	↓	↓	↓	↓	↓	↓	↓	↓	↓	↓	↓	↓	↓	↓	↓	↓	↓	↓	↓	↓	↓
D	First	2	2	↓	↓	↓	↓	↓	↓	↓	↓	↓	↓	↓	↓	↓	‡	0 2	0 2	0 3	0 4	1 5	2 7	3 8	5 10	7 12	11 17	↑	↑
	Second	2	4															0 2	0 3	0 4	1 5	4 7	6 9	8 12	12 16	18 21	26 30		
E	First	3	3	↓	↓	↓	↓	↓	↓	↓	↓	↓	↓	↓	↓	‡	0 2	0 2	0 3	0 4	1 5	2 7	3 8	5 10	7 12	11 17	↑	↑	↑
	Second	3	6														0 2	0 3	0 4	1 5	4 7	6 9	8 12	12 16	18 21	26 30			
F	First	5	5	↓	↓	↓	↓	↓	↓	↓	↓	↓	↓	↓	‡	0 2	0 2	0 3	0 4	1 5	2 7	3 8	5 10	7 12	11 17	↑	↑	↑	↑
	Second	5	10													0 2	0 3	0 4	1 5	4 7	6 9	8 12	12 16	18 21	26 30				
G	First	8	8	↓	↓	↓	↓	↓	↓	↓	↓	↓	↓	‡	0 2	0 2	0 3	0 4	1 5	2 7	3 8	5 10	7 12	11 17	↑	↑	↑	↑	↑
	Second	8	16												0 2	0 3	0 4	1 5	4 7	6 9	8 12	12 16	18 21	26 30					
H	First	13	13	↓	↓	↓	↓	↓	↓	↓	↓	↓	‡	0 2	0 2	0 3	0 4	1 5	2 7	3 8	5 10	7 12	11 17	↑	↑	↑	↑	↑	↑
	Second	13	26											0 2	0 3	0 4	1 5	4 7	6 9	8 12	12 16	18 21	26 30						
J	First	20	20	↓	↓	↓	↓	↓	↓	↓	↓	‡	0 2	0 2	0 3	0 4	1 5	2 7	3 8	5 10	7 12	11 17	↑	↑	↑	↑	↑	↑	↑
	Second	20	40										0 2	0 3	0 4	1 5	4 7	6 9	8 12	12 16	18 21	26 30							
K	First	32	32	↓	↓	↓	↓	↓	↓	↓	‡	0 2	0 2	0 3	0 4	1 5	2 7	3 8	5 10	7 12	11 17	↑	↑	↑	↑	↑	↑	↑	↑
	Second	32	64									0 2	0 3	0 4	1 5	4 7	6 9	8 12	12 16	18 21	26 30								
L	First	50	50	↓	↓	↓	↓	↓	↓	‡	0 2	0 2	0 3	0 4	1 5	2 7	3 8	5 10	7 12	11 17	↑	↑	↑	↑	↑	↑	↑	↑	↑
	Second	50	100								0 2	0 3	0 4	1 5	4 7	6 9	8 12	12 16	18 21	26 30									
M	First	80	80	↓	↓	↓	↓	↓	‡	0 2	0 2	0 3	0 4	1 5	2 7	3 8	5 10	7 12	11 17	↑	↑	↑	↑	↑	↑	↑	↑	↑	↑
	Second	80	160							0 2	0 3	0 4	1 5	4 7	6 9	8 12	12 16	18 21	26 30										
N	First	125	125	↓	↓	↓	↓	‡	0 2	0 2	0 3	0 4	1 5	2 7	3 8	5 10	7 12	11 17	↑	↑	↑	↑	↑	↑	↑	↑	↑	↑	↑
	Second	125	250						0 2	0 3	0 4	1 5	4 7	6 9	8 12	12 16	18 21	26 30											
P	First	200	200	↓	↓	↓	‡	0 2	0 2	0 3	0 4	1 5	2 7	3 8	5 10	7 12	11 17	↑	↑	↑	↑	↑	↑	↑	↑	↑	↑	↑	↑
	Second	200	400					0 2	0 3	0 4	1 5	4 7	6 9	8 12	12 16	18 21	26 30												
Q	First	315	315	↓	↓	‡	0 2	0 2	0 3	0 4	1 5	2 7	3 8	5 10	7 12	11 17	↑	↑	↑	↑	↑	↑	↑	↑	↑	↑	↑	↑	↑
	Second	315	630				0 2	0 3	0 4	1 5	4 7	6 9	8 12	12 16	18 21	26 30													
R	First	500	500	↓	‡	0 2	0 2	0 3	0 4	1 5	2 7	3 8	5 10	7 12	11 17	↑	↑	↑	↑	↑	↑	↑	↑	↑	↑	↑	↑	↑	↑
	Second	1,000	1,500			0 2	0 3	0 4	1 5	4 7	6 9	8 12	12 16	18 21	26 30														

↓ = use first sampling plan below arrow. If sample size equals or exceeds lot or batch size, do 100% inspection.
↑ = use first sampling plan above arrow.
Ac = acceptance number.
Re = rejection number.
† If, after the second sample, the acceptance number has been exceeded but the rejection number has not been reached, accept the lot but reinstate normal inspection.
‡ Use corresponding single sampling plan (or alternatively, use double sampling plan below, when available.)

Table R Master table for normal inspection (multiple sampling)—MIL-STD-105D (ABC Standard)

Sample size code letter	Sample	Sample size	Cumulative sample size	0.010	0.015	0.025	0.040	0.065	0.10	0.15	0.25	0.40	0.65	1.0	1.5	2.5	4.0	6.5	10	15	25	40	65	100	150	250	400	650	1,000
				Acceptable quality levels (normal inspection)																									
				Ac Re	Ac Re	Ac Re	Ac Re	Ac Re	Ac Re	Ac Re	Ac Re	Ac Re	Ac Re	Ac Re	Ac Re	Ac Re	Ac Re	Ac Re	Ac Re	Ac Re	Ac Re	Ac Re	Ac Re	Ac Re	Ac Re	Ac Re	Ac Re	Ac Re	Ac Re
A				↓	↓	↓	↓	↓	↓	↓	↓	↓	↓	↓	↓	↓	↓	†	↓	↓	†	†	†	†	†	†	†	†	†
B				↓	↓	↓	↓	↓	↓	↓	↓	↓	↓	↓	↓	↓	†	↑	↓	‡	‡	‡	‡	‡	‡	‡	‡	‡	‡
C				↓	↓	↓	↓	↓	↓	↓	↓	↓	↓	↓	↓	†	↑	↓	‡	‡	‡	‡	‡	‡	‡	‡	‡	‡	↑
D	First	2	2	↓	↓	↓	↓	↓	↓	↓	↓	↓	↓	↓	†	↑	↓	§ 2	§ 2	§ 3	§ 4	0 4	0 5	1 7	2 9	4 12	6 16	↑	↑
	Second	2	4															§ 2	0 3	0 3	1 5	1 6	3 8	4 10	7 14	11 19	17 27		
	Third	2	6															0 2	0 3	1 4	2 6	3 8	6 10	8 13	13 19	19 27	29 39		
	Fourth	2	8															0 3	1 4	2 5	3 7	5 10	8 13	12 17	19 25	27 34	40 49		
	Fifth	2	10															1 3	2 4	3 6	5 8	7 11	11 15	17 20	25 29	36 40	53 58		
	Sixth	2	12															1 3	3 5	4 6	7 9	10 12	14 17	21 23	31 33	45 47	65 68		
	Seventh	2	14															2 3	4 5	6 7	9 10	13 14	18 19	25 26	37 38	53 54	77 78		
E	First	3	3	↓	↓	↓	↓	↓	↓	↓	↓	↓	↓	†	↑	↓	§ 2	§ 2	§ 3	§ 4	0 4	0 5	1 7	2 9	4 12	6 16	↑	↑	↑
	Second	3	6														§ 2	0 3	0 3	1 5	1 6	3 8	4 10	7 14	11 19	17 27			
	Third	3	9														0 2	0 3	1 4	2 6	3 8	6 10	8 13	13 19	19 27	29 39			
	Fourth	3	12														0 3	1 4	3 5	3 7	5 10	8 13	12 17	19 25	27 34	40 49			
	Fifth	3	15														1 3	2 4	3 6	5 8	7 11	11 15	17 20	25 29	36 40	53 58			
	Sixth	3	18														1 3	3 5	4 6	7 9	10 12	14 17	21 23	31 33	45 47	65 68			
	Seventh	3	21														2 3	4 5	6 7	9 10	13 14	18 19	25 26	37 38	53 54	77 78			
F	First	5	5	↓	↓	↓	↓	↓	↓	↓	↓	↓	†	↑	↓	§ 2	§ 2	§ 3	§ 4	0 4	0 5	1 7	2 9	↑	↑	↑	↑	↑	↑
	Second	5	10													§ 2	0 3	0 3	1 5	1 6	3 8	4 10	7 14						
	Third	5	15													0 2	0 3	1 4	2 6	3 8	6 10	8 13	13 19						
	Fourth	5	20													0 3	1 4	2 5	3 7	5 10	8 13	12 17	19 25						
	Fifth	5	25													1 3	2 4	3 6	5 8	7 11	11 15	17 20	25 29						
	Sixth	5	30													1 3	3 5	4 6	7 9	10 12	14 17	21 23	31 33						
	Seventh	5	35													2 3	4 5	6 7	9 10	13 14	18 19	25 26	37 38						
G	First	8	8	↓	↓	↓	↓	↓	↓	↓	↓	†	↑	↓	§ 2	§ 2	§ 3	§ 4	0 4	0 5	1 7	2 9	↑	↑	↑	↑	↑	↑	↑
	Second	8	16												§ 2	0 3	0 3	1 5	1 6	3 8	4 10	7 14							
	Third	8	24												0 2	0 3	1 4	2 6	3 8	6 10	8 13	13 19							
	Fourth	8	32												0 3	1 4	2 5	3 7	5 10	8 13	12 17	19 25							
	Fifth	8	40												1 3	2 4	3 6	5 8	7 11	11 15	17 20	25 29							
	Sixth	8	48												1 3	3 5	4 6	7 9	10 12	14 17	21 23	31 33							
	Seventh	8	52												2 3	4 5	6 7	9 10	13 14	18 19	25 26	37 38							
H	First	13	13	↓	↓	↓	↓	↓	↓	↓	†	↑	↓	§ 2	§ 2	§ 3	§ 4	0 4	0 5	1 7	2 9	↑	↑	↑	↑	↑	↑	↑	↑
	Second	13	26											§ 2	0 3	0 3	1 5	1 6	3 8	4 10	7 14								
	Third	13	39											0 2	0 3	1 4	2 6	3 8	6 10	8 13	13 19								
	Fourth	13	52											0 3	1 4	2 5	3 7	5 10	8 13	12 17	19 25								
	Fifth	13	65											1 3	2 4	3 6	5 8	7 11	11 15	17 20	25 29								
	Sixth	13	78											1 3	3 5	4 6	7 9	10 12	14 17	21 23	31 33								
	Seventh	13	91											2 3	4 5	6 7	9 10	13 14	18 19	25 26	37 38								
J	First	20	20	↓	↓	↓	↓	↓	↓	†	↑	↓	§ 2	§ 2	§ 3	§ 4	0 4	0 5	1 7	2 9	↑	↑	↑	↑	↑	↑	↑	↑	↑
	Second	20	40										§ 2	0 3	0 3	1 5	1 6	3 8	4 10	7 14									
	Third	20	60										0 2	0 3	1 4	2 6	3 8	6 10	8 13	13 19									
	Fourth	20	70										0 3	1 4	2 5	3 7	5 10	8 13	12 17	19 25									
	Fifth	20	100										1 3	2 4	3 6	5 8	7 11	11 15	17 20	25 29									
	Sixth	20	120										1 3	3 5	4 6	7 9	10 12	14 17	21 23	31 33									
	Seventh	20	140										2 3	4 5	6 7	9 10	13 14	18 19	25 26	37 38									

↓ = use first sampling plan below arrow (refer to continuation of table on following page, when necessary). If sample size equals or exceeds lot or batch size, do 100 % inspection.
↑ = use first sampling plan above arrow.
Ac = acceptance number.
Re = rejection number.
† Use corresponding single sampling plan (or alternatively, use multiple sampling plan below, where available).
‡ Use corresponding double sampling plan (or alternatively, use multiple sampling plan below, where available).
§ Acceptance not permitted at this sample size.

Table R Master table for normal inspection (multiple sampling)—MIL-STD-105D (ABC Standard). (*Continued*)

Sample size code letter	Sample	Sample size	Cumulative sample size	0.010 Ac Re	0.015 Ac Re	0.025 Ac Re	0.040 Ac Re	0.065 Ac Re	0.10 Ac Re	0.15 Ac Re	0.25 Ac Re	0.40 Ac Re	0.65 Ac Re	1.0 Ac Re	1.5 Ac Re	2.5 Ac Re	4.0 Ac Re	6.5 Ac Re	10 Ac Re	15 Ac Re	25 Ac Re	40 Ac Re	65 Ac Re	100 Ac Re	150 Ac Re	250 Ac Re	400 Ac Re	650 Ac Re	1,000 Ac Re
K	First	32	32						↑			‡ 2	‡ 2	‡ 3	# 4	0 4	0 5	1 7	2 9	↑	↑	↑	↑	↑	↑	↑	↑	↑	↑
	Second	32	64									‡ 2	0 3	0 3	1 5	1 6	3 8	4 10	7 14										
	Third	32	96									0 2	0 3	1 4	2 6	3 8	6 10	8 13	13 19										
	Fourth	32	128									0 3	1 4	2 5	3 7	5 10	8 13	12 17	19 25										
	Fifth	32	160									1 3	2 4	3 6	5 8	7 11	11 15	17 20	25 29										
	Sixth	32	192								↓	1 3	3 5	4 6	7 9	10 12	14 17	21 23	31 33										
	Seventh	32	224									2 3	4 5	5 6	7 9	9 10	13 14	18 19	25 26	37 38									
L	First	50	50							↑		‡ 2	‡ 2	‡ 3	# 4	0 4	0 5	1 7	2 9	↑									
	Second	50	100									‡ 2	0 3	0 3	1 5	1 6	3 8	4 10	7 14										
	Third	50	150									0 2	0 3	1 4	2 6	3 8	6 10	8 13	13 19										
	Fourth	50	200									0 3	1 4	2 5	3 7	5 10	8 13	12 17	19 25										
	Fifth	50	250									1 3	2 4	3 6	5 8	7 11	11 15	17 20	25 29										
	Sixth	50	300									1 3	3 5	4 6	7 9	10 12	14 17	21 23	31 33										
	Seventh	50	350									2 3	4 5	5 6	7 9	9 10	13 14	18 19	25 26	37 38									
M	First	80	80					↑				‡ 2	‡ 2	‡ 3	# 4	0 4	0 5	1 7	2 9										
	Second	80	160									‡ 2	0 3	0 3	1 5	1 6	3 8	4 10	7 14										
	Third	80	240									0 2	0 3	1 4	2 6	3 8	6 10	8 13	13 19										
	Fourth	80	320									0 3	1 4	2 5	3 7	5 10	8 13	12 17	19 25										
	Fifth	80	400									1 3	2 4	3 6	5 8	7 11	11 15	17 20	25 29										
	Sixth	80	480									1 3	3 5	4 6	7 9	10 12	14 17	21 23	31 33										
	Seventh	80	560									2 3	4 5	5 6	7 9	9 10	13 14	18 19	25 26	37 38									
N	First	125	125			↑					‡ 2	‡ 2	‡ 3	# 4	0 4	0 5	1 7	2 9											
	Second	125	250								‡ 2	0 3	0 3	1 5	1 6	3 8	4 10	7 14											
	Third	125	375								0 2	0 3	1 4	2 6	3 8	6 10	8 13	13 19											
	Fourth	125	500								0 3	1 4	2 5	3 7	5 10	8 13	12 17	19 25											
	Fifth	125	625								1 3	2 4	3 6	5 8	7 11	11 15	17 20	25 29											
	Sixth	125	750								1 3	3 5	4 6	7 9	10 12	14 17	21 23	31 33											
	Seventh	125	875								2 3	4 5	5 6	7 9	9 10	13 14	18 19	25 26	37 38										
P	First	200	200		↑			‡ 2	‡ 2	‡ 3	# 4	0 4	0 5	1 7	2 9														
	Second	200	400					‡ 2	0 3	0 3	1 5	1 6	3 8	4 10	7 14														
	Third	200	600					0 2	0 3	1 4	2 6	3 8	6 10	8 13	13 19														
	Fourth	200	800					0 3	1 4	2 5	3 7	5 10	8 13	12 17	19 25														
	Fifth	200	1,000					1 3	2 4	3 6	5 8	7 11	11 15	17 20	25 29														
	Sixth	200	1,200					1 3	3 5	4 6	7 9	10 12	14 17	21 23	31 33														
	Seventh	200	1,400					2 3	4 5	5 6	7 9	9 10	13 14	18 19	25 26	37 38													
Q	First	315	315	↑			‡ 2	‡ 2	‡ 3	# 4	0 4	0 5	1 7	2 9															
	Second	315	630				‡ 2	0 3	0 3	1 5	1 6	3 8	4 10	7 14															
	Third	315	945				0 2	0 3	1 4	2 6	3 8	6 10	8 13	13 19															
	Fourth	315	1,260				0 3	1 4	2 5	3 7	5 10	8 13	12 17	19 25															
	Fifth	315	1,575				1 3	2 4	3 6	5 8	7 11	11 15	17 20	25 29															
	Sixth	315	1,890				1 3	3 5	4 6	7 9	10 12	14 17	21 23	31 33															
	Seventh	315	2,205				2 3	4 5	5 6	7 9	9 10	13 14	18 19	25 26	37 38														
R	First	500	500		↑	‡ 2	‡ 2	‡ 3	# 4	0 4	0 5	1 7	2 9																
	Second	500	1,000			‡ 2	0 3	0 3	1 5	1 6	3 8	4 10	7 14																
	Third	500	1,500			0 2	0 3	1 4	2 6	3 8	6 10	8 13	13 19																
	Fourth	500	2,000			0 3	1 4	2 5	3 7	5 10	8 13	12 17	19 25																
	Fifth	500	2,500			1 3	2 4	3 6	5 8	7 11	11 15	17 20	25 29																
	Sixth	500	3,000			1 3	3 5	4 6	7 9	10 12	14 17	21 23	31 33																
	Seventh	500	3,500			2 3	4 5	5 6	7 9	9 10	13 14	18 19	25 26	37 38															

↓ = use first sampling plan below arrow. If sample size equals or exceeds lot or batch size, do 100 % inspection.
↑ = use first sampling plan above arrow (refer to preceding page, when necessary).
Ac = acceptance number.
Re = rejection number.
† Use corresponding single sampling plan (or alternatively, use multiple plan below, where applicable).
‡ Acceptance not permitted at this sample size.

Table S Master table for tightened inspection (multiple sampling) — MIL-STD-105D (ABC Standard)

Acceptable quality levels (tightened inspection)

Sample size code letter	Sample	Sample size	Cumulative sample size	1.0 Ac Re	1.5 Ac Re	2.5 Ac Re	4.0 Ac Re	6.5 Ac Re	10 Ac Re	15 Ac Re	25 Ac Re	40 Ac Re	65 Ac Re	100 Ac Re	150 Ac Re	250 Ac Re	400 Ac Re
A																↓	↓ ↓
B																	
C																←	↑ ↑
D	First	2	2					↓	‡ 2	‡ 2	‡ 3	‡ 4	0 6	0 9	1 8	3 10	6 15
	Second	2	4						0 2	0 3	1 4	1 5	3 8	3 12	10 17	10 17	16 25
	Third	2	6						0 2	0 3	2 5	2 6	6 10	7 17	—	17 24	26 36
	Fourth	2	8						0 3	1 4	3 6	3 7	8 13	11 22	—	24 31	37 46
	Fifth	2	10						1 3	2 4	4 6?	5 8	11 15	14 25	—	31 37	49 55
	Sixth	2	12						1 3	3 5	—	7 9	14 17	18 27	—	37 43	61 64
	Seventh	2	14						2 3	4 5	—	9 10	18 19	21 22	32 33	48 49	72 73
E	First	3	3				↓	‡ 2	‡ 2	‡ 3	‡ 4	0 6	0 9	1 8	3 10	6 15	
	Second	3	6					0 2	0 3	1 4	1 5	3 8	3 12	10 17	10 17	16 25	
	Third	3	9					0 2	0 3	2 5	2 6	6 10	7 17	—	17 24	26 36	
	Fourth	3	12					0 3	1 4	3 6	3 7	8 13	11 22	—	24 31	37 46	
	Fifth	3	15					1 3	2 4	—	5 8	11 15	14 25	—	31 37	49 55	
	Sixth	3	18					1 3	3 5	—	7 9	14 17	18 27	—	37 43	61 64	
	Seventh	3	21					2 3	4 5	—	9 10	18 19	21 22	32 33	48 49	72 73	
F	First	5	5			↓	‡ 2	‡ 2	‡ 3	‡ 4	0 6	0 9	1 8	3 10	6 15		
	Second	5	10				0 2	0 3	1 4	1 5	3 8	3 12	10 17	10 17	16 25		
	Third	5	15				0 2	0 3	2 5	2 6	6 10	7 17	—	17 24	26 36		
	Fourth	5	20				0 3	1 4	3 6	3 7	8 13	11 22	—	24 31	37 46		
	Fifth	5	25				1 3	2 4	—	5 8	11 15	14 25	—	31 37	49 55		
	Sixth	5	30				1 3	3 5	—	7 9	14 17	18 27	—	37 43	61 64		
	Seventh	5	35				2 3	4 5	—	9 10	18 19	21 22	32 33	48 49	72 73		
G	First	8	8		↓	‡ 2	‡ 2	‡ 3	‡ 4	0 6	0 9	1 8	3 10	6 15			
	Second	8	16			0 2	0 3	1 4	1 5	3 8	3 12	10 17	10 17	16 25			
	Third	8	24			0 2	0 3	2 5	2 6	6 10	7 17	—	17 24	26 36			
	Fourth	8	32			0 3	1 4	3 6	3 7	8 13	11 22	—	24 31	37 46			
	Fifth	8	40			1 3	2 4	—	5 8	11 15	14 25	—	31 37	49 55			
	Sixth	8	48			1 3	3 5	—	7 9	14 17	18 27	—	37 43	61 64			
	Seventh	8	56			2 3	4 5	—	9 10	18 19	21 22	32 33	48 49	72 73			
H	First	13	13	↓	‡ 2	‡ 2	‡ 3	‡ 4	0 6	0 9	1 8	3 10	6 15				
	Second	13	26		0 2	0 3	1 4	1 5	3 8	3 12	10 17	10 17	16 25				
	Third	13	39		0 2	0 3	2 5	2 6	6 10	7 17	—	17 24	26 36				
	Fourth	13	52		0 3	1 4	3 6	3 7	8 13	11 22	—	24 31	37 46				
	Fifth	13	65		1 3	2 4	—	5 8	11 15	14 25	—	31 37	49 55				
	Sixth	13	78		1 3	3 5	—	7 9	14 17	18 27	—	37 43	61 64				
	Seventh	13	91		2 3	4 5	—	9 10	18 19	21 22	32 33	48 49	72 73				
J	First	20	20	‡ 2	‡ 2	‡ 3	‡ 4	0 6	0 9	1 8	3 10	6 15					
	Second	20	40	0 2	0 3	1 4	1 5	3 8	3 12	10 17	10 17	16 25					
	Third	20	60	0 2	0 3	2 5	2 6	6 10	7 17	—	17 24	26 36					
	Fourth	20	80	0 3	1 4	3 6	3 7	8 13	11 22	—	24 31	37 46					
	Fifth	20	100	1 3	2 4	—	5 8	11 15	14 25	—	31 37	49 55					
	Sixth	20	120	1 3	3 5	—	7 9	14 17	18 27	—	37 43	61 64					
	Seventh	20	140	2 3	4 5	—	9 10	18 19	21 22	32 33	48 49	72 73					

AQL columns 0.010, 0.015, 0.025, 0.040, 0.065, 0.10, 0.15, 0.25, 0.40, 0.65 (Ac Re) are indicated by directional arrows (↓ / → / ↑).

→ = use first sampling plan below arrow (refer to continuation of table on following page, when necessary). If sample size equals or exceeds lot or batch size, do 100 % inspection.

↑ = use first sampling plan above arrow.

Ac = acceptance number.

Re = rejection number.

* Use corresponding single sampling plan (or alternatively, use multiple sampling plan below, where available).

† Use corresponding double sampling plan (or alternatively, use multiple sampling plan below, where available).

‡ Acceptance not permitted at this sample size.

Table S Master table for tightened inspection (multiple sampling)—MIL-STD-105D (ABC Standard). (*Continued*)

Acceptable quality levels (tightened inspection). Each AQL column below shows the pair **Ac Re** (acceptance number / rejection number). Arrow cells: ↓ = use first sampling plan below arrow; ↑ = use first sampling plan above arrow; ← = use first sampling plan to the left (above).

Code	Sample	Sample size	Cumulative sample size	0.010	0.015	0.025	0.040	0.065	0.10	0.15	0.25	0.40	0.65	1.0	1.5	2.5	4.0	6.5	10	15	25	40	65	100	150	250	400	650	1,000
K	First	32	32	↓	↓	↓	↓	↓	↓	↓	↓	↓	‡ 2	‡ 2	‡ 3	‡ 4	‡ 6	‡ 6	‡ 8	←	←	←	←	←	←	←	←	←	←
K	Second	32	64	↓	↓	↓	↓	↓	↓	↓	↓	↓	0 3	0 3	0 3	1 5	1 7	3 9	6 12	←	←	←	←	←	←	←	←	←	←
K	Third	32	96	↓	↓	↓	↓	↓	↓	↓	↓	↓	0 3	0 3	1 4	2 6	3 9	6 14	12 17	←	←	←	←	←	←	←	←	←	←
K	Fourth	32	128	↓	↓	↓	↓	↓	↓	↓	↓	↓	1 3	1 4	2 5	3 7	5 11	10 17	17 22	←	←	←	←	←	←	←	←	←	←
K	Fifth	32	160	↓	↓	↓	↓	↓	↓	↓	↓	↓	1 3	2 4	3 6	5 8	7 13	13 19	22 25	←	←	←	←	←	←	←	←	←	←
K	Sixth	32	192	↓	↓	↓	↓	↓	↓	↓	↓	↓	2 3	3 5	4 6	7 9	10 14	17 21	27 29	←	←	←	←	←	←	←	←	←	←
K	Seventh	32	224	↓	↓	↓	↓	↓	↓	↓	↓	↓	2 3	4 5	6 7	9 10	14 15	21 22	32 33	←	←	←	←	←	←	←	←	←	←
L	First	50	50	↓	↓	↓	↓	↓	↓	↓	↓	‡ 2	‡ 2	‡ 3	‡ 4	‡ 6	‡ 6	‡ 8	←	←	←	←	←	←	←	←	←	←	←
L	Second	50	100	↓	↓	↓	↓	↓	↓	↓	↓	0 3	0 3	0 3	1 5	1 7	3 9	6 12	←	←	←	←	←	←	←	←	←	←	←
L	Third	50	150	↓	↓	↓	↓	↓	↓	↓	↓	0 3	0 3	1 4	2 6	3 9	6 14	12 17	←	←	←	←	←	←	←	←	←	←	←
L	Fourth	50	200	↓	↓	↓	↓	↓	↓	↓	↓	1 3	1 4	2 5	3 7	5 11	10 17	17 22	←	←	←	←	←	←	←	←	←	←	←
L	Fifth	50	250	↓	↓	↓	↓	↓	↓	↓	↓	1 3	2 4	3 6	5 8	7 13	13 19	22 25	←	←	←	←	←	←	←	←	←	←	←
L	Sixth	50	300	↓	↓	↓	↓	↓	↓	↓	↓	2 3	3 5	4 6	7 9	10 14	17 21	27 29	←	←	←	←	←	←	←	←	←	←	←
L	Seventh	50	350	↓	↓	↓	↓	↓	↓	↓	↓	2 3	4 5	6 7	9 10	14 15	21 22	32 33	←	←	←	←	←	←	←	←	←	←	←
M	First	80	80	↓	↓	↓	↓	↓	↓	↓	‡ 2	‡ 2	‡ 3	‡ 4	‡ 6	‡ 6	‡ 8	←	←	←	←	←	←	←	←	←	←	←	←
M	Second	80	160	↓	↓	↓	↓	↓	↓	↓	0 3	0 3	0 3	1 5	1 7	3 9	6 12	←	←	←	←	←	←	←	←	←	←	←	←
M	Third	80	240	↓	↓	↓	↓	↓	↓	↓	0 3	0 3	1 4	2 6	3 9	6 14	12 17	←	←	←	←	←	←	←	←	←	←	←	←
M	Fourth	80	320	↓	↓	↓	↓	↓	↓	↓	1 3	1 4	2 5	3 7	5 11	10 17	17 22	←	←	←	←	←	←	←	←	←	←	←	←
M	Fifth	80	400	↓	↓	↓	↓	↓	↓	↓	1 3	2 4	3 6	5 8	7 13	13 19	22 25	←	←	←	←	←	←	←	←	←	←	←	←
M	Sixth	80	480	↓	↓	↓	↓	↓	↓	↓	2 3	3 5	4 6	7 9	10 14	17 21	27 29	←	←	←	←	←	←	←	←	←	←	←	←
M	Seventh	80	560	↓	↓	↓	↓	↓	↓	↓	2 3	4 5	6 7	9 10	14 15	21 22	32 33	←	←	←	←	←	←	←	←	←	←	←	←
N	First	125	125	↓	↓	↓	↓	↓	↓	‡ 2	‡ 2	‡ 3	‡ 4	‡ 6	‡ 6	‡ 8	←	←	←	←	←	←	←	←	←	←	←	←	←
N	Second	125	250	↓	↓	↓	↓	↓	↓	0 3	0 3	0 3	1 5	1 7	3 9	6 12	←	←	←	←	←	←	←	←	←	←	←	←	←
N	Third	125	375	↓	↓	↓	↓	↓	↓	0 3	0 3	1 4	2 6	3 9	6 14	12 17	←	←	←	←	←	←	←	←	←	←	←	←	←
N	Fourth	125	500	↓	↓	↓	↓	↓	↓	1 3	1 4	2 5	3 7	5 11	10 17	17 22	←	←	←	←	←	←	←	←	←	←	←	←	←
N	Fifth	125	625	↓	↓	↓	↓	↓	↓	1 3	2 4	3 6	5 8	7 13	13 19	22 25	←	←	←	←	←	←	←	←	←	←	←	←	←
N	Sixth	125	750	↓	↓	↓	↓	↓	↓	2 3	3 5	4 6	7 9	10 14	17 21	27 29	←	←	←	←	←	←	←	←	←	←	←	←	←
N	Seventh	125	875	↓	↓	↓	↓	↓	↓	2 3	4 5	6 7	9 10	14 15	21 22	32 33	←	←	←	←	←	←	←	←	←	←	←	←	←
P	First	200	200	↓	↓	↓	↓	↓	‡ 2	‡ 2	‡ 3	‡ 4	‡ 6	‡ 6	‡ 8	←	←	←	←	←	←	←	←	←	←	←	←	←	←
P	Second	200	400	↓	↓	↓	↓	↓	0 3	0 3	0 3	1 5	1 7	3 9	6 12	←	←	←	←	←	←	←	←	←	←	←	←	←	←
P	Third	200	600	↓	↓	↓	↓	↓	0 3	0 3	1 4	2 6	3 9	6 14	12 17	←	←	←	←	←	←	←	←	←	←	←	←	←	←
P	Fourth	200	800	↓	↓	↓	↓	↓	1 3	1 4	2 5	3 7	5 11	10 17	17 22	←	←	←	←	←	←	←	←	←	←	←	←	←	←
P	Fifth	200	1,000	↓	↓	↓	↓	↓	1 3	2 4	3 6	5 8	7 13	13 19	22 25	←	←	←	←	←	←	←	←	←	←	←	←	←	←
P	Sixth	200	1,200	↓	↓	↓	↓	↓	2 3	3 5	4 6	7 9	10 14	17 21	27 29	←	←	←	←	←	←	←	←	←	←	←	←	←	←
P	Seventh	200	1,400	↓	↓	↓	↓	↓	2 3	4 5	6 7	9 10	14 15	21 22	32 33	←	←	←	←	←	←	←	←	←	←	←	←	←	←
Q	First	315	315	↓	↓	↓	↓	‡ 2	‡ 2	‡ 3	‡ 4	‡ 6	‡ 6	‡ 8	←	←	←	←	←	←	←	←	←	←	←	←	←	←	←
Q	Second	315	630	↓	↓	↓	↓	0 3	0 3	0 3	1 5	1 7	3 9	6 12	←	←	←	←	←	←	←	←	←	←	←	←	←	←	←
Q	Third	315	945	↓	↓	↓	↓	0 3	0 3	1 4	2 6	3 9	6 14	12 17	←	←	←	←	←	←	←	←	←	←	←	←	←	←	←
Q	Fourth	315	1,260	↓	↓	↓	↓	1 3	1 4	2 5	3 7	5 11	10 17	17 22	←	←	←	←	←	←	←	←	←	←	←	←	←	←	←
Q	Fifth	315	1,575	↓	↓	↓	↓	1 3	2 4	3 6	5 8	7 13	13 19	22 25	←	←	←	←	←	←	←	←	←	←	←	←	←	←	←
Q	Sixth	315	1,890	↓	↓	↓	↓	2 3	3 5	4 6	7 9	10 14	17 21	27 29	←	←	←	←	←	←	←	←	←	←	←	←	←	←	←
Q	Seventh	315	2,205	↓	↓	↓	↓	2 3	4 5	6 7	9 10	14 15	21 22	32 33	←	←	←	←	←	←	←	←	←	←	←	←	←	←	←
R	First	500	500	↓	↓	↓	‡ 2	‡ 2	‡ 3	‡ 4	‡ 6	‡ 6	‡ 8	←	←	←	←	←	←	←	←	←	←	←	←	←	←	←	←
R	Second	500	1,000	↓	↓	↓	0 3	0 3	0 3	1 5	1 7	3 9	6 12	←	←	←	←	←	←	←	←	←	←	←	←	←	←	←	←
R	Third	500	1,500	↓	↓	↓	0 3	0 3	1 4	2 6	3 9	6 14	12 17	←	←	←	←	←	←	←	←	←	←	←	←	←	←	←	←
R	Fourth	500	2,000	↓	↓	↓	1 3	1 4	2 5	3 7	5 11	10 17	17 22	←	←	←	←	←	←	←	←	←	←	←	←	←	←	←	←
R	Fifth	500	2,500	↓	↓	↓	1 3	2 4	3 6	5 8	7 13	13 19	22 25	←	←	←	←	←	←	←	←	←	←	←	←	←	←	←	←
R	Sixth	500	3,000	↓	↓	↓	2 3	3 5	4 6	7 9	10 14	17 21	27 29	←	←	←	←	←	←	←	←	←	←	←	←	←	←	←	←
R	Seventh	500	3,500	↓	↓	↓	2 3	4 5	6 7	9 10	14 15	21 22	32 33	←	←	←	←	←	←	←	←	←	←	←	←	←	←	←	←
S	First	800	800	↑	↑	‡ 2	‡ 2	‡ 3	‡ 4	‡ 6	‡ 6	‡ 8	←	←	←	←	←	←	←	←	←	←	←	←	←	←	←	←	←
S	Second	800	1,600	↑	↑	0 3	0 3	0 3	1 5	1 7	3 9	6 12	←	←	←	←	←	←	←	←	←	←	←	←	←	←	←	←	←
S	Third	800	2,400	↑	↑	0 3	0 3	1 4	2 6	3 9	6 14	12 17	←	←	←	←	←	←	←	←	←	←	←	←	←	←	←	←	←
S	Fourth	800	3,200	↑	↑	1 3	1 4	2 5	3 7	5 11	10 17	17 22	←	←	←	←	←	←	←	←	←	←	←	←	←	←	←	←	←
S	Fifth	800	4,000	↑	↑	1 3	2 4	3 6	5 8	7 13	13 19	22 25	←	←	←	←	←	←	←	←	←	←	←	←	←	←	←	←	←
S	Sixth	800	4,800	↑	↑	2 3	3 5	4 6	7 9	10 14	17 21	27 29	←	←	←	←	←	←	←	←	←	←	←	←	←	←	←	←	←
S	Seventh	800	5,600	↑	↑	2 3	4 5	6 7	9 10	14 15	21 22	32 33	←	←	←	←	←	←	←	←	←	←	←	←	←	←	←	←	←

↓ = use first sampling plan below arrow. If sample size equals or exceeds lot or batch size, do 100 % inspection.
↑ = use first sampling plan above arrow (refer to preceding page, when necessary).
Ac = acceptance number.
Re = rejection number.
† Use corresponding single sampling plan (or alternatively, use multiple sampling plan below, where available).
‡ Acceptance not permitted at this sample size.

Table T Master table for reduced inspection (multiple sampling)—MIL-STD-105D (ABC Standard)

Acceptable quality levels (reduced inspection) †

Sample size code letter	Sample	Sample size	Cumulative sample size	AQL data region
A				↓ (use first sampling plan below arrow) across low AQL columns
B				
C				
D				
E				
F	First	2	2	
	Second	2	4	
	Third	2	6	
	Fourth	2	8	
	Fifth	2	10	
	Sixth	2	12	
	Seventh	2	14	
G	First	3	3	
	Second	3	6	
	Third	3	9	
	Fourth	3	12	
	Fifth	3	15	
	Sixth	3	18	
	Seventh	3	21	
H	First	5	5	
	Second	5	10	
	Third	5	15	
	Fourth	5	20	
	Fifth	5	25	
	Sixth	5	30	
	Seventh	5	35	
J	First	8	8	
	Second	8	16	
	Third	8	24	
	Fourth	8	32	
	Fifth	8	40	
	Sixth	8	48	
	Seventh	8	56	
K	First	13	13	
	Second	13	26	
	Third	13	39	
	Fourth	13	52	
	Fifth	13	65	
	Sixth	13	78	
	Seventh	13	91	

AQL columns (each with Ac and Re sub-columns): 0.010, 0.015, 0.025, 0.040, 0.065, 0.10, 0.15, 0.25, 0.40, 0.65, 1.0, 1.5, 2.5, 4.0, 6.5, 10, 15, 25, 40, 65, 100, 150, 250, 400, 650, 1,000.

Acceptance (Ac) / Rejection (Re) numbers, diagonal data band (best reading of the dense numeric region):

Code	Sample	10 (Ac Re)	15 (Ac Re)	25 (Ac Re)	40 (Ac Re)	65 (Ac Re)
F	First	3	3	0 4	0 5	0 6
	Second	0 4	0 4	1 6	3 7	3 9
	Third	0 5	1 5	3 8	6 9	7 12
	Fourth	1 6	2 6	5 10	8 11	10 14
	Fifth	2 7	3 7	7 11	11 13	13 17
	Sixth	3 8	4 8	10 13	14 17	17 20
	Seventh	4 10	6 10	13 14	18 22	21 22

↓ = use first sampling plan below arrow (refer to continuation of table on following page, when necessary).
↑ = use first sampling plan above arrow.
Ac = acceptance number
Re = rejection number
† If, after the final sample, the acceptance number has been exceeded but the rejection number has not been reached, accept the lot but reinstate normal inspection.
‡ Use corresponding single sampling plan (or alternatively, use multiple sampling plan below, where available).
¶ Use corresponding double sampling plan (or alternatively, use multiple plan below, where available).
¶ Acceptance not permitted at this sample size.

If sample size equals, or exceeds lot or batch size, do 100 % inspection.

Table T Master table for reduced inspection (multiple sampling)—MIL-STD-105D (ABC Standard). (*Continued*)

Acceptable quality levels (reduced inspection)†

Sample size code letter	Sample	Sample size	Cumulative sample size
L	First	20	20
	Second	20	40
	Third	20	60
	Fourth	20	80
	Fifth	20	100
	Sixth	20	120
	Seventh	20	140
M	First	32	32
	Second	32	64
	Third	32	96
	Fourth	32	128
	Fifth	32	160
	Sixth	32	192
	Seventh	32	224
N	First	50	50
	Second	50	100
	Third	50	150
	Fourth	50	200
	Fifth	50	250
	Sixth	50	300
	Seventh	50	350
P	First	80	80
	Second	80	160
	Third	80	240
	Fourth	80	320
	Fifth	80	400
	Sixth	80	480
	Seventh	80	560
Q	First	125	125
	Second	125	250
	Third	125	375
	Fourth	125	500
	Fifth	125	625
	Sixth	125	750
	Seventh	125	875
R	First	200	200
	Second	200	400
	Third	200	600
	Fourth	200	800
	Fifth	200	1,000
	Sixth	200	1,200
	Seventh	200	1,400

↓ = use first sampling plan below arrow. If sample size equals, or exceeds, lot or batch size, do 100% inspection.
↑ = use first sampling plan above arrow (refer to preceding page when necessary).
Ac = acceptance number.
Re = rejection number.
† If, after the final sample, the acceptance number has been exceeded but the rejection number has not been reached, accept the lot but reinstate normal inspection.
‡ Use corresponding single sampling plan (or, alternatively, use multiple sampling plan below, where available).
§ Acceptance not permitted at this sample size.

Table U Average outgoing quality limit factors for normal inspection (single sampling)—MIL-STD-105D (ABC Standard)

Acceptable quality level

Code letter	Sample size	0.010	0.015	0.025	0.040	0.065	0.10	0.15	0.25	0.40	0.65	1.0	1.5	2.5	4.0	6.5	10	15	25	40	65	100	150	250	400	650	1,000
A	2															18	17	28	42	69	97	160	220	330	470	730	
B	3														12	11	17	27	46	65	110	150	220	310	490	720	1,100
C	5													7.4	6.5	11	15	24	39	63	90	130	190	290	430	660	1,100
D	8												4.6	4.2	6.9	9.7	16	24	40	56	82	120	180	270	410		
E	13											2.8	2.6	4.3	6.1	9.9	14	22	34	50	72	110	170	250			
F	20										1.8	1.7	2.7	3.9	6.3	9.0	13	21	33	47	73						
G	32									1.2	1.1	1.7	2.4	4.0	5.6	8.2	12	19	29	46							
H	50								0.74	0.67	1.1	1.6	2.5	3.6	5.2	7.5	12	18	29								
J	80							0.46	0.42	0.69	0.97	1.6	2.2	3.3	4.7	7.3											
K	125						0.29	0.27	0.44	0.62	1.00	1.4	2.1	3.0	4.7												
L	200					0.18	0.17	0.27	0.39	0.63	0.90	1.3	1.9	2.9													
M	315				0.12	0.11	0.17	0.24	0.40	0.56	0.82	1.2	1.8														
N	500			0.074	0.067	0.11	0.16	0.25	0.36	0.52	0.75	1.2															
P	800		0.046																								
Q	1,250	0.029																									
R	2,000			0.042	0.069	0.097	0.16	0.22	0.33	0.47	0.73																

NOTE: For the exact AOQL, the above values must be multiplied by $\left(1 - \dfrac{\text{sample size}}{\text{lot or batch size}}\right)$.

Table V Average outgoing quality limit factors for tightened inspection (single sampling)—MIL-STD-105D (ABC Standard)

Code letter	Sample size	Acceptable quality level																									
		0.010	0.015	0.025	0.040	0.065	0.10	0.15	0.25	0.40	0.65	1.0	1.5	2.5	4.0	6.5	10	15	25	40	65	100	150	250	400	650	1,000
A	2																			42	69	97	160	260	400	620	970
B	3																		28	46	65	110	170	270	410	650	1,100
C	5														7.4	12		17	27	39	63	100	160	250	390	610	
D	8																11	17	24	40	64	99	160	240	380		
E	13															6.5	11	15	24	40	61	95	150	240			
F	20											1.8	2.8	4.6	4.2	6.9	9.7	16	26	40	62						
G	32													2.6	4.3	6.1	9.9	16	25	39							
H	50												1.7	2.7	3.9	6.3	10	16	25								
J	80								0.46	0.74	1.2	1.1	1.7	2.4	4.0	6.4	9.9	16									
K	125										0.67	1.1	1.6	2.5	4.1	6.4	9.9										
L	200						0.18	0.29		0.42	0.69	0.97	1.6	2.6	4.0	6.2											
M	315					0.12			0.27	0.44	0.62	1.0	1.6	2.5	3.9												
N	500		0.029	0.046	0.074			0.17	0.27	0.39	0.63	1.0	1.6	2.5													
P	800					0.067	0.11	0.17	0.24	0.40	0.64	0.99	1.6														
Q	1,250					0.067	0.11	0.16	0.25	0.41	0.64	0.99															
R	2,000	0.018			0.042	0.069	0.097	0.16	0.26	0.40	0.62																
S	3,150		0.027																								

NOTE: For the exact AOQL, the above values must be multiplied by $\left(1 - \dfrac{\text{sample size}}{\text{lot or batch size}}\right)$.

Table W Limit numbers for reduced inspection—MIL-STD-105D (ABC Standard)

Number of sample units from last 10 lots or batches	Acceptable quality level																									
	0.010	0.015	0.025	0.040	0.065	0.10	0.15	0.25	0.40	0.65	1.0	1.5	2.5	4.0	6.5	10	15	25	40	65	100	150	250	400	650	1,000
20–29	†	†	†	†	†	†	†	†	†	†	†	†	†	†	†	0	0	2	4	8	14	22	40	68	115	181
30–49	†	†	†	†	†	†	†	†	†	†	†	†	†	†	0	0	1	3	7	13	22	36	63	105	178	277
50–79	†	†	†	†	†	†	†	†	†	†	†	†	†	0	0	2	3	7	14	25	40	63	110	181	301	
80–129	†	†	†	†	†	†	†	†	†	†	†	†	0	0	2	4	7	14	24	42	68	105	181	297		
130–199	†	†	†	†	†	†	†	†	†	†	†	0	0	2	4	7	13	25	42	72	115	177	301	490		
200–319	†	†	†	†	†	†	†	†	†	†	0	0	2	4	8	14	22	40	68	115	181	277	471			
320–499	†	†	†	†	†	†	†	†	†	0	0	1	4	8	14	24	39	68	113	189						
500–799	†	†	†	†	†	†	†	†	0	0	2	3	7	14	25	40	63	110	181							
800–1,249	†	†	†	†	†	†	†	0	0	2	4	7	14	24	42	68	105	181								
1,250–1,999	†	†	†	†	†	†	0	0	2	4	7	13	24	40	69	110	169									
2,000–3,149	†	†	†	†	†	0	0	2	4	8	14	22	40	68	115	181										
3,150–4,999	†	†	†	†	0	0	1	4	8	14	24	38	67	111	186											
5,000–7,999	†	†	†	0	0	2	3	7	14	25	40	63	110	181												
8,000–12,499	†	†	0	0	2	4	7	14	24	42	68	105	181													
12,500–19,999	†	0	0	2	4	7	13	24	40	69	110	169														
20,000–31,499	0	0	2	4	8	14	22	46	68	115	181															
31,500–49,999	0	1	4	8	14	24	38	67	111	186																
50,000 and over	2	3	7	14	25	40	63	110	181	301																

† Denotes that the number of sample units from the last 10 lots or batches is not sufficient for reduced inspection for this AQL. In this instance more than 10 lots or batches may be used for the calculation, provided that the lots or batches used are the most recent ones in sequence, that they have all been on normal inspection, and that none has been rejected while on original inspection.

Table X Some factors for use in acceptance sampling by variables

This table gives factors taken from " Sampling Inspection by Variables " by A. H. Bowker and H. P. Goode, McGraw-Hill Book Company, Inc., New York, 1952. These factors are representative of much more extensive sets of variables plans given in that volume. For a brief explanation of the use of these factors, see Chap. 17. The Bowker-Goode volume gives sample size code letters (not reproduced here) that correspond to those used in the attributes tables in the Columbia Statistical Research Group's (SRG's) volume "Sampling Inspection" and in JAN-STD-105. AQL classes also correspond to the AQL classes in these attributes tables, and the same definition of AQL ($100p_{0.95}$) is used. Each line of the following table gives factors for three different types of variables plans as well as the corresponding single sampling attributes plan. The four plans on any line have the same AQL class and are selected using the same sample size code letter. The OC curves of all plans on a given line match as closely as practicable under the restriction imposed by the use of standard sample sizes for each code letter for the one-sided variables plans. The Bowker-Goode volume gives full OC curves for all its unknown-sigma plans that relate to one-sided specifications.

Known-sigma plans for-one sided specifications				Unknown-sigma plans for one-sided specifications		Known-sigma plans for two-sided specifications		Single sampling attributes plan	
n	k'	$100p_{0.95}$	$100p_{0.10}$	n	k	n	$k'*$	n	c
5	1.748	0.65	12.00	7	1.636	3	1.587	10	0
5	1.522	1.20	17.15	7	1.449	4	1.404	30	1
5	1.278	2.20	24.03	7	1.242	4	1.201	20	1
5	1.117	3.20	29.34	7	1.107	5	1.070	15	1
5	1.027	3.90	32.50	7	1.053	5	1.017	10	1
5	1.015	4.00	32.93	7	0.969	5	0.935	10	1
6	1.812	0.65	9.87	10	1.757	4	1.720	15	0
6	1.586	1.20	14.40	10	1.562	5	1.529	30	1
6	1.343	2.20	20.63	10	1.400	5	1.303	20	1
6	1.272	2.60	22.71	10	1.287	6	1.162	15	1
6	1.181	3.20	25.54	10	1.186	6	1.119	15	1
6	0.973	5.00	32.63	10	0.994	7	1.060	15	2
7	2.105	0.32	5.26	13	1.957	5	1.927	20	0
7	1.862	0.65	8.41	13	1.764	5	1.736	55	1
7	1.635	1.20	12.49	13	1.583	6	1.557	30	1
7	1.432	2.00	17.16	13	1.472	6	1.448	20	1
7	1.392	2.20	18.19	13	1.371	7	1.348	20	1
7	1.177	3.60	24.41	13	1.189	8	1.169	20	2
7	1.084	4.40	27.43	13	1.132	8	1.113	20	2

Table X Some factors for use in acceptance sampling by variables. (*Continued*)

Known-sigma plans for one-sided specifications				Unknown-sigma plans for one-sided specifications		Known-sigma plans for two-sided specifications		Single sampling attributes plan	
n	k'	$100p_{0.95}$	$100p_{0.10}$	n	k	n	k'^*	n	c
9	2.300	0.22	3.06	16	2.116	5	2.090	30	0
9	2.178	0.32	4.00	16	2.018	6	1.994	150	1
9	1.935	0.65	6.57	16	1.822	6	1.799	55	1
9	1.709	1.20	10.00	16	1.694	7	1.672	30	1
9	1.466	2.20	14.95	16	1.437	8	1.418	30	2
9	1.363	2.80	17.47	16	1.378	8	1.360	30	2
9	1.226	3.80	21.22	16	1.217	9	1.201	30	3
9	1.158	4.40	23.25	16	1.180	10	1.164	30	3
11	2.433	0.17	2.03	20	2.246	6	2.225	40	0
11	2.352	0.22	2.47	20	2.180	6	2.159	225	1
11	2.231	0.32	3.26	20	2.080	7	2.060	150	1
11	1.988	0.65	5.46	20	1.880	7	1.861	55	1
11	1.761	1.20	8.46	20	1.749	8	1.732	40	1
11	1.518	2.20	12.89	20	1.504	10	1.489	40	2
11	1.400	2.90	15.54	20	1.388	10	1.374	40	3
11	1.356	3.20	16.61	20	1.351	11	1.337	40	3
11	1.210	4.40	20.51	20	1.218	12	1.205	40	4
13	2.579	0.12	1.31	25	2.395	7	2.378	55	0
13	2.473	0.17	1.71	25	2.306	7	2.289	300	1
13	2.392	0.22	2.09	25	2.239	7	2.222	225	1
13	2.270	0.32	2.78	25	2.137	8	2.121	150	1
13	2.028	0.65	4.72	25	1.933	9	1.918	55	1
13	1.781	1.20	7.42	25	1.756	10	1.742	55	2
13	1.558	2.20	11.46	25	1.569	11	1.556	55	3
13	1.539	2.30	11.83	25	1.504	12	1.492	55	3
13	1.396	3.20	14.90	25	1.385	13	1.373	55	4
13	1.250	4.40	18.56	25	1.261	14	1.250	55	5
16	2.828	0.06	0.61	35	2.653	8	2.640	750	1
16	2.624	0.12	1.06	35	2.480	9	2.467	450	1
16	2.518	0.17	1.40	35	2.389	9	2.377	300	1
16	2.437	0.22	1.72	35	2.319	10	2.307	225	1
16	2.315	0.32	2.30	35	2.234	10	2.222	150	1
16	2.073	0.65	3.99	35	2.031	12	2.020	75	1
16	1.846	1.20	6.36	35	1.811	13	1.795	75	2
16	1.664	1.90	8.96	35	1.672	15	1.662	75	3
16	1.532	2.60	11.28	35	1.552	16	1.543	75	4
16	1.351	3.90	15.13	35	1.390	18	1.381	75	6
16	1.253	4.80	17.54	35	1.284	19	1.276	75	7

Table Y Operating characteristics of certain unknown-sigma and known-sigma variables acceptance plans for one-sided specifications

In this table, n is the sample size for an unknown-sigma plan. The values of $p_{0.95}$, $p_{0.50}$, and $p_{0.10}$ apply to the unknown-sigma plans for the stated values of k and n. The symbol n^* is used to show the sample size for the known-sigma plan having an OC curve that comes closest to matching the OC curve of the given unknown-sigma plan when the k' of the known-sigma plan is made equal to the k of the given unknown-sigma plan. The information in this table is taken from W. G. Ireson, "Sampling Tables for Inspection by Variables," Technical Report No. 7, Applied Mathematics and Statistics Laboratory, Stanford University.

k	$100p_{0.95}$	$100p_{0.50}$	$100p_{0.10}$	n^*	$100p_{0.95}$	$100p_{0.50}$	$100p_{0.10}$	n^*
	$n = 5$				$n = 7$			
0.6	8.42	28.73	52.58	5	10.39	28.30	48.17	6
0.8	5.23	22.77	46.65	4	6.72	22.24	41.87	6
1.0	3.00	17.59	41.09	4	4.05	17.00	36.00	5
1.2	1.59	13.24	35.95	3	2.28	12.64	30.63	4
1.4	0.77	9.70	31.25	3	1.19	9.13	25.80	4
1.6	0.34	6.92	26.95	2	0.57	6.41	21.49	3
1.8	0.14	4.80	23.06	2	0.26	4.37	17.70	3
2.0	0.05	3.24	19.62	2	0.11	2.89	14.42	3
2.25	0.01	1.90	15.83	2	0.03	1.64	10.99	2
2.5	0.00	1.06	12.61	2	0.01	0.89	8.21	2
3.0	0.00	0.29	7.72	1	0.00	0.23	4.34	2
	$n = 10$				$n = 15$			
0.6	12.43	28.01	44.38	9	14.61	27.80	40.95	10
0.8	8.30	21.89	37.85	8	10.05	21.63	34.31	9
1.0	5.22	16.62	31.84	7	6.55	16.35	28.27	8
1.2	3.08	12.26	26.42	5	4.03	11.99	22.89	7
1.4	1.70	8.78	21.62	5	2.34	8.52	18.23	6
1.6	0.88	6.09	17.44	5	1.28	5.87	14.26	6
1.8	0.42	4.10	13.87	4	0.66	3.91	10.96	5
2.0	0.19	2.67	10.87	4	0.32	2.52	8.27	4
2.25	0.06	1.49	7.84	3	0.12	1.39	5.67	4
2.5	0.02	0.79	5.53	3	0.04	0.73	3.77	3
3.0	0.00	0.19	2.55	2	0.00	0.17	1.52	3

Table Y Operating characteristics of certain unknown-sigma and known-sigma variables acceptance plans for one-sided specifications. (*Continued*)

k	$100p_{0.95}$	$100p_{0.50}$	$100p_{0.10}$	n^*	$100p_{0.95}$	$100p_{0.50}$	$100p_{0.10}$	n^*
	$n = 20$				$n = 25$			
0.6	16.02	27.70	38.96	17	17.04	27.64	37.64	22
0.8	11.21	21.52	32.30	15	12.05	21.45	30.97	19
1.0	7.45	16.22	26.28	14	8.13	16.15	24.99	17
1.2	4.70	11.86	20.98	12	5.21	11.78	19.75	15
1.4	2.81	8.40	16.44	10	3.17	8.33	15.30	13
1.6	1.59	5.76	12.62	9	1.83	5.70	11.60	11
1.8	0.85	3.82	9.50	8	1.00	3.78	8.61	10
2.0	0.43	2.45	7.01	7	0.62	2.42	6.25	9
2.25	0.17	1.34	4.65	6	0.21	1.32	4.06	7
2.5	0.06	0.70	2.99	5	0.08	0.68	2.55	6
3.0	0.01	0.16	1.12	4	0.01	0.15	0.90	5
	$n = 30$				$n = 35$			
0.6	17.82	27.61	36.68	26	18.45	27.58	35.94	30
0.8	12.71	21.40	30.02	23	13.24	21.37	29.29	27
1.0	8.65	16.10	24.06	20	9.08	16.06	23.36	24
1.2	5.61	11.74	18.88	18	5.94	11.70	18.23	21
1.4	3.46	8.29	14.50	15	3.70	8.26	13.91	18
1.6	2.03	5.66	10.89	13	2.20	5.64	10.37	16
1.8	1.13	3.74	8.00	12	1.24	3.72	7.56	14
2.0	0.60	2.39	5.74	10	0.66	2.37	5.37	12
2.25	0.25	1.30	3.67	9	0.28	1.29	3.39	10
2.5	0.10	0.67	2.26	8	0.11	0.66	2.06	9
3.0	0.01	0.15	0.77	6	0.01	0.15	0.68	7
	$n = 40$				$n = 50$			
0.6	18.96	27.56	35.35	34	19.76	27.53	34.46	43
0.8	13.67	21.35	28.71	31	14.36	21.31	27.84	38
1.0	9.44	16.04	22.81	27	10.00	16.00	21.98	34
1.2	6.22	11.68	17.71	23	6.66	11.64	16.95	29
1.4	3.91	8.23	13.45	20	4.24	8.20	12.76	25
1.6	2.34	5.62	9.97	18	2.58	5.59	9.37	22
1.8	1.33	3.70	7.21	15	1.49	3.68	6.71	19
2.0	0.72	2.36	5.19	14	0.82	2.34	4.69	17
2.25	0.31	1.28	3.18	12	0.37	1.27	2.89	14
2.5	0.13	0.66	1.91	10	0.15	0.65	1.70	12
3.0	0.02	0.15	0.61	8	0.02	0.14	0.52	9

Table Z Random numbers*

10	09	73	25	33	76	52	01	35	86	34	67	35	48	76	80	95	90	91	17	39	29	27	49	45
37	54	20	48	05	64	89	47	42	96	24	80	52	40	37	20	63	61	04	02	00	82	29	16	65
08	42	26	89	53	19	64	50	93	03	23	20	90	25	60	15	95	33	47	64	35	08	03	36	06
99	01	90	25	29	09	37	67	07	15	38	31	13	11	65	88	67	67	43	97	04	43	62	76	59
12	80	79	99	70	80	15	73	61	47	64	03	23	66	53	98	95	11	68	77	12	17	17	68	33
66	06	57	47	17	34	07	27	68	50	36	69	73	61	70	65	81	33	98	85	11	19	92	91	70
31	06	01	08	05	45	57	18	24	06	35	30	34	26	14	86	79	90	74	39	23	40	30	97	32
85	26	97	76	02	02	05	16	56	92	68	66	57	48	18	73	05	38	52	47	18	62	38	85	79
63	57	33	21	35	05	32	54	70	48	90	55	35	75	48	28	46	82	87	09	83	49	12	56	24
73	79	64	57	53	03	52	96	47	78	35	80	83	42	82	60	93	52	03	44	35	27	38	84	35
98	52	01	77	67	14	90	56	86	07	22	10	94	05	58	60	97	09	34	33	50	50	07	39	98
11	80	50	54	31	39	80	82	77	32	50	72	56	82	48	29	40	52	42	01	52	77	56	78	51
83	45	29	96	34	06	28	89	80	83	13	74	67	00	78	18	47	54	06	10	68	71	17	78	17
88	68	54	02	00	86	50	75	84	01	36	76	66	79	51	90	36	47	64	93	29	60	91	10	62
99	59	46	73	48	87	51	76	49	69	91	82	60	89	28	93	78	56	13	68	23	47	83	41	13
65	48	11	76	74	17	46	85	09	50	58	04	77	69	74	73	03	95	71	86	40	21	81	65	44
80	12	43	56	35	17	72	70	80	15	45	31	82	23	74	21	11	57	82	53	14	38	55	37	63
74	35	09	98	17	77	40	27	72	14	43	23	60	02	10	45	52	16	42	37	96	28	60	26	55
69	91	62	68	03	66	25	22	91	48	36	93	68	72	03	76	62	11	39	90	94	40	05	64	18
09	89	32	05	05	14	22	56	85	14	46	42	75	67	88	96	29	77	88	22	54	38	21	45	98
91	49	91	45	23	68	47	92	76	86	46	16	28	35	54	94	75	08	99	23	37	08	92	00	48
80	33	69	45	98	26	94	03	68	58	70	29	73	41	35	53	14	03	33	40	42	05	08	23	41
44	10	48	19	49	85	15	74	79	54	32	97	92	65	75	57	60	04	08	81	22	22	20	64	13
12	55	07	37	42	11	10	00	20	40	12	86	07	46	97	96	64	48	94	39	28	70	72	58	15
63	60	64	93	29	16	50	53	44	84	40	21	95	25	63	43	65	17	70	82	07	20	73	17	90
61	19	69	04	46	26	45	74	77	74	51	92	43	37	29	65	39	45	95	93	42	58	26	05	27
15	47	44	52	66	95	27	07	99	53	59	36	78	38	48	82	39	61	01	18	33	21	15	94	66
94	55	72	85	73	67	89	75	43	87	54	62	24	44	31	91	19	04	25	92	92	92	74	59	73
42	48	11	62	13	97	34	40	87	21	16	86	84	87	67	03	07	11	20	59	25	70	14	66	70
23	52	37	83	17	73	20	88	98	37	68	93	59	14	16	26	25	22	96	63	05	52	28	25	62
04	49	35	24	94	75	24	63	38	24	45	86	25	10	25	61	96	27	93	35	65	33	71	24	72
00	54	99	76	54	64	05	18	81	59	96	11	96	38	96	54	69	28	23	91	23	28	72	95	29
35	96	31	53	07	26	89	80	93	54	33	35	13	54	62	77	97	45	00	24	90	10	33	93	33
59	80	80	83	91	45	42	72	68	42	83	60	94	97	00	13	02	12	48	92	78	56	52	01	06
46	05	88	52	36	01	39	00	22	86	77	28	14	40	77	93	91	08	36	47	70	61	74	29	41
32	17	90	05	97	87	37	92	52	41	05	56	70	70	07	86	74	31	71	57	85	39	41	18	38
69	23	46	14	06	20	11	74	52	04	15	95	66	00	00	18	74	39	24	23	97	11	89	63	38
19	56	54	14	30	01	75	87	53	79	40	41	92	15	85	66	67	43	68	06	84	96	28	52	07
45	15	51	49	38	19	47	60	72	46	43	66	79	45	43	59	04	79	00	33	20	82	66	95	41
94	86	43	19	94	36	16	81	08	51	34	88	88	15	53	01	54	03	54	56	05	01	45	11	76
98	08	62	48	26	45	24	02	84	04	44	99	90	88	96	39	09	47	34	07	35	44	13	18	80
33	18	51	62	32	41	94	15	09	49	89	43	54	85	81	88	69	54	19	94	37	54	87	30	43
80	95	10	04	06	96	38	27	07	74	20	15	12	33	87	25	01	62	52	98	94	62	46	11	71
79	75	24	91	40	71	96	12	82	96	69	86	10	25	91	74	85	22	05	39	00	38	75	95	79
18	63	33	25	37	98	14	50	65	71	31	01	02	46	74	05	45	56	14	27	77	93	89	19	36
74	02	94	39	02	77	55	73	22	70	97	79	01	71	19	52	52	75	80	21	80	81	45	17	48
54	17	84	56	11	80	99	33	71	43	05	33	51	29	69	56	12	71	92	55	36	04	09	03	24
11	66	44	98	83	52	07	98	48	27	59	38	17	15	39	09	97	33	34	40	88	46	12	33	56
48	32	47	79	28	31	24	96	47	10	02	29	53	68	70	32	30	75	75	46	15	02	00	99	94
69	07	49	41	38	87	63	79	19	76	35	58	40	44	01	10	51	82	16	15	01	84	87	69	38

* This table is reproduced with permission from tables of the RAND Corporation published in "A Million Random Digits with 100,000 Normal Deviates," Glencoe Free Press Division of The Macmillan Company, New York, 1955.

NAME INDEX

NAME INDEX

American National Standards Institute (ANSI),
53, 64n, 125n, 145, 256n
American Society for Quality Control (ASQC),
53, 64n, 155n, 156, 352, 363n, 418
American Society for Testing and Materials
(ASTM), 36n, 53, 85n
Ashley, R. L., 495n

Banzhof, R. A., 486n, 489n
Bazovsky, Igor, 536n
Beckwith, O. P., 337, 587
Bell, L. F., 340n, 536n, 590n
Bellinson, H. R., 415
Bell Telephone Laboratories, 103, 413
Bell Telephone System, 269
Bender, Arthur, Jr., 20, 537
Blanton, H. E., 570n
Bowker, A. H., 479–480, 505–509, 537n
Brinegar, C. S., 609n
Brugger, R. M., 486n, 489n
Bryan, J. G., 172n, 349

Calabro, S. R., 536n
Cameron, J. M., 451, 453
Campbell, G. A., 448n
Chateaneuf, Robert, 269, 270
Chorafas, D. M., 599n

Cisne, L. E., 405
Clifford, P. C., 287n, 288
Cocca, Omberto, 414n
Columbia Statistical Research Group, 374n,
413, 459n
Cone, A. F., 471n
Cowan, David, 155n, 156
Cowell, J. G., 595n

Darwin, C. G., 317, 319
Dean, Joel, 590n
Deming, W. E., 1, 33, 254, 277
De Morgan, 84
Dixon, W. J., 350
Dodge, H. F., 201, 202, 269, 271, 371, 374n, 391,
396–406, 408n, 412, 413n, 419, 421n, 438n,
465–471, 475–479, 483
Duncan, A. J., 87

Edwards, G. D., 20, 413n, 492
Ellis, E. W., 500n
Enell, J. W., 432
Epstein, Benjamin, 325, 552–553

Feigenbaum, A. V., 342
Ferrell, E. B., 288, 348
Freeman, H. A., 385n, 391n, 420n, 436n

SUBJECT INDEX

SUBJECT INDEX

ABC standard, 412–442
  graph showing average sample sizes (ASN) in,
    428
  Limiting Quality (LQ) tables for, 440–441
ABC Working Group, membership, 414*n*
Acceptable quality level (AQL):
  acceptance plans based on, 412–442, 465–468,
    486–488
  concept of, 413–415
    objections to, 415–416
  definitions, 418
  probabilities of accepting lots at, 418–419
  use of phrase by Columbia Statistical
    Research Group, 374*n*, 413
Acceptance based on number of defects,
    437–438
Acceptance costs, 581–582
Acceptance number, importance in determining
    shape of OC curve in attributes sampling,
    366–367, 369–371, 449–450, 454–455
Acceptance procedures, 7, 20–25, 359–571
  based on control chart, 134–136, 137, 502–504
  economic choice of, 583–585
  minimizing of total inspection in, 395–396,
    455–459
Acceptance/rectification scheme, meaning of,
    392–393

Acceptance sampling, 359–571
  conflicting interests of consumer and producer
    in, 368–369, 412–413, 467–468
  economic field for, 579–597
  indexing of plans by single point on OC
    curve, 374, 467
  introductory statements on, 7, 20–21
  for life testing, 534–571
  nonproduct applications of, 608–611
  randomness in, 383–384
  symbols used in, 362–363, 375, 428, 539,
    561, 567
  by variables, 492–529
Accuracy of method of measurement, 102–103,
    334–337
Addition theorem, 183
Adjustments of machines, too frequent,
    reduction of, 103, 107–109
AGREE Report, 534–536
Analytical procedure, effect of chance errors
    in, 336–337
AOQL (*see* Average outgoing quality limit)
AQL (*see* Acceptable quality level)
AQL and AOQL, difference in meanings of
    initials of, 414*n*
Army Ordnance tables, 413, 418, 435, 467*n*
Army Service Forces tables, 413, 435, 467*n*

677